AUSTRALIA CIRCUMNAVIGATED: THE VOYAGE OF MATTHEW FLINDERS IN HMS *INVESTIGATOR*, 1801–1803

VOLUME I

Edited by

KENNETH MORGAN

Published by
Ashgate
for
THE HAKLUYT SOCIETY
LONDON
2015

Published for The Hakluyt Society by

Ashgate Publishing Limited
Wey Court East
Union Road
Farnham
Surrey GU9 7PT
England

Ashgate Publishing Company
110 Cherry Street
Suite 3–1
Burlington, VT 05401–3818
USA

Ashgate website: http://www.ashgate.com
Hakuyt Society website: http://www.hakluyt.com

British Library Cataloguing in Publication Data
A catalogue record for this book is available from the British Library

Library of Congress Cataloguing-in-Publication Data
2014950201

ISBN 9781908145093 (hbk)
ISBN 9781908145116 (Two volume set)
ISBN 9781472460851 (ebk – PDF)
ISSN 0072 9396

Typeset by Waveney Typesetters, Wymondham, Norfolk

Printed in the United Kingdom by Henry Ling Limited,
at the Dorset Press, Dorchester, DT1 1HD

To Leigh, Ross and Vanessa Morgan
and to the memory of
Kenneth Albert Morgan and Clare Frances Morgan

WORKS ISSUED BY
THE HAKLUYT SOCIETY

Series Editors
Gloria Clifton
Joyce Lorimer

AUSTRALIA CIRCUMNAVIGATED:
THE VOYAGE OF MATTHEW FLINDERS
IN HMS *INVESTIGATOR*, 1801–1803
VOLUME I

THIRD SERIES
NO. 28

Portrait of Captain Matthew Flinders, RN, 1774–1814, by Toussaint Antoine de Chazal de Chamerel, 1806–7, Mauritius. Oil on canvas, 64.5 × 50.0 cm. Gift of David Roche in memory of his father, J. D. K. Roche, and the South Australian Government 2000. Art Gallery of South Australia, Adelaide.

CONTENTS

VOLUME I

LIST OF MAPS AND ILLUSTRATIONS

VOLUME I

Maps

Colour Plates

Figures

VOLUME II

Maps

Colour Plates

Between pages 274 and 275

Figures

PREFACE

This edition presents the edited text of two manuscripts written by Matthew Flinders in the period between 1803 and 1807. These comprise his fair journals in HMS *Investigator* on the first circumnavigatory voyage of Australia between 1801 and 1803 and a 'Memoir' that he wrote to accompany his journals and survey charts on this expedition. Both manuscripts are deposited among the Admiralty records at the National Archives, Kew, England; they have not been published before. The full title of the first volume of the journal (ADM 55/75) is: 'Journal of a Voyage to Terra Australis in His Majesty's Ship *Investigator* by Matthew Flinders Commander 1801–1802–1803–1804.' The full title of the second volume of the journal (ADM 55/76) is: 'Journal kept on board His Majesty's sloop *Investigator* by Matthew Flinders Comm*ander*, and afterwards in subsequent vessels and places, during the years 1801, 2, 3, 4, 5.' The title of the third volume of the journal (ADM 55/78) is '*Investigator* 1803'. Rough versions of Flinders's journal, which differ considerably from the fair versions edited here, are deposited among the Matthew Flinders Papers at the Mitchell Library, Sydney, Australia. The full title of the 'Memoir' (ADM 55/76) is 'A Memoir explaining the marks used in the charts of Australia constructed on board His Majestys ship *Investigator*; and the manner in which the latitude, longitude, and variation of the compass were obtained, corrected, and applied in their construction; With some new facts and additional observations upon these and other nautical subjects connected with Australia; by Matt*hew* Flinders, Late commander of the *Investigator*: a prisoner in the Isle of France.' Earlier, partial versions of the 'Memoir', which are not reproduced here, can be found at the United Kingdom Hydrographic Office, Ministry of Defence Archives, Taunton, and among the Royal Greenwich Observatory's Board of Longitude Papers at Cambridge University Library. This edition does not reproduce facsimile versions of the texts but it aims to present the manuscripts accurately and as fully as possible, with explanatory notes.

ACKNOWLEDGEMENTS

I would like to thank the following organizations who provided support for my research and other work involved in the preparation of this edition of the fair journals and memoir of Matthew Flinders: the Menzies Centre for Australian Studies, King's College, London, for an Australian Bicentennial Fellowship; the Scouloudi Foundation, Institute of Historical Research, University of London, for a Scouloudi Historical Award; the Harry & Grace Smith Fund of the Hakluyt Society for support for the production and publication of the maps.

I am grateful to the staff of the following archives and libraries for their help in providing the books, manuscripts and journals for the research underpinning these volumes: the National Archives, Kew; the National Maritime Museum, Greenwich; the British Library; the Royal Society; the Royal Geographical Society; the Natural History Museum, South Kensington; the Linnean Society, London; the Institute of Historical Research, University of London; the Royal Botanic Gardens Library, Kew; Cambridge University Library; the Scott Polar Research Institute, Cambridge; the United Kingdom Hydrographic Office, Ministry of Defence Archives, Taunton; the Lincolnshire Archives; the Bibliothèque municipal de Caen; the Mitchell Library, State Library of New South Wales; the National Library of Australia, Canberra; the State Library of Victoria, Melbourne; the Fisher Library, University of Sydney; the Baillieu Library, University of Melbourne; the State Library of South Australia, Adelaide; and the Allport Library, State Library of Tasmania, Hobart. The digitizing projects carried out by some of these libraries and archives have enabled me to maintain momentum on a large project by making available some of Flinders's manuscripts in electronic form. This is the place also to thank the many previous scholars of Matthew Flinders and his voyages for their insights into the maritime exploration of Australia. Brunel University granted me two terms of research leave in the academic year 2013–14 to complete the project.

Numerous individuals should be thanked for replying to my queries during the gestation of this project. Thanks are due to Miss Naomi Boneham, Captain R. J. Campbell, Lieutenant Commander Andrew C. F. David, the late Mr George Huxtable, Professor Andrew Lambert, Dr Nigel Rigby, Professor W. F. Ryan, Mr James M. S. Taylor, Professor Glyndwr Williams and Professor C. W. J. Withers. Dr Adrian Webb was my guide to the manuscript records at the United Kingdom Hydrographic Office. Dr Andrew S. Cook was a fount of knowledge on Flinders-Dalrymple-Arrowsmith queries. Mr Robert Cook and Ms Jocelyn Teh offered hospitality in Melbourne. Ms Judith Scurfield assisted me with map resources in Melbourne. Dr Martin Woods, Dr Brendan Whyte, Dr Susannah Helman and Ms Rachel Eddowes facilitated my map research at the National Library of Australia. Professor Alan Dench and Dr Frances Morphy offered their expertise on Aboriginal matters. Professor Campbell Macknight illuminated my understanding of the Makasar trepangers. Dr John Smedley and the staff at Ashgate

Publishing have cooperated constructively in the final stages of the project. Mr Barrie Fairhead expertly prepared the text and tables for typesetting. Dr C. Ian Jackson acted as a liaison scholar for the Hakluyt Society, and added important details to my editing of the text. His experience in editing scholarly texts assisted me considerably. Dr Gloria Clifton has worked with me in a cordial way to prepare the text for publication. Her editorial expertise and knowledge of scientific instruments has been most helpful. Captain M. K. Barritt has gone beyond his duties as President of the Hakluyt Society to provide important help with the transcription of the 'Memoir' and with the selection and presentation of maps for the volumes. He has also helped in many other ways to ensure that these volumes were completed.

LIST OF ABBREVIATIONS

A	Arnold
ADM	Admiralty
AH	Artificial Horizon
Alt	Altitude
Amp	Amplitude (an arc of the horizon from true east or west)
App or Appt	Apparent
Az	Azimuth (angular distance from north or south point of horizon)
Barom	Barometer
Bearing Book	United Kingdom Hydrographic Office, Ministry of Defence Archives, Taunton, 'Bearings taken on board His Majesty's ship *Investigator* whilst exploring the coasts of Terra Australis; by Matthew Flinders, Commander, 1801, 2, and 3', Data Book 22
BL	British Library
CO	Colonial Office
Com or Comp	Complement
Cor	Correction
CUL	Cambridge University Library
cwt	Hundredweight, equal to 112 lb or 50.8 kg
DR	Dead Reckoning
E	Earnshaw
E^t	East
fms	Fathoms
h	Hours
HRA	Frederick Watson, ed., *Historical Records of Australia*, Sydney, 1914–25
HRNSW	F. M. Bladen, ed., *Historical Records of New South Wales*, Sydney, 1892–1901
Ins	Inches
LL or LL^b	Lower limb
ML	Mitchell Library, Sydney
NLA	National Library of Australia, Canberra
NMM	National Maritime Museum, Greenwich
obs	Observed
OED	*Oxford English Dictionay*
P	Parallax
QLD	Queensland
R	Ramsden [instrument by], or Refraction
Rough Journal	Mitchell Library, Sydney, Matthew Flinders Papers, Private Journal of Matthew Flinders, 2 vols.

Semid	Semi-diameter
SLV	State Library of Victoria, Melbourne
Sup or Supp	Supplement
TK	Timekeeper
Ther	Thermometer
T	Troughton
TNA	The National Archives, Kew
UKHO	United Kingdom Hydrographic Office, Ministry of Defence Archives, Taunton
UL or L^b	Upper limb
Var	Variation
VOC	Vereenigde Oostindische Compagnie ['United East India Company' = the Dutch East India Company]

Symbols

☉   Sun or Sunday
☽   Moon upper limb, or Monday
☾   Moon lower limb
♂   Mars, or Tuesday
☿   Mercury, or Wednesday
♃   Jupiter, or Thursday
♀   Venus, or Friday
♄   Saturn, or Saturday
✳   Star
⚓   Anchor, or anchorage
☌   Conjunction

Weights and Measures

Foot	=	30.48 centimetres
Gallon	=	4.55 litres
Inch	=	2.54 centimetres
Mile	=	1.61 kilometres
Ounce	=	28.35 grams
Pint	=	0.55 litres
Pound	=	453.59 grams
Ton	=	1,015.87 kilograms
Yard	=	91.44 centimetres

GLOSSARY

Backstays: Long ropes leading aft from the mastheads and supporting the masts against the forward thrust of the sails.

Baricoes: Small casks for use in ships, often to carry water.

Beam compass: A compass with a beam and sliding sockets or cursors (also called trammel points) for drawing and dividing circles larger than those made by regular compasses. It can be used to make measurements by rotating each point 180° until the desired measurement is reached.

Binnacle: A wooden case or box containing the compass.

Bitts: Strong posts of oak fixed upright in the fore part of a ship and bolted securely to the beams to fasten the cables as a ship rides at anchor.

Boatswain: The officer who superintends the ship's sails, rigging, canvas, anchors, cables and cordage.

Booms: Spaces where spare spars are stowed.

Bowers: Anchors carried at the bow and in constant working use.

Braces: Ropes secured to the yards and used to square or traverse them horizontally.

Breechings: Heavy ropes shackled to the side of a vessel to secure the carriages of cannon.

Bridle: The upper end of a fixed mooring laid in a harbour.

Cable tier: The part of the ship (in the hold or between decks) where the cables were coiled away.

Carronades: Short, smoothbore cast iron cannons.

Chain-plate bolts: The bolts at the lower end of the chain plate, which fasten it to the vessel's side.

Clinch: The attachment of a cable to the ring of an anchor by a half hitch with the end stopped back to its own part by seizings.

Close reef: The last reefs of the sails being taken in.

Courses: The lowest square sail on each mast.

Coxswain: The helmsman of a boat, also in charge of its crew.

Cross-jack yard: The lower yard on the mizzen mast of a square-rigged ship.

Crosstree: One of two horizontal timber crosspieces at the upper ends of the lower masts.

Cutter: A ship's boat pulling four to six oars and with one or two lugsails.

Dredge: A drag-net consisting of a bag supported by an iron frame.

Ducks: Light clothes worn by sailors in warm climates.

Eye-bolt: An iron bolt driven into a timber or beam with an eye in the protruding end to which ropes or tackles can be fastened.

Flood tide: The incoming or rising tide.

Forehold: The part of the hold before the fore hatchway.

Fore topmast head: The upper part of the fore topmast, to which the heel of the fore topgallant mast is secured.

Foretopsail: Topsails set on the foremast.

Futtock: A curved timber that forms a rib in the frame of a ship.

Gig: A light ship's boat, usually reserved for use by the captain.

Grapnel: A small anchor with three or four arms.

Ground tier: The lowest tier of water casks in a vessel's hold.

Gun tackle: A purchase formed of a single sheave block and a double sheave block used to haul a muzzle-loading gun back out through its port after it had been fired and reloaded.

Half pike: A short pike used to repel boarders.

Haliards: The ropes or tackles used to hoist or lower a sail or yard.

Hand lead: A cylinder of lead with a hollow in the base, attached to a line about 25 fathoms in length with strips of leather and different cloths twisted into the strands at intervals, used to take soundings in shallow water.

Hawse: The part of a vessel's bow in which the hawseholes are cut.

Hawsehole: A smooth cylindrical aperture in the bow through which the anchor cable is passed.

Hawsers: Thick cables or ropes used in mooring or towing ships.

Hogshead: One of several units of measure used for wine or other commodities. The number of gallons of wine in a hogshead varied according to the type of wine.

Iron knees: Timbers or metal brackets fashioned into an angle to provide strengthening and support at the junction of major components (especially frames and deck beams) in a wooden vessel.

Jews harp: The shackle for joining a chain-cable to the anchor ring.

Jib: A triangular staysail set ahead of the foremast.

Jib boom: A spar used to extend the length of the bowsprit. The higher and fore-end of the flying jib boom is the foremost extent of a ship.

Junk: Pieces of old cordage.

Kedge: A light anchor used for warping a vessel.

Larboard: The left side of a ship when one is facing the bow.

Leadsman: The person heaving the lead line in taking soundings.

Lee tide: A tidal stream which runs in the same direction as the wind is blowing, forcing a ship to leeward of the intended track.

Lodging knees: Right-angled wooden brackets fixed at the junctions of beams and the timbers of the hull.

Log board: A board comprising two parts closing together like a book. The direction of the wind and the course of the ship during each hour of the day and night were entered in its columns and transferred to the logbook.

Log ship: A piece of wood about 6 inches across secured at two corners to the end of the log-line.

Long guns: A longer cannon than the carronade.

Lower yards: The yards permanently fixed in position at the top of the lower masts.

Lugger: A small sailing vessel with lugsails (four-cornered sails) set on two or more masts.

Mainsail: The principal and lowest sail on the main mast of a vessel.

Messenger: A large cable-laid rope with its ends lashed together to form a loop which is passed round the capstan and secured to the cable with nippers (q.v.) to heave up the anchor.

Mizen topsail: A square sail on the mizen mast.

Muskets: Smooth-bore weapons firing round balls.

Musquetoon: Shorter-barrelled version of the musket, particularly used by navies.

Nipper: A short length of rope used to secure an anchor cable to the messenger.

Petty officers: Officers equivalent in rank to a sergeant or corporal, whose status lay between commissioned and warrant officers, on the one hand, and the ordinary seamen, on the other.

Plain sails: The sails normally carried in ordinary weather.

Points: Short lengths of line attached to a sail in order to reef or reduce the area of the sail by securing them round the yard.

Preventer: Any rope used as an additional stay for standing or running rigging, or used to limit the movement of some fitting or spar.

Quarter deck: A raised deck behind the main mast of a sailing ship.

Riders: Timbers laid to bind a ship and give additional strength.

Riggers: Men employed on ships to fit the standing and running rigging, or to dismantle them.

Rounding of the cables: The winding of old ropes round the part of a cable lying in the hawse to prevent it chafing.

Royals: Light sails spread immediately above the top-gallant sails.

Running rigging: Moving as opposed to static rigging, used for raising, lowering and adjusting the sails.

Seine: A large fishing-net forming a bag with the upper end buoyed and the lower end weighted.

Sheet anchor: A large extra bower anchor always ready for immediate use in an emergency.

Shroud: Standing rigging running from masthead to ship's side and supporting a mast laterally.

Sinnet: Braided cordage.

Six pounders: Cannons using shot weighing 6 lb.

Sleepers: Heavy floor timbers in a ship's bottom.

Sliding keel: Retractable keel to prevent drifting to leeward.

Spanker: A gaff-rigged fore-and-aft sail, usually the aftermost sail of a ship.

Spar: Any mast, yard or boom.

Splinter netting: Rope net rigged for protection from falling masts and yards.

Station bills: These bills summarized the duties of the personnel on board ship. They were usually posted in the crew's quarters so that individuals could check their tasks. The station bill was often referred to as the muster roll.

Staysails: Fore-and-aft (usually triangular) rigged sails.

Stemson: A piece of curved timber bolted to the stem and keelson at their junction near the bow of a wooden vessel.

Stern chases: Cannons mounted in the stern of the ship.

Stern post: A vertical timber on the after end of the keel on which the rudder is mounted.

Stoppers: Lengths of rope belayed at one end and used to take the strain off a loaded cable so that the part thus no longer under tension can be handled freely.

Streams: Anchors carried at the stern and used in narrow channels where there is no room for the ship to swing with the tide.

Studding sails: Fine weather sails set outside the square sails.

Supplement: The supplement was the amount by which an angle was less than 180°, and was normally calculated from a second observation as a check on the first.

Sweeps: Long oars used in calm seas.

Swivels: Small cannon mounted on a pivot and swivelled by hand to bear on the enemy.

Taffrel: The upper part of a ship's stern timbers.

Tier: The compartment below decks where cable and rope were stored.

Top gallant mast: The third mast above the deck.

Topsail: A square sail rigged above the course and below the topgallant sail.

Topsail yard: A yard used to spread the head of a topsail and the foot of a topgallant sail.

Trawl heads: Iron fittings on the ends of the trawl beam.

Tree nails: Cylindrical pins driven through the sides and bottom of a vessel to secure and bind her planking and timbers together.

Turn: One passage of a rope around a fitting.

Tye: A thick rope for hoisting a yard to set the sail.

Wad: Old rope yarn rolled into a ball and rammed in to hold shot in place in the gun barrel.

Warp: To move a ship into position by hauling on a rope fastened to a buoy or anchor.

Warrant officers: A disparate group of literate professionals in the Navy, holding a warrant from the Navy Board, with specialist functions such as purser, master, chaplain or surgeon.

Wear ship: To alter course by turning away from the wind.

Whaleboat: A wooden boat, pointed at both ends, normally between 26 and 56 feet (about 8–18 metres) in length, originally designed for chasing whales, but often carried on survey ships for exploring areas of coastline or shallow water.

Woomera: A throwing-stick used by Aborigines to increase the speed of a spear when it is hurled.

INTRODUCTION

This edition provides the first annotated published account of Matthew Flinders's fair journals in HMS *Investigator* during his circumnavigation of Australia between 1801 and 1803. This was one of the most notable voyages of exploration undertaken by a British navigator, and, at the time, it was the most comprehensive survey ever made of Australia's coastline. Flinders, aided by a party of scientific gentlemen, proved that Australia was a continent, added considerably to geographical and hydrographical knowledge of Australian shores, islands and waters, and contributed significantly to the extension of knowledge about Australia's animals, flora and fauna. Flinders's voyage, and his Australian survey, was unfortunately cut short by misfortune. In August 1803 the *Investigator* reached Port Jackson after an anti-clockwise voyage around Australia only to be deemed unseaworthy. Flinders and some of his crew were transferred to another vessel, the *Porpoise*, which was wrecked off the coast of what is now Queensland a few weeks after it had sailed northward from Port Jackson. Flinders returned to Port Jackson in a cutter, negotiated for the use of another vessel, and proceeded northward in the *Cumberland* to rescue his shipmates. Having achieved that goal, he sent some crew back to Port Jackson but sailed with others through Torres Strait and back towards England. He hoped the Admiralty would provide another vessel to enable him to return to Australia to complete his survey. That never happened. Further misfortune befell Flinders, including six and a half years' detention at the Ile de France between 1803 and 1810.[1] After he finally returned to England in late 1810, he wrote his magnum opus on his voyage. Entitled *A Voyage to Terra Australis,* this comprised two large volumes and an atlas. It was published in 1814 a few days before Flinders's death from a severe bladder complaint at the age of forty.[2]

The fair journals, transcribed and annotated in these volumes, were compiled from Flinders's rough journals in the *Investigator*. These manuscripts, other documents compiled by Flinders, and associated logs and journals by others on board the ship, are described in the textual introduction. Flinders's fair journals are the most comprehensive of these documents. They are the best surviving record of his daily observations on the voyage and include a fair amount of detail that was summarized in *A Voyage to Terra Australis*. But additional material appears in the journals that is not replicated in the published voyage account. This is particularly the case with the detailed astronomical data and with the extensive 'additional remarks' and 'general remarks' that Flinders appended to most of his daily entries. To understand the progress and the achievements

---

[1] Flinders's life and career are the subject of many books, including Scott, *The Life of Matthew Flinders*; Mack, *Matthew Flinders*; Ingleton, *Matthew Flinders*; Estensen, *The Life of Matthew Flinders*; and Morgan, *Matthew Flinders*.

[2] Estensen, *The Life of Matthew Flinders*, p. 470. For the most authoritative analysis of the medical symptoms of Flinders's final illness, see Milazzo, 'Flinders' Last Illness', pp. 506–11.

of the voyage, one needs to consult the fair journals, the rough journals and *A Voyage to Terra Australis*, along with the other primary documents referred to in the textual introduction. As far as ships' logs and journals are concerned, only the fair journals in the *Investigator* are included in this edition. The journals of the *Porpoise* and *Cumberland* are not reproduced because they contributed very little to Flinders's nautical survey of Australia's coasts and offshore islands. But one other substantial document is transcribed and edited for the first time. This is a 'Memoir' written by Flinders during his captivity at the Ile de France. This document includes detailed navigational and astronomical data directly related to Flinders's charts and to his fair journals. It is included in these volumes because of the light it throws on Flinders's professional methods.

1.   Background to the Voyage

Matthew Flinders (1774–1814) was born into a solid, respectable, middle-class family in the small market town of Donington, Lincolnshire. His father, also called Matthew, was a doctor who served as the town's general practitioner and, as was common in the eighteenth century, as a 'man mid-wife'.[1] His mother gave birth to ten children, of whom five were living at the time of her death from nervous weakness in 1783. Dr Flinders remarried soon afterwards to a widow, Elizabeth Ellis, with whom he had two daughters.[2] Dr Flinders was keen that his son should be educated for a professional career, preferably following in his own footsteps. Accordingly, he sent Matthew to local schools where he studied Latin, mathematics and grammar. Matthew became a keen reader, and was particularly fascinated by the maritime atmosphere of Defoe's *Robinson Crusoe*.[3] His father purchased books for him to study arithmetic, geometry, trigonometry, geography, astronomy and navigation.[4]

Though none of his family came from a maritime background, Matthew Flinders decided as a teenager that he wished to pursue a naval career. In 1789 he left his father, stepmother and the rest of his close-knit family in Lincolnshire to take up his first naval position. This was acquired through the patronage of Thomas Pasley, a frigate captain, via an introduction by Flinders's cousin Henrietta, a young governess in the Pasley household.[5] In 1790–91 Flinders learned about seamanship and the routines of shipboard life, working mainly at Chatham dockyard and on shore. Pasley recommended Flinders to William Bligh (of the *Bounty*) who was about to embark on a second voyage to transport breadfruit from Tahiti to the Caribbean (as a potential staple food for plantation slaves). Flinders set sail with Bligh in the *Providence* on 3 August 1791. The voyage, which delivered breadfruit to St Vincent and Jamaica, lasted exactly two years. Flinders kept a detailed journal, and learned much about navigation and nautical surveying from Bligh. During the voyage, Flinders gained first-hand acquaintance of the

---

[1] Information on the medical work of Dr Flinders is presented in Beardsley and Bennett, eds, *'Gratefull to Providence'*; Burnby, 'The Flinders Family', pp. 51–2; Burnby, 'Some Flinders Family History', pp. 61–6; and Loudon, *Medical Care and the General Practitioner*, pp. 94–5, 102–9.

[2] Beardsley and Bennett, eds, *'Gratefull to Providence'*, I, pp. 136, 143; Burnby, 'The Flinders Family', p. 58.

[3] Clarke, 'Biographical Memoir of Captain Matthew Flinders', p. 178.

[4] Scott, *The Life of Matthew Flinders*, pp. 11–13.

[5] Ibid., pp. 13–14.

challenges of navigating Australian waters. He encountered the trials and tribulations of sailing through Torres Strait for the first time, and helped Bligh with his chart of the strait.[1] Flinders drew a chart to accompany his log on the voyage. This was entitled 'A Chart of the Passage between New Holland and New Guinea as seen in His Majesty's ship Providence in 1792'.[2]

After completing the voyage in the *Providence*, Flinders was invited by Pasley to join the third-rate warship *Bellerophon*, of which he was commander. Flinders enlisted on 7 September 1793 as an able seaman. He was upgraded to midshipman in less than a month. The vessel joined the Channel Fleet to protect Britain against France during the revolutionary wars. In 1794 Flinders participated in his only naval battle. This was the famous Glorious First of June, a sea battle that raged for a week before a British victory was secured. Pasley, now a Rear-Admiral of the Blue, had a leg blown off by French cannon fire during the engagement. Flinders recorded in his journal a detailed account of the engagements with the French fleet, and drew six perpendicular views of the British and French fleets in different positions. Flinders arrived home in June 1794, with hopes of further advancement in his career to a naval lieutenant.[3]

At the age of twenty, Flinders had assumed the main physical characteristics of his young adulthood. Some of his particular features were recorded on a pro forma filled in by a family member after his death. This noted that Flinders was a 'slight and active' man of pale complexion, around 5 feet 7 inches tall, with dark hair and dark-brown eyes. He displayed 'extreme energy & activity', and had 'very keen senses & observation'.[4] Isabella Tyler, the half-sister of Flinders's future wife, noted that the navigator's figure was 'well proportioned', and that he had 'a light and buoyant step. His chin rather projecting. His lips thin & compressed, nose inclining to aquiline' and 'eyes commanding, amounting at times to sternness'. His manner was pleasant and cheerful.[5] Neither the pro forma nor the biographical sketch provided details on Flinders's penchant for maritime discovery, but the navigator's own words filled the gap. Flinders was ambitious to join a voyage that would enable him to travel on the oceans; as he himself expressed it, he was 'led by his passion for exploring new countries, to embrace the opportunity of going out upon a station, which of all others, presented the most ample field for his favourite pursuit'.[6]

Through a friendship with Henry Waterhouse, who had been first lieutenant in the *Bellerophon*, Flinders was appointed senior master's mate on the *Reliance*, which was taking a new governor, John Hunter, out to the fledgling colony of New South Wales.[7] He was expected to serve on ships based in Port Jackson for four or five years. He thought

---

[1] This is a well-documented voyage. Among the secondary sources that describe Flinders's role on this expedition are Darby, 'Bligh's Disciple', pp. 401–11, and Salmond, *Bligh*, pp. 224–5. Flinders's writings on the voyage include TNA, ADM 55/97–8, Flinders, Log in the *Providence*, and NMM, Flinders Papers FLI/8/A, Portion of a Journal on HMS *Providence*.

[2] This is deposited at NMM, Flinders Papers, FLI/15/1.

[3] Estensen, *The Life of Matthew Flinders*, pp. 33–5; NMM, Flinders Papers, FLI/8/B, Journal in the *Bellerophon*, 7 September 1793–15 July 1794, ff. 32v–33r, 35r; Willis, *The Glorious First of June*, pp. 147, 155, 161, 165, 178, 190.

[4] These quotations are taken from a completed pro forma in Galton's *Record of Family Faculties* reproduced in Russell, 'Flinders Re-Visited', p. 7.

[5] NMM, Flinders Papers, FLI/107, Isabella Tyler, 'Biographical Outline of Captain and Mrs Flinders', 1852.

[6] Flinders, *A Voyage to Terra Australis*, I, p. xcvi.

[7] Estensen, *The Life of Matthew Flinders*, pp. 38–9.

he would have a better chance of promotion than if he stayed in the home service, as he was the oldest petty officer in the *Reliance*.[1] Flinders was embarking for the last of the world's habitable continents to be explored by Europeans. *Terra Australis Incognita* – the unknown southern land – had formed part of the imaginative world of geographers and philosophers since ancient times. Portuguese and Spanish navigators in the sixteenth century had sailed across the Pacific from Peru in search of a large continent in the southern hemisphere but they did not reach Australia. The first known landfall in Australia was by the Dutch sailor Willem Janszoon on the 66-foot-long *Duyfken* in 1606; he touched at the Cape York peninsula.[2] His compatriot Abel Janszoon Tasman made two voyages in 1642 and 1644 to determine whether Australia (which he named New Holland) was part of a large southern land. On his first voyage, he discovered and named Van Diemen's Land – modern Tasmania – though he did not realize it was an island. The second voyage was devoted to mapping and charting the north-west Australian coast.[3]

Landfalls by other Dutch and English voyagers became more common in the later seventeenth century. But these did not lead to any plans for a colonial settlement in New Holland. Indeed, the English buccaneer and adventurer William Dampier warned against settlement in Western Australia owing to the arid conditions there. This was based on his brief landfall in the *Cygnet* at King Sound, north-west Australia, in January 1688.[4] During the eighteenth century, European interest in *Terra Australis* was influenced by the scientific curiosity of the Enlightenment; but this progressed slowly up to 1770. Enlightenment thinking emphasized human progress via greater discovery of the globe. Scientific curiosity and maritime exploration together stimulated the expansion of geographical, botanical, zoological and ethnographical knowledge. Britain and France were at the forefront of voyages of discovery to the Pacific after 1750 through the work of the Royal Society in London, the patronage of Sir Joseph Banks for collectors of new knowledge, and the Admiralty's and Board of Longitude's interest in oceanic exploration.[5] Nevertheless, by the late 1760s the framework of knowledge about Australia had not progressed significantly since the time of Dampier.[6]

Britain established a stronger interest in Australia in the wake of James Cook's first great voyage of exploration to the Pacific. On the voyage of the *Endeavour*, Cook spent eight days at Botany Bay and Sydney harbour. He then sailed up the east coast of Australia, landing on Possession Island off the northern tip of the Cape York peninsula on 22 August 1770, when he claimed the land he had explored and charted for Britain. New South Wales was his name for this territory. Banks sailed with Cook, and was favourably impressed with the prospects for settlement in and around Botany Bay. Cook never returned to the Australian mainland on his two subsequent Pacific voyages, and the British government did not quickly follow up the claim to New South Wales with a further expedition or attempt at settlement. Matters changed considerably, however,

[1] Beardsley and Bennett, eds, *'Gratefull to Providence'*, II, pp. 141–2.

[2] Burningham, 'Duyfken: Charting a Sea of Misconceptions'.

[3] Sharp, *The Voyages of Abel Janszoon Tasman*.

[4] Marchant, *An Island unto Itself*, pp. 72–3.

[5] For a summary of these developments, see Morgan, *Australia*, pp. 8–9. Detailed treatments include Wood, *The Discovery of Australia*; Eisler, *The Furthest Shore*; Estensen, *Discovery*; and Powell, *Northern Voyages*, pp. 11–36.

[6] Williams, 'New Holland to New South Wales', p. 140, and Williams, 'From Dampier to Cook', pp. 12–23.

after the end of the American War of Independence in 1783. With prisons and hulks full of convicted felons and with no obvious or available place to send them into exile, the government of the Younger Pitt eventually decided to establish a convict colony in New South Wales. Banks played a significant part in persuading the government that this was an appropriate place for settling a colony. Whether the British government established the Botany Bay colony primarily to dump convicts as far away from Britain as possible, or whether they had commercial or strategic motives for settling a colony in Australia, is still disputed by historians. Whatever the mixture of reasons, the first fleet of eleven naval vessels carrying convicts guarded by marines set sail from Portsmouth in May 1787 and arrived in Sydney harbour on 26 January 1788. The colony they established there was the destination for Flinders's forthcoming voyage in the *Reliance* in the summer of 1794.[1]

Flinders's stay in Port Jackson between 1795 and 1800 was divided between essential naval duties he was required to carry out on the *Reliance* and opportunities for exploration. With Governor Hunter's support, Flinders and his friend George Bass, a surgeon who had also sailed in the *Reliance* to Port Jackson, had the chance to explore the coast of New South Wales. In late October 1795 Flinders and Bass took a small craft called the *Tom Thumb* – only about 9–10 feet long – on a short expedition of nine days from Port Jackson towards Botany Bay. They then explored the inland course of George's River for twenty miles.[2] Flinders and Bass followed up this short excursion with another voyage in a second craft called the *Tom Thumb*, not more than 12 feet long. This expedition (from 25 March to 1 April 1796) sailed south from Port Jackson as far as the Martin Isles, located off modern Port Kembla.[3] Flinders's charts of the area covered in the second *Tom Thumb* voyage indicated his ability in preparing graphic illustrations. They were sent back to England along with a recent topographical plan prepared by Charles Grimes, the Deputy Surveyor General of New South Wales. These were combined and published in London on 12 March 1799 by the private cartographer Aaron Arrowsmith as *A Topographical Plan of the Settlement of New South Wales, Including Port Jackson, Botany Bay and Broken Bay. Surveyed by Messrs Grimes and Flinders – Communicated by Lt. Col. Paterson of the New South Wales Corps*.[4] This engraved map was the first separately issued publication to show the spread of settlement in Sydney and the first published chart by Flinders.

Governor Hunter dispatched Bass in an open whaleboat to sail southwards from Port Jackson on a voyage intended to determine whether, as was suspected, a strait existed off the south-eastern end of New South Wales. Maps then in use showed Van Diemen's Land joined to the mainland.[5] But if a strait existed, ships sailing along Australia's southern coast would shorten the sea route to Port Jackson by nearly 700 miles because they would no longer need to follow a track around the southern end of Van Diemen's Land.[6] Flinders was unable to join this expedition owing to his duties on the *Reliance*. Bass

---

[1] Morgan, *Australia*, pp. 10, 13–14.

[2] Estensen, *The Life of Matthew Flinders*, pp. 52–3; Sprod, ed., *Van Diemen's Land Revealed*, p. 7; Bowden, ed., *Matthew Flinders' Narrative of Tom Thumb's Cruise to Canoe Rivulet*, p. 1.

[3] King, 'Bass and Flinders and the Voyages of the two "Tom Thumbs"', p. 83.

[4] Estensen, *The Life of Matthew Flinders*, pp. 60–61. For an online digital version of the map, see www.nla.gov.au/apps/cdview/?pi=nla.map-rm711.

[5] Tooley, *The Mapping of Australia*, p. xiii.

[6] Estensen, *The Life of George Bass*, pp. 115–16.

was therefore dispatched by Hunter with six volunteers and six weeks' provisions to undertake the voyage, which lasted from 3 December 1797 until 25 February 1798. Bass and his party examined Twofold Bay, discovered Western Port, and found that Jervis Bay appeared to be the best harbour between Port Jackson and Western Port.[1] Bass sailed through Bass Strait, though at the time he did not know for certain that that was the case. In *A Voyage to Terra Australis*, Flinders paid tribute to the achievements of Bass on this whaleboat voyage, noting that his friend had sailed along 600 miles of coast in a small boat 'exposed to the buffeting of an open sea' and had returned in 'no doubt about the existence of a wide strait separating Van Diemen's Land from New South Wales'.[2]

While Bass was on his whaleboat voyage, Flinders volunteered to join the *Francis* on a voyage from Port Jackson to rescue the survivors and cargo of the *Sydney Cove*, a merchant vessel in a sinking condition that had run on to a beach near Preservation Island in Bass Strait.[3] After returning from this expedition and conferring with Bass after his return from the whaleboat voyage, Flinders reported to Hunter his discovery of the Kent Group of islands and his hydrographical surveying of the Furneaux Group. Flinders drafted the first sketch to delineate modern Victoria's shoreline from the eastern entrance of Bass Strait to Western Port. He incorporated Bass's whaleboat material into his sketch plan, at Hunter's request, but gave due credit to Bass.[4] Hunter considered that proof of the existence of Bass Strait was a matter of some importance. He informed Banks of his long-held belief that Van Diemen's Land was an island.[5] Hunter promptly fitted out the sloop *Norfolk* under Flinders's command, with Bass on board, to ascertain whether the strait existed. The *Norfolk* was a vessel of 25 tons, some 35 feet in length and 11 feet in the beam. Flinders was supplied with a theodolite, azimuth compass and brass sextant, but he was not given a chronometer. Twelve weeks were allocated for the expedition.[6]

The voyage of the *Norfolk* lasted from 7 October 1798 until 11 January 1799. Flinders and Bass both wrote journals on the voyage. Many geographical features they encountered had not been seen by previous navigators.[7] The voyage's main achievements were to circumnavigate Van Diemen's Land for the first time, proving beyond doubt that it was an island, and to confirm that an extensive strait separated New South Wales from Van Diemen's Land. Flinders and Bass examined Port Dalrymple and the Tamar Estuary, in the northern part of Van Diemen's Land. They also sailed into the Derwent River, on

[1] Ibid., pp. 79–91; Cole and Cole, *Mr Bass's Western Port*; Bass's journal of the whaleboat voyage in Bladen, ed., *HRNSW*, III, pp. 312–33.

[2] Flinders, *A Voyage to Terra Australis*, I, p. cxix. This and other voyages through Bass Strait are illuminated on the map 'Early Navigators of Bass Strait 1770–1803' at www.anzmaps.org/publications.

[3] Henderson, *Maritime Archaeology in Australia*, pp. 41–3.

[4] Flinders, 'Narrative of an Expedition to the Furneauxs Islands', pp. 12–13; Aurosseau, 'Flinders' Voyage in the Francis', p. 112.

[5] ML, Banks Papers, series 38.09, Hunter to Banks, 25 July 1798.

[6] Estensen, *The Life of Matthew Flinders*, pp. 72–3.

[7] Flinders's original journal of this voyage is no longer extant. A clerical copy of the journal is available in manuscript at ML. The journal (Flinders, 'Narrative of the Expedition of the Colonial Sloop *Norfolk*') has been published in Bladen, ed., *HRNSW*, III, pp. 769–818, and, along with Bass's journal (Bass, 'Journal ... from notes made on board the Colonial Sloop *Norfolk* in 1798 and 1799'), in Sprod, ed., *Van Diemen's Land Revealed*, pp. 23–106. Flinders later published a revised account of the *Norfolk*'s circumnavigation of Van Diemen's Land in *A Voyage to Terra Australis*, I, pp. cxxxviii–cxciii.

the southern side of the island, reaching the site of what is now Hobart. Flinders and Bass produced a joint sketch of Bass Strait.[1] On Flinders's recommendation, Governor Hunter gave the strait its name in honour of Bass's whaleboat voyage. It was originally called 'Bass's Strait', but soon became known as Bass Strait.[2]

Flinders knew that much of Australia's southern coast from Western Port westwards to King George Sound had yet to be explored. He thought the discovery of Bass Strait would encourage further voyages to identify bights and places of shelter along that coast. Proving that Bass Strait existed was the most important geographical discovery in Australian waters since the days of Cook. News of Flinders's and Bass's voyaging there was well received by Governor Hunter in Port Jackson and, eventually, by Banks in Britain.[3] Bass and Flinders parted company after the voyage in the *Norfolk*. Bass transferred his employment from being a naval surgeon to assisting the merchant Charles Bishop in his commercial trade between New South Wales and China.[4] Flinders, for his part, undertook a further short voyage in the *Norfolk* (8 July–21 August 1799) to explore coastal parts of northern New South Wales.[5] Flinders and Bass, having been good friends, went their separate ways; they never met again.[6]

Flinders publicized the circumnavigation of Van Diemen's Land in a pamphlet entitled *Observations on the Coasts of Van Diemen's Land, on Bass's Strait and its islands, and on Parts of the Coast of New South Wales: intended to accompany the charts of the late discoveries in those countries*. This was published in 1801 with a dedication to Banks, applauding his zealous promotion of nautical and geographical knowledge. It was accompanied by three charts, including a chart of Van Diemen's Land and Bass Strait that the London map engraver Aaron Arrowsmith had already published separately on 16 June 1800. Flinders and Arrowsmith were agreed that advances in the geographical knowledge of Australia had to be based on verifiable information derived from fieldwork and exploration: only reputable sources could be trusted to produce accurate maps, and all conjectural information should be disregarded.[7] This jointly-held view informed Flinders's circumnavigation of Australia in the *Investigator*.

In London, Banks had been hoping to support a major voyage to explore more of the unknown coasts of New Holland. This might locate large rivers that could be navigated into the interior of Australia, and locate objects of commerce to benefit the mother country.[8] He recommended that Flinders – 'A Countryman of mine, a Man of activity

---

[1] UKHO, Matthew Flinders and George Bass, 'Parts between New South Wales and Van Diemen's Land'. For a reproduction of, and commentary on, the sketch, see Cole and Cole, *Mr Bass's Western Port*, pp. 62–4.

[2] Flinders, *A Voyage to Terra Australis*, I, p. 119.

[3] Scott, *The Life of Matthew Flinders*, p. 102.

[4] Estensen, *The Life of George Bass*, pp. 93, 95, 121–2.

[5] For a descriptive account of this voyage, see Collins, *An Account of the English Colony in New South Wales*, II, pp. 225–63. For Flinders's journal for this voyage, see ML, Matthew Flinders, Journal in the *Norfolk* sloop, 1799, MS C211/2. A digitized version of the manuscript and a transcript are available online at http://acms.sl.news.gov.au/transcript/2012/D14130/a002.html#a002009. See also Smith, 'Matthew Flinders and the North Coast of New South Wales', pp. 163–8.

[6] Estensen, *The Life of Matthew Flinders*, pp. 91–2.

[7] Verner, 'The Arrowsmith Firm', pp. 1–7. The Arrowsmith charts are *A Chart of Bass's Strait and Van Dieman's Land* (1800) and *A Chart of Bass's Strait between New South Wales and Van Diemen's Land* (1801). See also Faden, *Chart of Bass's Strait*.

[8] Mackay, 'In the Shadow of Cook', p. 106.

& information, who is already there' – should be entrusted with the command of such a vessel.[1] Philip Gidley King, a former naval captain, friend of Banks, and subsequently third governor of New South Wales, also suggested to Banks that Flinders would be a suitable commander for a surveying voyage in Australian waters.[2] In a letter to Banks, Governor Hunter, himself an accomplished hydrographical surveyor, had praised Flinders's maritime surveying in New South Wales.[3] While he was still in Port Jackson, Flinders knew such a voyage under his command was contemplated: 'We are now given to understand,' he wrote to a friend on 17 January 1800, 'that it is the contemplation of Government to send out one or two vessels to carry on the examination of this still immense ('still immense' even when Van Diemen's Land was found to be separated) Island, the command of which, report has given to me'.[4]

Flinders was near the end of his duties in New South Wales when he wrote this letter. On 3 March 1800 he sailed in the *Reliance* back to England after an absence of five and a half years. Shortly after arriving at Portsmouth, Flinders wrote a bold letter to Banks, whom he knew was the single most important person in London acting as a patron and conduit for voyages of exploration. Flinders's letter of 6 September 1800 – probably the most important one he ever wrote – referred to his charts of Van Diemen's Land and Bass Strait and discussed his work in surveying the coast of New South Wales. It emphasized the importance of a further, more ambitious voyage to promote British imperial and maritime interests and to extend knowledge of Australian geography and natural history. Flinders's letter also provided a knowledgeable account of how the exploration of the shores of New South Wales and New Holland should be completed.[5]

Flinders's letter referred to a conjecture that 'a still larger than Bass's Strait dismembers New Holland'.[6] This was a widely discussed idea at the time, stemming from distrust about the accuracy of maps depicting Australia: it was not based upon any prior, verifiable suggestion that a north–south strait split Australia in two. Governor King referred to the possible existence of such a strait to Banks and to Evan Nepean at the Admiralty.[7] Hunter had similarly referred to the possibility of a dividing strait running southwards from the Gulf of Carpentaria.[8] Flinders inserted the remark as an additional enticement to Banks's curiosity, for Banks was interested in finding a route into the interior of Australia. It has been argued that Flinders deliberately dangled a carrot to gain Banks's interest, while knowing that contemporary maps depicted a continuous coastline for Australia with no suggestion of a possible strait into the interior.[9] But one should not discount the widely-held belief that existing maps included errors. Though such a strait

[1] Banks to John King, 15 May 1798, in Chambers, ed., *The Indian and Pacific Correspondence*, IV, p. 502, and also in Watson, ed., *HRA*, series 1, II, pp. 231–2.

[2] Philip Gidley King to Banks, 20 March 1799, in Chambers, ed., *The Indian and Pacific Correspondence*, V, pp. 60–61.

[3] Hunter to Banks, 20 February 1800, in Chambers, ed., *The Indian and Pacific Correspondence*, V, p. 159.

[4] NMM, Flinders papers, FLI/08a, Flinders to Pulteney Malcolm, 17 January 1800.

[5] Flinders to Banks, 6 September 1800, in Brunton, ed., *Matthew Flinders*, pp. 50–52. Most of this letter is also transcribed in Mack, *Matthew Flinders*, pp. 43–5.

[6] Flinders to Banks, 6 September 1800, in Brunton, ed., *Matthew Flinders*, p. 51.

[7] Philip Gidley King to Banks, 28 September 1800, and to Nepean, 31 December 1800, in Bladen, ed., *HRNSW*, IV, pp. 207, 701.

[8] Hunter to Banks, 1 June 1799, in Chambers, ed., *The Indian and Pacific Correspondence*, V, pp. 85–8.

[9] Gerritsen, 'Getting the Strait Facts Straight', pp. 11–21.

was never found, the search for one leading to an inland sea preoccupied explorers of Australia until well into the nineteenth century.[1]

Flinders's letter to Banks was timely; it has been suggested that, without Banks's support, the proposal for an expedition to Australia stood little chance of being accepted.[2] Banks recommended Flinders as commander of the voyage by contacting Earl Spencer, the First Lord of the Admiralty.[3] A ship was soon found for the voyage and Banks began to draw up plans for appointing personnel for the expedition.[4] Between December 1800 and June 1801 Banks took the lead in recruiting men for the voyage, playing a significant role in the appointment of the scientific gentlemen. It was as a result of Banks's efforts that Robert Brown was engaged as botanist, Peter Good as gardener, Ferdinand Bauer as botanical artist and William Westall as landscape artist. Brown was connected with the Linnean Society in London, and became one of Banks's main protégés. Banks was attracted by Brown's enthusiasm for natural history. Good had previously worked on plants at Kew Gardens. Bauer, a gifted botanical artist, was the brother of Franz Bauer, whose work at Kew Gardens was known to Banks. Westall, the landscape and figure painter, was recommended to Banks by Benjamin West, the President of the Royal Academy. Banks also liaised with the Admiralty, the Navy Board, the Board of Longitude and the East India Company about the provisions, payments and astronomical and navigational equipment needed for the voyage. The only choice among the scientists for the *Investigator* that was not made by Banks was the astronomer John Crosley. He was selected by the Admiralty, on the advice of the Astronomer Royal.[5]

The intention was that the *Investigator* should survey Australia's coast and offshore islands and undertake a thorough investigation of botany, zoology and geology by a team of scientific gentlemen. Flinders himself was to oversee their work and to carry out detailed hydrographical surveys, charting and recording the progress of the voyage in journals. Flinders greatly appreciated Banks's 'zealous exertions to promote geographical and nautical knowledge', his 'encouragement of men employed in the cultivation of the sciences that tend to this improvement', and the countenance he had shown towards Flinders.[6] Banks, for his part, was delighted at Flinders's appointment to command the expedition. 'I give you sincere joy at the attainment of your wish in your appointment of Commander,' he wrote to Flinders. He added: 'I have long known that it was Certain, but I am glad it is now placed beyond the Reach of accident'.[7] Flinders was joined on the voyage by his younger brother Samuel Ward Flinders, who had previously accompanied him to New South Wales in the 1790s.[8]

---

[1] Cumpston, *The Inland Sea and the Great River*.

[2] Rigby, '"The whole of the surveying department rested on me"', p. 263.

[3] Banks to George John Spencer, [December 1800], in Chambers, ed., *The Letters of Sir Joseph Banks*, pp. 219–20.

[4] ML, Banks Papers, series 63.01 and 63.03, Memorandum written by Banks, 12 December 1800, and 'Original Establishment proposd [*sic*]', 12 December 1800.

[5] Morgan, 'Sir Joseph Banks and the *Investigator* expedition', pp. 235–64; CUL, Royal Greenwich Observatory, Board of Longitude Papers, RGO 35/55, Nevil Maskelyne to Banks, 23 January 1801.

[6] Quoted in Scott, *The Life of Matthew Flinders*, p. 123.

[7] Banks to Flinders, 19 February 1801, in Chambers, ed., *The Indian and Pacific Correspondence*, V, p. 279.

[8] Estensen, *The Life of Matthew Flinders*, pp. 109–10.

2. The *Investigator*

The *Investigator* was built as a collier at Monkwearmouth, near Sunderland, in County Durham in 1795 by Henry Rudd. Originally named the *Fram*, this vessel of 334 tons was 100 feet long, about 29 feet on the beam, with a draught of around 14 feet and 19 feet depth of hold. She was a three-masted, square-sterned ship built to ply the route from the north-eastern coalfields around East Anglia to London.[1] The Navy Board purchased the ship at Deptford in April 1798 and renamed her the *Xenophon*. The vessel was converted to an armed sloop.[2] This mainly involved building a gun deck beneath her main deck and cutting large gun ports in her sides. The gun ports were needed to hold twenty 32-pounder and two 18-pounder carronades. Over the next two years the *Xenophon* was deployed with the Channel Fleet on convoy escort duties in and out of the Nore. In late November 1800 the ship arrived at Sheerness with instructions for her defects to be repaired.[3]

Banks drew up a shortlist of possible new names for the *Xenophon* on this important voyage of discovery. One of his suggestions, the *Investigator*, was selected by the Admiralty, which, on 19 January 1801, ordered the Navy Board to prepare this vessel for an expedition to the southern hemisphere.[4] Deploying a converted collier for a voyage of discovery had famous precedents in the ships used by Cook for his voyages of Pacific exploration. To prepare the vessel for a long ocean voyage, copper sheathing took place, as was then becoming common in the navy, to protect the hull from being destroyed by the *teredo navalis*. As it was anticipated the load taken by the *Investigator* would weigh down the vessel in the water, an additional two planks were sheathed to cope with the weight of the extra stores. Flinders requested that this should be done after taking advice from Isaac Coffin, the resident naval commissioner at Sheerness.[5] Coffin oversaw the fitting out of the *Investigator*, dealing with her masts, spars, stores and guns.[6]

Whether the ship's timbers were properly caulked and checked for a long voyage is unknown, as there is little correspondence between the Sheerness dockyard and the Navy Board about the ship.[7] The repairs were undertaken swiftly, but it is possible that not all of the iron bolts and fittings were replaced with copper ones and that the vessel may have been coppered over rotten timbers.[8] After repairs were made, the *Investigator* was described in Admiralty records as 'fitting out for a voyage to remote parts'.[9] The

---

[1] Ashley, *The Indomitable Captain Matthew Flinders*, p. 21.

[2] TNA, ADM 180/23, Dimension Book, ff. 90, 113.

[3] TNA, ADM 2/293/484, Admiralty Out-Letters, Instructions to the Navy Board, 21 November 1800, and ADM 8/81, Admiralty List Book.

[4] Mackay, *In the Wake of Cook*, p. 3. For a detailed discussion of the ship, see Geeson and Sexton, 'H. M. Sloop *Investigator*', pp. 275–98.

[5] Geeson and Sexton, 'H.M. Sloop *Investigator*', p. 288.

[6] TNA, ADM 106/3556/71, 75, 82, 116, 117, Sheerness Yard letters, 1800–01.

[7] Rigby, '"Not at all a Particular Ship"', pp. 19–21; Ashley, *The Indomitable Captain Matthew Flinders*, pp. 21–6; Ingleton, 'Flinders as Cartographer', p. 67. Only two plans of the *Investigator* are known. These cover the gun and quarter decks: see NMM, Ship Plans 6223, box 66, I, and Figures 2 and 3 below (pp. 104, 140). There are no known pictures of the *Investigator*, but a model of the ship is displayed at the South Australian Maritime Museum. A detailed diagram showing a longitudinal section of the *Investigator* is included in Ingleton, *Matthew Flinders*, p. 430.

[8] Ashley, 'HMS Investigator – a "copper-bottomed" ship?', pp. 271–88; Ashley, *The Indomitable Captain Matthew Flinders*, pp. 23–4.

[9] TNA, ADM 8/81, Admiralty List Book.

Investigator carried a launch, two cutters, a gig and a whaleboat for exploration of inlets, rivers and creeks along the shoreline of Terra Australis. It carried eighteen 32-pounder carronades and two 18-pound guns for chase.[1] Flinders had reservations about the suitability of the *Investigator* for its voyage of exploration. Before the voyage began, as he was about to sail the ship from Spithead to Portsmouth harbour, he noted that she 'does not appear to be a strong ship, and I fear the taking her into dock in her present deep state may tend to make her weaker'.[2]

3. The Instructions for the Voyage

The Admiralty's orders for the voyage closely followed the recommendations originally made by Banks. Flinders was instructed to make 'a complete examination and survey' of the coast of New Holland. The *Investigator* was to sail along the south coast of Australia, putting in at King George Sound if necessary for refreshments and water, and to proceed along 130° east of longitude to Bass Strait and from thence to Sydney Cove. After refitting the ship, taking on board fresh provisions and consulting the governor of New South Wales about the best means of surveying the coast, Flinders was to begin the survey by sailing in a clockwise direction from Port Jackson, back through Bass Strait. Flinders was to have the use of the *Lady Nelson* as a tender. This vessel had already been sent from London to Port Jackson specifically for use in coastal exploration there.[3] Flinders was given the option of surveying the south coast either by proceeding westward to King George Sound or to sail to that location and return eastward along the southern coast to undertake the survey. The whole of the coast was to be examined for any rivers or inlets and for signs of soil fertility and of indigenous inhabitants of the land. It was important to take accurate astronomical observations, to note the timing and extent of tides, and to calculate the geographical coordinates of bays, harbours, islands and other landmarks.[4]

This was only the first stage of a comprehensive survey of Australia's coastline. The Admiralty instructions instructed Flinders to explore Australia's north-west coast, where it was hoped harbours would be found, and then to examine the Gulf of Carpentaria and the land to its west, between 130° and 139° longitude; to survey Torres Strait; and to examine the rest of the north, west and north-west coasts of Australia. The instructions made it clear that these coasts should be investigated, along with the bank between Timor and the Trial Rocks, whose location was unknown but thought to be a few days' sail from Timor. The English ship *Trial* had been wrecked on these rocks in 1622.[5] Flinders was instructed to ascertain whether East India Company ships could call at Timor on outward-bound voyages to China, Indonesia and the Far East at a time when British trade with these widely scattered areas was conducted under the monopoly of the Company. After completing these surveys, the *Investigator* was to turn to a careful investigation of the east coast from Cape Flattery to the Bay of Inlets, already surveyed

---

[1] Geeson and Sexton, 'H.M. Sloop *Investigator*', pp. 291–2.

[2] TNA, ADM 1/1800, Admiralty Captains' letters, Flinders to Evan Nepean, 9 June 1801.

[3] Instructions for Philip Gidley King regarding the *Lady Nelson*, 1800, in Chambers, ed., *The Indian and Pacific Correspondence*, V, pp. 143–6.

[4] Details taken from below, entry for 17 July 1801, pp. 126–31.

[5] Lee, 'The First Sighting of Australia by the English', pp. 273–80; Henn, 'The Tryal Rocks', pp. 38–43.

by Captain Cook in the *Endeavour* in 1770. Implicit in the instructions, though not stated directly, was the need to sail as near to the shore as possible. Flinders was reminded that the circumnavigation was as much connected with accruing knowledge about the natural world as it was concerned with geography and hydrography; and that he should allow time for the botanist, the other scientific gentlemen and the painter to undertake their work in relation to Australia's natural history. That is why the *Investigator* carried a plant cabin to collect plants, trees and shrubs found during the survey for transfer to the Royal Gardens at Kew.[1]

These were ambitious and strict instructions, and it may be that the Admiralty had not fully considered the mileage to be covered or the time available for the voyage: to perform his instructions to the letter would have taken Flinders longer than a three-year voyage could manage. An awkward part of the orders, from the practical point of view, was the instruction for Flinders to sail eastwards along the southern coast of Australia to Port Jackson before starting his survey but then to begin that by voyaging along that same coast – a distance of over 1,600 nautical miles. On receiving his sailing orders, Flinders immediately wrote to his patron, Banks, to note that 'the Admiralty have not thought it good to permit me to circumnavigate New Holland in the way that <u>appears to me</u> best suited to expedition and safety'. Nevertheless, he reported to Banks that he was happy with the adjustment of the crew to the ship and that the voyage 'may see the examination of New Holland performed in the way that will be most gratifying to you'.[2]

A couple of weeks before writing this letter, Flinders had suggested to Banks that delays in starting the *Investigator*'s voyage meant that he would not arrive on Australia's south coast in the summer, and therefore that stormy seas might obstruct a survey of that coast as the Admiralty instructed, that is, in a westward direction after first sailing to Sydney Cove. Flinders added that if his orders did not forbid it, he would 'examine the south coast more minutely in my first run along it; and if anything material should present itself, as a strait, gulph, or very large river, shall employ as much time in its examination as the remaining part of the summer may then consist of; for I consider it very material to the success of the voyage, and to its early completion, that we should be upon the northern coasts in winter and the southern ones in summer'.[3] Before the *Investigator* expedition began, Governor Philip Gidley King had also written to Banks about prioritizing a survey of the southern coast.[4] It is not known whether Banks discussed Flinders's proposed alteration with the Admiralty; but he did not write back to Flinders to dissuade him from altering the sailing orders.[5]

4. The Circumnavigation of *Terra Australis*

a. *The Voyage out to Australia*

More than six months passed before the ship was ready to begin her voyage. On 25 January 1801 Flinders mustered the ship's company and read his commission from the

---

[1] Details taken from below, entry for 17 July 1801, pp. 126–31; Estensen, *The Life of Matthew Flinders*, p. 273.
[2] Flinders to Banks, 17 July 1801, in Chambers, ed., *The Indian and Pacific Correspondence*, V, p. 369.
[3] Flinders to Banks, 5 July 1801, ibid., V, p. 368.
[4] ML, Banks Papers, series 39.059, King to Banks, 3 May 1800.
[5] Scott, *The Life of Matthew Flinders*, p. 130.

Admiralty as lieutenant on the *Investigator*, which he had received six days earlier.[1] While the vessel was at Sheerness, routine naval duties took place. These included receiving the boatswain's and carpenter's stores, clearing the holds to receive coals, taking on board beer, bread and provisions from lighters, dealing with the anchors, fitting gun tackles and breechings, and so forth.[2] In April Flinders was granted ten days' leave of absence to go to London to hasten the supply of the mathematical instruments, forward the ordering of stationery and books, buy some articles for presents and barter, and write letters to the Governor of New South Wales relating to the *Lady Nelson*.[3] Flinders requested some financial support from the East India Company, and was gratified to be awarded £1,200 in table money for the voyage.[4] A brief period of leave enabled Flinders to make a swift journey to Lincolnshire to marry Ann Chappelle, with whom he had conducted a warm friendship for some years. The marriage was held at St Nicholas Church, Partney, on 17 April 1801. Flinders hoped to take his wife with him on his expedition to Terra Australis.[5]

On 27 May the *Investigator* sailed from the Thames Estuary to an anchorage at the Downs. A couple of days later a bad nautical error occurred. The person taking the lead line in making soundings left the chains without anyone replacing him. As a result, the ship hit a sandbank in daylight. Flinders, who was in the company of his wife, at once went up from his cabin to the quarterdeck and ordered boats to be lowered to sound around the ship. He realized he should have been on deck to watch the pilotage. He sailed back to the Downs and reported the ship's grounding to the Admiralty. Flinders managed to extricate himself from what appeared to be slack discipline by arguing that the chart of the channel supplied to him by Arrowsmith did not show a sandbank called the Roar.[6] Banks's support was needed to clear up the problems caused.[7] The *Investigator* set sail again on 30 May and reached Spithead on 2 June.[8]

On 15 June Flinders was pleased to receive John Thistle on board ship as master.[9] Flinders had a high regard for Thistle, who had been on the *Reliance*, with Bass on the whaleboat voyage into Bass Strait, and with Flinders on both expeditions in the *Norfolk*. A less happy occurrence for Flinders was that his wife Ann, feeling unwell and in a convalescent state, was taken home to Lincolnshire by her stepfather: it had become apparent that her presence on the *Investigator*'s expedition would not be tolerated by the Admiralty.[10] Indeed, Banks had warned Flinders that taking one's spouse on such a voyage contravened naval discipline and that, if the Lords Commissioners of the Admiralty were

---

[1] See below, p. 99.

[2] See below, pp. 100–12.

[3] ML, *Investigator* Rough Journal, I, 5 April 1801, f. 21.

[4] BL, India Office Records, Court of Directors: Miscellaneous Letters Received, E/1/104, Flinders to W. Ramsay, 12 May 1801, f. 208, and Committee of Correspondence: Miscellanies no. 41, E/1/237, W. Ramsay to Flinders, 14 May 1801, f. 535.

[5] Estensen, *The Life of Matthew Flinders*, pp. 153–4. Flinders was worried about his father's displeasure because he had not formally asked for his consent to marry Ann: see Lincolnshire Archives, Flinders Correspondence, Flinders to Dr Matthew Flinders, 10 July 1801.

[6] Flinders to Banks, 6 June 1801, in Bladen, ed., *HRNSW*, IV, p. 385.

[7] Banks to Flinders, June 1801, ibid., IV, p. 387.

[8] Estensen, *The Life of Matthew Flinders*, pp. 160–63.

[9] See below, p. 122.

[10] Royal Geographical Society, London, Sir John Franklin Collection, SJF/1, Flinders to Thomas Franklin, 7 July 1801.

to hear of her being in New South Wales, they would immediately order Flinders to be superseded.[1] Flinders decided to leave his wife in England in order to avoid their 'ill opinion'.[2] The parting of the young couple was a matter of sorrow after barely three months of marriage. Flinders wrote several letters to Ann while the *Investigator* waited to sail. He was committed to the voyage, and realized he would have to leave her behind in England.[3]

The delay in the start of the voyage arose partly from the pressures involved in preparing ships for sea when many naval vessels demanded attention during the war with France, and partly from the illness of Nepean, the Secretary of the Admiralty, who had to authorize all the paperwork connected with the expedition. Flinders himself thought the Admiralty had not promoted the voyage with the same energy as they did when Earl Spencer headed the Admiralty Board (Spencer had been succeeded by the Earl of St Vincent on 19 February). More important than these reasons for delay, however, was the need to wait for a French passport to arrive, as a guarantee that the *Investigator* would have a safe passage across the oceans.[4] Finally, on 17 July Flinders received his instructions for the voyage from the Admiralty along with some other papers, including the passport from the French Republic signed by the minister of the marine and of the colonies, to prevent the *Investigator* being seized by any French ships and to permit Flinders to put into any French-controlled ports to refit as necessary. The document was made out specifically for the *Investigator*. Other papers included extracts from a memoir written by Alexander Dalrymple on the winds around Australia and a letter from the Duke of Portland to the governor of New South Wales, relating to the brig *Lady Nelson*.[5]

The *Investigator* sailed from Spithead on 18 July 1801. Over the next few days she followed a course past the Isle of Wight and along the English Channel out into the Atlantic. A careful watch for enemy vessels was maintained, as Britain and France were at war. A different pressing cause for concern became apparent: while approaching Porto Santo, the easternmost island of the Madeiran archipelago, on 30 July, Flinders noted that they had 'the mortification to find that the ship makes two inches of water per hour'.[6] He dropped a boat down the side of the ship to examine the seams and butts near the water's edge, but could find no cause of the leak.[7] The ship continued its voyage safely, but the leak had raised concerns about what might happen later in the expedition.

The first proper port of call on the voyage was the roadstead at Funchal, Madeira. The *Investigator* arrived there to find British naval vessels in the bay with men from the 85th regiment of the army. These forces had been dispatched to Madeira in case there was a French invasion of the island. The administration of Madeira remained in Portuguese

[1] Banks to Flinders, 21 May 1801, in Bladen, ed., *HRNSW*, IV, p. 372.

[2] Flinders to Banks, 3 June 1801, ibid., IV, p. 381.

[3] Estensen, *The Life of Matthew Flinders*, pp. 162, 164–5.

[4] Austin, *The Voyage of the Investigator*, p. 56; Royal Geographical Society, Sir John Franklin Collection, SJF/1, Flinders to Thomas Franklin, 7 July 1801. The application to the French government for the passport is discussed in BL, Add MS 31169, Sir John Jervis letterbook (1801–6), St Vincent Papers, John Jervis to Andrew Hammond, 20 March 1801, f. 104.

[5] See below, entry for 17 July 1801, pp. 126–31; TNA, ADM 7/708, Journal of Matthew Flinders, f. 54; ML, *Investigator* Rough Journal, I, 17 July 1801, f. 59.

[6] See below, p. 152.

[7] See below, p. 154.

hands despite this British army presence.[1] Flinders landed and waited upon both the British consul and the governor of Madeira. The brief stopover was an opportunity to take on board fresh beef, water and wine. The botanist and the other scientific gentlemen had three days on shore for botanical investigations. Madeira was familiar to British naturalists. Sir Hans Sloane, physician and collector of curiosities, had called there in 1687 en route to Jamaica. Banks and the Swedish naturalist Daniel Solander had collected there, as part of the *Endeavour* voyage in 1768. Banks's collector Francis Masson – the first botanical collector sent out from Kew – had also visited the island in 1776 and 1783. Robert Brown had studied Masson's writings on Madeiran botany before leaving London for the present voyage. Unfortunately, the botanical excursion was fairly unproductive. Brown was disappointed to find scarcely any new plants and very few additions to the flora of the island.[2] He described eighteen plants on his Madeiran slips; only seven of these plants have been traced.[3]

After the departure from Madeira, the *Investigator* sailed past the Cape Verde Islands, which Flinders had previously seen in the *Reliance* in 1795 on his first voyage to Australia. The ship continued its voyage southward uneventfully. It continued to leak, gaining two inches of water per hour, but Flinders was not unduly concerned as the leaks were confined to her upper works.[4] Flinders was prepared for dealing with the expected south-westerly winds near the Equator. He knew the longitudes where Cook and La Pérouse had crossed the line of the Equator, and, to verify his position, consulted Arrowsmith's *Chart of the World on Mercator's Projection ...* (1790) and the geographical notes of the Comte de Fleurieu, a noted French geographer and hydrographer, that were prefixed to La Pérouse's voyage.[5]

To offer the ship's company some amusement, Flinders allowed them to carry out the well-known initiation ritual associated with crossing the Equator. This was a merry ceremony in which costumes were worn. King Neptune and his attendants came on deck and all those who had crossed the line before shaved the heads of all the officers and seamen who had not. Seamen were allowed as much grog as they could drink.[6] Seaman Samuel Smith reported that 'the greatest part of the Officers & Men was shaved, not having cross'd the line before'.[7] It is not clear whether Flinders participated in the ritual. The ceremony was rowdy and disorderly. Peter Good noted that, amidst the turbulence, some sailors were insolent to the officers.[8] At a muster on the following day, Flinders admonished the sailors and blamed himself for allowing so much alcohol to be consumed.[9]

Strong winds accentuated the weakness of the ship, and so Flinders rearranged the carronades and the vessel's upper works to lighten the load and to lessen the shaking of

---

[1] Gregory, *The Beneficent Usurpers*, p. 47.

[2] Brown, 6 August 1801, in Vallance, Moore and Groves, eds, *Nature's Investigator*, p. 59.

[3] Moore, 'Some aspects of the work of Robert Brown', pp. 384, 387–8.

[4] TNA, ADM 1/1800, Admiralty Captains' letters, Flinders to Evan Nepean, 5 August 1801, and below, p. 156.

[5] See below, p. 174.

[6] See below, p. 179; Flinders, *A Voyage to Terra Australis*, I, p. 40; Scott Polar Research Institute, Cambridge: Sir John Franklin Collection, MS 248/304, John Franklin to his father, 22 October 1801.

[7] Entry for 19 September 1801 in Monteath, ed., *Sailing with Flinders*, p. 27.

[8] Entry for 7 September 1801 in Edwards, ed., *The Journal of Peter Good*, p. 40.

[9] Estensen, *The Life of Matthew Flinders*, pp. 172–3.

the timber that allowed water to seep through.[1] This settled the *Investigator* for the rest of the voyage down to the Cape of Good Hope, but it was potentially worrying because it was unpredictable for how long the ship could continue without further problems. Flinders remained focused on the route followed, closely comparing the ship's sailing direction with that of previous voyages, notably by Cook, for which he had information to hand. At the end of September he and his officers looked out for Saxemberg Island, mentioned in Fleurieu's geographical notes mentioned above. This island was reportedly discovered in 1670 by John Lindestz Lindeman, a Dutchman. Its coordinates were said to be 30°45′S and 19°40′W. Lindeman had made a sketch of the island, showing it to be low-lying with a mountain in the middle. Flinders searched for the island, could not find it, and decided to press ahead for the Cape. He was right not to linger, both for the sake of his voyage and because the island is non-existent: Lindeman had probably mistaken stationary clouds on the horizon that are common in this part of the Atlantic for a distant island.[2]

In the early hours of 17 October 1801, the *Investigator* sighted the high land of the Cape of Good Hope. This was a key point in world maritime sea routes as the meeting place of the Atlantic and Indian Oceans. On the next day the master of the *Lancaster*, an East India Company ship that served as the flagship at the Cape, came on board to conduct Flinders and his ship to her anchorage in Simon's Bay, an embayment within False Bay.[3] Flinders had decided in advance not to put into Table Bay owing to the heavy gales that occurred there late in the year and the danger of shipwreck. Simon's Bay, by contrast, offered a safe anchorage at all seasons.[4] The voyage from Spithead to the Cape had taken 144 days. Bauer reported to his brother that 'throughout the entire voyage so far we seldom had a dry cabin because water was coming in everywhere through the sides of the upper middle deck despite the fact that during this time we were not exposed to any great storm'.[5]

The Cape of Good Hope was the main scheduled port of call on the *Investigator*'s voyage out to Australia. Virtually every vessel sent out from a European port to the Indian Ocean in the age of sail called at the Cape. The Dutch East India Company (VOC) had been installed there since 1652, but Britain had seized the Cape in 1795. This had been partly for strategic reasons (mainly to stymie French plans to occupy it) during the French revolutionary wars; but it also occurred for political and commercial reasons. France had overrun the Netherlands in 1795, and had established the Batavian Republic there as an ally. Therefore Britain needed control of the Cape to keep sea lanes open for its East India Company, merchant and naval vessels sailing from the Atlantic to the Indian Ocean and vice versa. The Dutch were also a threat to British commerce and settlements in India and the Pacific. Though the Cape was restored to Dutch control on 1 October 1801, just over two weeks before Flinders arrived there, in accordance with the Treaty of Amiens, a strong British military and naval presence remained there under the command of Sir Roger Curtis.[6] Flinders had previously been at the Cape for seven weeks in 1791, when

[1] Ibid., p. 172.
[2] Stommel, *Lost Islands*, pp. 22–5.
[3] See below, pp. 203–4; Flinders, *A Voyage to Terra Australis*, I, pp. 36–8.
[4] Estensen, *The Life of Matthew Flinders*, p. 173.
[5] Ferdinand Bauer to Franz Bauer, 23 January 1802, in Norst, *Ferdinand Bauer*, p. 100.
[6] Arkin, 'John Company at the Cape', pp. 177–344.

sailing with Bligh in the *Providence*, and later in January 1797, when he successfully took an examination for the rank of lieutenant.[1]

Essential repairs were carried out on the *Investigator* at the Cape. Curtis authorized complete assistance for a thorough caulking on the inside and the outside of the vessel. New stores for the voyage across the Indian Ocean were loaded on board ship as well as a week's allowance of fruit and vegetables from the naval hospital in Cape Town.[2] The stopover at the Cape was the last opportunity to check the scientific instruments for longitude before starting the Australian survey. On 18 October Flinders and his brother Samuel accompanied the astronomer Crosley on shore to find a convenient place to set up a tent observatory and marquee. Work continued at the observatory on shore, which was guarded by marines, until 1 November. The aim was to gather accurate geographical coordinates so that the site could be used as a reference point by future navigators.[3]

Crosley was an experienced astronomer. He had spent three years (1789–92) at the Royal Observatory, Greenwich, as an assistant to Dr Nevil Maskelyne, the Astronomer Royal.[4] During the *Investigator*'s voyage from England to the Cape, Crosley had made regular astronomical observations.[5] Unfortunately, he had been feeling unwell with rheumatism and gout since the ship had left Madeira and it was decided he should leave the voyage. Crosley returned to England, taking with him two defective chronometers.[6] Flinders realized it would take too long for another astronomer to be sent out from England, and no suitable substitute could be found at the Cape.[7] Thus Flinders began to acquaint himself in every leisure moment with knowledge of astronomy and with the scientific instruments on board ship. Samuel Flinders was given the main responsibility for dealing with astronomical calculations for the rest of the voyage, with his brother overseeing his work.[8]

Crosley's departure was a major loss for the voyage because the expertise necessary for making astronomical calculations, and judgment about where measurements might best be taken, could not be carried out so well by someone who lacked the requisite professional training. Nevertheless, Flinders aimed to ensure that, with his younger brother's help, these problems were overcome. The astronomical tasks taken on by Matthew and Samuel Flinders were divided, according to the Board of Longitude's instructions, into observations to be made on shipboard and those to be made on shore.[9]

The botanical investigations carried out by the scientific gentlemen at the Cape were partly determined by the location of the *Investigator*'s anchorage in the sheltered cove of Simon's Bay. From there the botanists had easy access to the southern part of the Cape peninsula. This had scientific advantages because that area had been poorly explored botanically by the early nineteenth century. By contrast, the botany of the Table Bay area

---

[1] See above, pp. 2, 5.

[2] See below, p. 208; Flinders, *A Voyage to Terra Australis*, I, p. 42.

[3] See below, pp. 205–7.

[4] Croarken, 'Astronomical Labourers', p. 291.

[5] CUL, Royal Greenwich Observatory, Board of Longitude Papers, Papers of Nevil Maskelyne, RGO 4/186, Observations made by John Crosley.

[6] Howse, *Nevil Maskelyne*, p. 187.

[7] Flinders to Banks, 29 October 1801, in Bladen, ed., *HRNSW*, IV, p. 601.

[8] See below, p. 208. For the handling of the scientific instruments on the voyage, see Phillips, 'Remembering Matthew Flinders', pp. 115–16.

[9] For the instructions, see below, pp. 209–11.

had been scrutinized since the Dutch arrived at the Cape in 1652 and was the subject of a detailed scientific literature, notably by some Linnaean pupils. The timing of the *Investigator*'s visit was also favourable for botanizing because Flinders and his scientific gentlemen arrived there in late spring, the peak flowering time for geophytes and shrubs. Brown undertook a detailed exploration of the Cape's flora and fauna. He gathered lichens, mosses, ferns and flowering plants, including orchids. He collected and made habitat observations on twenty-four of the forty-one species of Proteaceae, a family of plants he was to come across in Australia.[1] This was the plant group about which he was to write his most notable scientific paper.[2] To keep the plants fresh on his excursions, Brown and his fellow scientists used tightly-lidded tin boxes. They treated and dried the plants after returning to the ship.[3]

Flinders tried to leave the Cape of Good Hope on 3 November 1801. A south-easterly gale delayed sailing, but two days later the *Investigator* set out from the Cape for King George Sound, Western Australia; Port Jackson, however, was its 'proper rendezvous'.[4] The voyage across the Indian Ocean was uneventful. The *Investigator* proceeded at a rate of 140 miles per day. On 6 December first sight was made of the Australian continent. The ship had reached Australia after a trouble-free thirty-two days from the Cape of Good Hope. The *Investigator* sailed past Cape Leeuwin, the south-westernmost point of Australia. Flinders had a copy of the French explorer D'Entrecasteaux's chart of this landfall, dating from 1792 when he was on an expedition searching for the lost explorer La Pérouse.[5] Late at night on 8 December the *Investigator* anchored in King George Sound, a large, fine natural anchorage comprising forty-two square miles. It is the location of the present-day town of Albany.[6] On their way into Princess Royal Harbour, situated on the west side of the Sound, Flinders stopped at Seal Island in order to search for a sealed bottle and parchment left by the English naval officer George Vancouver to commemorate his visit there on 11 October 1791; but nothing was found.[7]

b. *From Cape Leeuwin to St Peter and St Francis Islands*

The only navigators who had seen any part of south-western Australia before Flinders were the Dutch explorer Pieter Nuyts in 1626–7, engaged on a Dutch East India Company voyage to map part of the south Australian coast; the Frenchman Louis Aleno de St Aloüarn who anchored near Cape Leeuwin in 1772 and who claimed possession of Western Australia for France; Vancouver on his Pacific expedition in the *Cape Chatham* in 1791; and D'Entrecasteaux, commander of the French ships *Recherche* and *Espérance* in 1792 on a rescue mission to search for the vanished La Pérouse expedition.[8] The

[1] Rourke, 'Getting There', p. 30.

[2] Brown, 'On the Proteaceae of Jussieu', pp. 15–226.

[3] Rourke, 'Getting There', p. 27.

[4] Scott Polar Research Institute, Sir John Franklin Collection, MS 248/304, John Franklin to his father, 22 October 1801.

[5] Scott, *The Life of Matthew Flinders*, p. 147; and below, p. 234.

[6] Flinders provides a detailed account of the passage to the first anchorage in King George Sound in *A Voyage to Terra Australis*, I, pp. 50–53.

[7] See below, p. 242.

[8] Scott, *The Life of Matthew Flinders*, p. 147; Godard and de Kerros, *1772: The French Annexation of New Holland*. La Pérouse had sailed from Port Jackson on 10 March 1788, bound for New Caledonia and eventually Australia's western and southern coasts, but neither he nor his men were seen again.

subsequent extensive coastline, from the beginning of the Great Australian Bight, to almost the border of modern Victoria, had never been explored. It was referred to as 'the unknown coast'. In 1800 it was one of the largest stretches of coast in the habitable earth still to be discovered.[1]

Flinders and his company remained at King George Sound for nearly a month, between 8 December 1801 and 5 January 1802. Flinders selected this anchorage to prepare for the examination of Australia's south coast for several reasons: it offered secure shelter; the masts could be stripped; the rigging and sails put in order; and communication could be made with the shore without the interference of the elements.[2] Before setting out to explore the unknown coast, Flinders examined King George Sound and the two harbours that were adjacent to it – Princess Royal Harbour and Oyster Harbour.[3] He had Vancouver's account of his voyage to aid him in his survey, and found it to be as good as could have been achieved given that it was constructed hastily.[4] Flinders also had (by courtesy of Dalrymple) the charts prepared by the hydrographer and cartographer Charles-François Beautemps-Beaupré on D'Entrecasteaux's voyage. He found these to be excellent, even though he drew up more detailed charts of his own.[5]

On 9 December Flinders examined Princess Royal Harbour, on the west side of King George Sound, as a convenient place to gather wood and water and refit the ship.[6] He took a boat to examine Oyster Harbour, an inner cove to the north of the Sound that Vancouver had named on account of the many oysters found there.[7] Flinders made several sets of astronomical observations and surveyed King George Sound, using Vancouver's survey as a basis for a more thorough investigation.[8] The scientific gentlemen botanized in and around the Sound and continued their work on the next stage of the voyage, which focused on Lucky Bay and the Archipelago of the Recherche. These visits, occurring in summer, came long after the peak spring flowering period for Western Australia's southern flora. Brown and his colleagues collected more than 500 species of plants from the Albany area and another 100 from Lucky Bay and the islands of the Archipelago of the Recherche. These collections are crucial for the elucidation of the status of Western Australian plants. Brown named twenty-six genera that are endemic to Western Australia. At the species level, some 1,450 names of vascular plants published later by Brown are applied to Western Australia.[9]

The first encounter with Aborigines on the voyage occurred at King George Sound. In 1791 Vancouver had mentioned smokes, huts and drying fish in the vicinity, but never saw any people.[10] Flinders's party were more fortunate in seeing native people. The Aborigines were fascinated by the ship's company. They approached the tents of Flinders's men,

---

[1] Scott, *Terre Napoléon*, p. 27.

[2] Flinders, *A Voyage to Terra Australis*, I, p. 53; Milne, 'The Albany Perspective', p. 177.

[3] Flinders, *A Voyage to Terra Australis*, I, p. 73.

[4] See below, p. 238.

[5] Scott, *The Life of Matthew Flinders*, p. 148.

[6] See below, pp. 240–2.

[7] See below, pp. 242–3; Lamb, ed., *The Voyage of George Vancouver*, I, p. 338.

[8] Estensen, *The Life of Matthew Flinders*, p. 180.

[9] Keighery and Gibson, 'The Flinders Expedition in Western Australia', pp. 105–7. The Australian plant genera named by Brown are listed in ibid., pp. 108–9.

[10] Milne, 'The Albany Perspective', p. 177.

undertook some parleying and exchanged some of their implements for manufactured iron-ware.[1] This encounter between Flinders's party and the Aborigines is discussed further below.[2] On 3 January 1802 a change in wind direction enabled Flinders to take the *Investigator* out of Princess Royal Harbour into King George Sound. Five days later he reached the Recherche archipelago, comprising around 130 granite islands and rocky islets. Situated in crystal clear water, they cover a distance of 143 miles from west to east and stretch up to thirty-one miles offshore. Flinders knew many of these islands had never been explored or named. D'Entrecasteaux had named the archipelago after one of his ships, and had landed on at least one of them; but he encountered stormy weather and needed to continue sailing towards Van Diemen's Land, so he did not conduct a thorough survey of these islands.[3]

Brown noted in his diary that the islands in the Archipelago of the Recherche – then referred to as D'Entrecasteaux's islands – were 'more considerable than laid down in the French chart' compiled by Beautemps-Beaupré.[4] This was excusable: as Flinders later explained, charting was difficult in this vicinity owing to a 'labyrinth of islands and rocks'.[5] It required great skill to take accurate bearings of the various islands before the ship's position changed. Moreover, sailing between the rocks and breakers in the archipelago was dangerous as gales were frequent there.[6] Flinders did not intend to spend much time exploring these islands, however, because he found Beautemps-Beaupré's chart to be very accurate and because he wanted to reach the unknown coast of South Australia before the summer was too far advanced.[7]

In the event, because the botanists wanted to do some collecting and then adverse winds occurred, Flinders remained in and near the Archipelago of the Recherche for several days. A couple of days were spent exploring Middle Island, the largest island they had yet seen in the archipelago. Flinders and his associates visited Goose Island, situated in the bay on the north side of Middle Island, where they saw western grey kangaroos, geese, penguins and ducks.[8] The *Investigator* left Middle Island on 17 January to enter the Great Australian Bight (later given its name by Flinders).[9] Flinders was now sailing in waters that marked the limit of previous exploration. In 1791 Vancouver had reached Termination Island, the southernmost of the Archipelago of the Recherche, before abandoning his survey in favour of proceeding to investigate the north-west Pacific region. Brown noted that over the next ten days the *Investigator* passed 'a very uninteresting coast without the least appearance of inlet, harbour or shelter'.[10] By 28 January, at the head of the Great Australian Bight, the *Investigator*, then situated about longitude 133° east, reached the limits of the Australian mainland explored by D'Entrecasteaux in 1792.[11]

---

[1] Flinders includes more commentary on these Aborigines in *A Voyage to Terra Australis*, I, pp. 58–9, 66–7.

[2] See below, pp. 61–2.

[3] Austin, *The Voyage of the Investigator*, p. 85.

[4] Vallance, Moore and Groves, eds, *Nature's Investigator*, p. 110. The Admiralty had supplied Flinders with copies of maps from D'Entrecasteaux's voyage that had been seized by Britain when that expedition was disbanded in 1795. Sankey, 'The Cartography of the Baudin Expedition', p. 8.

[5] Flinders, *A Voyage to Terra Australis*, I, p. 79.

[6] See below, p. 265.

[7] See below, p. 272.

[8] See below, pp. 272–5; Vallance, Moore and Groves, eds, *Nature's Investigator*, pp. 116–17.

[9] Ibid., pp. 109–18.

[10] Ibid., p. 118.

[11] Austin, *The Voyage of the Investigator*, p. 85.

Flinders headed for the islands of St Peter and St Francis, the last landmarks seen by Pieter Nuyts, the highest ranking official on the VOC ship *'t Gulden Zeepaard* [*Golden Seahorse*], under the command of François Thijssen, in 1627.[1] This vessel was sailing towards the VOC's headquarters in Batavia when it encountered strong south-westerly winds which blew it off course. By accident, the ship reached the south Australian coast and sailed east as far as today's Ceduna before turning back to sail to Batavia. Flinders noted that Nuyts's discovery ended with these islands, and that 'the coast abreast of the islands and further eastward is totally unknown'.[2] The *Investigator* stayed for a week in the Nuyts archipelago. Flinders took angles from two stations on St Francis Island. He detected twelve islands in the archipelago. Navigation was difficult because these islands appeared to be lower than those of the Archipelago of the Recherche, though reefs were not so abundant.[3] Hazy weather rendered the mainland shore indistinct, while shallow water prevented Flinders from sailing near to the coast. These factors hampered the completion of his running survey in this area.[4]

There was no point in delaying the voyage in this vicinity. On 9 February the *Investigator* left her anchorage in Petrel Bay, on St Francis Island, and continued her voyage eastwards. Entering Spencer Gulf, which had not been explored before, she anchored off the north-western shore of what Flinders later called Thistle Island.[5] No water was found there. Flinders sent the master, John Thistle, with a boat and crew to find an anchorage near the mainland from which water could be obtained. The boat was last seen at dusk on its return voyage. It then disappeared. Robert Fowler took a cutter to search for the lost boat party, but this returned alone. On 22 February Fowler and other crew members landed in what became known as Memory Cove and found the wreck of the boat, bottom up, several pieces of the boat and an oar on the shore, and the boat's compass floating in the water. None of the missing crew was found. These were the first fatalities on the *Investigator*'s voyage. Those lost were Thistle, the midshipman and the coxswain of the boat, and five others. Thistle's death was keenly felt by Flinders. They had sailed together previously, as mentioned above. Thistle had been closely involved with Flinders's daily business on the *Investigator*, as master of the ship and as someone who often deputized for Flinders at the binnacle to make astronomical calculations.[6]

The *Investigator* remained for two days at Memory Cove. A boat journey northwards along the coast led to Flinders finding a small keg that had belonged to Thistle and some fragments of the boat. On 24 February Flinders sent on shore an inscription on a plate of copper recording the loss of Thistle and his boat party, ending with the warning 'Nautici cavete!' ('Sailors beware!'). Flinders named the point of land where Thistle's boat had foundered Cape Catastrophe. After several days spent searching for the lost crew, Flinders resumed his survey. On 25 February he anchored in a bay that he later named Port Lincoln in honour of his native county.[7] Over the preceding few days, Flinders and

---

[1] Schilder, 'From Secret to Common Knowledge', p. 78.

[2] See below, p. 292.

[3] ML, *Investigator* Rough Journal, I, entry for 5 February 1802, f. 313.

[4] Tiley, *Australian Navigators*, p. 147.

[5] Vallance, Moore and Groves, eds, *Nature's Investigator*, pp. 138–40.

[6] Ibid., pp. 140–41; Flinders, *A Voyage to Terra Australis*, I, pp. 133–6; Edwards, ed., *The Journal of Peter Good*, p. 60.

[7] Flinders, *A Voyage to Terra Australis*, I, p. 142.

his crew had frequently discussed what they might find as they sailed along the unknown coast – 'large rivers, deep inlets, inland seas, and passages to the Gulph of Carpentaria are the phrases most current in our conversations'.[1] Flinders ventured on shore to take bearings from Stamford Hill, overlooking the bay, and the naturalists landed to examine the surrounding area.[2] During eight days at Port Lincoln, Brown gathered eighty-eight plant collections and thirty-seven seed collections, a larger haul than he made at any other location in South Australia.[3]

On 6 March the *Investigator* left Port Lincoln and took a course to the north-east, anchoring in the evening at Kirkby Island in Spencer Gulf. Flinders noted twelve other isles that he named the Sir Joseph Banks Group of Islands after his patron.[4] Flinders named numerous islands in the area after his Lincolnshire associations – Partney Island, Revesby Island and Spilsby Island.[5] As the ship proceeded to the head of Spencer Gulf, shoal water was evident on both sides of the *Investigator*. This led to the supposition that they were 'sailing up the channel of a considerable river'.[6] This proved not to be the case. Flinders was disappointed that he had failed to find a major waterway penetrating the continent in Spencer Gulf.[7]

Flinders continued his survey of Spencer Gulf until 20 March. On the following day, the *Investigator* anchored off Kangaroo Island. This was a place of refuge from south-westerly gales.[8] Flinders thought the island had not been explored previously. A couple of days' stay on the island enabled Brown and the botanists to collect further plant specimens and to observe the wildlife, which included kangaroos, wallabies, brown pigeons, parrots and seals. Flinders and his party shot thirty-one kangaroos, brought them on board ship, skinned and cleaned them, and then offered the meat as a feast to crew that had existed on salt provisions for four months. Flinders appropriately named the location Kangaroo Island.[9]

On 24 March the *Investigator* left Kangaroo Island and sailed towards the mainland coast near Cape Spencer. A few days later the ship entered Gulf St Vincent, which Flinders was the first explorer to identify. He hoped the mouth of a major river would be found in an estuary. The convergence of Spencer Gulf and Gulf St Vincent alerted him to the possibility that a river could be found in this vicinity.[10] On 30 March Brown accompanied Flinders in the cutter to the head of the Gulf St Vincent to ascertain whether any river could be found. Flinders had noticed the absence of a tide on the previous evening, however, and this meant there was little chance of finding a river nearby that would offer access to the interior of the continent.[11] He did not find a river at his landing place: the inlet

---

[1] See below, p. 314.
[2] Vallance, Moore and Groves, eds, *Nature's Investigator*, pp. 145–6.
[3] Barker, 'The Botanical Legacy of 1802', p. 10.
[4] Flinders, *A Voyage to Terra Australis*, I, pp. 151–4.
[5] Austin, *The Voyage of the Investigator*, p. 99.
[6] Vallance, Moore and Groves, eds, *Nature's Investigator*, p. 152.
[7] Estensen, *The Life of Matthew Flinders*, p. 194.
[8] Ibid., pp. 163–5.
[9] See below, p. 342.
[10] Perry, 'Seasons for Exploration', p. 55.
[11] Vallance, Moore and Groves, eds, *Nature's Investigator*, pp. 169–71; Flinders, *A Voyage to Terra Australis*, I, p. 8.

appeared to close about six or seven miles from the head of the Gulf.[1] The approach of winter induced Flinders to finish the examination of the south coast before the weather and a lack of necessary supplies obliged him to make haste to Port Jackson.[2]

c. From Encounter Bay to Port Jackson

In a remarkable coincidence, in the early afternoon of 8 April 1802 Flinders saw a ship ahead and showed her colours. Flinders was sailing off the south Australian coast, and the meeting was unexpected. He later called its location Encounter Bay.[3] At first, Flinders thought the ship might be an English sealer or whaler, as such ships had been active in southerly voyages from Port Jackson for several years.[4] But as the two vessels drew nearer, Flinders recognized the unknown ship as *Le Géographe*, commanded by Nicolas Baudin, also engaged on a voyage of exploration to Australia, backed by Napoleon Bonaparte. Flinders knew about the Baudin expedition through Banks, who had obtained passports for Baudin to conduct a scientific voyage of discovery in Australian waters.[5] Baudin, however, knew nothing about Flinders's expedition. Flinders was sailing in an easterly direction while Baudin was proceeding in a westerly direction, having surveyed parts of Van Diemen's Land and a relatively small section of the Victorian and southern Australian coasts.[6]

At daylight Flinders went on board *Le Géographe*, where he and Baudin met for the first time. The meeting was private; only Robert Brown, the naturalist, accompanied Flinders. Neither Flinders nor Baudin knew that a truce in the Napoleonic Wars between Britain and France had occurred in October 1801, for they had both begun their voyages months beforehand. Neither did the commanders know that the truce had been confirmed by the Peace of Amiens of 27 March 1802. They must have approached one another with circumspection, and needed to show the passports they had been provided with as a diplomatic precaution for a safe passage in the event of an encounter with the enemy in wartime.[7] Flinders requested to see, and was shown, the passport carried by Baudin. He then handed his passport to Baudin, who gave it back without looking at it. During the meeting Flinders therefore knew he was speaking to Baudin whereas the French commander was unaware of Flinders's identity. Baudin wrote in his journal, however, that the name of the English commander was made clear on this occasion, and Flinders 'expressed great satisfaction at this agreeable meeting, but was extremely reserved on all other matters'. On the next day, 9 April, Flinders went aboard the French vessel for a second meeting. On this occasion Baudin showed greater awareness of his English counterpart and was inquisitive about the voyage of the *Investigator*.[8]

---

[1] See below, p. 351; Flinders, *A Voyage to Terra Australis*, I, pp. 177–80.

[2] See below, p. 359.

[3] Flinders, *A Voyage to Terra Australis*, I, p. 195. Encounter Bay is situated off the coast of the present-day town of Victor Harbor. The position of the meeting was 35°40′S, 138°58′E.

[4] Steven, *Trade, Tactics and Territory*, pp. 64–105.

[5] Starbuck, 'Sir Joseph Banks and the Baudin Expedition', pp. 59–60.

[6] For helpful material on Flinders and Baudin at Encounter Bay, see www.slsa.gov.au/encounter/baudin/maps.htm.

[7] Fornasiero, Monteath and West-Sooby, *Encountering Terra Australis*, p. 154.

[8] For details of the meeting between the English and French vessels, see ML, *Investigator* Rough Journal, I, 8 and 9 April 1802, ff. 432–435; Flinders, *A Voyage to Terra Australis*, I, pp. 188–90; *Journal of Post Captain Nicolas Baudin*, trans., Cornell, pp. 379–80 (quotation on p. 380); Fornasiero, Monteath and West-Sooby, 'Hydrographic Reputations', p. 18; and below, pp. 362, 364–5.

Conversations between Flinders and Baudin were conducted mainly in English. Flinders had no French but Baudin spoke enough English to be understood.[1] Flinders and Baudin discussed what they had so far achieved on their respective voyages. There were no signs of resentment by either commander of the other's achievements. Nor is there evidence of either man withholding information or indulging in sleight of hand in describing the progress of their voyages. The cordial nature and open exchange of information at these meetings suggests that neither party had strategic imperatives in their voyages: these were mainly geographical and scientific explorations. Baudin's expedition originally had twenty-two scientists, draughtsmen, gardeners and artists, while the *Investigator* carried a larger scientific complement than any other British voyage of exploration since 1768.[2] Despite the courtesy of the meetings between Flinders and Baudin, however, both commanders knew their respective nations were rivals for strategic and commercial advantage in the Pacific.[3]

During their meetings, Flinders learned that the French had visited western Australia, where they examined the coast between Cape Leeuwin and Edels Land. The French expedition had explored the southern and eastern parts of Van Diemen's Land, and had examined the south Australian coast from Cape Banks to Encounter Bay. Baudin and his company had not found any inlets or rivers along that coast where they could anchor, especially near Western Port. He reported that *Le Géographe* had been separated in a heavy gale from its companion ship, *Le Naturaliste*, in Bass Strait. Flinders enquired whether Baudin had come across a large island (King Island) in the western entrance to Bass Strait, but the Frenchman had not seen it and 'seemed much to doubt its existence'.[4] At the second meeting Flinders presented Baudin with three charts lately published by Arrowsmith of London on Bass Strait and Van Diemen's Land and a copy of his *Observations on the Coasts of Van Diemen's Land, on Bass's Strait and its Islands, and on Part of the Coasts of New South Wales: intended to accompany the charts of the late discoveries in those countries* (1801). Baudin spoke about Bass Strait at both meetings.[5]

Baudin, for his part, learned that the English vessel had been sent on a mission similar to his own, and that Flinders had left England eight months after Baudin had sailed from France. The French commander was informed that Flinders and his party had explored the south-west coast of Australia from Cape Leeuwin in an eastward direction; that they had surveyed the coast along to Encounter Bay, including Kangaroo Island; and that Flinders was the creator of the chart of Bass Strait in Baudin's possession. This had been copied in Paris from an English print. Baudin showed this chart to Flinders on their first meeting. According to Flinders, the French commander did not realize he was speaking to the compiler of the chart until their second meeting. Baudin's account is different: in his journal and in a letter to the French Minister of the Marine, he stated that he knew Flinders's name at the start of their first meeting. Baudin showed Flinders finished and coloured charts he had made of Van Diemen's Land and paintings of the Aborigines

---

[1] Flinders, *A Voyage to Terra Australis*, I, p. 190. Brown, however, noted 'the extreme badness' of Baudin's English (Vallance, Moore and Groves, eds, *Nature's Investigator*, p. 178).

[2] Mackay, 'In the Shadow of Cook', pp. 103–4, and Mackay, *In the Wake of Cook*, p. 4; Frost, *The Global Reach of Empire*, p. 237.

[3] Gascoigne, *Encountering the Pacific*, p. 347.

[4] ML, *Investigator* Rough Journal, I, 9 April 1802, f. 435.

[5] Ibid., I, 9 April 1802, f. 434; and below, pp. 364–5.

there. According to Flinders, Baudin 'appeared to be somewhat mortified' to learn about the English exploration of the south Australian coast. The English presence at Encounter Bay did not give Baudin 'any great pleasure'.[1]

The ships parted after two days, Flinders continuing in an easterly direction, Baudin following a westerly course. Soon after leaving Encounter Bay, the *Investigator* sailed eastwards into choppy waters. Flinders wanted to survey the five degrees of the unknown coast between Encounter Bay and the entrance to Bass Strait – the shoreline already explored by *Le Géographe*. He came upon barren land, saw no harbours, and found no evidence of running water. He confirmed Baudin's observation that this land was barren, for not 'even the worst parts of Nuyts' Land exceed it in sterility'.[2] Climatic conditions worsened. Squalls of rain and hazy weather, with occasional outbreaks of lightning, made navigation difficult and 'common prudence' obliged the ship to keep a distance from the mainland shore. Extra sails were put up to help the ship cope with strong winds.[3] A gale blew from the south-west which, as Flinders later stated, 'obliged us to push on for Bass's Straits, without attending minutely to the formation of the coast'.[4] At this stage of the voyage, the *Investigator* had sailed for forty weeks from England; the need for fresh food, water and repairs was pressing. Flinders had hoped to recommence exploring the mainland at Cape Bridgewater, but the winds were unfavourable so he abandoned any thought of doing so.[5]

Inclement weather forced Flinders to sail further from the mainland than he would have liked, but in so doing he came across King Island at the opening of Bass Strait, a large island unseen by the French. This was Flinders's first major discovery after the meeting with *Le Géographe*. Flinders knew it was likely that an island would be found in this location. Before leaving New South Wales in 1799, he had received an account of this island lying to the north-west of Hunter's Isles, the southern part of it having been seen in 1798 by Captain William Reid in a sealing vessel.[6] Flinders and his small party explored parts of the island cursorily in a day. It was too densely wooded for them to penetrate more than half a mile from the shore.[7] The most important feature of this brief excursion consisted of botanical collection, for Brown gathered 'a greater variety of plants upon this island than upon any one we have yet seen'.[8]

Judging the weather to be fine, on the next day Flinders steered the *Investigator* towards the mainland to trace as much as possible of the remaining part of the south coast before setting off for Port Jackson. He sighted land and a large circular bay. The *Investigator* had arrived at what became Port Phillip – the site of modern Melbourne. Flinders was surprised to come across this large port and bay on the mainland opposite King Island because Baudin made no mention of it even though 'he had had fine winds and weather

---

[1] Most of these details are in ML, *Investigator* Rough Journal, I, 8 and 9 April 1802, ff. 433–435, but some are based on the testimony of Brown and Hyacynthe de Bougainville (a midshipman on the *Géographe*) in Baldwin, 'Flinders and the French', p. 54, and Vallance, Moore and Groves, eds, *Nature's Investigator*, pp. 179, 189 n.4. Bougainville was not present at the meetings.

[2] Flinders, *A Voyage to Terra Australis*, I, p. 201.

[3] ML, *Investigator* Rough Journal, I, 14–20 April 1802 (quotation from 20 April), ff. 442–453.

[4] Flinders to the Admiralty, 11 May 1802, in Bladen, ed., *HRNSW*, IV, p. 749.

[5] Flinders, *A Voyage to Terra Australis*, I, p. 208.

[6] Ibid., I, p. 205; Scott, *The Life of Matthew Flinders*, p. 169.

[7] Edwards, ed., *The Journal of Peter Good*, p. 74.

[8] ML, *Investigator* Rough Journal, I, 24 April 1802, f. 459; and below, pp. 378–9.

to run along it'.[1] Flinders congratulated himself on having made 'a new and useful discovery'.[2] The entrance to the bay proved difficult to navigate. Though it was two miles wide, the deep channel was only about one mile and the tides flowed into a single channel. On his chart of the entrance to Port Phillip, Flinders marked the 'strong tide ripplings' and he also noted extensive shoals on the southern side of the bay above the Mornington Peninsula.[3] Whenever an ebb tide coincided with a south-west gale, it was dangerous for a ship to pass through this entrance, which had a general tidal range of 3–5 feet. Then, about three miles from the entrance, the ship had to contend with shoal water. The *Investigator* ran aground here. This was the third time this had happened since the ship left England.[4]

Flinders decided to examine Port Phillip Bay. This was worthwhile, in his view, because he thought he had discovered a part of the Australian coastline that had not previously been explored.[5] Flinders and his party, including Brown, Bauer and Westall, rambled over the heathlands of the Mornington Peninsula. They landed where Portsea now stands, and also visited Swan Bay. Coasting around the port in the *Investigator* proved slow because of unfavourable winds and the strong possibility of going aground. Flinders therefore abandoned the idea of examining the port in the ship, which was directed back to the entrance. Instead, he took a small party on a cutter. They spent four days investigating the extent of the bay, which they estimated could be no less than fifty or sixty miles round. They climbed a mountain named Arthur's Seat, about 1,000 feet high, on the eastern side of Port Phillip Bay. Flinders examined the northern part of the Bellarine Peninsula. His party also went on shore on the west side of the bay to climb a granite mountain which Flinders called Station Peak.[6]

Conscious of impending winter weather and the need to replenish his ship's provisions, and aware that the coast to the east of Western Port was already charted, Flinders sailed towards Port Jackson.[7] He took less than a week to reach that destination on 9 May. He was in a hurry because of winter gales. On arrival at Port Jackson, he noted that the officers and the crew were in better health than on the day they left Spithead. They were also in good spirits. The fresh colour and healthy complexion of many among the ship's company was noted by those who welcomed the vessel.[8] On 10 May Flinders and his crew received the news that peace between Britain and France had been concluded in October 1801.[9]

Evidence of the French voyage of exploration to the south seas was immediately apparent, for, on arrival at Sydney Cove, Flinders came across the *Le Naturaliste*, which had been at Port Jackson since 24 April. He told its captain about Baudin's intention to come there. Flinders also saw the *Lady Nelson* riding in Sydney Cove and soon found out

[1] Flinders to Banks, 20 May 1802, in Bladen, ed., *HRNSW*, IV, p. 755.

[2] Flinders, *A Voyage to Terra Australis*, I, p. 212.

[3] Austin, *Matthew Flinders: On the Victorian Coast*, p. 34; Flinders, *A Voyage to Terra Australis, Atlas*, plate VI.

[4] ML, *Investigator* Rough Journal, I, 27 April 1802, f. 464; Ingleton, *Matthew Flinders*, p. 157.

[5] For detailed consideration of Flinders's stay at this location, see Fowler, 'The Work of Captain Matthew Flinders in Port Phillip', pp. 20–32.

[6] Edwards, ed., *The Journal of Peter Good*, p. 77; Austin, *Matthew Flinders: on the Victorian Coast*, p. 40; Scott, *The Life of Matthew Flinders*, pp. 172–3.

[7] Ingleton, *Matthew Flinders*, p. 159.

[8] Flinders, *A Voyage to Terra Australis*, I, pp. 226–7.

[9] Edwards, ed., *The Journal of Peter Good*, p. 79.

that this vessel had pre-empted his discovery of parts of King Island and Port Phillip. This ship, as mentioned above, had been sent out from England by the Admiralty in 1800 to survey parts of the unexplored Australian coast.[1] In late 1801 and early 1802 Governor Philip Gidley King of New South Wales had sent her under John Murray to Bass Strait, expecting the ship to fall in with the *Investigator*. Murray had explored the east, north and south-east sides of King Island, and had discovered a spacious harbour on the mainland coast which Governor King named Port Phillip.[2] Flinders acknowledged this prior discovery of Port Phillip, though he noted that Murray had only made a cursory examination of the bay.[3] While at Port Jackson Flinders also found that, on a voyage of the *Lady Nelson* in 1800–1801, James Grant had discovered Cape Bridgewater and Cape Schanck on the south Australian coast. Flinders had thought Baudin deserved credit for these discoveries, but he now stood corrected and acknowledged the fact immediately, as he always did in such circumstances.[4]

The *Investigator* spent most of May and all of June 1802 in Sydney harbour. Flinders was technically under the orders of Governor King, who assisted him considerably during this time. The main purposes of the stay were to refresh the ship's company; to repair the leaky vessel; to complete the provisions for a year's expedition around Australia; to examine the stores on board; to complete the charts of the south coast and send copies to the Admiralty; to ascertain the errors of the timekeepers in longitude; to recruit extra crew and to get another boat to replace one lost; to set up a greenhouse for the exotic plants gathered; and to consult with King about the best way to follow his instructions for the circumnavigatory voyage.[5]

The ship's company of the *Investigator* immediately began preparing the vessel for the next stage of her voyage. Flinders received an agreement from Governor King that he could engage some convicts to make up deficiencies in the ship's company. These men were granted a conditional pardon and given provisional freedom while they were in New South Wales.[6] Baudin and *Le Géographe* entered Port Jackson on 21 June with a crew suffering from severe debilitation and scurvy, stemming from lack of vitamin C during 110 continuous days at sea. Only twelve men were capable of working the ship.[7] Fortunately for Baudin and his crew, help was at hand. Governor King dispatched a party of British seamen to bring the vessel into harbour, where the French seamen were given food and a cordial welcome.[8] Flinders and his ship's company fraternized and dined with their French counterparts while they overlapped in Port Jackson.[9] Nevertheless, the British governor had suspicions about the French motives for sailing in Australian waters.

[1] Steven, *First Impressions*, pp. 70–71.

[2] Governor King to Banks, 5 June 1802, in Bladen, ed., *HRNSW*, IV, pp. 782–3.

[3] Flinders to Banks, 20 May 1802, ibid., IV, p. 755.

[4] ML, *Investigator* Rough Journal, I, 10 May 1802, f. 524; Scott, 'English and French Navigators on the Victorian Coast', pp. 159–62; Currey, ed., *John Murray*; Lipscombe, *On Austral Shores*, pp. 35, 74–5, 80–81. For an argument that Baudin should be credited with discovery of this part of the Victorian coast, see Lipscombe, 'Two Continents or One?', pp. 32–3, 36–7.

[5] ML, *Investigator* Rough Journal, I, 22 July 1802, ff. 508–509.

[6] See below, vol. II, pp. 5–6.

[7] Brown, *Ill-Starred Captains*, pp. 478–9; Scott, *The Life of Matthew Flinders*, p. 177. For Baudin's stay in Sydney, see Sankey, 'The Baudin Expedition in Port Jackson', pp. 5–36, and Starbuck, *Baudin, Napoleon and the Exploration of Australia*, pp. 25–43.

[8] Frost, *The Global Reach of Empire*, p. 240.

[9] Hambly, ed., *Pierre Bernard Milius, Last Commander of the Baudin Expedition*, p. 168.

He thought they might be planning a settlement somewhere in the Bass Strait region, though he conceded that he did not have definite knowledge of their political intentions.[1]

Flinders met Baudin on the two days following the arrival of *Le Géographe* at Sydney. Flinders scrupulously set out the respective claims to the discovery of the south Australian coast. He and Baudin agreed to call the south-west cape of New Holland Cape Leeuwin, thinking that the Dutch, who had discovered it, would not object. Flinders then claimed his own area of discovery to stretch from the south coast of Nuyts to Encounter Bay. Baudin had vested in himself and the French nation about 150 miles of coast from Encounter Bay (35°43′) to Cape Northumberland (38°3′). Grant had priority of discovery from Cape Northumberland to Western Port. Bass discovered the coast from Western Port to Point Hicks. Murray claimed the discovery of the Port Phillip area.[2]

d. *The East Coast and Torres Strait*

Setting sail from Sydney Cove on 21 July 1802, the *Investigator* was accompanied by the *Lady Nelson* as a tender. This was in conjunction with Admiralty orders conveyed to Governor King, who authorized Flinders to take the *Lady Nelson* under his command on 15 July 1802. Flinders was given the freedom to deploy that sixty-ton brig as he saw fit for as long as its service was helpful to his survey. In the event of parting from the *Investigator*, the *Lady Nelson* was instructed to anchor near Sandy Cape in Herveys Bay and remain one day; if she missed the *Investigator*, she was to sail to Thirsty Sound and anchor there until the ships made a rendezvous. Once the utility of the *Lady Nelson* had ended, the vessel was to return to Port Jackson. Apart from the company of the *Lady Nelson*, Flinders also had the use of a newly constructed rowing boat, 28 feet 7 inches long, with eight oars, constructed by Thomas Moore, master boatbuilder in the dockyard at Port Jackson.[3]

The voyage of the *Investigator* up the east coast of Australia lasted from late July to the end of October 1802. This was a coastline of 2,000 miles, following a long shallow curve from Sydney to Cape York. Over half of that distance lay in the tropics. For many hundreds of miles, the voyage near the coast was made difficult by the rocky islets and coral cays of the Great Barrier Reef. It would be necessary for the *Investigator* and the *Lady Nelson* to proceed in tandem to overcome the navigational challenges of this route northwards. The *Lady Nelson*, it was also supposed, would be sufficiently small to penetrate any river openings.[4] The east coast of Australia, unlike much of the southern coast, was not virgin territory for navigators. Flinders himself had previously sailed from Port Jackson as far north as Moreton Bay in the *Norfolk* in 1799. More significantly, Cook had sailed up the east coast on the *Endeavour* in 1770 and had described and charted a good deal of that coast.[5]

---

[1] Governor King to Banks, 5 June 1802, in Bladen, ed., *HRNSW*, IV, p. 786. François Péron's draft Memoir on the British settlement at Port Jackson indicates that King's suspicions were not unfounded. Fornasiero and West-Sooby, eds, *French Designs on Colonial New South Wales*.

[2] ML, *Investigator* Rough Journal, I, 9 May 1802, ff. 525–527. When in 1807 François Péron published the first volume of his account of the Baudin expedition, he claimed for France the south Australian coastline from Nuyts archipelago to Western Port and named it Terre Napoléon (*Voyage de Découvertes aux Terres Australes*, I, p. 325). Flinders referred to this false claim in *A Voyage to Terra Australis*, I, p. 191.

[3] See below, vol. II, p. 6. The boat was about 28 feet long.

[4] Scott, *The Life of Matthew Flinders*, p. 191.

[5] Beaglehole, *The Life of Captain James Cook*, pp. 226–56; David, 'Cook and the Cartography of Australia', pp. 47–59.

Flinders was fully aware of Cook's track and his achievements. This was the one part of the *Investigator*'s voyage where Flinders literally sailed in the wake of Cook. Flinders was determined to make his own significant contribution, however, to the exploration and charting of the east coast. He knew Cook's exploratory survey had been undertaken without a chronometer, and he wanted to improve on the accuracy of his illustrious predecessor in charting that part of Australia. Flinders was bold enough to think he could re-survey the east coast and still have time to undertake a detailed investigation of the Gulf of Carpentaria.[1]

A few days' sail north of Port Jackson, Flinders found the *Lady Nelson* had parted from the *Investigator* and was nowhere to be seen. This was the beginning of a familiar pattern, for the brig frequently lagged behind the *Investigator* – which soon proved a hindrance. On 27 July the *Investigator* was in the neighbourhood of Double Island Point and Wide Bay, and Flinders wanted to explore what appeared to be a passage leading towards the shore because Cook had only seen this part of the coast indistinctly. The absence of the *Lady Nelson* made this impossible. It was in this location near the Great Sandy Peninsula that Flinders thought the southern limit of the Great Barrier Reef began under the water's surface.[2] On 30 July the *Lady Nelson* saw the *Investigator* bearing north-west at a distance of ten or eleven miles. When the vessels anchored near one another, Flinders questioned Murray about his sailing over the past week and concluded that he was inexperienced at keeping his ship close to the shore and negotiating adverse currents.[3]

Flinders had surveyed the area around Hervey Bay in the *Norfolk* in 1799. He decided to resume surveying where he had left off on that voyage.[4] Sailing past Bustard Bay, the *Investigator* proceeded northwards, but Flinders missed the entrance to the Burnett River where the town of Bundaberg now stands.[5] The *Investigator* anchored at the northern entrance to Port Curtis on 5 August. The scientific gentlemen landed from the ship and soon came across a group of Aborigines. Several attempts were made to approach them, but they remained at a distance, watching the gentlemen. A little later the Aborigines attacked the party with a war whoop and a discharge of stones. The party retreated but Brown ordered a musket to be fired, and, on hearing this, the Aborigines retreated.[6] After dealing with this encounter, Brown and his colleagues were able to conduct their botanizing. They identified forty-eight plants in this location.[7]

While the botanical party was on shore, Flinders took a boat to explore the passage between Curtis Island and the mainland (near today's Gladstone) and took bearings on Quoin Island.[8] Encountering dense mangrove swamps, covered inlets and several muddy islands, he was convinced there was no navigable river; but in fact one of the openings he saw was the Fitzroy River. Today this leads up, over thirty-five miles, to the city of Rockhampton.[9] Ascending West Arm Hill on Mackenzie Island, Flinders observed four

---

[1] Estensen, *The Life of Matthew Flinders*, p. 239.

[2] Bowen and Bowen, *The Great Barrier Reef*, p. 63.

[3] Flinders, *A Voyage to Terra Australis*, II, p. 9; Lee, *The Logbooks of Lady Nelson*, p. 165.

[4] See below, vol. II, p. 25.

[5] Austin, *The Voyage of the Investigator*, p. 150.

[6] Entry for 5 August 1802 in Vallance, Moore and Groves, eds, *Nature's Investigator*, p. 238.

[7] Ibid., pp. 239–40, 242.

[8] Flinders, *A Voyage to Terra Australis*, II, pp. 15–17.

[9] Austin, *The Voyage of the Investigator*, p. 151.

different places where the water opened through the shores of the bay into the mainland; but they did not appear to be large openings.[1] Flinders's verdict on Keppel Bay was that it was 'not of much value, either as a place for a future colony, or for ships to procure refreshment'.[2]

On 18 August the *Investigator* and the *Lady Nelson* left Keppel Bay and sailed north past Cape Manifold and the Herveys Isles, both of which Westall sketched.[3] Three days later, Flinders anchored at Entrance Island, near Port Bowen (now Port Clinton), which had escaped Cook's view.[4] Flinders considered Port Bowen to lack a secure anchorage; it was only suitable for ships needing to put in there in an emergency. The land surrounding the port, in his opinion, was stony, sandy, and unfit for cultivation.[5] The next day the *Investigator* proceeded into Shoalwater Bay, which Cook had discovered and named in May 1770.[6] Flinders continued his survey there until 4 September, allowing the botanists time to carry out their investigations. He then sailed to Thirsty Sound and anchored the *Investigator* at Pier Head, near its entrance. This was where Cook had used an azimuth compass to take bearings, and found the needle differed from its true position by more than 30°.[7] Flinders took an extensive set of angles here to determine the difference by experiment. He was anxious to follow Cook in observing the variations of the needle because his longitude on the *Investigator* 'was getting more eastward from captain Cook as we advanced along the coast'.[8]

Flinders examined some of the Northumberland Isles, and concluded that ships might procure pines from them for ship masts. He was unimpressed with the potential of Thirsty Sound as a harbour: it was subject to north-east and east winds coming in from the ocean and there seemed to be insufficient shelter for ships.[9] On 13 September the *Lady Nelson* ran aground suddenly near Upper Head, on the mainland, and it was clear she could advance no further and would be stranded at low water: her main keel was broken and her small bower cable parted. After repairs took place, Flinders and Brown sailed in the *Lady Nelson* to the head of Broad Sound to complete the examination of these waters.[10] The *Lady Nelson* grounded a second time on 17 September. While she was again being repaired, Flinders sailed in the *Investigator* from Broad Sound to examine the western entrance to Thirsty Sound. He was held up on both the outward and return journeys by difficult navigation through shoals.[11]

Flinders thought the area was the best neighbourhood he had come across for a settlement on Australia's east coast north of Port Jackson. The high rise of the tide made Broad Sound suitable for the construction of ships and docks; the abundant pines would

[1] See below, vol. II, p. 38.

[2] See below, vol. II, p. 48.

[3] Flinders, *A Voyage to Terra Australis*, *Atlas*, plate XVIII, views 6 and 7.

[4] See below, vol. II, p. 54.

[5] See below, vol. II, p. 56.

[6] Flinders, *A Voyage to Terra Australis*, II, pp. 40–41.

[7] Beaglehole, ed., *The Journals of Captain James Cook*, I, p. 331.

[8] Flinders, *A Voyage to Terra Australis*, II, pp. 54–5.

[9] Ibid., II, p. 57; and below, vol. II, p. 78.

[10] Flinders, *A Voyage to Terra Australis*, II, pp. 270–01; and below, vol. II, pp. 86–8.

[11] Vallance, Moore and Groves, eds, *Nature's Investigator*, pp. 274–6; Flinders, *A Voyage to Terra Australis*, II, pp. 69–70.

make good masts; the extensive eucalyptus was available for ship timbers; and the hot climate would be appropriate for the cultivation of cotton, sugar, coffee or tobacco. He speculated that there might be an opening somewhere along the coast just examined that would possibly lead into the Gulf of Carpentaria or the equivalent of a Mediterranean sea.[1] That he could offer such an observation is testimony to the information that still needed to be gathered about Australia's geography, notably whether it was intersected by passages or rivers from one part of the continent to another.

Leaving Broad Sound on 27 September, the *Investigator* proceeded northwards near the Percy Isles, stopping briefly at Middle Island for botanical investigation, and sighted the first reefs among the Great Barrier Reef at midday on 5 October.[2] In his published account, Flinders referred to the reef forming 'a barrier to the coast'.[3] Flinders knew about several voyages that had sailed through the reefs within the previous thirty years. Principally, there was the example of Cook in the *Endeavour*, which had left a legacy of charts showing the explorer's track through the reefs.[4] Flinders was dependent on Cook's survey for most of his own voyaging through the Great Barrier Reef, but a blank space on the charts existed for the stretch of 220 miles between Cape Flattery to Cape Weymouth which Cook, sailing away from the coast, had not seen. Flinders hoped to find a way through the barrier, but he did not know several thousand reefs stretched for more than 1,250 miles from Hervey Bay up to Papua New Guinea.[5] Navigation through the reefs to find a passage to the open sea would be difficult and time-consuming. Flinders knew that the *Endeavour* had stuck fast on the south side of Endeavour Reef on 11 June 1770 and that the repairs had taken seven weeks before the ship could sail again.[6]

Flinders's intention was to use his chart of 1801 to head for the westernmost part of the reefs seen by Captain William Campbell in the *Deptford* in 1797 and Captain Swain in the *Eliza* in 1798.[7] Flinders wanted to trace their continuation across the Bay of Inlets before quitting the coast to head for Torres Strait.[8] Knowing that Cook had already charted the Whitsunday Islands, and taking into account the lateness of the season and the desire to reach the Gulf of Carpentaria before the north-west monsoon began, Flinders looked for a shortcut towards the top of the Cape York peninsula by breaking off the coast and heading seaward.[9] After sailing northwards for another couple of days, he was convinced there was now a good prospect of sailing out of the Great Barrier Reef without interruption. He decided to reverse his intentions for the *Lady Nelson*: as he wrote on one of his charts, 'sent the *Lady Nelson*, tender, back to Port Jackson, expecting no further impediment from the reefs'.[10]

---

[1] See below, vol. II, p. 93–5.

[2] Vallance, Moore and Groves, eds, *Nature's Investigator*, pp. 278–83.

[3] Flinders, *A Voyage to Terra Australis*, II, p. 83.

[4] For modern maps and the track of Cook's voyage up the east coast of Australia, see Robson, *Captain Cook's World*, maps 1.22–1.32.

[5] Estensen, *The Life of Matthew Flinders*, pp. 232–3, 493.

[6] Robson, *Captain Cook's World*, map 1.28.

[7] Estensen, *The Life of Matthew Flinders*, pp. 232–3.

[8] See below, vol. II, p. 106.

[9] Foley, 'Through the Barrier', p. 173.

[10] TNA, ADM 352/487, Chart of Terra Australis by Matthew Flinders, Commander of HMS *Investigator*, 1802, Sheet 8, Australia, East Coast: Queensland: Bustard Bay to Cape Sandwich, Admiralty Hydrographic Department, Original Surveys.

Flinders had additional reasons for this parting of the ways between the *Investigator* and the *Lady Nelson*. As there were no more spare anchors for the consort should she run aground or hit a reef and stores might run low, it would be unsafe for that ship to continue sailing with the *Investigator*. In addition, the *Lady Nelson* had lagged behind her sister ship for most of the voyage from Port Jackson and might be the cause of further, unwanted delays.[1] Flinders apparently did not consult Murray over this decision: the news was conveyed to Murray by Fowler when he visited the *Lady Nelson*.[2] An exchange of a few crew members between the *Investigator* and the *Lady Nelson* took place, and a launch was transferred from the latter to the former.[3]

Having bade the *Lady Nelson* farewell, Flinders steered the *Investigator* on 18 October between Round Reef and Tideway Reef and aimed for a gap between Ross Reef and Block Reef. But he was forced to turn back when the water shoaled suddenly. He then headed for a gap near Block Reef, but that also proved impassable. On the following day, Flinders sailed past Hook Reef, Bait Reef, Seagull Reef and then proceeded to the north-west between Faith Reef and Hope Reef.[4] Flinders had now sailed about 500 miles inside the Reef.[5] In a straight line, this amounted to nearly 350 miles 'and in all this space, there seems no large opening'.[6]

On 20 October around 4 o'clock, however, Flinders reported there were no reefs in sight. In his journal Good recorded that 'past noon a considerable swell & heavy sea ... indicated we were clear of the Reefs'.[7] An exit had been found through the Great Barrier Reef via a course now known as Flinders Passage. This lay in latitude 18°45' south and longitude 148°10' east.[8] It was the southernmost of the passages used by ships sailing through the Barrier Reef, but it involved treacherous navigation. Though still often used nowadays because it is one of the few safe passages through the reefs, it has been referred to as 'a tortuous and commercially useless path'.[9] Flinders had not travelled the full length of the Great Barrier Reef, but he had followed the outer route of the Reef with more persistence than any previous navigator. He was uncertain whether the reefs he had traversed were connected 'with the labyrinth of captain Cook', but he suspected they reached as far north as Torres Strait.[10]

Four days' sailing north from Flinders Passage brought the *Investigator* towards Torres Strait and a landfall at the Murray Islands.[11] Flinders steered the ship well away from reefs, and did not examine the coast between Cape Grafton and Cape Flattery because

---

[1] See below, vol. II, pp. 107–8.; Flinders, *A Voyage to Terra Australis*, II, p. 96.

[2] Lee, *The Logbooks of Lady Nelson*, p. 200.

[3] Flinders's and Murray's accounts differ about which crew members were transferred: see below, vol. II, p. 124, and Lee, *The Logbooks of Lady Nelson*, p. 201.

[4] TNA, ADM 352/486, Admiralty Hydrographic Department, Original Surveys, Chart of Terra Australis by Matthew Flinders, Commander of HMS *Investigator*, 1803, East Coast, Sheet 4, Queensland; Cape Grafton to Cape Manifold.

[5] Bowen and Bowen, *The Great Barrier Reef*, p. 64.

[6] Flinders, *A Voyage to Terra Australis*, I, p. 102.

[7] Edwards, ed., *The Journal of Peter Good*, p. 96.

[8] Vallance, Moore and Groves, eds, *Nature's Investigator*, p. 289; Flinders, *A Voyage to Terra Australis*, II, pp. 99–100.

[9] Scott, *The Life of Matthew Flinders*, p. 193; Foley, 'Through the Barrier', p. 175 (quotation).

[10] Bowen and Bowen, *The Great Barrier Reef*, p. 65; Flinders, *A Voyage to Terra Australis*, I, p. 102.

[11] Flinders, *A Voyage to Terra Australis*, II, pp. 105–6.

Cook had already done so thoroughly.[1] The condition of the ship caused concern, for it was leaking four inches of water per hour.[2] The *Investigator* anchored at Maer, the largest of the three Murray Islands. From the ship, Brown reported that they could see huts and many people on the beach, with canoes. They were not Aborigines but Melanesians. Some of these people sailed out in their canoes to the ship and exchanged coconuts, bananas, water in bamboo cane, bracelets, ornaments and bows and arrows for iron products such as hatchets.[3] The Murray Islanders carried spears, but were not hostile. Nevertheless, Flinders was wary of them because he knew that at least five men on the merchant ship *Shaw Hormazier* had been killed in 1793 by Papuan warriors when it was sailing along the south coast of New Guinea towards Timor.[4] Flinders ordered his marines to remain under arms, watching the motions of each canoe. The Melanesians were not afraid, though they were surprised to come across Flinders and his company.[5]

Continuing to sail towards Torres Strait, Flinders knew from the work of previous navigators that reefs would be encountered and so he followed a course close to the Cape York peninsula.[6] On 31 October he anchored at Wednesday Island, where Bligh had once stopped, and took bearings.[7] The *Investigator* was now at the entrance to Torres Strait. Flinders proceeded with caution owing to the formidable navigational dangers there. Torres Strait links two mainly separate tidal systems, one operating within the Gulf of Carpentaria and Arafura Sea to the west and the other within the Gulf of Papua and the Coral Sea to the east. Differences between the ocean tides within these seas cause complex tidal dynamics throughout Torres Strait. Shallow waters and coral reefs modify the hydrodynamics further.[8]

Despite hazards to navigation, Flinders concluded, after finding clear water for most of his passage, that the challenges of sailing through the strait were much less formidable than steering a passage through the Great Barrier Reef. Flinders sailed through Torres Strait in six days, but he believed it could have been accomplished in three.[9] Flinders had with him his own chart, drafted in 1792, that showed the track of the *Providence* under Bligh through the Strait.[10] He avoided Bligh's track and kept away from the south side of the strait, knowing from Cook's chart and the wreck of the *Pandora* in 1791 that that would prove a dangerous and tortuous route. Instead, he opted for a central route through

---

[1] Cook's and Flinders's tracks in this vicinity are marked on TNA, ADM 352/485, Admiralty Hydrographic Department, Original Surveys, Chart of Terra Australis by Matthew Flinders, Commander of HMS *Investigator*, 1803, East Coast, Sheet 5: Queensland: Cape Flattery to Cape Grafton.

[2] See below, vol. II, p. 140.

[3] TNA, ADM 352/481, Admiralty Hydrographic Department, Original Surveys, Chart of Terra Australis by Matthew Flinders, Commander of HMS *Investigator*, 1806, Australia, North Coast, and Papua New Guinea, South Coast: Queensland: Torres Strait, Louisiade Archipelago.

[4] Flinders, *A Voyage to Terra Australis*, I, pp. xxv, xxxiv–xxxix. Reference to the attack by Aborigines on the crew of this vessel is made in BL, Stowe MS 794, Matthew Alt, Log of the *Chesterfield*, 1793–4, entry for 11 July 1793. The *Chesterfield* sailed together with the *Shaw Hormazier*.

[5] Entries for 29 and 30 October 1802 (quotation) in Vallance, Moore and Groves, eds, *Nature's Investigator*, pp. 291–2; and below, vol. II, p. 142. The canoes are depicted in a plate in Flinders, *A Voyage to Terra Australis*, II, p. 110.

[6] Flinders, *A Voyage to Terra Australis*, II, p. 112.

[7] Ibid., II, pp. 116–18. For Westall's sketch of this vicinity, see ibid., *Atlas*, plate XV, no. 12.

[8] Kaye, *The Torres Strait*, pp. 4–5; Babbage, *The Strategic Significance of Torres Strait*, pp. 55, 169.

[9] Flinders, *A Voyage to Terra Australis*, II, p. 214; and below, vol. II, p. 142.

[10] NMM, Flinders Papers, FLI/15, Flinders, 'A Chart of the Passage between New Holland and New Guinea as seen in His Majesty's ship Providence in 1792'; Flinders, *A Voyage to Terra Australis*, II, p. 121.

the Strait, and established that this was the safest way of taking ships from the Pacific to the Gulf of Carpentaria.[1] Flinders reported to Banks that finding a safe route through Torres Strait was one of the main navigational achievements of his expedition.[2]

The Admiralty had requested a detailed survey of Torres Strait. But Flinders only made a sketchy investigation of the strait owing to the state of his ship, the navigational difficulties encountered and a later arrival in Torres Strait than he wanted, with the impending north-west monsoon season in the offing. He intended to return in the following year to find a more direct passage into Torres Strait to the south of Murray's Islands, and to have the assistance of the *Lady Nelson* in making a survey of the strait.[3] This return visit to Torres Strait never occurred. But even though Flinders had not investigated the strait with the thoroughness he would have liked to achieve, his route through these dangerous waters was a significant navigational advance. It proved important for future navigators, who could save weeks on their voyage by following a similar track. Governor King acknowledged that this route was 'a matter of great universal benefit'.[4]

e. *The Gulf of Carpentaria and the North Coast*

Dutch navigators had explored part of the Gulf of Carpentaria in the seventeenth century. In 1606 Willem Janszoon in the *Duyfken* surveyed the Cape York peninsula on the east side of the Gulf as far as Cape Keerweer (Cape Turnaround in English) before turning north across Torres Strait and finding barrier reefs off the southern coast of New Guinea. The *Duyfken*'s logbooks were lost in the seventeenth century, and no certain explanation indicated why Janszoon did not persist with exploring the Gulf of Carpentaria.[5] Several subsequent Dutch expeditions followed and charted part of the Gulf coast. They included Jan Carstensz's command of two ships, the *Pera* and the *Arnhem*, which in 1623 discovered the west coast of Cape York peninsula for about 3°21' latitude beyond Cape Keerweer.[6]

By the turn of the nineteenth century, the Gulf was a remote area for Europeans: Flinders was the first navigator to enter it in forty-six years.[7] He intended to examine it minutely, as no explorer had identified its main coastal features. Several maps of Australia printed between 1798 and 1802 showed a continuous gulf coast. These included *A New Chart of the World on Wright's or Mercator's Projection in which are exhibited ... tracks ... Byron, Wallis, Carteret and Cook ... La Pérouse*, published by Laurie & Whittle in 1800, and *New Holland*, published by Cadell & Davies in 1802.[8] Arrowsmith's engraved *Chart of the Pacific Ocean ...*, however, which Flinders had with him in the *Investigator*, did not include the Arnhem Land coastline but suggested its shape with a line of soundings.[9] The factual basis on which Australia's shoreline was marked on these maps was open to

---

[1] See entry for 8 April 1803 below, vol. II, p. 149. The *Pandora* was the naval vessel sent from England to search for Bligh's *Bounty* and her mutineers.

[2] Flinders to Banks, 28 March 1803, in Bladen, ed., *HRNSW*, V, p. 78. Attempts to find a safe route through Torres Strait are examined in Morgan, 'From Cook to Flinders'.

[3] Flinders, *A Voyage to Terra Australis*, II, p. 123.

[4] Austin, *The Voyage of the Investigator*, pp. 156–7.

[5] Burningham, 'Duyfken: Charting a Sea of Misconceptions'; Gerritsen, *The Duyfken*.

[6] Sharp, *The Discovery of Australia*, p. 52; Austin, 'Flinders on the Northern Coast', p. 3.

[7] Estensen, *The Life of Matthew Flinders*, p. 246.

[8] Gerritsen, 'Getting the Straight Facts Straight', pp. 12–13.

[9] Wood, 'Successive States', p. 11.

question. There was speculation that the Dutch charts, on which they were based, were inaccurate; and that a great strait leading into the interior might be found somewhere in the Gulf of Carpentaria even though no trace of such a thing appeared on the Dutch charts.[1] As Flinders later noted, 'the real form of this gulph remained in as great doubt with geographers' as that of Torres Strait.[2]

Flinders's running survey of the Gulf of Carpentaria occurred between 3 November 1802 and 6 March 1803. To help examine the coast of the Gulf of Carpentaria, Flinders had a copy of an old Dutch chart even though he did not have access to the detailed narratives of Dutch voyagers who explored this coastline between 1623 and 1644. Dalrymple had supplied the Dutch chart to Flinders. It was a copy of the French cartographer Melchisédec Thévonot's 1663 map, which incorporated the discoveries of Tasman and other Dutch explorers.[3] This map was reissued in constantly augmented editions over the next thirty years.[4] It included a number of rivers that the Dutch had discovered in the Gulf of Carpentaria, mainly on the voyage of the *Duyfken*. The Thévonot map was the only detailed map of the Gulf of Carpentaria that Flinders had with him in the *Investigator*. It proved problematic, however, in identifying landmarks along the coast of the Gulf because it had inaccuracies and relatively few names and details.[5] Flinders later stated that this map 'was considered little better than a representation of fairy land'.[6]

Flinders, ironically, in his desire to avoid sailing around the Gulf in the monsoon season, arrived on Australia's north coast at the end of the dry season when the rivers experienced their minimum flow.[7] In early November, his attempt to identify three rivers proved inconclusive. First, he did not see an opening that corresponded to the Van Spult River of the Dutch chart; if it existed, it would be very small and only accessible to boats. Second, he saw an entrance about two miles wide that he supposed to be the Batavia River of the Dutch chart; but he was unable to explore it because a large shoal immediately near its entrance made it impossible to navigate. Third, he saw a small opening that he supposed to be the Coen River of earlier Dutch visitors. He entered it on the whaleboat, but again found an entrance blocked by shoals and only a narrow winding channel beyond.[8] This was the only river that Flinders identified on the north coast.[9] The visit to the shore was made at the request of the botanical gentlemen. Brown listed various plants collected here.[10] This was the only landing by the *Investigator* on the eastern side of the Gulf of Carpentaria.[11]

[1] Tiley, *Australian Navigators*, p. 147.

[2] Flinders, *A Voyage to Terra Australis*, I, p. xlvi.

[3] Estensen, *The Life of Matthew Flinders*, p. 247. The Dutch charts are discussed in Jack, *Northmost Australia*, I, pp. 133–4. The Thévonot map is reproduced as an inset to Flinders, *A Voyage to Terra Australis, Atlas*, plate XIV, north coast, sheet II. See also 'South Land to New Holland: Dutch Charting of Australia 1606–1756', http://pandora.nla.gov.au/pan/60542/20060914-0000/www.nla.gov.au/exhibitions/southland/ intro.html.

[4] Ash, 'French Mischief: A Foxy Map of New Holland', p. 1.

[5] Høgenhoff, *Sweers Islands Unveiled*, p. 25.

[6] Flinders, *A Voyage to Terra Australis*, II, p. 135.

[7] Perry, 'Seasons for Exploration', pp. 52–3, 55.

[8] See below, vol. II, p. 157; Flinders, *A Voyage to Terra Australis*, II, p. 127.

[9] Perry, 'Seasons for Exploration', p. 55. The Coen River is now called the Pennefather River. This is where the *Duyfken* made the first known Australian landfall by a European ship, in 1606.

[10] See the list in Vallance, Moore and Groves, eds, *Nature's Investigator*, pp. 304–7.

[11] Ibid., p. 303.

On 9 November Flinders entered Albatross Bay, but the water was too shallow for the *Investigator* to sail near the shore. This probably accounts for his missing the mouth of the Holroyd River and its tributary, the Kendall River.[1] It was impossible to get the *Investigator* nearer than two miles from the coast along this section of the Gulf of Carpentaria. The seventeenth-century Dutch vessels, by contrast, were smaller in tonnage and lighter in draft, and had been able to sail closer to the shore.[2] The shallow water persisted. Flinders concluded, perhaps prematurely, that this would lead to the termination of the Gulf as represented in the old Dutch chart 'and disappointed the hopes found of a strait or passage leading out at some other part of Terra Australis'.[3] The flat monotony of the shore was referred to by Flinders as 'a tediously uniform coast' that had few hills, points, and islands that could be distinguished as fixed points for his survey.[4] In the 400 miles sailed since losing sight of the Prince of Wales Isles, he had not seen any land as high as a ship's masthead.[5] Continuing in a clockwise direction down the eastern shore of the Gulf, Flinders sighted a slight projection near where the Dutch had marked Staaten River, but he was unable to locate it.[6] 'If the latitude of Staten River is 17° south,' he noted in his fair journal, 'this opening must be it, but it is a profanation of the term to call such places as these rivers.'[7]

On 16 November Sweers Island was discovered near the head of the Gulf of Carpentaria. This was named by Flinders after Cornelius Sweers, a member of the Dutch Council in Batavia in 1644 and a signatory to Tasman's orders. Though the ship anchored there for the night, Flinders initially thought he was lying off a part of the mainland because no island was marked in the Dutch chart near that location.[8] The *Investigator* remained anchored between Sweers Island and the nearby (and much larger) Bentinck Island for three days. Flinders later called this well-sheltered passage Investigator's Road. He thought it would be the best place for a ship to anchor in the Gulf of Carpentaria if an expedition was ever planned into the interior of Terra Australis.[9]

The *Investigator* remained at anchor in this location for a week because its bad timbers needed caulking. This allowed the botanical gentlemen further time to explore the natural productions of Bentinck and Sweers islands.[10] The carpenters undertaking the caulking accidentally discovered that one of the timbers was rotten. Further examination showed that this was a more general problem.[11] To identify the extent of the rotten timbers, Flinders ordered the master and chief carpenter – John Aken and Russell Mart – to examine the physical state of the *Investigator* and to inform him about whether the leaks would impede the progress of the voyage.[12]

---

[1] Ibid., p. 308; see below, vol. II, p. 160.
[2] Ingleton, *Matthew Flinders*, p. 208.
[3] Flinders, *A Voyage to Terra Australis*, II, p. 129.
[4] See below, vol. II, p. 162.
[5] ML, *Investigator* Rough Journal, II, 29 December 1802, f. 245.
[6] Flinders, *A Voyage to Terra Australis*, II, pp. 131–2. The river does exist.
[7] See below, vol. II, p. 166.
[8] Flinders, *A Voyage to Terra Australis*, II, pp. 133–5.
[9] Ibid., II, pp. 139–40, p. 146.
[10] See below, vol. II, pp. 171–81.
[11] Brown, 22–28 November 1802, in Vallance, Moore and Groves, eds, *Nature's Investigator*, p. 314.
[12] See below, vol. II, pp. 179–80.

Aken and Mart immediately carried out their examination of the ship. Within two days, they presented a detailed written report that caused great concern to Flinders. Plenty of rotting timbers had been found, and it was suspected that the inside parts of the ship replicated this problem. The master and the carpenter offered considered answers to Flinders's four questions. First, the *Investigator* was making ten inches of water per hour in a common fresh breeze and would hardly escape foundering if a strong gale were encountered. Aken and Mart concluded that the vessel was 'totally unfit to encounter too much bad weather'. Second, if the ship came upon the shore in unfavourable circumstances, she would immediately break into pieces: it was much more dangerous for the ship to get aground in her present state than if she were sound. Third, the vessel could not bear heaving down in any circumstances and laying her on shore would lead to vast repairs. Fourth, Aken had experience of several ships of the same kind and condition that had rotted very quickly after the first damage to timbers occurred. Aken and Mart concluded: 'it is our joint opinion that in twelve months there will be scarcely a sound timber in her; but that if she remains in fine weather and happens [to have] no accident, she may run six months longer without much risk'.[1]

Flinders was mortified to receive the report, as it placed his ambitious voyage in jeopardy. His reaction to the report on the precarious fabric of the *Investigator* indicated a crucial change in the objectives of the voyage:

> From this dreadful state of the ship, I find the complete examination of the extensive country, which is one of the nearest objects to my heart, to be greatly impeded if not wholly frustrated. I have hitherto considered, that my business is to make so accurate an examination of the shores of New Holland and New South Wales, that there shall be no necessity for any further navigator to come after me; and with this object always in view ... I have kept ever close in with the land that nothing might escape our notice.

He added he had always adopted the plan that 'nothing of importance should have been left for future discovery upon any of the shores of this great, and in many points, interesting country ... but with a ship which cannot encounter bad weather ... I do not know how to prosecute so great an undertaking'.[2]

Geoffrey Ingleton has criticized Flinders's ambitions for the voyage, arguing that the facts presented by Aken and Mart about the *Investigator*'s condition had rudely shattered the 'over-optimistic and irrational expectations' for complete fulfilment of the voyage.[3] A case can be made that over-optimism characterized the intentions of the voyage, and that the initial Admiralty instructions, and the selection of the *Investigator*, had created unrealistic expectations. Yet a charge of 'irrational' is hard to justify. This voyage was the main goal of Flinders's life and career; he had enough self-awareness to realize the perils of continuing the voyage when, as here in the Gulf of Carpentaria, the odds were stacked against him. But he made a rational decision to proceed with the voyage and to reassess the options available to him, should the condition of the ship deteriorate. There was no possibility of turning back eastwards and heading back through Torres Strait owing to the prevalence of storms there at that time of year and summer cyclones on the east coast. He therefore continued with his survey of the Gulf, hoping he could sail north in the shelter

---

[1] See below, vol. II, pp. 182–3.
[2] See below, vol. II, p. 184.
[3] Ingleton, *Matthew Flinders*, p. 210.

of its western shore while the monsoon weather continued and until the arrival of the south-east trade winds in April 1803.[1]

A landing was made on Bountiful Island on 3 December. Flinders took bearings on a hill that was later called Mount Flinders by J. Lort Stokes, sailing on the *Beagle* in 1841.[2] Proceeding out to sea, the *Investigator* spent several days sailing westwards, anchoring each night. At sunset on 10 December Flinders noticed a hillock to the west-north-west of the ship and thought it must be the River Van Alphen marked on the old Dutch chart. It was, in fact, what is now the Calvert River.[3] Shortly afterwards Flinders saw another small opening that was called Tasmans River in the old chart; but he could not see any passage into it for a ship. This was probably today's Robinson River.[4]

Flinders had now surveyed enough of the Gulf of Carpentaria to form some conclusions about previous exploration of that area. 'I have now no doubt but that the whole of the Gulph of Carpentaria has really undergone an examination of some former period,' he wrote in his fair journal, 'and I believe that the old Dutch charts contain a faithful delineation of what was seen; but it seems to me evident, that the head and western part of the gulph, as far as we have advanced, have been examined but superficially, for in every point of minuteness the old chart is miserably deficient, though the general formation bears a striking resemblance.'[5]

The *Investigator* continued on a westerly course and survived three small incidents of grounding. On 13 December the ship reached what Flinders later called the Sir Edward Pellew group of islands and spent the next two weeks exploring them.[6] The north-east monsoon had started. Conditions for continuing the survey were treacherous, with heavy squalls, thunder, lightning, high heat (about 85° Fahrenheit) and excessive humidity. The *Investigator* moved several times to new anchorages among the Pellew group and landings were made on Vanderlin Island, Urquhart Islet, North Island and Wheatley Islet. Flinders took the whaleboat to explore the waters between these islands. He discovered and named Centre Island.[7] Near North Island Flinders saw two broken bark canoes and a piece of black rope made of a vegetable substance resembling horse hair. He concluded that this was gomuti, which was much used for making ropes, cords and cables in the Moluccas. He inferred that these remains had been left by visitors to this vicinity from elsewhere rather than being used by Aborigines.[8] On Wheatley Islet Flinders and his companions found a small shade made of palm trees, with part of a bamboo cane lying near it.[9] On North Island Brown reported seeing thirty-eight fire places with pieces of bamboo, coconut shells, small fragments of blue striped calico, a few baskets and small pieces of

---

[1] Austin, *The Voyage of the Investigator*, p. 163; Estensen, *The Life of Matthew Flinders*, p. 253.

[2] Brown, 3, 4 and 6 December 1802, in Vallance, Moore and Groves, eds, *Nature's Investigator*, pp. 317, 319, 320.

[3] Brown, 10 December 1802, ibid., p. 322; Flinders, *A Voyage to Terra Australis*, II, p. 160. There is still uncertainty about the exact location of Australian rivers named by the Dutch: see Høgenhoff, *Sweers Islands Unveiled*, pp. 24–7.

[4] See below, vol. II, p. 201; Vallance, Moore and Groves, eds, *Nature's Investigator*, p. 323.

[5] See below, vol. II, p. 198.

[6] Flinders named them after the admiral who helped him gain his release from the Ile de France in 1810. Ingleton, *Matthew Flinders*, p. 213.

[7] Vallance, Moore and Groves, eds, *Nature's Investigator*, pp. 326–31.

[8] See below, vol. II, p. 208.

[9] See below, vol. II, p. 211.

wood cut by an edged tool.[1] Flinders suspected that the visitors were from China, but he had no idea why they were drawn to the Gulf.[2]

After sailing around Groote Eylandt between 5 and 14 January, Flinders and his scientific gentlemen landed on a small island to take bearings. Deep chasms in the cliffs made it difficult to reach the top; the location was thus called Chasm Island.[3] An important find on this island comprised some Aboriginal art in caverns, consisting of drawings of porpoises, turtle, kangaroos and a human hand. Westall took a boat out to Chasm Island and identified the representation of a kangaroo with a file of thirty-two people following after it, apparently done in charcoal. Flinders thought this painting had a symbolic meaning because the leader of the chase after the kangaroo was nearly twice as tall as the others.[4] Westall copied the paintings and made a watercolour copy of the scene with the kangaroo hunt.[5] This is the first known European discovery of Aboriginal rock and cave paintings.[6]

Owing to the 'alarming state of the ship', Flinders did not think it feasible to stay longer in and near Groote Eylandt.[7] On 1 February the ship took a north-east direction to anchor in Caledon Bay. This was marked on the Dutch chart as near the eastern extremity of Arnhem Land. Flinders called the place Arnhem South Bay.[8] The *Investigator* departed from Caledon Bay on 10 February and on the following day passed Cape Arnhem, the point at which the ship sailed out of the Gulf of Carpentaria.[9] Flinders was expecting to meet the French expedition led by Baudin in the Gulf. He had conferred several times with Baudin about this when they were both at Port Jackson in 1802. But there was no rendezvous. Baudin had sailed from Port Jackson on 18 November 1802 in a clockwise direction towards Prince George's Sound.[10]

The *Investigator* had one of its most notable encounters when, on 17 February, it came across some Malay trepangers in the English Company Islands, situated to the north of the peninsula between Melville Bay and Arnhem Bay. 'About 3 PM,' Brown wrote in his diary, 'not a little astonishd to see 6 small vessels at anchor under a small neighbouring island'.[11] The vessels were Malay praus from Makassar, on the island of Sulawesi, formerly the territory of the Rajahs of Bone. Praus were the ships used in the Makasar trepang fleet.[12] This encounter with the trepangers is discussed further below.[13]

Having left the anchorage at Malay Road on 27 February, and after a brief grounding on a sand bank, the *Investigator* continued to Arnhem Bay.[14] On 5 March, near the Wessel

---

[1] Brown, 23 December 1802, in Vallance, Moore and Groves, eds, *Nature's Investigator*, p. 331.

[2] See below, vol. II, pp. 212, 220; Macknight, *The Voyage to Marege'*, p. 52.

[3] Austin, 'Flinders on the Northern Coast', p. 7.

[4] See below, vol. II, pp. 241, 243; Flinders, *A Voyage to Terra Australis*, II, p. 189.

[5] Nos 100 and 101 in Perry and Simpson, eds, *Drawings by William Westall*; Findlay, *Arcadian Quest*, pp. 14–15, 39. See also Clarke and Frederick, 'The Mark of Marvellous Ideas', pp. 155–7.

[6] See McCarthy, 'The cave paintings of Groote Eylandt and Chasm Island', pp. 297–414.

[7] See below, vol. II, p. 230.

[8] Vallance, Moore and Groves, eds, *Nature's Investigator*, p. 352.

[9] Brown, 10 and 11 February 1803, ibid.; Edwards, ed., *The Journal of Peter Good*, pp. 116–17.

[10] 'The Baudin Legacy', timeline <http://sydney.edu.au/arts/research/baudin/voyage/timeline.shtml >.

[11] Brown, 17 February 1803, in Vallance, Moore and Groves, eds, *Nature's Investigator*, p. 368.

[12] UKHO, OD 76, Matthew Flinders, 'Information collected from the Malay Praos met with on February 17th 1803 near Cape Arnhem'. This is a transcription of Flinders's information rather than an original document.

[13] See below, pp. 62–3. Trepang are also known as sea cucumbers.

[14] Vallance, Moore and Groves, eds, *Nature's Investigator*, pp. 376–80.

Islands, Flinders terminated his coastal survey of Australia owing to concerns about the seaworthiness of the *Investigator*. With an exhausted crew and attacks of scurvy, there seemed little option other than to sail for Timor in his rotting ship.[1] Flinders asked surgeon Bell to report on the medical condition of the crew. Bell found twenty-two men had symptoms of scurvy and that diarrhoea was a common complaint. He recommended a course of lime juice as an anti-scorbutic measure for scurvy.[2]

It could be argued that Flinders had carried on the survey too long in the Gulf of Carpentaria without refreshing the crew. There had been indications for some time that the length of the voyage, wet weather and humid conditions had caused problems for the sailors. Yet Flinders felt a duty to complete the survey and his personal ambition compelled him to carry out the methodical work each day for as long as possible. He wanted sufficiently detailed charts to send back to the Admiralty to record his many findings on this voyage of exploration. He also no doubt remembered his own intention to examine Australia's coast so minutely that no future navigator would need to redo the work. There now loomed large the possibility that he might not be able to continue the survey along a large stretch of coast, from the Gulf of Carpentaria to King George Sound. Nevertheless, for all the reasons outlined above, his prime duty was to get the *Investigator* and her crew safely back to Port Jackson. That would permit the charts and descriptions of Australia's coastal landform and its flora, fauna and minerals to be stored safely. It would also enable Flinders, or so he hoped, to have his ship repaired and to resume his survey.

f. *The Return to Port Jackson*

The *Investigator* left the mainland coast and the offshore islands near Arnhem Bay on 6 March 1803. She sailed generally northwards past the Cunningham Islands and continued at sea until reaching New Year Island six days later.[3] This had been seen in 1792 by John McCluer of the East India Company Bombay marine service, who had been sent from London in August 1790 as the captain of the *Panther* to the Sir Edward Pellew Islands.[4] Ever since leaving Arnhem Bay, the winds had been light, variable and 'commonly foul'. This made sailing slower than hoped for. Flinders became worried that, if such conditions continued, the ship's passage would be further delayed and the winter season would begin before the *Investigator* proceeded along the south coast and through Bass Strait. Given that consideration and the surgeon's concerns over the health of the crew, Flinders decided to put in at Timor for refreshment.[5]

By 28 March the *Investigator* was in sight of Timor, which Flinders had called at once before, in the *Providence* in 1792. Coming through the Semau Strait to Kupang from the southwards, Flinders saw two ships. They turned out to be a Dutch brig and an American vessel. The captains of both ships came on board the *Investigator* to exchange information. Flinders sent his brother ashore to inform the Dutch governor of Kupang of their arrival and needs. Flinders met the governor, who spoke no English. Fortunately, the captain of

[1] Brown, 5 March 1803, ibid., p. 382; Austin, 'Flinders on the Northern Coast', p. 9.
[2] Estensen, *The Life of Matthew Flinders*, pp. 268–9.
[3] Flinders, *A Voyage to Terra Australis*, II, pp. 246–8.
[4] David, 'As it Was', n.p.
[5] See below, vol. II, pp. 323–5.

the Dutch vessel in the harbour, who did speak English, acted as translator.[1] Flinders and his ship's company were welcomed and helped by the Dutch on Timor. Fresh fruit, beef and vegetables were brought on board the *Investigator*, which was thoroughly cleaned while lying in harbour. Rice, arrack and water were also gathered over the next few days as well as gulah, to be used as molasses for spruce beer in lieu of oatmeal.[2]

The *Investigator* left Timor on 8 April. Sailing past the island of Savu, Flinders decided to search for a bank extending from the Trial Rocks towards Timor. This was part of the Admiralty instructions for the voyage.[3] Flinders thought the *Investigator* was still seaworthy enough to allow for a few days' delay on the voyage to Port Jackson. The Trial Rocks were named after the English ship *Trial*, which was wrecked there in 1622. Dampier had sought to find them on a voyage in 1700, but without success. Flinders had a copy of Arrowsmith's *Chart of the Pacific Ocean ...*, which included the soundings made by two East Indiamen near the rocks. He also knew about Dalrymple's description of the rocks, published in 1782, which was based on details supplied by a sloop sent from Batavia.[4] Despite these aids, Flinders spent several days fruitlessly searching for the rocks. He abandoned the search on 27 April, by which time he had ten men suffering from diarrhoea and many others who were feeling ill. He attributed their bad health to the rainy weather experienced since leaving Timor and the transition from warm, humid conditions to a more temperate region.[5]

The location of the Trial Rocks continued to puzzle later navigators during the nineteenth century: at least four groups of non-existent islands were charted in the area. It was not until 1928 that they were properly located at 20°17′S, 115°23′E, north-west of the Monte Bello Islands.[6] After the failure to locate the Trial Rocks, the voyage continued southwards, well away from the shore, and with the express intention of reaching Port Jackson expeditiously. Owing to the state of the ship and the crew's health, Flinders was unable to conduct a running survey of the north-west and west coasts of Australia. Thus his circumnavigation failed to examine long swathes of Australia's shores from Timor to Cape Leeuwin. That detailed work was left for the naval officer and hydrographer Philip Parker King to complete between 1818 and 1822.[7] Flinders and his company were fortunate that the winds encountered on this leg of the voyage were mainly southerlies, keeping the damaged starboard bow of the ship out of the water.[8]

Cape Leeuwin was sighted in mid-May. Flinders intended to sail to the Archipelago of the Recherche, to complete the survey he had conducted there in January 1802, and to obtain geese at Goose Island Bay for the sick, seals for lamp oil, and salt from the lake on Middle Island.[9] His chart of the archipelago had not identified many islands in the

---

[1] See below, vol. II, p. 330.

[2] See below, vol. II, p. 331.

[3] Flinders, *A Voyage to Terra Australis*, II, pp. 261–2; Vallance, Moore and Groves, eds, *Nature's Investigator*, p. 403.

[4] See below, vol. II, pp. 350–60.

[5] See below, vol. II, pp. 359–60.

[6] Vallance, Moore and Groves, eds, *Nature's Investigator*, p. 404; Henn, 'The Tryal Rocks', pp. 38–43. In 1969 an exploration team found the wreck of the *Tryall* on Ritchie Reef.

[7] King, *Narrative of a Survey*.

[8] Austin, *The Voyage of the Investigator*, p. 177.

[9] Flinders, *A Voyage to Terra Australis*, II, pp. 264–5.

group, and he now wanted to skirt along its southern islands in order to produce a more detailed and accurate chart. The arrival of the *Investigator* at Goose Island Bay was accompanied by a report of the death of the boatswain, Charles Douglas, from fever and dysentery. This was the first death of a sailor from illness on the voyage. Many other crew members were then on the sick list suffering from the same complaint.[1] The gardener Peter Good was among those who were ill; he stopped writing his journal on arrival at Middle Island.[2] Douglas was buried on Middle Island; the quartermaster, William Hillier, died there; and the surgeon had fourteen on his sick list.[3]

Flinders was suffering from scorbutic sores on his feet and legs, and could hardly walk on shore. The salt in the lake on Middle Island had been diluted by recent rains. Fresh water could not be obtained. Flinders therefore proceeded with the voyage. He had not seen the south and west sides of Kangaroo Island on his previous visit there in 1802. He wanted to complete his survey of those parts of the island, but this proved impossible. Owing to the poor health of the ship's company and his own incapacity, Flinders abandoned his plan to explore the south side of Kangaroo Island and the coast between Cape Northumberland and Cape Bridgewater so that he could make swift progress towards Bass Strait.[4]

On 26 May Flinders passed Port Lincoln and recorded the death of James Greenhalgh, Sergeant of Marines, from dysentery. Fifteen men were then on the sick list, but the worst sufferers were getting better.[5] Sickness among the ship's company had caused tension between Flinders and surgeon Bell. Around this stage of the voyage, Bell had indicated his displeasure at the delays in returning to Port Jackson: he criticized his commander in writing for spending too long trying to complete his survey on the north coast and neglecting his prime responsibility for the health of his crew. Flinders responded to the criticisms with three letters replying to Bell's accusations. He was angry with Bell's suggestion that he was delaying the voyage back to Port Jackson. He stated that Bell's accusations were inappropriate in calling into question the commander's duties on the voyage. Bell had challenged Flinders's authority as commander, and Flinders felt the necessity to put him down by drawing attention to some of the surgeon's unhelpful actions during the voyage.[6]

Bell had touched a raw nerve by criticizing Flinders's actions as commander. In one sense, he was bringing to the surface Flinders's own anxieties about reaching Port Jackson safely and expeditiously while trying to carry out as much of his survey as possible. Flinders wrote in his fair journal:

> It grieves me to be obliged to pass Kangaroo Island and the part of the coast west from Cape Otway without completing their examination, since without it my chart of the south east must ever remain imperfect. It is not so much my own ill health that prevents me from doing this, as the sickly state of many of my ships company; no less than 18

[1] See below, vol. II, p. 371.
[2] Edwards, ed., *The Journal of Peter Good*, p. 122.
[3] Flinders, *A Voyage to Terra Australis*, II, pp. 267–9.
[4] See below, vol. II, p. 377.
[5] Flinders, *A Voyage to Terra Australis*, II, p. 269; and below, vol. II, p. 375.
[6] ML, Flinders letterbook (1801–6), Flinders to Bell, 27, 29, 30 May 1803. Bell's letters to Flinders appear not to be extant.

being now in the sick list, of whom three or four are considered to be dangerous: add to which our complement is seven men short.[1]

Each day the ship was cleaned and aired with stoves to try to prevent further loss of life.[2] But the deteriorating health of the crew remained serious: the quartermaster, John Draper, died of dysentery on 2 June.[3]

Sailing through Bass Strait, Flinders abandoned plans to correct the longitudes along the north coast of Van Diemen's Land and to connect them with the observations made of King Island and the north side of the strait when sailing in the *Norfolk*. It was a 'great mortification' to him to forego the chance to add to the details of his chart dealing with Bass Strait, but this was offset by the need to ensure that the sick crew could have 'a speedy arrival in port'.[4] Another member of the crew, Thomas Smith, died. On 9 June the *Investigator* reached Sydney Cove and found several vessels riding there, including the *Lady Nelson*.[5] Flinders immediately arranged for twelve sick crew members to be placed in the colonial hospital in Port Jackson. Four were too exhausted to be removed and died within a few days. They included Peter Good, who died of dysentery.[6] An addition to the *Investigator*'s complement was the astronomer James Inman. He had been sent out by the Board of Longitude to Port Jackson to replace the astronomer Crosley, who had left the expedition at the Cape of Good Hope. Inman had arrived at Sydney in July 1802, and had waited nearly a year for the *Investigator* to arrive there. He began checking the survey data gathered on the voyage by setting up an observatory at Garden Island in Sydney harbour.[7]

At Port Jackson, Flinders learned of his father's death. His joy at arriving safely in port and receiving letters from family and friends was tempered by this sad news. Further, Flinders expected to find Bass at Port Jackson, but was disappointed to find he was absent.[8] However, he did contact Charles Bishop, the business associate of Bass, who had kept two letters for Flinders. Bishop was downhearted because his business venture with Bass had failed, and Bass had left Port Jackson with a contract to import pork from the Pacific Islands. This proved a successful voyage. But in early February 1803 Bass set out on another Pacific voyage from Sydney Cove and, unknown to Flinders or Governor King, disappeared without trace.[9] Flinders read two letters Bass had left for him there, and then wrote to Bass informing him of the *Investigator*'s voyage, the discovery of a safe passage through Torres Strait, the minute examination of the Gulf of Carpentaria, and his hopes for advancement in his naval career. He alluded to the competition of the French voyage under Baudin's command to Terra Australis, but considered that any comparisons between that expedition and his own would work to his advantage. His own efforts in hydrography and geography, which Bass would see confirmed when Flinders's charts were printed, were superior to the 'very vague and inconclusive' work in these fields

---

[1] See below, vol. II, p. 377.
[2] See below, vol. II, pp. 377–81.
[3] Flinders, *A Voyage to Terra Australis*, II, p. 271.
[4] See below, vol. II, p. 379.
[5] See below, vol. II, pp. 383–4.
[6] *New South Wales Advertiser*, 1 no. 16, 19 June 1803.
[7] Flinders, *A Voyage to Terra Australis*, II, p. 272; Ingleton, *Matthew Flinders*, pp. 228, 236.
[8] Flinders, *A Voyage to Terra Australis*, II, pp. 199, 201–2.
[9] Estensen, *The Life of Matthew Flinders*, pp. 286–8.

on the French expedition. The letter ends with the words 'God bless you, my dear Bass; remember me, and believe me to be your very sincere and affectionate friend'.[1] This was Flinders's last letter to Bass: the two men never met again.

Arriving in port after such a long voyage provided an opportunity to write letters to London about the progress of the survey and the state of the *Investigator*. Flinders requested that Governor King approve of a detailed examination of the vessel.[2] King agreed to this at once. Within two days, a thorough investigation of the ship had been undertaken by William Scott, of the *Porpoise*, Edward Hanmore Palmer, commander of the *Bridgewater*, and Thomas Moore, the master boatbuilder in the colony. Their signed report to the governor came to an unequivocal conclusion: the ship was so defective 'that she is not worth repairing in any country, and that it is impossible in this country to put her in a state fit for going to sea'.[3] Flinders only had two vessels from which to select: the naval vessel *Porpoise* and another ship, the *Rolla*, which would have to be purchased for £11,500. The *Porpoise* was a vessel of 308 tons burden but would need to sail with a tender to accommodate all of the *Investigator*'s equipment. The *Rolla* was a vessel of 440 tons that had brought out convicts from Cork to Port Jackson.[4] The *Porpoise* was currently engaged on a voyage to Van Diemen's Land. The *Rolla* would take far less time to fit out for a voyage.[5]

Governor King was not prepared to pay the sum required for the *Rolla*. He was amenable to the use of the *Porpoise*, however, and suggested that she sail in company with the *Lady Nelson*. This was not what Flinders hoped to hear, given his previous problems with that tender.[6] The *Porpoise* left for Van Diemen's Land on 19 June.[7] Flinders drafted a letter to Banks, outlining his plans for completing his survey of Australia's coasts. He set down a timetable in which the *Porpoise* would arrive at the Cape of Good Hope in July 1805, having parted at Timor from the *Lady Nelson*, which would return to Port Jackson. Arrangements were made for keeping the botanical collections gathered on the *Investigator* in Sydney until they could be sent to London.[8]

The *Porpoise* returned from her visit to Van Diemen's Land on 3 July. On the following day, the *Lady Nelson* arrived at Port Jackson from the same expedition, though she had only sailed as far as Twofold Bay where she lost her main keel and was forced to come back to Sydney Cove.[9] Flinders asked King to authorize a survey of the *Porpoise*. This was carried out expeditiously by Aken, Mart and Moore. They stated that it would take a year to make the necessary repairs to the ship for a voyage at sea intended to last for two and a half years.[10] After considering various courses of action, the option of waiting a year in Port Jackson for the *Porpoise* to be repaired was rejected in favour of Flinders going back to England with the hope of returning with a better ship. Flinders asked King to fit out

---

[1] Scott, *The Life of Matthew Flinders*, pp. 202–3.

[2] Flinders to King, 10 June 1803, in Watson, ed., *HRA*, first series, IV, pp. 370–71.

[3] Flinders, *A Voyage to Terra Australis*, II, pp. 274–5.

[4] Estensen, *The Life of Matthew Flinders*, p. 285.

[5] Flinders to King, 15 June 1803, in Watson, ed., *HRA*, first series, IV, pp. 375–6; Vallance, Moore and Groves, eds, *Nature's Investigator*, p. 411.

[6] King to Flinders, 16 June 1803, in Watson, ed., *HRA*, first series, IV, pp. 376–7.

[7] *Sydney Gazette*, 19 June 1803, p. 4.

[8] Ingleton, *Matthew Flinders*, p. 234.

[9] *Sydney Gazette*, 10 July 1803.

[0] Flinders to King, 6 July 1803, in Watson, ed., *HRA*, first series, IV, pp. 377–8.

the *Porpoise* for sea expeditiously, with a route planned through Torres Strait. This would offer Flinders 'a second opportunity of seeing whether this Strait can safely become a common passage for Ships from the Pacific to the Indian Ocean'.[1] King acted immediately to support Flinders's request by writing to the commander of the *Porpoise*, with instructions to prepare the ship for departure from Port Jackson on 1 August for a voyage to England via Torres Strait. Flinders was to sail on her as a passenger with as many of the officers and crew of the *Investigator* as the ship could carry.[2]

After Flinders's various options had been discussed and a plan agreed for his return to England, the position of the scientific gentlemen needed clarification. Should they return with Flinders, or should they remain in New South Wales to continue their botanical work? Brown wrote to Flinders, explaining that Bauer, Allen and himself would be best employed by remaining in Australia and awaiting Flinders's return. This would give them further opportunities to examine flora, fauna and minerals and to sketch and paint plants and wildlife. Brown added they would have more favourable seasons for undertaking the botanical collections than they had experienced during the voyage in the *Investigator*. Allen would have the opportunity to examine minerals in the mountainous interior parts of New South Wales. Brown's request concluded by stating that, if they received no instructions from the Admiralty within eighteen months, they would then take a voyage back to England.[3] Flinders readily agreed to Brown's arguments that he and his immediate scientific colleagues should remain in New South Wales to continue their work. Flinders decided to leave eighteen months' provisions for them while he was away.[4]

The *Investigator* was taken out of commission. Most of the ship's company were discharged into the *Porpoise*. Flinders had mooring chains laid in Sydney Cove to secure the *Investigator* as a hulk to be used as a store ship.[5] Robert Fowler was given a warrant to serve as commander of the *Porpoise*, with Flinders travelling as a passenger.[6] On 22 July 1803 the *Investigator* was decommissioned and, at sunset, Flinders hauled down its pendant. This marked the end of the *Investigator*'s voyage.[7]

5. The Wreck of the *Porpoise*

On 10 August 1803 Flinders sailed out of Sydney harbour as a passenger in the *Porpoise* accompanied by the *Cato*, commanded by John Park, and *Bridgewater*, under Edward Hanmore Palmer. Governor King and his party followed the ships to Sydney Heads where Flinders took leave of his 'respected friend' and 'received his dispatches for England'.[8] The vessels proceeded safely and uneventfully northwards, crossing the Tropic of Capricorn on 17 August when they were about 320 miles east of Keppel Bay. A sandbank was sighted towards nightfall on that day, but it caused little alarm because it

[1] Flinders to King, 11 July 1803, ibid., IV, pp. 381–2.
[2] King to William Scott, 12 July 1803, ibid., IV, pp. 382–3.
[3] Brown to Flinders, 13 July 1803, in Bladen, ed., *HRNSW*, V, pp. 170–71.
[4] BL, Add MS 32439, Flinders to Brown, 17 July 1803, f. 102.
[5] *Sydney Gazette*, 17 July 1803, p. 2, 24 July 1803, p. 3.
[6] King, Warrant to Lt. Fowler, 20 July 1803, in Watson, ed., *HRA*, first series, IV, pp. 386–7.
[7] Vallance, Moore and Groves, eds, *Nature's Investigator*, p. 416. For the subsequent history of the *Investigator*, see Ashley, *The Indomitable Captain Matthew Flinders*, p. 37.
[8] Flinders, *A Voyage to Terra Australis*, II, p. 297.

seemed to be well away from the dangers of the Great Barrier Reef. A decision was made to progress with the ships through the night 'under easy working sail'.[1]

Unexpectedly, breakers were suddenly sighted ahead to the north-east of Sandy Cape and the *Porpoise* struck a reef. The foremast fell over the side of the ship. Spray flew all over the vessel. Unable to get a gun fired or a light shown in the confusion that ensued, the crew gave a collective shout to warn the two other ships in the party. The *Cato* steered to avoid the *Bridgewater* but failed to tack properly because of missing stays and then struck the reef. The *Bridgewater*, however, cleared the barrier.[2] Flinders consulted with Fowler, and told him he would take his charts, logs and bearing book in a small boat to the *Bridgewater*. He would then attempt to rescue the crew of the *Porpoise* as soon as possible.[3]

Masts had fallen off the *Porpoise* and she lay in shallow water on a coral reef. All her hatches, containing the stores and provisions, remained closed. The decks and bulkheads of the *Cato* were broken and everything inside her had been washed away. It was later found that the ships had been damaged on sand cays and coral reefs subsequently known collectively as Wreck Reef. Provisions, stores and water were taken to a nearby dry bank 'with great hardship & Difficulty'.[4] Ninety-four men from the *Porpoise* and the *Cato* were stranded on the sandbank.[5] After two clear days, no sight was made of the *Bridgewater*, on which the ships' company were relying for a rescue. Hopes began to fall that Captain Palmer of that vessel would find the wrecked crew and take them aboard his ship.[6]

By 22 August, all hope of seeing the *Bridgewater* had vanished. What had happened to that vessel? Months later Captain Palmer sent a report to the Admiralty explaining his interpretation of events. He had sailed northwards after sighting the wrecks of the *Cato* and *Porpoise*, and decided he could not reach the reef in sufficient time to find survivors. Palmer, according to an officer on his ship, assembled his officers and asked them if it was prudent at night-time, with heavy surf, to provide assistance to the *Porpoise*, and they agreed it would be better to wait for daylight to help. The weather was tempestuous on the next day and too violent to send anyone to the wrecked vessels. The *Cato* and the *Porpoise* were seen, but Palmer concluded, without searching to confirm his supposition, that everyone on board the ships had perished.[7] He then sailed in the *Bridgewater* up the east coast of Australia and around the north side of New Guinea to Batavia and thence to Tellicherry in south-west India. There he issued a statement on what had happened to *The Orphan*, a Calcutta newspaper.[8]

Flinders gathered the officers of his company together to determine the best way out of their predicament. They readily agreed with his plan that he should sail in a cutter with

[1] TNA, ADM 55/78, Log of the *Porpoise*, 18 August 1803.

[2] Ibid., 18 August 1803.

[3] Ibid.; Flinders, 'Account of the wreck of the *Porpoise* and *Cato*', enclosure no. 3 in King to Evan Nepean, 17 September 1803, in Watson, ed., *HRA*, IV, p. 402. A vivid account of the wreck by a member of the crew is given in 'Narrative of the Wreck of His Majesty's Ship Porpoise', 1806, pp. 135–9, and 1807, pp. 53–7. This contemporary account has been printed in Purdie, *Narrative of the Wreck of HMS Porpoise*.

[4] Monteath, ed., *Sailing with Flinders*, p. 67.

[5] TNA, ADM 55/78, Log of the *Porpoise*, 18–19 August 1803; Estensen, *The Life of Matthew Flinders*, p. 295. Westall's drawing of the sandbank at Wreck Reef is available as R1992 at NLA.

[6] TNA, ADM 55/78, Log of the *Porpoise*, 21 August 1803.

[7] Clarke, 'Biographical Memoir of Captain Matthew Flinders', p. 185.

[8] Estensen, *The Life of Matthew Flinders*, p. 299; E. H. Palmer, account published in *The Orphan*, Calcutta, 3 February 1804, in Flinders, *A Voyage to Terra Australis*, II, p. 307.

Park and a small party of men to Port Jackson to secure from Governor King a vessel to rescue those stranded on Wreck Reef. It was also decided that the seven or eight carpenters who were among the stranded company should build a vessel to take everyone back to Sydney in two months' time if Flinders was unable to get a ship to rescue them. Enough provisions had been saved to leave at Wreck Reef for the company's sustenance during Flinders's absence.[1] On 26 August, Flinders, Park and fourteen men bade farewell to their shipmates on Wreck Reef with three cheers, and began their voyage in the cutter to Port Jackson. Flinders and Park took it in turns to take watches at the helm, and had to rely on guesswork for distances. The voyage proceeded safely to Port Jackson, arriving there on 9 September.[2] The governor and officers at Port Jackson reportedly greeted him with the name 'Indefatigable' on account of his persistence in steering the cutter back to Sydney Cove.[3] Flinders wrote a letter to Governor King, explaining the circumstances under which the *Porpoise* was wrecked.[4] He also published an account of the wreck in the *Sydney Gazette and New South Wales Advertiser* (18 September 1803).

6. The Voyage of the *Cumberland*

Governor King acted swiftly to order the *Rolla* to convey the stranded crew to China, accompanied by the colonial schooner *Francis*, which was to be used to carry stores and carronades saved from the *Porpoise*. King ordered another colonial schooner, the *Cumberland*, to return immediately from the Hawkesbury River to Sydney Cove to take Flinders to Wreck Reef to prepare the stranded seamen for their passage in the *Rolla*. King assured Flinders of prompt help and commended him for his journey of over 700 miles in an open boat to secure assistance for the safe recovery of his shipmates on Wreck Reef. King hoped the commander of the *Bridgewater* would 'for the honour of humanity' eventually explain why he had thought the abandoned men of the *Porpoise* and the *Cato* had perished on the reef. King ordered that the *Cumberland* should be provided with provisions for six months for ten officers and a crew. King gave Flinders a set of letters to deliver to the Admiralty in London.[5] Flinders then prepared for his departure, offering farewells to Brown, Bauer and other members of the *Investigator*'s crew who remained in Sydney. Flinders did not know that the Peace of Amiens had ended and that Britain and France had been at war since May 1803.[6]

The *Cumberland*, *Rolla* and *Francis* sailed from Sydney Cove on 20 September. Despite squally weather, they managed to stay near one another to proceed northwards to Wreck Reef.[7] Flinders wrote a letter to Governor King while at sea, informing him of their progress. Flinders reported on the deficiencies of the *Cumberland*: it lacked top gallant

---

[1] TNA, ADM 55/78, Log of the *Porpoise*, 22 August 1803. For a list of the stores, see Scott, *The Life of Matthew Flinders*, p. 210.

[2] TNA, ADM 55/78, Log of the *Porpoise*, 26–27, 30 August, 2 and 9 September 1803.

[3] Clarke, 'Biographical Memoir of Captain Matthew Flinders', p. 191.

[4] Flinders to Philip Gidley King, 9 September 1803, in Brunton, ed., *Matthew Flinders*, pp. 107–8.

[5] King to Flinders, 17 September 1803, in Vallance, Moore and Groves, eds, *Nature's Investigator*, p. 438.

[6] Estensen, *The Life of Matthew Flinders*, p. 305.

[7] TNA, ADM 55/78, Log of the *Cumberland*, 20 September 1803. Fowler kept a log on the *Rolla*: see TNA, ADM 55/77.

sails and double reefed top sails and was 'exceedingly crank' (i.e. easily keeled over by the wind). The *Cumberland* was also very leaky: water flowed onto the cabin floor and the crew were uncomfortable, being dry only when at anchor. Flinders was concerned about the loss of time that would be incurred in writing and chart-drawing on the voyage to England. His intention was to transfer at Cape Town to a faster sailing vessel if one were available for a more expeditious conveyance home.[1] Ingleton has suggested that Flinders's decision to stay with the *Cumberland* was 'the paramount mistake of his career': he should have sent that leaky ship back to Port Jackson and taken a passage with the *Rolla* to Canton.[2] But, at the time, Flinders could not have envisaged the problems he was to encounter at the Ile de France, and the suggestion that he made a decisive mistake in his choice of ship is only apparent with hindsight.

The vessels reached Wreck Reef on 7 October after a six-week voyage from Port Jackson. The stranded seamen fired a salute of thirteen guns on seeing Flinders, who was cheered when he stepped on shore.[3] 'Never were three cheers more heartily given,' Flinders wrote to King, 'than those I received on landing at the bank; and the expressions of their joy did not stop there, but they fired a salute of guns also, having got the carronades on shore.'[4] The *Porpoise* lay intact on the reef and all the stranded ship's company were in good health and spirits.[5] They had spent time exploring neighbouring reefs and sand cays, fishing and hunting for turtle and birds' eggs.[6] Flinders selected his crew for the *Cumberland*. They comprised John Aken (acting master), Edward Charrington (acting boatswain), John Elder (acting master at arms), George Alder (carpenter's mate of the *Porpoise*) and the following seamen who had sailed in the *Investigator*: John Wood, Henry Lewis, Francis Smith, William Smith, James Carter and Jacob Tippet. Flinders gave them a day to decide whether they wanted to make the long voyage back to England; only one man declined.[7] On 11 October Flinders went on board the *Rolla* to take leave of his former officers and crew.[8] The *Rolla* had a safe voyage to Canton, and in 1804 the remainder of the ship's company who had sailed in the *Investigator* returned to England in a company of thirty-one merchant vessels. Flinders's brother Samuel was among the passengers.[9]

Flinders and his company in the *Cumberland* set out from Wreck Reef for Torres Strait on 12 October.[10] They passed through the strait uneventfully. On 10 November the ship reached Kupang and Flinders sent Aken ashore to meet the governor of Timor. He learned that the *Le Géographe* had been at Kupang in May 1803. The *Bridgewater* had not stopped there. Flinders was supplied with wood, water and provisions for his voyage across the Indian Ocean. On 15 November Flinders set sail from Kupang, hoping to avoid the north-west monsoon.[11] The ship made good progress across the ocean towards

---

[1] Flinders to King, 24 September 1803, in Brunton, ed., *Matthew Flinders*, pp. 108–9.
[2] Ingleton, 'Flinders as Cartographer', p. 72.
[3] Monteath, ed., *Sailing with Flinders*, p. 68.
[4] Flinders to King, 24 September 1803, in Brunton, ed., *Matthew Flinders*, pp. 109–10.
[5] TNA, ADM 55/78, Log of the *Cumberland*, 8 October 1803.
[6] Estensen, *The Life of Matthew Flinders*, p. 307.
[7] Ibid., p. 308; TNA, ADM 55/78, Log of the *Cumberland*, 10 October 1803.
[8] TNA, ADM 55/78, Log of the *Cumberland*, 11 October 1803.
[9] Scott, *The Life of Matthew Flinders*, pp. 217–18.
[0] TNA, ADM 55/78, Log of the *Cumberland*, 12 October 1803.
[11] Ibid., 10–15 November 1803.

the Cape of Good Hope. However, it had been decided before the *Cumberland* left Sydney that, on account of the vessel's small size and the sheer length of the voyage, there should be a stopover at the Ile de France (Mauritius). This would give Flinders the opportunity to decide whether the vessel was seaworthy enough to continue the voyage to England or whether the *Cumberland* should be sold there or freighted back to Sydney. Governor King had indicated in conversation with Flinders that he was not in favour of the ship stopping at the Ile de France, partly because of possible hurricanes in that vicinity, but more because he did not want to encourage relations between a French colony and Port Jackson in case war might be resumed.[1]

Given that stopping at the Ile de France would only involve sailing 200 miles away from the course for the Cape, Flinders decided to set aside King's concerns and to stop there for several reasons. The upper part of the *Cumberland* was very leaky; the pump for the water was wearing out; and the ship needed to be caulked. Wood, water and provisions were needed. There was also the possibility of finding a homeward-bound ship there for a convenient and expeditious passage to England.[2] On 15 December, the *Cumberland* anchored on the south-west coast of the Ile de France at the Baye du Cap. Flinders saw a man on shore with a plume in his hat and some soldiers with muskets. He sent Aken on shore with the French passport and some letters. Aken's brief conversation with the officer, Major D'Unienville, confirmed Flinders's fear that war had resumed between Britain and France. The arrival of a French officer who spoke English confirmed that this had happened. Flinders was required to hand over his passport and commission for the *Investigator*, whereupon the district commandant, Etienne Bolger, stated that the passport was not for the *Cumberland* and demanded an explanation. Flinders was then instructed to sail in the *Cumberland* to Port Louis.[3]

7. Detention at the Ile de France

Flinders decided to contact the governor of the island immediately to show his passport and to request that he could make repairs to the *Cumberland*. On arriving at government house Flinders was eventually shown into a room where he saw two French officers sitting at a table, one of whom was the governor Charles Mathieu Isadore Decaen. An interpreter was present: Flinders spoke little French, and Decaen could speak no English. After virtually no pleasantries, the French governor demanded to see the passport. He asked Flinders imperiously for the reason why he had called at the Ile de France in a small schooner with a passport for another vessel, the *Investigator*. Flinders briefly explained the circumstances that had led him to change vessel in Port Jackson and the purpose of the present voyage. Decaen was annoyed and impatient with this explanation; he could not believe that the governor of New South Wales had authorized a voyage across the Indian Ocean in so small a vessel as the *Cumberland*. Waving his arms and raising his voice, Decaen stated 'Vous m'en imposez, monsieur!' The French governor looked at Flinders's passport and commission, and handed him back the documents. Flinders was

---

[1] Flinders, *A Voyage to Terra Australis*, II, p. 191.
[2] TNA, ADM 55/78, Log of the *Cumberland*, 4 December 1803.
[3] Flinders, *A Voyage to Terra Australis*, II, pp. 207–8.

escorted by military officers to his ship and ordered to hand over his passport, papers, letters and charts.[1]

Decaen had a strict cast of mind and was a strong patriot. Appointed by Napoleon, he had only arrived in the Ile de France to become governor four months before Flinders reached the island. Stubborn and strong-willed, he intended to preserve the Ile de France as a French stronghold in the Indian Ocean while war continued. Flinders thus encountered a formidable opponent. Decaen kept his cards close to his chest and remained silent to any requests made of him by Flinders, giving no hints for his motives in detaining the English explorer other than that he suspected he might be a spy.[2] Decaen already had information about Flinders (of which the English navigator was unaware) that cast a suspicious light on the arrival of the *Cumberland* at the Ile de France. François Péron, the scientist on Baudin's voyage, who arrived there some months before Flinders, presented Decaen with a detailed report of the British colony at Sydney Cove. Included in the report was a brief comment to the effect that the English navigator Flinders was currently sailing in the South Pacific looking for a strong military position from which British forces might pressurize rich Spanish possessions in South America.[3] Péron's remarks suggested that Flinders was engaged on a political mission.[4] Péron left the Ile de France only two days before Flinders's arrival.[5]

Matters were not likely to be resolved quickly in the wake of the meeting between Flinders and Decaen. Flinders was given lodging on shore, where he stayed for a night. He was indignant at his abrupt treatment by Decaen. On the next day, he was visited by an aide-de-camp, Lieutenant Colonel Louis Auguste Fulcher de Monistrol. Flinders was asked by a German secretary who spoke some English to answer a series of questions about the nature and purpose of his voyage. The interrogation continued for six hours. The questions were read from a paper dictated by Decaen. Flinders's replies were written down in French translated from his English replies.[6] Flinders was asked to justify why the *Cumberland* had entered port at the Ile de France rather than sailing to the Cape of Good Hope. He decided that the best strategy, in these difficult circumstances, was to allow Decaen to see his third logbook giving details of the instructions from Governor King and the details of the *Cumberland*'s progress from Port Jackson to Port Louis.[7]

Flinders was surprised, considering this tense situation, to receive an invitation to dine with Decaen. Flinders's pride and anger had been roused by his treatment at Port Louis. He was suspicious of Decaen's offer, and felt insulted. He therefore declined the invitation.[8] Flinders acted unwisely in refusing the invitation to dinner: a diplomatic approach would have been a better course to follow. 'By offending Decaen,' Jean

---

[1] Ibid., II, p. 210; Estensen, *The Life of Matthew Flinders*, pp. 321–2 (quotation on p. 321). The French translates as 'You are imposing on me, Sir!'

[2] Scott, *The Life of Matthew Flinders*, pp. 222–30.

[3] Brown, 'Friends of Humanity', p. 58.

[4] Horner, *The French Reconnaisance*, p. 322.

[5] Prentout, *L'Ile de France sous Decaen*, p. 661.

[6] The original documents, dated 19 December 1803, are in the Bibliothèque municipale de Caen, Papiers Decaen, tome 84. Some of the questions and answers are included in Scott, *The Life of Matthew Flinders*, pp. 233–6. For a full transcript of the interrogation, see Brown and Dooley, eds, *Matthew Flinders Private Journal*, pp. 489–93. See also Auzoux, 'L'Arrestation du Capitaine Flinders', pp. 481–515.

[7] Flinders, *A Voyage to Terra Australis*, II, p. 212.

[8] The reasons for declining the invitation are outlined in ibid., II, p. 212.

Fornasiero has written, Flinders 'had met with a steeliness even greater than his own'.[1] Decaen considered that Flinders had violated his understanding of neutrality and that he should be detained under suspicion and the ship's company of the *Cumberland* kept under military control in a prison ship in Port Louis harbour. Flinders's remaining papers were placed in a trunk and taken away by the French officers. Flinders was stunned by this treatment, and realized he was being held as a spy. He wrote a formal letter to Decaen to protest at his confinement. It was wrong to accuse him of breaching neutrality, he argued, because his supposition (with no knowledge to the contrary) was that Britain and France were still at peace. He asked Decaen to reconsider his decision to detain him as a prisoner.[2]

Flinders was attended in his confinement by a surgeon, who treated his scorbutic ulcers, and he was visited by aides to Decaen who treated him civilly. Flinders again requested access to his papers and charts. This was complied with partially. He was permitted to go to government house and take his private letters and papers, his journal of bearings and astronomical observations, two log books and charts needed for compiling his own chart of the Gulf of Carpentaria. But he was not allowed access to two boxes of despatches from Governor King and Colonel Paterson. Nor was he able to see his third log book, which included information on the various vessels with which he had been involved over the previous six months and which also had his remarks on Torres Strait and the Gulf of Carpentaria. Flinders wrote to Decaen to request the return of the third log book, but he received no answer. However, other printed books that had been seized were returned to him.[3]

Flinders served a long detention at the Ile de France. For six and a half years, he was kept on the island by Decaen, and for much of the time he was effectively a prisoner. Naturally this caused anguish and distress to Flinders, who wanted to return to England to be reunited with his wife and family and who still had hopes of gaining another ship from the Admiralty to complete his examination of Australia's coasts. Although Flinders occasionally lapsed into despondency at his unfortunate fate, his loneliness was relieved by the friends he made at the Ile de France and their efforts to sustain his mental and physical well-being. Nor was the long Mauritian sojourn wasted in terms of Flinders's attention to the findings of his expedition on the *Investigator*. He worked methodically and systematically at his charts; his servant John Elder transcribed his voyage account into a fair copy; and Flinders started to write a 'Memoir' explaining his navigational achievements in Australian waters.[4]

In April 1805 Decaen approved of Flinders's application to move away from Port Louis. Several possible locations were suggested for him to take up residence. Eventually, Flinders chose to live on the Le Refuge plantation of Madame d'Arifat at Vacoas. This was situated on Plaines Wilhelms in the centre of the island. He remained there from 25 August 1805 until 29 March 1810.[5] Flinders described Madame d'Arifat as 'an elderly widow lady, of an excellent understanding and disposition, and respectable character'. He soon made friends with her eldest daughter, Delphine, and her eldest son, Paul David

[1] Fornasiero, 'Of rivalry and reputation', p. 171.

[2] Flinders, *A Voyage to Terra Australis*, II, pp. 214–15; Scott, *The Life of Matthew Flinders*, p. 243.

[3] Bibliothèque municipale de Caen, Papiers Decaen, tome 84, Flinders to Decaen, 9 January 1804.

[4] Flinders, *A Voyage to Terra Australis*, II, p. 223.

[5] Carter, *Companions of Misfortune*, p. 42; Flinders to Banks, 8 December 1806, in Brunton, ed., *Matthew Flinders*, p. 173.

Labauve.[1] Flinders promised to obey Decaen's insistence that he should not stray beyond two leagues from this residence. Flinders was accompanied to the D'Arifat residence by Aken and Elder; they lived in one pavilion near to the main house on the plantation and he lived in the other. These new living quarters provided Flinders with welcome access to fresh air and walks for exercise.[2]

By the middle of 1805, Flinders hoped to receive despatches from France informing him he was no longer to be kept as a prisoner.[3] But no such missives arrived and, as long as the war continued, Flinders saw no prospect of his release: the French government was too preoccupied with their Continental war to set aside time to deal with his case.[4] Flinders wrote to influential people to help him in his plight. Letters were dispatched to Banks, the Admiralty, Fleurieu, Denis Decrès, Sir Edward Pellew and others.[5] Flinders sent to the French Minister of the Marine a detailed explanation of the circumstances in which he arrived at the Ile de France and of his detainment. He appealed to the French government to act on his behalf in the face of Decaen's continued inaction.[6] Flinders wrote many other letters to officials in France about his situation. It is unclear how many of these were received in Paris, but most of them appear to have been unanswered.[7] Governor King wrote to Decaen from Port Jackson, stating that the only reason for detaining Flinders would be if he had not observed the strictest neutrality in wartime.[8]

Though preoccupied with trying to secure his release from confinement in the Ile de France, Flinders nevertheless found a circle of French friends among the cultivated people he encountered. His closest French friend was the merchant Thomi Pitot de la Beaujardière, an influential member of the Société des Sciences ets Arts de l'Ile de France, which was mainly devoted to science and natural history.[9] Pitot visited Flinders at the Maison Despaux in August 1804; he lent books and music to Flinders; and behaved cordially towards the English navigator.[10] Flinders also became acquainted with other Francophone Mauritians, especially during his long stay on the d'Arifat plantation. There were many occasions when he dined with these people and experienced their warm hospitality. He learned French while living there, and after a couple of years was able to converse fluently in that language and also to write letters in French.[11] Flinders also

---

[1] Flinders to Ann Flinders, 20 November 1805, in Brunton, ed., *Matthew Flinders*, pp. 134–5.

[2] Entries for 23, 27, 30 August 1804 and 10 October 1805, in Brown and Dooley, eds, *Matthew Flinders Private Journal*, pp. 80, 84, 86, 96.

[3] ML, Flinders to Ann Flinders, 7 July 1805, MLDOC 1579.

[4] Entry for 17–19 February 1806 in Brown and Dooley, eds, *Matthew Flinders Private Journal*, p. 116.

[5] Flinders to Elizabeth Flinders, 13 April 1806, *La Trobe Library Journal*, 1974, p. 2; Flinders to Banks, 20 March 1806, 28 July 1806, 1 July 1807, in Bladen, ed., *HRNSW*, VI, pp. 48–9, 116, 273; ML, MS A 1590, Matthew Flinders, Memorial to the Comte de Fleurieu, 11 March 1805, available at http://acms.sl.nsw.gov.au/album/. Decrès was Napoleon's Minister of the Navy. Pellew was then commander of the British fleet in the Indian Ocean.

[6] SLV, John J. Shillinglaw Papers, Matthew Flinders Public Letters and Papers (1807–14), MS 6730, box 341, Memorial of Flinders to the Minister of the Marine and Colonies of France, 15 September 1808.

[7] Repeated letters, some in French and others in English, are found in ibid. Further French material dealing with Flinders's detention at the Ile de France is discussed in Baldwin, 'The Flinders dossier', pp. 135–47.

[8] Bibliothèque municipale de Caen, Papiers Decaen, tome 84, King to Decaen, 5 June 1805.

[9] Pineo, *In the Grips of the Eagle*, pp. 124–6.

[10] Entry for 10 August 1804 in Brown and Dooley, eds, *Matthew Flinders Private Journal*, p. 40.

[11] For some examples of the latter, see Flinders to Thomi Pitot, 24 September and 18 October 1805, in Brunton, ed., *Matthew Flinders*, pp. 131–3. For a list of Flinders's hosts and hostesses on Mauritius, see http://library.flinders.edu.au/resources/collection/special/hitchcock/app_1.php.

cultivated Francophone friends at the Ile de France to help him with his geographical and scientific endeavours.[1]

Flinders's long Mauritian stay gave him ample time for reading and reflection. He had always been an assiduous reader and, on his circumnavigation of Terra Australis, he regularly spent evenings reading and writing. These endeavours were undertaken largely in relation to the books necessary for him to construct his voyage account and to read the work of geographers and previous explorers of Australia's shoreline. Flinders's writing skills were also deepened during his detention. His private journal, with almost daily entries, includes some 234,000 words. Its main literary quality, as Gillian Dooley has emphasized, is the ability to analyse his plight in a rationally detached way.[2] For his own edification, Flinders wrote an extended description of his cat, Trim, who had been with him on his voyages since the mid-1790s and who was still his pet while at the Ile de France.[3] Flinders was also an assiduous correspondent, writing letters to his wife, Banks, and a wide circle of family, friends and professional acquaintances.[4]

Flinders's writing in captivity also included a considerable amount of work on his charts and voyage account. His 'Memoir' dealt with the hydrographical, astronomical and geographical findings of the *Investigator* expedition. Flinders began to write an account of the construction of the charts and a short account of the impacts of winds, tides and currents on magnetism aboard ships. With clerical assistance, he worked on writing up for the Admiralty a fair copy of his logbook and journal to replace the daily logbook and journal spoiled during the shipwreck of the *Porpoise*.[5]

Flinders made arrangements to distribute these documents to his patrons and supporters whenever an opportunity permitted. In August 1804 he sent material to Philip Gidley King and to the Admiralty as well as his General Chart to Sir Joseph Banks. In May 1805 he handed over papers to Aken, who had been released from his parole at the Ile de France. Aken left there on 19 May.[6] In July 1806 Flinders sent a narrative of his treatment at the Ile de France to England. In July 1807 he despatched further papers to England under the care of his servant Elder, who was released from his Mauritian detention in that month and sailed on a ship bound to Baltimore.[7] Flinders had the satisfaction of seeing his paper on the uses of the marine barometer published in the *Philosophical Transactions of the Royal Society* for 1806.[8]

Flinders's mind was still pondering the continuing mysteries of Australia's geography while he remained in confinement. He realized that further exploration of the north and west coasts and of the interior of the continent was still needed before a full, accurate

[1] Bréelle, 'The Scientific Crucible of Île de France', pp. 1–24.

[2] Dooley, 'The Uses of Adversity', p. 88. See also Austin, 'Matthew Flinders as an Author', pp. 39–46, and Dooley, 'Matthew Flinders's Private Journal', pp. 122–32.

[3] Flinders, *A Biographical Tribute to the Memory of Trim*.

[4] Good selections of his letters are Brunton, ed., *Matthew Flinders*, and Retter and Sinclair, eds, *Letters to Ann*.

[5] Entries for 16–18 May, 15 October 1804, in Brown and Dooley, eds, *Matthew Flinders Private Journal*, pp. 33, 48. The spoiled items are the rough journals deposited at ML and available at http://acms.sl.nsw.gov.au/item/.

[6] Entry for 19 May 1805 in Brown and Dooley, eds, *Matthew Flinders Private Journal*, p. 63.

[7] Pineo, *In the Grips of the Eagle*, pp. 121, 127; CUL, Royal Greenwich Observatory, Board of Longitude Papers, RGO 14/51, ff. 171–173, Flinders to Banks, 23 August 1804; entries for 18 May 1805, 30 June–1 July and 7 July 1807, in Brown and Dooley, eds, *Matthew Flinders Private Journal*, pp. 64, 169–70; Flinders to Banks, 28 July 1806, 1 July 1807, in Bladen, ed., *HRNSW*, VI, pp. 116, 273.

[8] Entry for 19 August 1808 in Brown and Dooley, eds, *Matthew Flinders Private Journal*, p. 225.

knowledge of Australian geography was achieved. 'Think there must certainly be some river or large opening upon the north-west coast of Australia' he mused in his private journal, hoping that the Admiralty would not give any passports to French ships to embark on voyages of discovery while he was kept a prisoner. He added:

> Cannot conceive how it is that there should be no copy of Tasmans chart of that coast remaining, spoken of by Dampier. If there is an opening near the Rosemary Isles, a settlement there would be advantageous for the East India company, on account of the high tides, and the proximity of the position to the Spice Islands, as a place for their ships to touch at and take in spices for China, as a naval station for the eastern cruisers, and to counteract the armaments of the French at this island: determine to propose it to the company on my return ... If there should be no great opening on the N.W. coast, it would be desirable to explore by land from the head of the great inlet on the south coast [i.e. Spencer Gulf], and from Port Phillip.[1]

Flinders received news of the death of Nicolas Baudin on the Ile de France.[2] He was mortified to read, in a copy of the *Moniteur* for July 1808, that part of Australia's south coast that he had discovered, in addition to some of that coast first seen by James Grant and Baudin, was to be called Terre Napoléon; that Kangaroo Island was to be termed the Isle Decrès; that Spencer Gulf and Gulf St Vincent were to be called Golphe Bonaparte and Golphe Josephine. Flinders was always scrupulous about first discoverers of territory having the right to name the places they had come across, and he was keen to find out who had authorized these 'encroachments' on his discoveries.[3] He was indignant about the French adoption of the name Terre Napoléon for parts of Australia's south coast discovered by Grant and himself, considering the appellation 'an injustice to our nation in general, and to me in particular'.[4] Flinders did not attack Péron but assumed that the Napoleonic regime had forced the French scientist to promote Terre Napoleon as the name for the south coast.[5] Others echoed his views. Thus a review of Péron's account of the Baudin expedition later referred to the 'audacious attempt ... to rob Captain Flinders of the well-earned merit of his nautical labours and discoveries'.[6] It was probably small compensation to Flinders to learn in due course that the naming of the unknown coast as Terre Napoléon had caused difficulties for Péron and Louis Claude de Freycinet, the two French writers responsible for the circulation of the term.[7]

Flinders's release from the Ile de France came in 1810. Lord Minto, Governor General of India, sent Hugh Hope, a commissary of prisoners, to negotiate this outcome.[8] Hope patiently dealt with Decaen for a couple of months, and managed to persuade him that Flinders should be granted his freedom. It is not known why he succeeded after many others had failed. But apart from Hope's diplomatic skills, it may be that the French governor felt threatened by British military initiatives, and rumours of an impending attack, against the Ile de France. Decaen probably thought he would be well rid of

[1] Entry for 18 August 1805, ibid., p. 77.
[2] Entry for 3 May 1806, ibid., p. 123.
[3] Entry for 7 January 1809, ibid., p. 241.
[4] Flinders to Banks, 28 February 1809, in Bladen, ed., *HRNSW*, VII, p. 52.
[5] Fornasiero and West-Sooby, 'Doing it by the Book', p. 148.
[6] *The Quarterly Review*, XXXIII, April 1817, p. 229.
[7] Horner, *The French Reconaissance*, pp. 3–16.
[8] Carter, *Companions of Misfortune*, p. 17.

Flinders if he needed to negotiate with the British.[1] On 28 March 1810 Flinders received a letter from Monistrol stating that Decaen had granted him liberty to return to England on condition that he did not act in a hostile way towards France and her allies during the present war. Flinders did not wish to see Decaen before leaving as he did not want 'to accept of any civility from a man whose conduct has been such as has his to me'. Flinders sailed from the harbour of Port Napoléon on 13 June in the *Harriet* and transferred to the *Otter*, which sailed to the Cape of Good Hope.[2] He arrived back in England in October 1810.

8.   Flinders as a Naval Commander

Flinders had great ambitions for his career as a naval commander and maritime explorer. He wanted to achieve fame, and believed that his achievements should lead to promotion on merit. He knew that patronage was the key to a successful naval career. Fortunately for him, the Navy was a profession that did not require the application of influence or money.[3] He had gained patronage as a young midshipman from Sir Thomas Pasley. Before the *Investigator* voyage began, he had been promoted to lieutenant. Banks was to serve as his patron on the *Investigator* expedition, with governors Hunter and King of New South Wales providing full backing for Flinders's endeavours.[4] Before gaining the command of the *Investigator*, he indicated that he was tired of serving in the Navy for a pittance and wanted to be his own master.[5] He expressed his ambitions succinctly: 'I am fully determined never to serve as a common lieutenant in a common ship, unless in case of necessity; and I am doubtful whether even a vessel upon the survey of New Holland, unaccompanied by promotion, or emolument to the general run of service, will tempt me'.[6] To his wife-to-be, he speculated that the future was uncertain for his career: 'I may now perhaps make a bold dash forward, or may remain a poor lieutenant all my life.'[7]

   The expectation of career advancement and recognition for his achievements as a maritime explorer was a strong motivating factor in Flinders's personality. When detained at the Ile de France, he wrote to Banks as follows:

> I have too much ambition to rest in the unnoticed idle order of mankind. Since neither birth nor fortune have favoured me, my actions shall speak to the world. In the regular service of the Navy there are too many competitors for fame. I have therefore chosen a branch which, though less rewarded by rank and fortune, is yet little less in celebrity. In this the candidates are fewer, and in this, if adverse fortune does not oppose me, I will succeed; and although I cannot rival the immortalized name of Cook, yet if persevering industry, joined to what ability I may possess, can accomplish it, then I will secure the second place.[8]

---

[1] Flinders to Hugh Hope, 13 March 1810, in Brunton, ed., *Matthew Flinders*, p. 196.

[2] Flinders to Charles Desbassayns, 16 April 1810, ibid., p. 198; entry for 14 June 1810 in Brown and Dooley, eds, *Matthew Flinders Private Journal*, p. 314.

[3] Rodger, *The Wooden World*, p. 124.

[4] Morgan, 'Sir Joseph Banks as Patron of the *Investigator* Expedition', pp. 235–64.

[5] Flinders to Christopher Smith, 14 February 1800, in Brunton, ed., *Matthew Flinders*, pp. 41–3.

[6] ML, Waterhouse Family Collection, Flinders to George Bass, 15–21 February 1800, http://www.acmssearch.sl.nsw.gov.au/search/itemDetailPaged.cgi?itemID=412971.

[7] Flinders to Ann Chappelle, 18 December 1800, in Brunton, ed., *Matthew Flinders*, pp. 54–6.

[8] Flinders to Banks, 12 July 1804, in Bladen, ed., *HRNSW*, V, pp. 397–8.

Promotion and acclaim for his endeavours, however, came slowly. He was worried that he would never have the opportunity to complete his examination of Australia or obtain promotion as recompense of what he had achieved in the *Investigator*.[1] Arriving back in England after the long detention in the Ile de France, he hoped the Admiralty would award him a promotion from the time he had been first detained there.[2] He was disappointed to be informed, however, that, according to the rules of office, he could only be awarded a promotion to post-captain backdated to 7 May 1810, the date when Charles Philip Yorke became the new Lord Commissioner of the Admiralty.[3]

As indicated above, Flinders modelled his naval career on James Cook, following his skills as a navigator and as a commander who exercised good judgement and care over the health and well-being of his ship's company. Flinders placed Cook on a pedestal, and considered his leadership in the *Investigator* could never exceed his hero's achievements but would be regarded as a worthy successor.[4] Ernest Scott referred to Flinders as 'the nautical grandson of Cook'.[5] Flinders himself saw himself as following in Cook's wake: nobody could replicate his achievements because 'the great harvest is reaped, and the gleanings only are reserved for us'.[6] Flinders followed Cook's example in fitting out the *Investigator* and in his sailing directions, use of running surveys and shipboard routine.[7] When Flinders drew attention to his own discoveries during his circumnavigation of Australia, he was careful to explain that his survey of the east coast followed Cook's track and findings to complete 'what that great navigator had not had time to examine' beyond Cape Palmerston.[8]

After being appointed commander of the *Investigator*, Flinders issued detailed orders to the boatswain, gunner and carpenter, and to the gentlemen of the quarter deck.[9] Like Cook, Flinders maintained firm discipline on board ship, handing out punishments where necessary. Before the *Investigator*'s voyage began, Flinders established his authority by ordering floggings of crew members who were disobedient or who had tried to desert ship.[10] Similar punishments occurred from time to time during the circumnavigation of Australia, but not frequently.[11] Flinders, unlike Bligh, did not inflict excessive verbal lashings on his ship's company. But he reprimanded those who did not perform their duties promptly and punctiliously. His younger brother, Samuel, was reproached several times for his slack behaviour.[12] Flinders allowed his crew to relax when traditional ceremonies were observed, such as the rituals associated with crossing the equator on the voyage out down the Atlantic towards the Cape of Good Hope. But on this occasion he spoke afterwards to the ship's company about their excessive drinking and found fault

---

[1] Flinders to Banks, 18 January 1810, ibid., V, p. 276.

[2] Flinders to Banks, 25 October 1810, ibid., VII, p. 436.

[3] ML, Matthew Flinders letterbook (1810–14), Flinders to Commissioner Shield, 1 February 1811; NMM, Flinders letters, FLI/03, John Barrow to Flinders, 26 October 1810.

[4] For Flinders's assessment of Cook as a navigator, see below, vol. II, pp. 479, 482.

[5] Scott, *The Life of Matthew Flinders*, p. 140.

[6] Flinders to Charles Baudin, 12 September 1808, in Brunton, ed., *Matthew Flinders*, p. 189.

[7] Mackay, 'In the Shadow of Cook', p. 108.

[8] ML, Matthew Flinders letterbook (1810–14), Flinders to J. S. Clarke, 21 May 1813.

[9] See below, pp. 141–4.

[10] See below, pp. 100, 109–10, 113–14.

[11] See below, pp. 198, 234, 250, 406, 408, 411, 416, vol. II, 65, 105, 123, 262, 264, 282, 356.

[12] Estensen, *The Life of Matthew Flinders*, pp. 184, 288.

with himself for not anticipating such laxity.[1] When detained at the Ile de France, he reflected on the best way of exercising authority as a naval commander. 'The great requisites,' he informed his brother, 'are activity and equality of temper: justice, with severity in one hand and recompense in the other, seldom fail of producing the desired effect, and are infallible when joined to amenity of manner.'[2]

Flinders paid scrupulous attention to a weekly cleaning of the *Investigator*, and to following Cook's advice on the food and anti-scorbutic measures necessary to keep the ship's company healthy. The areas beneath deck were cleaned each week and aired with stoves.[3] Flinders ensured that the ship's company had a hot breakfast and hot soup for dinner.[4] Fresh meat, such as porpoise, kangaroo, swan and turtle, was occasionally served as a special treat for dinner, often as part of a communal feast.[5] Lime juice and sugar were issued as anti-scorbutic measures in warm weather and sauerkraut was given to the crew when the weather was cooler.[6] Flinders had absorbed the value of these health initiatives long before his voyage began, for he wrote out Cook's recommendations when he was sailing in the *Providence* with Bligh in 1791.[7] The net result of Flinders's careful handling of these matters was that there were no deaths from scurvy on the *Investigator* expedition. Moreover, overall mortality statistics on the voyage were very favourable compared with other voyages of discovery of the late eighteenth and early nineteenth centuries: Flinders lost a quarter of his men on the voyage whereas for Cook and D'Entrecasteaux the loss was nearer 40 per cent of the ship's company.[8]

Flinders stated that it had been a prime objective of the outward voyage to arrive at the Cape of Good Hope with a healthy crew. This was motivated partly by concern for the ship's company but also by the need to avoid delays. Flinders was pleased to report, on arriving at the Cape, that nobody was on the sick list.[9] The only serious ill health among the crew occurred in the last stage of the voyage from north-west Australia around the west and south Australian coasts to Port Jackson. Contaminated water, probably from Timor, affected the crew's health, leading to dysentery and a number of deaths.[10] This caused the only major recorded dispute between Flinders and his crew. Surgeon Bell warned Flinders about the health risks to the crew as dysentery began to spread but Flinders stubbornly insisted on continuing the circumnavigation, only yielding to further pressure from Bell when several deaths occurred.[11]

Flinders exercised brave leadership on occasions when it was required during the expeditionary voyage. When the *Investigator* was experiencing difficulty sailing through the entangled coral reefs of the Great Barrier Reef, Flinders gave clear orders for how to

---

[1] See below, p. 179.

[2] Flinders to Samuel Flinders, 25 October 1808, in Brunton, ed., *Matthew Flinders*, p. 193.

[3] See below, pp. 152, 164, 171, 173, 178, 181–2, 186, 188–9, 195, 198–9, 232, 280, 306, 371, vol. II, 137, 242, 352, 366, 375, 377, 380–1.

[4] See below, p. 176, vol. II, pp. 192, 201–2.

[5] See below, pp. 198, 205–7, 215, 344, vol. II, 329–30, 349, 353, 387, 389; Fornasiero and West-Sooby, 'An Appetite for Discovery', p. 24.

[6] See below, pp. 177, 193, 220, 229–30, 232, 260, 280, 282–3, 295, vol. II, pp. 51, 135, 166, 172, 225, 247, 256, 267–8, 321–2, 326, 358, 363, 376–7.

[7] TNA, ADM 55/97, Flinders, Log in the *Providence*, f. 49.

[8] Williams, 'Scurvy on the Pacific Voyages in the age of Cook', pp. 37–46; Fornasiero, 'Of rivalry and reputation', p. 175.

[9] See below, p. 202.   [10] Estensen, *The Life of Matthew Flinders*, p. 273.   [11] See below, vol. II, p. 376.

steer the ship to safety and found, for the first time, a safe passage through the reefs that became known as Flinders Passage.[1] When the *Porpoise* was wrecked off the Queensland coast, Flinders set out in a small launch with a few crew members to undertake an arduous voyage back to Port Jackson where he negotiated for the use of another vessel and then sailed back to Wreck Reef to rescue the remaining stranded crew.[2]

Decision-making was a critical matter for someone to be a successful naval commander. Flinders's first major decision was to depart from his Admiralty orders by beginning the survey of Australia's coasts at King George Sound, working from there along the south coast of Australia, rather than obeying orders to begin his survey work at Port Jackson. This seems a justified decision because it enabled him to survey the unknown south coast before the Baudin expedition and before the weather turned for the worse in Bass Strait and along the south coast.[3] Flinders's decision to send back the *Lady Nelson* to Port Jackson when it had accompanied the *Investigator* halfway up the Queensland coast was more controversial, but probably justified.[4] The *Lady Nelson*'s slowness had held up the *Investigator*, and the loss of several anchors, with no more available, was likely to hinder further progress. On the other hand, this decision meant that Flinders no longer had the support of a tender for the difficult passage through Torres Strait and for the survey of the Gulf of Carpentaria. Flinders's stubborn refusal to curtail the expedition when he reached Arnhem Land and the crew were suffering from serious sickness and he himself had scorbutic sores on his legs, can be viewed more critically. He put the lives of some of his crew at risk, but was reluctant to end the voyage prematurely because this was probably his one chance to complete his survey.[5]

Flinders did not frequently mention his fellow crew members in his journals or letters; that would not have been expected in compiling a ship's journal for the Admiralty. But he occasionally allowed his feelings towards the ship's company to be expressed. One such occasion was his lament for the loss of his trusted associate John Thistle and other crew at Memory Cove, off the coast of South Australia. In writing about these deaths, Flinders showed compassion for their loss.[6] The deaths of Thistle and his companions 'made the deepest impression at the time'.[7] During the *Investigator*'s voyage, Flinders gave particular help to a young member of the crew, John Franklin, who later achieved status as Governor of Van Diemen's Land and as an Arctic explorer. Flinders regarded the then teenager as having excellent potential, and instructed him in different aspects of navigation to prepare him for promotion. Franklin, according to Brown, was 'the most promising young gentleman on the quarterdeck' while serving in the *Investigator*.[8] After he returned to London, Flinders was solicitous about what had happened to his former crew members in the *Investigator*. He recommended his brother and the midshipman Sherrard Lound for promotion.[9] The only person on the voyage with whom he appears to have had strained relations was surgeon Bell

[1] See below, vol. II, p. 131.

[2] Estensen, *The Life of Matthew Flinders*, pp. 292–307.

[3] See above, p. 126, n. 5.

[4] See below, vol. II, p. 125.

[5] See below, vol. II, pp. 324–5.

[6] See below, pp. 318–19.

[7] Scott Polar Research Institute, Cambridge: Thomas H. Manning Polar Archives, Sir John Franklin Collection, MS 248/293, John Franklin, 'Some Observations on Captain Flinders' Voyage', 13 December 1840.

[8] Ibid., MS 248/304 and MS 248/296/2, John Franklin to his father, 22 October 1801, and Robert Brown to John Franklin, 25 August 1814.

[9] ML, Matthew Flinders letterbook (1810–14), Flinders to Frederic Edgcumbe, 16 April 1811.

– a result of their conflicting views about whether to continue the survey along the coast of North Australia after serious illness broke out among the crew.[1]

9. Encounters with Aborigines

Flinders and his shipboard colleagues encountered Aborigines at various stages of the *Investigator*'s voyage. Flinders made numerous observations about these indigenous people whom he usually referred to as 'Indians' but also called 'New Hollanders' and 'Australians'.[2] Brown and Good also wrote about the Aborigines and Westall sketched several of them. Flinders had prior knowledge of Aborigines from his voyages in the *Tom Thumb* south of Sydney in March 1796 and in the *Norfolk* north of Sydney to Hervey Bay in July 1799.[3] He had the advantage of taking a helpful Aboriginal man, Bongaree, with him on those voyages and for part of the *Investigator*'s expedition.[4]

Brown, Good, Westall and the crew of the *Investigator*, however, had not encountered Aborigines before. They were fascinated by their encounters with them. At King George Sound, soon after the *Investigator* made its first Australian landfall, Westall drew an Aborigine: the native obliged by baring his body to the waist so that the painter could finish his sketch.[5] Another native allowed Brown and an associate to examine him physically, accompanying this with naming different parts of his body.[6] Surgeon Bell made an anthropological chart of the largest native they saw.[7] Later in the voyage, in the Gulf of Carpentaria, Westall sketched the dead body of an Aborigine on the beach at Morgans Island and Brown, at Blue Mud Bay, wrote down a lengthy list of the names of Aborigines and their words for plants and parts of the body. The meanings of many words were recorded correctly but there are some mistranslations.[8]

The extent of the encounters with Aborigines on the *Investigator* expedition was greater than on Cook's voyage on the *Endeavour*, the one previous British voyage of discovery to explore Australia's coast in some detail. Flinders and his colleagues came across Aborigines at King George Sound, Port Phillip, Sandy Cape and in the Gulf of Carpentaria.[9] But whereas Cook offered philosophical reflections about the state of happiness of the Aborigines in New South Wales, Flinders and his colleagues did not follow suit.[10] Nor did

---

[1] See above, vol. II, pp. 324, 376.

[2] See below, pp. 137, 257, vol. II, pp. 67, 141, 230, 251–4, 266–7, 290, 295, 300.

[3] Estensen, *The Live of Matthew Flinders*, pp. 55–61, 96–106.

[4] Bongaree's sailing with Flinders is described in Smith, *King Bungaree*, pp. 26–64. Flinders's encounters with Aborigines are discussed in Davis, 'Encountering Aboriginal knowledge', pp. 29–50, and Douglas, *Science, Voyages and Encounters in Oceania*, pp. 106–60.

[5] Vallance, Moore and Groves, eds, *Nature's Investigator*, p. 105. One sketch of a King George Sound native is reproduced in Perry and Simpson, eds, *Drawings by William Westall*, no. 12.

[6] Edwards, ed., *The Journal of Peter Good*, p. 52.

[7] Austin, *The Voyage of the Investigator*, p. 83.

[8] See below, vol. II, p. 251; Edwards, ed., *The Journal of Peter Good*, p. 112; Morphy, 'Encountering Aborigines', p. 158.

[9] See below, pp. 247, 250–1, 257–8, 388–91, vol. II, pp. 19, 23–4, 30, 159, 175–6, 186, 251–4, 266, 269–71, 273–5, 295.

[10] For Cook's encounter with Aborigines, see Williams, '"Far More Happier than We Europeans"', pp. 499–512. Flinders did not know, however, about Cook's reflections on the Aborigines as his remarks were not published until the later 19th century.

they provide the level of fascinating detail about the personal characteristics of Aborigines that the Baudin expedition gathered, with the help of an anthropologist on board *Le Géographe*.[1] But Flinders and his associates nevertheless offered perceptive comments on the indigenous people they came across. Flinders reported that neither the males nor the females among the Aborigines he encountered at Caledon Bay wore clothing; that all the men had been circumcised; and that the upper left tooth of the men had been knocked out as a rite of puberty.[2] Flinders was fascinated by the Aboriginal cave paintings that he saw on Chasm Island at the north end of Groote Eylandt, in the Gulf of Carpentaria. Westall's painting of a line of figures on one of these cave paintings probably represents a ceremonial re-enactment of an ancestral turtle-hunters' dance. [3]

Flinders and his associates were particularly interested in the similarities and differences they perceived in the appearance and behaviour of Aborigines in different localities. Brown noted that the Aborigines seen at Allen Island, in the Gulf of Carpentaria, 'very exactly resembled those of Port Jackson & the East coast', though they were uncommonly tall.[4] Flinders offered a similar description of these people.[5] At Port Phillip, where natives were only sighted for a short time, Flinders could not understand the language of the Aborigines but noted that it differed considerably from that spoken by natives at Port Jackson.[6] At King George Sound, Flinders drew attention to the different words used for the same objects by natives at Port Jackson and Van Diemen's Land.[7] He found their language was very different from the Aboriginal words he had previously heard at Botany Bay and Broken Bay – an accurate reflection of the considerable variation in Aboriginal language and dialects in different parts of Australia.[8] Flinders thought the behaviour of the Aborigines he came across at Caledon Bay differed much from those he had observed at Port Jackson; the chief difference lay in the propensity of those in the Gulf of Carpentaria to steal iron axes or hatchets.[9]

Communication between the British explorers and the Aborigines was made difficult because, in several localities, the natives deliberately kept their distance from Flinders and his associates. Flinders was unsurprised when this happened – as, for example, at Spencer Gulf – because he always found Aborigines generally avoided those most anxious to communicate with them.[10] Often the shyness displayed by the indigenous people must have resulted from lack of familiarity with visitors from the outside world. At Princess Royal Harbour, for instance, Smith noted in his diary that 'on our first interview with them, they seem'd surprised, which gave us reason to think they had never before seen Europeans'.[11] Flinders had recourse to sending his trusted Aboriginal crew member, Bongaree, to communicate with indigenous people; but invariably he could not make himself understood by them, and vice versa. At Sandy Cape, when Bongaree, stripped

[1] See Konishi, 'Depicting Sexuality' and Sankey, 'The Aborigines of Port Jackson as seen by the Baudin Expedition', pp. 98–125.

[2] See below, p. 257, vol. II, p. 273.

[3] Morphy, 'Encountering Aborigines', p. 156.

[4] Brown, entry for 20 November 1802 in Vallance, Moore and Groves, eds, *Nature's Investigator*, p. 302.

[5] See below, vol. II, p. 175.

[6] See below, p. 258.

[7] Scott, *The Life of Matthew Flinders*, p. 148.

[8] See below, p. 258.

[9] See below, vol. II, p. 274.

[10] See below, pp. 246, 323.

[11] Monteath, ed., *Sailing with Flinders*, p. 35.

naked as the natives were, tried to communicate with the Aborigines he could not understand a word of their language and further mystification followed when Bongaree used his woomera to throw a spear and the natives watched with incomprehension.[1]

Most encounters between Flinders and his party and different groups of Aborigines were friendly and peaceful. At King George Sound Aborigines approached the tents of the European visitors, undertook some parleying and exchanged some of their implements for manufactured ironware.[2] At Sandy Cape about thirty Aborigines followed Flinders and his party back to their ship. On the shore Flinders gave them presents of red caps and tomahawks, while the Aborigines handed over some buckets and nets.[3] When Flinders and some companions landed on the beach at Allen Island, in the Gulf of Carpentaria, friendly signs were made to the natives and an exchange of gifts followed. The Aborigines accepted some red worsted caps, a hatchet and an adze and, in return, they offered two spears and a throwing stick.[4]

The meetings between the personnel from the *Investigator* and the Aborigines, however, were not all examples of sweetness and light. Occasionally clashes occurred. On such occasions, Flinders tried to defuse the friction. At Port Curtis, on the Queensland coast, a skirmish took place with Aborigines after they attacked Flinders's crew with a war whoop and a discharge of stones. This was the first unfriendly encounter with the Aborigines on the voyage.[5] On Morgan Island six of them surprised Westall and a wooding party in a canoe. The master and some associates chased the Aborigines. Flinders, however, disapproved of this decision even though he thought the natives had staged a premeditated attack.[6] At Caledon Bay relations between the ship's company and local people deteriorated after Flinders detained an Aborigine called Woga in retaliation for an axe being stolen. But though there was a tense encounter between both groups at the head of Grays Bay on 8 February 1803, Flinders calmed down the situation by ordering Woga to be released.[7]

Encounters between Flinders and his associates and the Aborigines were compromised by misunderstandings of gesture and language. The best example of this in the entire voyage occurred at King George Sound when, after the marines landed on the shore, they staged a military parade. The Aborigines watched their red coats with white belts and their exercises, with fife and drum, with delight. The volleys of firing did not scare them. Curiosity and astonishment were conjured up in the 'vociferation and wild gestures' of the Aborigines.[8] They made several attempts to take the fife, but this was resisted obstinately. Further firing by the marines caused the natives 'to Dance & hollow unmercifully'.[9] This military exercise by the marines appears to have been staged to assess

---

[1] See below, vol. II, p. 23.

[2] See below, pp. 249–51, 257–8; and Flinders, *A Voyage to Terra Australis*, I, pp. 58–9, 66–7.

[3] See below, vol. II, p. 23.

[4] See below, vol. II, p. 175; and Flinders, *A Voyage to Terra Australis*, II, pp. 137–9.

[5] Edwards, ed., *The Journal of Peter Good*, pp. 83–4; entry for 5 August 1802 in Vallance, Moore and Groves, eds, *Nature's Investigator*, p. 238.

[6] See below, vol. II, pp. 250–6; and Flinders, *A Voyage to Terra Australis*, II, pp. 197–200.

[7] Flinders, *A Voyage to Terra Australis*, II, pp. 209–10. Westall sketched an Aborigine called 'Woogah', who was presumably the same person: see nos. 105 and 106 in Perry and Simpson, eds, *Drawings by William Westall*, n.p.

[8] See below, p. 251, n. 1.

[9] Monteath, ed., *Sailing with Flinders*, p. 35.

the Aborigines' responses. It occurred partly because the marines and the Aborigines lacked a common language. The Aborigines appear to have interpreted the military drill as an appropriate contact ritual. In 1908 the anthropologist Daisy Bates met an elderly man near Albany called Nebinyan. He told her that the Nyungar Aborigines of King George Sound believed that Flinders and his party were ghosts of their own dead ancestors who had returned from Kooranup, the home of the dead across the sea. They thought the full dress parade of the marines was a Kooranup ceremony. The ritual was considered sacred, to be handed down the generations.[1]

10.   The Makasar Trepangers

After several days spent in the vicinity of Melville Bay, in the Arafura Sea, the *Investigator* had one of its most notable encounters when, on 17 February 1803, it came across Malay trepangers in the English Company Islands, situated to the north of the peninsula between Melville Bay and Arnhem Bay. 'About 3 PM,' Brown wrote in his diary, 'not a little astonishd to see 6 small vessels at anchor under a small neighbouring island.'[2] Flinders and his crew hoisted their pendant and ensign and each of the small vessels hung out a small white flag. Flinders sent his brother in an armed boat to find out who they were, and ordered his crew to be ready to fire muskets if necessary. 'Every motion in the whale boat, and in the vessel alongside which she was lying,' Flinders wrote, 'was closely watched with our glasses, but all seemed to pass quietly; and on the return of lieutenant Flinders, we learned that they were prows from Makassar.'[3]

John Mulvaney referred to this meeting as 'a symbolic moment in Australian protohistory, when Asian and European first met in territorial waters'.[4] The vessels were Malay praus from Makassar, on Sulawesi. Praus were the ships used in the Makasar trepang fleet and what Flinders saw was probably a small type of prau called a pajala. Flinders went on board the prau of Pobassoo, the principal chief.[5] Pobassoo, whom Brown referred to as 'the old commodore', was the first known Asian in Australia's prehistory.[6] The Malay crew had muskets but not bows or poisoned arrows.[7] Westall made sketches of the praus and their crews and drew Pobassoo's portrait.[8]

When Flinders first saw the praus, he found it difficult to imagine what they might be, but had no doubt that they contained the same people of whom he had seen so many marks in the Gulf of Carpentaria. He had supposed they would be Chinese, but it crossed his mind that they might be pirates. Flinders was able to communicate with them through Abraham Williams, a Javanese cook on the *Investigator*.[9] The six praus were part of a larger fleet of sixty containing one thousand men that had sailed two months earlier from Makassar, which was

---

[1] Carter, *Living in a New Country*, pp. 161–2; White, 'Birth and Death of a Ceremony', pp. 33–42.

[2] Brown, entry for 17 February 1803, in Vallance, Moore and Groves, eds, *Nature's Investigator*, p. 368.

[3] Flinders, *A Voyage to Terra Australis*, II, p. 136.

[4] Mulvaney, *The Prehistory of Australia*, p. 17.

[5] UKHO, OD 76, Matthew Flinders, 'Information collected from the Malay Praos met with on February 17th 1803 near Cape Arnhem', Australia south and east coasts, and Torres Strait, thence to Timor.

[6] Mulvaney, *The Prehistory of Australia*, p. 19.

[7] Brown, 18 February 1803, in Vallance, Moore and Groves, eds, *Nature's Investigator*, p. 371. Makasars were known for their use of ippo poison (from the Upas tree) on bamboo arrows.

[8] Estensen, *The Life of Matthew Flinders*, p. 265.

[9] For information on Williams, see Thomas, 'Interpreting the Macassans', pp. 69–93.

under direct Dutch rule. The other praus were lying in different places to the westward, in parties of five or six together. The object of their expedition was to procure trepang (sometimes called sea cucumbers). The crews did this by diving into water of three to eight fathoms' depth where these marine animals were abundant. Each prau could carry 100,000 trepang, which were preserved by splitting the animal on one side, boiling it and pressing it with stones after which it was dried in the sun. The trepang were carried to Timor and sold to Chinese ships.[1] Nearly all Australian trepang was exported to China. Makasar traders took advantage of favourable monsoonal winds blowing them towards Marege' (the Makasar name for Australia's Top End) in December and back to Sulawesi in about April. This trade involved selling about thirty varieties of trepang at Makassar. It was largely organized without any direct British or European involvement.[2] The trade continued throughout the nineteenth century; the last prau from the Arnhem Land coast returned to Makassar in 1907.[3]

Pobassoo told Flinders that he had been among the first of the Malays to trade for trepang on the coast of New Holland twenty years beforehand. It is not clear, however, whether this referred to a trade conducted at Arnhem Land or on the north-west Australian coast.[4] Pobassoo had never seen another European ship on this coast before. He had been wounded in the knee by a native spear on a previous visit to these shores in a skirmish between the Makasars and the Aborigines.[5] Flinders asked Pobassoo a series of questions that might throw light on the *Investigator*'s voyage. But he found Pobassoo's knowledge of Terra Australis was limited apart from the same coasts visited previously with the trepang fleet. Pobassoo did not know about the British settlement at Port Jackson. He and the other Malay sailors had no charts, using a small compass in a box to direct their course at sea, unassisted by any astronomical observations. They carried about a month's water to sea along with food for provisions. They did not know of any rivers or openings leading far into northern Australia.[6] Flinders told Pobassoo about Baudin's expedition, and explained that *Le Géographe* and *Le Naturaliste* might soon reach this stretch of coast. In the event of that happening, Flinders addressed a short note to them which he gave Pobassoo to hand to them. Flinders named Malay Road and Pobassoo Island to commemorate the encounter with the trepangers.[7] Flinders recorded his meeting with the Makasars in detail partly because he thought the East India Company might want to enter into the trade in trepang with the Chinese market.[8]

11. Scientific Achievements

After the unseaworthy *Investigator* reached Sydney in June 1803, while Flinders negotiated with Governor King for a replacement vessel, Brown and Bauer decided it would waste too much time for them to return to England with Flinders: they wanted to

---

[1] See below, vol. II, p. 288; UKHO, OD 76, Flinders, 'Information collected from the Malay Praos'. See also Blair and Hall, 'Travelling the "Malay Road"', pp. 205–26.

[2] Ganter, 'China and the Beginning of Australian History', pp. 36–7, and *Mixed Relations*, p. 4.

[3] Macknight, 'Harvesting the memory', pp. 136–7.

[4] Ibid.

[5] Estensen, *The Life of Matthew Flinders*, p. 266.

[6] See below, vol. II, pp. 289–90.

[7] Brown, 18 February 1803, in Vallance, Moore and Groves, eds, *Nature's Investigator*, p. 372.

[8] Gascoigne, *Encountering the Pacific*, p. 350.

continue their scientific work in Australia. On 17 July Flinders approved of their plan to stay in the colony: 'your present application is very laudable and judicious,' he wrote to them, 'and is further proof of your zeal in prosecuting the service you have undertaken to perform'. Flinders intended to leave eighteen months' provisions in the charge of the commissary at Port Jackson for their convenience while he was abroad.[1]

Brown, Bauer, Westall and Allen remained in Port Jackson with some servants. Governor King offered them accommodation.[2] Thus, although the curtailment of the *Investigator*'s voyage was disastrous in terms of Flinders's ambition to complete his coastal survey of Terra Australis, it benefited the scientific gentlemen by allowing them more time to explore some interior parts of the Australian continent. No doubt Brown was determined to make amends for the loss of many of his best plant specimens when the *Porpoise* was lost on Wreck Reef in August 1803.[3]

Brown decided it was time to write a long letter to Banks about the expedition. He expressed disappointment at their findings: they had found no navigable rivers; they had seen no mountains of great height; and they had not strayed more than a few miles inland on any part of the Australian coast. 'The interior of New Holland,' he wrote, 'is as completely unknown as ever.' The litany of disappointment continued: there had been few zoological finds; mineralogy had been a barren field; and even botany had fallen short of expectations. Along the south coast, from Cape Leeuwin to Bass Strait, the only places where examination was not too late in the season for plants were King George Sound and Lucky Bay. Their exploration of the east coast, from Sandy Cape to Broad Sound, suffered from being undertaken too early in the season. Altogether, Brown had observed around 2,000 species of plants in Australia, of which 700 or 800 were nondescript. He had so far described 1,600 plants gathered, but all the descriptions needed to be checked and rewritten. Brown intended to retain many plants to complete the descriptions.[4]

Brown's storm-bound stay in the Kent Group of Islands in Bass Strait gave him time to write a letter to Banks that he sent on the *Calcutta*, encountered at sea and bound to Port Jackson. Brown explained that this vessel would take most of his collection of plants and seeds back to England, including the items rescued from Wreck Reef. His samples from birds, quadrupeds and minerals were insufficiently arranged or packed to send them to England at present.[5] The *Calcutta* took aboard twelve puncheons of dried specimens and four boxes of seeds in Port Jackson; these arrived safely in England.[6]

Brown also reported that some plants collected in very dry weather had already died, and that others would probably not survive the long voyage back to England in the reassembled plant cabin on the *Porpoise*. He had lacked sufficiently good plant boxes for his collections, and suggested that Flinders had not been as concerned about this aspect of the *Investigator*'s voyage as he could have been. This is a somewhat unfair comment as

---

[1] BL, Add MS 32349, Flinders to Brown and Bauer, 17 July 1803, f. 102.

[2] Brown and Bauer to Flinders, 13 July 1803, in Bladen, ed., *HRNSW*, V, p. 170.

[3] Edwards, 'Botany of the Flinders voyage', p. 148. See also Edwards, 'Robert Brown', pp. 385–407.

[4] Brown to Banks, 6 August 1803, in Vallance, Moore and Groves, eds, *Nature's Investigator*, pp. 417–19. Banks duly received the twelve casks of plants: see Banks to Brown, 30 August 1804, in Bladen, ed., *HRNSW*, V, pp. 461–2.

[5] Brown to Banks, 30 December 1803, in Chambers, ed., *The Indian and Pacific Correspondence*, VI, pp. 306–7.

[6] Edwards, 'Botany of the Flinders voyage', p. 148.

Flinders had always tried to allow sufficient time for the scientific gentlemen to do their work. When reading Brown's letters, one has to remember he was temperamentally gloomy and tended to make matters seem worse than they were. To conclude his letter, however, Brown offered more positive suggestions about the work yet to be accomplished in Australia. He intended to examine the neighbourhood of Port Jackson for plants; to spend time in the Blue Mountains; to explore the flora and fauna of Hunter River; and to visit Van Diemen's Land. He hoped these expeditions would yield new plant species. He would spend the rest of his time in New South Wales finishing and recopying his descriptions.[1] Brown hoped the visit to Van Diemen's Land, which had not been explored on the *Investigator*'s voyage, would yield 'many cryptogamic novelties' among the ferns and mosses.[2]

Bauer was not a frequent letter writer, but he also decided this was an appropriate time to inform Banks of his contribution to the expedition so far and his intention to remain in New South Wales working alongside Brown. Bauer reported to Banks that he had made more than 1,000 sketches of plants and 200 of animals. None of them were yet finished, however, so he did not send any back to England with Flinders in the *Porpoise*.[3] Bauer also wrote to his eldest brother Joseph Anton Bauer, based in Vienna, reporting his safety in Sydney and his intention to stay there for the next twelve to eighteen months while Flinders sought to acquire a new ship to continue the expedition.[4]

Brown and Bauer were respectively botanizing and sketching in the Sydney area in June and July 1803.[5] This work continued during August and September, when the localities visited extended to cover Parramatta, George's River, the Hawkesbury River and parts of the Blue Mountains. Sometimes Brown and Bauer accompanied one another, but frequently they independently visited different locations.[6] This activity was interrupted by the unwelcome news, in mid-September, that the *Porpoise* had run aground at Wreck Reef and that the garden and plant specimens on board the ship were totally lost. Brown referred to these losses as 'irreparable'. He had duplicates of many specimens but the ones lost were the best he had. Many were from the south coast and were the most valuable specimens collected during the voyage. Brown consulted with Flinders and King and was at least reassured that boxes containing the seeds sent on the *Porpoise* were enclosed in strong cases. Thus most of the seeds should have been preserved.[7]

Brown and Bauer continued their work in and around Sydney during October and November 1803.[8] A new departure soon occurred, however, because Governor King indicated his intention to send Brown and another naturalist to Risdon Cove, Van Diemen's Land, where a small settlement (about four miles north of Hobart) had just been made by a party accompanying Lieutenant John Bowen.[9] Brown left for Van

---

[1] Brown to Banks, 6 August 1803, in Vallance, Moore and Groves, eds, *Nature's Investigator*, pp. 419–21.

[2] BL, Add MS 32439, Brown to Charles Greville, 6 August 1803, ff. 121–124. Extracts from this letter are printed in Bladen, ed., *HRNSW*, V, pp. 185–7.

[3] Bauer to Banks, 8 August 1803, in Chambers, ed., *The Indian and Pacific Correspondence*, VI, p. 280.

[4] Bauer to Joseph Anton Bauer, 8 August 1803, in Norst, *Ferdinand Bauer*, p. 108.

[5] Vallance, Moore and Groves, eds, *Nature's Investigator*, p. 433.

[6] Ibid., pp. 433–43.

[7] Brown to Banks, [16] September 1803, ibid., pp. 438–9.

[8] For details see ibid., pp. 444–58.

[9] King to John Bowen, 18 October 1803, in Bladen, ed., *HRNSW*, V, pp. 243–6.

Diemen's Land on 28 November. Bauer visited Norfolk Island for seven months where he undertook some pencil landscape drawings.[1] The *Lady Nelson*, in which Brown sailed, encountered bad weather in Bass Strait and had to seek shelter at East Cove, Deal Island, in the Kent Group on 11 December. Inclement weather kept Brown there for almost three weeks. During this time he collected various marine algae, plants and rock specimens.[2] Brown sailed from Deal Island to Port Dalrymple, on the northern side of Van Diemen's Land, on 1 January 1804. When the *Investigator*'s expedition began, it was not intended that Brown should visit Van Diemen's Land; but the changed circumstances now offered the opportunity to botanize there.[3]

After arriving at Port Dalrymple, Brown saw kangaroos, wallabies and black swans. He had materials written by Bass and Flinders, from their voyage in the *Norfolk*, to help him find his bearings.[4] Brown encountered Aborigines that resembled the indigenous people of New South Wales 'in their persons & colour'.[5] He also began a vocabulary of Tasmanian Aboriginal language for the Risdon area.[6] After nearly three weeks spent exploring Port Dalrymple and the River Tamar, Brown sailed in the *Lady Nelson* to the Port Phillip settlement on mainland Australia, but he soon returned to Van Diemen's Land, staying at Risdon Cove for almost six months.[7] The main areas for collection were Risdon Cove, Sullivans Cove and Mount Wellington. Storm Bay and Bruny Island were visited. There was an attempt to reach the headwaters of the Huon River. Some of the excursions were by boat up the River Derwent; others involved trekking across rugged countryside.[8] Brown arrived in southern Van Diemen's Land when the summer season was already well advanced and the hills were dry and brown. Most of the new species he found came from Table Mountain, which he ascended ten times.[9]

Brown gathered 733 plants in Van Diemen's Land, including 230 specimens from the Port Dalrymple area and 248 specimens from the River Derwent and Mount Wellington. The plant groups represented among these collections included lichens, ferns, conifers, Casuarinaceae, Leguminosae, Fagaceae, Myrtaceae, Asteraceae and grasses.[10] This was a considerable haul, but Brown characteristically reported his findings to Banks in a grumpy way, pointing out the hindrances to his botanical excursions. He was worried (without having any details) that repeated French visits to Van Diemen's Land had pre-empted many of his plant discoveries.[11] Brown finally left the island on the *Ocean*, with his plant collections, on 9 August and arrived back at Port Jackson on

---

[1] Moore, 'The Pencil Landscape Drawings', pp. 213–20.

[2] Vallance, 'Jupiter Botanicus in the Bush', p. 79; Vallance, Moore and Groves, eds, *Nature's Investigator*, pp. 460–63.

[3] Vallance, Moore and Groves, eds, *Nature's Investigator*, p. 459.

[4] Ibid., p. 464.

[5] Brown, entry for 4 January 1804, ibid., p. 469.

[6] Moore, 'Some aspects of the work of Robert Brown', p. 132.

[7] Vallance, Moore and Groves, eds, *Nature's Investigator*, pp. 464–81.

[8] For the detailed itinerary, see Moore, 'Some aspects of the work of the botanist Robert Brown', pp. 135–9, 144.

[9] Edwards, 'Botany of the Flinders voyage', p. 149.

[10] Ibid., p. 139; Vallance, Moore and Groves, eds, *Nature's Investigator*, p. 459.

[11] Brown to Banks, 12 December 1804, in Chambers, ed., *The Indian and Pacific Correspondence*, VI, pp. 387–9.

24 August.[1] Just before his return there, Bauer went to Norfolk Island, where, during a stay of eight months, he made the first important survey of the flora of that island. Unfortunately, few of the plants he collected in Norfolk Island are extant. Bauer also undertook excursions to Newcastle, the Blue Mountains and the south coast of New South Wales.[2]

Preparations were made at Port Jackson for Brown and Bauer's return to England. Though the *Investigator* had proved unseaworthy for Flinders and members of his crew to continue their exploration of Australia's shoreline, extensive repairs were carried out to make her fit for another voyage. Her upper deck was removed, which effectively reduced her overall tonnage by half. New rigging was installed. Two masts were placed on the ship instead of the original three. This meant that the *Investigator* would now sail as a brig. Brown agreed, with some reluctance, to return home on the ship with his herbarium, which was the least perishable part of his plant collection: he was concerned that the unfitness of the after-hold on the ship would damage the specimens through humidity or exposure to water. Living plants were left with Banks's collector George Caley at Parramatta. Brown and Bauer returned to England on the *Investigator* in October 1805. They sailed around Cape Horn in difficult winter weather to Liverpool without any stops en route.[3] Brown noted that 'this extensive Voyage was performed in four months & sixteen days in the crazy low cut down *Investigator*, perhaps the most deplorable Ship in all the World'.[4]

Thirty-eight cases of natural history specimens and drawings from the voyage were landed at Liverpool on 13 October 1805.[5] Brown appealed to Banks's librarian and curator Jonas Dryander (a former pupil of Linnaeus) to have the collection transferred to London. Banks paid the cost of carriage by waggon, and presented a claim for £87 to the Admiralty.[6] Dryander informed Banks of the circumstances of Brown and Bauer's arrival.[7] On 5 November 1805 Brown and Bauer reported to the Admiralty in London to signal the official end to their participation in the *Investigator* expedition. They were not received by officials there owing to celebrations taking place to mark the British naval victory at the Battle of Trafalgar a couple of weeks earlier.[8]

Altogether Brown collected 3,600 specimens of plants, one case of insects, three boxes of minerals and about 150 dried skins of birds in Australia. His rough estimate of his plant collection suggested that he had gathered 700 species from the south coast of Australia; 500 from the east coast; another 500 from the north-east coast; 1,000 from Port Jackson and its neighbourhood; 700 from Van Diemen's Land; and 200 from Timor.[9] Brown wanted to arrange and describe the plants himself, but preferred to

[1] Vallance, 'Jupiter Botanicus in the Bush', p. 82.

[2] Edwards, 'Botany of the Flinders voyage', pp. 149, 155; Norst, 'Recognition and Renaissance', p. 300.

[3] Williams, *Naturalists at Sea*, p. 228; Chambers, ed., *The Letters of Sir Joseph Banks*, p. 260; Brown to Philip Gidley King, 11 May 1805, in Bladen, ed., *HRNSW*, V, p. 619.

[4] Brown, entry for 16 July 1805, in Vallance, Moore and Groves, eds, *Nature's Investigator*, p. 594.

[5] Brown to Banks, 13 October 1805, in Bladen, ed., *HRNSW*, V, pp. 711–12.

[6] Brown to Marsden, 5 November 1805, and to Dryander, 29 October 1805, in Vallance, Moore and Groves, eds, *Nature's Investigator*, pp. 603–5; BL, Add. MS 32439, ff. 244–245.

[7] Dryander to Banks, 7 November 1805, in Vallance, Moore and Groves, eds, *Nature's Investigator*, p. 605. Brown's account of the income and expenditure related to the *Investigator* voyage is included in ibid., pp. 606–7.

[8] Watts, Pomfrett and Mabberley, *An Exquisite Eye*, p. 21.

[9] Banks to Marsden, 3 January 1806, in Bladen, ed., *HRNSW*, V, p. 181.

transfer the arrangement of the birds, insects and minerals to experts with more knowledge in those branches of natural history.[1] The seeds had already been sent to the Royal Gardens, Kew, where they constituted 'a large portion of the newest ornaments of that extensive & possibly unparalleld collection'.[2] Brown's animal specimens from Terra Australis included twenty-three mammals, including five different kangaroo species, an echidna and three bats. He also brought back to England 217 samples of birds (150 species), 39 fish, 33 reptiles and amphibians, a platypus, and 29 invertebrates other than insects.[3] He eventually presented 358 zoological species to the British Museum, of which 246 were insects.[4] Bauer had undertaken 2,073 sketches of plants, fungi and animals in Australia, and needed time to complete them.[5]

Banks reported on the collections to the Admiralty. He estimated it would take Brown and Bauer three years to arrange the plants in systematic order and to finish the most interesting sketches. Brown's collections were currently held in the herbarium at Banks's London home. Bauer retained his sketches. Banks asked the Admiralty to continue to pay Brown's and Bauer's salaries so that they could complete their work from the voyage. Banks, who would oversee this enterprise, indicated that Brown had been very successful in collecting

> the vegetable produce of the Earth & preparing dried specimens of every species of Plant in such a manner as to ensure a perfect & critical examination of their natural structure & constituent parts when they can at leisure be compar[e]d with Books & Specimens already deposited in Collections at home.

He also requested that orders be issued by the Admiralty for the deposit of minerals, quadrupeds, birds and insects among the collections of the British Museum.[6]

Brown distributed many zoological and mineralogical specimens to friends who would work on them rather than allowing them to be deposited at the Admiralty's offices, where they might be neglected. The botanical samples were forwarded to Banks's house in Soho Square.[7] Brown had kept his notebooks, in which he had jotted down the plants collected on his Australian field excursions, and the rewritten descriptions on slips of paper: these now form part of his substantial slip catalogue in the Botany Department of the Natural History Museum, London.[8] In January 1806 Brown was appointed as the first librarian of the Linnean Society of London. He had sufficient time in this position to consider the botanical issues raised by the *Investigator* expedition. He continued to be paid by the Admiralty until the end of 1810.[9] From 1805 onwards Brown received two days' pay per week from the Navy Board and two days' pay from the Linnean Society as its clerk, librarian and housekeeper.[10]

[1] On the insects see Kirby, 'New Species of Insects collected in New Holland', pp. 454–82.

[2] Banks to Marsden, [25] January 1806, in Chambers, ed., *The Indian and Pacific Correspondence*, VII, pp. 117–20.

[3] Watts, Pomfrett and Mabberley, *An Exquisite Eye*, p. 22.

[4] Wheeler, 'The Zoological Manuscripts of Robert Brown', p. 419.

[5] TNA, ADM1/4379, Admiralty Correspondence and Papers. [Banks] to Marsden, January 1806.

[6] Banks to Secretary Marsden, January 1806, in Bladen, ed., *HRNSW*, VI, pp. 16–19. For Banks's handling of the plant species, drawings and minerals sent back from the *Investigator*'s voyage, see Chambers, *Joseph Banks and the British Museum*, pp. 53–7.

[7] Miller, 'Joseph Banks, empire, and "centers of calculation" in late Hanoverian London', p. 29.

[8] Edwards, 'Botany of the Flinders Voyage', pp. 145, 147.

[9] Mabberley, *Jupiter Botanicus*, p. 177.

[10] Groves, 'Procrastination or Unpredictable Circumstances?', p. 130.

In the period 1806–10 Brown was based at Gerrard Street, Soho, a stone's throw from Banks's London residence in Soho Square. He regularly consulted with Banks and Dryander over the classification of his Australian natural history findings. Brown took four months after arriving back in England in November 1805 to examine the general arrangement of his plant specimens. With Dryander's help, he selected specimens for public collection. He had already gone through the first eight classes of the Linnaean system by June 1807. By that time he had re-examined the species, completed his descriptions, and had tried to ascertain the affinities of 546 new species and 688 species altogether. The number of species applicable to useful purposes was very small. 'The Interesting Novelties to the Botanist are however numerous,' he pointed out to Banks, '& are chiefly contained in the natural orders of *Protacae, Rubiacea, Companulcae* & *Orchidea*, each of which has afforded several new genera.'[1]

By June 1809 Brown reported to Banks that he had now described 1,600 plants, and had begun to prepare a prodromus, with full details of the genera. He hoped the French botanists would not anticipate this by publishing their findings about New Holland.[2] Around this time, Bauer submitted to Banks a catalogue of his finished Australian drawings.[3] Bauer had originally made pencil sketches and kept a colour record of the plants he collected. Banks explained that these sketches were 'prepared in such a manner by reference to a table of colours as to enable him to finish them at his leisure with perfect accuracy'.[4] Bauer's colour code was linked to the many sets of numbers on his sketches, but the secret of his code has never been found.[5]

By April 1811 Banks was able to inform the Admiralty of Brown and Bauer's progress. Brown had completed his arrangement and classification of Australia's flora and fauna; he had finished one volume and was working on a second. Bauer had completed 150 of the 2000 drawings that Banks thought were most interesting for the advancement of botany and zoology. Among the Australian creatures sketched by Bauer were koala bears, the duck-billed platypus, the wombat, the butterfly cod fish, the southern bell frog and the black-footed rock wallaby.[6] Banks referred to their being completed 'in a state of masterly excellence'. Bauer decided to issue his work first in fasciscles (small separate sections) because of the relative slow progress of his finished work. He then intended to bring the fasciscles together in a completed edition.[7] Brown's laborious work and Bauer's elaborate drawings – each one taking more than a week to finish – had slowed up progress, but Banks hoped that the Admiralty would pay the salaries of Brown and Bauer until the end of 1811. Banks noted that the public already had access to 'the advantages of the discoveries in Natural History made under the liberal equipment of the *Investigator*'.[8]

---

[1] Brown to Banks, 18 June 1807, in Chambers, ed., *The Indian and Pacific Correspondence*, VII, pp. 265–6.

[2] Brown to Banks, 2 June 1809, ibid., VII, p. 453.

[3] BL, Add. MS 32439, ff. 288–291, n.d. but 1809.

[4] Edwards, 'Botany of the Flinders voyage', p. 160; TNA, ADM 1/4379, Admiralty Correspondence and Papers, Banks to Marsden, January 1806. For a list of the finished drawings and where they were published, see Britten, 'Ferdinand Bauer's Drawings of Australian Plants', pp. 140–46. See also Plates 2 and 3 below, between pp. 200 and 201.

[5] Norst, 'Recognition and Renaissance', p. 299.

[6] For reproductions of Bauer's drawings of these animals, see Mabberley, 'The Legacy of Flinders' Naturalist', pp. 54–5. See also Plate 4 below, and Plate 8, vol. II, between pp. 274 and 275.

[7] Bowen and Bowen, *The Great Barrier Reef*, p. 73.

[8] BL, Add MS 32439, ff. 319–320, Banks to [the Admiralty], 30 April 1811.

Brown was particularly interested in the Protea family of plants, which are common in the region of the Great Barrier Reef and, indeed, throughout Australia: 44 genera out of a world total of 75 are found in Australia. The Protea family included the Waratah, Hakea, Grevillea, Banksia, Dryandra, Lomatia, Stenocarpus, Telopea and Macadamia genera. Brown used the microscope to examine pollen grains as an important determining factor in assigning the taxonomy of these genera. In 1809 he read a paper to the Linnean Society titled 'On the natural orders of the plants called Proteaceae'. Brown also had a special interest in orchids: while in the Port Jackson area, he discovered nearly a quarter of the Australian species known today. Brown's pollen studies were new branches of Botany while his microscopy laid foundations for the modern approach to plant anatomy.[1] Overall, Brown was the first botanist to identify and describe over a third of the 12,000 plant species known in Australia today.[2] Brown also provided the first significant treatment of Australian grasses. His work is still a major point of reference for scholars working on Australian grass diversity.[3]

Brown was influenced by the newly published work by Lamarck, which questioned the categories of classification adopted by Jussieu.[4] Brown had found there was no system he could adopt that had already decided on the classification or arrangement of Australian flora. He tried a new approach by gathering a variety of plants in various stages of development as well as in their fully mature state. This enabled him to classify them in accordance with the anatomy and physiology of their parts. He liaised closely with Bauer in order to achieve his classifications by close perusal of the botanical artist's detailed watercolours of floral and seed structure.[5]

In 1810 Brown, now Banks's librarian, produced a volume on his Australian field investigations entitled *Prodromus Florae Novae Hollandiae et Insulae Van-Dieman, exhibens characters planterum quas innis 1802–1805 ... collegit descripsit R. Brown*. This was only a quarter of the text that Brown planned to write. He was not yet ready to publish his entire Australian findings; the work involved in labelling, classifying and describing his collections was extremely time-consuming even though he was an industrious man. David Mabberley has suggested two alternative explanations for Brown deciding to publish only a portion of his *Prodromus* at this juncture. One is that the Admiralty was becoming impatient with the dissemination of the scientific results of the *Investigator* expedition and Brown's salary, paid by the Admiralty, was scheduled to terminate soon. Brown may therefore have felt pressure to publish some of his botanical findings. Another possibility is that Banks advised publication at this point to encourage the Admiralty to extend Brown's employment.[6]

Unfortunately, the *Prodromus* had extremely poor sales. Only twenty-six copies were bought. The fact that it had neither an index nor any illustrations did not help it to attract public interest. Moreover, it was written in Latin whereas popular works on botany in England were then being published in English.[7] Brown, in dismay at the lack of interest

[1] Mabberley, 'The Legacy of Flinders' Naturalist', pp. 58, 63.
[2] Austin, *The Voyage of the Investigator*, p. 199.
[3] Clark, 'The Grasses', p. 509.
[4] Bowen and Bowen, *The Great Barrier Reef*, p. 72; Brown, 'On the Proteaceae of Jussieu', pp. 15–226.
[5] Steven, *First Impressions*, p. 74.
[6] Mabberley, *Jupiter Botanicus*, p. 161.
[7] Ibid., p. 162.

in Australian flora, withdrew it from sale. He decided not to publish the remainder of the work.[1] Lack of sales was unconnected to the volume's botanical importance. Brown had produced a scholarly work of great influence on subsequent botanical scholarship. His *Prodromus* described 464 genera and about 1,000 species.[2] 'In point of novelty of plant forms and structures which it describes, accuracy of details, precision of language, wealth of observations and far-reaching view of classification,' commented Sir Joseph Dalton Hooker, Darwin's closest friend and an eminent Victorian pioneer of geographical botany, 'it maintains to this day the unique position which was assigned to it on its appearance.'[3]

Brown published 'General remarks, geographical and systematical, on the botany of Terra Australis' as an appendix to Flinders's *A Voyage to Terra Australis* in 1814. He worked on a second volume of his own major work but failed to complete it. In 1830 he published a short supplement to the *Prodromus* entitled *Supplementum Primum Prodromi Florae Novae Hollandiae*. Brown was still working on the botanical specimens from the *Investigator* expedition when Banks died in 1820. His plant collections from Australia had turned into a lifetime's work. Brown resigned his Linnean Society post in May 1822 after he had acquired the lease of Banks's old house in Soho Square. He became the first keeper at the new Banksian department at the British Museum. The first set of Brown's Australian collection is now housed in the Natural History Museum, London.[4] Brown's important contributions to Australian botany were recognized in the early 1980s when the National Herbarium of New South Wales was opened in the Robert Brown building in Sydney's Royal Botanic Gardens. Research teams there still work on many matters related to plant classification and ecology which Brown pioneered.[5]

In 1806 Brown wondered in a letter whether Bauer's drawings would ever be published.[6] The sheer amount of work need to complete the drawings gave the impression that the work would take years to complete. Bauer's field sketches were usually life-size representations of plants. They were encoded with an elaborate system of numbers for later colouring, but the pigments Bauer used for his colour drawings are unknown.[7] Bauer had access to Brown's and Banks's herbaria in London. He also checked his sketches with living plants grown at Kew. His finished plant drawings are notable for their botanical accuracy of the smallest and intricate parts of plant structure. They depicted not just the general form of the plant but the flowers, leaves, seeds, stamens, pollen grains and root structures. His drawings have a three-dimensional quality. They are very fine examples of artistic achievement as well as scientific accuracy.[8] Bauer's watercolours are highly refined

---

[1] Williams, *Naturalists at Sea*, p. 229; Edwards, 'Botany of the Flinders voyage', pp. 152–3.

[2] Mabberley, *Jupiter Botanicus*, p. 164.

[3] Hooker, *The Botany of the Antarctic voyage of H.M.S. Erebus and Terror*, Part III, Vol. 1, p. cxiv.

[4] Mabberley, *Jupiter Botanicus*, p. 265; Vallance, Moore and Groves, eds, *Nature's Investigator*, p. 10. The subsequent fate of Brown's specimens, from the death of Banks in 1820 to the present, is outlined in Groves, 'Procrastination or Unpredictable Circumstances?', pp. 131–6.

[5] Mabberley, 'The Legacy of Flinders' Naturalist', p. 57.

[6] Mabberley, *Jupiter Botanicus*, p. 132.

[7] Lack and Ibáñez, 'Recording Colour', pp. 87–100; Mabberley and Moore, 'Catalogue ... of the Australian botanical drawings of Ferdinand Bauer', pp. 83, 85.

[8] Watts, Pomfrett and Mabberley, *An Exquisite Eye*, pp. 27–8.

and precise depiction of plants. He was one of the first artists to depict the complete reproductive system of each plant.[1]

The dissemination of Bauer's paintings was held up when Banks refused to fund a flora including the coloured plates. Ten of Bauer's engraved plates were included in the atlas accompanying *A Voyage to Terra Australis*. Bauer also published, at his own expense, some of his best botanical illustrations and engravings in *Illustrationes Florae Novae Hollandiae: sive icons generum quae* in *Prodromo Florae Novae Hollandiae et Insulae Van-Diemen descripsit Robertus Brown/Ferdinandi Bauer* (1813–16).[2] They were hand-coloured to an excellent standard and Bauer himself prepared the engraved plates. But, as with Brown's *Prodromus*, they sold only a few copies. Bauer completed his botanical drawings for publication between 1806 and 1819 in accordance with Admiralty instructions. His finished watercolour paintings were housed in the Admiralty Library until 1843 and then transferred to the British Museum. They are now in the Natural History Museum, London. Bauer himself returned to live in Vienna in 1814.[3] Most of his sketches of Australian flora and fauna were acquired by the Austrian Imperial Museum, and are now kept in Vienna's Natural History Museum.[4]

Brown's botanical findings were significant when viewed within a regional Australian context. He gathered plants from all of today's six Australian states.[5] His 727 collections of plants in the *Investigator* from Western Australia included more than 500 species from the Albany area and another 100 from Lucky Bay and the islands of the Archipelago of the Recherche. Brown named 26 genera that are endemic to Western Australia. At the species level, 1,450 names of vascular plants published by Brown are Western Australian. Brown's plant collections remain important for the elucidation of the status of Western Australian plants.[6] In Victoria, Brown only examined the extreme southern portion of Port Phillip Bay, the first botanist to do so.[7] This visit to the Mornington Peninsula came late in the summer season when few plants were in bloom, but Brown still identified 96 species, in 74 genera, of plants he collected in Victoria.[8] He made 108 collections in Port Phillip Bay; 27 of these were destined to become type specimens. Some 61 per cent of the taxa recognized by Brown on Victorian soil are still represented by his own name and circumscription.[9] Brown's plant collections from South Australia were the first made by a trained botanist in that area. The *Investigator* expedition accounted for around 300 plant collections in twelve collecting localities along the South Australian coastline. Brown and Good were responsible for

---

[1] Norst, 'Recognition and Renaissance', pp. 300, 304.

[2] Barker, 'The Botanical Legacy of 1802', p. 9.

[3] Norst, *Ferdinand Bauer*, pp. 84–7; Edwards, 'Botany of the Flinders voyage', p. 161. See also Mabberley and Moore, 'Catalogue ... of the Australian botanical drawings of Ferdinand Bauer', pp. 81–225. Twenty-five of Bauer's finished plant drawings are reproduced in Stearn, *The Australian Flower Paintings of Ferdinand Bauer*.

[4] The complicated dissemination of Bauer's *Investigator* drawings is summarized in Mabberley and Moore, 'Catalogue ... of the Australian botanical drawings of Ferdinand Bauer', pp. 87–9.

[5] Burbridge, 'Robert Brown's Australian Collecting Localities', pp. 229–33.

[6] Keighery and Gibson, 'The Flinders Expedition in Western Australia', pp. 105–9.

[7] Watts, Pomfrett and Mabberley, *An Exquisite Eye*, p. 18.

[8] Willis, 'Robert Brown's Collectings in Victoria', pp. 51–4.

[9] Hewson, *Brunonia Australis*, pp. 2–4.

most of the herbarium specimens from South Australia, but Bauer also contributed to this work.[1]

12. Artistic Achievements

While still in Australia, William Westall grumbled to Banks that the voyage in the *Investigator* had not met his expectations: he complained of the coast of Terra Australis not having sufficient variety to employ his 'pencil with any advantage to myself or my employers'.[2] Westall's frank letter to Banks expressing his disappointment at the barren landscapes of Australia received a frosty reception from the President of the Royal Society.[3] Perhaps this sour judgement partly stemmed from the misfortune of seeing much of his topographic and descriptive artwork either lost or severely water-damaged in the wreck of the *Porpoise* in 1803.[4] Nevertheless Westall had kept around 160 sketches, drawings and watercolours; these were returned to England on 1 August 1804 by Robert Fowler, formerly first lieutenant of the *Investigator*, and transferred first to the Admiralty.[5]

It was only in 1809 that Banks obtained a commission for Westall to prepare oil paintings that could be used to illustrate Flinders's published voyage account. Banks made the point to the Admiralty that the French had published the results of the artists sent out on their voyages of discovery, but that Britain had been dilatory in carrying this out. Henry Phipps, Lord Mulgrave, the First Lord of the Admiralty, responded to this criticism by asking Banks to oversee arrangements for getting Westall's drawings and pictures painted. Banks agreed and Westall met Mulgrave in June 1809 to finalize the commission.[6] But problems arose. Westall completed two paintings from the voyage but then, after submitting a third painting, he received a letter from Mulgrave advising him that the Admiralty commission was only intended to cover two works of art.[7]

Between 1809 and 1812 Westall made nine paintings that were engraved in copperplate for *A Voyage to Terra Australis*. Eight of these paintings were based on oil paintings Westall had undertaken for the Admiralty art collection; the remaining illustration, entitled *View of Port Jackson from the South Head*, was based on Westall's watercolour of that title. Three of the oil paintings were exhibited at the Royal Academy in 1812. They attracted attention because of their novel depiction of a continent which few Europeans had visited.[8] The engraved illustrations featured in *A Voyage to Terra*

[1] Barker, 'The Botanical Legacy of 1802', pp. 9–10, 29.

[2] Westall to Banks, 31 January 1804, in Chambers, ed., *The Indian and Pacific Correspondence*, VI, pp. 310–11.

[3] Monteath, 'Contradictory Encounters', p. 48.

[4] Bowen and Bowen, *The Great Barrier Reef*, p. 71.

[5] Findlay, *Arcadian Quest*, pp. 14–16.

[6] Smith, *European Vision and the South Pacific*, p. 196; entry for 7 June 1809 in Cave, ed., *The Diary of Joseph Farington. Volume 9*, p. 3481.

[7] CUL, Australasia Miscellanea, Royal Commonwealth Society Collections, RCMS 278/19/1, Westall to J. W. Croker, 26 June 1810.

[8] Smith, *European Vision and the South Pacific*, pp. 196–7.

Australis were issued separately by Rudolf Ackermann in February 1814, about five months before Flinders's voyage account was published, in de-luxe and cheaper editions.[1] Westall's Australian art also appeared in his pencil field drawings on paper and some oil paintings on canvas.[2]

Westall undertook sketches of the Australian coastal landscape as well as drawing examples of Australian flora and fauna. He exercised a certain amount of artistic licence in these drawings. Thus, Westall's view of King George Sound in *A Voyage to Terra Australis* includes drawings of trees seen by the artist at Port Jackson and in Spencer Gulf. Similarly, Westall's view of Wreck-Reef Bank, taken at low water, which is also reproduced in *A Voyage to Terra Australis*, depicts uncovered reefs whereas Flinders himself noted that in reality the tide always covered them. Westall ranged beyond his official brief to undertake drawings of Aborigines, including two sketches of a native in Spencer Gulf and the body of an Aborigine shot on Morgan Island. He was the first European artist to make images of the indigenous cave paintings seen at Chasm Island in the Gulf of Carpentaria. He also drew a portrait of Pobassoo, the leader of the Makasar trepangers that Flinders and his company encountered in Arnhem Land.[3]

As Bernard Smith has shown, Westall's sketches while serving in the *Investigator* reflected absorption of the concerns of the scientific gentlemen aboard ship and the main focal points of Flinders as commander of the voyage. Brown and Bauer's influence can be detected in Westall's detailed rendering of vegetation in his Australian landscapes, while Flinders's interest in geology and coastal survey appears to have influenced Westall's sketching of the terrain. Though Westall never revisited Australia and painted scenes from many other locations, he never forgot his sketches from the *Investigator* expedition. When he died in 1850 he was working on a painting of *Wreck Reef a few days after the Wreck of the Porpoise and the Cato*, now on loan to the National Maritime Museum, Greenwich, from the Ministry of Defence.[4]

13. The Astronomical Data

The Admiralty selected John Crosley as the astronomer for the *Investigator* expedition, following the recommendation of Nevil Maskelyne, the Astronomer Royal. Between 1795 and 1797 Crosley had sailed on a surveying voyage in the *Providence* to the North Pacific, under the command of William Broughton. He was employed by the Board of Longitude. His was the only choice among the scientists made for the expedition for which Banks did not play a part.[5] A good astronomer was vital for ascertaining the position of the ship throughout the voyage and for expert knowledge of the scientific instruments. Banks was especially concerned about this professional position as he realized Vancouver had compromised his round-the-world expedition between 1791 and

---

[1] Findlay, *Arcadian Quest*, pp. 14–16.
[2] Stehn and George, 'Artist in a New Land', pp. 87–8.
[3] Monteath, 'Contradictory Encounters', pp. 50–53; Bonyhady, *Images in Opposition*, p. 87.
[4] Smith, *European Vision and the South Pacific*, pp. 191, 197.
[5] CUL, Royal Greenwich Observatory, Board of Longitude Papers, RGO 35/55, Maskelyne to Banks, 23 January 1801; Estensen, *The Life of Matthew Flinders*, pp. 145–7; David, ed., *William Robert Broughton's Voyage*, p. xxx.

1795 by sailing without an astronomer.[1] Crosley was an experienced astronomer who had spent three years (1789–92) at the Royal Observatory, Greenwich, as an assistant to Maskelyne.[2] During the *Investigator*'s voyage from England to the Cape of Good Hope, he made regular astronomical observations.[3] Unfortunately, it was decided at the Cape that his rheumatic pain was sufficiently bad for him to leave the voyage. He therefore returned to England.[4]

Flinders realized it would take too long for another astronomer to be dispatched from England and no suitable substitute could be found at the Cape. Another astronomer sent out by the Board of Longitude would not reach Port Jackson for twelve months or the *Investigator* for eighteen, by which time most of the survey of Australia's coasts (it was hoped) would be completed. Flinders therefore decided that that he and his brother should acquire the knowledge to carry out the astronomical tasks.[5] Samuel Flinders was given the main responsibility for dealing with astronomical calculations for the rest of the voyage, with his brother overseeing his work.[6] The Board of Longitude, after hearing of Crosley's illness, made preparations to send out a Cambridge mathematician, James Inman, as a replacement. Inman sailed on the *Glatton* but did not arrive at Port Jackson until April 1803, when the *Investigator* had largely finished its survey of Australia's coastline.[7]

Crosley's departure was a major loss for the voyage. The astronomical calculations, and judgement about where measurements might best be taken, could not be carried out so well by someone without the requisite professional training. Nevertheless, Flinders aimed to ensure, with his younger brother's help, that these problems were overcome. The Board of Longitude had supplied numerous scientific instruments for use on the voyage and a full set of instructions for astronomical calculations. These were now handed over to Flinders by Crosley. The instruments included a highly accurate astronomical long-case clock built by Thomas Earnshaw in 1791. It had been used by Vancouver on his Pacific voyage of 1791–5, and was now to be deployed on the *Investigator* to check the timekeeping of the chronometers. In addition, there were two box chronometers by John Arnold (nos. 82 and 176), a further two chronometers by Thomas Earnshaw (nos. 520 and 543), a version of Hadley's sextant, a universal theodolite made by Jesse Ramsden, a sextant made by John Dollond, several barometers and thermometers, Nairne and Blunt's dipping needle, an azimuth compass, various mathematical tables, and Murdoch Mackenzie's *Treatise of Maritim* [sic] *Surveying* and Charles Hutton's *Mathematical Tables*, which had been published for the Board of Longitude.[8] These instruments were all made by leading

---

[1] Banks to Flinders, 19 February 1801, in Chambers, ed., *The Indian and Pacific Correspondence*, V, p. 279. Vancouver set out on his voyage of 1791 without an astronomer, but after sailing from England he changed his mind and applied to the Board of Longitude for one. The astronomer selected then died before he could join the expedition. Lamb, ed., *The Voyage of George Vancouver*, I, pp. 32, 51.

[2] Croarken, 'Astronomical Labourers', p. 291.

[3] CUL, Royal Greenwich Observatory, Board of Longitude Papers, Papers of Nevil Maskelyne, RGO 4/186, Observations made by John Crosley.

[4] Howse, *Nevil Maskelyne*, p. 187.

[5] Natural History Museum, London, Dawson Turner Collection, Flinders to Banks, 29 October 1801; Dawson, ed., *The Banks Letters*, p. 328.

[6] See below, pp. 253, 256, 300, vol. II, pp. 8, 75, 271, 297, 302, 347, 373, 419.

[7] Howse, *Nevil Maskelyne*, p. 187.

[8] For a complete list of the scientific instruments supplied by the Board of Longitude, see below, pp. 211–12.

instrument makers based in London in the late eighteenth century.[1] Crosley took home with him Earnshaw's watch no. 465 and Troughton's reflecting circle no. 74, both of which Flinders considered a loss to the voyage.[2]

The astronomical tasks taken on by Matthew and Samuel Flinders were divided, according to the Board of Longitude's instructions, into observations made on ship board and those made on shore. Every day on board ship, the instructions explained, there should be observations of the meridian altitudes of the sun for finding latitude and longitude. Hadley's sextant was used for this purpose. Other instructions were to wind up the chronometers every day, as soon as possible after noon, and to compare them and note their respective times. Longitude could then be computed from comparing the watches with the apparent time of day from the morning and afternoon altitudes of the sun. Also on board ship there were instructions to observe the variation of the compass, the inclination of the dipping needle and the height of the thermometers, to keep a ship journal, and to calculate the latitude and longitude of the positions of head lands, islands and harbours.[3]

The expectations for observations on shore were equally demanding. The tent observatory and astronomical clock were to be set up wherever possible on land and Hadley's sextant and the universal theodolite used to take equal altitudes of the sun and fixed stars to determine the accuracy of the astronomical clock. The chronometers were to be wound up every day. Observation of the meridian altitudes of the sun and the heights of the portable thermometers and barometers needed to be checked daily. The eclipses of Jupiter's first satellite and occultation of fixed stars by the moon were to be recorded to compute the timing of the astronomical clock and to calculate longitude. The variations in the compass and the inclination of the dipping needle were to be observed. There was also the instruction to observe the height of the tides, especially the difference between the day and night tides. Books recording all these observations were to be kept, and the principal observations sent back to the Astronomer Royal.[4]

Flinders and his associates had to master the complexities of calculating longitude by taking lunar observations. The arithmetic needed to calculate such observations required considerable expertise: one had to allow for atmospheric refraction and for lunar parallax. Thus, the sun and the stars always appeared to be higher than they really were whereas the moon always appeared to be lower. Five steps were required to calculate longitude by lunar observations. First, several observations, preferably by more than one observer, were needed to calculate the lunar distance between the moon and the sun or a star, the altitude of the moon above the horizon and the altitude of the sun or star. A sextant was used to measure the lunar distances. Second, a calculation was made of the measured angles and times of the observations. Third, the local apparent time was found from the measured altitude of the sun or star. Fourth, the lunar distance between the centres of the sun and moon was calculated from readings taken by the sextant that provided the distance between their limbs (or outer edges). This adjustment in arithmetic counteracted the effects of refraction and parallax. Fifth, one had to find Greenwich apparent time by

[1] See Clifton, *Directory of British Scientific Instrument Makers*.
[2] Flinders, *A Voyage to Terra Australis*, I, p. 41.
[3] The instructions are given below: see p. 209.
[4] See below, p. 210.

consulting lunar distance tables. These stages enabled the navigator to calculate longitude, namely the difference between local apparent time and Greenwich apparent time expressed in degrees, minutes and seconds of arc.[1]

Though he had no formal astronomical training, Flinders worked in his usual methodical and precise way to gather astronomical data. His journals include virtually daily evidence of the painstaking care with which he approached his astronomical duties. His brother, Samuel, also played an active role in making calculations.[2] After the *Investigator*'s voyage ended, Bauer noted that Flinders's 'great and constant occupation ... in the Geographical department' left him little time to attend to astronomy.[3] Flinders himself was worried that Maskelyne would find fault with his astronomical data because he had had no training in that branch of knowledge and was fully absorbed in his surveying when sailing around Australia's coast. The occultation of stars, of Jupiter's satellites and of the aurora australis could not be recorded with the same exactitude and timeliness that a qualified astronomer would bring to the task. Unfortunately, there were occasions during the voyage where Samuel forgot to wind up the chronometers, leading to erroneous astronomical readings. Matthew Flinders was furious when this happened, and reprimanded his bother over his laxness. There were further problems. Several scientific instruments needed repair during the voyage. No-one on board ship had the practical expertise to undertake this work; nor would it have been easy, given that the ship was away from readily supplied parts. Flinders reported that only two of his five timekeepers (Earnshaw E520 and E543) were reliable for readings of longitude; the three Arnold chronometers (nos 82, 176 and 1736) had all proven unreliable.[4]

Inman joined the *Investigator* as astronomer at Port Jackson in June 1803 after the circumnavigation of Australia had ended prematurely. He set up the Tent Observatory on Garden Island, in Sydney's harbour, and found the universal theodolite was useless and the astronomical clock in need of repairs. He found Earnshaw's E543 kept bad time, though the E520 timekeeper was rather better. There was no possibility of mending the universal theodolite in New South Wales.[5] As he could not carry out his professional work properly and the circumnavigation had been suspended, Inman sailed with the *Rolla* to China and England rather than accompanying Flinders on the *Cumberland*. This was after the *Rolla* had sailed from Port Jackson to Wreck Reef, where Flinders handed over for safe keeping the instruments belonging to the Board of Longitude.[6]

The tale of woe associated with the astronomical data continued long after the separate returns to England of the two Flinders brothers. It was clear that the data would need to be completely recalculated before Flinders could publish his charts and his voyage account. This was necessary owing to errors in the published *Nautical Almanac* that had

---

[1] This draws upon Howse, 'The Lunar-Distance Method of Measuring Longitude', pp. 150–51, 157–8.

[2] Extensive surviving material detailing Samuel's handling of the astronomical data can be found in CUL, Royal Greenwich Observatory, Board of Longitude Papers, RGO 14/65, Reduction of the Astronomical Observations made in the voyage of the *Investigator* 1801–1805 by Samuel Ward Flinders, second lieutenant.

[3] CUL, Royal Greenwich Observatory, Board of Longitude Papers, RGO 14/68, ff. 31r–v, Bauer to [Samuel Ward] Flinders, 11 May 1806.

[4] CUL, ibid., RGO 14/68, ff. 17r–18v, Flinders to Dr Maskelyne, 25 May 1802.

[5] CUL, ibid., RGO 14/68, ff. 175r–181v, Account by James Inman of his work as astronomer.

[6] CUL, ibid., RGO, 14/68, f. 174v, List of instruments belonging to the Board of Longitude put into the hands of James Inman on Wreck Reef by Captain Flinders, 8 October 1803.

been taken on the voyage. Samuel wanted to be involved with the recalculations, and, since he was now on half-pay, he requested payment for this work.[1] In 1806 he sent a memorial to the Board of Longitude asking for additional back pay for having taken over the duties relating to nautical astronomy for most of the *Investigator*'s voyage.[2] Nothing happened. Six years later he petitioned the Board of Longitude for remuneration.[3] Matthew Flinders wanted the astronomical data redone partly to preserve his own reputation, but the problems caused by his brother's interventions with the Board of Longitude led to Banks's displeasure.[4] The astronomical work was eventually allocated to Crosley, but even with his expertise it took two years to recalculate the data. This delayed Flinders in the task of reconstructing his charts, as correct astronomical data were needed for their plotting.[5]

14. Surveying, Nautical Astronomy and Hydrography

To improve knowledge of Australia's coastal geography, Flinders deployed a range of skills that demonstrated his command of thorough preparation through background reading, careful recording of daily occurrences during the voyage, an understanding of nautical astronomy, hydrographical expertise, an ability to undertake running surveys, accurate construction of survey sheets, charts and maps, and painstaking efforts to ensure that a published atlas was produced to accompany a highly detailed voyage account. Flinders was a very capable synthesizer, and the range of skills he used to achieve his cartographical improvements to Australia's geography can be explained in sequence.[6]

Flinders had a detailed library on board the *Investigator* that he studied very carefully in order to determine prior knowledge of Terra Australis. Banks had loaned him a copy of the manuscript journal he had compiled during the voyage of the *Endeavour* with Cook. He had also provided Flinders with many volumes on 'the South Seas' from his own library. Dalrymple had furnished Flinders with additional volumes and charts, and also supplied him with a 'memoir' on the winds and weather in the oceans surrounding Australia. He gave Flinders copies of charts of the Archipelago of the Recherche compiled by the celebrated French hydrographer Beautemps-Beaupré. Flinders had access to Astley's *Travels*, to Cook's and Vancouver's charts, to Fleurieu's geographical notes prefixed to La Pérouse's voyage account, to Arrowsmith's General Chart of the World and Chart of the Pacific Ocean, and to the Thévonot chart of the

---

[1] CUL, ibid., RGO 14/68, ff. 55r–56r, Samuel Ward Flinders to John Pond, 10 September 1811.

[2] CUL, ibid., RGO 14/68, f. 33r–v, Memorial of Samuel Ward Flinders to the Commissioners of Longitude, April 1806.

[3] CUL, ibid., RGO 14/68, ff. 62r–63r, Petition of Samuel Ward Flinders to the Commissioners of Longitude, 2 December 1812.

[4] ML, Matthew Flinders letterbook (1810–1814), Flinders to Lt. Flinders, 22 February 1813.

[5] CUL, Royal Greenwich Observatory, Board of Longitude Papers, RGO 14/68, f. 67r, John Crosley to the Commissioners of Longitude, 3 March 1814; Scott Polar Research Institute, Matthew Flinders Collection, MS 383/7, Flinders to John Franklin, 18 November 1812.

[6] Flinders's surveying techniques are briefly described in Ferrar, 'The Graphical Records of Matthew Flinders's Voyage to Terra Australis', pp. 94–103.

Gulf of Carpentaria.[1] Flinders found these items invaluable when sailing around Australia for the compilation of his logbooks, journals and charts. Flinders approached the business of maritime discovery in a scholarly manner, and was scrupulous in his acknowledgement of others who had made important discoveries.[2]

Flinders deployed the intellectual capital associated with his voyage in other ways. He kept a rough journal during the circumnavigation of his daily sailing routines. Partly conceived as a log, with information on the tides, the course followed by the vessel, and the winds, and partly put together as a journal with discursive 'general remarks' or 'additional remarks', this served as one of the foundations needed to prepare his charts and survey sheets.[3] It was rather more extensive in scope than the sort of logbook usually kept by navigators.[4] Flinders's rough journal was damaged in the wreck of the *Porpoise* off the Queensland coast in September 1803.[5] He therefore instructed his clerk John Olive to prepare a fair copy while he was detained at the Ile de France.

Flinders combined his intellectual and practical skills in his handling of nautical astronomy, surveying and hydrography, which provided essential information for his voyage account and his charts and maps. Far from thinking he was omniscient in his grasp of scientific practices, Flinders acknowledged his own lack of training in nautical astronomy.[6] Yet he and his brother assumed responsibility for calculating and recording all the data on longitude and latitude. These data needed substantial correction after he returned to England.[7] Flinders was on firmer ground with his grasp of nautical surveying. He had been taught the rudiments of constructing maritime charts by William Bligh, who in turn had been instructed in marine surveying by James Cook.[8] There was therefore a tradition of skilful surveying techniques being handed down from one navigator to another. In 1791 Flinders had sailed on Bligh's second breadfruit voyage from Tahiti to the Caribbean, during which he assisted Bligh in drawing a chart of the sailing routes through Torres Strait.[9] Before setting out on the *Investigator* expedition, Flinders had also helped his friend convert an eye sketch of Bass Strait into a chart and had drawn survey sheets of their circumnavigation of Van Diemen's Land in 1799 that were later consolidated into charts published by Arrowsmith, as mentioned above.[10]

---

[1] The books and charts supplied to Flinders are noted in Flinders, *A Voyage to Terra Australis*, I, pp. 5–6. The significance of Beautemps-Beaupré's hydrographical surveying is discussed in Pearson, '"Nothing left undone"'; Chapuis, *A la mer comme au ciel*; and Chapuis, 'L'emergence des nouvelles cartes marines.'

[2] For some possible exceptions to this rule see Gooch, 'Puzzling over the Early Flinders' Charts', pp. 5–22.

[3] The *Investigator*'s rough log and journal is deposited at ML.

[4] Some of the other logbooks kept during the voyage are much less extensive: e.g. that of Robert Fowler discussed below, pp. 93–4.

[5] Entries for 16–18 May, 15 October 1804, in Brown and Dooley, eds, *Matthew Flinders Private Journal*, pp. 33, 48.

[6] CUL, Royal Greenwich Observatory, Board of Longitude Papers, RGO 14/68, ff. 17r–18r, Flinders to Dr Maskelyne, 25 May 1802.

[7] CUL, ibid., RGO 14/68, f. 67r, John Crosley to the Commissioners of Longitude, 3 March 1814.

[8] NMM, Flinders Papers, FLI/05, Service Papers of Captain Matthew Flinders: Memoir of official services.

[9] Estensen, *The Life of Matthew Flinders*, p. 20. The chart is at NMM, Flinders Papers, FLI/15/1.

[10] Flinders's published chart is reproduced as an insert to Sprod, ed., *Van Diemen's Land Revealed*. For discussion of this chart in relation to Flinders's survey sheet and Bass's eye sketch, which is not extant, see Cole and Cole, *Mr Bass's Western Port*, pp. 62–76.

Flinders's hydrographical expertise was vital for plotting the track of the *Investigator* and for indicating soundings for future navigators. Hydrographical data gathered during the running surveys that characterized the voyage also provided essential information for maps, charts and survey sheets. Cook and Vancouver had both practised running surveys, which involved examining and charting long stretches of coastline as one sailed along them. Using the principle of intersection, bearings of prominent points were recorded at regular intervals and plotted on the ship's track through the water and then developed into triangles from which one could calculate distance and position and, through this means, the shape of the coast. Flinders mainly used an azimuth compass to take bearings rather than a quadrant (which Cook and Vancouver had preferred). The ship's track was plotted each hour by dead reckoning, which involved recording the ship's compass course with adjustments for wind, current, and compass variation. Dead reckoning needed to lay down precise geographical coordinates to be accurate. Flinders established latitude by measurements of the altitude of heavenly bodies as they crossed the observer's meridian.[1] He calculated longitude by the method of lunar distances. This measured angular distances between the sun and the moon and one of the ten fixed stars. These were then compared with the data tabulated in the *Nautical Almanac* and with the times they occurred on the Greenwich meridian.

To conduct running surveys, Flinders sailed as closely as possible to the shore. When he had the opportunity to set up fixed stations on shore, he took more precise astronomical observations with the various scientific instruments supplied by the Board of Longitude referred to above.[2] At various points along Australia's coast – at King George Sound and Port Lincoln, for example – Flinders measured a base line in order to provide scale for his survey.[3] Flinders was aware of magnetism affecting the compass readings on board ship. He therefore adjusted the record of his bearings before plotting his survey sheets.[4] To record accurately what was seen and what remained conjectural, he marked the track of the *Investigator* with a solid line, shaded the parts of the coast he had seen, but used a dotted line for what was still to be confirmed.[5] He did not have time during a running survey to gather extensive data on tides over a period of time; he had to resort to snapshots, as it were, by noting the time of high water and the extent of the tidal range. In some areas, such as the Gulf of Carpentaria, he recognized that mixed tides were common – following partly a semi-diurnal and partly a diurnal cycle. He inserted such observations on his survey sheets.[6] Flinders's survey sheets also contained comments on vegetation, Aboriginal settlements and geology.[7]

---

[1] For detailed information, see below, vol. II, pp. 407–14.

[2] Chapter 4 of the 'Memoir' discusses the fixed stations. For the scientific instruments, see below, pp. 211–12.

[3] See below, pp. 248, 321.

[4] For an analysis of the problem of magnetism and the ship's head, see below, vol. II, pp. 456–67.

[5] Rigby, '"The whole of the surveying department rested on me"', pp. 267–9.

[6] This is evident on TNA, ADM 352/548, Admiralty Hydrographic Department, Original Surveys, Chart of Australia, North Coast: Northern Territory and Queensland: Gulf of Carpentaria, 1803, and ADM 352/549, Chart of Australia, North Coast: Northern Territory; Arnhem Land; Gulf of Carpentaria; English Company Islands to Groote Eylandt.

[7] See Flinders's survey sheets at TNA, ADM 352/477–569.

15. Survey Sheets and Charts

Flinders began work drawing charts from his survey sheets while in captivity at the Ile de France.[1] By September 1804 he had completed his general chart of Terra Australis and that of the Gulf of Carpentaria.[2] By mid-October in the same year he had finished drawing his charts; the last one to be completed was one of Bass Strait. By then, he had begun to write an account of the construction of the charts and a short account of the impacts of winds, tides and currents on magnetism aboard ships. With clerical assistance, Flinders prepared for the Admiralty a fair copy of his logbook and journal to replace the daily logbook and journal spoiled during the shipwreck of the *Porpoise*.[3] Flinders also instructed Aken, the former master of the *Investigator*, to copy a book that contained details of the survey operations and bearings undertaken in the exploration of Australia's coast. This became known as the 'Bearing Book'. It includes entries in chronological order for virtually each day of the voyage, noting geographical landmarks and recording astronomical bearings and soundings.[4]

Flinders spent much time at the Ile de France preparing charts or survey sheets to depict his main geographical findings from his running surveys around Australia's coast. Drawing on prior authorities, in terms of their books and charts, and on his rough journal, evidence gathered on latitude and longitude, and astronomical calculations, he synthesized his findings on charts that included comprehensive details on his discoveries. He combined what he knew from intensive study with his own practical investigations. Flinders was influenced by the skilled nautical surveying of Beautemps-Beaupré. He extended the French hydrographer's charting of the Archipelago of the Recherche by taking more observations and more soundings[5] and later praised the Beautemps-Beaupré's charts of the south-east part of Van Diemen's Land as combining 'scientific accuracy and minuteness of detail, with an uncommon degree of neatness in the execution: they contain some of the finest specimens of marine surveying, perhaps ever made in a new country'.[6]

In the 'Memoir' he prepared while kept in detention, Flinders explained his methods for constructing his charts. He had prepared rough survey sheets when stretches of the coast were seen during the voyage. He then redrew the details when time permitted, incorporating information from his log books and journals and his observation and bearing book. The charts were usually plotted on a scale of four inches to one degree of longitude but, for harbours and places of significance, he used a scale of twelve inches per degree of longitude. For two localities, King George Sound and Torres Strait, he drew on a much larger scale in order to include detailed soundings. He explained in the 'Memoir' his markings on the charts for fixed points in his survey, for rocks and shoals, for current

---

[1] For an appraisal of his methods and findings, see Barritt, 'Matthew Flinders's Survey Practices and Records', pp. 1–15.

[2] Entry for 2 September 1804 in Brown and Dooley, eds, *Matthew Flinders Private Journal*, p. 43. The General Chart can be seen at http://acms.sl.nsw.gov.au/item/.

[3] Entries for 16–18 May, 15 October 1804, in Brown and Dooley, eds, *Matthew Flinders Private Journal*, pp. 33, 48. The spoiled items are the rough journals deposited at ML and available at http://acms.sl.nsw.gov.au/item/.

[4] The Bearing Book is deposited at UKHO. See below, p. 93.

[5] Pearson, '"Nothing left undone"', p. 30.

[6] Flinders, *A Voyage to Terra Australis*, I, p. xciii.

and tides, and a set of symbols used for navigational details along the ship's track. The overall aim was to ensure the sheets were as accurate as possible for future navigators; and, as always, Flinders was meticulous in distinguishing what was verified from what was known conjecturally.[1]

Flinders's survey sheets included several innovations on previous practice by most hydrographers. He showed the fixed points of his survey on land and the places from which bearings were taken. He distinguished between night-time and daytime tracks, something Dalrymple had suggested to him. He made it clear which parts of the coast he had examined and those parts copied from other sources. He similarly distinguished his own soundings from those recorded by other hydrographers. He differentiated his own place names from those conferred by other explorers. He used arrows to indicate the strength of the tides, currents and winds.[2] Flinders also drew the tracks of other voyages that had sailed in Australian waters, where such information was available to him, and he offered succinct commentaries in boxes to explain the context of voyaging on some survey sheets. Thus, for example, Flinders's large-scale plot of Torres Strait included the tracks followed by the *Endeavour* (1770), the *Pandora* (1791), the *Investigator* (1802) and the *Cumberland* (1803). This showed that Cook had sailed much closer to the northern tip of the Cape York peninsula than the other vessels.[3] Flinders's chart of Bass Strait showed the track and discoveries made in the *Norfolk* (1798) and by John Murray in the *Lady Nelson* (1801) and also noted which explorers had examined King Island in the years from 1798 to 1802.[4]

16. *A Voyage to Terra Australis* and the *Atlas*

Flinders did not have the opportunity, or the authorization from the Admiralty, to compose and publish a voyage account or his charts until he returned to England from the Ile de France in late 1810, but it was quickly agreed in January 1811 that he should proceed expeditiously in both tasks. The Admiralty considered the *Investigator* expedition to have a comparable public interest to Cook's voyages forty years earlier. The Commissioners of the Admiralty therefore authorized Banks to superintend the draughtsmen and engravers employed to help with the task, and requested that he take charge of the sketches, charts, journals and other manuscripts in their possession that Flinders had returned to them while abroad.[5] The expectation was that printing costs be paid out of the proceeds of the work.[6] Banks arranged for the Admiralty to pay the expense of the charts and engravings for Flinders's voyage account.[7] In keeping with the publication of Pacific voyages undertaken by Byron, Wallis, Carteret and Cook, it was

[1] See below, vol. II, pp. 408–12.

[2] Perry, 'Matthew Flinders and the Charting of the Australian Coast', p. 2, and below, vol. II, p. 414.

[3] TNA, ADM 352/482, Admiralty Hydrographic Department, Original Surveys, Matthew Flinders, Chart of Australia: North Coast and Papua New Guinea, South Coast: Queensland: Torres Strait, 1803.

[4] TNA, ADM 352/563/1, Admiralty Hydrographic Department, Original Surveys.

[5] Entry for 16 January 1811 in Brown and Dooley, eds, *Matthew Flinders Private Journal*, p. 341.

[6] Entry for 13 January 1811, ibid., p. 341; John Barrow to Banks, 15 January 1811 (two letters), in Bladen, ed., *HRNSW*, VII, pp. 487–8.

[7] ML, Matthew Flinders letterbook (1810–14), Flinders to S. H. Greig, 22 February 1813.

expected that Flinders's volumes would be detailed tomes addressed to a professional readership.[1]

It was recognized that there would be rivalry with the French over the new discoveries in Australia. De Freycinet, who had sailed on Baudin's expedition, assumed responsibility for publishing the cartography of the official account of that expedition after the death of Péron in 1810. He published the first full map of Australia in 1811. This incorporated the discoveries made by Baudin's expedition but took no account of Flinders's discoveries on the south coast.[2] Flinders wanted to publish his own atlas partly to show that he had discovered far more of the unknown south coast of Australia than Baudin, and that English nomenclature should be applied to the coastal features identified. But he scrupulously included French place names from Cape Jervis to Cape Bridgewater on the south coast to acknowledge Baudin's prior discovery of that coastline.[3]

Banks took the lead in commissioning and paying the engravers for Flinders's *Atlas*; he also appointed a printer (the bookseller George Nicol) and publisher. Flinders regularly visited Banks's home in Soho Square to discuss progress on the volumes. Through Banks's influence, the Arrowsmith firm were contacted to publish the charts and atlas. Flinders informed Banks of his discussions with these private map-makers and print sellers over the scale of the charts of the Australian coast. Flinders had maintained a cordial relationship with Arrowsmiths since they published his charts of Bass Strait and Van Diemen's Land in 1800–1801.[4] The arrangement made with Arrowsmith over the publication was for eleven large charts and four smaller ones to be produced as an atlas to accompany a detailed voyage account. Flinders determined the scales of the charts and the number of copper plates needed.[5] The fair sheets were drafted at four inches to a degree of longitude, from which reductions were made and engraved for plates in the atlas accompanying *A Voyage to Terra Australis*.[6] Flinders did not consult with Thomas Hurd, the Admiralty Hydrographer, over these arrangements. This was probably because his charts were not being published by the Admiralty. But Flinders did liaise with Hurd over the supply of plates of his charts to the Navy.[7]

To refine the survey sheets he had drafted at the Ile de France into finished charts, Flinders continued his long-established method of gathering all relevant cartographical information done by others and then synthesizing such findings with his own written record of the voyage. While based in London, Flinders used D'Entrecasteaux's chart of the Archipelago of the Recherche; he checked John Murray's log kept in Bass Strait; borrowed Francis Barrallier's sketches of Western Port and Hunter's River from the Hydrographic Office; discussed with Charles Grimes his examination of the upper part of Port Dalrymple, Van Diemen's Land; incorporated Captain Heywood's soundings

[1] Payne, 'The Publication and Readership of Voyage Journals', pp. 176–7.

[2] Gerritsen and Reynders, 'The Freycinet Map of 1811', pp. 1–11; Perry, *The Discovery of Australia*, p. 91. The second edition of Freycinet's charts, published in 1824, removed the French names for Terre Napoléon in favour of Flinders's names, except those bestowed by Baudin by right of discovery: see Terry, 'Global Roaming', pp. 208–9.

[3] Gerritsen, 'Terra Australis or Australia', p. 225.

[4] Wood, 'Successive States', p. 7.

[5] Entries for 22 and 26 January 1811 in Brown and Dooley, eds, *Matthew Flinders Private Journal*, p. 343; Estensen, *The Life of Matthew Flinders*, p. 442.

[6] Estensen, *The Life of Matthew Flinders*, p. 442.

[7] Webb, 'The Expansion of British Naval Hydrographic Administration', p. 230.

onto his chart of Timor; and obtained from Banks copies of the first volume of Cook's second Pacific voyage, Tasman's journal of his first voyage, an account of Hamilton's *Pandora* voyage, and Péron's account of the Baudin expedition. Flinders also borrowed his own journals of the *Providence* voyage from the Admiralty. He enquired at Banks's house about the charts announced but not published in the atlas that accompanied Péron's account of the Baudin expedition, but found they had not been published.[1] Admiral John Hunter brought Flinders a copy of Bass's whaleboat journal.[2] To prepare final versions of his charts, Flinders examined papers prepared by Philip Gidley King and William Paterson, lent to him by their widows, and consulted Hunter and the Banksian collector George Caley about inland parts of New South Wales.[3] The enquiries are typical of Flinders's methodical approach to establishing the context for his own achievements on the *Investigator* expedition. They are also consistent with his concern for accuracy and appropriate credits for individual acts of discovery. The main source of vital information that Flinders could not acquire was his third logbook and journal, covering the voyage of the *Cumberland*, which had been confiscated by Decaen.[4]

Flinders gave detailed attention to providing names for the geographical features he had surveyed along Australia's shoreline. His manuscript journals had often designated features by symbols, letters and numbers. But in his voyage account and his charts, he supplied names largely based on his British connections. During his various explorations in Australia, Flinders named 347 places. Most of these were given names for inclusion in *A Voyage to Terra Australis*. Flinders's names can be grouped into nine categories: those named after geographical and geological features and after plants or animals are the first two; a third category comprised senior officers of the Admiralty or East India Company or major British public figures; three categories honoured those connected with navigation and voyages of discovery; two categories assigned names after Flinders's family, friends and acquaintances; and the final category included names connected with ethnography and human geography. Flinders's nomenclature on Australia's south coast replaced the French names given by Péron and Freycinet. When applying names to the various features of Australian coastal geography that he discovered, Flinders named nowhere after himself.[5]

There were disagreements over the name to be attached to the Australian continent. Banks, Arrowsmith and Brown did not approve of the designation Terra Australis and used the name New Holland in their publications. Flinders, however, used the name Terra Australis on his charts from the time he was confined at the Ile de France, and he considered it would now be difficult to make alterations. He was aware of several previous

[1] Entries for 6 January 1811, 6 and 14 February 1811, 9 March 1811, 13 and 19 May 1811, 3 and 10 June 1811, 20 September 1811, 8 November 1811, 27 February 1812, in Brown and Dooley, eds, *Matthew Flinders Private Journal*, pp. 339–40, 344–5, 349, 360–61, 363–4, 377, 383, 396. Barrallier was a French-born explorer who explored Bass Strait in March 1801 and the Hunter River in June 1801. Peter Heywood was a British naval officer who accompanied Bligh in the *Bounty* and later sailed in the *Pandora* to rescue the *Bounty*'s mutineers.

[2] Entry for 18 July 1812, in Brown and Dooley, eds, *Matthew Flinders Private Journal*, p. 415.

[3] Estensen, *The Life of Matthew Flinders*, p. 443.

[4] ML, Matthew Flinders letterbook (1810–14), Flinders to Charles Desbassyns, 14 July 1812; Horner, 'The Missing Third Journal of Flinders', p. 40.

[5] For a detailed discussion, see Bréelle, 'Matthew Flinders's Australian Toponomy', pp. 1–41.

writers who had used the term Terra Australis.[1] In 1804 he had expressed a preference for using either Terra Australis or Australia on the basis that the existing names of New Holland and New South Wales did not acknowledge the totality of the continent.[2] After he returned to England, Flinders eventually persuaded Banks that Terra Australis was an appropriate name to represent the existing New Holland and New South Wales by a collective name, though his own preference would have been to convert it to Australia.[3]

During the last few months of his life, in the first half of 1814, when he was experiencing considerable pain in his bladder, Flinders worked around the clock to finish his voyage account and the charts for his atlas.[4] Arrowsmith brought him a set of proofs of all the charts for the atlas on 29 June 1814, and Flinders approved of the engraving.[5] Flinders only just lived long enough to know that his book and atlas were published in July 1814.[6] The plates included in the atlas that accompanied *A Voyage to Terra Australis* included a general chart of Terra Australis (Plate I), six charts of the coast of South Australia (Plates II–VII), five charts of the east coast (Plates VIII–XII), and two charts of the north coast (Plates XIII–XIV). No sheets relating to the north-west and west coasts were included because, as mentioned above, Flinders was unable to survey those part of Australia's shoreline during his voyage in the *Investigator*.[7]

The plates in the atlas are testimony to Flinders's scholarly and practical skills. He incorporated information on the track of the *Investigator* and of other ships that had sailed around Australia's coastline. Thus, for example, Plate X (East Coast, Sheet III) includes the tracks of ships Flinders himself sailed in (the *Norfolk*, the *Investigator*, the *Porpoise* and the *Cumberland*) as well as ships associated with his voyaging (the *Rolla*, the *Francis*, the *Cato* and the *Bridgewater*) and the track of Cook's *Endeavour*. Flinders scrupulously noted the discoverers of various parts of Australia's shores on the sheets. Thus Plate VII (South Coast, Sheet VI) acknowledged the discoveries made by Furneaux, Cook, D'Entrecasteaux and Cox in Van Diemen's Land and credited Baudin as the discoverer of Great Oyster Bay on the east coast of that island. Where names had been assigned to places on Dutch charts, Flinders retained their names. He also included important details for navigators, including notes on soundings, currents, winds, weather and the nature of the sea floor.[8]

To prepare the atlas accompanying *A Voyage to Terra Australis*, Flinders drew upon all the sources he had consulted as well as his survey sheets he had prepared during the voyage of the *Investigator* and at the Ile de France. The charts took account of the reconstruction of the astronomical data completed by Crosley. This enabled the maps to be drawn according to correct geographical coordinates. Flinders also showed an awareness of

---

[1] Scott, *The Life of Matthew Flinders*, pp. 304–10; Healey, 'The Origins of the name "Australia"', pp. 95, 104.

[2] Flinders to Samuel Flinders, 4 November 1804, in Brunton, ed., *Matthew Flinders*, p. 117.

[3] Entry for 19 August 1813 in Brown and Dooley, eds, *Matthew Flinders Private Journal*, p. 451; ML, Matthew Flinders letterbook (1810–14), Flinders to Banks, 17 August 1813; Flinders, *A Voyage to Terra Australis*, I, p. iii.

[4] ML, Matthew Flinders letterbook (1810–14), Flinders to Banks, 19 April 1814.

[5] Entry for 29 June 1814 in Brown and Dooley, eds, *Matthew Flinders Private Journal*, p. 484. The copperplates used for the engravings are deposited at the Royal Naval Museum, Portsmouth.

[6] ML, Matthew Flinders letterbook (1810–14), Ann Flinders to Thomi Pitot, 29 July 1814.

[7] Flinders, *A Voyage to Terra Australis*, Atlas.

[8] Ibid.; Perry and Prescott, *A Guide to Maps of Australia*, pp. 166–71. John Henry Cox charted Great Oyster Bay, Maria Island and Marion Bay on the east coast of Van Diemen's Land in 1789 aboard the brig *Mercury*.

information gathered on Australian coastal geography over the decade or so since the *Investigator* voyage ended. With his passion for precision and the deployment of new knowledge, Flinders had used a methodology that synthesized all that could then be known, from practical fieldwork and scholarly research, about the shape of the Australian continent and the details of its coastal geography. He had managed to combine geographical and navigational data effectively to advance knowledge of a part of the world where certain knowledge was limited when he began his naval career. It was fitting that Flinders should liaise with Arrowsmith, a private cartographic firm that prided itself on excluding all doubtful information and on presenting the most up-to-date geographical knowledge as soon as it was available.[1] It was also appropriate that Flinders's general chart should include Australia alongside Terra Australis. The name Australia was soon taken up as an appropriate term for the continent by Governor Lachlan Macquarie.[2] The General Chart was not superseded until the era of aerial surveys.

Flinders's survey work, supported by subsequent voyage accounts and maps, was later extended by Philip Parker King's and John Lort Stokes's surveys of north-west and west Australia.[3] The atlas accompanying *A Voyage to Terra Australis* became known, however, as the most accurate representation of Australia as soon as it was published. Arrowsmith's 'Chart of the Pacific Ocean' also helped at once to show Flinders's discoveries relating to Australian coastal geography. Thus Arrowsmith's printing in 1814 of a revised version of his chart incorporated discoveries made by Flinders in the *Investigator*: it included Flinders's charting and naming of Australia's south coast and Spencer Gulf, Gulf St Vincent and Kangaroo Island; it named Bass Strait and included King Island; and the Gulf of Carpentaria is as Flinders charted it. Subsequent amendments and additions were made to the chart in its 1820 version and its final printed version in 1832.[4]

Shortly after Flinders died, John Franklin, who sailed in the *Investigator*, succinctly summed up Flinders's contribution to the improvement of geographical knowledge about Australia in *A Voyage to Terra Australis* and its atlas:

> He has related Facts and Circumstances with the utmost accuracy ... his observations are reduced with the greatest nicety and precision; they, together with his charts which certainly are very superior, will gain for him what he most desired, the character of a good navigator and a man of perseverance and science and procure that respect for his memory which I think he deserves.[5]

For his part, Flinders worked assiduously on finishing his book and charts, which he found a laborious task.[6] This is unsurprising when one considers that the charts had to be compiled meticulously from various sources and that the book comprised two large volumes of about 400,000 words. Flinders drafted a long historical introduction that covered the history of maritime discovery to Australia before his own expedition. The main part of the book, however, provided a chronological narrative of the *Investigator*'s

[1] Baigent, 'Arrowsmith, Aaron the elder', pp. 524–5.

[2] Ward, *Finding Australia*, p. 392.

[3] King, *Narrative of a Survey*; Stokes, *Discoveries in Australia*.

[4] Wood, 'Successive States', pp. 12–15.

[5] Scott Polar Research Institute, Cambridge: Sir John Franklin Collection, MS 248/296/5, John Franklin to Robert Brown, 9 June 1815.

[6] ML, Matthew Flinders letterbook (1810–14), Flinders to James Wiles, 5 March 1812.

voyage, the wreck of the *Porpoise*, and the voyage of the *Cumberland*. The book included appendices on coastal longitudes, the compass errors caused by magnetism, and Brown's discussion of Australian botany. Flinders felt under pressure to complete his book and atlas, admitting that he was 'pressed, on every side, to the same effect'; when nothing intervened, he was writing from ten o'clock in the morning until ten at night.[1] He was so absorbed in preparing his book and charts that he gave little thought to his future. He realized, however, that he would not sail on another voyage of discovery, and he had no desire to serve on a ship in the common line of service. He expected to retire to Lincolnshire and live with his wife and daughter on a small income, dividing his time between his garden and his study.[2] This never occurred because of his death just after completing *A Voyage to Terra Australis*.

The evidence presented in *A Voyage to Terra Australis* and its atlas, along with the artistic achievements of Bauer and Westall and the scientific findings of Brown, should be consulted with the details of the fair journal and 'Memoir' edited in these volumes to gain a comprehensive view of Flinders's achievements in the maritime exploration of Australia. Flinders conceived of his work in a holistic way, and all these strands of information accumulated painstakingly as a result of the *Investigator* expedition were significant in advancing navigational, geographical and scientific knowledge of Australia. After the 1814 printing of the *Atlas*, the Hydrographic Office claimed the plates and subsequently issued copies of all of them. The first Hydrographic Office printing of the entire *Atlas* was in the 1820s. The General Chart and eleven of the thirteen detailed charts were printed with corrections up to 1822. Philip Parker King's completion of the survey of Australia's coasts between 1818 and 1822 explored parts of the north-east, north and west parts of the coast not seen by Flinders. King produced eight charts. After these were completed in 1825, the whole of Australia's coast was covered by Admiralty charts.[3]

---

[1] ML, ibid., Flinders to Madame Darifat, 16 December 1811. Flinders's interest in compass deviations caused by magnetism is discussed in Cotter, 'Matthew Flinders and Ship Magnetism', pp. 123–34.

[2] Flinders to Thomi Pitot, 8 March 1812, in Riviere, ed., *My dear friend*, p. 57.

[3] Perry, 'Matthew Flinders and the Charting of the Australian Coast', pp. 4–6.

TEXTUAL INTRODUCTION

1.   The Fair Journals and the 'Memoir'

The principal sources transcribed and edited in this edition comprise the fair copy of Flinders's journals in the *Investigator* and a 'Memoir', which was intended to explain major features of his voyage and to be used in conjunction with his charts and journals. These documents are deposited among the Admiralty Records at the National Archives, Kew.[1] The fair journals were compiled from the rough copy of Flinders's journals (discussed below) and his associated charts and other papers to which he had access while detained at the Ile de France. Flinders composed the fair journals (with the assistance of his servant John Elder) partly because his rough journals had been damaged during the wreck of the *Porpoise* and partly because he had more-or-less uninterrupted time to devote to the task. He also wanted to record details of the voyage while they were fresh in his memory and to correct parts of his rough journals.[2] The 'Memoir' was also compiled while Flinders was a prisoner at the Ile de France. Elder again assisted Flinders in this task.[3] Its purpose was to set in context the hydrographical practices he had used to compile his survey sheets and charts and to write down his thoughts on nautical matters he had grappled with during his circumnavigation of Australia. The 'Memoir' would provide essential context about the construction of the charts, should the Admiralty wish to publish them.[4]

Flinders gave the fair copy of the first volume of the *Investigator*'s journal and the first five chapters of the 'Memoir', dated 14 May 1805, to John Aken, who had been the master in the *Investigator* and the *Cumberland*, to take back to England.[5] Flinders informed the Secretary of the Admiralty that the originals of his surveys were not quite finished and that the 'Memoir' was incomplete and in a crude state. He hoped the Astronomer Royal, Dr Nevil Maskelyne, would be able to check his nautical

[1] TNA, ADM 55/75–6, 78. The 'Memoir' follows part of the journals in ADM55/76. These documents are available online as part of Centre for Environmental Data Archival website, http://badc.nerc.ac.uk/view/. A partial copy of the fair journal is deposited among the Royal Greenwich Observatory MSS in the Board of Longitude Papers at CUL: see RGO 14/64, Logbook, Observations and Memoir of HMS *Investigator*, ff. 5r–106v (with gaps). This includes daily log entries for most, but not all, days between 1 November 1801 and 31 January 1803, interspersed with many meteorological and lunar observations, a good many of which are not included in the fair journals. The document is available online at http://cudl.lib.cam.ac.uk/view/MS-RGO-00014-00064.

[2] Entries for 16–18 May, 15 October 1804, 14 September 1805, 9–10 March 1807, in Brown and Dooley, eds, *Matthew Flinders Private Journal*, pp. 33, 48, 90, 158.

[3] Entries for 11 January, 17 March 1807, ibid., pp. 150, 159.

[4] Entry for 1–2 May 1805, ibid., p. 63. For descriptions of these manuscript charts, see Ingleton, *Matthew Flinders*, pp. 436–42.

[5] Flinders, *A Voyage to Terra Australis*, II, p. 238.

astronomy in that unpublished account for accuracy.[1] Flinders explained to his patron, Banks, that:

> this logbook contains an account of all our transactions, remarks, boat-excursions on surveying, astronomical observations &c in short, almost the whole that I have to relate concerning the voyage so far; general observations upon the winds, tides, currents &c excepted. This book, Sir Joseph, with the charts and memoir, I am extremely anxious you should see, because you will then be able to form a just judgement of my exertions and success in prosecuting the investigation of New Holland.[2]

Flinders had another motive for submitting these materials via Aken to London: he hoped that their arrival, with evidence of assiduous surveying, would induce the Admiralty to promote him to post-captain.[3] The documents were duly submitted to the Admiralty for Dr Maskelyne's inspection in March 1806.[4] After Aken's departure from the Ile de France, Flinders worked on a fuller version of his 'Memoir', concentrating on two remaining chapters dealing with the winds that prevailed upon the coasts of Australia and upon the currents.[5]

Flinders sent the second volume of the *Investigator*'s fair journal and a corrected copy of the eight chapters of the 'Memoir' to England with Elder in June 1807, after his trusted servant had received permission to leave the Ile de France.[6] He explained that the eight chapters should be attached to his charts in the event 'of their being published without or previously to the voyage of the *Investigator*'.[7] Flinders also entrusted to Elder letters to Dalrymple, Banks, the Admiralty and his family, and three newly constructed charts.[8] The documents, along with charts and books, were to be delivered to W. A. Standert, Flinders's agent in London. Elder arrived in London in January 1808.[9] Flinders asked his brother to let him know whether Elder and the copy of the fair journal arrived safely in London.[10] He could not submit to London the third volume of his logbook and journal because it was confiscated by Governor Decaen at the Ile de France and never handed back to Flinders.[11]

The fair journal is contained in three Admiralty volumes. ADM 55/75 and ADM 55/76 are bound volumes with hard covers measuring 388 mm × 240 mm. ADM 55/75

---

[1] ML, Matthew Flinders Public Letters, Flinders to William Marsden, 13 May 1805.

[2] Flinders to Ann Flinders, 15 May 1805, and to Banks, 16 May 1805, in Brunton, ed., *Matthew Flinders*, pp. 125–6. The letter to Banks is also published in Bladen, ed., *HRNSW*, V, pp. 623–5.

[3] Flinders to Samuel Ward Flinders, 29 March 1806, in Brunton, ed., *Matthew Flinders*, p. 147.

[4] Flinders, *A Voyage to Terra Australis*, II, p. 411; TNA, ADM 1/3523, 'Memoir explaining the construction of the Charts of Australia with remarks upon the Observations of the Latitude & Longitude by Capt. Flinders', f. 150.

[5] Entry for 17 November 1807, in Brown and Dooley, eds, *Matthew Flinders Private Journal*, p. 192.

[6] Flinders to Banks, 1 July 1807, in Bladen, ed., *HRNSW*, VI, p. 273; Flinders, *A Voyage to Terra Australis*, II, p. 262.

[7] ML, Matthew Flinders Public Letters (1805–7), Flinders to William Marsden, 30 June 1807.

[8] NMM, Flinders Papers, FLI/12, Journal and Letterbook of Matthew Flinders (1806–7), f. 198.

[9] Flinders to Charles Baudin, 12 September 1808, in Brunton, ed., *Matthew Flinders*, p. 191; entry for 30 June and 1 July 1807, in Brown and Dooley, eds, *Matthew Flinders: Private Journal*, p. 169.

[10] Flinders to Samuel Ward Flinders, 25 October 1808, in Brunton, ed., *Matthew Flinders*, p. 194. By the time this letter was written, the journals, books, letters and papers had already been delivered by Elder to Standert: see NMM, Flinders Papers, FLI/28, John Elder to Mrs Flinders, 3 February 1808.

[11] See above, p. 51.

is entitled 'Journal of a Voyage to Terra Australis in His Majesty's Ship *Investigator* by Matthew Flinders Commander 1801–1802–1803–1804'. It comprises 1 blank folio + 486 numbered folios covering the period from 25 January 1801 to 13 March 1803. The title page has a Hydrographic Office stamped mark. At some time after the document was compiled, the folios were renumbered to 251 double pages. ADM 55/76 is entitled 'Journal kept on board His Majestys sloop *Investigator* by Matthew Flinders Commander, and afterwards in subsequent vessels and places, during the years 1801, 2, 3, 4, 5', followed by 1 blank folio. It covers the period from 14 March 1803 to 10 June 1803 and includes 62 folios with text. Once again, renumbering has occurred sometime after the document was written: this produces 35 double pages. The renumbered pages 36–136 are blank. The 'Memoir' (see below) is included at the other end of the volume. ADM 55/78 is a much smaller volume, measuring 200 mm × 160 mm. It has a title page with '*Investigator* 1803', then 1 blank folio and 26 double pages, covering the period from 11 June 1803 until 22 July 1803. The remainder of the volume comprises daily logbook entries for the *Cumberland* and the *Porpoise*.

Flinders's fair journals conform partly to the usual layout of a ship's logbook but also contain additional features that are more commonly found in journals. The Dutch East India Company developed the first logbooks in their present form in the seventeenth century; they were first mentioned in English in 1697. Logbooks derived from the use of the log-line, or piece of weighted wood attached to a length of cord, which was thrown overboard to determine the distance travelled by a ship. Logbooks were intended to provide codified accurate information about a voyage through daily entries.[1] Flinders's fair journals include a daily log entry, beginning at midday and ending at the following midday. This followed standard nautical practice. Thus, the p.m. reading preceding the a.m. reading takes the date and day from the civil one that followed twelve hours later. The a.m. days and dates are therefore identical for both sea and civil reckonings. When the ship was in harbour, the log reverted to civil time by extending a twenty-four-hour period into thirty-six hours.[2]

The format of the fair journals follows a standard pattern for the log account. On the left-hand side of the page, the journals have columns recording Hours, Knots, Fathoms, Courses, Winds, Soundings, Leeway and Officers of the Watch. Boxes are often inserted giving thermometer and barometer readings and detailed material on the calculations for latitude and longitude. At the bottom of each daily log entry, there is usually a set of columns providing data on the ship's course and distance, the latitude by dead reckoning and by observation, the longitude by dead reckoning and according to the timekeepers, the variation allowed, the set or current, the error of the timekeepers, and thermometer and barometer readings. The fact that the fair journals were transcribed by Elder is apparent from the occasional use of the third-person singular, with Flinders referred to as 'the commander'.

Sea journals were a hybrid genre. They were invariably compiled by the commander of a voyage, but other officers also sometimes wrote such journals. Sea journals provide diverse categories of information and allowed greater scope for reflections on a voyage than the standard format of a logbook.[3] Flinders's fair journals include a full account of

[1] Sankey, 'Writing the Voyage of Scientific Exploration', pp. 402, 404.
[2] Cole and Cole, *Mr Bass's Western Port*, p. 14.
[3] Sankey, 'Writing the Voyage of Scientific Exploration', p. 406.

his interests and preoccupations as a maritime explorer. He extended the range of information included in daily log entries considerably by including 'additional remarks' or 'general remarks' in his fair journals. These sections, which usually follow a daily log entry, provide discursive observations on his surveying and investigations, and they sometimes cover several days at a time. The 'additional remarks' and 'general remarks' offer a more complete record of the voyage than the logbook entries. Another feature of Flinders's fair journals is that they include various instructions and letters that were important for the progress of the voyage, lists of the ship's company, and inventories of the scientific instruments carried in the *Investigator*. These documents, some of which can be found in manuscript elsewhere, are usually interspersed among the logbook and journal entries at appropriate points.[1]

Entries in the fair journals often insert letters, numbers or symbols, or a combination of these, for features of the Australian coastline. Flinders used this method of identifying landmarks because most of them had never been named by Europeans. It was not until he began to write *A Voyage to Terra Australis* in 1811 that he supplied most of the names. Most of the letters and numbers are given in English, but the Greek alphabet and Greek numbers are also used. Flinders explained the use of these letters, numbers and symbols in his 'Memoir.' He applied capital letters to features on land, such as capes, points and harbours, and small letters to islands. Clusters of islands were often noted by a small letter followed by a number.[2] Letters, numbers and symbols are used more frequently for parts of Australia's coast that had not previously been explored, such as much of the 'unknown' south coast and the Gulf of Carpentaria, than for sections of the coast where nomenclature had already been supplied, as with the east coast that Cook had surveyed in the *Endeavour* in 1770. The extent of the unnamed landscape features in Flinders's fair journals, however, can be grasped by noting that only 14 out of approximately 135 coastal features named by Flinders received their names at the time of discovery between January and April 1802.[3] Flinders also used a combination of letters, numbers and symbols, incidentally, in annotating his survey sheets of the *Investigator*'s voyage.[4]

Some of the coastal features represented by letters, numbers and symbols can be identified by comparing the journals with *A Voyage to Terra Australis*. Previous historians have identified the locations of some places and geographical features, and I have drawn upon their findings.[5] In many instances, however, the letters, numbers and symbols used by Flinders have not been pinpointed by previous scholars. In order to identify them, I have used various sources, including the Bearing Book (see below), volume 2 of Yule's *Australia Directory*, covering the east coast and Torres Strait, the Australian Government's NATMAP series, and two nautical publications that provide up-to-date information, and geographical coordinates, for the main features along Australia's coast – *Sailing Directions (Enroute): North, West and South Coasts of Australia* and *Sailing Directions (Enroute): East Coast of Australia and New Zealand*. A thorough and

[1] See below, pp. 126–36, 211–12, vol. II, pp. 390–400.

[2] See below, vol. II, p. 414.

[3] Brown and Cornell, 'Legacy of the Encounter', p. 10.

[4] Bréelle, 'Matthew Flinders's Australian Toponymy', p. 8.

[5] See the footnotes throughout Vallance, Moore and Groves, eds, *Nature's Investigator*; Cooper, *The Unknown Coast*, pp. 134–5; Bréelle, 'Matthew Flinders's Australian Toponymy', pp. 1–40; Stearn, 'Introduction', pp. xxi–xxiv; and Burbidge, 'Robert Brown's Australian Collecting Localities', pp. 231–3.

systematic search through these sources yielded hundreds of identifications, but in some cases the letters, numbers and symbols used by Flinders have never been replaced with a name. This is particularly the case with islets and rocks, notably in the Gulf of Carpentaria.

Several versions of Flinders's 'Memoir' survive in manuscript. The first five chapters are preserved among the Royal Greenwich Observatory's records. At the end of the preface is a pencil marking indicating that the manuscript was unfinished, dated 10 May 1805. A pencilled note at the end of chapter 5 states that it is necessary that Dr Maskelyne should provide expert opinion for its revision.[1] Chapters 6 and 7 exist in manuscript form among the Ministry of Defence Archives.[2] The fullest copy, which is presented in this edition, incorporates a fair number of emendations and additions within the text. It is included in the second volume of Flinders's fair journal in the *Investigator* (ADM 55/76, ff. 137–188). In all, there are 103 pages of text. These comprise a title page, a Preface of two folios, a blank folio, and then the 'Memoir', consisting of 100 folios. This 'Memoir' is not contained in the Mitchell Library's Rough Journals discussed below. The full title of the 'Memoir' edited in this volume is: 'A Memoir explaining the marks used in the charts of Australia constructed on board His Majestys ship *Investigator*; and the manner in which the latitude, longitude, and variation of the compass were obtained, corrected, and applied in their construction; With some new facts and additional observations upon these and other nautical subjects connected with Australia; by Matthew Flinders, Late commander of the *Investigator*: a prisoner in the Isle of France.'

There are innumerable differences between the three extant manuscript copies of the 'Memoir', indicating that Flinders revisited and redrafted the material on various occasions. Many changes consist of alternative words, phrases and changes in punctuation. In the fullest version of the 'Memoir' reproduced in this edition there are also a good many complete paragraphs added to the two unfinished versions. These alterations are far too numerous to cite by chapter and verse; but it is clear that Flinders intended the ADM document to be the final version. The 'Memoir', it should be remembered, was intended to be seen by the Admiralty along with Flinders's charts, in order to establish his activities, achievements and methodology in gathering geographical and scientific data during the *Investigator*'s expedition.

2.   Flinders's Rough Journals

These two volumes are the original manuscript journals that Flinders compiled with the aid of his clerk, John Olive, during the voyage in the *Investigator*. They were presented in 1922 by Flinders's grandson, Sir William Flinders Petrie, to the Mitchell Library, Sydney, where they are still deposited. Volume 1 (527 folios) covers 19 January 1801 to 22 July 1802 and Volume 2 (550 folios) covers 24 July 1802 to 10 June 1803. Both volumes are

---

[1] CUL, Board of Longitude Papers, RGO 14/64, ff. 213r–247v (available online at http://cudl.lib.cam.ac.uk/view/MS-RGO-00014-00064).

[2] UKHO, OD 779, ff. 596–613. The back page of this volume (f. 614) is annotated, in black ink, in what looks like Dalrymple's hand, 'Papers relative to New Holland Rec 28 dec 1805 Flinders'. A more recent annotation in red pencil, 'Ba1', indicates that this document was at some stage taken from volume 69 of the Remark Books in the second series of Miscellaneous Papers.

available as digitized copies, with an unannotated transcription in the Matthew Flinders Collection, James Fairfax electronic archive (www.sl.nsw.gov.au/flinders/manuscripts/). The transcription retains Flinders's spelling and punctuation; it does not include any tables from the original volumes or the astronomical and navigational data. The only material additional to the journals itself in these documents is a fourteen-page text at the end of the second volume entitled 'General observations upon the rates and errors of the time-keepers No 543 and No 520, and the necessary corrections to be applied to their longitudes during the circumnavigation of New Holland in 1802 and 1803'.

Though, as mentioned above, these journals were damaged in the wreck of the *Porpoise*, most of their pages are quite well preserved. They include a fair number of 'additional remarks' and 'general remarks', but these are sometimes indecipherable. The punctuation used in the rough journals is rather hit-and-miss. In comparison with the fair journals, there are also numerous crossings-out. A good deal of information overlaps the rough journals and the fair journals, but the latter provide a fuller account of the *Investigator*'s expedition. In my edited text of the fair journals, I have footnoted statements from the rough journals that add to the material presented in the fair journals.

3. The Bearing Book

This is a unique document that Flinders compiled for several of his voyages in Australian waters, including those in the *Norfolk* and the *Investigator*. Aken copied it for Flinders and brought it back to London from the Ile de France in 1805.[1] It is deposited at the UK Hydrographic Office, Ministry of Defence Archives, Taunton.[2] The title on the volume is 'Bearings taken on board His Majesty's ship *Investigator* whilst exploring the coasts of Terra Australis; by Matthew Flinders Commander 1801, 2, and 3'. This copy was largely made by Aken. Flinders's 'Memoir' stated that the 'Bearing Book' contained 'all the bearings and angles that were taken, whether on shore or on board, entered in a regular chronological order; as also the boat-soundings, and occasional eye-sketches of particular parts'.[3] Many daily entries in the 'Bearing Book' contain a considerable amount of data on soundings and bearings. They use the letters, numbers and symbols that Flinders deployed in his fair journals. In some cases, they are accompanied by a name that Flinders had devised for a particular coastal or island feature. Though the Bearing Book is not reproduced in this edition, it contains significant hydrographical and astronomical information that could be used for detailed scholarly investigation.[4]

4. Other Primary Voyage Sources Compiled during the *Investigator* Expedition

Several of these sources survive, and add informative details to the material presented in the manuscripts written by Flinders during the expedition. Robert Fowler kept a log that

[1] Flinders, *A Voyage to Terra Australis*, II, p. 238.
[2] UKHO, Data Book 22.
[3] See below, vol. II, p. 407.
[4] Though there has been little published analysis of the Bearing Book, a good start has been made in Barritt, 'Matthew Flinders's Survey Practices and Records', pp. 1–15.

provides daily entries and nautical details, but he did not add the discursive material that Flinders included in his fair and rough journals. Fowler's log, however, provides virtually no information that cannot be found in Flinders's journals.[1]

The gardener, Peter Good, kept a journal inscribed 'Remarks &c. on Board his Majesty's ship *Investigator* during a voyage of Discovery by Peter Good'. This exists in several versions among the manuscripts preserved at the Natural History Museum, London. The fullest version was edited for publication in 1981 by Phyllis Edwards.[2] It includes brief daily entries for the period from 18 July 1801 to 17 May 1803. It is naturally strong on botany, but also includes nautical information. Succinct annotation is provided.

A seaman on the voyage, Samuel Smith, kept a journal that includes interesting observations on Australian flora and fauna and Aborigines in particular. The original manuscript is deposited at the Mitchell Library, Sydney. It has a watermark dated 1813, and it appears that Smith wrote up his journal at least a decade after the *Investigator*'s voyage. There is a published edition of this document.[3] Neither Bauer nor Westall wrote journals during the *Investigator* expedition. Logbooks are available for the tender *Lady Nelson* that accompanied the *Investigator* during its survey of the east coast. The original documents are kept at the National Archives, Kew.[4]

Robert Brown's diary is an extensive source of information on the *Investigator* expedition. This has been reconstructed painstakingly from the original manuscripts at the Natural History Museum, London, and has been published in a scholarly edition.[5] Brown kept daily entries during the voyage, and continued his diary after the *Investigator* was decommissioned in July 1803. He provides expert information on botany, zoology, geology and mineralogy, and includes fascinating entries dealing with the general objectives of the voyage and the encounters with Aboriginal groups. The published edition has been produced meticulously, with very helpful maps of many Australian localities. The scholarly apparatus to the edition is substantial, and has been of inestimable benefit for my own edition.

5.   The Edited Text

In accordance with the rules and guidelines of the Hakluyt Society, this edition does not seek to present a facsimile version of the fair journals and the 'Memoir'. But it does aim to render most of Flinders's original texts accurately and as comprehensively as can be realistically achieved. Editorial decisions have been taken to make certain omissions in the presentation of the fair journals. Columns on the left-hand side of the page in the daily log entries are omitted. Thus the columns with information on Hours, Knots, Fathoms, Courses, Winds, Soundings, Leeway and Officers of the Watch are not included. Readers can readily consult these data in the original manuscripts, which, as mentioned above, are available online. Some of this information is also provided elsewhere in the daily log entries. Flinders frequently singled out particular hours in his log entries, for example,

---

[1] Fowler's log is found at TNA, ADM 55/77.
[2] Edwards, ed., *The Journal of Peter Good*.
[3] Monteath, ed., *Sailing with Flinders*.
[4] TNA, ADM 52/4170. For extensive selections from this source, see Lee, *The Logbooks of Lady Nelson*.
[5] Vallance, Moore and Groves, eds, *Nature's Investigator*.

and the course is summarized in a box at the end of most daily entries. Information on latitude within the log entries is retained, but it was decided to omit the complex calculations found therein for longitude. This does not mean that evidence on daily coordinates is omitted from the edition: the box entries for most days give the latitude and longitude by dead reckoning and according to the timekeepers, and all information on coordinates in the 'additional remarks' and the 'general remarks' is retained. Readers wanting more details on these matters can consult the online records of the Board of Longitude, which include much data submitted on the nautical astronomy of the *Investigator*'s expedition.[1] No omissions are made in the transcription and editing of the 'Memoir'.

Flinders's handwriting, and that of his clerks, is legible and relatively easy to read for an early nineteenth-century text. Capitalization is easy to discern and sentences are properly punctuated. Spellings sometimes differ from modern British usage. Certain words fall regularly into this category. 'Lightening' is often used for 'lightning', 'kanguroo' for 'kangaroo', and 'center' for 'centre'. In such cases, a footnote identifies the correct modern spelling on the first occasion the word is used and then it is assumed that readers will have picked this up. Individual odd spellings are followed by '*sic*' in square brackets. Omitted letters are included in italics within words. All ships' names are italicized to help the reader to identify vessels with certainty. Flinders implies where paragraphs should be inserted in his log entries by leaving sufficient blank space. I have inserted paragraphing accordingly. The 'additional remarks' and 'general remarks' already have paragraphs, so this has been followed. Headings to daily log entries are retained, but rendered in bold type. It has not proven possible to identify many numbered anchorages used in these headings. Folio numbers (using Flinders's original numbering not the later renumbering) are retained in brackets, for two reasons. One is that Flinders and his clerks occasionally cross-referenced material by reference to folio numbers. The second reason is that the chronological order of the text occasionally departs from a precise numerical folio sequence. In such cases, I have rearranged the text into the correct order and have indicated in a footnote that this has been done.

6.   Place Names

A final word is necessary about the nomenclature used for place names in this edition. It was not possible to rely on the edited text of the journals for place names on the maps because the journals use letters, numbers and symbols for many features of Australia's coastal landscape. Flinders supplied place names for all of these features in *A Voyage to Terra Australis* and its accompanying atlas. Some places had already been given names by Cook, Vancouver and French and Dutch explorers. However, these place names have often been modified so that modern usage can differ from the original designations. A good example would be Flinders's use of King George's Sound or King George III's Sound for what is today called King George Sound. I considered that a consistent approach was needed in this edition. Although it would be an interesting exercise to compare the English, Dutch and French versions of place names for Australia's coastal features and to

[1] See above, p. 88, n. 1.

indicate which ones have survived and which ones have disappeared in modern usage, this is not the right place for such an enquiry. I decided it was not realistic to explain the variations in detail in the footnotes to this edition because that would overload what is already full documentation. For consistency, therefore, the following procedures are followed in respect to the nomenclature in this edition: place names on the maps follow the designations given in *A Voyage to Terra Australis* and its atlas, whereas place names in footnotes and in square brackets in the text after letters, symbols and numbers follow modern usage.

JOURNAL OF A VOYAGE TO TERRA AUSTRALIS IN HIS MAJESTY'S SHIP *INVESTIGATOR* BY MATTHEW FLINDERS COMMANDER

Part 1: From England to Sydney Cove and Port Jackson, Australia, January 1801–July 1802

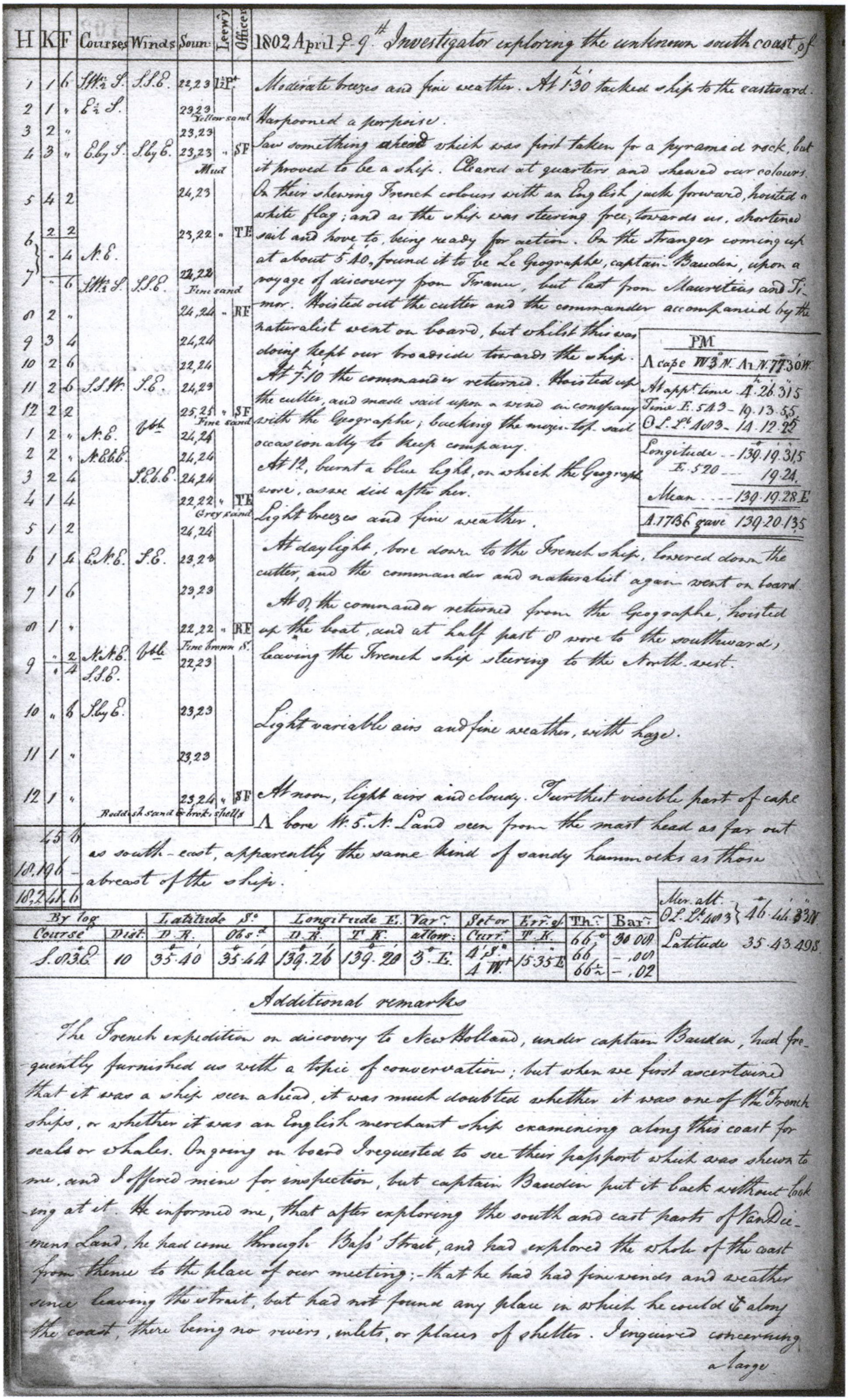

H	K	F	Courses	Winds	Soun:	Leew'y	Officer	1802 April 8-9th Investigator exploring the unknown south coast of
1	1	6	SWb½S.	S.S.E.	22,23	1½P.t		Moderate breezes and fine weather. At 1:30 tacked ship to the eastward.
2	1	"	E½S.		23,23 Yellow sand			Harpooned a porpoise.
3	2	"			23,23			Saw something ahead which was first taken for a pyramed rock, but
4	3	"	Eby S.	Sby E.	23,23 Mud	"	SF	it proved to be a ship. Cleared at quarters and shewed our colours.
5	4	2			24,23			On their shewing French colours with an English jack forward, hoisted a white flag; and as the ship was steering free, towards us, shortened
6	2	2			23,22	"	TF	sail and hove to, being ready for action. On the stranger coming up
	-	4	N.E.					at about 5h 40, found it to be Le Geographe, captain Baudin, upon a
7	-	6	SWbS.	S.S.E.	22,22 Fine sand			voyage of discovery from France, but last from Mauritius and Timor. Hoisted out the cutter and the commander accompanied by the
8	2	"			24,24	-	RF	naturalist went on board, but whilst this was
9	3	4			24,24			doing kept our broadside towards the ship.
10	2	6			22,24			At 7:10 the commander returned. Hoisted up
11	2	6	S.S.W.	S.E.	24,23			the cutter, and made sail upon a wind in company
12	2	2			25,25 Fine sand	"	SF	with the Geographe; backing the mizen-top-sail
1	2	"	N.E.	Ebb	24,25			occasionally to keep company.
2	2	"	NEbE.		24,24			At 12, burnt a blue light, on which the Geographe
3	2	4		S.EbE.	24,24			wore, as we did after her.
4	1	4			22,22 Grey sand	"	TF	Light breezes and fine weather.
5	1	2			24,24			
6	1	4	EbN.E.	S.E.	23,24			At daylight, bore down to the French ship, lowered down the cutter, and the commander and naturalist again went on board.
7	1	6			23,23			
8	1	"			22,22 Fine brown S.d	"	RF	At 8, the commander returned from the Geographe, hoisted up the boat, and at half past 8 wore to the southward,
9	"	2	N.N.E.	Ebb	22,23			leaving the French ship steering to the North-west.
	"	4	S.S.E.					
10	"	6	SbyE.		23,23			Light variable airs and fine weather, with haze.
11	1	"			23,23			
12	1	"			23,24 Reddish sand & broke shells	"	SF	At noon, light airs and cloudy. Furthest visible part of cape A bore W. 5°N. Land seen from the mast head as far out

PM	
A cape W3°N. Az N.77°30'W.	
At appt time	4.26.315
Time E. 543	19.13.55
O.L. Ld 403	14.12.25
Longitude	139.19.315
E. 520	19.24
Mean	139.19.28 E
A.1736 gave	139.20.135

45 6 as south-east, apparently the same kind of sandy hammocks as those
18.19 6 - abreast of the ship.
18.24 4.6

Mer. alt. O.L. Ld 403 } 46.44.33 N.
Latitude 35.43.49 S.

By log Course	Dist.	Latitude S.o D.R.	Obs.d	Longitude E. D.R.	T.K.	Var.n allow.	Set or Curr.t	Err. of T.K.	Th.	Bar.
S.83E.	10	35.40	35.44	139.26	139.20	3° E.	4 S. 4 W.	15.35 E	66° 66 66½	30.00 -.00 -.02

Additional remarks

The French expedition on discovery to New Holland, under captain Baudin, had frequently furnished us with a topic of conversation; but when we first ascertained that it was a ship seen ahead, it was much doubted whether it was one of the French ships, or whether it was an English merchant ship examining along this coast for seals or whales. On going on board I requested to see their passport which was shewn to me, and I offered mine for inspection, but captain Baudin put it back without looking at it. He informed me, that after exploring the south and east parts of Van Diemens Land, he had come through Bass' Strait, and had explored the whole of the coast from thence to the place of our meeting; that he had had fine winds and weather since leaving the strait, but had not found any place in which he could & along the coast, there being no rivers, inlets, or places of shelter. I enquired concerning

a large

Figure 1. Matthew Flinders, Entry for 9 April 1802, Fair Journal of the *Investigator*, ADM 55/75, f. 192. Courtesy of the National Archives, Kew.

JOURNAL OF A VOYAGE TO TERRA AUSTRALIS IN HIS MAJESTY'S SHIP *INVESTIGATOR* BY MATTHEW FLINDERS COMMANDER

1801

[ADM 55/75]

[f. 1] His Majestys ship *Xenophon*[1] of 334 tons and 75 men, having undergone a thorough examination and been newly coppered[2] in dock at Sheerness,[3] was pitched upon to proceed upon a voyage of discovery to the South Seas; and on January 19 a commission was signed by the Lords Commissioners of the Admiralty for Matthew Flinders, late second lieutenant of His Majestys ship *Reliance*[4] to be lieutenant of the *Investigator,* to which name the *Xenophon* was changed by this commission; and being the senior officer, I took the command, and John Henry Martin[5] *Esquire* considered himself to be superseded.

Sunday 25 January

AM.[6] Mustered the ships company and read my commission as lieutenant.[7] Received fresh beef. Snow at times.[8]

Monday 26 January

Moderate breezes with snow. AM. Surveyed the pursers stores. Employed occasionally.[9]

---

[1] For the previous history of this vessel, see above, p. 10.

[2] From the 1750s onwards, copper plates were applied to some merchant and naval vessels to prevent teredo worms and marine weeds from fouling vessels' hulls. After the American War of Independence the Royal Navy attempted to copper bottom the entire fleet. Harris, 'Copper and Shipping in the Eighteenth Century', pp. 550–68, and Knight, 'The Introduction of Copper Sheathing into the Royal Navy'. pp. 299–309.

[3] The ship was then moored in Sheerness harbour. NMM, ADM/L/Y/55, 'Journal of Proceedings on board His Majesty's sloop *Xenophon* kept by Lieutenant Robert Fowler'.

[4] Flinders had been appointed senior master's mate on the *Reliance* on 10 August 1794. This ship was about to embark on a voyage taking out a new governor, John Hunter, to New South Wales. The *Reliance* arrived at Port Jackson in September 1795. During the voyage to Australia, Flinders was promoted to acting lieutenant after the 2nd lieutenant left the ship at Rio de Janeiro owing to ill health. While staying at the Cape of Good Hope, following a voyage of the *Reliance* there from Port Jackson, Flinders passed and received his certificate for lieutenant on 24 January 1797. After being attached to the vessel for five-and-a-half years, Flinders sailed home on the *Reliance*, arriving at Plymouth on 27 August 1800. Bowden, *George Bass*, p. 27; Estensen, *The Life of Matthew Flinders*, pp. 110–11; ML, Banks Papers, series 37.28, Henry Waterhouse to Arthur Phillip, 24 October 1795; Beardsley and Bennett, *'Gratefull to Providence'*, II, p. 182.

[5] John Henry Martin (1753–1823) had sailed on Cook's third Pacific voyage in the *Discovery* and the *Resolution.* He was given command of the *Xenophon* for operations in the North Sea in 1800. Robson, 'John Henry Martin'.

[6] For an explanation of references to times of the day in the journal, see above, p. 90.

[7] The Commission would have been signed by two Lords Commissioners of the Admiralty and a Secretary.

[8] Rough journal, I, f. 2, adds: 'Applied to have the present master superseded, which was acceded to, and the choice left entirely to me.'

[9] i.e. as circumstances required. Rough journal, I, f. 2, adds: 'Applied for Joseph Robinott to supersede the present cook, which was complied with & his warrant given[.]'

Tuesday 27 January
Fresh breezes and cloudy. Held surveys on boatswains and carpenters stores. Fresh breezes and cloudy.[1]

Wednesday 28 January
Prepared to throw out the shingle ballast to receive coals: otherwise employed occasionally.

Thursday 29 January
Strong breezes in the morning which prevented us from moving to moorings nearer in shore. Moored ship again and struck topmasts. Received fresh beef. 516 lbs.

Friday 30 January
Transported the ship to her moorings, and took them in. Employed throwing the shingle ballast into a lighter. Received fresh beef 179 lbs. Launched the six-oared cutter.[2]

Saturday 31 January
Employed clearing the holds to receive coals.

Sunday 1 February
AM. Mustered the ships company and read the articles of war.[3] Received beer and bread per lighter.

Monday 2 February
Returned our cables (one excepted) and hawsers.[4] AM. Employed on shore about the cables, and drawing boatswains stores.

Tuesday 3 February
Employed taking in 35¼ chaldrons[5] of coals, in which the ground tier[6] is to be stowed. Received 164 lbs fresh beef.

Wednesday 4 February
Received two chords[7] of wood. Employed in the holds stowing the ground tier. AM. Read the articles of war and punished John Fuller marine, with 12 lashes for contempt to his serjeant.[8] Washed and aired below.

---

[1] Rough journal, I, f. 2, adds: 'Applied to the Commissioners of the victualling for our casks to be new, and to prepare 18 months salt and 12 of dry provisions; as also for the usual allowance of extra articles[.]'

[2] Rough journal, I, f. 5, adds: 'Made application to the Commissioners of the victualling for water casks, being the second; and to the Sick and Hurt Board for a medical man to be sent down to us[.]' The Sick and Hurt Board was responsible for medical services in the Royal Navy between 1715 and 1806.

[3] This was necessary because Britain and France had been at war since 1 February 1793. It was also common practice to read out the Articles of War publicly when a new ship was commissioned. The Articles of War, originally established in the 1650s, served as the law practised in the Royal Navy.

[4] i.e. thick cables or ropes used in mooring or towing ships.

[5] A dry English measure of volume, not a weight, that was used in the coal industry from the 13th century onwards. A London chaldron of coal weighed about 28 cwt. Hutton, *A Philosophical and Mathematical Dictionary*, p. 302.

[6] The lowest tier of water casks in a vessel's hold.

[7] A chord is a unit of measure of dry volume for wood, usually amounting to 128 cubic feet.

[8] Flogging was a common punishment in the Navy until it was suspended in peacetime in 1871 and suspended altogether in 1879, though technically it can still be reintroduced in wartime. Winton, 'Life and Education in a Technically Evolving Navy', p. 265.

Thursday 5 February

Moderate and cloudy. Employed in the holds and in occasional duties.

Friday 6 February

Received orders to take on board as much stores and provisions as the *Investigator* could stow with all expedition and repair to the Nore,[1] keeping the ship ready for sailing; also a new establishment for the ship, amounting to 83 including 15 marines.[2] Returned various carpenters stores. Joiners from the yard employed as usual, and shipwrights cutting scuttles[3] in the ports.[4]

Saturday 7 February

Fresh breezes and cloudy. Returned some boatswains and carpenters stores. Employed slinging buoys &c. &c. on board. Received 339 lbs of fresh beef.[5]

Sunday 8 February

Received some boatswains stores. Mustered the people & saw them clean.

Monday 9 February

Received 18 tons of water. Employed in the holds.

Tuesday 10 February

Fresh breezes and cloudy. Shipwrights and joiners employed on board about various jobs. Returned all the provisions in the ship, a small quantity for present use excepted. AM. Got off our anchors, making together 5 bowers,[6] 2 streams[7] and 2 kedges.[8] Received 106 lbs of fresh beef.

[f. 2] Wednesday 11 February

Fresh breezes and rainy at times. Employed occasionally on board the ship.

---

[1] A sandbank at the end of the Thames Estuary where the River Thames meets the North Sea, extending between Shoeburyness and Sheerness in Kent.

[2] Thus, eight more men were placed on board than on the *Xenophon* (see above, p. 99). At this stage no commander was listed but Flinders pressed for this over the next few days, and was successful. Estensen, *The Life of Matthew Flinders*, p. 141.

[3] i.e. holes.

[4] Rough journal, I, f. 5, adds: 'Received orders to take on board as much stores and provisions as the *Investigator* could store, with all expedition, and repair to the Nore, keeping the ship ready for sailing. Received also a new establishment for the ship, amounting to 83 including 15 marines. Warrant officers being allowed by this new order, I applied for Charles Douglas the boatswains mate to be Boatswain, and Russel Mart of Sheerness Yard to be carpenter, which was complied with; but my application for John Whitewood to be acting gunner was not. I requested also of my Lords Commissioners that such men, who from age or other cause should be found unfit for such a voyage as the present intended should be discharged, and the complement filled up with healthy young men who should be volunteers; and in consequence, *Vice Admiral* Graeme received orders to act accordingly, so soon as we should go out to the Nore[.]'

[5] Rough journal, I, f. 7, adds: 'Informed the Victualling Board that the ship was waiting for water casks, and applied for some additions and alterations in the provisions they had ordered[.] Applied to the Navy Board, for two carronades to be mounted abaft, and for our launch to be fitted so as to receive one of them; both of which were complied with[.]'

[6] Anchors carried at the bow.

[7] Anchors used in narrow channels to prevent the vessel's stern moving with the tide.

[8] Light anchors used for warping a vessel.

Thursday 12 February
Carpenters &c as usual. D*itt*o Weather with snow.[1]

Friday 13 February
Discharged the clerk and 3 Men into His Majestys boat *Explosion*[2] after John Martin my predecessor. Employed on board occasionally.[3]

Saturday 14 February
Fresh breezes with hail and snow. An officer and men at the yard drawing stores. Cleared out the sail room and overhauled the few sails on board and found that the mice had got them. Received 114 lbs of fresh beef.

Sunday 15 February
Fresh breezes with rain and hail. Received boatswains stores. Mustered the ships company.

Monday 16 February
Employed at the dock yard drawing the boatswains stores. Carpenters &c on board.[4]

Tuesday 17 February
Fresh breezes and cloudy. Received a lighter loaded with boatswains stores. Employed at the yard. Received 146 lbs of fresh beef.

Wednesday 18 February
Employed variously. Mr. Robert Purdie Surgeon's mate joined. Employed at the yard and occasionally.

Thursday 19 February
Read my commission as Commander.[5] Employed as necessary. Entered Mr. James Woolsey.[6]

Friday 20 February
Received two lighter-loads of provisions. Employed at the yard and in the holds.[7]

---

[1] Rough journal, I, f. 7, adds: 'Informed the victualling board that we were still waiting for water and provisions; and applied for coopers tools, weights and measures, which were given[.]'

[2] TNA, ADM 8/81, Admiralty List Book, The *Explosion*, H. S. Butt commander, 67 men, commissioned on 8 August 1797, was at the Nore fitted for the Channel service.

[3] Rough journal, I, f. 7, adds: 'Applied to have the present master surveyed for sick quarters; and to the Board of Ordnance for cylinder powder, and a chest of fireworks[.]'

[4] Rough journal, I, f. 9, adds: 'Applied to the Victualling Board for permission to draw for 2 years necessary money. 18 m*onths* granted[.]'

[5] Sir Joseph Banks had influenced the Admiralty in securing Flinders's appointment as commander. The commission authorizing promotion to this rank was dated 16 February 1801. Estensen, *The Life of Matthew Flinders*, pp. 141–2.

[6] Rough journal, I, f. 9, adds: 'Applied to the Navy Board for one of the two whale boats, which had been built at Deptford for us, to be exchanged for a 4-oared boat to be built at Queenborough according to my directions. Rejected at first, but complied about 3 weeks afterwards[.]'

[7] Rough journal, I, f. 9, adds: 'Informed the Victualling Board that such hand mills as I had applied for, could be procured at Port Jackson for £4 or 6; on which they ordered me to procure two[.]'

Saturday 21 February
Fresh breezes and cloudy. Received boatswains carpenters and pursers stores. Employed stowing them away. Received 270 lbs of fresh beef.[1]

Sunday 22 February
Employed as above.

Monday 23 February
Fresh breezes with rain. Employed in the holds. AM. Received a variety of provisions.

Tuesday 24 February
Received more provisions for sea and 168 lbs of fresh beef. Employed stowing away provisions.

Wednesday 25 February
Employed in the holds. Carpenters &c. on board.

Thursday 26 February
Strong breezes with rain. Got top gallant masts[2] down upon deck and struck lower yards.[3] Employed occasionally.

Friday 27 February
Yard Carpenters &c. on board. Employed putting the ship to rights. Entered Mr Kennet Sinclair. Received fresh beef.

Saturday 28 February
Unstowed the forehold,[4] got up 6 tons of iron ballast and placed it abaft to trim[5] the ship.

Sunday 1 March
Fresh breezes with rain. Employed in the forehold. Mustered the ships company.

Monday 2 March
Fine weather. Employed variously. Received 265 lbs of fresh beef.

Tuesday 3 March
Fresh breezes and cloudy. Employed making points for the new sails.[6]

---

[1] Rough journal, I, f. 9, adds: 'Obtained 10 days leave of absence; which was afterwards extended to 14 on application. My business in town was partly to forward the providing of the requisite instruments, books, charts, stationary [sic], articles for presents and barter &c &c &c.'

[2] These held square-rigged sails immediately above the topsails.

[3] These parts of the rigging are permanently fixed in position at the top of lower masts.

[4] i.e. the forward part of a hold of a ship.

[5] i.e. to get the ship ready for sailing with regard to ballast, sails and yards.

[6] See the Glossary, p. xxiii.

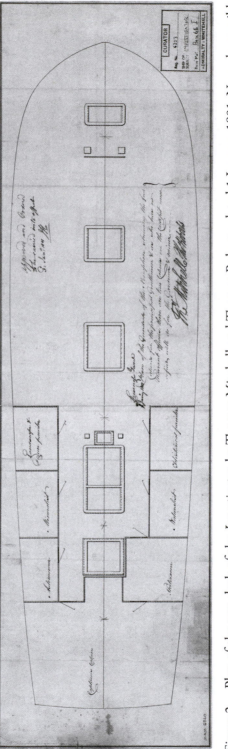

Figure 2. Plan of the gun deck of the *Investigator*, by Thomas Mitchell and Thomas Roberts, dated 1 January 1801. No scale, possibly 1:48. © National Maritime Museum, Greenwich, London.

Wednesday 4 March
Received water. Employed on board in the holds and fitting gun tackles[1] and breechings.[2]

Thursday 5 March
People employed in the dock yard and in the holds. Carpenters and painters on board. Received spare spars.[3]

Friday 6 March
Employed stowing the booms.[4] AM. People employed principally in the dock yard. Answered the signal for weekly accounts as usual this day.

[f. 3] **Saturday 7 March**
Moderate and cloudy. Received water per lighter. Employed in the holds. Received 251 lbs of fresh beef.

Sunday 8 March
Employed as before, and in receiving 7 bower cables.[5]

Monday 9 March
Fresh breezes and cloudy. Employ[ed] stowing away various stores.[6]

Tuesday 10 March
Carpenters and joiners on board. People employed at the dockyard, and in various duties on board. Received 243 lbs of fresh beef.

Wednesday 11 March
Employed getting off sundry stores, and in occasional duties on board.

Thursday 12 March
Received sundry stores and 4 tons of beer. Returned hops and molasses which we were unable to stow. Shipwrights coppering the ship a streak higher up.

Friday 13 March
Fresh breezes and squally. Struck lower yards and top gallant masts. Employed in the yard and stowing away stores. Coiled shroud hawsers &c in the magazine. Received 8 men from His Majesty's ship *Hydra*.[7] Answered signal for weekly accounts.

---

[1] Made of two single-sheave blocks and used to haul muzzle-loading guns back into the battery after the guns had been fired and reloaded.

[2] i.e. heavy ropes shackled to the side of a vessel to secure the carriages of cannon.

[3] Round poles of wood or metal.

[4] Spars at the foot of sails.

[5] i.e. belonging to the bower anchor.

[6] Rough journal, I, f. 13, adds: 'Wrote to the Board of Ordnance to hurry the gun carriages, musquets &c &c nothing of which was yet received; and also to the Admiralty for 8 men, volunteers from H.M.S. *Hydra*, both of which were complied with, as also to have Mr Gray superseded whom they had appointed as gunner[.]'

[7] TNA, ADM 8/81, Admiralty List Book, the *Hydra*, Hon. C. Paget commander, 284 men, was at Sheerness refitting for the Channel service.

Saturday 14 March
Received 105 lbs of fresh beef and 12 six pounders[1] and 2 eighteen-pound carronades[2] and gunners stores; also a proportion of our sails.

Sunday 15 March
Rainy weather. Employed fitting up the guns. Bent sails.

Monday 16 March
Employed coiling away hawsers &c. AM. Received 65 half barrels of powder and stowed it away. Washed below.

Tuesday 17 March
Employed stowing shot cases &c in the light room, the ship being much by the head.[3] AM. Began painting the ship. Received a variety of fireworks from Woolwich[4] with directions. Received 275 lbs of fresh beef 6 lbs short of weight.

Wednesday 18 March
Strong breezes. Struck lower yards. Employed occasionally on board, being unable to get anything from the yard. Painters employed.[5]

Thursday 19 March
Fresh breezes. Received some small stores. Opened a cask of pork, contents 53 pieces, 1 short. Answered the signal for a midshipman.[6]

Friday 20 March
Squally. Got off 4 tons of iron ballast to bring the ship by the stern. AM. Received some stores. Employed lashing and securing. Entered the Astronomer and servant (Mr John Crosley and Thomas White).[7]

Saturday 21 March
Heavy squalls. Struck lower yards per signal. AM. Employed occasionally. Hauled up the cutter to repair. Received 224 lbs of fresh beef.

---

[1] i.e. cannons using shot weighing 6 lbs.

[2] Short, smoothbore cast-iron cannons. They were first introduced in 1776 by the Carron ironworks at Falkirk, Scotland. Tucker, 'The Carronade', pp. 15–23.

[3] i.e. the bow.

[4] i.e. from the Royal Arsenal, Woolwich.

[5] Rough journal, I, f. 15, adds: 'Informed the Navy Board of the difficulty I found in obtaining a master, and submitted it to them whether some additional pay or encouragement ought not to be given. In answer they agree to give 3 *shillings* per day more than the rate allows, in lieu of all pilotage.'

[6] A commissioned officer of the lowest rank who normally served for seven years on the lower deck.

[7] Rough journal, I, f. 15, adds: 'Entered Mr Crossley, Astronomer & his servant, as supernumeraries. Applied for a survey on surgeons stores.' John Crosley had been an assistant at the Royal Observatory, Greenwich. He had worked for three years as assistant to the Astronomer Royal, Nevil Maskelyne, and had been the astronomer on William Robert Broughton's voyage in the *Providence* to the North Pacific between 1795 and 1797. Flinders, *A Voyage to Terra Australis*, I, p. 255; Howse, *Nevil Maskelyne*, p. 156; David, ed., *William Robert Broughton's Voyage*, p. 269.

Sunday 22 March

Received a five-oared whale boat[1] from the dock yard. AM. Restored the booms. Received a four-oared whaleboat from the yard. Employed cleaning the ship.

Monday 23 March

Employed as in the morning. AM. Brought off the launch (a 32-gun frigate) and a spare rudder in parts. Received 20 baricoes.[2] Loosed sails to dry.

Tuesday 24 March

Employed stowing away the rudder in the quarters, and spars. AM. loosed sails: otherwise employed occasionally.

Wednesday 25 March

Squally with rain. Furled sails. AM. Fine weather. Loosed sails. Received 198 lbs of fresh beef.

Thursday 26 March

Hoisted in the launch and furled sails. AM. Received beer and water, and returned empty casks. Employed cleaning ship and securing for sea.[3]

[f. 4] Friday 27 March

AM. Thick weather and almost calm. At 7, made signal with pilot for a gun. At 8 slipped the moorings and made sail out of the harbour. At 11, brought to at the little Nore,[4] and furled sails in 11 fathoms water with small bower. Answered the signal for weekly accounts.

Saturday 28 March

Thick weather and almost calm. Veered away with the ebb and moored ship: the Garrison Point[5] bearing SW about 1¼ mile. Employed rounding the cables.[6] AM. Cleared below and loosed all sails to dry. Employed painting the cables. Received 269 lbs of fresh beef.

Sunday 29 March

Light airs and fine weather. Employed pointing cables and about occasional jobs. AM. Mustered the ships company, and read the Articles of War. Answered signal for all lieutenants. Loosed sails to dry, and washed and cleared below.

---

[1] A relatively narrow open boat that is pointed at both ends, enabling it to move forwards or backwards equally well. Whaleboats could be used for work along beaches.

[2] Small casks for use in ships, often to carry water.

[3] Rough journal, I, f. 15, adds: 'Applied to the board of Ordnance for Francis Jennings to be appointed Armourer, which was complied with and his warrant inclosed to me[.]'

[4] An anchorage off Sheerness (51°27′N and 0°45′E). Rough journal, I, f. 17, adds: 'Reported the *Investigator* at the Nore waiting their Lordships orders, being ready for sea; and informed them of no books, charts, instruments, stationary, articles for presents and barter, or the men of science, having joined. Received for answer, that the men of science had been hastened down to join.'

[5] Fortifications at Garrison Point, Sheerness, were first installed by Henry VIII to protect the River Medway from invasions at sea. They were remodelled and augmented after the Anglo-Dutch War of 1665–7 to protect the naval dockyard being built at Sheerness. The fortifications were only completed in 1685. Sheerness was one of the bases of the Royal Navy's Nore command.

[6] This involved binding the cables with old rope to protect them against chafing.

Monday 30 March

Furled sails. Part of the people on shore on leave. AM. Fitting travelling backstays[1] and making boats fenders &c.

Tuesday 31 March

Moderate and fine weather. Discharged 8 men into His Majesty's ship *Zealand*,[2] per order of vice-admiral Graeme;[3] and received 8 volunteers for the voyage in lieu.[4] Employed in various jobs in securing for sea, and about the rigging. Received 218 lbs of fresh beef.

Wednesday 1 April

Carpenters on board from the yard. Employed working up junk[5] &c.[6]

Thursday 2 April

Received 4 tons of water. AM. Loosed sails to dry and scrubbed hammocks. Employed working up junk and in various occasional jobs.[7]

Friday 3 April

Furled sails: employed otherwise as above. AM. Washed below, and secured ballast in the after part of the ship. Our carpenters putting together the spare rudder for shipping. Answered the signal for the guard and weekly accounts. Came in His Majestys brigs *Express* & *Advice*,[8] and out of the harbour the *Vesuve*[9] and *Plumper*.[10]

Saturday 4 April

Moderate and fine weather. Employed working up junk, and putting the spare rudder together. AM. Returned the guard, received 269 lbs of fresh beef. Unshipped the rudder and tried to ship the spare one, but could not.

---

[1] The pieces of standing rigging running from the mast to the ship's transom.

[2] TNA, ADM 8/81, Admiralty List Book, the *Zealand*, Vice Admiral Graeme and William Mitchell commanders, 491 men, was a receiving ship at Chatham, Sheerness, the Nore and the River Medway.

[3] Admiral Alexander Graeme (d. 5 Aug. 1818) was commander-in chief of the Navy at the Nore between 30 June 1799 and 11 July 1802, http://inchbrakie.tripod.com/abookofthegraemes/id64.html.

[4] Eleven volunteers were recruited from the *Zealand* from at least 250 on board who were willing to join the *Investigator* after being informed of the nature of her voyage. Flinders, *A Voyage to Terra Australis*, I, p. 126.

[5] i.e. pieces of old cordage.

[6] Rough journal, I, f. 19, adds: 'Sent up the two-monthly books, up to 26th last, and a sick ticket, with two allotments; and letter advising the Navy Board of them and requesting an acknowledgment of their receipt[.]'

[7] Rough journal, I, f. 19, adds: 'Received an admiralty order, to receive on board Mr Rennell and victual him as a supernumerary.'

[8] TNA, ADM 8/81, Admiralty List Book: the *Express*, Robert Sayes commander, 30 men, was based in the River Thames; the *Advice*, William Robertson commander, 30 men, was at the Nore.

[9] TNA, ADM 51/4514, Admiralty Captains' Logs: the *Vesuve*, a gun brig captured from the French.

[10] TNA, ADM 8/81, Admiralty List Book: the *Plumper*, H. W. Barrett commander, 50 men, was a troop ship.

Sunday 5 April

Shipped the rudder again, and hoisted in the spare one to be examined. AM. Mustered the ships company, and gave part of them leave.[1]

Monday 6 April

Fresh breezes and cloudy weather. AM. Fine weather. Up top gallant yards as usual. Carpenters came off from the yard to examine the spare rudder and compare it with the old which we unshipped for them. Having made the requisite alterations, we hoisted it out, and shipped it without difficulty. Punished Thomas Leach marine for absenting himself beyond his leave, with 12 lashes. Answered the signal and took the guard.

Tuesday 7 April

Fresh breezes and cloudy. Hoisted in the spare rudder, took it to pieces and restored it on the quarters. Came out of the harbour His Majestys ship *Camilla*.[2] AM. Returned the guard.[3] Employed berthing the hammocks, and working up junk.

Wednesday 8 April

Strong breezes and squally. Employed working up junk. Struck top gallant masts. AM. Up top gallant masts and yards, and mended sails. Employed otherwise working up junk.

[f. 5] Thursday 9 April

Fresh breezes and cloudy. Employed making points and ropes. Mustered the ships company. AM. Received 3 tons of beer and of water per lighter.

Friday 10 April

Employed working up junk. AM. struck top gallant masts. Answered the signal to take guard and for weekly accounts. Cleared hawse and mustered per Clerk of the Cheque.[4]

Saturday 11 April

Employed as before. Came out of the harbour His Majestys ships *Ruby* and *Ranger*;[5] and sailed the former. Received 205 lbs of fresh beef. Employed airing the sails.

[1] Rough journal, I, f. 21, adds: 'By desire of Sir *Joseph Banks* applied to V*ice* Ad*miral* Graeme for leave of absence from the 9th to the 19th following, which was granted. Whilst in London, my publick employments were to hasten the mathematical instruments, forward the ordering of the necessary stationary and books, and articles for presents and barter; and put some necessary letters to the gove*rnor* of New South Wales under weigh; particularly relating to the brig *Lady Nelson*, a colonial vessel, but commanded by L*ieutenant* James Grant commander of the *Supply* hulk there I obtained through the kindness of Mr Dalrymple the Hydrographer, every certain information relating to new Holland, which I brought down with me; and copies of every chart lodged in the Admiralty Office were prepared for me and afterwards sent down; that is, such as related to the objects of our intended research[.]'

[2] TNA, ADM 8/81, Admiralty List Book: the *Camilla*, Robert Larkan commander, 155 men, was at Sheerness fitting for foreign service.

[3] Refers to taking on and relinquishing the 'row guard' during the night in a dockyard.

[4] An official responsible for a dockyard's financial and administrative affairs. He reported to the dockyard's commissioner, who was nominally a member of the Navy Board.

[5] TNA, ADM 8/81, Admiralty List Book: the *Ruby*, Admiral Lutwidge and John Bazeley commanders, 491 men, was at the Downs. The sloop *Ranger*, John Little commander, 121 men, was commissioned into A squadron under the command of Sir H. Parker on 21 November 1794.

Sunday 12 April

Fresh breezes and cloudy. Employed about the sails &c. AM. Squally with snow.

Monday 13 April

Fresh breezes and squally. Employed staying the masts and setting up rigging. Took the guard per signal.[1]

Tuesday 14 April

Squally weather. A boat belonging to the *Mary*, hired cutter,[2] picked up 2 of the crew of a boat which had been upset in the mouth of the harbour and brought them to us; found they belonged to the *Griper* gunbrig.[3] AM. More moderate. Sent the 2 men on board their ship and returned the guard. Employed working up junk, and fixing the splinter netting[4] afresh.

Wednesday 15 April

Fresh breezes and cloudy weather. AM. Up top-gallant masts. Received carpenters stocks and 306 lbs of fresh beef; short of weight 6 lbs. Loosed sails.

Thursday 16 April

Furled sails. Employed working up junk.[5]

Friday 17 April[6]

Fresh breezes and cloudy. AM. Fine weather. Dried small sails, and mended the rounding of the cables.

Saturday 18 April

Received 251 lbs of fresh beef: short of weight 6 lbs. Cleared hawse. AM. Fine weather. Sent the top-gallant masts down and unrove the rigging. Punished William Brown, seaman with 12 lashes for neglect of duty; and Olloff Wastream with 8 lashes for leaving the boat on duty. Sent a boat on duty to His Majesty's ship *Ruby* below the great Nore.[7]

Sunday 19 April

Returned the top-gallant mast rigging to the yard, and received new. Employed fitting it. Cleared hawse. Mustered per clerk of the checque [*sic*]. AM. Up top-gallant masts and set up the rigging. Answered the signal for all lieutenants.

---

[1] Refers to taking on the 'row guard' during the night in a dockyard.

[2] A vessel of 105 tons by builder's measurement, armed with twelve-pounders and carronades. Winfield, *British Warships in the Age of Sail*, p. 390.

[3] TNA, ADM 8/81, Admiralty List Book: the *Griper*, William Graham commander, 50 men, was a troop ship.

[4] Rigged to protect the ship from falling masts and yards.

[5] Rough journal, I, f. 25, adds: 'Applied from London to have my leave of absence extending until such time as the instruments &c &c should be ready and every necessary arrangement made; it being considerd that my presence may be more useful in London than at Sheerness. In answer, the Admiralty extended my leave one week, or until the 26th.'

[6] Flinders was on a short leave from the Admiralty. On this day he married Ann Chappelle at St Nicholas Church, Partney, Lincolnshire.

[7] An anchorage off Sheerness (51°28′N and 0°48′E).

Monday 20 April

Light airs. Employed staying the top and top-gallant masts and setting up the rigging. Shipwrights from the yard employed on board.

Tuesday 21 April

Employed occasionally. Received 3 tons of beer, and 4 of water, and 242 lbs of fresh beef. Employed cleaning the lighter.

Wednesday 22 April

Fresh breezes and cloudy. Opened beef No. 62. Contents 42 pieces. Washed below. Employed as necessary.

Thursday 23 April

Employed making points and rope bands. AM. Loosed sails to dry.

Friday 24 April

Furled sails; otherwise employed as before. Received 238 lbs of fresh beef. Answered signal for weekly accounts.

[f. 6] Saturday 25 April

Mustered the ships company per clerk of the checque. Washed below. Loosed sails, and took the guard per signal.[1]

Sunday 26 April

Furled sails. Employed as necessary. AM. Cleared hawse. Mustered the ships company and read the articles of war.

Monday 27 April

Arrived and anchored His Majestys ship *Isis*.[2] AM. Washed below and cleared hawse. Took the guard per signal. Employed working up junk.

Tuesday 28 April

Fresh breezes and fine weather. Rowed guard. Loosed sails to dry. Received 275 lbs of fresh beef.

Wednesday 29 April

Employed about the rigging, making fenders for the boats and in other occasional jobs: took the guard per signal.

---

[1] Rough journal, I, f. 27, adds: 'Represented to the admiralty that the guns now on board were more than sufficient to combat Indians, and that they prevented us from carrying the quantity of present use water that was requisite; and understanding that a passport was to be obtained and was now daily expected, I begged leave to request "that their Lordships will be pleased to order, that ten of the twelve long six-pounders now on board may be taken out; and that in lieu, the ship may be supplied with six twelve-pound carronades and two more swivels; which guns, in addition to two eighteen-pound carronades now on board, I consider to be sufficient to repel the attack of any Indians with whom we are likely to meet." I also requested to be supplied with a pocket time piece.'

[2] TNA, ADM 8/81, Admiralty List Book, the *Isis*, James Walker commander, 343 men, was at the Downs.

Thursday 30 April

Fine weather. Employed principally working up junk. Returned the guard.

Friday 1 May

Employed as before and occasionally. Took the guard per signal. Received 300 lbs of fresh beef, 3 lbs short.[1]

Saturday 2 May

Moderate with showers of rain. AM. Fine weather. People washing their cloaths. Returned the guard.

Sunday 3 May

Employed variously. AM. Up top-gallant yards &c as usual every fine morning. Took the guard per signal. Punished Richard Hetherly with 12 lashes for quitting the boat and staying on shore without leave.

Monday 4 May

Light winds and fine weather. Employed working up junk, and in various duties. Returned the guard.

Tuesday 5 May

Cloudy. AM. Moderate and clear. Took the guard per signal. Cleared hawse. Received 326 lbs of fresh beef, 6 lbs short of weight. Loosed sails to dry.[2]

Wednesday 6 May

Moderate and cloudy. Furled sails. Employed making mats. Anchored here: His Majestys gun brig *Manly*.[3] AM. Returned the guard. Employed working up junk.

Thursday 7 May

Served half allowance of spirits, having no beer on board, though demanded 8 days. AM. Took guard per signal. Employed about the rigging and other necessary jobs.

---

[1] Rough journal, I, f. 27, adds: 'Wrote to the Victualling Board requesting to know the proportion of wheat which ought to be issued in lieu of bread; whether one pound and a half of wheat for one pound of bread would be proper; or if not, begged to receive their instructions upon the subject. Answer. One pound and a quarter to be issued for a pound of bread[.]'

[2] Rough journal, I, f. 29, adds: 'Wrote to J. Mathews Esq*uire*, Agent Victualler at Chatham, stating the shortness of weight in the fresh beef which had been as follows March 20 lbs, April 39 [lbs] May 5th 9 lb; and requested that caution might be given to the boatmen, that the weight of beef might hereafter agree. Answer, that the master of the brig would take oath, that none had ever been cut off in his vessel; that the quarters were weighed in presence of 3 clerks, and not until the beef was cold. (Note, the letter had some effect, for the next beef was 5 lb greater than charged).' Another note adds: 'May 5. Wrote to the Admiralty requesting them to order the *Investigator* to be paid in six months wages; the resident Commissioner (Coffin) having objected to paying her until sailing orders were arrived. This was complied with.' The reference is to Isaac Coffin, the resident Commissioner of the Navy Board and later a vice-admiral. Laughton, rev. Gwyn, 'Coffin, Sir Isaac', pp. 397–9.

[3] TNA, ADM 8/81, Admiralty List Book: the *Manly*, John Clements commander, 50 men, was a troop ship.

Friday 8 May

Fresh breezes and fine weather. Received 3 tons of beer and 5 of water. AM. Answered the signal for weekly accounts and returned the guard.[1]

Saturday 9 May

Moderate breezes. Received 277 lbs of fresh beef, 5 lbs excess of weight. AM. Watched below. Punished Thomas White with 18 lashes for staying several days on shore beyond his leave. Employed working up junk. Took the guard per signal.[2]

Sunday 10 May

Fresh breezes and cloudy. Punished Thomas Brown with 24 lashes and Thomas Reynolds with 18 lashes for exceeding their leave 6 days and running from their Officer. AM. Mustered the ships company and read the articles of war.[3]

[f. 7] Monday 11 May

Moderate and clear weather. AM. Loosed small sails to dry. Took the guard per signal. Received 304 lbs of fresh beef. Employed as necessary.[4]

Tuesday 12 May

Moderate and cloudy. Sent 15 men to His Majestys brig *Advice*, per order of Vice Admiral Graeme. Cleared hawse. AM. Fresh breezes and clear. Returned the guard. Received beer and water per lighter.

Wednesday 13 May

Working up junk. AM. Commissioner Coffin came on board, and paid the ship up to 30 June last. Took the guard per signal.

Thursday 14 May

Fresh breezes and cloudy. Sailed into the harbour His Majestys ship *Arrow*,[6] and came out the *Bittern*[7] and anchor'd here. AM. Light airs and cloudy. Unmoored ship, hove short on the small bower, and received a pilot on board. At 9 weighed and made sail for the

---

[1] Rough journal, I, f. 29, adds: 'Wrote to the Navy Board requesting them to stop the Allotment of William Kemble Marine, he being discharged as being a deserter from the Inniskilling or 6th dragoon regiment.'

[2] Rough journal, I, f. 31, adds: 'May 9th. Received a letter from the Navy Board, charging me with various Mathematical &c instruments as in the letter is expressed; all of which had been received the preceding day[.]'

[3] Rough journal, I, f. 31, adds: 'Wrote to the Navy Board, representing, that from the greatest part of H.M. ships being at sea I was not able to find a fit person, a volunteer, to fill the office of master; and requested them "to select an officer whose character at the Board is such as to be presumptive proof, that his abilities and conduct will enable him to be a useful assistant to me in carrying on the service in which we are about to engage." I represented that perfection in Astronomy was not absolutely requisite so much as sobriety, activity, a desire to be useful, and good knowledge and experience in common seamanship and navigation[.]'

[4] Rough journal, I, f. 31, adds: 'Wrote to the Navy Board for documents for 6 men, claiming pay for different ships, and for permission to antidate the entry of Mr S. W. Flinders [his brother]. Complied with in answer[.]'

[6] TNA, ADM 8/81, Admiralty List Book: the *Arrow*, William Bolton commander, 140 men, was at the Downs.

[7] TNA, ADM 8/81, Admiralty List Book: the sloop *Bittern,* 121 men, Edward Kittoe commander, was commissioned into a squadron under the command of Admiral Sir Hyde Parker on 8 October 1794.

great Nore; but the wind being too light for the flood tide[1] to be stemmed, and becoming more scant, dropped the best bower in 15 fathoms. The garrison point bearing SW. Veered to a third of a cable on the weather becoming squally.[2]

Friday 15 May
Fresh breezes and squally with heavy showers of hail and rain. At ½ past noon weighed and made sail. Tacked ship occasionally. At 3 came to with the small bower in 5 fathoms, and moored ship. Furled sails, and returned the 15 men to the *Advice* who had come on board to receive their pay. Lying here His Majestys ship *Zealand*, Vice Admiral Graeme, and several small ships. The extremes of Sheppy Island[3] SEbS and the Garrison Point at Sheerness West. Waited on the commanding officer to report the ship. AM. squally with rain at times. Answered the signal for weekly accounts. Employed as necessary.

Saturday 16 May
Strong breezes. Struck top-gallant masts. AM. Fresh breezes and fine weather. Hoisted out the launch and made other preparations for getting out the guns, according to my letter of the 28 of April. Received 323 lbs of fresh beef.[4]

Sunday 17 May
Fresh breezes and cloudy. Anchored here from the harbour His Majestys ship *Hydra*. Employed in occasional duties. AM. Took the guard per signal.[5]

Monday 18 May
Cloudy with hard rain. AM. Returned the guard. Sailed His Majestys ship *Blenheim* for Yarmouth.[6] Received 121 lbs of fresh beef. Employed as necessary.

Tuesday 19 May
Calm with rain. Sailed His Majestys ship *Hydra*. Punished Thomas Smith with 18 lashes for leaving his boat, being coxswain,[7] and attempting to desert. AM. Fine. Loosed sails to dry. Shipwrights on board from the yard to fit ports for the Carronades.

[f. 8] **Wednesday 20 May**
Fine weather. Furled sails. Otherwise employed as necessary. AM. Employed getting out ten of the twelve long six pounders, with their accompanying stores; and receiving in lieu six twelve-pound carronades, and two more swivels with their shot and other stores.[8]

---

[1] i.e. the incoming or rising tide.

[2] Rough journal, I, f. 31, adds: 'Received orders from Vice Admiral Graeme to proceed with the sloop under my command to the Nore so soon as paid; and to give the ships company no opportunity of desertion. Received a large chest of Stationary from the Navy Office, and three French voyages of Discovery.'

[3] The Isle of Sheppey (51°24′N, 00°50′E), situated off the north coast of Kent, in the Thames estuary, some 46 miles east of London.

[4] Rough journal, I, f. 33, adds: 'Applied to the Navy Board for permission to pay five men bounty, who claim it; and also four others who come to us as prest from the *Zealand*. In answer, they only permit one.'

[5] Rough journal, I, f. 33, adds: 'Applied to the victualling for provisions to complete our stock; having received intelligence from Sir Joseph Banks that we might expect to sail shortly, which were sent on 22nd.'

[6] TNA, ADM 8/81, Admiralty List Book: the *Blenheim*, P. T. Bower commander, 590 men, was at Chatham fitting for Channel service.

[7] i.e. in charge of the boat's navigation and steering.

[8] This was done because carronades were lighter than six-pounders and could be placed on the upper deck, creating more space below to carry extra supplies of fresh water. Flinders, *A Voyage to Terra Australis,* I, p. 5.

<u>Our arms are now as follows</u>

Carronades eighteen pounders			stern chases[1]	Two	No.	
Ditto	twelve	„	on both sides	Six	„	
Long guns[2]	Six	„	to shift	Two	„	
Swivels[3]	half	„	to shift	Six		
Musquetoons[4]			to shift	Two		
Muskets,[5] black, independent of Marines				Forty		
Pistols			Fifteen	Pair		
Cutlasses				Thirty	No.	
Tomahawks				Twenty		
Half pikes[6]				Thirty		

Besides several pairs of pistols, double and single barrelled guns with and without bayonets, belonging to individuals. Seven shipwrights from the yard victualled on board.

Thursday 21 May

Light winds and cloudy. Employed stowing away gunners stores. AM. Employed in jobs about the rigging and occasionally Answered the signal 219.[7]

Friday 22 May

Received per lighter from Deptford 13 tons of water, 1 ton of flour, and 300 lbs of cheese; also beer for personal use. Employed stowing provisions in the places formerly occupied by the guns. AM. Received per lighter from the Navy Office[8] various extra articles for our own use and for presents to the inhabitants of New Holland and the South-Sea Islands.[9] Answered the signal for weekly accounts.[10]

[1] Cannons mounted in the stern of the ship.

[2] A longer cannon than the carronade.

[3] Shackles used to set up anchors.

[4] Shorter-barrelled version of the musket, particularly used by navies.

[5] Smooth-bore weapons firing round balls.

[6] A short pike used to board ships; a spontoon.

[7] Flinders is answering a flag signal that refers him to a numerical code. The instructions conveyed by the code were listed in Edles, *Signal Book for Ships of War*. Rough journal, I, f. 35, adds: 'May 21. Applied to the Admiralty to have the officers and crew paid up to the end of the month previous to sailing, and also for two months advance; to be paid at the last port we might be at.'

[8] Situated in the heart of the City of London, this carried out 'civil service' functions such as handling and recording bills of exchange, signing tickets for payment for invalids, dealing with the Pay Office, attending the Navy Board, and so forth. Rodger, *The Command of the Ocean*, pp. 296–7.

[9] In *A Voyage to Terra Australis*, I, pp. 5–6, Flinders noted that the 'extra articles' comprised a set of astronomical and surveying instruments for use by him and his officers; most of the published books and charts on the maritime exploration of 'the South Seas', presented by Sir Joseph Banks; and hydrographical writings by Alexander Dalrymple. 'New Holland' was frequently applied as a name to the whole of Australia after the Dutch explorer Abel Tasman referred to that continent as Nova Hollandia (after Holland) in 1644; but after the British settlement of New South Wales in 1788, it was often used to refer to parts of Australia (including the western half) that were not under British sovereignty. Its usage here suggests, however, that Flinders considered New Holland to be the entire Australian continent. 'South-Sea Islands' refers to the South Pacific Ocean.

[10] Rough journal, I, f. 35, adds: 'Applied to Vice Admiral Graeme for two marines to complete our establishment. Received letter from Secretary of East India Directors informing me of their intention to give the gentlemen of the *Investigator* and myself £1200 for table-money: half of which I am at liberty to draw for immediately and the rest at the end of the voyage.'

Saturday 23 May

Light winds and fine weather. AM. Took the guard per signal. Employed securing the water casks in the places formerly occupied by the guns. Came out of harbour, a line of battle ship a frigate and corvette belonging to the Prince of Orange.[1]

Sunday 24 May

Moderate and clear. Answered the signal for a lieutenant. Received some boatswain[2] and carpenters stores to complete. Employed preparing for sea. AM. Returned the guard. Employed as before.[3]

Monday 25 May

Received back from the *Advice* brig 12 of the men out of the 15 lent her; the remaining three having found means to desert. Sailed to the southward the Dutch men of war[4] and the brig *Driver*.[5] James Grice, one of the carpenters, unfortunately fell overboard; and notwithstanding that great exertions were made to save him, was drowned. AM. Fresh breezes and cloudy. Employed as before preparing for sea.

Tuesday 26 May

Fresh breezes and fine weather. Robert Chapman, marine absented himself without leave from the boat. At 3 brought the pilot (Mr Gibbs of Queenborough[6]) on board. Hoisted up the boats and at 5, when the ship swung to the flood, unmoored, and hove in to half a cable. AM. At half past 12 light breezes. Weighed and made sail, lying to for considerable intervals drifting with the tide till daylight, as also to clear our buoy. The flood making at 6, came to with the best bower in 4 fathoms, the buoy of the Oaze[7] bearing NWbW. 2 cables length. The Knob[8] SSb½E. The Dutch ships at anchor about 1 mile SbE of us. Light air with rain at times. Shorten[e]d in the cable.[9]

[1] i.e. the stadtholder of the Netherlands. From the mid-16th century Dutch rulers held this position in connection with Orange, a small principality in southern France. Rough journal, I, f. 37, adds: 'May 23. Received orders from my lords Commissioners to proceed to Spithead without loss of time. Dated 22nd. Which I immediately acknowledged the receipt of.'

[2] i.e. supervisor of the unlicensed members of the ship's deck.

[3] Rough journal, I, f. 37, adds: 'Received the private signals from Vice Admiral Graeme, consisting of the Private Signals by day and night, the Signals to be made to Signal Posts, the Signals denoting the signal posts along the coast, the Day and Night signals established between cruizers and those posts, and the signals to be made at those posts together with their signification, being six papers: the receipt of which I immediately acknowledged[.]'

[4] The Dutch Republic was part of the First Coalition that opposed revolutionary France in 1792. It was overrun in 1795 by French forces and the Batavian Republic – a client of the French Republic – was established. An Anglo-Russian force invaded North Holland in August 1799 and forced the French-controlled Dutch fleet to surrender. A number of the Dutch ships were later purchased by the British from the Dutch stadtholder, and this may explain the reference here to Dutch men of war in British waters. TNA, ADM 8/81, covering the stations of naval vessels under British control in the first half of 1801, identifies a number of Dutch vessels under British naval command. James, *The Naval History of Great Britain*, II, p. 310.

[5] TNA, ADM 8/81, Admiralty List Book: the *Driver*, 80 men, James Dunbar commander, was part of A squadron under the command of Sir Hyde Parker.

[6] A small town (51°25′N, 0°44′E) on the Isle of Sheppey, two miles south of Sheerness.

[7] The Oaze Channel is situated between the Nore and the North Foreland.

[8] The Knob Channel lies in the Thames estuary.

[9] Rough journal, I, f. 39, adds: 'Mr Gibbs of Queenborough[.] Received P.M. 285 lbs of fresh beef[.]'

[f. 9] **Wednesday 27 May**

Light airs with rain at intervals. At 3 weighed and made sail, at 4 came to in 12 fathoms with the best bower. At 6 light breezes. Weighed and made sail over the flats[1] for the Queens Channel.[2] At half past 8 came to with the best bower. The pans[3] and beacon NNW about 2 miles. AM. Light breezes. At 3 weighed and made sail for the Downs.[4] At 8 fresh breezes. At half past 8 came to with the best bower in 8 fathoms and veered to half a cable. Upper Deal church WbS and Walmer Castle SW. Went on shore to wait on Admiral Lutwidge.[5] At noon. Fresh breezes and cloudy weather.

Thursday 28 May[6]

Down Channel. Fresh breezes and cloudy. Returned the old cutter and received a new one from George Lawrence Esq*uire* the naval storekeeper in lieu. Having this intention the boat had not been exchanged at Sheerness. At 3 the ebb tide[7] began to make, when we weighed and made sail to work out of the Downs and down channel. Tacked occasionally between the Goodwin[8] and South Foreland,[9] and lay to some time for a boat with refreshments. At 8 the South EbN½N (by compass) and the Town of Folkstone [Folkestone] NW about 3 miles. Tacked ship off shore.

Tacked, stretching along the coast to stem the tide. Variable breezes and cloudy with squalls. Spoke the cutter *Earl Spencer*.[10] In top-gallant sails and 1 reef of the mizzen topsail.[11] At 1, tacked ship and also at 4. At 6 tacked and set staysails[12] and top gallant sails. At 8 fresh breezes and cloudy weather. Down staysails and tacked ship. In top gallant sails and 2nd reef of the foretopsail.[13] At 10 tacked off the town of Hythe. At noon moderate breezes with fine weather. Set the main top gallant sails. The South Foreland bore NE½E and Folkstone North 7 or 8 miles. Tacked ship in shore. Several vessels in sight.

[f. 10] **Friday 29 May**

SWbW. Squally. Double reefed the main topsail.[14] At 2 and ½ past 3, tacked ship. At 4 made sail the wind being more moderate. South Foreland EbN. At 6 the ship touched the

[1] i.e. the Kentish flats, just offshore from Whitstable, Kent.

[2] Provides access to the Thames Estuary for vessels approaching from the east or south-east. It lies on the north side of Margate Sand and terminates at the east edge of the Flats. Moore, *The Coaster's Companion*, p. 9.

[3] A reference to Pan Sands, situated between the Nore and the North Foreland. Ibid., p. 11.

[4] The Downs (51°13′N, 1°27′E) is a roadstead between the North and South Foreland, off the east Kent coast. It was a permanent base for sailing warships patrolling the North Sea. Lying between the Straits of Dover and the Thames Estuary, the Downs was also a place where merchant sailing ships could wait for an easterly wind to take them up to London or into the English Channel.

[5] At this time Skeffington Lutwidge (*c.*1735–1814) was Admiral of the Blue and commander in chief in the Downs. Admirals took rank according to the colour of their squadron. They were ranked in the order red (as senior), white and blue. *London Gazette*, no. 15324 (30 December 1800), pp. 2–3.

[6] Once they were at sea, Flinders used planetary symbols for the days of the week, but for the sake of clarity they have been converted to words, except in tables. See Abbreviations, p. xx.

[7] i.e. lowering the water level.

[8] Goodwin Sands (51°14′N, 1°35′E).

[9] Near Dover.

[10] This vessel was of 163 tons according to the builder's measurement. It was armed with six-pounders, twelve-pounders and carronades. Winfield, *British Warships in the Age of Sail*, p. 390.

[11] A fore-and-aft sail on the mizzen mast.

[12] Fore-and-aft (usually triangular) rigged sails.

[13] Topsails set on the foremast.

[14] A square sail rigged above the course sail and below the topgallant sail.

ground, hove all aback. The leadsman[1] having found no bottom with 15 fathoms at ¼ before six, had left the chains without being relieved, and the supposed distance of the land by the Officer of the watch being six miles, the lead had not been attended to minutely at the time.[2]

Low[e]red down the boats, sent one of them to sound round the ship, and put a kedge and hawser into the other.[3] There was 2½ and 2¾ fathoms to the eastward of us, whilst we had but 13 feet along side; we therefore got her head that way, the ship being afloat forward, and by fitting everything, she drew over, and the water gradually deepened to 5 and 7 fathoms steering upon an east course, and from that to SEbE. The bearings taken on the bank or immediately after the ship was clear, were as follows. Dungeness lighthouse SW. Lidd church WbS.½S. Town of Hythe NWbN. Folkstone ENE. Extreme of the cliffy head[4] near Dover E½N. The least possible distance from the nearest shore a little north of Hythe was, in the commanders estimation, 2½ miles; but it was guessed to be nearer 4 miles. Fortunately the water remained smooth, the ship had little motion, and did not appear to have received any injury; as she made no more water than she did before the circumstance happened. It should seem that it was low water about the time that the ship was upon the bank and at the height of the spring tides. Note. I afterwards found this bank laid down in the other charts and called the Roar.[5] Our erroneous chart is that of John Hamilton Moore.[6]

At 8 stood offshore having passed over the shoal. At ½ past 9 tacked in shore to get out of the flood tide. At ½ past 11 tacked to the Northward and double-reefed the fore and main topsails. South Foreland SEbE. Dungeness[7] WSW.

At 2 tacked, seeing the foreland light bearing NWbW½W. Close reefed the fore and mizen topsails.

At 4, strong breezes with thick weather and rain. Put the helm[8] up and ran for the Downs. Struck top gallant masts.

---

[1] The person taking the lead line in making soundings.

[2] Robert Fowler was the leadsman who was not relieved after his duty. No one was in place to call soundings. The pilot had been left at the Downs. There was no master on the vessel. Nobody on board the *Investigator* had an acquaintance with the navigation of the English Channel. At the time Flinders was below deck in his cabin with his wife. Arguably, he should have been on deck to watch the pilotage. This incident was reported to the Admiralty. An enquiry established that the Hydrographic Office held no survey of the coast between the South Foreland and the Oaze. Banks was 'mortified' to hear about the grounding and had to defend Flinders's seamanship to the Admiralty. Estensen, *The Life of Matthew Flinders*, pp. 160–61; Flinders, *A Voyage to Terra Australis*, I, p. 127; TNA, ADM 1/3522, Admiralty Letters from the Hydrographer of the Navy, Alexander Dalrymple to Evan Nepean, 8 June 1801; Banks to Flinders, 5 June 1801, in Bladen, *HRNSW*, IV, pp. 383–4.

[3] This paragraph is included after the next one in the manuscript, but Flinders indicated that it should be placed here.

[4] i.e. the White Cliffs of Dover.

[5] The Roar was a sand ridge that lay nearly parallel to the shoreline. It appeared on two charts of 1797 but Flinders had not been given these. Estensen, *The Life of Matthew Flinders*, p. 161.

[6] John Hamilton Moore (1738–1807) was a teacher of, and author on, navigation and hydrographer to the Duke of Clarence. His charts were widely used by the Admiralty in the late 18th century. Flinders probably used Moore's *Chart of the British Channel*. See also Moore's *The New Practical Navigator*, and Cotter, 'John Hamilton Moore and Nathaniel Bowditch', pp. 323–6.

[7] A headland in south-east Kent (50°55′N, 0°58′E).

[8] i.e. the steering gear of a ship.

At 7, came to the South Foreland SW½W. Veered to half a cable; and when the lee tide made, to a whole one.

Answered the signal for weekly accounts. Found riding here the *Overyssel*,[1] Admiral Lutwidge, the 3 Dutch men of war, and several English.

[f. 11] Saturday 30 May

Fresh breezes and cloudy with rain. At 1, the Admiral and other of His Majestys ships as also the Dutch ships fixed a royal salute on the anniversary of the Restoration.[2] At 2 moored a cable each way. Wrote to Admiral Lutwidge informing him of the desertion of the carpenter of the *Trent*[3] who had been sent on board at the Nore for a passage. At 12 moderate breezes and cloudy. AM. At 4 fresh breezes and cloudy weather. Unmoored ship. Swayed up top-gallant masts and yards and hoisted up the boat. At 7 weighed and made sail. At 8, abreast of the South Forland, and 1 mile distant. Set studding sails and royals and shifted them occasionally. The Dutch men of war weighed a little before us, but we came up with them when carrying all sail; although the *Xenophon* was the worst sailing ship that could be met with, before coppered.[4] Noon light breezes and hazy weather. The lighthouse on Dungeness bore NbW. about 2 leagues. The Dutch ships in company and several small vessels in sight.

Sunday 31 May

Light breezes and cloudy. Bent the spanker[5] and mizzen top gallant sail. Beachy Head[6] WNW about 4 Leagues. Exercised great guns and fired. At 8, Beachy Head NNW about 3 leagues. Sounded in 16½ fathoms stones and broken shells. Stowed staysails. Light airs inclinable to calms. The effects of James Grice De*ceas*ed sold at the mast this PM.[7] Took in studding sails on the wind shifting. At ½ past 3 Beachy Head. NNW about 3 leagues. Hazy with rain. Sounded in 20 fathoms stones. Passed a frigate on the other tack and shewed our colours. Moderate and cloudy with rain. At ¼ past 9 sounded in 25 fathoms speckled sand and stones, and tacked ship. Set staysails. Made sail occasionally. Light breezes and hazy, with constant rain. No land in sight.

Monday 1 June

Light airs with constant rain. At ¼ past 3 sounded in 35 fathoms. Beachy Head NEbE 4 or 5 leagues. At 6 Beachy Head EbN½N about 6 leagues. At ½ past 1 tacked ship and sounded in 28 fathoms brown sand and stones. In royals and staysails. At 9 tacked ship.

---

[1] TNA, ADM 8/81, Admiralty List Book, the *Overyssel*, 491 men, a third-rate ship, was at the Downs under the command of Admiral Lutwidge. The vessel was commissioned on 9 July 1796.

[2] Charles II had entered London on 29 May 1660 to restore the Stuart monarchy after nine years' exile on the Continent.

[3] HMS *Trent* was built at Woolwich dockyard and commissioned in March 1796. It was a fifth-rate vessel of 925 tons. Winfield, *British Warships in the Age of Sail*, p. 148.

[4] The *Xenophon* was 'old and unsound' and had been patched and caulked for this voyage of discovery. She was apparently the best ship that the Admiralty could spare at the time. Scott, *The Life of Matthew Flinders*, p. 125.

[5] A gaff-rigged fore-and-aft sail.

[6] A chalk headland near Eastbourne, Sussex (50°44′N, 0°14′E).

[7] When a sailor died on board, or was drowned, his effects were sold at the mast by auction, and the produce charged against the purchasers' names on the ship's books.

At 10 sounded in 32 fathoms. Moderate breezes and cloudy. Sounded in 35 fathoms; broken shells and stones. Thick weather with rain. It cleared a little. Saw the Isle of Wight to windward. At 8, Isle of Wight N½W to St. Catherine's point.[1] NNW¾W. At 9, in royals. At 11, sounded in 33 fathoms. At noon light airs and cloudy. Isle of Wight. South point NWbW. Land about Selsea.[2] N¼W. Tacked ship.

[f. 12] **Tuesday 2 June**

Moderate and fine weather. Made more sail. Fresh breezes. In royals and tacked ship. Sounded in 35 fathoms, stones. Exercised great guns and small arms and fired 2 rounds of powder. At 8, Culver Cliff[3] NW½W 2 or 3 miles. At ¼ past 9, anchored in St. Helens road[4] in 8½ fathoms with the best bower, and veered to ⅓ of a cable. Found here His Majestys ships *Hannibal*[5] and *Hydra*.

Cabin with rain. AM. At 5, weighed and made sail with a light haze, but at 6 anchored being calm. Buoy of the Warner[6] NNE 1 mile. At ½ past 6 answered signal 275 by shewing our number (750). At 8, weighed and made sail. At 10 came to at Spithead. Variable breezes with dull cloudy weather and rain. Veered to a whole cable but finding we were likely to overlay a ship, hove in again and waited for the tide on St. Helens. Went on shore to wait upon Mark Milbank Esq*uire*, Admiral of the White and commander in chief here,[7] to shew my orders and take a weekly account.

Wednesday 3 June

Rainy weather. Hove up the best bower and dropped in shore. Moored a cable each way. South sea Castle[8] E½N. Black-house point NEbE. AM. Fine weather and rainy showers alternately. Loosed sails. Employed making wads and then necessary duties.[9]

Thursday 4 June

Cloudy with rain at times. Furled sails. Employed as in the morning. Answered signal for all lieutenants. AM. Employed making wads and plats, working up junk.[10]

---

[1] The southernmost point on the Isle of Wight (50°34′N, 1°17′W).

[2] Selsey (50°44′N, 0°47′W), Sussex.

[3] On the east end of the Isle of Wight (50°40′N, 1°06′W).

[4] An advanced anchorage to Spithead, located on the eastern side of the Isle of Wight. It guarded the approaches to Portsmouth harbour and the naval dockyard there.

[5] TNA, ADM 8/81, Admiralty List Book: the *Hannibal*, Solo Ferris commander, 590 men, was at Portsmouth fitting out for Channel service.

[6] A sea channel entrance to Portsmouth. Moore, *The New Practical Navigator*, p. 303.

[7] Mark Milbanke (1724–1805), a naval officer who was Governor of Newfoundland (1789–92) and later commander-in-chief at Portsmouth between 1799 and 1803. The Admiral of the White was effectively the second-in-command of the whole fleet. Laughton, rev. Morriss, 'Milbanke, Mark', p. 103; Thompson, 'Milbanke, Mark', pp. 595–6.

[8] A fort at the southern end of Portsea Island that protected the town and harbour of Portsmouth (50°47′N, 1°05′W).

[9] Rough journal, I, f. 47, adds: 'Received an order from the Navy Board to send up Pay Books &c up to May 31; and an answer relative to my application of May 12, for a master, hoping that I should find one here and that they would give a warrant immediately and put him on the list from the date of it, after passing. Wrote in favour of Mr John Thistle of the *Buffalo*[.]'

[10] Rough journal, I, f. 47, adds: 'Received an order to send up a list and descriptions of three men who had deserted from the Advice, as also the attendant circumstances; which I complied with on the 5th.'

Friday 5 June

At 1 fired a salute of 19 guns, in honour of His Majesty's birthday.[1] Answered the signal for a midshipman. AM. Employed making wads and plats for the cables. Answered the signal for weekly accounts.[2]

Saturday 6 June

Employed on jobs about the rigging, and as before. AM. Carpenters repairing the cutter. Opened a cask of beef, contents 42 pieces: right. Received 278 lbs of fresh beef.

Sunday 7 June

Answered the signal for all lieutenants. Employed making mats &c. AM. Received 3 tons of beer, and 5 of water per lighter. Returned empty casks.

Monday 8 June

Employed stowing water &c. AM. Working up junk into wads, plats and mats.[3]

Tuesday 9 June

Fine weather. Employed working up junk as before. Mustered per clerk of the checque. AM. Employed as before and occasionally.[4]

Wednesday 10 June

Moderate and fine weather. Answered the signal for a midshipman. Employed preparing to go into harbour. AM. Light airs and calms. At 4, unmoored and a pilot came on board. Made the signal for assistance with 2 guns. Set sail; sent our boat ahead to tow, and two launches from the *Royal William* and *Puissant*.[5] At ½ past 8 made fast alongside a lump at moorings in the harbour. At 9 returned all the powder into a lump, and afterwards warped[6] the ship over and into dock by the assistance of riggers.[7] Hoisted up two boats and kept one cutter without the dock gates. Got down top gallant masts and yards and lower yards. Employed clearing ship. Light airs with warm fine weather. Thermometer 72°.[8]

---

[1] George III was born on 5 June 1738.

[2] Rough journal, I, f. 47, adds: 'Sent up Pay and monthly books, as also some powers of Attorney and Tickets.'

[3] Rough journal, I, f. 47, adds: 'Applied to the Sick and Hurt Board for Instructions relative to seamen sent on shore in foreign parts'.

[4] Rough journal, I, f. 47, adds: 'Received orders to proceed into Portsmouth Harbour, to dock the ship and get her defects repaired with expedition and return to Spithead; the receipt of which I immediately acknowledged, inclosing the carpenters certificate. See Letter 58[.] Received orders from Admiral Milbank to send any men suspected of intending to desert on board the Royal William.'

[5] TNA, ADM 8/81, Admiralty List Book: the *Royal William*, Admiral Milbank and Francis Pickman commanders, 424 men, and the *Puissant*, William Syme commander, 153 men, were receiving ships at Portsmouth and Spithead.

[6] i.e. moved the ship into position by hauling on a rope fastened to a buoy or anchor.

[7] i.e. workers specializing in moving heavy objects in harbours and docks.

[8] Rough journal, I, f. 49, adds: 'The orders marked as received yesterday were received this PM. by the midshipman. Immediately went on shore to bespeak a pilot, and also a hoy to receive our powder; and settled with the dockyard officers to take the ship into dock by the same time that should bring us into the harbour. But found in the morning that no preparations were made. Whilst getting out the powder, I pressed them very anxiously to take her in this tide, and they complied.'

Thursday 11 June

Returned some boatswains stores, and received others in lieu. On examining the ships bottom as soon as the tide was out, it was found that she had received no injury, and the water was therefore let into the dock as the tide rose. AM. Up lower yards and top gallant masts. At 11, cast off: hauled out of dock, and having a pilot on board made sail out of harbour and at noon came to anchor with the best bower at Spithead[1] in 6 fathoms, and moored a cable each way, South Sea Castle bearing EbS and Block house NEbN.[2]

[f. 13] **Friday 12 June**

Employed cleaning ship. Received our powder back from the hoy. AM. Fresh breezes. Answered the signal for weekly accounts. Carpenters from the yard making a sky light and fitting hammock stantions[3] in the waste. People making small mats &c.

Saturday 13 June

Fresh breezes and cloudy. Received 268 lbs of fresh beef. Employed working up junk.

Sunday 14 June

Mended the rounding of the cables. AM. Mustered the ships company and read the articles of war.[4]

Monday 15 June

Fresh breezes and fine weather. Answered the signal for a midshipman. AM. Sailmakers fitting waste hammock cloths. Mustered for clerk of the checque. Entered Mr John Thistle Master.

Tuesday 16 June

Fresh breezes and cloudy weather. Employed making mats for various purposes. AM. Received 156 lbs of fresh beef. Carpenters &c employed in their respective duties.

Wednesday 17 June

Employed working up junk into mats &c, and upon other occasional duties.

Thursday 18 June

Answered the signal for a lieutenant, and received a draft of 7 men from His Majesty's ship *Royal William*. Cleared hawse. AM. Commissioner Sir Charles Saxton[5] came on

---

[1] An area of the Solent protected from all winds except those from the south-east. Named after the Spit, a sandbank stretching south from the Hampshire shore for three miles.

[2] Rough journal, I, f. 49, adds: 'Received an order from the admiralty reinforcing their former order to go into dock. Reported the ship having been into dock, and was now at Spithead waiting their Lordships further orders. Wrote to the Navy Board to request two months advance might be given to ships company, as well as paying them up to May 31. This was complied with, and the officers were allowed to draw for three in advance.'

[3] i.e. stanchions (upright bars or posts).

[4] Rough journal, I, f. 51, adds: 'Applied to the admiralty to have our complement filled up; and amongst the 7 wanted to have a sailmaker and 2 carpenters crew included; as also to receive their Lordships directions concerning the mode of bearing the men of science &c on *Investigator*s books. To this the answer was, that both would be complied with when my sailing orders were issued[.]'

[5] Resident Commissioner of the Navy at Portsmouth, then the principal naval dockyard, between 1789 and 1806. Laughton, rev. Morriss, 'Saxton, Sir Charles', p. 153.

board and paid the petty officers[1] and ships company up to May 31st; and 2 months advance to them and to the warrant officers.[2]

Friday 19 June

Fresh breezes with fine weather. Received 5 tons of water, and one of beer, to complete for sea. Received an order to attend the solicitor of the Admiralty in London. AM. Punished James Leech and Thomas White with 8 and 18 lashes for drunkenness and neglect of duty. Answered the signal for weekly accounts. Employed working up junk.[3]

Saturday 20 June

Moderate and fine weather. Received 239 lbs of fresh beef. Set up the standing rigging. Employed otherwise on junk.

Sunday 21 June

Answered the signal for all lieutenants. AM. Scrubbed hammocks and mustered the ships company.

Monday 22 June

Fresh breezes and cloudy. AM. Employed working up junk and in various occupations.

Tuesday 23 June

Employed as before. Received 201 lbs of fresh beef. Moderate breezes and hazy.

Wednesday 24 June

Fine weather. Employed as necessary. Mustered clerk of the checque.

Thursday 25 June

Light winds and fine weather. Received 170 lbs of fresh beef. Employed in occasional duties.

Friday 26 June

Moderate and cloudy. Received 6 tons of water and 2 of beer. Punished Thomas Smith seaman with 24 lashes for riotous behaviour and fighting. Returned empty casks to the lighter.

---

[1] i.e. inferior officers whose status lay between the commissioned and warrant officers, on the one hand, and the ordinary seamen, on the other.

[2] Warrant officers were a disparate group of literate professionals in the Navy. They had specialist functions such as master, chaplain, purser and surgeon. For the authorities who examined, warranted and were responsible for warrant officers, see Rodger, *Naval Records for Genealogists*, p. 6. Rough journal, I, f. 51, adds: 'Received 164 lbs of fresh beef[.]'

[3] Rough journal, I, f. 53, adds: 'Received an order through the Commander in chief here to go up to town on admiralty leave; went on shore in the evening accordingly, and in the morning set off in a post chaise for London. On the Wednesday following, I answered to certain Interrogatories relative to a prosecution against a commander of a ship called the *Andersons*, who had deserted the convoy of His *Majestys Ship Reliance* in September last, of which ship I was then second lieutenant. On Thursday, my business with the Solicitor was concluded. During the above time, I had frequently attended at the Admiralty Office to attempt the forwarding of the issuing of our sailing orders, but to little effect, the multiplicity of business in general preventing my voice from being heard[.]'

Saturday 27 June

Light airs and hazy. Received 385 lbs of fresh beef. Cleared hawse.[1] Punished 3 men with 12 lashes each for attempting to desert. Mustered the ships company and read the articles of war.

Sunday 28 June

Calms. AM. Fresh breezes. Entered William Carter and employed in various duties.[2]

Monday 29 June

Light breezes with fine weather. Employed in the main hold. Mustered for clerk of the checque.

Tuesday 30 June

Moderate with rain at times. People employed in the after hold and coal hole. AM. Received 280 lbs of fresh beef. Cleared hawse.

[f. 14] Wednesday 1 July

Constant showers of rain. AM. Received 3 tons of beer and one of water. Returned empty casks. Employed as necessary.

Thursday 2 July

Light airs with showers of rain. Employed working up junk and in occasional jobs.

Friday 3 July

Light breezes and cloudy. AM. Loosed sails to dry. Answered signal for all lieutenants. Strong breezes with showers. Furled sails.

Saturday 4 July

Fresh breezes and fine weather. Loosed sails to dry. Answered signal for a lieutenant. Furled sails. Received 322 lbs of fresh beef.

Sunday 5 July

Sent a boat with a mate and 12 men to assist His Majestys ship *Malta*[3] by order of the

---

[1] Part of a vessel's bow in which the hawseholes are cut.

[2] Rough journal, I, f. 55, adds: 'Wrote the letter N°. 64 to the admiralty, requesting instructions relative to the conduct which I am to observe towards French ships, in consequence of the passport; as also towards the ships of other nations with whom the United Kingdoms are at war. Also, whether the taking such letters as the post master might put on board for the *Cape of Good* Hope, would be any infringement upon neutrality, if such was to be the conduct of the *Investigator*. The letter concludes with observing, "that since the end of March last, the advancement of the seasons makes every days delay in sailing of bad consequence to the success of the voyage for which the *Investigator* had been fitted." During the months that the ship has been waiting, both at the Nore and at this place for sailing orders, I constantly had the people exercised with the T*op Gallan*t yards whenever the weather would permit; and endeavoured to bring the ships company under good order and government, to which indeed the majority of them were well inclined; but some of the heedless occasionally fell under the lash, though not a man in the ship ever showed any signs of an ill disposition to a proper subjection to their officers, or to living sociably with each other. Some desertions prevent me from permitting any to go on shore upon leave, since the payment of the ship[.]'

[3] TNA, ADM 8/81, Admiralty List Book: the *Malta*, Albert Bertie commander, 738 men, was fitting and mooring for Channel service at Portsmouth and Spithead.

admiral. Employed occasionally. AM. Fresh breezes with variable weather. Received the mate and the men from the *Malta*. Fine weather.

Monday 6 July
Fresh breezes and cloudy weather. Answered the signal for all lieutenants. AM. Drizzling rain. Employed in occasional duties.

Tuesday 7 July
Moderate with cloudy weather. AM. Received 181 lbs of fresh beef. People employed principally working up junk.

Wednesday 8 July
Moderate and cloudy. AM. Fresh gales. Got the sheet anchor[1] over the side.

Thursday 9 July
Fresh gales with rain at times. AM. struck lower yards and top gallant masts. AM. Sent a mate and 12 men to assist His Majestys ship *Malta* out of harbour, per signal. Received 161 lbs of fresh beef. Served out spirits this day, having no beer on board. Discharged William Carter (ord*inary*) into His Majestys ship *Royal William*, being a deserter from the *Wolverene*.[2]

Friday 10 July
Strong breezes and cloudy. Our men returned from the *Malta*. AM. Up lower yards and top gallant masts. Sent the mate and men again to His Majestys ship *Malta*, being ordered by signal. Received 3 tons of beer and 3 tons of water, and returned empty casks. Mustered the ships company per clerk of the checque.

Saturday 11 July
Furled sails which had been loosed in the morning to dry. Received our men from the *Malta*, she having anchored at Spithead. AM. Received 364 lbs of fresh beef. People imployed working up junk. Drizzling rain.

Sunday 12 July
Fresh gales and squally with rain. AM. Mustered the ships company and saw them all clean.

Monday 13 July
Moderate and cloudy. Answered the signal for all lieutenants. AM. Loosed sails to dry. Received 16 bags of bread and 3 firkins[3] of butter to complete for sea. Employed stowing it away and occasionally.

---

[1] A large extra anchor for use in an emergency.
[2] TNA, ADM 8/81, Admiralty List Book: the *Wolvereen*, John Wright commander, 70 men, was fitted out for Channel service at Portsmouth and Spithead.
[3] Firkins were small wooden tubs or casks.

Tuesday 14 July

Rainy weather. Furled sails. Entered Nathaniel Wright (LM).[1] Answered the signal for all lieutenants. AM. Light breezes and fine weather. Received 302 lbs of fresh beef. Loosed sails to dry. Sent a boat manned and armed to attend the execution of one of the *Hermione*s mutineers[2] on board the *Puissant* sheer hulk, at Spithead.

Wednesday 15 July

Furled sails. AM. Moderate with rain. Sent a boat manned and armed to attend punishment, round the fleet. Employed as necessary.

Thursday 16 July

Fine weather. Discharged Francis Le Begle (AB)[3] into the *Puissant* by the admirals order being ruptured. AM. Loosed sails. Cleared hawse. Received 162 lbs of fresh beef.

Friday 17 July

Furled sails. Mended the rounding of the cables. Squally with Thunder and lightening,[4] accompanied with large hail and heavy rain. AM. Answ[e]red the signal for weekly accounts. Employed upon occasional duties. Received sailing orders &c &c as hereafter follow.[5]

[f. 15] Paper No. 1
Instructions for the *Investigators* voyage[6]
By the Commissioners for executing the office of Lord High Admiral of the United Kingdom of Great Britain and Ireland &c

---

[1] i.e. landsman.

[2] Refers to a mutiny on HMS *Hermione* in 1797. British officials conducted an extended search for those involved, many of whom had signed on American merchantmen and naval vessels. The mutineer referred to here was Henry Poulson. Frykman, 'The Mutiny on the Hermione', pp. 159–87.

[3] i.e. able-bodied seaman.

[4] Flinders frequently uses this spelling for 'lightning'.

[5] In a letter written on this day Flinders, who wanted to survey the southern coast soon after he reached Australia, indicated that he was not in full accord with his instructions: 'The Admiralty have not thought good to permit me to circumnavigate New Holland in the way that appears to me best suited to expedition and safety' (quoted in Scott, *The Life of Matthew Flinders*, p. 130). Rough Journal, I, f. 59, notes: 'This morning I received sailing orders and thirteen pages of instructions, together with the following papers: An order to victual the astronomer and servant. A passport from the French Republic signed by the minister of the marine and of the colonies, to prevent our being molested by any of the ships of the republic, and permitting us to put into any of their ports to refit as necessary; on condition that we in no way give offence to them or their allies. A memoir from Mr Dalrymple relating to the winds, on which the instructions are partly founded. An extract of a letter written by the Duke of Portland to the governor of New South Wales, relating to the *Lady Nelson* brig. An Answer to my letter No. 64 written July 2. Wrote to the Admiralty acknowledging the receipt of the above, and requesting that twelve months provisions of all species might be sent out to Port Jackson by the first opportunity, for the *Investigator*: to be lodged in the government storehouses for our sole use.'

[6] I have omitted some words in boxes in the manuscript that repeat parts of the instructions. These instructions can also be found at NMM, Flinders Papers, FLI/3/22. These Admiralty instructions were closely based on Banks's draft version: see ML, Banks Papers, series 63.39, 'Draft of Instructions for the *Investigator*', March 1801.

Whereas the sloop under your command has been fitted and stored for a voyage to remote parts; And whereas it is our intention that you should proceed in her to the coast of New Holland, for the purpose of making a complete examination and survey of the said coast, on the eastern side of which His Majestys colony of New South Wales is situated;[1] You are hereby required and directed to put to sea the first favourable opportunity of wind and weather, and proceed with as little delay as possible in execution of the service above-mentioned, repairing in the first place to Madeira and the Cape of Good Hope,[2] in order to take on board such supplies of water and livestock as you may be in want of.

Having so done you are to make the best of your way to the coast of New Holland, running down the said coast from 130° degrees of east longitude to Bass' Strait[3] (putting if you shall find it necessary into King George the thirds Harbour[4] for refreshments and water, previous to your commencing the survey)[5] and on your arrival on the coast use your best endeavours to discover such harbours as may be in those parts; and in case you should discover any creek or opening likely to lead to an inland sea or strait, you are at liberty either to examine it, or not, as you shall judge it most expedient, until a more favourable opportunity shall enable you so to do.[6]

When it shall appear to you necessary, you are to repair to Sydney Cove for the purpose of refreshing your people, refitting the sloop under your command, and consulting with the governor of New South Wales upon the best means of carrying on the survey of the coast; and having received from him such information as he may be able to communicate,

---

[1] Captain James Cook, sailing in the *Endeavour*, took possession of the east coast of New Holland in Britain's name on 22 August 1770 without permission from the local inhabitants. Cook named the territory New South Wales because it reminded him of South Wales. Captain Arthur Phillip took formal possession of New South Wales on behalf of the British government when he arrived in Botany Bay with the First Fleet of convicts on 26 January 1788. Kingston, *A History of New South Wales*, p. 1.

[2] This was the main port of call for vessels sailing from the Atlantic Ocean into the Indian Ocean. The currents of the two oceans meet at a point that fluctuates between Cape Agulhas (about 93 miles to the ESE of the Cape of Good Hope) and Cape Point (about ¾ mile east of the Cape of Good Hope).

[3] 130°E longitude marked the western edge of the Great Australian Bight. Bass Strait separated Van Diemen's Land (modern Tasmania) from the Australian mainland. The surgeon and navigator George Bass had visited the north side of Bass Strait in an open whaleboat, from Port Jackson, in January 1797. Flinders and Bass confirmed the existence of Bass Strait in their voyage in the colonial sloop *Norfolk* in December 1798. Flinders, *Observations on the Coasts of Van Diemen's Land*, pp. 33–4; Sprod, ed., *Van Diemen's Land Revealed*, pp. 40–48, 93.

[4] Sailing ships seeking to reach the east coast of Australia from the Cape of Good Hope followed the wind system across the Indian Ocean to west Australia; they then headed for the south-western tip of New Holland and continued eastwards to the south of the Australian mainland. Around 1800 King George Sound, as it is now called, was the only known haven along the south-western coast of New Holland. It had been discovered a decade earlier by Captain George Vancouver as part of a voyage that mainly surveyed the Pacific coast of North America. King George Sound, an inlet of the Indian Ocean, has a surface area of 35 square miles. Vallance, Moore and Groves, eds, *Nature's Investigator*, p. 86.

[5] The instructions below make it clear that Flinders was not expected to begin his survey voyaging of the Australian coast until he had reached Port Jackson.

[6] Maritime explorers were repeatedly admonished to search for rivers and an inland sea in their voyaging around the Australian continent. Before the voyage of the *Investigator*, exploration of Australia's coast had not yet found any substantial rivers; yet there was speculation that such rivers, if found, would flow into an inland sea or strait through the centre of the continent. Lipscombe, 'Two Continents or One?', pp. 24–5.

and taken under your command the *Lady Nelson* tender,[1] which you may expect to find at Sydney Cove, you are to recommence your survey by first diligently examining the coast from Bass' Strait to King George the thirds Harbour, which you may do either by proceeding along shore to the westward, or, in case you should think it more expedient, by proceeding first to King Georges Sound and carrying on your survey from thence to the eastward.

You are to repair from time to time, when the season will no longer admit of your [f. 16] carrying on the survey, to Sydney Cove, from whence you are to return in the execution of these Instructions, so soon as circumstances will enable you to do so.

You are to be very diligent in your examination of the said coast, and to take particular care to insert in your journal every circumstance that may be useful to a full and complete knowledge thereof; noting the winds and the weather which usually prevail there at different seasons of the year, the productions and comparative fertility of the soil, and the manners and customs of the inhabitants of such parts as you may be able to explore; fixing in all cases, when in your power, the true positions in latitude and longitude of remarkable Head Lands, Bays, and Harbours, by astronomical observations, and noting the variation of the needle,[2] and the right direction and course of the tides and currents, as well as the perpendicular height of the tides; and in case during your survey, any river should be discovered, you are either to proceed yourself in the tender, or to direct her commander to enter it; and proceed as far up as circumstances will permit; carefully laying down the course and the banks thereof, and noting the soundings; going on shore as often as it shall appear probable that any considerable variation has taken place, either in the productions of the soil or the customs of the inhabitants, examining the country as far inland as shall be thought prudent to venture with the small number of persons who can be spared from the charge of the vessel, wherever there appears to be a probability of discovering anything useful to the commerce or manufactures of the United Kingdom.

When you shall have completely examined the whole of the coast from Bass's Strait to King George the thirds Harbour, you are, at such time as may be suitable for the purpose (which may be seen on a reference to Mr. Dalrymples memoir, and extract of which accompanied this)[3] to proceed to and explore the north-west coast of New Holland,

---

[1] By instructions from the Admiralty, the governor of New South Wales placed HMS *Lady Nelson*, a 60-ton brig, as a tender at Flinders's disposal. This vessel had sailed from the River Thames on 13 January 1800 and had reached Port Jackson on 16 December 1800. Between 6 March and 14 May 1801 the *Lady Nelson* under James Grant surveyed the south-eastern coast of Australia via Bass Strait as far as Western Port. In late 1801 and early 1802 the *Lady Nelson*, commanded by John Murray, explored parts of King Island in Bass Strait and discovered a spacious harbour on the mainland coast that was named Port Phillip. TNA, ADM 1/4187, Admiralty Letters from Secretaries of State, Order from the Admiralty Office, April 1801; Vallance, Moore and Groves, eds, *Nature's Investigator*, p. 225; Currey, *John Murray, H.M. Survey Vessel Lady Nelson and the Discovery of Port Phillip*, pp. 7–13.

[2] i.e. the deviation of the direction of a magnetic needle from the true north and south line. Also called the declination of the needle. It is measured by an arc of the horizon, intercepted between the true and magnetic meridian. Harding, 'Observations on the Variation of the Needle', pp. 107–18.

[3] For further reference to this memoir, see below, pp. 132–3.

where, from the extreme height of the tides observed by Dampier,[1] it is probable that valuable harbours may be discovered.

Having performed this service you are carefully to examine the Gulph of Carpentaria, and the parts to the westward thereof, between the 130th and 139th degrees of east longitude; taking care to seize the earliest opportunity to do so, when the seasons and the prevalent winds may be favourable to visiting those seas.[2] When you shall have explored the Gulph of Carpentaria and the parts to the westward thereof, you are to proceed to a careful investigation and accurate survey of Torres Strait;[3] and when that shall have been completed, you are to examine and survey the whole of the remainder of the north, the west, and the north-west coasts of New Holland, and especially those parts of the coast most likely to be fallen in with by East-India ships in their outward-bound passages.[4] [f. 17] And you are to examine as particularly as circumstances will allow, the bank which extends itself from the Trial Rocks towards Timor,[5] in the hope that by ascertaining the depth and nature of the soundings thereon, great advantage may arise to the East India Company ships, in case that passage should hereafter be frequented by them.[6]

So soon as you shall have completed the whole of these surveys and examinations as above directed, you are to proceed to and examine very carefully the east coast of New Holland seen by captain Cook, from Cape Flattery[7] to the Bay of Inlets;[8] and in order to refresh your people and gain the advantage of sanity to the painters,[9] you are at liberty to touch at the Fejees[10] or some other of the islands in the South Seas.

During the course of the survey, you are to use the tender under your command as much as possible, moving the *Investigator* onwards from one harbour to another as they

---

[1] A reference to William Dampier's expedition to New Holland in the *Roebuck* in 1699. His comment on the tides is reported in Major, *Early Voyages to Terra Australis*, p. 107.

[2] According to Governor Arthur Phillip's Commission as Governor of New South Wales in 1787, the eastern boundary of New South Wales lay at 135°E longitude. The Gulf of Carpentaria has generally shallow water. Tropical depressions and cyclones occur on this part of the Australian coast, which is close to the Equator. Cyclones in this region move very erratically and mainly form from lows within the monsoon trough from November to April.

[3] Named after Luis Vaz de Torres, a Spanish pilot who participated in the first European navigation of the strait in 1606. Torres Strait separates the Australian continent's northernmost point – the Cape York peninsula – from New Guinea. Torres was the first navigator to prove that New Guinea was not the northern peninsula of a southern continent. There are at least 274 small islands in Torres Strait. Hilder, *The Voyage of Torres*.

[4] These would be mainly bound for China. The East India Company had granted money towards the voyage. Banks had informed Flinders that 'the real reason for the allowance is to encourage the men of science to discover such things as will be useful to the Commerce of India & you to find new passages'. ML, Banks Papers, series 65.16, Banks to Flinders, 1 May 1801.

[5] This sounds easier than it was: the exact location of the Trial Rocks between Timor and Australia was unknown at the time and Flinders later spent twelve days in April 1803 unsuccessfully looking for them. Estensen, *The Life of Matthew Flinders*, p. 273.

[6] East India Company ships returning home from China sometimes sailed through the Ombai Straits west of Timor.

[7] Cape Flattery (14°56'S, 145°20'E) is between North and South Direction Island and Three Islands, situated off the coast of Queensland.

[8] Discovered by James Cook on 28 May 1770 and named the Bay of Inlets – a name no longer used – this is the area from Cape Palmerston to Cape Townshend, including Shoalwater Bay (22°23'S, 150°24'E), on the central Queensland coast.

[9] i.e. help the mental well-being of the painters.

[10] i.e. the Fiji islands.

shall be discovered in order that the Naturalists may have time to range about and collect the produce of the earth; and the painters allowed time to finish as many of their works as they possibly can on the spot where they may have been began: And when you shall have completed the whole of the surveys and examinations as above mentioned, you are to lose no time in returning with the sloop under your command to England for further orders, touching on your way, if necessary, at the Cape of Good Hope, and repairing with as little delay as possible to Spithead, and transmit to our secretary an account of your arrival.

During your continuance on the service above mentioned, you are, by all proper opportunities to send to our secretary for our information accounts of your proceedings and copies of the surveys and drawings which you shall have made, and such papers as the Naturalist and the Painters employed on board may think proper to send home; and upon your arrival in England you are immediately to repair to this office in order to lay before us a full account of your proceedings in the whole course of your voyage; taking care before you leave the sloop to demand from the officers and petty officers the log books and journals which they may have kept, and such drawings and charts as they may have taken, and to seal them.

And whereas you have been furnished with a plant cabin for the purpose of depositing therein such plants, trees, shrubs &c. as may be collected during the survey above mentioned, you are, when you arrive at Sydney Cove to cause the said plant cabin to be fitted up by the carpenter of the sloop you command, according to the intention of its construction; and you are to cause boxes for containing earth to be placed thereon, in the same manner as was done in the plant cabin carried out by the *Porpoise* store ship, which plant cabin you will find at Sydney Cove. You are to place the said plant cabin with the boxes of earth contained in it under the charge and care of the Naturalist and Gardener[1] [f. 18] and to cause to be planted therein, during the survey, such plants, trees, shrubs &c. as they make think suitable for the Royal Garden at Kew:[2] and you are, as often as you return to Sydney Cove, to cause the said plants to be deposited in the governors garden under his charge, there to remain until you sail for Europe: and so soon as you shall be preparing to return home, you are to cause the small plant cabin to be removed from the sloops quarter deck, and the one brought out by the *Porpoise* (which is something larger) to be placed there in its stead; in this last mentioned cabin the Naturalist and Gardener are to place the plants, trees, shrubs &c. which may have been collected during the survey, in order to their being brought home for His Majesty; and you are, so soon as the sloop shall arrive at any port in England, to give notice of her arrival to His Majestys botanic gardens at Kew, and to transmit to him a list and state of the said plants &c. which the gardener employed under your orders is to furnish you with for that purpose.

---

[1] The prefabricated plant cabin was carried by the *Investigator* from England and, as these instructions stated, it was not assembled until the vessel reached Sydney in May 1802. The plant cabin was large and heavy and placed directly over the tiller ropes. The *Porpoise*, under the governor of New South Wales's direction, was placed at Flinders' disposal when he reached Sydney. Estensen, *The Life of Matthew Flinders*, p. 212; Rigby, 'The Politics and Pragmatics of Seaborne Plant Transportation', p. 96.

[2] i.e. the Royal Botanic Gardens, Kew, much improved by George III.

Given under our hands the 22d of June 1801
St. Vincent[1]
T. Trowbridge[2]
J. Markham[3]
To Matthew Flinders esquire Commander of His Majestys sloop *Investigator* at Spithead
By command of their Lordships
Evan Nepean[4]

Paper No. 2 relating to the *Lady Nelson*

To Evan Nepean Esquire   Whitehall 15 July 1801
Sir
I am directed by the Duke of Portland[5] to transmit to you herewith an extract of a letter which His Grace has written to Governor King,[6] relative to putting the *Lady Nelson* under the command of captain Flinders, to assist him in prosecuting the objects of his voyage of discovery. I am to desire that you will lay the same before the Lords Commissioners of the Admiralty for the information of their Lordships.
I am &c. &c. &c.
J. King[7]

Extract of a letter from the Duke of Portland to Governor King dated Whitehall 26 June 1801
'You will receive this by captain Flinders, who is about to proceed on a voyage of discoveries in His Majestys ship *Investigator*. As his attention will be in a more particular manner directed to New Holland, and as it may enable him to execute the object of his voyage with more success if he is accompanied by the *Lady Nelson*, I am to desire you will place that vessel under his command, provided the public service of your government will allow of your so doing.'

---

[1] John Jervis, 1st Earl of St Vincent (1735–1823), First Lord of the Admiralty between 1801 and 1804, had been a Whig MP between 1783 and 1794 for Launceston, Great Yarmouth and Wycombe. Crimmin, 'Jervis, John', pp. 67–76.

[2] Sir Thomas Troubridge (?1758–1807) was a Lord of the Admiralty between 1801 and 1804. He was promoted to Rear-Admiral in 1804. Crimmin, 'Troubridge, Sir Thomas', pp. 435–40.

[3] John Markham, Lord of the Admiralty, 1801–4 and 1806–7. He was a Whig MP for Portsmouth in the years 1801–18 and 1820–26. Laughton rev. Morriss, 'Markham, John', pp. 693–4.

[4] Sir Evan Nepean (1752–1822), British politician and colonial administrator, MP for Queenborough and later Bridport, was under-secretary of state in the Home Office (1782–94) and secretary to the Admiralty Board (1795–1804). He was created baronet in 1804 and became a Lord of the Admiralty from 1804 to 1806. Parsons, 'Nepean, Evan', p. 281; Sparrow, 'Nepean, Sir Evan', pp. 425–6.

[5] William Cavendish Bentinck, 3rd Duke of Portland, was prime minister of Britain in 1783 and 1807–9 and Home Secretary between 1801 and 1804. Wilkinson, 'Bentinck, William Henry Cavendish Cavendish', pp. 261–9.

[6] Philip Gidley King (1758–1808), a naval officer, became lieutenant governor of New South Wales on 28 September 1800. He had his position upgraded to governor in 1802, a position he retained until August 1806. Shaw, 'King, Philip Gidley', pp. 55–61.

[7] John King, an under-secretary at the Home Office. Estensen, *The Life of Matthew Flinders*, p. 94.

From Mr. Dalrymples memoir relating to the voyage of the *Investigator*[1]

[f. 19] 'The only inference that can be made of the winds and weather to be expected on an unfrequented coast is from the analogy of nature.

Within the tropics, near land, the monsoons or periodical winds prevail; in north latitude from April to October the SW monsoon blows, and during this season in south latitude the SE winds: In north latitude from October to April the NE and in that season in south latitude the NW monsoon prevails; not that the winds are constant in those points, the direction of the coast gives a direction to the wind, and calms and variable winds are common near the change of the monsoons: which change is often introduced by a violent gale denominated the breaking up of the monsoon: And on the skirts of the general trade wind, that trade contending with the monsoon produces hurricanes and typhoons which I conceive are the same and from the same cause: Another circumstance necessary to be attended to, is, that within the tropics, the monsoon blowing on the coast produces rainy weather, and when blowing from over the land it produces land and sea breezes. The Malabar and Coromandel Coast in the same latitude have rainy weather in contrary monsoons, the former with the SW the latter with the NE, the east coast of the Bay of Bengal with the SW monsoon, the coast of Cochin-China with the NE. The south coast of China and the west coast of the Philipines with the SW monsoon: And where the coast is not opposed to the monsoon, such as the north part of the West side of the Bay of Bengal, there is a kind of anomalous monsoon, the weather partaking partly of both.[2]

This rule does not extend to coasts beyond the tropics: the southern extremity of Africa is nearly in the same latitude with the Land of Nuyts;[3] both have land to the north and an extensive ocean to the south; In one instance certainly, and in the other probably, reaching to the frozen polar regions. What difference the projecting point forming the north side of Bass's Strait, and Van Diemen's Land,[4] may occasion, it must be left to future experience to determine; we can at present only reason on general analogy.

On the south coast of Africa, the SE winds are prevalent in their summer months, from October to March, and the NW wind in their winter months from March to October; not that the winds are to be considered to be invariable. It is at all times dangerous to be on a lee shore, but a lee shore on an unknown coast is hazardous in the last extreme.[5] Off the Cape of Good Hope the SE winds blow with great violence; but during the height of the gale by rising instead of falling. In the winter months the winds from the northwestward make the coast a weather shore, so that a vessel may keep close in with the land or stand off to sea at will. In the tropical regions the reason is still stronger to avoid approaching the land with the monsoon that blows on upon the coast; but to

---

[1] Flinders also refers in *A Voyage to Terra Australis*, I, p. 12, to receiving this memoir by the hydrographer Alexander Dalrymple (1737–1808), but it is unknown whether this was printed. It has not been found anywhere but here. Vallance, Moore and Groves, eds, *Nature's Investigator*, p. 46 n. 5.

[2] Monsoons were and are an annual part of the tropical wet climate of these Asian regions. Heavy rainfall occurs between May and December in the south-west monsoon. October to January is the main period for the north-east monsoon.

[3] A part of the south Australian coast named after Pieter Nuyts, the highest ranking person on board a Dutch East India Company vessel headed for Batavia which accidentally came upon this coast on 26 January 1627.

[4] The original name used by Europeans for Tasmania. In 1642 the Dutch explorer Abel Janszoon Tasman, the first European to sight the island, named it after his sponsor, Anthony van Diemen, the governor of the Dutch East Indies.

[5] A lee shore is one that is to the side of a vessel, meaning the wind is blowing the ship towards the shore.

chuse the land and sea breezes for that purpose, though it is most commodious to go with the monsoon, as some would necessarily be lost in time.'[1]

[f. 20] <u>Paper No. 4 French passport</u>[2]

Premier Consul de la République Française sur le compte qui lui a été rendu de la demande faite par le Lord Hawkesbury au Citoyen Otto,[3] Commissionaire du Gouvernement Française à Londres, d'un Passeport pour le Corvette *Investigator*, dont le signalement est ci-après, expédiée par le Gouvernement Anglais sous le commandement du capitaine Matthew Flinders pour un voyage découverte dans la mer Pacifique, ayant décidé que ce Passeport seroit accordé et que cette expedition, dont l'objet est d'étendre les connaissances humaines et d'assurer davantage les progrès de la science nautique et de la géographie, trouverait de la part du Gouvernement Français la sureté et la protection nécessaires.

Le Ministre de la Marine et des Colonies[4] ordonne en conséquence à tous les Commandants des Bâtiments de guerre de la République à ses Agens dans toutes les Colonies Françaises, aux Commandants des Bâtiments, porteurs de Lettres de Marque et à tous autres qu'il appartendra, de laisser passer librement et sans empêchement, la dite Corvette *Investigator*, ses Officiers, Equipage, et effets, pendant la durée de leur voyage de leur permettre d'aborder dans les différents ports de la République, tant en Europe que dans les autres parties du Monde, soit qu'ils soient forcés par le mauvais temps d'y chercher un réfuge, soit qu'ils viennent y reclamer les secours et les moyens de réparation nécessaires pour continuer leur voyage. Il est bien entendu, cependant, qu'ils ne trouveront ainsi protection et assistance, qui dans le cas où ils ne se seront pas volontairement détournés de la route qu'ils doivent suivre, qu'ils n'auront commis, ou qu'ils n'annonçeront l'intention de commettre aucune hostilité contre la République Française et ses alliés, qu'ils n'auront procuré ou cherché à procurer aucun secours à ses enemies, et qu'ils ne s'occuperont d'aucune espèce de commerce, ni de contraband.

Fait à Paris le quatre Prairial an neuf de la République Française.[5] Le minister de la Marine et des Colonies.

Signé Forfait[6]

Par le minister de la marine et des colonies

---

[1] The severity of winds near the Cape of Good Hope made passing around it difficult for sailing vessels.

[2] For an English translation, see Appendix 2, vol. II, p. 511. Flinders asked for this passport in February 1801 to assure the safety of the *Investigator*, devoted to geographical exploration and scientific work, in any encounter with the French. The foreign secretary, Lord Hawkesbury, requested the passport in May 1801 and it arrived in London on 23 June. Flinders did not understand French, and had the passport translated for him while on board the *Investigator*. The passport, issued by the Minister of Marine and the Colonies on behalf of the French government, instructed French naval officers to assist Flinders and his ship during any encounter, if so required, unless the English ship committed any hostile act towards the French or trafficked in merchandise or contraband. Estensen, *The Life of Matthew Flinders*, pp. 141, 148, 168; Scott, *The Life of Matthew Flinders*, p. 132. The original document is deposited at NMM, FLI/3/21.

[3] Lord Hawkesbury was the foreign secretary under Addington's government. He took this courtesy title in 1796 and became Lord Liverpool on the death of his father in 1808. He was prime minister between 1812 and 1827. Citizen Otto was the French government representative in London and commissioner for the exchange of French prisoners. Hawkesbury and Otto liaised over the provisions of the Peace of Amiens in 1801. Gash, 'Jenkinson, Robert Banks, second earl of Liverpool', pp. 983–90.

[4] From 1791 onwards this minister was entrusted with control of the French Navy and colonies.

[5] Prairial was the ninth month of the French Republican calendar (in effect from 1793 to 1805). It ran from 20 May to 18 June.

[6] Pierre Alexandre Laurent Forfait was Minister of Marine and the Colonies between November 1799 and October 1801.

Signalement de la Corvette
Chs. M. Jurien[1]
La Corvette l'*Investigator* est du port
326 tonneaux. Son Equipage est composé de 83 hommes, outre cinq hommes de lettres
Son artillerie est de   6 Carronades de 12
                           2 ditto   de 18
                           2 canons   de 6
                           2 pierriers[2]
Le soussigné Commissaire du Gouvernement Français à Londres, certifie le signalement conforme à la note qui lui a été communiquée par le ministère de sa Majesté Britannique. Londres le 4 Messidor An 9[3]
Otto

[f. 21] Paper No. 5 Conduct to enemies
Admiralty Office 16 July 1801
Sir
Having laid before my Lords Commissioners of the Admiralty your letter to me of the 2nd instant: I am commanded by their Lordships to acquaint you, in answer thereto, that you are to act in all respects towards French ships as if the two countries were not at war; and with respect to the ships and vessels of other powers with which the country is at war, you are to avoid if possible having any communication with them; and not to take letters or packets other than such as you may receive from this office, or the office of His Majestys secretary of state. I am,
Sir,
Your very humble servant
Evan Nepean
Capt*ain* Flinders – *Investigator* Spithead

Paper No. 6 Terms of agreement between the Admiralty and men of science employed on board the *Investigator*[4]
In order to prevent all misunderstandings between the Lords Commissioners for executing the office of Lord High Admiral of the United Kingdoms, and the persons employed by their Lordships as scientific assistants on board His Majestys ship the *Investigator*, for the purpose of exploring the country of New Holland, their Lordships have been pleased to issue the following instructions and commands, to be obeyed by all persons so employed: and it is expected that every person so employed do sign his name to the same in testimony of his acquiescence in the terms in which their Lordships are pleased to employ him.
1st Their Lordships require every person employed as a scientific assistant on board the *Investigator*, to render voluntary obedience to the commander of the ship, in all orders he shall from time to time issue for the direction of the conduct of his crew, or any part thereof.

[1] Charles-Marie Jurien (1763–1836) was a member of the French naval administration.
[2] i.e. cannon designed to throw stone and marble shot.
[3] This was the ninth year of the French Republican calendar. Messidor was its tenth month, beginning on 19 June and ending on 18 July.
[4] I have omitted the brief comments in a box placed by the side of the numbered points in the manuscript.

2nd Their Lordships require that all persons so employed do on all occasions conduct themselves peaceably, quietly, and civilly to each other; each readily assisting the other in his respective department to the utmost of his ability, in such manner as will best promote the success of the public service in which they are jointly engaged and unite their individual endeavours into one general result.

3rdly Their Lordships require the Draughtsman employed for natural history[1] to pay due attention to the directions he shall receive from the Naturalist[2] and the Draughtsman employed for landscape and figures[3] to pay regard to the opinion of the Commander, in the choice of objects most fitting to be delineated, and their Lordships moreover require the gardiner[4] and the miner[5] to pay obedience to the Naturalist, in all such orders as he shall think fit to give them.

4thly Their Lordships consider the salary allotted to each person employed as a full compensation for the whole of his time;[6] they therefore expect that all journals, remarks, memorandums, drawings, sketches, collections of natural history, and of habits, [f. 22] arms, utensils, ornaments &c. of every kind, to be delivered up on the return of the ship to such persons as their Lordships shall direct to receive them.

5thly In order, however, to encourage the persons engaged in this undertaking to exert themselves to the utmost in accomplishing the object of their mission, their Lordships hereby declare, that if the information collected during the voyage is deemed of sufficient importance, it is their Lordships intention to cause it to be published in the form of a narrative, drawn up by the Commander, on a plan similar to that pursued in the publication of captain Cook's voyages and to give such pecuniary assistance as their Lordships shall see fitting, for the engraving of charts, plans, views, figures &c and that in such case, the most interesting observations of natural history and the most remarkable views of land and delineations of people &c. will be inserting therein.[7]

6thly their Lordships moreover declare, that in case the persons employed in the undertaking as scientific assistants are industrious in their several departments, civil and obliging to each other, and co-operate on all occasions, in making the general work in which they are engaged complete, by assisting each other and uniting their efforts for the advantage of the public, it is intended that the profit derived from the sale of the said publication shall be divided between the Commander and the Assistants, in proportion to the good conduct each shall have held during the voyage, and the comparative advantage the publication shall, in the opinion of their Lordships, derive from the labours of each individual.[8]

---

[1] Ferdinand Bauer.

[2] Robert Brown.

[3] William Westall.

[4] Peter Good.

[5] John Allen.

[6] Inserted at the bottom of the page: 'Naturalist 400 *Guineas* per an*num*: Draughtsmen 300 *Guineas*: Gardener and Miner 100 *Guineas* per annum.'

[7] Flinders did not begin writing *A Voyage to Terra Australis* until 1811 after he had returned to London from imprisonment in the Ile de France. The Admiralty furnished Flinders with half-pay while he was writing it, and paid for the reproduction of the charts that accompanied the book. Public interest and politics had determined the publication of Cook's three Pacific voyages in versions by John Hawkesworth (volume 1), published in 1773, and John Douglas (volumes 2 and 3), published in 1777 and 1784. Estensen, *The Life of Matthew Flinders*, pp. 441–2.

[8] No specific financial arrangements were ever made for this remuneration. Ibid., p. 441.

7thly their Lordships moreover declare, that after such descriptions and sketches as shall be found necessary for the illustration and embellishment of the intended publication, shall have been selected by such persons as their Lordships shall be pleased to appoint; and such specimens of natural history, arms, implements, habits, ornaments &c. as their Lordships think fitting shall have been applied to such purposes as their Lordships shall approve, the remainder of the descriptions of plants and of animals &c. and the sketches of all kinds shall be at the disposal of the persons who have made them for the purpose of being published by them whenever it is thought proper, at their own risk, and for their own advantage; provided, however, that all such drawings as shall be finished during the voyage, and such sketches as their Lordships shall order to be finished after the return of the ship shall be considered as the property of the public and lodged in the depôt of the Admiralty when required so to be; and that the remainder of the collections of natural history, arms, habits, implements, ornaments &c. shall be at the disposal of the persons who have collected them; all this, however, on condition that each person shall during the voyage have behaved himself with propriety to the rest; their Lordships reserving to themselves the power of punishing all deviations from good humour and perfect harmony among parties, by withholding from the persons offending such parts of the benefits we described as they shall think proper.[1]

[f. 23] We the undersigned Robert Brown, naturalist, &c. in testimony of our concurrence in the above terms, and as a pledge of our obedience to all such instructions and commands as their Lordships shall be pleased to issue to us during the time we shall be in their Lordships employ, have signed our names to this engagement on the 29th day of April in the year of our Lord 1801

Robert Brown	naturalist
Ferdinand Bauer	botanic draughtsman
William Westall	landscape & figure painter
Peter Good	gardener
John Allen	miner

---

[1] The work of these specialists reached the public domain in various ways. William Westall's drawings on the voyage of the *Investigator* remained in his family's hands until the late 19th century. They were bought by the Royal Commonwealth Society in 1899 and sold to the National Library of Australia in 1968. They were reproduced in print in Perry and Simpson, *Drawings by William Westall* (1962). In 1809 the Admiralty commissioned Westall to produce nine oil paintings of Australian scenes from the voyage. These became the basis for engravings in *A Voyage to Terra Australis*. Westall published the engravings separately as *Views of Australian Scenery*. Bauer returned to England in 1805 with eleven cases of drawings containing over 1,500 Australian plants. The Admiralty continued to employ him so that he could publish an account of his travels. Between 1806 and 1813 he published fifty sets of his *Illustrationes Florae Novae Hollandiae*. His finished paintings were acquired by the Admiralty and transferred to the British Museum in 1843. They are described in Mabberley and Moore, 'Catalogue ... of the Australian Botanical Drawings of Ferdinand Bauer'. Bauer returned to live in Vienna in 1814 and most of his sketches are now in the Natural History Museum there. Peter Good died during the *Investigator's* voyage (on 12 June 1802) and his plants were incorporated into Robert Brown's collection. Good's journal on the *Investigator* has been published as Edwards, ed., *The Journal of Peter Good*. Brown was employed by the Linnean Society in London in 1805 and in 1810 he became Sir Joseph Banks's librarian for a decade until Banks died. He published a major work on Australian plants in 1810: *Prodromus Florae Novae Hollandiae et Insulae Van-Diemen*. He transferred Banks' collection to the British Museum in 1827, and directed their oversight. His personal collections were acquired by the British Museum in 1876. His journal on board the *Investigator* has been published as Vallance, Moore and Groves, eds, *Nature's Investigator*.

Note. This was not one of the papers enclosed to me from the Admiralty, but I think it necessary to insert it, from its importance to the intended voyage.   *Matthew Flinders*.

Paper No. 7 List of articles for presents and barter with Indians,[1] and for the convenience and use of the Commander and gentlemen employed on board the *Investigator*, supplied by Alexander Davison Esq*uire* by order of the Honourable Navy Board.[2]

A D

No.			
1	1 case containing	1 Marquee and 3 bell tents	
2	1 ditto	3 Canteens with every necessary for Excursions	
3	1 ditto	50 strings blue beads: 50 red: 50 white: 50 ditto of yellow beads	
4	bale	100 blankets: 100 yards red baize: 10 red caps: 10 yards gartering: 100 yards linen	
5 to 7	3 kegs	6 cwt. of lead shot No. 1 in bags of 56 lbs each	
8 to 10	3 ditto	6 cwt. Ditto No. 2	ditto
11 to 13	3 ditto	5 cwt. Ditto No. 4	ditto
14 to 17	4 ditto	6 cwt. Ditto No. 6 and dust ditto	
18 to 22	5 ditto	10 cwt. Large buck	
23 to 27	5 ditto	10 cwt. Ditto Small buck	
28 to 32	5 ditto	10 cwt. Ditto Swan	
33 to 35	3 ditto	1000 lbs lead for casting into shot	
36	1 Case	2 pairs of shot molds	
37	1 Cask	42 of 4d. nails	
39	1 ditto	13 of 10d. ditto	
40	1 ditto	8 of 20d. ditto	
41 to 43	3 ditto	5 cwt. of bar iron	
44	1 ditto	2 cwt. of steel	
45	1 Case	200 tohees[3] and 50 small adzes	
46	1 ditto	1000 needles, 100 combs and 5 lbs of red thread	
47	1 ditto	5 Cross-cut saws	
48	1 ditto	5 Pitt saws	
49	1 Cask	180 Hatchets	
50	1 ditto	120 ditto and 48 hammers	
51	1 ditto	16 Hammers, 100 shoe knives: 500 pocket ditto 300 scissors; 50 axes, and 200 files	
52	1 ditto	100 Handsaws and 36 hammers	
53 & 54	2 cases	480 looking glasses; 200 rings, and 100 pair of Earrings	
55	1 ditto	144 yellow medals and 50 white medals of His Majesty	

and for which the Commander signed a receipt May 22 1801

[1] i.e. Aborigines.

[2] This may have been Alexander Davison, a contracting agent and friend of Horatio Nelson. From 1546 to 1831 the Navy Board was a body separate from the Admiralty. It was responsible for the administrative affairs of the Navy, including the building and repairs of naval ships and their supplies. Pool, *Navy Board Contracts*, p. ix.

[3] These are pieces of thin bar iron about 6 inches long, sharpened at one end, and turned a little at the other. They are meant to be a substitute for an adze. Admiralty to [the Navy Board], 15 April 1801, in Bladen, ed., *HRNSW*, IV, p. 345.

[f. 24] <u>Paper No. 8 List</u>

of instruments, books and stationary, supplied for the use of the commander of the *Investigator* by the Honourable Navy Board

Instruments from Troughtons[1]

Surveying chain, graduated to $\frac{1}{1000}$	1
Riding scales of ebony, of 3 and 5 feet	2
Thermometers	2
Pocket d*itto*	1
Horizons of quicksilver, in cases[2]	2
Instruments, large case	1
Beam compass[3]	1
Graduating scales of ivory[4]	set 1
Compass, Walkers new invented	1
D*itto* Common azimuth, upon Walkers construction[5]	1

Pocket chronometer from Arnold (No. 1736) for the purpose of in the tender or in boats, up rivers and other inlets.[6] Instruments are altogether unconnected with the large and expensive set furnished to Mr. John Crosley, astronomer, by the Board of Longitude.[7]

[f. 25] **Saturday 18 July 1801**

Light airs and cloudy with rain at times. Employed lashing and securing for sea. Received 3 tons of beer and 4 tons of water to complete. AM. At 4 made the signal and unmoored

---

[1] Edward Troughton, then the leading British maker of navigational, surveying and astronomical instruments. McConnell, 'Troughton, Edward', pp. 442–4.

[2] A mercurial artificial horizon used mainly with the sextant for observing the double altitude of a celestial body.

[3] A compass with a beam and sliding sockets or cursors (also called trammel points) for drawing and dividing circles larger than those made by regular compasses. It can be used to make measurements by rotating each point 180° until the desired measurement is reached.

[4] Lines of graduation were more legible using ivory (or boxwood) scales, which is why they were included among these instruments. Warren, *A Manual of Drafting Instruments and Operations*, p. 27.

[5] An azimuth is a horizontal angle between a reference point, usually North, and a celestial object, measured along the observer's horizon. An azimuth compass measures in degrees an angle clockwise from the north. True North is 0° or 360°. East is 90°. South is 180°. West is 270°. The azimuth compass was used for important magnetic experiments that Flinders undertook along the coast of South Australia. Ralph Walker, a seaman with an interest in navigational problems, travelled to London in 1794 to promote his meridional and azimuth compass to the Board of Longitude. This compass was widely used on vessels in the 19th century. It had a sundial attachment to find true north from the Sun. Comparing this with the needle's direction gave the magnetic variation and a possible means of determining longitude. Flinders had met Walker when his azimuth compass was on trial in HMS *Providence*. Flinders, *A Voyage to Terra Australis*, I, p. 199; Walker, *A Treatise on Magnetism*; Howse, *Greenwich Time and the Discovery of the Longitude*; Dunn and Higgitt, *Finding Longitude*, p. 181.

[6] John Arnold of London designed this instrument. He was the first person to popularize the name chronometer. The watch was supplied to Flinders by the Navy Board. See ML, Matthew Flinders letterbook (1801–6), Matthew Flinders to Dr. Maskelyne F.R.S., 25 May 1802. On Arnold, see Betts, 'Arnold, John', pp. 435–6.

[7] A British government body composed of twenty-two admirals and scientists, though usually only a dozen at most attended meetings. It was formed in 1714 to solve the problem of finding longitude at sea, and was dissolved in 1828. After John Harrison had designed a marine chronometer that solved the problem of finding longitude at sea, the work of the Board became broader to encompass other aspects of navigation. From the 1770s onwards it was concerned with disseminating accurate naval charts, testing chronometers, rewarding instrument makers, and promoting observation of the southern skies. Johnson, 'The Board of Longitude', pp. 63–9. For the scientific instruments furnished to Crosley, see below, pp. 211–12.

ship. Received 360 lbs of fresh beef, as also 2 barrels of pease, 2 half hogsheads of oatmeal, and one of cheese, completing up to 12 months. At 10, made the signal and weighed. Hoisted up and secured 2 of the boats. Peter Cartwright (ord*inary*) absented himself without leave. At noon passed St. Helens road. Light airs and fine with haze. Discharged George Webb from the books to the civil power, he having been taken out by a writ for 37£, some time since. Thomas White having been checked twice without leave, we sail with 4 men short of complement.

A list of the *Investigator*s ships company agreeable to the establishment ordered for her on February 6 and as now filled up.

Supernumeraries borne by order				Complement continued		
John Crosley	astronomer, and servant	2			number brought up	10
Robert Brown	naturalist, and servant	2		James Wolsey		
Ferdinand Bauer	nat*ural* hist*ory* painter and d*itto*	2		Thomas Bell	gentlemen of the quarter deck being two more than allowed	8
William Westall	lan*dscape* and fi*gure* painter & d*itto*	2		Nathaniel Bell		
Peter Good	gardener	1		Kennet Sinclair		
John Allen	miner	_1_		Sherrard Ph*ilip* Lound		
		10		John Olive	clerk	1
				Cook and mate		2
Complement				Sailmaker and mate		2
Matthew Flinders	commander	1		Armourer		1
Robert Fowler	lieutenants	2		Master at arms		1
Sam*uel* Ward Flinders				Boatswains mates		2
John Thistle	master	1		Carpenters mates		2
Hugh Bell	surgeon	2		Gunners mates		1
Robert Purdie	assistant			Carpenters crew		2
Charles Douglas	boatswain	1		Quarter masters		4
Robert Colpits	gunner	1		Able and ordinary seamen & landsmen		35
Russell Mart	carpenter	1			Serjeant Greenhalgh	1
Thomas Evans	gentlemen of the quarter deck[1]			Marines	Corporal	1
William Taylor					Drummer	1
John Franklin					Privates	_12_
		_10_			Complement	83

But we are now deficient of complement as under				
Sailmaker	1		Cooks mate	1
Master at arms	1		Carpenters crew	_1_
Quarter masters	2		Deficiency	6

which being combined with the usual deficiency of a widows man[2] and the two young gentlemen in addition, leaves the number of people on board to be eighty-eight,[3] with which we now sail.[4]

[1] A raised deck behind the main mast of a sailing ship. This was traditionally where the Captain commanded his vessel, with his principal officers.

[2] This was a fictitious seaman kept on the books of Royal Navy ships in the 18th and early 19th centuries in order to make payments to families of dead crew members. This financial arrangement helped widows from being left destitute following the death of their seafaring husbands.

[3] The numbers in the right-hand column do not tally with the names: they appear to include servants and assistants who are unnamed. If one adds together the numbers in the column and deducts the deficiency of six plus the widow's man, the total does come to 88.

[4] A full list of the ship's company is given in Appendix 1, vol. II, pp. 506–10.

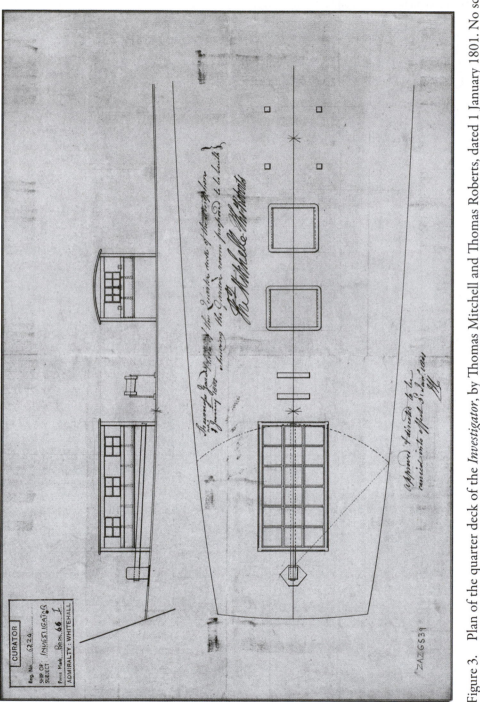

Figure 3. Plan of the quarter deck of the *Investigator*, by Thomas Mitchell and Thomas Roberts, dated 1 January 1801. No scale, possibly 1:48. © National Maritime Museum, Greenwich, London.

[f. 26] On going to sea I judged it necessary to issue the following orders.

To Mr. Charles Douglas, boatswain, to Mr. Robert Colpitts, gunman, and Mr. Russel Mart, carpenter, of His Majestys ship *Investigator*.

By Matthew Flinders esq*uire* Commander of His Majestys ship *Investigator*

The length of time that the present voyage may be expected to require, making a particular care of the stores a matter of the first importance. It is my directions to Mr. Charles Douglas, boatswain, to Mr. Robert Colpitts gunner and Mr. Russel Mart carpenter of His Majestys sloop *Investigator*, under my command, that they do not issue any stores of any kind, however small the quantity, to any officer or man whatever without my permission; and if any officer sees the necessity of replacing anything that may be deficient, or to apply stores to any use that may be wanted, he is requested to mention it to the commander for his approbation, before he orders the warrant officer to issue, since it cannot be complied with in consequence of this order. It is however to be understood that in case of imminent danger or immediate necessity, where timely application cannot be made to me that the commanding officer is authorized to give such orders relative to the stores as he may judge necessary, and as if this order had not been given.

Given under my hand this 18 July 1801 at sea

(Signed) Matthew Flinders[1]

To the officers of the quarter deck I issued the following instructions for the regulation of their general conduct; and 1st to the officer of the watch

On relieving the deck, particularly at night, he is to see that the look-out is attended to, that the ropes are properly belayed[2] and coiled fair, and that the sails are properly trimmed: for he is not to permit a sail to remain set in a slovenly or improper manner because he found it so. The weather lifts, braces,[3] and backstays are recommended to his constant attention, more especially when it blows fresh.

2nd The watch is to be mustered at the first quarter hour of the watch; and if any are absent the officer is himself to inquire into the cause, and to punish the absentees moderately or to excuse their attendance, as shall appear to him proper. In cases of repeated or material neglect, he is referred to the second article of his instructions. The people are to be mustered at any other time or times in the watch, if the officer suspects that any are about.

3rd One man at least is to be kept looking out at night; and in particular cases by day also; and never to be taken off but upon some particular emergency,[4] and replaced as soon as possible. The day lookout is to be at the fore top-mast head, and when it is not constant,

---

[1] Flinders, *A Voyage to Terra Australis*, I, p. 154, noted that stores were placed on board ship for the long voyage: 'So soon as my sailing orders were received, demands were sent on shore for provisions to replace what had been consumed at Spithead; and they came on board the next morning, when the ship was unmoored. We were able to stow a proportion of provisions for twelve months, bread excepted, of which only seven months could be taken, including a part in flour. Of salt meat I took for eighteen months, knowing that little reliance could be had on the colony in New South Wales for that article; and further to guard against any detriment to the voyage from the want of provisions, I left an application to the Admiralty for a general supply, for twelve months; to be sent after me, and lodged in the store houses at Port Jackson for our sole use.'

[2] i.e. turning the rope to secure it.

[3] Ropes belonging to the yards of a ship.

[4] A note adds: 'In a small ship where there are only 35 seamen, cases may occur that will make it necessary to call in the assistance of even the man at the look-out, for a short time.'

a man is to be sent up to look well round every two hours, as also before dark and at daylight.

4th He is strictly to forbid any person from taking off the attention of the helmsman from the steerage of the ship.

5th It is expected that from his own observation he shall know the course which the ship has been steered for each hour, that he may be able to correct any inaccuracies that have been made in marking the log board;[1] and he is to notice [f. 27] whether the mate of the watch applies to the quarter master or helmsman for an account of the ships course, and if he does observe it, he is to reprimand him for the inattention that makes an application to them necessary.

6th He is constantly to inform the Commander of any material alteration in the wind or weather, and not to make any alteration of consequence in the quantity of sail without his knowledge, unless in cases of immediate necessity. With respect to alterations in the course, he is referred to the 4th article of his instructions.

7th The officer of the watch is desired to put the initials of his name upon the logboard at the end of his watch: and is expected to answer for the correctness of what is there marked. If he suspects the accuracy of the copy in the log book, he may examine it before it is brought in to me, which will be regularly done before one o'clock.

8th The height of the thermometer in the shade is to be marked at the end of each watch, both by night and by day. At noon, a bucket of sea water is to be drawn and the thermometer immersed into it; and its height marked on the logboard also. At daylight and at noon, the height of the marine barometer is to be marked[2] in its column on the board.

9th At the earliest opportunity every morning watch, the topsail sheets are to be housed home, and all the sails hoisted up fair and properly trimmed. The upper decks are to be washed when the weather will permit; and at seven bells,[3] the hammocks to be piped up[4] and the between-decks swept out. It is expected of the officer of the morning watch, that he use every exertion to have the sails, the upper and lower decks, the ropes and hammocks, in a proper state for the people to go to breakfast at eight o'clock. When circumstances will permit they are to be allowed one hour to breakfast.

10th He is to take care that the boatswain and carpenter, or their mates, do examine the state of the rigging, the masts and yards, before the hammocks are piped up. The captains of the tops and of the after-guard are to accompany the boatswain or mate in his examination; and whatever is amiss is to be reported to the officer, and repaired as soon as possible.

11th The officer of the morning watch, and his mates and midshipmen, are to attend to any duty that may be required from the watch below during the day. The lower deck is to be washed and aired, or cleaned, in the best manner that the weather and the duty of the ship will permit; and the officer is to report to me when such cleaning is done, that I may inspect into it.

[1] A board comprising two parts closing together like a book. The direction of the wind and the course of the ship during each hour of the day and night were entered in its columns and transferred to the logbook.

[2] At bottom of page: 'It was afterwards ordered to be marked at 8 PM also.'

[3] Bells were rung in numerical sequence (up to eight bells) at each half an hour of a four-hour watch. Watches were usually timed with a thirty-minute hourglass. Bells would be struck every time the glass was turned.

[4] i.e. aired.

12th The hammocks are to be piped down[1] at 6 pm: and afterwards the ship pumped out, the decks swept (and wetted when within the tropics) and the ropes coiled fair for performing any evolution during the night; these necessary duties are to be performed before 8 pm.

13th He is desired to be very particular in mentioning to the officer that relieves him, the exact state of the sails, and the orders that may have been left with him, and every other thing which it may be necessary for him to know: And generally, an account of the ships situation at noon each day is expected from the commissioned officers of the ship; and it is wished that this situation may be found by astronomical observation as often as possible. Attention to this branch of science from the principal officers is of consequence in the present voyage, both from its utility and as an example to the inferior officers.

[f. 28] As the Commander expects that when an officer receives an order he will never lose sight of it until not only the letter of it, but also the intention and spirit of the order are fulfilled; so he requests that the officers will never permit the petty officers or men either to neglect any duty which they may have ordered, or to execute it any otherwise than completely and expeditiously. A due attention to these points is the very essence of discipline and good order; and therefore the Commander begs to press it upon the consideration of the officers very particularly.

From the mates and midshipmen of the ship much is expected.

1st In relieving the watch, they are expected to show an example of alertness to the men. They are not to leave the deck without being relieved, or having the permission of the officers of the watch so to do, who in that case is answerable for their duty; and this indulgence is not to be abused. They are to be attentive to the orders given by the officer, which they are not only to repeat, but to see them executed; and when a particular duty is ordered, the mate or midshipman who is appointed to superintend is in most cases to report when it is executed. They are expected to give manual assistance when circumstances require it; and when a topsail is reefed, or any material duty going on in the top, the senior midshipman is to attend there. The duty of the mizzen top is solely to be done by the younger gentlemen, as far as their strength will enable them to do it. Upon all duties, the Commander expects to see them forward and active, and anxious to give every assistance to their power.

2nd They are never to take off the attention of the helmsman by talking to him, or otherwise.

3rd A days work is expected from the masters mates, and from every midshipman who has any expectation of being rated. It is to contain the situation by log, the observed latitude as taken and worked by themselves, and the longitude by any astronomical observation that they may be master of. Such as are unacquainted, it behoves to apply themselves, and those whose application entitles them to notice will be permitted to work in the cabin, and will have every assistance from the astronomer and commander, to make them perfect in this part of their profession. They will also be initiated into the manner of making marine surveys and constructing charts; by which means they may make themselves useful in the voyage, and lay a foundation for their own future promotion.

4th On the first day of every month, the mates and such midshipmen as expect to be rated, are desired to send in their journals to the Commander for his inspection; as also

---

[1] This was the signal to go below deck and retire for the night.

a complete watch bill, quarter bill, station bills[1] for tacking and unmooring ship; and an order book, in which the present orders are to be inserted, as also such as may be hereafter given out.

Given this 18th day of July at sea 1801

Mat*th*ew Flinders

Note: The longitude by time-keeper in this log book as far as Madeira is found by means of Arnolds watch No. 1736, supplied to me by the Navy Board.

From Portsmouth Academy,[2] the error of N*o*. 1736 from mean Greenwich time was given me, on Au*gust* 17 1801 at noon 0 hours 2′ 37.81″ slow

And its rate of losing per day 4′41″[3]

[f. 28a] <u>Explanation of the articles contained in this log</u>

The time is usually dated according to the custom at sea, which makes Sunday begin immediately after the sun has passed the meridian on Saturday, and concludes it with the suns transit on Sunday at noon; so that the sea day begins twelve hours before the civil or natural day, and also ends twelve hours before it ends.[4] Sometimes I found it most convenient in detailing the transactions and remarks in harbour, to conform to the common mode of reckoning, by the natural day; but whenever the time is changed, it is always distinctly noted; so that it is to be understood, that the days are marked by the sea reckoning when it is not otherwise expressed.

Astronomers reckon their day not to begin until noon, the first commencement of Saturday being the moment that the sun is upon the meridian on Saturday, and it terminates on Sunday the instant <u>before</u> the sun is upon the meridian again.[5] Astronomical time, then, is twelve hours later than civil time, as log or sea time is twelve hours before it; but as seamen make the extant of noon to be the end of their day, and the astronomer makes it the commencement of his, it is evident that they agree in their reckonings at noon, but will date one day different at every other time: Thus, Saturday at noon is the same point of time by the seaman, the civilian, and the astronomer, but one hour afterwards the seaman will date Sunday at 1 pm, whilst the astronomer calls it Saturday at 1 hour.

The astronomical observations made at sea are inserted in the log of that day in which they were taken; but when in harbour, I usually deferred entering the observations to the end of our day, and then brought them all into one point of view; and in this case, they

---

[1] These bills summarized the duties of the personnel on board ship. They were usually posted in the crew's quarters so that individuals could check their tasks. The station bill was often referred to as the muster roll.

[2] i.e. the Royal Naval Academy. See Sullivan, 'The Royal Naval Academy at Portsmouth', pp. 311–26.

[3] Refers to the errors of the chronometer, i.e. how many seconds it was behind or ahead of Greenwich meantime on a particular date, and its rate, i.e. how many seconds it was gaining or losing on Greenwich each day. The rate could be deduced from the error during an ocean passage but only if the longitudes at both ends were accurately known. Otherwise, the rate could be deduced from the way the error changed over a stay of several days in port.

[4] Until 1805 ships' logs observed nautical time (i.e. beginning and ending at noon): they were written up at midday with the proceedings of the p.m. of the day before and a.m. of that day. Robertson, rev. Wales, *Elements of Navigation*, II, pp. 315–16.

[5] Thus astronomical time is counted continuously from noon through twenty-four hours until the following noon.

are dated according to astronomical time: but to prevent mistakes, the column of Time in such cases is always marked Astronomical time.

My object has been to follow the sea time in relating transactions and observations at sea: civil time, in relating the daily [f. 28b] occurrences and remarks in harbour; and astronomical time when detailing observations and treating upon subjects wholly astronomical.[1] 2nd the points of the compass marked in the columns of Courses, Winds, Tide, are magnetic, without any allowance for variation. In the tide, it is the point of the compass that the water runs to, that is marked: or it is the course of the tide.[2]

3rd The Soundings are marked in fathoms, and without any reduction for the rise of tide, but the quarter fathoms are generally excluded; thus 5¼ is marked 5, 4¾ is marked 4½ &c; and in the early parts of the log, the half fathoms have also been frequently dropped: At all times I have been careful not to mark the depth of water too great; and in the charts, though not in this log, the soundings are reduced to low water.

4th All the bearings contained in the remarks are magnetic, as given by the compass, unless it is otherwise particularly expressed: These bearings are always of objects that are in sight.

5th The bearings given in the column of astronomical observations are reduced to the true compass, the variation having been allowed upon them.[3]

6th The altitudes given in the astronomical observations are corrected only for the dip, and error of the instrument, and are therefore apparent altitudes. When the circle was used, the altitude is the mean result [f. 28c] from using both handles; unless it is otherwise mentioned, and then D: signifies the direct and In: the inverting handle. When the center of the sun or moon is given, it is the mean result of an equal number of altitudes of the upper and lower limits: but this relates not to lunar observations.[4]

7th It may be taken as a general rule, that the astronomical observations were taken by the commander when no name is expressed, the naming of other observations has, however, been sometimes neglected. Another general rule is that all observations made with Troughtons circle or with his sextant No 483 were taken by the commander; and those with 482 or 488, or with Ramsdens 932 were taken by lieutenant Flinders;[5] there

---

[1] Flinders suggested in a note here how this complexity in time reckoning might be simplified: 'This confusion in the modes of reckoning might, I should think, be in some measure obviated. The seaman is under the necessity of making noon the end of his day, that he may correct his last 24 hours run by the observation for the latitude; and I am not aware of any great inconvenience that would arise to the astronomer in making noon the termination, instead of the commencement, of his day. Such an agreement would be a considerable accommodation to the young navigator; but as each of these modes have had their origin in their respective utility, we may despair of seeing it brought about. Should it ever take place, it will be from the liberality of astronomers, whose superior knowledge will make them surmount with greater care the inconvenience which in the first cases are unavoidably attendant upon a change, even from worse to better.'

[2] Sailors described tides in relation to the compass point on which the new moon stood when the tide was full.

[3] Refers to magnetic variation.

[4] To calculate the true latitude of a celestial body, one adds the parallactic angle to the apparent altitude and from the sum deducts the refraction of the rays of light by the terrestrial atmosphere.

[5] i.e. Samuel Ward Flinders, Matthew's brother. In 1788 Edward Troughton patented his pillar-framed sextant comprising double flat bars connected by pillars. This design was popular and copied by many other instrument makers. Jesse Ramsden was one of the principal British manufacturers of scientific instruments in the second half of the 18th century. His sextant no. 932, issued to Flinders by the Board of Longitude in 1801, was a thirteen-year-old instrument. Stimson, 'The Influence of the Royal Observatory at Greenwich upon the Design of 17th and 18th century Angle-Measuring Instruments at Sea', pp. 123–30; McConnell, *Jesse Ramsden*, p. 7.

are, however, some few exceptions to both these, which, though sometimes not expressed, may be discovered with a little attention.

8th The quantities applied to the longitude of the timekeepers to reduce it to noon are sometimes deduced from the log, and sometimes from bearings, the latter being always preferred when it could be conveniently obtained.

9th The Course by log for the twenty four hours is the true course, with the variation allowed; as is the bearings of places on the columns of Bearing & distance.

10th The Latitude by dead reckoning[1] is brought on from the last observation only, but the Longitude by dead reckoning is continued from one port or place of departure to another.

11th The Longitude by *Timekeeper* is sometimes by one time keeper and sometimes taken from many. This will always be learned from the column of astronomical observations where the time keepers then in use are specified.

12th The column of Variation allowed is the variation that has been applied to the different courses in the log to obtain the true course for the twenty four hours: It may not always be correct, but at the time it was supposed to be so.

13th The miles contained in the column of Set or Current are the whole differences [f. 28d] between the log on one part, and the observation for the latitude and the longitude by time keepers on the other. Currents or tides are doubtless the principal cause of these differences, especially when they are considerable; but errors in the log may occasion a part and sometimes even the whole of them; as they may at other times counteract the current, and thus reduce the quantity; but what is marked in the column is done on the supposition that the log has been correctly kept, and the general course and distance with the astronomical observations truly calculated.

14th The Error of *Timekeeper* is the last thing inserted in the log, and therefore the columns of current and bearing and distance do not include it. This error is most commonly found by dividing the quantity which the time keepers have erred between one port and another by the number of days on the passage; from hence a daily error results, the accumulation of which forms the Error of the time keepers as inserted daily.[2] The marks against the quantity in these columns express the manner in which the quantity is to be applied to the longitude by time keepers in order to obtain the correct longitude at that noon; or otherwise it is marked E*ast* or W*est*; and when it is east the error is to be subtracted; when west, to be added.

In lunar observations, when the altitudes are said to be 'from proportion' they were obtained in this manner; one altitude of each object was taken, and the corresponding time by time keeper noted, before the distances were observed, and the same thing was done afterwards; then by means of the differences between the times and altitudes before and after the distances, the altitudes of the objects at the middle time of the distances are obtained by common proportion.

---

[1] Dead reckoning (the common abbreviation for deduced reckoning) is most important for projecting the position of ships into the immediate future and for avoiding navigational hazards. It is a mathematical calculation based on direction, distance, and elapsed time.

[2] Flinders added in a note here: 'For a more particular explanation of the different modes in which these errors are sometimes found, see pages 221 to 224, and other places.'

[f. 29] Sunday 19 July 1801 from Spithead

Moderate breezes with fine weather. Culver Cliff N30°W about 5 leagues. Tacked ship and reefed the fore and mizzen topsails. Sounded in 20 fathoms. Needles point[1] North about 4 miles. Needles point NbW about 4 leagues. Light airs with fine weather. Tacked ship, outreefs and made all sail. Sounded in 27 fathoms. Cleaned below, and mustered the ships company. Set the larboard studding sails. Light breezes and hazy weather. Needles point NE¾N. Some small vessels astern but no sight of Alderny,[2] which by the latitude is not farther distant than the Needles.

☉ lower limb by *time keeper* Reflec*ting* Circle No 74	60°27′31″S
Latitude	50°12′21″N

Monday 20 July 1801 towards Madeira

Light breezes and fine weather. The spanker boom[3] being rotten was carried away by being leaned upon. The carpenters employed repairing it, and the cutter which was stove. Found 32 fathoms. St. Albans Head NNE.[4] No bottom with 30 fathoms. Light breezes with fine weather. Carrying all sail. Several sail of merchant ships in sight. Exercised the watch below at small arms. At noon, land supposed to be the Start,[5] bore NWbW½W. Light breezes and fine weather. Several sail of vessels in sight.

Var*iation* per Amp*litude*	28°43′W
Mer*idian* Alt*itude* ☉ lower limb	60°34′16″S
Latitude	49°55′00″N

[f. 30] Tuesday 21 July 1801 HM sloop *Investigator*

Light breezes and fine weather. Took departure from the Start, bearing NbE. 5 or 6 leagues. Bolt tail[6] bore NbW. Bent and set the spanker, the boom being repaired. Served slops and tobacco. Steady pleasant breezes with fine weather. Start Point 50°9′N 3°51′W. *Ditt*o weather. Stowed the anchors and unbent the cables. Worked between decks. Employed in placing the boats more conveniently in the quarters. At noon, moderate breezes and fine weather. Set larboard studding sails. A sail in sight, south.

☉ Lo*we*r Limb by Troughton Circle No 74	61°3′55″
Latitude	49°14′2″

Wednesday 22 July

Hazy weather. Made the private signal[7] to four three-decked men of war; and answered their signal No. 275 and 84. In studding sails. Spoke the *Windsor Castle* Vice Admiral Mitchell[8] and went on board by desire. At 5½ returned. Cheered the admirals ship and

---

[1] A narrow chalky peninsula on the west of the Isle of Wight, with 395 foot cliffs. A lighthouse was erected here by Trinity House in 1786 to warn ships of the rocks on their approach to Portsmouth and Southampton water.

[2] The most northerly of the British Channel islands (49°42′N, 2°11′W), part of the bailiwick of Guernsey.

[3] i.e. a boom to which the spanker (fore-and-aft) sail is attached.

[4] St Alban's Head (50°34′N, 2°03′W) is 3 miles south-west of Swanage, Dorset. Flinders, *A Voyage to Terra Australis*, I, p. 156, includes observations on the variation of the compass off St Alban's Head.

[5] Start Point (50°13′N, 3°38′W), Devon.

[6] A headland in Devon (50°14′N, 3°52′W).

[7] i.e. a custom-designed flag to identify the owner of a ship. Such a signal would only be understood by other captains having the same key.

[8] Sir Andrew Mitchell (1757–1806) was a Vice Admiral of the Blue in the Royal Navy. In 1799 he was given the command at Sheerness. Laughton, rev. Webb, 'Mitchell, Sir Andrew', pp. 391–2.

made all sail again. Exercised great guns and small arms and fired 4 rounds. Fresh breezes and fine weather. Several sail in sight. Moderate and hazy weather. Made and shifted sail occasionally. Employed in little jobs about the rigging. Exercised the marines at small arms. Light breezes with fine weather.

Meri*dian* alt*itude* ☉ centre	62°10′13″S
Latitude	47°55′54″N

[f. 31] Thursday 23 July from England towards Madeira

Moderate and fine weather, a little hazy. A strange sail in the SSW. Fresh breezes and cloudy. At 8, two luggers,[1] apparently privateers, hove in sight. NWbW. They fired a shot to leeward, shewed English colours and steered towards us, one ahead and the other a stern. Towards 9, they fired 2 guns, perhaps to bring us to. We had hoisted the pendant and ensign,[2] and now took in all studding sails and cleared for action, but still kept on our course. Seeing our preparations, at 9 they hauled to the wind. Exercised marines at small arms with powder. Made all sail again. Steady breezes and hazy weather.

Meri*dian* alt*itude* ☉ Lower Limb Troughton	63°40′7″
Latitude	46°13′52″

By log		Latitude North		Longitude West						
Course	Distance	DR	Obs	DR	TK 1736	Var allowed	Set or current	Barom below	Bearings &c	Error of TK
S37°W	117	46°23′	46°14′	9°16′	8°32′	28W	9S 10E	30.18 30.11	Cape Finisterre S9°W 204 miles	+10′8″

Friday 24 July

Fresh breezes and cloudy. In royals and top gallant sails. At dusk in fore top gallant sail. Double reefed the fore and mizzen topsails, and bent the main sail. Fresh breezes with dull hazy weather. Strong breezes and cloudy with heavy rain. In all studding sails. In main top gallant sail. Strong breezes with some running. Double reefed the main topsail. Bent the main staysail. A considerable sea from the NE. Fine weather. Set the jib, mainsail, main top mast staysail, and top gallant sails; and out 2nd reef of the main topsail. At noon strong breezes and fine weather, with haze. No vessels or land in sight.

Meri*dian* Alt*itude* ☉ Lower Limb	65°52′28″S
Latitude	43°48′7″N

By log		Latitude North		Longitude West						
Course	Distance	DR	Obs	DR	TK 1736	Var allowed	Set or current	Barom below	Bearings &c	Error of TK
S28°	171	43°43′	43°48′	11°10′	10°21′	28°W	5N 2E	30.02 30.19	Cape Finisterre S39°E	+12′2″

[1] Small sailing vessels with lugsails (four-cornered sails) set on two or more masts.

[2] A pendant is usually triangular in shape whereas a naval ensign has an oblong shape, resembling a flag and distinguishing a nation.

[f. 32] Saturday 25 July HM sloop *Investigator*

Fresh breezes with squally weather. Made more sail. Set fore topmast and lower studding sails. More moderate. Set royals and main top gallant studding sails. Carried away the fore top gallant mast, got another up and rigged it and set the sail again. Set jib[1] and staysails and took in the main royal and top gallant and studding sails. Fresh breezes and cloudy weather. Took in studding sails occasionally. Moderate breezes and cloudy weather. Washed ship below and sailed with stoves. Noon, fine weather. Carrying all sail.

Meri*dian* alt*itude* ☉ Lowe*r* Lim*b* T*roughton* Circle inwa*rd*   67°46′10″S[2]
Lat*itude*   41°42′32″N

		Latitude North		Longitude West						
Course	Distance	DR	Obs	DR	TK 1736	Var allowed	Set or current	Barom below	Bearings &c	Error of TK
S29°W	146	41°40′	41°43′	12°46′	11°45′	27°W	3N 13E	30.34 30.36	Funchal Road S26°W 202 leagues	+14′4″

Sunday 26 July

Light breezes with fine weather. The reefs out and studding sails set. Cloudy weather. At 10½ saw a vessel standing towards us. Made the private signal, which not being answered, took in all studding sails and cleared at quarters. At 11 fired a shot across her, tacked ship and spoke a brig from Lisbon to Stockholm. At 11½ made all sail again. Fresh breezes and cloudy. In all but fore topmast studding sail. Saw a brig standing to the eastward. In fore topmast studding sail. Squally with rain at times. In top gallant sails. Variable airs with cloudy weather. Set top gallant sails and royals. D*itt*o. Weather. Cloudy weather with haze. No observation at noon for the latitude.

		Latitude North		Longitude West						
Course	Distance	DR	Obs	DR	TK	Var allowed	Set or current	Barom below	Bearings &c	Error of TK
S30°W	86	40°28′	–	13°42′	–	26°W	8½°S 1½°W	30.22 30.20	–	–

[f. 33] Monday 27 July from England towards Madeira

Moderate breezes and cloudy weather. Set the staysails. In royals and mizzen top gallant sail. Saw 2 sail steering to the northeastward. Squally. In first reefs, otherwise made and shortened sail occasionally. Fresh breezes and cloudy weather. Moderate breezes. Set starboard studding sails and royals. Fine weather. Aired below with stores. Employed

---

[1] A triangular staysail set ahead of the foremast.

[2] Troughton's reflecting circle had three handles which could be fixed in different positions, facing both inwards and outwards, for ease of observation. It was usual to take several observations of the same object using different parts of the circular scale and average them, to increase accuracy. Photographs and a description of a similar instrument to the one used by Flinders can be seen on the National Maritime Museum website (http://collections.rmg.co.uk/collections/objects/42283.html).

pointing a new foresail, painting the cutter over the quarter, and airing some boatswains stores. Exercised the watch below at small arms. Moderate breezes and cloudy. Carrying all sail.

Meri*dian* alt*itude* ☉ Lowe*r* Lim*b* Troug*hton* Circle	70°39′55.5″
Latitude	38°23′21″N

By log		Latitude North		Longitude West						
Course	Distance	DR	Obs	DR	TK	Var allowed	Set or current	Barom below	Bearings &c	Error of TK
S26°W	121	38°39′	38°23′	14°50′	13°46′	24°W	8½S 1½W	30.25 30.19	Funchal Road in Madeira S26°W 128 leagues	+17′6″

Tuesday 28 July

Moderate breezes and fine weather. Employed pointing a second suit of sails. Moderate and cloudy weather. Hauled up for an hour to get a fair sight of Antares[1] and the Moon, for lunars.[2] See following page. Took in all the studding sails. Set mizzen to gallant sail. A sail in sight NbW. Cloudy weather. Employed pointing a second suit of sails. At noon, the strange sail ahead carrying studding sails and steering about south. Moderate breezes and fine weather.

Meri*dian* alt*itude* ☉ up*per* limb	72°39′16″
Latitude	36°40′44″

By log		Latitude North		Longitude West						
Course	Distance	DR	Obs	DR	TK 1736	Var allowed	Set or current	Barom below	Bearings &c	Error of TK
S20°W	98	36°51′	36°41′	15°31′	14°32′ 14°53′	25°W	10S 5W	30.20 30.15	Funchal Road S29°W 278 miles	+19′3″
				Lunars						

[f. 34] Being much surprised at the magnitude of west variation, and doubting whether a change of place did not materially affect the compasses, Mr Thistle took the following sets of variations upon the booms between the fore and main masts, and I took the following on the center of the binnacle. Place of obser*vatio*n Latitude 38° 01′N Longitude 14° 00′W By time keeper.

---

[1] A brilliant constellation set within the Milky Way. Its red colour is similar to that of Mars.
[2] i.e. lunar distances, to determine longitude at sea.

On the binnacle			On the boom		
Mag Azimuth	Sun (apparent)	Variation West	Mag Azimuth	Sun center (true)	Variation West
N 52°00′W 51 7	15°33′ 14 45	25°38′ Walker No 1 25 56 ditto turned 25 47 mean	N 56°20′W 57 4	19°35′ 18 28	22 00 Walker No 1 22 34 turned 22 17 mean
N 50°50′W 49 53	13°51′ 13 6	25 33 Adams compass[1] 25 55 turned 25 44 mean	N 56°50′W 57 35	17 07 16 22	21 48 Adams compass 20 29 turned 21 9 mean
N 49°25′W 49 45	12 14 11 47	26 5 Walker No 2 25 5 turned 25 35 mean	N 56°50′W 58 30	15 24 14 6	20 34 Walker No 2 17 56 turned 19 15 mean
N 49°53′W 48 25	10 47 10 10	24 10 Walker No 3 25 11 turned 24 41 mean	N 54°55′W 53 50	13 33 13 7	21 05 Walker No 3 21 50 turned 21 27 mean
Mean of six variations By inspection		25 46 Walker Compass	No variation taken by inspection of Walkers compass on the boom		
N 47°10′W 45 50	8° 51′ 8 17	25 24 Ditto 26 18 turned	N 54°20′W 53 5	11 41 10 55	26 16 Walker Compass 20 55 turned 20 35 mean
Whole mean		25 34 West	Whole mean		20 57 West

Towards midnight observed distances of star Antares from moon's far limb

Apparent time of observations deducted from the following altitudes for the timekeeper 10 hours 48′00″	Apparent time 2nd set 11 hours 2′8″
	Apparent calculated 12 hours 6′0″
apparent altitude observed 13 hours 49′22″	Moon center observed 23 hours 14′49″
Moon center 20 hours 58′7″	Incorrect distance 91 hours 20′53″
Distance Time Keeper No. 74 incorrect (of limbs)	Longitude 8 hours 12′ A.M. 14 hours 56′45″W
	Both sets 14 hours 49′29″W
91 hours 13′43″	+ 3′20″
Error of tables in longitude 7′45″	At noon July 28 14 hours 52′49″W
Longitude at 8 hours 12′ A.M. 14 hours 42′12″	

Wednesday 29 July

Moderate breezes with fine weather. Set the top gallant and fore topmast studding sails. In top gallant studding sails. In first one of the topsails. Fresh breezes and cloudy weather. Fresh breezes with light airs alternately, with dark cloudy weather. Squally with rain. In jib, staysails, top gallant sail, mainsail and spanker. Made sail again gradually, as the wind permitted. Set starboard studding sails and royals. Out first reefs. Cleaned between decks and aired with stoves. Employed pointing sails. Moderate breezes with fine weather. Looking out for the eight stones, but see nothing.[2]

[1] An azimuth compass made by George Adams, a mathematical instrument and globe maker in London.
[2] The 'eight stones' were a natural hazard in the Atlantic Ocean to the north of Madeira.

Mer*idian* alt*itude* ☉ Center T*roughtons Circle*   74°14'9"S
Latitude   34°36'6"N

| By log | | Latitude North | | Longitude West | | | | | | |
Course	Distance	DR	Obs	DR	TK	Var allowed	Set or current	Barom below	Bearings &c	Error of TK
S13°W	118	34°46'	34°46'	16°4' Lunars	15°7' 15°28'	24°W	10S 2W	30.04 30.10	Island Porto Santo[1] S33½°W 110 by lunars	+21'2"

[f. 35] Thursday 30 July from England towards Madeira

Light breezes with fine weather. Carrying all sail but fore studding sail which was now set. We have the mortification to find the ship makes two inches of water per hour. This leak commenced yesterday and keeps increasing something.[2] Saw a strange sail to the ESE. At half past two, having run to near the latitude of a rock or shoal off Porto Santo, hove to and tried the soundings with 70 fathoms, but got no ground. Light breezes and fine weather, with a swell from the NW. Cleaned below and aired with stoves. Mustered the ships company. At noon light breezes with fine weather. All the plain sails[3] set, the royals excepted.

Mer*idian* alt*itude*   75°15'8"S
Latitude   33°5'0"N

| By log | | Latitude North | | Longitude West | | | | | | |
Course	Distance	DR	Obs	DR	TK	Var allowed	Set or current	Barom below	Bearings &c	Error of TK
S5°W	81	33°15'	33°5' by lunars	16°13' oppos	15°9' 15°18'	23°W	10S 7E	30.06 30.17	Porto Santo by lunars W7°S 20 leagues	+22'9"

---

[1] The northernmost and easternmost island of the Madeira archipelago (33°4'N, 16°20'W), known to the Portuguese since 1420. Situated 31 miles north-east of Madeira Island.

[2] Perhaps an error for 'increasing somewhat'.

[3] i.e. any of the working sails of a vessel.

Observations of ☉ east ☽ taken AM July 30 by the commander

TK No 1736	☉Lower Limb	☽Upper Limb	Observed Distance uncorrected	No of sights	Instrument Used	Longitude West
	Apparent altitudes from proportion					
24h3′23″	34°40′42″	28°3′5″	115°32′30.5″	4	T Circle 74 both handles[1]	15°18′45″
21h14′35.6″	37°00′54″	25°50′54″	115°27′39.6″	5	T Sextant No 482	15°18′28.5″
21h21′50.8″	38°31′10″	24°11′6″	115°24′11″	5	Ditto 483	15°24′03″
21h28′47″	39°53′42″	23°2′50″	115°21′33″	4	Circle 74 both handles	15°12′30″
					Mean longitude	15°18′27″W[2] 0′36″
					At noon July 30	15°17′51″W
21h34′35.5″	41°10′49″	Apparent time	20h31′29.9″	2	Circle 74 both handles	15°9′40.5″W 36″
					At noon July 30	15°9′4.5″

Time keeper to the east of these lunar observations   8′46.5″

To reduce the lunars up to Funchal by the new error and rates found there, see page before August 8

The Connaisance des temps[3] calls Funchal in 16°56′00″W

Time keeper	21h34′35.5″
New error	+ 5′53.61″
Mean Greenwich time	21h40′29.11″
Ships ditto	20h37′31.58″
Error longitude by TK	15°44′24″ = 1h2′57.61″
	17°6′15″ Longitude Funchal
	1°21′51″ λ to Funchal
	15°17′51″ Lunars
	16°39′42″W Longitude of Funchal by these lunars; but see page 39.

[f. 36] Friday 31 July from England

Moderate breezes with fine weather. At 1½ tacked ship but finding a heavy swell stopping her way and the ship lying up very ill. Tacked again to the southward. Saw land from the mast head to the NW (by compass) supposed to be Porto Santo.

Light breezes with fine weather. Light airs and calms. A still long swell from the NNW. Saw land supposed to be Porto Santo. NWbN. Bent the cables, and afterwards cleaned

[1] The standard arrangement when taking altitudes with a reflecting circle was to have two handles attached on opposite sides of the instrument, so that a number of measurements could be taken in quick succession at different points on the circle and averaged.

[2] A note adds: '–16.1′ error of timekeeper.'

[3] A reference to the French nautical almanac, with astronomical observations, which first appeared in Paris in 1679. It was reprinted and used many times down to the early 20th century. The context of this publication is discussed in Boistel, *L'astronomie nautique au XVIIIe siècle en France*.

below. At noon light airs and fine weather. Find the ship makes less water this 12 hours, being more upright.[1]

Meridian altitude ☉ center by Troughtons Circle with both handles   75°48′54″S
Latitude   32°32′24″

		Latitude North		Longitude West						
Course	Distance	DR	Obs	DR	TK 1736	Var allowed	Set or current	Barom below	Bearings &c	Error of TK
S31°W	28	32°41′	32°32′	16°30′	15°16′	2 points	9S 10E	30.09 30.10	Dezertas seen WNW by compass	+24′7″

Saturday 1 August

Landed down the boat, and examined the seams and butts near the waters edge to find the cause of the leak, but could find none, except the seams being somewhat open. Picked up a small hawks-bill turtle. At 4 sounded with 200 fathoms but found no bottom: the middle line breaking, lost the head and 2 lines. Hoisted up the boat. On a light air springing up at 6 made sail, but the long northerly swell stops the ships way considerably.

Light airs and cloudy. We find the ship now make 3 inches only in 12 hours, which I attribute to her being upright; the leak or leaks appearing to be above the waters edge. Saw the land and made sail for it. At 6, the southernmost Dezerta. WbN½N. Porto Santo N½W Northernmost Dezerta NW½W apparently from 6 to 7 leagues distant.[2]

Light breezes with fine weather. All sail set that would draw. On the wind shifting to the southward, hauled up to windward of the Dezertas. Saw a turtle, lowered down the boat but was too late. At noon, extremes of the Dezertas N71° to 41°W off shore 8 or 9 miles. East extreme of Madeira N31°W Porto Santo N13°E.

Meridian altitude Sun Lower Limb Sextant 482   75°24′57″S
Latitude   32°24′39″N
South end of South Dezerta W2°S 3 leagues   20″N
Latitude of South Dezerta   32°24′19″N

		Latitude North		Longitude West				
Course	Distance	DR	Obs	DR	TK 1736	Var allowed	Set or current	Barom below
W4°N	20	32°30′	32°25′	16°46′	–	2 points	5S 6W	30.14 30.20

[1] Flinders, *A Voyage to Terra Australis*, I, p. 157, notes: 'we had the mortification to find the ship beginning to leak so soon as the channel was cleared, and in the last three days she had admitted three inches of water per hour. The seams appeared sufficiently bad, especially under the counter and at the butt ends, for the leak to be attributable to them; and as less water came in when the ship was upright than when heeling to a beam wind, I hoped the cause need not be sought lower down.'

[2] The three uninhabited Desertas islands lie 15½ miles off the eastern tip of Madeira island (32°40′N, 16°45′W). The two referred to here are Deserta Grande (32°32′N, 16°31′W) and Bugió (32°25′N, 16°29′W).

[f. 37] Sunday 2 August towards Madeira, in the *Investigator*

Light airs and fine weather. Caught another small turtle. In studding sails, and up courses. At dusk, the south point of the south Dezerta. N56°W about 3 leagues. Easternmost part of the Island Madeira N24°W. Light airs inclinable to calm. Set studding sails. Drizzling rain at times. South end of the southernmost Dezerta NNE 2 or 3 leagues. Extremes of Madeira N½W to NNW½W. Lowered down the cutter and went in her with the naturalist and draftsman to examine the nearest Dezerta.[1] At noon, sultry weather. Extremes of the Dezertas N30°½ & probably W to N47½E distance about 3 or 4 leagues.[2]

		Latitude North		Longitude West						
Course	Distance	DR	Obs	DR	TK	Var allowed	Set or current	Barom below	Bearings &c	Error of TK
W4°N	19½	32°24′	32°11′ by JT	17°9′	16°7′ by JT	21°	13S 6W	30.19 30.23		+28′2″

Monday 3 August

Calm with cloudy weather. Light airs. Saw a strange brig NNW. At 6 moderate and cloudy. The Dezertas NE½N to ENE. Shewed a blue light for the boat and tacked ship. Shortened sail. At 9 the boat came on board. Hoisted her up and made sail on the starboard tack. Center of Madeira NbE about 4 leagues. Being taken aback, filled and stood to the eastward. Light breezes and cloudy at 4½ tacked ship.

Fresh breezes at times from NE which is the bare wind in the offing. At other times light airs from the SW and off the land. The swell from the *North* Eastward. Working up into Funchal Bay[3] the tide or current running to the NE observed an English man of war (supposed the *Argo*[4]) a transport and several small vessels in the road. At noon Funchal NNW 7 or 8 miles.

---

[1] This was Bugió. Vallance, Moore and Groves, eds, *Nature's Investigator*, p. 55.

[2] Rough Journal, I, f. 85, adds: 'The weather being fine and calm this morning, accompanied by Mr Brown, Mr Bauer and *Lieutenant* Flinders, I took the cutter and went away from the ship with the intention of examining the southmost of the rocky island, called Dezertas. In our way, we saw a great number of brown gulls with white breasts. I shot seven of these and the first, to our surprise, had about 1½ fms of brass wire bound round one wing. There were smaller birds flying round, resembling the sooty petrel. We left the ship at 9½, but owing to the distance being more than we expected, did not get on shore until 3 o clock, on the SW part of the island. The cliffs overhang, but there was a low ledge under them upon which we landed with difficulty. The shore was too barren to produce amusement even to a naturalist. There appeared to be fish near the rocks but we could only stop to eat. The deep water prevailed almost under the shade of the cliffs. The mass was somewhat stratified irregularly, and had a mixture of iron stone. The base underneath was black and honeycombed, and had certainly been in the fire. I judged it to be basaltic. We found no water in the spot where we landed, or any signs of inhabitants, a few small birds about the cliffs excepted, like canaries. A gully amongst the cliffs appeared to have been cut out by streams and water from the top, during rains. We did not get on board until 9 in the evening. We saw no turtle either going or returning.' Further details on this short expedition are supplied in Flinders, *A Voyage to Terra Australis*, I, p. 157.

[3] Funchal (32°38′N, 16°55′W), the capital city of Madeira, was the first proper port of call for the *Investigator*. Its bay was an open roadstead.

[4] Bowen took command of this fifth-rate naval vessel in March 1798, Laughton, rev. Lambert, 'Bowen, James', pp. 911–12.

By log		Latitude North		Longitude West						
Course	Distance	DR	Obs	DR	TK	Var allowed	Set or current	Barom below	Bearings &c	Error of TK
-	-	-	-	-	-	-	-	30.22 30.31	-	-

[f. 38] **Tuesday 4 August from England into Funchal Road**

Light airs off the land and from the SW and fresh breezes from the NE. Working up the bay. At 2 lowered down the boats and sent them ahead to tow. A Portuguese ship of war and an American brig working in at the same time. Guard boat from the *Argo* came on board. At 4 came to with the boat lower in 22 fathoms and moored with a kedge. Brazen head[1] S71°E Loo Fort[2] N12°W being N85°W offshore ¼ or ½ mile. Waited upon captain Bowen[3] of His Majestys Ship *Argo*, and sent an officer to wait upon the governor. Keeled the ship in the evening to ascertain the quantity of water that she will admit at the lower seams in the larboard side; and found that she took more than 3 inches per hour.

AM. Light airs off the land. Carpenters employed caulking two seams above the copper all round the ship. Struck the fore and main topmasts, examined the rigging and got up other masts. Sent empty casks on shore to be filled with water by Portuguese boats. The commander waited upon His Excellency the governor of Madeira.[4]

By log		Latitude North		Longitude West		
Course	Distance	DR	Obs	DR	TK 1736	Error of TK
			32°30'		16°22'42" +33'18" 16°56'00"	33'18"

Wednesday 5 August

Moderate sea breezes with fine weather. Employed rigging the topmasts. AM. light land breezes during the night and sea breezes about 8 AM. Received 6 tons of water by the Portuguese boats and sent empty casks on shore. Unlashed the casks on the lower deck, washed and aired with stoves. Received 212 lbs of fresh beef. Employed scraping the topmasts and as before mentioned.[5]

---

[1] The eastern entrance to Funchal Bay, also known as Garajao.

[2] On Loo Rock, by the western shore of Funchal Bay.

[3] James Bowen (1751–1835), later a rear-admiral. He was the commander of the British regiment on Madeira at the time. Vallance, Moore and Groves, eds, *Nature's Investigator*, p. 57; Laughton, rev. Lambert, 'Bowen, James', pp. 911–12.

[4] During the friendly British occupation of Madeira in the French revolutionary and Napoleonic wars, William Henry Clinton, a British colonel, served as governor of Madeira between July 1801 and March 1802. Healey, 'Clinton, Sir William Henry', pp. 153–4; Gregory, *The Beneficent Usurpers*, p. 48.

[5] Rough Journal, I, f. 89, adds: 'The preceding AM I waited upon the consul, Joseph Pringle es*quire* and arranged matters for our being supplied with fresh beef, water, and a small quantity of wine. A Portuguese boat was immediately sent off for the water casks, and a bullock ordered to be killed for tomorrow morning. The

Thursday 6 August

Light hazes and cloudy: heavy clouds hanging over the mountains at the back of the town. Carpenters employed caulking the ship as before. Employed principally in cleaning on the lower deck resecuring the casks, getting the shut cable out of the forehold upon the lower deck and putting casks and various things in its place. Got the bread up out of the bread room to examine it and to air them. Started seven puncheons of bread from the lower deck into the bread room, and sent the casks on shore to be filled with water. Received 3 tons of water by a shore boat. Arrived His Majestys ships *Carysfort* and *Voltigeur*.[1] AM. Received 2 Hogsheads[2] of wine for the ships use. Employed in the breadroom and holds.[3]

Friday 7 August

Light winds with cloudy weather. Employed setting up the main and main topmast rigging and in lashing and securing above and below for sea. Weighed the kedge anchor and waited only for five puncheons of water to put to sea; having received 250 lbs more of fresh beef. AM. Variable breezes but afterwards moderate sea breeze. Employed cleaning the ship. Loosed the topsails and fired two guns to hurry off our water and sent twice on shore after it. Entered Richard Stanley (ord*inary* seaman). At 11½ *hours* the five puncheons of water came alongside and we began clearing; but a flurry of wind coming on, the ship drove and we were obligded [*sic*] to break off fill the sails and heave at the capstan for fear of driving too near the shore. On the wind lulling again, cleared the boat, sent her away and about noon weighed and made sail with light sea breeze.

Sailed for England the *Alexander* transport No. 144 under convoy of His Majestys ship *Voltigeur*. Sent home monthly books &c by the transport.

[f. 38a] General remarks, omitted

To get into Funchal Bay, the best mode is to come between the east end of Madeira and the Dezertas. If a ship hauls close round Brazen Head she will lose the NE wind and be becalmed; she must then tow into the bay as we did; but by giving the head a good berth

---

consul announced my intention of paying my respects to His Excellency the governor, who appointed 2 o clock this day for the interview. I accordingly waited upon him in form, being introduced by the consul, who, as I spoke neither Portuguese nor French, interpreted between us. His Excellency expressed his readiness to give us every assistance, and permitted our scientific gentlemen to make excursions into, and examine the productions of, the island; which permission he had deferred giving when applied for by the officer who first waited upon him. During the short interview, I made no mention of saluting, from there being a senior officer in the road.'

[1] Captain James Bowen was in charge of this group of British vessels, which arrived at Funchal nine days before the *Investigator*. Colonel Clinton and the 85th regiment were on board the transport ships. Flinders, *A Voyage to Terra Australis*, I, p. 159. The *Voltigeur* had brought dispatches from the court at Lisbon, authorizing the governor of Madeira to receive the British troops. Flinders, *A Voyage to Terra Australis*, I, p. 160.

[2] One of several units of measure used for wine. The number of gallons of wine in a hogshead varied by the type of wine.

[3] Rough Journal, I, ff. 89–91, adds: 'In consequence of permission given by the governor, the naturalist and his assistants and the two draftsmen set off on Wednesday morning upon an excursion to the Pico Ruivo, the highest part of the island. They made some collections and sketches; but unfortunately when they were coming off on Thursday night, there was a great surf upon the shore, their boat filled, and the produce of their two days labour was mostly destroyed ... On our first arrival in the road, there was so little surf that we always landed upon the stony beach, about the center of the town; but the easterly winds then blowing very strong, in the offing, caused a swell to roll in, and it was with great caution only that we could land there with safety. The general landing place is at the back of the Loo fort.'

so as to keep the NE wind in the sails until abreast of the town, or even a little west of it, she will then get a light south west wind from the sea which will run her up to the anchorage. This sea breeze prevails 3 or 4 miles out on the south side of the island, from nine or ten in the morning in summertime to sunset. At night, if a ship wishes to get in, as she very well may, it is best to haul close round Brazen Head and tow in under the lie of the land.

The *Argo* anchored very far within the ground marked on Mr. Johnston's chart of Madeira;[1] nay, on her first arrival she ran in close to the town and came to in 7 fathoms; as did the *Carysfort*, but further to the east, off Fort St. Diego (the titular saint of the island). It was told me that there were many anchors lying in the place where the *Investigator* lay, but although we drove at least a quarter of a mile, when getting under weigh, we did not hook any.

On our first arrival, there was so little surf that we always landed upon the stony beach near the center of the town; but the easterly winds blowing strong in the offing caused a swell to roll in, and it was with great caution only that we could afterwards land there in safety. The landing place used in all seasons is at the back of the Loo fort.

The appearance of the town of Funchal from the bay is pretty and picturesque; it acquires this from being placed at the feet of those majestic hills that occupy all the central parts of the island. Behind the town, and considerably raised above it, are the country houses of many of the richer inhabitants, situated amongst groups of trees and surrounded by vineyards; these, with a convent dedicated to Nossa Seignora del Monte,[2] which is white but partly hid by the green foliage of the vines and trees, as indeed are the houses, add very much to its appearance. The town is rather large, and there was more trade and activity in it than I expected to see: The students of the college and the different ecclesiastics appear to form no inconsiderable part of the superior class of its inhabitants.[3] Several British merchants reside here, who besides their houses of business in the town have country houses behind it. I visited the hospitable seat of Mr. Murdoch[4] and thought it the prettiest place I had ever seen. The house of Joseph Pringle Esq*uire* the British consul[5] was my home when on shore, and indeed the hospitality of our countrymen prevented me from experiencing the accommodation which is afforded to strangers by a house in the town dignified with the name of hotel. Some of our gentlemen complained of it being miserable enough even without the addition of such swarms of fleas and other vermin with which they were annoyed.

---

[1] The chart was drawn by William Johnston, probably the person of that name who was a partner in Newton, Gordon & Johnston (1777–91), the oldest company in the Madeira wine trade. The abbreviated title of the chart is *Geo-Hydrographic Survey of the Isle of Madeira with the Dezertas and Porto Santo Islands geometrically taken in the year 1788. By William Johnston Esq[ui]r[e]*. This was published by W. Faden, Geographer to the King, in London in 1791.

[2] Dedicated to Our Lady of the Mount, the patron saint of Madeira.

[3] The Jesuits took precedence among the predominantly Catholic religious groups in Madeira. They had a college in Funchal. Hancock, *Oceans of Wine*, pp. 10, 29.

[4] Thomas Murdoch, A distributor of wine on Madeira. In 1791 he joined the Funchal firm of Newton, Gordon, Murdoch & Co. Ibid., p. 366; Gregory, *The Beneficent Usurpers*, p. 47.

[5] From 1754 Whitehall allowed Madeirans to elect a British representative to this position. Joseph Pringle was part of a merchant network in Madeira which dominated the consulship there in this period. Hancock, *Oceans of Wine*, pp. 144, 194, 483 n.26.

[f. 38b] One of my first requests to His Excellency the governor was to permit our scientific gentlemen to visit the island and examine its natural productions; but this was declined until my visit was paid, when after an explanation of what objects they had in view, the permission was immediately granted. On Wednesday morning the gentlemen with the assistants and servants set off with a guide to mount the Pico Ruivo, which is the highest top of the island and said to be 5067 feet above the level of the sea.[1] The labour of the journey and heat of the weather disabled them from reaching the summit so as to get back by Thursday evening as I appointed them. They made some collections and sketches, but unfortunately these got wetted and almost destroyed by the swamping of a boat in the surf when they were coming off to the ship.[2]

His Majestys Ships *Argo*, *Carysfort*, and *Falcon*, with transports, had arrived here about nine days before us, with the 85th regiment under the command of Colonel Clinton; and immediately made dispositions for attacking the town in case of resistance.[3] The commanders of the squadron and of the troops then informed the governor that His Britannic Majesty considering the probability of an attack upon the island from the French in the present fluctuating state of politics had sent troops to assist in the defence of the island, and they demanded permission for the troops to land. A council was called by the governor when it being agreed that although they should be inclined, yet no effectual resistance could be made to the English force, his assent was given for the troops to land with their tents and a place assigned for the encampment to the west of the town. The English troops were also admitted into the Loo fort and that of St. Diego which between them command the bay and the town. No alteration took place in the administration of government, the Portuguese colours were kept flying, and the trade of the town still continued in its former channel. Some little jealousy had subsisted between the Portuguese and the British, nor was the governor quite satisfied that his conduct would be approved; but the arrival of the sloop of war which came in at the same time we did, but did not anchor, had dissipated it was said the governors apprehensions by his intelligence of peace being concluded between Spain and Portugal, but that war was continued with France.[4] I understood that in consequence, war was declared against France in the town of Funchal on Wednesday evening. The *Voltigeur* brought dispatches from the court of Lisbon ordering the governor to give admission to the British troops, and it was now expected that everything relating to the defence of the island would be put into the hands of the British, as it is requisite it should be, since it appears that their

[1] It is actually 6,107 feet above sea level.

[2] Robert Brown was disappointed to find 'hardly a single new plant & scarc[e]ly any additions to Flora of the Island' made by Sir Joseph Banks when he stopped at Madeira (13–18 September 1768) on the *Endeavour* voyage. Vallance, Moore and Groves, eds, *Nature's Investigator*, p. 59.

[3] Nine days before the *Investigator* arrived at Madeira, a British force had landed there to defend the island against the French after asking the island governor's permission. The Portuguese governor of Madeira was José Manuel de Camara. While Flinders was there an order arrived from Lisbon directing acceptance of the foreign troops, which were in a precarious position as defenders. The *Argo* was a ship of the line and the other vessels were a frigate and brigantine. Ibid., pp. 57–8; Gregory, *The Beneficent Usurpers*, p. 48.

[4] During the summer of 1801 Portugal was under great pressure to join France and Spain in the latter's conflict with Britain. Spain invaded Portugal but disagreements were sorted out in a peace treaty between the two Iberian powers. The administration of Madeira remained in Portuguese hands despite the British army presence on the island. Gregory, *The Beneficent Usurpers*, p. 47.

magazines, ports, gun carriages &c. are in a state almost incapable of defence; and were the Portuguese left to themselves would most probably remain so.

[f. 39] The prices charged for our ships supplies are as follows. Water sent on board in shore boats at 7/6 per ton. Wine of a tolerable quality at 5/8 per gallon besides charges for the casks and boat hire. Fresh beef at 10d per lb which was tolerably good meat, but very ill dressed. The best Madeira was 42£ per pipe.[1] Fruit and onions were procured here in abundance and very cheap.

My occupations leaving me no time to attend to astronomical observations, I can only say that Mr. Crosley made the latitude of the ship by a single meridional altitude on board, to be 32°37′44″ North.

The timekeeper No. 1736 differed from the longitude of Funchal given in the Requisite Tables 43′32″ to the eastward; so that a part of the difference of longitude called current has been the error of the time-keeper. Its present rate of losing was found to be 11.45″, and its error 0 *hours* 7′14.95″ slower than the mean Greenwich time, at noon there August 6 1801, calling the longitude of Funchal 17°6′15″W.

To ascertain the longitude of Funchal Bay
By Mr. Crosleys observations the time keepers gave it as follows.

Arnold box *Time Keeper*	82	15°29′13″W
Ditto	176	16°16′5″
Ditto	1736	16°22′42″
Earnshaws watch	465	16°54′26″
Ditto box *Time Keeper*	520	16°41′25″
Ditto	543	16°51′56″
Mean of 3 best		6°49′16″W

By making use of Earnshaws 465[2] to reduce the preceding lunars of July 30 and the following ones of August 17 the longitude of Funchal will be as follows.

Longitude by 465 July 30 AM. was	15°29′55.5″W
By lunars east	15°18′27″
Lunars to the east	11′28.5″
which being applied to what 465 shewed at Funchal will give the longitude of that place	16°42′57.5″W
By sun west moon August 17 found in the same manner, the longitude of Funchal is	16°58′28″
Mean	16°50′43″W
Observations of east on August 2 taken by Mr. Crosley, 6 sets, ordered as above	16°32′7.5″ + 27′30″
Observations of west on August 14 & 16 4 sets by Mr. Crosley, reduced as above	16°54′11″ + 4′15″
Mean by Mr. Crosley	16°43′9″W
Mean of all	16°46′56″W

P. S.
From all the above observations it seems to be evident that the longitude 16°56′W of Funchal given by the Connaissance des Temps is nearer to the truth than the 17°6′15″

---

[1] This was considerably more than the mean price of £21 per pipe demanded by Madeira wine growers of exporters in Funchal between 1793 and 1801. Hancock, *Oceans of Wine*, p. 71.
[2] This was a pocket timekeeper, made by Thomas Earnshaw of London.

Figure 4.   H3940 Box chronometer, serial No. 520, brass / wood / steel / glass, made by Thomas Earnshaw, London, England, 1801, used by Captain Matthew Flinders, 1801–3. Collection: Powerhouse Museum, Sydney. Photo: Marinco Kojdanovski.

West given by the requisite Tables; and taking this to be the case the error of Arnolds watch No. 1736 on our arrival will be 33′18″ of longitude to the east; which being contracted between July 17th at Greenwich noon and August 4 at 21 hours (astronomical account) will give the daily error of the watch in longitude to have been 1′46.4″ to the eastward, whence the quantities contained in the preceding columns entitled Error of *Time Keeper* are deduced.

Note. The longitude 16°56′ of the Connaissance des temps is from observations of Jupiters satellites.[1] Now I have before found, that lunar observations do often, if not always, give a longitude more easterly than Jupiters satellites, even to 15′ of longitude; I am therefore of opinion that the mean of the above results will be the longitude of Funchal, nearly as correct as lunar observations will give it, in the present state of the lunar tables.

[f. 40] Saturday 8 August from Madeira

Finding the ship set in shore by the tide, and not being able to keep the ships head out after we lost the SW wind, towed with the boat until we got the true offing wind. Strong breezes. In top gallant sails and close reefed the fore and main topsails and handed the mizzen. At 3 took our departure Funchal town NbE 3 leagues, having previously hoisted up the boats and stowed the anchors. At 6 more steady and moderate; set jib and mizzen topsail and out close reef of the fore topsail.

Strong breezes and cloudy with some following sea. In jib and mainsail.[2] Moderate breezes with rain. Set mainsail &c. Out 3rd and 2nd reefs of the fore and main, and 1st reef of the mizzen topsails. Out 1st reefs of the main and mizzen topsails. Fresh breezes and cloudy. Cleared below and aired with stores. Set fore-topmast and fore studding sails. Moderate breezes and cloudy weather. We find the ship continues to admit water but at the rate of an inch per hour only. A very dull observation taken today but not thought worthy of notice.

		By log		Latitude North		Longitude West					
Course	Distance	DR	Obs	DR	TK	Var allowed	Set or current	Barom below	Bearings &c	Error of TK
S13°W	161½	30°1′	–	17°48′	–	20°W	16N 2E	30.22 30.22		

Sunday 9 August

Moderate breezes and cloudy weather. Set all studding sails &c that would draw. Shifted studding sails occasionally. At dusk, in royals and 1st reef of fore and mizzen topsails. In studding sails. Fresh breezes and cloudy weather with haze. Took in the top gallant sails. Fresh breezes and cloudy. Set top gallant sails. Saw the Island of Palma SE½E 10 or 12 leagues.[3] Set studding sails. Last 2 log lines. Several Albacores[4] about. Served out lines and hooks to the officers and ships company. Cleaned below and mustered the people clean. Served lemon juice and sugar in the grog. Light breezes and hazy weather.

Meridian altitude Sun Lower Limb Theodolite Circle direct[5]   77°19′25″S

Latitude   28°21′33″N

---

[1] Jupiter has the largest number of satellites in the solar system. In 1610 Galileo observed four of these moons and proved them to be the first objects to orbit a body that was neither the Earth nor the Sun.

[2] The most important sail, raised on the main mast of a vessel.

[3] Las Palmas (28°7′N, 15°25′W) in the Canary Islands.

[4] A species of tuna.

[5] The theodolite had a vertical circular scale and telescopes, with coloured filters, for viewing the sun or landmark and taking its altitude directly from the circle, as opposed to a sextant which used a reflected image.

		Latitude North		Longitude West						
By log										
Course	Distance	DR	Obs	DR	TK 1736	Var allowed	Set or current	Barom below	Bearings &c	Error of TK
S26°W	144	27°51′	28°22′	18°59′	18°55′	19°W	15N 2E	30.06 30.08	Town of Ferro[1] S60°E 10 miles	−8′

[f. 41] Monday 10 August towards Cape of Good Hope

Moderate breezes and hazy: shifted studding sails occasionally. Wetted decks. Many flying fish. In royals. Took in the starboard studding sails and set jib and staysails. Set the starboard studding sails again. Moderate breezes. Dew falling. Light breezes and fine weather. Set the main royal. The after main top mast crosstree[2] having lifted from the trestle tree. At 9 took in all the sail on the main mast. Got down top gallant mast and struck the topmast. Lifted the rigging, secured the crosstree, swayed up all again, set up the rigging, and at noon, made all sail as before. Moderate breezes with fine weather. Several flying fish about the ship.

		Latitude North		Longitude West						
By log										
Course	Distance	DR	Obs	DR	TK 1736	Var allowed	Set or current	Barom below	Bearings &c	Error of TK
S27°W	121½	26°34′	26°37′	20°01′	19°55′	18°W	3N 2E	30.03 30.09	St Antonio[3] SW end S27°W	−7′

Tuesday 11 August

Moderate breezes with fine weather, all sail set. Variation per azimuth on the binnacle by Mr. Thistle 19°33′W. Steady moderate breezes and cloudy weather. In larboard fore topmast studding sail and main royal. Steady breezes and fine weather. Set the large studding sail called a logic.[4] Found the spanker boom to be sprung in two places. Sailmakers employed making a second logic. Cleared [sic] below. Steady breezes and fine weather.

---

[1] Ferro (El Hierro) (27°45′N, 18°1′W) is an island rather than a town. It is the smallest and most westerly of the Canary Islands.

[2] One of two horizontal crosspieces at the upper ends of the lower masts.

[3] The north-westernmost of the Cape Verde Islands (17°05′N, 25°10′W). Flinders provides more detail about passing the island in *A Voyage to Terra Australis*, I, pp. 25–6.

[4] This was intended to increase the speed of the ship.

	By log	Latitude North		Longitude West						
Course	Distance	DR	Obs	DR	TK 1736	Var allowed	Set or current	Barom below	Bearings &c	Bearing & distance
S27°W	142	24°30′	24°34′	21°13′	21°3′	18°W	4N 4E	30.10 30.13	SW end of the island St Antonio S28°W dist*ant* 171 leagues	–6′

[f. 42] Wednesday 12 August From Madeira

Steady breezes with fine weather. Began to serve one of the casks of wine to the ships company, received at Madeira. Steady breezes and cloudy weather, with haze. Took in the mizzen royal. Took in and set the main top gallant studding sail occasionally. In starboard studding sails and set the main topmast staysail and mainsail. Cleaned below and aired the cockpits with stoves. Fresh breezes and cloudy.

Me*ridian* alt*itude* Sun *Lowe*r *Lim*b circle direct   82°28′54″
Latitude   22°18′48″

	By log	Latitude North		Longitude West						
Course	Distance	DR	Obs	DR	TK	Var allowed	Set or current	Barom below	Bearings &c	Error of TK
S27°W	155	22°16′	22°19′	22°30′	22°21′	18°W	3N 1W	30.11 30.12	St Antonio bears S27½W 120 leagues	–5′

Thursday 13 August

Steady breezes and fine weather. Set staysails between the masts. Lost two log lines. Set the jib. Cloudy with drizzling rain. In all studding sails in a squall. Set the studding sails again. Fresh breezes and cloudy with haze. Cleaned between decks and aired with stoves. Moderate breezes and cloudy weather.

Me*ridian Altitude* ☉ *Lowe*r *Lim*b Circle direct   84°27′38″
Latitude   20°01′49″N

	By log	Latitude North		Longitude West						
Course	Distance	DR	Obs	DR	TK	Var allowed	Set or current	Barom below	Bearings &c	Error of TK
S28°W	159	19°59′	20°2′	23°50′	23°50′	17°W	3N 9W	30.09 30.00	SW end of St Antonio S27°W 68 leagues	–3′

[f. 43] Friday 14 August towards the Cape of Good Hope

Light breezes and hazy. Set the mizzen top gallant sail and fore top gallant studding sail. Fresh breezes with drizzling rain. Took in the main royal. Lost 2 log lines off the reel and a log ship. Set the jib. Fresh breezes and cloudy. Squally. In lower and top gallant studding sails and mizzen top gallant sail. Set studding sails again at daylight. Fresh breezes and cloudy with haze. Cleaned below and aired with stoves. In studding sails. Exercised great guns and small arms. At noon fresh breezes and fine weather, with haze; many flying fish about. Some swell from the eastward.

Meridian Altitude ☉ Lower Limb Circle direct handle[1]   86°2′35″S
Latitude   18°8′25″N

		Latitude North		Longitude West						
Course	Distance	DR	Obs	DR	TK 1736	Var allowed	Set or current	Barom below	Bearings &c	Bearing & distance
S29°W	155½	17°46′	18°8′	25°10′ marked by 465	25°11′ 25°5′	16°W	22N 1W	29.95 29.98	SW end of St Antonio S5°W 68 miles	–2′

Saturday 15 August

Fresh breezes and cloudy weather. On hauling closer to the wind, took 1st reef in the main and mizzen topsails. Opened No. 41 beef cask contained 42 pieces short 8 lbs. Variation per azimuth observed. by Mr. Thistle 13°51′ West. Light airs and fine weather. Looking out for the island of St. Antonio. Hazy. At 12 hours ½ saw the land and steered for the westernmost part, leaving SW under topsails. At 2 hours, saw some lights on shore, at 3½ hours made more sail on the wind slackening. At 4 set the westernmost land SWbW apparently 6 or 7 miles but at daylight found ourselves not more than 4 or 5 from it, as we saw the surf on the rocks. Sounded with 75 fathoms.

At 8 light airs and calms with following swell. Extremes E½N to SSW½W off the nearest shore 4 miles. Saw a boat rowing in shore: hoisted a white ensign but they did not come near us. Cleaned and aired below. Sailmakers putting a 4th reef in a new main topsail. Hoisted the whale boat[2] on board to repair her. Extremes E½N to SSW off shore to the SE about 4 miles. Hazy with clouds over the land. Light variable airs and calms. Easterly swell running.

		Latitude North		Longitude West						
Course	Distance	DR	Obs	DR	TK 1736	Var allowed	Set or current	Barom below	Bearings &c	Error of TK
S28°W	60	17°4′	–	25°24′	–	14°W	1S 4W	30.00 30.04		

[1] The handles on a reflecting circle could be placed in different positions for direct and inverted observations.
[2] This was carried on the *Investigator*, and used for excursions along rivers and creeks.

[f. 44] The Island St. Antonio is of considerable height; so much so as to be seen 15 or more leagues. It appears to be rocky and excessively barren, from the sea; although it is said that the vallies are fertile, producing various fruits &c. From one of the gullies I traced a path with the glass,[1] leading over the hills; but except the boat, the light seen last night, and this path, we saw no other traces of inhabitants on this north west side, which appears to be the greatest length of the island. A very scanty portion of vegetation seemed to be sprinkled over a considerable portion of the island. From the north extreme, the north west point, which is a steep bluff, lies W½S by compass from thence to the SW extreme, which slopes from the high land to a low point. The coast seems to lie about WSW not less than 4 or 5 leagues. The south point runs sloping down from the high land also to a low point, and opened from the southwest point at south, perhaps 2 leagues asunder. Between these lies something of a bay, which may be that mentioned in Astleys voyages;[2] but we did not see the sandy beach or any symptoms of that fertility about the Island there spoken of. The principal village is said to be some days journey from this bay, so that a vessel may be there several days and nobody know it. Some land, perhaps St. Lucia,[3] opened from the south, point at SEbE½E at 5 *hours* 20′ PM. From the unlucky circumstance of losing the observation for the latitude, I can say nothing of its situation from our present observation. When on His Majestys ship *Supply* on March 21st 1795 I made the high land on the SW part of the island to lie in 17°00′ N and by the time-keeper corrected in 25°17′W but Mr. Crosley made its longitude at the same time by lunar observations (88 sights) to be 25°12′W which I take.[4] This high land is perhaps the highest part of the island, and seems to be about 5 miles within the Southwestern extreme; and about 2 inland from the north-west side of the island. There were several birds about.

Sunday 16 August
An easterly swell drifting the ship along the land: At 2, a breeze springing up, made all sail. Employed painting the 4th reef of the main topsail. The high land of the SW part of St Antonio bearing NEbE 4 leagues. In 1st reef of the topsails. In studding sails and braced up. Fine weather. Set top gallant studding sails. In starboard studding sails and set the staysails. Moderate and fine weather. Sent up every moveable from the lower deck; then washed and aired with stoves there and in the cockpits. Saw all the ships company clean then mustered and read the articles of war to them. The people dined upon deck today. At noon, moderate and fine weather.

Mer*idian* Alt*itude* ☉ Lowe*r Lim*b Circle direct	87°35′19.5″
Latitude	15°58′13″N

---

[1] i.e. telescope.

[2] See Astley, *A New General Collection of Voyages and Travels*, I, p. 674. Astley calls it 'Saint Anthony'.

[3] Santa Luzia is one of the Cape Verde Islands (16°45′N, 24°44′W).

[4] The *Reliance* and the *Supply*, a tender, were purchased for the Navy Board in 1793. On 16 February 1795 these ships left Plymouth Sound as part of a large fleet bound into the Atlantic Ocean. Flinders was the senior master's mate on the *Reliance*, taking him on his first voyage to Australia. He used the sextant and timekeeper to observe locations on the Canary and Cape Verde Islands en route to Rio de Janeiro. Estensen, *The Life of Matthew Flinders*, pp. 39–42.

| By log | | Latitude North | | Longitude West | | | | | | |
Course	Distance	DR	Obs	DR	TK 1736	Var allowed	Set or current	Barom below	Bearings &c	Error of TK
S5°W	63	16°01′	15°58′	25°30′ lunars	25°39′ 25°39′	13°W	2S 4W	30.02 30.09	Penedo de St Pedro[1] S6°E distant 303 leagues	–

[f. 45] Monday 17 August towards the Cape of Good Hope

Moderate and fine weather. Carrying top gallant sails and fore topmast studding sails. Took on the fore studding sail. Moderate and Cloudy. Light hazes and fine. Up mainsail. Out all reefs. Set royals and fore studding sail. Light breezes. Cleaned below. Sailmakers putting 3rd reef into a new mizzen topsail. Carpenters repairing the gig.[2] At noon, light breezes and fine weather, with haze. All sail set: Water very smooth.

Meridian Altitude ☉ *Lower Limb* direct   88°34′22″S
Latitude   14°40′07″N

| By log | | Latitude North | | Longitude West | | | | | | |
Course	Distance	DR	Obs	DR	TK	Var allowed	Set or current	Barom below	Bearings &c	Error of TK
S10°E	78	14°41′	14°40′	25°16′	25°32′ SF	12°W	1S 7W	30.07 30.09	Penedo de St Pedro S6½°E distant 267 leagues	–

Tuesday 18 August

Steady breezes and fine weather. Broached No. 17 brandy: marked 83 gallons 6½ short. Cloudy. In all studding sails to pick up a man that had fallen overboard. In 1st reef of the topsails and made sail again. Lightening [*sic*] from the southward. Light airs with heavy showers of rain: thunder and lightning about. Shortened sail. Set top gallant sails and mainsail. Light airs with a long southerly swell; fixed the lightening conductor. Lowered down the cutter[3] to try the current. She rode by 12 deep-sea and hand leads with 400 fathoms of line and found the log ship[4] drift N½E about ½ knot per hour. At noon tacked ship. Light airs and cloudy weather.

[1] An uninhabited small islet: see below, p. 174.
[2] This was a long, light ship's boat, usually reserved for use by the ship's captain.
[3] A ship's boat (usually single-masted) with double-banked oars and one or two lugsails.
[4] The wooden chip of a chip log, for holding the end of the log line.

By log		Latitude North		Longitude West						
Course	Distance	DR	Obs	DR	TK	Var allowed	Set or current	Barom below	Bearings &c	Error of TK
S13°E	52	13°49′	–	25°4′	–	12°W	2N 2W	30.02 30.04		

[f. 46] Wednesday 19 August from Madeira

Light airs and calms, with a swell from the southward. Hoisted up and scoured the boat. Variable airs with threatening weather. In top gallant sails. Fresh breezes with rain at times. Set top gallant sails and staysails. Light and fresh breezes alternately, with thick cloudy weather and drizzling rain. Out 1st reef of the mizzen topsail. Showers of rain occasionally. Aired between decks with stoves. Squally. In top-gallant sails and set them occasionally. Took 1st reef in the mizzen topsail. At noon moderate breezes with cloudy [weather]. The southerly swell still continues, but takes a direction somewhat from the westward.

By log		Latitude North		Longitude West						
Course	Distance	DR	Obs	DR	TK	Var allowed	Set or current	Barom below	Bearings &c	Error of TK
S38°E	32	13°24′	–	24°44′	–	1 Pt W	3N 2W	30.02 30.04		

Thursday 20 August

Variable winds and weather; drizzling rain at times. Saw the appearance of land NEbN.[1] Light breezes and cloudy: southerly swell still continuing. Up courses.[2] Lightning in NE quarter. Squally. In top gallant sails. Set courses and staysails (lower). Fresh breezes and fine weather. Set top gallant sails and upper staysails. Light breezes with rain at times. Set the starboard studding sails. Cleaned below and sent up everything to be dried. Exercised the watch below and the boats crews in the use of small arms.[3] At noon light breezes and hazy weather. A swell from the SW-ward. Served tobacco to the people.

Supplement altitude ☉ Lower Limb Sextant 482   90°30′56″N
Latitude   12°46′57″N

By log		Latitude North		Longitude West						
Course	Distance	DR	Obs	DR	TK	Var allowed	Set or current	Barom below	Bearings &c	Error of TK
S35°E	55	12°30′	12°47′	24°12′	24°34′	1 Pt	2N 1W	30.05 30.05	Penedo de St Pedro S3°E 238 miles	+5′

[1] Possibly Brava and Fogo in the Cape Verde Islands. Vallance, Moore and Groves, eds, *Nature's Investigator*, p. 60; Edwards, ed., *The Journal of Peter Good*, p. 38.

[2] The lowest square sail on each mast.

[3] Refers to firearms practice by the sailors. Edwards, ed., *The Journal of Peter Good*, p. 38.

[f. 47] **Friday 21 August towards the Cape of Good Hope**

Moderate breezes and cloudy with showers at times. Set royals and larboard studding sails. At 3, in lower studding sails, royals and mizzen top gallant sail. Fresh breezes and cloudy. Set fore studding sail. Light breezes and cloudy, with flashes of lightning. Heavy claps of thunder with vivid lightning. Two electric balls of fire fell or struck near us.[1] Shortened sail. Constant heavy rain with thunder and lightning. Caught near a ton of water by spreading the awning. The water was only fit for the stock and for washing. Fine weather. Made sail. At noon light airs and cloudy weather. All the plain sails set. Some swell from the southward. Put the officers and gentlemen to four watches to give them more time for applying to astronomy, surveying and drawing; all of which are necessary requisites to the due execution of the service in which we are employed.[2]

By Mr Thistle

| Meridian altitude ☉ Lower Limb | 89°19′46″N |
| Latitude | 11°47′45″N |

By log		Latitude North		Longitude West						
Course	Distance	DR	Obs	DR	TK	Var allowed	Set or current	Barom below	Bearings &c	Error of TK
S22°E	65	11°47′	11°48′	23°47′	–	11°W	1N	29.87 30.05		

Saturday 22 August

Light airs nearly calm. The southerly swell still runs long. Trimmed sails and set studding sails, on the breeze springing up. In studding sails, courses and staysails, preparing for a shift of wind. Light airs. Set staysails. Set the upper studding sails and main royal. Fine weather with haze. Cleaned well below. Opened all the scuttles, sprinkled with vinegar, and aired with stoves. Exercised the boats crews at small arms with powder. Lemon juice and sugar continue to be served as before. People dined upon deck, leaving the lower deck to get a thorough airing. Note. During the calm I got out the dipping needle, and as far as the motion of the ship would allow me to be correct, the inclination of the north end is 40°.[3] Meridian altitude 89°7′16″N Latitude 11°15′18″N.

[1] The nature, and even the existence, of ball lightning remains a scientific dispute. Here, however, Flinders may have used the term loosely, to refer to conventional lightning strikes.

[2] Rough Journal, I, f. 111, adds: 'This morning I gave the following order to the officers and gentlemen of the ship. The Commander being pleased with the attention that the superior officers of the ship have hitherto paid to astronomical observations, hereby directs, that during the continuance of the ship in the tropical latitudes, or until further orders, that the officers keep every fourth watch in the following rotation 1st *Lieutenant* Fowler Mr. Wolsey Mr. Lound 2nd *Lieutenant* Flinders Mr. Evans Mr. N. Bell [3rd] Mr. Thistle master Mr. Taylor Mr. T. Bell [4th] Mr. Colpitts Gun*ner* Mr. Franklin Mr. Sinclair. It is to be understood, that this arrangement is made solely with the intention of giving the officers further time to attend to astronomy, surveying, drawing, and gaining information upon such subjects as may tend to qualify them in the first degree for executing well the arduous service in which we are engaged; and the Commander therefore trusts that this accession of leisure will be applied to the purpose for which it is given. The gentlemen of the quarter deck are included in the same order, and from the same motives.'

[3] Magnetic dip or magnetic inclination is the angle made by a compass needle with the horizontal at any point on the Earth's surface. This was used to determine latitude. The range of dip is from -90° to 90°. The north end of a compass needle points downwards in the northern hemisphere (positive dip) and upwards in the southern hemisphere (negative dip). While detained in the Ile de France in 1804, Flinders wrote a detailed paper on differences in the direction of the magnetic needle during the voyage. See Flinders, 'Concerning the Differences in the Magnetic Needle', pp. 186–97.

Mer*idian* alt*itude* ☉ Lowe*r Lim*b S 483   89°7′16″N
Latitude   11°15′10″N

| By log | | Latitude North | | Longitude West | | | | | | |
Course	Distance	DR	Obs	DR	TK	Var allowed	Set or current	Barom below	Bearings &c	Error of TK
S22°E	16½	11°33′	11°15′	23°41′ By No 465	24°1′	11°W	18S	30.05 30.07	Penedo de St Pedro bears South 207 leagues	+5′

[f. 48] **Sunday 23 August** *Investigator* **from Madeira**
Calm; very light variable airs at times. The swell still continues from the southward. Broached a cask of pork No. 25, contents 53 pieces, short 16 lbs. Light breezes with rain at times. Light breezes and cloudy. Fresh breezes and squally; ship plunging a good deal to the head swell. In top gallant sails and staysails and double reefed the fore topsail. At noon variable breezes with constant rain; weather thick and duly set the main top gallant sail.[1] The difference between the thermometer upon deck and below probably arises from the inhalations from the former, being wet.

| By log | | Latitude North | | Longitude West | | | | | | |
Course	Distance	DR	Obs	DR	TK	Var allowed	Set or current	Barom below	Bearings &c	Error of TK
S38°E	39	10°45′	–	23°17′	–	10°W	2S 24E	29.98 30.03		

Monday 24 August
Variable breezes with hard rain. In main top gallant sail. Ship pitching considerably to a swell from the south-ward. In main topmast staysail. A swallow flying about the ship for these two days past.[2] Moderate breezes with fine weather.

We find that since the ship has been upon a wind on the starboard tack, she makes two inches of water per hour, as before we went into Madeira.[3]

At 12, cloudy weather. Set fore top-gallant sail and staysails. Out 1st reef of the mizzen topsail. Fitted new slings to the main yard, the old having been carried away. Cleaned below and aired with stoves. Dried the people's cloaths. At noon moderate breezes with fine weather. Swell considerably abated.

---

[1] Eight hours of 'excessive heavy rain' occurred: Edwards, ed., *The Journal of Peter Good*, p. 39.
[2] Probably the European swallow (*Hirundo rustica*) on migration. Flinders, *A Voyage to Terra Australis*, I, p. 127.
[3] Flinders noted his concern at the leaking of the ship in ibid., I, p. 27.

Meridian Altitude ☽ Lower Limb S 484   65°57′46″S
Latitude   10°31′2″
                                             −18′40″
At 29h 21′   10°12′22″
                                            − 4′54″
Noon   10°7′28″N
Variation by azimuth   12°45′00″W
by Mr Thistle

By log		Latitude North		Longitude West						
Course	Distance	DR	Obs	DR	TK	Var allowed	Set or current	Barom below	Bearings &c	Error of TK
S50°E	41	10°10′	10°7′	22°20′	21°51′ No 465	1 Pt	1S 25E	30.01 30.05		+5′

[f. 49] Tuesday 25 August towards the Cape of Good Hope

Moderate breezes with cloudy but not thick weather. Out 2nd reef of the fore top sail and set the studding sail. At dusk, in fore topmast studding sail and took a reef in the fore and mizzen topsails. Moderate breezes and cloudy. Ditto weather. Steady breezes: the weather cloudy but not thick. Out 2nd reef of the fore topsail, and set the studding sail; and let the 1st reef out of the mizzen topsail. Cleaned below, washed with vinegar and aired with stoves. Our little friend, the swallow, still keeps about the ship. Pleasant breezes with thin cloudy weather.

Meridian Altitude ☉ Lower Limb Circle direct   87°33′25″N
Latitude   8°40′8″

By log		Latitude North		Longitude West						
Course	Distance	DR	Obs	DR	TK	Var allowed	Set or current	Barom below	Bearings &c	Error of TK
S32°W	99	8°43′	8°40′	21°28′	20°40′ No 465	1 Pt	3S 19E	30.04 30.06	Penedo de St Pedro S23° West	+5′

Wednesday 26 August

Moderate breezes with light cloudy weather. Ship continues to make two inches of water per hour; but as we are satisfied of its being near the waters edge, it gives me little uneasiness. Ditto weather. Drum and fife playing as usual to the people, who generally have a dance to some kind of play every evening. Ditto weather, took in staysails between the masts. Our friend the swallow was missing this morning; two days afterwards it was found dead in my stateroom, under a bureau. Employed getting the cables out of the main hold, to get at vinegar salt &c. which was stowed under them. Moderate breezes with fine weather, much clearer than we have had it lately.

Meridian altitude Sun Lower Limb Circle direct	86°39'25"
Latitude	7°25'27"

	By log		Latitude North		Longitude West						
Course	Distance	DR	Obs	DR	TK 465	Var allowed	Set or current	Barom below	Bearings &c	Bearing & distance
S43°W	89	7°35'	7°25'	20°26'	19°10'	11°W	10S 28E	30.04 30.07	Penedo de St Pedro S41°W 150 leagues	–6'

[f. 50] Thursday 27 August *Investigator* from Madeira

Steady breezes and cloudy weather. Employed getting cables into the main hold from between decks, and coiling the cables upon deck in their place. By this alteration we gained room in the hold, have the tiers more convenient for working the cables, and do not lose any room on the lower deck.[1]

Moderate breezes and cloudy but not unpleasant weather. After breakfast, took in all the sail from the top mast, stayed it and set up the rigging afresh, then made sail under single reefs &c as before. At noon, steady breezes and cloudy weather, which keeps off much of the heat and notwithstanding the height of the thermometer we find the temperature very pleasant.

Meridian altitude ☉ Lower Limb Circle direct	85°55'22"N
Latitude	6°20'32"N

	By log		Latitude North		Longitude West						
Course	Distance	DR	Obs	DR	TK	Var allowed	Set or current	Barom below	Bearings &c	Error of TK
S44°W	78½	6°29'	6°21'	19°31'	18°1'SF	11°W	8S 14E	30.10 30.10	Penedo de St Pedro S48°W 161 leagues	+5'

Friday 28 August

Moderate breezes with cloudy weather. A swell from the SSE seems to announce the neighbourhood of the SE trade wind.[2] The ship pitching considerably, took in top gallant sails and double reefed the fore topsail. Fresh breezes and squally; hauled down the jib. Caught a noddy.[3] Instead of the top of his head being white, it was a reddish brown.

---

[1] Cable tiers were the part of the ship used to store spare rigging and cables in the hold or between decks.

[2] Trade winds, used by captains for centuries to sail ships across the oceans, blow from the south-east in the southern hemisphere.

[3] A tropical seabird (tern) of the family Sternidae.

Moderate and cloudy weather. *Ditto* weather. *Ditto* weather. Finding the ship pitched considerably, and fearing the rains and calms that prevail in the neighbourhood of the African coast, tacked ship at 11 on her falling off to leeward of SE. At noon, moderate breezes and cloudy weather. Set the jib and top gallant sails.

| Meridian altitude ☉ Lower Limb Circle direct | 85°42′33″N |
| Latitude | 5°46′43″N |

	By log									
		Latitude North		Longitude West						
Course	Distance	DR	Obs	DR	TK 465	Var allowed	Set or current	Barom below	Bearings &c	Error of TK
S38°E	69	5°45′	5°47′	18°32′	16°50′SF	10W	2N 12E	30.10 30.07	Penedo de St Pedro S56°W 173 leagues	+6′

[f. 51] Saturday 29 August towards the Cape of Good Hope

Moderate breezes and cloudy weather. Rove a new tiller rope, the old one being carried away. Tacked to the SE. Tacked again to the westward, finding the ship continued to lie up so ill. Passed about 3 miles to windward of a strange sail, on the other tack. On the ship falling off, tacked at one to the south-eastward. Light breezes and cloudy, with some haze. Cleaned well below and aired with stoves. Got up the armourers forge. *Ditto* weather. The water considerably smoother than it has usually been lately.

| Meridian Altitude ☉ Lower Limb Circle direct | 85°30′29″N |
| Latitude | 4°52′40″ |

	By log									
		Latitude North		Longitude West						
Course	Distance	DR	Obs	DR	TK	Var allowed	Set or current	Barom below	Bearings &c	Error of TK
South	16	5°30′	5°32′	18°32′	16°38′ SF Th[1]	10W	2N 12E	30.08 30.10	Penedo de St Pedro S59° West 172 leagues	+6′

Sunday 30 August

Light breezes and cloudy weather. Heavy clouds hanging to the eastward. Fine weather. Fresh breezes and cloudy. Cleaned below. Mustered the ships company at quarters, and their stations for tacking and unmooring ship; and saw them all clean. At noon, light

---

[1] Samuel Flinders with a theodolite.

breezes and cloudy weather; with some head swell. Weeks expenditure of water is 3 tons. Remaining 52.

Vari*ation* per azim*uth* observed by Mr Thistle on the starboard quarter

Meri*dian* alt*itude* ☉ Lo*we*r L*imb* C*ircle* direct   85°30′29″N

Latitude   4°52′4″N

| | | Latitude North | | Longitude West | | | | | | |
Course	Distance	DR	Obs	DR	TK	Var allowed	Set or current	Barom below	Bearings &c	Error of TK
S61°E	60	5°3′	4°52′	17°40′	15°38′	1 Point	11S 8E	30.10 30.14	Penedo de St Pedro S65°W 185 leagues	+6′

[f. 52] <u>Some remarks upon the winds</u>

I find but one good parallel to our south-westerly winds in these regions, which is in Captain Cooks 2nd voyage. They carried him so far to the eastward that he crossed the line in about 9° West.[1]

The voyage of Pérouse indeed affords something like it, and time of year was not very different; but he does not seem, from his table or routes to have had them so constantly from the SW.[2]

I am myself an advocate of crossing the equator well to the west, as from 24° to 27° but this wind from the SW militates much against it; however, it favours a desire I have to ascertain the situation of one or both of the islands called Sable Island or St Pauls, and Penedo de St Pedro; as also an isle neighbouring to the former.[3] My knowledge of these is intirely gained from Arrowsmiths general chart, and from the geographical notes of M. Fleurieu, prefixed to Pérouse's voyage.[4] The latter from M. d'Après supposes its longitude to be near 27° West, whilst Arrowsmith places it in 24°;

[1] Flinders had access on board the *Investigator* to details of Cook's voyages in Hawkesworth, *An Account of the Voyages undertaken … for making Discoveries in the Southern Hemisphere*. Cook crossed the Equator on the first *Resolution* voyage on 8 September 1772 at 0°18′S, 8°58′W. Beaglehole, ed., *The Journals of Captain James Cook*, II, p. 36.

[2] The entry for La Pérouse crossing the Equator is in Dunmore, *Journal of la Pérouse*, I, p. 19. This does not comment on his course or the winds.

[3] Flinders did not sight these two uninhabited small islets (0°55′N, 29°21′W) because the *Investigator* crossed the Equator at 17°W. Vallance, Moore and Groves, eds, *Nature's Investigator*, p. 63.

[4] Aaron Arrowsmith (1750–1823) was an English commercial cartographer who published a *Chart of the World on Mercator's Projection, exhibiting all the new discoveries to the present time: with the tracks of the most distinguished Navigators since 1700, carefully collected from the best charts, maps, voyages, &c. extant* (1790) and *A Chart of the South Pacific* (1798). Reference to a 'general chart' here suggests that Flinders had the former in mind here. Charles Pierre Claret, Comte de Fleurieu (1738–1810), was a noted French geographer, hydrographer and politician. He was Director of Ports and Arsenals in France under Louis XVI, a position to which he was appointed in 1776. He oversaw the planning and drew the charts for La Pérouse's voyage and added a learned volume of analysis on the main oceanic voyagers since Christopher Columbus. Flinders wrote a 'Memorial to the Comte de Fleurieu' on 11 March 1805. This is preserved in manuscript at ML. Dunmore, *Journal of La Pérouse*, I, p. 10.

and the tracks of Captain Cook pass so near over the former situation, that I incline towards the latter.[1]

Monday 31 August

Moderate breezes and cloudy with haze. Opened a cask of beef No. 54 contents 42 pieces. 16 lbs short. *Ditto* weather. Thick to the eastward. Water very luminous about the ships bows and where the waves break. Showers of rain. Moderate and dull cloudy weather, with rain at times. Employed getting the other three cables out of the main hold upon the lower deck and putting casks from the deck into the hold. Moderate breezes with dull cloudy weather.

Meridian altitude ☉ Lower Limb Circle direct	85°21′19″N
Latitude	4°21′19″N

	By log			Latitude North		Longitude West				
Course	Distance	DR	Obs	DR	TK	Var allowed	Set or current	Barom below	Bearings &c
S57°E	75	4°11′	4°21′	16°37′	–	12W	10N 12E	30.10 30.10	No observations could be taken for the longitude today and that for latitude was not a good one.

[f. 53] Tuesday 1 September towards the Cape of Good Hope

Moderate breezes and cloudy weather. A swell setting in from the SW ward. At 6½ *hours* took in the *Fore Top* gallant sails. Same luminous appearance in the water as last night. The ship now makes more than 2 inches of water per hour if not more than three: and it seems to increase. Fresh breezes and cloudy. Took in middle and top gallant staysails. *Ditto* weather; ship pitching a good deal to the SW swell. In main top gallant sail. Employed recoiling one of the cables on the lower deck, in a shorter coil. Moderate breezes and dull cloudy weather: no observations could be taken this morning or noon. Ship pitching to the swell and uneasy.

Meridian Altitude ☉ Lower Limb Circle direct	85°21′19″N
Latitude	4°21′19″N

	By log			Latitude North		Longitude West				
Course	Distance	DR	Obs	DR	TK	Var allowed	Set or current	Barom below	Bearings &c	Error of TK
S68°E	79	3°51′	–	22°20′	15°24′	14Wt	12N 13E	30.09 30.08		

---

[1] Jean-Baptiste Nicolas Denis d'Après de Mannevillette (1707–80), astronomer and hydrographer, headed the French East India Company's map library at Lorient from 1762 to 1780. His *Neptune Oriental* (1745) appeared in an English version as *The East India Pilot* (1782). Dunmore, *Journal of La Pérouse*, I, p. 23.

Wednesday 2 September

Moderate breezes and cloudy weather. Find the ship increase her rate of admitting water. Drizzling rain. Fresh breezes with threatening weather. In 2nd reef of the fore, and 1st reef of the mizzen topsails. Double reefed the main topsail. Find the ship admits more than five inches of water per hour. Fresh breezes and squally. In jib. Several of men of war birds hovering about.[1] Cleaned below and aired with stoves. Employed making points and gaskets. Noon. Fresh breezes and cloudy, with a considerable swell from the SSW.[2]

Meridian Altitude ☉ Lower Limb Circle direct   85°37′54″N
Latitude   3°54′25″N

By log		Latitude North		Longitude West						
Course	Distance	DR	Obs	DR	TK	Var allowed	Set or current	Barom below	Bearings &c	Bearing & distance
S74°E	79½	3°29′	3°54′	14°8′	11°28′	15°W	13N 13E	30.08 30.10	Cape Palmas[3] from the chart W4°N 121 leagues	+6′

[f. 54] From the circumstance of our being too late to save any great portion of the summer season for the examination of the south coast of New Holland, and the necessity therefrom arising to remain as little time as possible at the Cape of Good Hope, I was induced still further to consider of means to preserve the health of our people, that no delay might arise from waiting at the Cape to reestablish their health.[4] On consulting with the surgeon we made the following alterations in their victualling.

Oatmeal boiled for breakfast, four days instead of three; and rice being served now in lieu of cheese, it was boiled for breakfast on the other three days.

Pease boiled for dinner four days in the week as usual; and on the other three days, we propose to give one pint of portable soup to each man, consisting of two ounces of the soup, two ounces of scotch barley, and such onions pepper &c as the messes might have to add to it, with a sufficiency of water. Thus the people would have a hot breakfast every day and also hot soup every day for dinner, besides the usual meat allowed them.

On examining into the surgeons stores almost the whole of the barley was found to be spoiled; and when the portable broth was boiled by itself, no person chused to take it; I therefore directed that each man should be served with two ounces of it, in

---

[1] Frigate birds. Flinders saw either the great frigatebird (*Fregata minor*) or possibly the magnificent frigatebird (*F. magnificens*). Vallance, Moore and Groves, eds, *Nature's Investigator*, p. 61.

[2] Flinders later observed that the strength of the south-western winds drove his course eastward nearer to the African coast 'much against my inclination', and that Cook and La Pérouse's voyages of exploration had experienced similarly strong winds in the South Atlantic Ocean. Flinders, *A Voyage to Terra Australis*, I, p. 139.

[3] A headland (4°22′N, 7°43′W) on the extreme south-east end of the coast of Liberia, West Africa.

[4] This reveals Flinders's awareness of the threat of storms and turbulent seas along the south Australian coast during autumn and winter in the southern hemisphere.

the cake, three times per week; threatening those who took it and wasted it, with punishment.

I did not think it necessary to issue sour krout so long as the lime juice and sugar continued to be issued to them; but purposed to change these so soon as the weather should become somewhat cooler.[1]

Thursday 3 September

Fresh breezes and cloudy weather. Moderate breezes with fine weather. Out 2nd reef of the main topsail and set top gallant sails and jib. At 6, tacked ship to the westward, on which we found the ship easier, the swell being from about south; and she does not admit so much water on the starboard side. At 8, in top gallant sails. Fresh breezes with fine weather. Took in the jib. Only seven inches water made the last four hours. Set the jib and top gallant sails. Fresh breezes and cloudy weather. Many men of war birds hovering near the ship and darting at the flying fish sometimes.[2] Our shooters sometimes struck the birds but did not bring them down. A small albacore hooked this morning.[3] At noon fresh breezes and fine weather.

Meridian Altitude ☉ *Lower Limb Circle* direct	85°47'36"N
Latitude	3°42'15"N

		Latitude North		Longitude West						
Course	Distance	DR	Obs	DR	TK	Var allowed	Set or current	Barom below	Bearings &c	Error of TK
S59°W	59	3°24'	3°42'	14°59'	11°54'	15W	18N 25E	30.03 30.05	Penedo de St Pedro S77°W 248 leagues	+6'

[f. 55] **Friday 4 September**

Moderate breezes and hazy weather. Drizzling rain at times. Fresh breezes and squally. Took in top gallant sails. Many fish about the ship. Moderate breezes and hazy. Set top gallant sails. Several men of war birds about the ship. Employed in the after hold. Moderate breezes and cloudy with haze. Water smoother than it has been lately.

Meridian altitude ☉ *Lower Limb Circle* direct	85°27'19"N
Latitude	2°59'46"N

---

[1] Flinders proudly reported these changes in provisions and victualling, undertaken to preserve the health of the officers and men en route to the Cape of Good Hope. He explained that 'sour krout' [sauerkraut] and vinegar were preferred as antiscorbutics in higher latitudes and lime juice and sugar within the tropics. Scott, *The Life of Matthew Flinders*, pp. 140–41.

[2] Flying fish were probably fish of the Exocoetidae. Vallance, Moore and Groves, eds, *Nature's Investigator*, p. 61.

[3] A warm-water fish (*Thunnus alalunga*). Ibid., p. 60.

By log		Latitude South		Longitude East						
Course	Distance	DR	Obs	DR	TK	Var allowed	Set or current	Barom below	Bearings &c	Error of TK
S59°W	86	2°50′	3°00′	16°13′	13°3′	14W	2N 5E	30.04 30.05	Penedo de St Pedro S79°W dist*ance* 223 leagues	+7′

Saturday 5 September

Moderate breezes and cloudy weather. Employed in the after hold. A bonito caught.[1]
Fresh breezes. Took in the fore top-gallant sail. Let the second reef out of the fore topsail.
Employed in the fore holds. Moderate breezes and cloudy weather.
*Meri*dian *Al*titude ☉ *Lowe*r *Lim*b *C*ircle direct   85°2′25″N
Latitude   2°12′33″N

By log		Latitude North		Longitude West						
Course	Distance	DR	Obs	DR	TK	Var allowed	Set or current	Barom below	Bearings &c	Error of TK
S60°W	89	2°15′	2°13′	17°31′	14°21′	14W	2S –	– 30.07	Sable Island S59°W	+7′

[f. 56] Sunday 6 September

Moderate breezes with cloudy weather. Set the top gallant sails. Wetted the decks as usual
every evening since leaving Madeira. Took in the fore top-gallant sail. Fresh breezes and
cloudy. In main top-gallant sail. At daylight set the top-gallant sails. Several men of war birds
and flying fish about the ship. Moderate breezes and cloudy weather. Cleaned below and
aired with stoves; afterwards mustered the ships company and saw them clean.[2] Cloudy but
not unpleasant weather. Last weeks expenditure of water 2⅓ tons remaining 49⅔ tons.
*Meri*dian alt*itude* ☉ *Lowe*r *Lim*b *C*ircle direct   81°41′28″N
Latitude   1°29′14″N

By log		Latitude South		Longitude East						
Course	Distance	DR	Obs	DR	TK	Var allowed	Set or current	Barom below	Bearings &c	Error of TK
S63°W	86	1°34′	1°29′	18°48′	15°49′ Lt Th*istle*	14W	5S 11W	– 30.09	Sable Island S57°W distance 210 miles	+7′

---

[1] Another warm-water fish (*Katsumonus pelamis*). Ibid.
[2] These actions were in the standing orders of the ship. Scott, *The Life of Matthew Flinders*, p. 140.

Monday 7 September

Moderate breezes and cloudy weather. Let the reefs out of the topsails. Struck a large porpoise, which yielded us 6 gallons of oil and more than 1½ lbs. of flesh per man.[1] In 1st reef at dusk. Fine weather. Light breezes and cloudy weather. Out 1st reef of the mizzen topsail, set royals and top gallant studding sails. Shortened sail, hove to, lowered down one of the cutters and hoisted her in upon deck; then made sail again. Moderate breezes with fine weather.

| *Meridian Altitude* ☉ *Lower Limb* Circle | 84°17′29″N |
| Latitude | 0°42′40″N |

| | By log | | | Latitude North | | Longitude West | | | | | |
Course	Distance	DR	Obs	DR	TK 465	Var allowed	Set or current	Barom below	Bearings &c	Error of TK
S46°W	80	0°34′	0°43′	19°45′	16°38′	13W	9N 8E	30.07 30.10	Sable Island S62°W distance 144 miles	+7′

[f. 57] **Tuesday 8 September from Madeira towards the Cape of Good Hope**

Moderate and fine weather. In order to give the ships company a days amusement I permitted the ceremony of shaving and ducking as usual on crossing the equator, to be performed in its full latitude. At the conclusion, they had as much grog given them as they could drink, the ship having been previously put under snug sail.[2] After the ceremony, hoisted the cutter upon the quarter again.[3]

Cloudy weather, with spitting rain at times. Moderate breezes and cloudy weather, some swell from the southward. Set top gallant sails, jib and staysails. Lost a log line. Cloudy with haze. Cleaned below and aired with stoves. *Ditto* weather. No birds about or any indication of land during this day.

| *Meridian Altitude* ☉ *Lower Limb* Circle direct | 83°40′00″N |
| Latitude | 0°17′26″S |

---

[1] This female porpoise was dissected, studied and sketched on board ship. Vallance, Moore and Groves, eds, *Nature's Investigator*, p. 62.

[2] i.e. a vessel well prepared in its rigging and sails to weather a storm.

[3] Flinders reported the crossing of the Equator – the third time he had done so – in *A Voyage to Terra Australis*, I, p. 40. Crossing the Equator was associated with a merry ceremony in which King Neptune and his attendants came on board and those who had crossed the line before shaved the heads of all the officers and seamen who had not. Sailors traditionally got drunk on this occasion. Seaman Samuel Smith reported that 'the greatest part of the Officers and Men was shaved'. Good wrote: 'the Captain very handsomely and humanely admonished the Sailors respecting their conduct the proceeding [*sic*] evening and took the blame on himself for having permitted them to have so much liquor and that as they had abused that indulgence they must not expect any more leniency.' Edwards, ed., *The Journal of Peter Good*, p. 40; Estensen, *The Life of Matthew Flinders*, pp. 172–3; Monteath, ed., *Sailing with Flinders*, p. 27. The initiation ritual described here when naval ships cross the Equator is still followed in today's navies, though it is mimed with the shaving brush armed with some form of sticky and noxious concoction that is glutinous and difficult to remove from skin and hair.

By log		Latitude South		Longitude West						
Course	Distance	DR	Obs	DR	TK	Var allowed	Set or current	Barom below	Bearings &c	Error of TK
S22°W	75½	0°27′	0°17′	20°13′	17°00′	13°W	10N 6E	– 30.10	Sable Island W4°S distant 105 miles	+7′

Wednesday 9 September

Moderate trade [wind] with fine weather. At 1 hour 15″ bore away to make Isle Sable or St. Paul, and set studding sails. At dusk, took in all sail, the three topsails excepted; afterwards clawed down the fore and mizzen topsails to curtail the rate of sailing. A warrant officer looking out upon the forecastle. Fine weather. At daylight, hoisted the topsails and made all sail. Opened a cask of beef No. 55, contents 42 pieces, but it was 32 pounds short of weight. Steady trade wind with fine weather. Cleaned the ship well below and afterwards opened out and aired all the bedding, as also the peoples clothing. At noon, *ditto* weather. Some swell from the southward. No birds about or any indications of being near land.[1]

Mer*idian* alt*itude* ☉ Lowe*r* Lim*b* by *Circle* direct handle   83°36′38″
Latitude   0°43′29″S

By log		Latitude South		Longitude East						
Course	Distance	DR	Obs	DR	TK	Var allowed	Set or current	Barom below	Bearings &c	Error of TK
S74°W	101	0°44′	0°43′	21°50′	18°28′	13W	1N 9E	30.08 30.09	Sable Isle by TK N44°W 25 miles	+7′

[1] Rough Journal, I, f. 133, adds: 'At 4, this afternoon, I judged the ship to be in the latitude of this isle, or perhaps somewhat to the south of it, as it is given in the geographical notes, prefatory to Perouses voyages. I ordered the ship to be steered west at that time, allowing the variation to counteract the northerly current, which from the last two days experience I expected would attend us; in this however, I was deceived, or else the bad steerage counteracted it. At dusk I regulated the sail so as that the part of the horizon behind us to which our view should extend in the morning should meet with that of the preceding evening before us. I allowed six leagues each way to be the distance at which any land ought to be seen in a clear evening to the west, and morning to the east, and the view in these points was very distinct at these times. The three warrant officers were now ordered to keep watch forward, and to have the charge of the lookout at night. In the day, a man was kept constantly at the masthead, and the mate of the watch went up also at the conclusion of the watch, and a report made to me by the officer, whether land or anything was in sight or not. At noon, the latitude showed that no current had prevailed, and that therefore we were now too far to the south; the ship was ordered to be kept to the northward until we should reach the latitude of 30′, when we steered in that parallel, looking out for land.'

[f. 58] **Thursday 10 September** *Investigator* **searching for Isle Sable**
Moderate breezes with fine weather. Set the starboard studding sails. Innumerable quantities of flying fish about the ship and many bonetos. At dusk shortened sail to the three topsails and braced them bye: keeping a sharp look ahead for the island. Moderate and cloudy. Opened pork No. 16 this PM. Contents 53 pieces, but short of weight 10 lbs. At daylight, made all sail. Three birds seen, of a whiteish colour, as also a man of war bird. Clearer weather. Cleaned the ship below and aired with stoves. A long still swell from the southward. Moderate breezes and fine weather. No birds about.

| *Meridian Altitude* ☉ *Lower Limb* Circle | 84°20′51″N |
| Latitude | 0°22′6″S |

By log		Latitude South		Longitude West						
Course	Distance	DR	Obs	DR	TK	Var allowed	Set or current	Barom below	Bearings &c	Error of TK
N81°W	84	0°31′	0°22′	23°13′	19°58′ By officers	13W	9N 7W	30.07 30.09	*Cape* St Augustine Brazil[1] S61°W 352 leagues	+7′

Friday 11 September
Moderate breezes with fine weather. Took in the studding sails, and at 2, hauled to the wind, having given up the search after Isle Sable. Took in the mizzen top-gallant sail and staysails. Moderate breezes with fine weather, the southerly swell still continuing. Took in the main top sail and unbent it; shifted the yard and bent the sail in which we have put a 4th reef, and at 11 *hours* 30′ set the top sail and top gallant sail again. Steady trade wind, with fine weather. A swell still running from the southward.

Supplement altitude ☉ *Upper Limb* Circle Direct	95°53′36″S
Latitude	1°31′16″S
☉ *Lower Limb* by Mr Crosley	83°33′0″N
Latitude	1°32′46″S
Mean latitude	1°32′1″S

By log		Latitude South		Longitude West						
Course	Distance	DR	Obs	DR	TK	Var allowed	Set or current	Barom below	Bearings &c	Error of TK
S41°W	102	1°39′	1°32′	24°19′	21°6′	13°W	7N 2W	30.08 30.13	Cape St Augustine S63°W 322 leagues	+7′

[1] Cabo de Santo Agostinho (8°17′S, 35°1′W), about 22 miles south of Recife, Brazil.

[f. 59] <u>Additional remarks</u>

On coming into the latitude of Isle Sable on the 9th PM. I ordered the ship to be steered west in order to make it, allowing the variation to the south to counteract the current to the north which we had experienced on the two preceding days.

At dusk, I regulated the sail so as that we should not run more than 12 leagues during the night; for with the clear weather that we had, I supposed we should see any land six leagues ahead at night and six astern in the morning from the mast head; by this means the two visible horizons would nearly meet and nothing in that latitude and longitude would escape being seen.

Our lookout was regulated thus. A man was kept constantly at the mast head during the day and the mate of every watch went up previous to leaving the deck. At night, the three warrant officers had charge of the lookout upon the forecastle.

In this manner we continued to run until Thursday the 10th at noon, from the longitude of 17° to 20°W, when seeing no indications of land I gave up all hope of finding Sable or St Pauls Island. Last year I had crossed the equator in 20°26′W and in 1795 in longitude 21°13′; and very lately, Mr. Thistle, when master of the *Buffalo*, had crossed the parallel of 25′ south in 22°12′W without seeing any particular indications of land.[1] If the island had lain to the westward of 22°12′ and within 25°W it must have been repeatedly seen, for ships are crossing the equator in that parallel constantly; I therefore think that there is no island lying between 17° and 25° of west longitude, between the equator and half a degree of south latitude.

To the eastward of 17° we have the track of the French commodore Pérouse at the distance of one degree; it is therefore not probable that Sable Isle will be found to the west of 16°; more especially as the man-of-war birds, which had attended us for several days before, quitted us about the ship from 11½° to 16° of west longitude, and as there are great objections to its lying in or on the west side of the latter, I think we may say with some confidence, that, if there is such an isle as Sable or St. Paul in latitude 25′ south or thereabout, it will most probably be found to lie between the longitudes of 10° and 15° west.[2]

[f. 60] **Saturday 12 September *Investigator* from Madeira**

Fresh breezes and fine weather. The carpenters employed making a spanker from out of a fore-topsail yard. Saw a gannet and a blackish bird like a sheerwater. At dusk, single reefed the main and mizzen and double reefed the fore topsail. Took in the top-gallant sails.

Fresh breezes and cloudy, with a southerly swell which makes the ship plunge a little. She now admits more than 5 inches of water per hour when in this larboard tack, yet we have hitherto [been] reckoning the starboard to be the lightest side. These are distressing facts at the commencement of a long voyage. Cleaned below and aired with stoves. The

---

[1] John Thistle, who was master on the *Investigator*, was recruited by Flinders at Spithead on 3 June 1801. Thistle had previously sailed with Flinders on both *Norfolk* expeditions to circumnavigate Van Diemen's Land (1798) and explore the Australian coast north of Sydney to Hervey's Bay (1799). Thistle arrived at Spithead in late May 1801 on HMS *Buffalo*, returning home on a voyage from Sydney. Estensen, *The Life of Matthew Flinders*, p. 162.

[2] Flinders summarized his search for Sable Island in *A Voyage to Terra Australis*, I, p. 140.

sailmakers employed repairing the old main top sail and putting a 4th reef into it. At noon, a fresh trade wind and cloudy weather, with a swell from the southward.

| Meridian altitude ☉ Lower Limb Circle direct | 82°28′35″N |
| Latitude | 3°0′9″S |

| | By log | Latitude South | | Longitude West | | | | | | |
Course	Distance	DR	Obs	DR	TK	Var allowed	Set or current	Barom below	Bearings &c	Error of TK
S31°W	110	3°6′	3°0′	25°16′	22°5′	12W	6N 2W	30.10 30.08	Cape St Augustine S67°W 294 leagues	+8′

Sunday 13 September

Fresh breezes and cloudy, with squalls at times and spitting rain: Took in top gallant Sails and staysails. Rounded in the weather braces,[1] so as to keep the sails well full with the wind abeam. Set and took in top-gallant sails as the squally weather made necessary. Squally at times, with cloudy weather. A considerable sea running from the south-eastward, on which account I allow a quarter point leeway. At 8, strong breezes and squally with spitting rain: took in the top-gallant sails. Cleaned the ship below, and afterwards mustered the ships company and saw them clean. A swallow seen and two sheerwaters, and a gannet is now flying about the ship. Moderate breezes and cloudy weather with haze. Set top-gallant sails. Weeks expenditure of water 2¼ tons remaining 47¼.

| Meridian altitude ☉ Lower Limb Circle direct | 81°8′16″N |
| Latitude | 4°43′34″S |

| | By log | Latitude South | | Longitude West | | | | | | |
Course	Distance	DR	Obs	DR	TK	Var allowed	Set or current	Barom below	Bearings &c	Error of TK
S11°W	120	4°49′	4°44′	26°8′	23°9′ By RF[2] SF[3] JT[4]	11W	5N 12W	30.08 30.11	Cape St Augustine S72°W 260 leagues	+8′

[f. 61] Monday 14 September towards the Cape of Good Hope

Moderate breezes with hazy weather. Employed about various duties, lightening the ships upper works. Fresh breezes and cloudy. We perceived the water to be much smoother between 6 and 8 o clock; afterwards, the swell and the motion of the ship became the same as before. Squally weather. Took in top gallant Sails.

---

[1] i.e. ropes on the windward side of the ship.
[2] Robert Fowler.   [3] Samuel Flinders.   [4] John Thistle.

Ditto weather. Took in the main top mast stay sail. In a strong squall, took in the jib and mizzen stay sail and kept the ship away for a little time. At daylight, set the sails last taken in. Moderate breezes, but squally at times. Cleared away in the after hold, and struck the two 18 pound carronades down there, having first payed[1] them over with a mixture of tar, grease &c. boiled together, in order to preserve them.[2] The weather being more steady at noon, set the top-gallant sails. A sheerwater seen.

Meridian alt*itude* ☉ Lowe*r Lim*b Circle direct 79°51′55″N
Latitude 6°23′1″S

	By log	Latitude South		Longitude East						
Course	Distance	DR	Obs	DR	TK	Var allowed	Set or current	Barom below	Error of TK	
S30½°W	119	6°26′	6°23′	27°8′	24°29′ 24°36′ ☉ west ☾	10W	3N 20W	30.07 30.08	+8′	The swell from the southeastward still continuing

Additional remarks

The fresh winds that now attend us, and the sea that is running in consequence, are what I did not expect to meet with in these latitudes, and in strong language tell us of the weakness of the ship. For these last two days the ship has been kept with the wind abeam, by which means she does not plunge and work so much, and we gain in distance; but even now, the blows of the sea make her tremble in every part, and make it necessary to take into serious consideration the means of lightening her upper works as much as possible. The eighteen-pound carronades, stern chases, we struck into the after hold, as before mentioned. The spare rudder, which for want of room had hitherto been stowed in the main and mizzen channels, we took within the ship; as also trawl heads[3] &c. which had also been stowed in the channels. Several boxes of shot that had been placed abaft to trim the ship were now sent below, and the guns were run in to the innermost part of their carriages. Many things had also been stowed upon the booms[4] with the spare spars, so that there was a great weight raised there over the boats, which doubtless had assisted to strain the ship. This weight we now reduced very much although indeed the ship is so full that we scarcely know where to stow the surplus. By shaking the empty water casks, however, in the between decks some room was made, and by putting what we could below and bringing other heavy articles into the central parts of the ship, we eased her considerably, and prepared as far as was possible to encounter the bad weather that seems already to have made a commencement.

[1] Refers to spreading them with this mixture. 'Pay' was a type of pitch.

[2] Flinders's rearrangement of the carronades and the ship's upper works was intended to lighten the load on the upper part of the ship and to mitigate the shaking of timber in an attempt to reduce water seeping in. Estensen, *The Life of Matthew Flinders*, p. 172.

[3] Situated at end of the trawl beam and used to sink nets.

[4] A spar (pole) along the bottom of a fore and aft rigged sail that greatly improves control of the angle and shape of the sail.

[f. 62] **Tuesday 15 September** *Investigator* **from Madeira**

Squally at times, with fine intervals of clear weather. Moderate breezes in general, but squally at times. Took in top gallant sails and jib, and double reefed the main topsail. Strong and moderate breezes alternately, with cloudy weather. Squally at times. Employed the people in small jobs about the rigging and in lightening the booms of oars &c. Moderate trade wind, with passing clouds and spitting rain. Swell still running from the SE ward.

Meridian altitude ☉ Lower Limb Circle Direct	78°45'21"N
Latitude	7°53'50"S

This is not a good observation

	By log		Latitude South		Longitude East						
Course	Distance	DR	Obs	DR	TK	Var allowed	Set or current	Barom below	Bearings &c	Error of TK
S26°W	111	8°3'	7°54'	27°57'	25°30'	9W 12W	8W	30.06 30.09	Isle Trinidad[1] S13½°W 260 leagues	+8'

Wednesday 16 September

Moderate breezes and cloudy weather. Set top-gallant sails. Employed stowing boats oars in the channels in lieu of heavier things. Fresh breezes and squally weather. Took in top-gallant sails. Ditto weather. Strong squalls at times. Set top gallant sails. Squally with rain. Took them in again. Sailmakers employed putting a third reef in the oldest mizzen top-sail. Fresh breezes and hazy weather. A brisk-running sea from the south-eastward.

AM. Variation Azimuth 4 sets taken by Lt Flinders on binnacle	7°50'W
Observation latitude by means of Lieutenant Flinders and Mr Thistle	9°56'15"S

	By log		Latitude South		Longitude West						
Course	Distance	DR	Obs	DR	TK	Var allowed	Set or current	Barom below	Bearings &c	Error of TK
S17°W	120	9°49'	9°56'	28°37'	26°15' by RF JT	7W	7S 5W	30.11 30.12	Isle Trinidad S12°W 216 leagues	+8'

[f. 63] **Thursday 17 September towards the Cape of Good Hope**

Fresh breezes and cloudy weather. Set the mizzen top gallant sail. Squally with spitting rain. Took in the *Main* top-gallant sail and top-mast-stay sail; and the jib occasionally. Fresh breezes and cloudy weather. Set top-gallant sails and *Main* top-mast-stay sail. Ditto

---

[1] An island in the South Atlantic Ocean (20°31'S, 29°19'W). Flinders had access to Captain D'Auvergne's plan of Trinidad (1782). Flinders, *A Voyage to Terra Australis*, I, p. 142.

weather, with smoother water. Took in and set top gallant sails as the wind permitted. Cleaned the ship below and aired with stoves. Mustered the ships company and saw them clean. Fresh breezes and fine weather. The sea runs now further aft and not so violently as before.

Observed latitude by Lt Flinders 12°3′45″S

	By log	Latitude South		Longitude West						
Course	Distance	DR	Obs	DR	TK	Var allowed	Set or current	Barom below	Bearings &c	Error of TK
S24°W	138½	12°2′	12°3′	29°34′	27°26′	6°W	1S 14W	30.09 30.15	Isle Trinidad S8°W 172 leagues	+8′

Friday 18 September

Fresh breezes and cloudy weather. Some sea running from the eastward, on which account a ¼ point leeway is allowed. Squally weather at times. Took in the top gallant sails. Spitting rain. Set top gallant sails. Fresh breezes and hazy weather. Ditto weather. Bent and set the spanker. Armourer employ'd at his forge. Ditto weather, with the same kind of sea running from the eastward.

Meridian altitude ☉ Lower Limb Circle Direct   73°16′50″N
Latitude   14°31′10″S

	By log	Latitude South		Longitude West						
Course	Distance	DR	Obs	DR	TK	Var allowed	Set or current	Barom below	Bearings &c	Error of TK
S12°W	155	14°34′	14°31′	30°7′	28°14′	4W	3N 15W	30.10 30.15	Isle Trinidad S3½°W 120 leagues	+8′

[f. 64] **Saturday 19 September *Investigator* from Madeira**

Moderate breezes and cloudy weather. Let out the second reefs. Unbent the main top sail, and rebent the old one in which the sailmakers have lately put a 4th reef. Double reefed the top sails, at dusk. Took in the spanker. Fresh breezes and cloudy weather. Set the spanker, and the middle and top-gallant stay-sails.

Moderate breezes and fine weather. Let out 2nd reefs and set the mizzen top-gallant sail. Cleaned the ship well below, and aired with stoves. Aired the marines clothing. At 11, shortened sail and shifted the gig for painting. At noon, moderate and fine weather, with tolerably smooth water.

Meridian altitude ☉ Lower Limb Circle direct   71°30′18″N
Latitude   16°41′43″

By log		Latitude South		Longitude East						
Course	Distance	DR	Obs	DR	TK	Var allowed	Set or current	Barom below	Bearings &c	Error of TK
S3°E	128	16°39'	16°41'	30°0'	28°12'	3W	2S 5W	30.22 30.24	Isle Trinidad S6°W 77 leagues	+9'

Sunday 20 September

Moderate and cloudy weather. Bent the old mizzen top sail in which a 3rd reef is lately put. Took the first reef in the mizzen top sail. Fine weather with haze. Light breezes and cloudy. Exercised great guns and swivels. Hove a salt-provision cask overboard for a mark, worked the ship round it, and fired each gun and swivel at it in the ship; being two rounds of powder and one of shot. At noon, light breezes and cloudy. Made all sail again upon our course. Expenditure of water last week 2¾ tons: remaining 44½ tons.

By log		Latitude South		Longitude West						
Course	Distance	DR	Obs	DR	TK	Var allowed	Set or current	Barom below	Bearings &c	Error of TK
S4°W	91	18°12'	18°19' By SF JT	30°07'	28°24' By SF JT	3W	7S 5W	30.28 30.33	Isle Trinidad (SE end) S5°W 44 leagues	+9'

[f. 65] Monday 21 September towards the Cape of Good Hope

Light airs approaching to a calm. Light breeze. Fine weather with a pleasant breeze. Light breezes and cloudy weather. Light airs. Employed setting up the rigging where necessary, fore and aft. Sunk an inclosed bucket 200 fathoms deep, and found the water at the depth to be 2° colder than at the surface.[1] Caught a small dolphin.[2] At noon, light airs and fine weather, with haze.

Meridian altitude ☉ Lower Limb Circle direct	69°38'55"N
Latitude	19°19'10"S

By log		Latitude South		Longitude West						
Course	Distance	DR	Obs	DR	TK 465	Var allowed	Set or current	Barom below	Bearings &c	Error of TK
S8°W	50½	19°9'	19°19'	30°14'	28°33'	10S 2W	3W	30.28 30.28	Isle Trinidad S3°W 24 leagues	+9'

[1] This was done to test water temperature and salinity at depth. Edwards, ed., *The Journal of Peter Good*, p. 41.
[2] Not a cetacean but the dolphinfish (*Coryphaena hippuris*). Vallance, Moore and Groves, eds, *Nature's Investigator*, p. 68.

Tuesday 22 September

Light airs and fine weather with an easterly swell. Several gannets[1] flying about, and many blubbers[2] in the water. Light airs and cloudy weather. The weather too cloudy to allow of lunar observations being taken. Not able to observe anything of the lunar eclipse, the weather being too cloudy.[3] Calm and hazy, with a swell from the eastward. Many gannets about the ship, and some man-of-war birds and sheerwater[4] were seen. Cleaned the ship well below and aired with stoves. Unbent the fore topsail to be repaired, and bent a new one. At 11, heavy rain, which continued until noon, with very light airs.

Variation Azimuth observed by Mr Thistle on binnacle   4°27′W
Amplitude by Ditto   4°33′W

		By log		Latitude South	Longitude West					
Course	Distance	DR	Obs	DR	TK	Var allowed	Set or current	Barom below	Bearings &c	Error of TK
S23°W	18½	19°36′	–	30°22′	–	3W	1N 3W	30.27 30.26	No observations could be procured this morning	

[f. 66] **Wednesday 23 September** *Investigator* **passing the island Trinidad**[5]

Rainy weather, with a rising swell from the southward. On a breeze springing up at 4, trimmed sails, and tacked to the eastward. Took in staysails and top-gallant sails. Fresh breezes and cloudy. At 9 hours 15′ tacked ship, at which time the cross-jack yard[6] being rotten was sprung by the flap of the sail. Squally at times, with some head swell. Moderate and fine weather. Set top gallant sails and stay sails. Many gannets and some other birds seen; and at 6 hours 15′ we saw the isle Trinidad the centre of Trinidad SSW¼W. Got up a spare fore topsail yard[7] for a cross-jack yard, which obliged us to take in the mizzen top sail. At noon, light breezes and fine weather. Set the mizzen topsail again. A peaked rock near the eastern extreme bore S21°W. The bluff western extreme, which opened off soon after and is the Eddystone rock,[8] Leeward 4° to the right, and a rock of Martim Vas 49°43′ to the left from the main top.[9]

Meridian altitude ☉ Lower Limb Circle direct   69°44′3″N
Latitude   20°0′52″S

[1] Birds of the family Sulidae. Ibid., p. 69.

[2] i.e. jellyfish or medusas.

[3] This was a total lunar eclipse at 7.19 universal time.

[4] Probably either the Manx shearwater or the great shearwater (*Puffinus gravis*). Vallance, Moore and Groves, eds, *Nature's Investigator*, p. 69.

[5] Now known as Trinidade (20°31′S, 29°19′W), an island in the South Atlantic Ocean off Brazil.

[6] The lower yard on the mizen mast of a square-rigged ship.

[7] A square yard used to spread the foot of a topsail where no course is set.

[8] This was a rock off Trinidade Island that resembled the British Eddystone.

[9] Martim Vaz is a tiny island in the South Atlantic Ocean (20°50′S, 28°85′W). Flinders, *A Voyage to Terra Australis*, I, p. 142.

	By log	Latitude South		Longitude West					
Course	Distance	DR	Obs	DR	TK	Var allowed	Set or current	Barom below	Error of TK
S31°W	33	20°4'	20°1'	30°39'	29°5' 28°53' by ☾	3W	2N 4W	30.22 30.29	+9'

[f. 67] **Thursday 24 September**

Moderate breezes and cloudy weather, with a southerly swell. The old fore topsail being repaired, bent it again. Some sheerwaters about, and several gannets flying towards the land. At 8, the centre of Trinidad bore SEbE½E; and at 11 it bore true east.

Fresh breezes and fine weather. Took in the fore top gallant sail to ease the ship in plunging to the headswell. At daybreak Trinidad was still in sight and bore N62°E. Set the fore top gallant sail. Light breezes and fine weather. Got up all the sails out of the other sail room, and aired the place with stoves. Mustered the ships company & saw them clean. At noon, moderate breezes and fine weather, with a swell from the southward.

Meridian altitude ☉ Lower Limb Circle direct	68°56'46"N
Latitude	21°11'39"S

	By log	Latitude South		Longitude West						
Course	Distance	DR	Obs	DR	TK	Var allowed	Set or current	Barom below	Bearing & distance	Error of TK
S38°W	80	21°4'	21°12'	31°32'	30°3' by SF JT	2W	8S 2W	30.28 30.35	Cape Frio[1] S81°W 221 leagues	+9'

Additional remarks

On October 21[2] at the Cape of Good Hope the errors of these three timekeepers were found as under

A1736   2°27'13.3"E

Error taken at Madeira   10'15"

In 76 days   2°37'28.3"E

E 465 in 96 days   0°10'59.2"E

E 543   0°39'21.5"E

The above errors of the time-keepers found at the Cape of Good Hope[3] being proportioned to the time of the two sets of altitudes, and applied to the longitudes given at this time by the time-keepers, will give Trinidad as under

[1] Situated in Namibia (18°27'S, 12°1'E).

[2] An indication that this journal was written up later than the voyage, as this is out of place chronologically.

[3] See below, p. 213.

Longitudes by *Time Keepers*	First set			Second set		
	A 1736	E 465	E 543	A 1736	E 465	E 543
At the above set altitudes	20°3′12″	29°15′15″	28°55′9″	20°6′51″	29°19′12″	28°58′48″
Reduction to the Eddystone	+2.20	+2.20	+2.20	−1.15	−1.15	−1.15
	28 5 32	29 17 35	28 57 29	28 5 36	29 17 15	28 57 33
Incorrect longitude of the Eddystone rock, by 2 sets				28 5 34	29 17 46	28 57 31
Errors of *Time Keepers* at this time, as found afterwards at the Cape				+1 40 41.2	+9 7.2	+29 17.3
Longitude of the Eddystone rock by time keepers				29 46 15	29 26 53	29 26 48

Distances of α Aquilae[1] west of ☽s far, and Aldebaran[2] east of ☽s near limb reduced to 2nd set of altitudes

Apparent time	By calculation		Apparent distance of limbs	Longitude West	Instrument used	
	Apparent altitude	Apparent ☽ centre				
10h54′14″ 11h 8′ 8″	34° 7′10″	41°48′38″	84°20′32″	28°55′45″	Circle No 74	
12h41′43″ 53′46″	31°10′ 2″	44°13′34″	24′40″	29° 6′25″	Sextant No 482	
	24°35′26″	56° 3′17″	43°14′19″	29°20′45″	C	74
	27° 1′ 8″	56°46′33″	10′40″	4′ 0″	S	482

Mean by Circle	29° 8′15″
Mean longitude by 4 sets	29° 6′43″ West
	−1′15″
Eddystone Rock by these 4 sets	29° 5′28″
Mean Error of tables	+15′45″
	29°21′13″

Friday 25 September

Moderate breezes and cloudy weather. Employed in airing the sails and sailroom. Fresh breezes and cloudy weather. A considerable swell from the southward, which makes the ship pitch a good deal. Moderate with fine weather. Light breezes, with a southerly swell. Cleaned the ship below. Got up the sails out of the middle sail room, aired them, and got stoves in the sail room. Light breezes and fine weather. All the plain sails set.

Meridian altitude ☉ Lower Limb Circle direct 67°49′45″N
Latitude 22°42′8″S

By log		Latitude South		Longitude West						
Course	Distance	DR	Obs	DR	TK	Var allowed	Set or current	Barom below	Bearing & distance	Error of TK
S21°W	87	22°33′	22°42′	32°06′	30°36′	2°W	9S 1E	30.33 30.33	Cape Frio W1°S 207 leagues	+9′

[1] A constellation in the northern sky that lies just to the north of the celestial Equator.
[2] An orange giant star located about 65 light years away in the zodiac constellation of Taurus. It is one of the brightest stars in the night sky.

[f. 68] Saturday 26 September

Light breezes and fine weather, with a swell from the southward. Let out 1st reefs and set mizzen topgallant sail. Took in the first reefs in the top sails. Moderate breezes and cloudy weather. Light airs with rain, but soon after a fresh breeze sprung up with cloudy weather. Fresh breezes with rain. Took in top gallant sails and the small staysails, but at 10, set them again. Saw a sheerwater. Moderate breezes and cloudy weather. Set the spanker, mizzen top gallant sail, and fore-top-mast studding sail. Some southerly swell still running.

Meridian altitude ☉ Lower Limb Circle direct	66°37′21″N
Latitude	24°17′55″S

	By log	Latitude South		Longitude West						
Course	Distance	DR	Obs	DR	TK	Var allowed	Set or current	Barom below	Bearing & distance	Error of TK
S13°W	87	24°7′	24°18′	31°44′	30°15′	1W	11S 1W	30.10 30.13	Cape of Good Hope S76½°E 873 leagues	+9′

Sunday 27 September

Fresh breezes and cloudy. Set the mizzen top-gallant sail, and the fore-top-mast and lower studding sails. Double reefed the mizzen top-sails and hauled down the staysails and spanker. Took in the studding sails, in doing which the lower standing boom was carried away. Lightening [sic] in the south-west quarter. Took in top-gallant sails. Heavy rain with thunder and lightening: Double reefed the fore topsail. Fresh gales and rainy weather. More moderate with cloudy weather. Set top gallant sails, and the fore top-mast and lower studding sails. Rove a new tiller rope. Mustered the ships company and saw them clean. Fresh breezes and cloudy with a following sea. Saw a white-billed sheerwater. Expenditure of water last week 2½ tons: remaining 42.

Meridian altitude ☉ Lower Limb Circle direct	64°33′19″N
Latitude	26°45′23″S

	By log	Latitude South		Longitude West						
Course	Distance	DR	Obs	DR	TK	Var allowed	Set or current	Barom below	Bearing & distance	Error of TK
S22°E	164	26°50′	26°45′	30°37′	29°1′	1W	5N 7E	29.98 29.83 29.82	Cape of Good Hope S79°E 832 leagues	+9′

[f. 69] **Monday 28 September Towards the Cape of Good Hope**

Fresh breezes with rain at times. In a sudden squall the fore topmast studding sail boom was carried: on which, took in studding sails and top gallant sails, but set them again soon afterwards. Took in studding sails. Lost four log lines off the reel. A strange sail in sight to the south-south-west. Double-reefed the main and close-reefed the mizzen top sail. Fresh breezes with fine starlight weather; but with lightening in different parts of the heavens. Cloudy. Heavy claps of thunder with lightening all round; and at 2 squalls of wind and rain came on and obliged us to take in top-gallant sails, main sail, and jib.

Set top-gallant sails, but took them in again presently; the frequent return of the squalls also obliged us to bear away at times. At 7 hours 30′ a heavy squall obliged us to close down the topsails for a time, and we had several repetitions of this during the morning, though between the squalls the weather was fine. At noon, fine weather, with a sea running from the westward. Ship under double-reefed topsails & courses. Some sheerwaters and a pintado bird[1] seen.

Meridian altitude ☉ Lower Limb Circle direct   62°49′55″N
Latitude   28°52′6″S

By log		Latitude South		Longitude West						
Course	Distance	DR	Obs	DR	TK	Var allowed	Set or current	Barom below	Bearing & distance	Error of TK
S28½°E	157	29°3′	28°52′	29°12′	27°20′	2W	11N 16E	29.82 29.78 29.84	Cape of Good Hope S82°E 786 leagues	+10′

Tuesday 29 September

Fresh breezes and squally weather, with rain at times. Many pintado birds and sheerwaters in the wake of the ship, and some white-bellied birds resembling a wood cock in shape and size.

Treble-reefed the fore and mizzen top-sails at dusk, the weather being squally at times; but at 8 the weather was fine. Fresh breezes and fine. Finding the barometer rising, let out 3rd reefs, and set the jib and mizzen stay-sail. Fresh breezes and cloudy. Set top-gallant sails at daylight. Moderate & fine; the swell considerably abated. Some sheerwaters, pintados, and diamond-winged albatrosses about. Out 2nd reefs. Found a leak in the larboard sail room, and got the sails up to dry. Unbent the fore top-sail to be repaired and bent a new one. Moderate breezes and fine weather, with haze.

Meridian altitude ☉ Lower Limb Circle direct   61°3′18″N
Latitude   31°2′4″S

---

[1] The pintado or Cape pigeon (also Cape petrel).

By log		Latitude South		Longitude West						
Course	Distance	DR	Obs	DR	TK	Var allowed	Set or current	Barom below	Bearing & distance	Error of TK
S26°E	151	31°8′	31°2′	27°56′	25°50′ By SF JT	3W	6N 14E	29.26 30.02 30.05	Cape of Good Hope S85°E 747 leagues	+10′

[f. 70] Wednesday 30 September *Investigator* from Madeira

Finding the ship to the south of Saxemberg Island,[1] steered something northward to get into its parallel, and set the fore and fore-top-mast studding sails; but the wind freshening took them in soon after. Albatrosses, sheerwaters, and pintados about. Double reefed the top-sails and took in the stay sails and jib. It was reported to me that the ship passed by a turtle this PM.

Fresh breezes and cloudy, with a following sea, but rather inclining from the south. Fine weather. At daylight, let out 2nd reefs and set the fore and fore-top-mast studding sails. There is now a swell from the WNW but the long under swell comes from the SW. Sailmakers repairing the old fore top-sail. Sauer-krout and vinegar served to the ships company. At noon, fresh breezes and hazy weather. Many pintado-birds about the ship.

Meridian altitude ☉ Lower Limb Circle direct	61°47′41″N
Latitude	30°40′54″S

By log		Latitude South		Longitude West							
Course	Distance	DR	Obs	DR	TK	Var allowed	Set or current	Ther deck	Barom below	Bearing & distance	Error of TK
N84°E	164½	30°45′	30°41′	24°45′	22°36′	4W	4N 3E	64° 64° 69°	30.05 30.00 30.00	Cape of Good Hope S84°E 696 leagues	+10′

Thursday 1 October

Fresh breezes and cloudy, with spitting rain at times. The old fore-top sail being repaired, bent it, and set it 2nd reefed. Many pintado birds and a few sooty petrels about the ship. Took in the studding sails and double-reefed the main top-sail at dusk. A long heavy swell rolling from the SW ward. Dull hazy weather, with showers of rain at times. Fresh breezes and cloudy. Set the main sail; and at daylight let out second reefs and set the studding sails forward. Light breezes and cloudy: Cleaned the ship below and aired with stoves.

[1] Flinders, *A Voyage to Terra Australis*, I, p. 34, noted that this day he looked out for the supposed Saxemberg Island, a phantom island that appeared intermittently on charts from the late 17th century to the early 19th century.

Mustered the people and saw them as usual on this day. Light breezes and fine weather, with haze. A long swell from the south-west.

Meridian altitude ☉ Lower Limb Circle direct	62°17′31″
Latitude	30°34′12″

		By log		Latitude South	Longitude West						
Course	Distance	DR	Obs	DR	TK	Var allowed	Set or current	Ther deck	Barom below	Bearing & distance	Error of TK
S88°W	129	30°45′	30°34′	22°16′	20°18′ by SF JT	6W	11N 11E	63° 60° 69°	– 30.04 30.07	Cape of Good Hope S83°E 657 leagues	+10′

[f. 71] Friday 2 October towards the Cape of Good Hope

Moderate breezes and fine weather, with a long swell from the south-westward. Took in the small studding sails, and set the fore-and-aft sails. Light breezes; Took in the studding sails &c. The ship tossed about unpleasantly by the south-west swell, during the calm. On a breeze springing up, set top-gallant sails and main sail. Light breezes and cloudy. At daylight set the larboard studding sails forward. Finding the cross trees at the main top-mast had sprung, sent down the top-gallant yard and mast, struck the top-mast, and fitted new cross-trees. The swell somewhat abated. Fresh breezes and cloudy weather. Many pintado birds about the ship.

Meridian altitude ☉ Lower Limb Circle	62°14′12″N
Latitude	31°16′46″S

		By log		Latitude South	Longitude West						
Course	Distance	DR	Obs	DR	TK	Var allowed	Set or current	Ther deck	Barom below	Bearing & distance	Error of TK
S64°E	97	31°16′	31°17′	20°34′	18°29′	7W	1S 7E	62° 60° 66°	– 30.09 30.02	Cape of Good Hope S84°E 622 leagues	+10′

Additional remarks upon Saxemberg Island

From the geographical notes prefixed to the voyage of La Pérouse by Fleurieu, I learn that this island was discovered by John Lindestz Lindeman, a Hollander, in 1670.[1] It is said

---

[1] Lindestz reportedly discovered this non-existent island and made a sketch of it, showing it to be low-lying with a mountain in the middle. His illusory Saxemburgh Island probably consisted of stationary clouds that are common on the horizon in this part of the Atlantic Ocean, and are easily mistaken for distant islands. Stommel, *Lost Islands*, pp. 22–5.

to lie in 30°45′S and in about the longitude of 19°40′W. It does not appear that this island has been seen since, although many ships have sought for it. Its supposed situation has frequently been made by single ships going to India, and they have steered east from it, several degrees, but without seeing land. This being the case I thought it probable it might be further west than its assigned situation, and therefore determined to try on that side. On the 29th we had passed its latitude a few miles and were 6° to the west; getting then back into its parallel, we steered eastward, keeping the same strict lookout as when searching for Sable or St. Pauls Isle; but my hope of finding it was not so strong as to induce me to shorten the rate of sailing in the night so much as in the preceding instance. The turtle that it was reported me, had been passed by on the 30th PM gave me some hopes of finding Saxemberg but afterwards we had no signs of the neighbourhood of land but such as are common in all the southern oceans without side the tropic. This afternoon we passed within a very few miles of its assigned situation, and giving up then all hope of seeing it we steered on our course for the Cape of Good Hope.

Had Saxemberg laid between 26° and 20° in the latitude of 30°35′, or nearly, it must have fallen under our inspection; and the track of captain Cook in his third voyage crosses the parallel about half a degree to the west of this space,[1] and as before observed, those of many ships for several degrees westward: it is therefore most probable that it does not lie between 15° and 27° of west longitude, and I think equally so, that it does not exist at all.

[f. 72] **Saturday 3 October _Investigator_ from Madeira**
Fresh breezes and cloudy weather. Swayed up the main-top and top-gallant masts, and set the sails. Took in studding-sails and spanker, and double-reefed the top-sails. Strong breezes. Took in top-gallant sails, and treble-reefed the fore and mizzen top-sails; afterwards took in the jib and main sail, the weather becoming squally with rain. Strong breezes and squally, with heavy rain, until the wind shifted to the southward, when the weather cleared and gradually became fine. At daybreak, let the 3rd reef out of the fore top-sail, and set the jib and main sail. Strong breezes and cloudy weather. Cleaned the ship below and aired with stoves. The south-westerly swell makes the ship work a good deal, and occasions both the decks and ships sides to leak very much. At noon, strong breezes and cloudy. Many pintados about.

| Meridian altitude ☉ lower limb Sextant No 483 | 61°7′51″N |
| Latitude | 30°30′11″S |

	By log	Latitude South		Longitude West							
Course	Distance	DR	Obs	DR	TK	Var allowed	Set or current	Ther	Barom below	Bearing & distance	Error of TK
S65½°E	182	32°32′	32°30′	17°19′	15°17′	8W	2N 7E	64° 59° 62°	29.93 29.88 29.88	Cape of Good Hope S86°E 560 leagues	+10′

---

[1] A reference to Cook sailing here in the _Resolution_ on 7 August 1776. Beaglehole, ed., _The Journals of Captain James Cook_, III, p. 15.

Sunday 4 October

Fresh breezes and cloudy weather, with a long, high swell from the south-westward. People employed making points. Under double-reefed top-sails, which, as the barometer was rising, were not further reduced at dusk. Fresh breezes with thick cloudy weather. Light breezes. Let out 2nd reefs, set staysails, top-gall*ant* sails, spanker, and fore studding sails. A high sea rolling in from the SW which by the flapping of the lower studding sail carried away one of the sweeps, which had been used for a lower standing boom. Mustered the ships company, saw them clean, and read the articles of war to them. Lowered down a boat to pick up a pintado-bird for the naturalist to examine. Noon, light airs and dull cloudy weather. Weeks expenditure of water 2⅔ tons; Remaining in the ship 39⅓d.

The anchorage under Tristan d'Acunha has according to the *Lion*[1]

Latitude   37°6′S

Longitude   11°43′W

	By log			Latitude South		Longitude West						
Course	Distance	DR	Obs	DR	TK	Var allowed	Set or current	Ther	Barom below	Bearing & distance	Error of TK
S65°E	132	33°26′	–	14°56′	–	9W	3N 4E	58° 56° 61°	29.93 30.03 30.04	Tristan d'Acunha[2] S13°E 75 leagues	+10′

[f. 73] Monday 5 October towards the Cape of Good Hope

Light airs with dull cloudy weather. Set the main topsail. Calm at times with rain. Caught an albatross whose extent of wing was 9′9″; and two sooty-coloured birds marked with white in the fore part of the head. The naturalist places these last in the tribe Procularia, and thinks them a variety of sheerwater.[3]

     Light breezes with thick rainy weather. The south-westerly swell which still runs, throws the ship something to windward, on which account no leeway is allowed. Fresh breezes and hazy. Drizzling rain. Double-reefed the top-sails. Took in top-gall*ant* sails. Third-reefed the top sails. At noon, fresh breezes and hazy. The southwesterly swell being almost beaten down, the water is tolerably smooth.

Mer*idian altitude* ☉ Lowe*r Lim*b Sex*tant* 483   60°0′26″N

Latitude   34°23′51″S

	By log			Latitude South		Longitude West						
Course	Distance	DR	Obs	DR	TK	Var allowed	Set or current	Ther	Barom below	Bearing & distance	Error of TK
S41°E	85	34°30′	34°24′	13°48′	11°28′	9W	3N 4E	54° 56° 58°	– 30.00 30.02	Tristan d'Acunha S4°W 54 leagues	+11′

[1] The *Lion*, commanded by Sir Erasmus Gower, carried George Macartney on the first British Embassy to China in 1792–93.

[2] The main island of a remote group of volcanic islands in the South Atlantic Ocean (37°07′S, 12°17′W).

[3] Probably the Manx shearwater or the great shearwater. Vallance, Moore and Groves, eds, *Nature's Investigator*, p. 69.

Tuesday 6 October

Fresh breezes with thick hazy weather. Many pintado birds about the ship, and a cape hen was seen.[1] Strong breezes, and a sea rising from the eastward. Single-reefed the courses. Moderate, and hazy weather. Set the jib and main-top stay-sail. Thick cloudy weather. Let the third reefs out of the top-sails; and at daybreak, let the reef out of the courses and the 2nd reef out of the top-sails, and set the spanker, staysails and larboard studding sails. Light breezes and fine weather: Let the 1st reefs out to be aired, and loosed the small sails in the tops. Cleaned the ship below and aired with stoves. Got up the slop shoes to be aired, they being found getting mouldy, and some few partly spoiled.

Meridian altitude ☉ Lower Limb Circle   59°31′11″N
Latitude   35°16′7″S

By log		Latitude South		Longitude West							
Course	Distance	DR	Obs	DR	TK	Var allowed	Set or current	Ther	Barom below	Bearing & distance	Error of TK
S61°E	93	35°9′	35°16′	12°9′	9°35′	10W	10S 14E	57° 59° 68°	– 30.00 30.05	Cape of Good Hope N88°E 459 leagues	+11′

[f. 74] **Wednesday 7 October *Investigator* from Madeira**

Light breezes, and fine weather; with occasional fogs sprouting over and then clearing away again: at 4, it continued thick. At dusk, took in studding-sails, two reefs in the fore and mizzen and one in the main top-sail; and afterwards took in the upper staysails and spanker. Fresh breezes and thick weather, with drizzling rain. Took in top gallant sails. Hazy weather. At daylight, set the top-gallant sails. Fresh breezes with dull hazy weather. Cleaned the ship below. Many pintados and a few other oceanic birds about. At noon, moderate and hazy. Saw a stream of small petrels passing the ship, but at too great a distance to distinguish the species.

Meridian altitude ☉ Lower Limb Sextant 483   59°57′56″N
Latitude   35°12′12″S

By log		Latitude South		Longitude West							
Course	Distance	DR	Obs	DR	TK	Var allowed	Set or current	Ther	Barom below	Bearing & distance	Error of TK
East	160½	35°16′	35°12′	12°9′	8°52′	1 Pt	4N 9E	61° 60° 60°	– 30.03 30.07	Cape of Good Hope N88°E 403 leagues	+11′

[1] A large seabird (*Procellaria aequinoctialis*), dark brown to black, with some white on the chin. Common in the seas around the Cape of Good Hope.

Thursday 8 October

Fresh breezes and hazy weather. Set the fore and fore-top-mast studding-sails. Took in the fore studding sail, and at dusk the top-mast ditto. Cut up pork No. 20, contents 53 pieces which it answered. Took in the upper staysails. Strong breezes and cloudy weather. Took in top-gallant sails. Ditto weather. Set top-gallant sails, spanker & stay-sails. Fresh breezes and fine weather with haze. Cleaned the ship below and aired with stoves. Painted the 4th reef of a new fore top-sail. Mustered the ships company & saw them clean. Strong breezes and fine weather. Pintado birds and some small grey petrels about the ship.

Meridian altitude ☉ center Circle   60°42′24″N

Latitude   35°6′53″S

	By log	Latitude South		Longitude West							
Course	Distance	DR	Obs	DR	TK	Var allowed	Set or current	Ther	Barom below	Bearing &c	Error of TK
N88½°E	185	35°7′	35°7′	5°6′	2°17′	13W	– 6E	59° 59° 61°	– 30.09 30.10	Cape of Good Hope N88°E 339 leagues	+11′

[f. 75] Friday 9 October towards the Cape of Good Hope

Fresh breezes and cloudy weather, with a following sea from the NW. Took in top gallant sails. Punished Thomas Flint, seaman, and Andrew Hobson, marine; the first with 12, and the last with six lashes, for fighting. At dusk, double-reefed the main top-sail. Strong breezes, with dull cloudy weather. Ditto weather. More moderate. Set the middle and main topmast staysails, and afterwards top-gallant sails. Cloudy weather, with haze. A few pintados about the ship. Passed by several patches of sea weed. People employed sinneting oars, making boats fenders, and others were preparing the boats for active service. Fresh breezes and hazy, with misty rain at times. The swell from the north-west which still runs, seems to prevent the rising of the sea from the NbyE, for the water continues smooth.

	By log	Latitude South		Longitude East							
Course	Distance	DR	Obs	DR	TK	Var allowed	Set or current	Ther	Barom below	Bearing & distance	Error of TK
S83½°E	192	35°29′	–	1°13′	–	16°W	5N 6E	58° 57° 58°	– 30.09 30.14	No observations could be obtained this AM	

Saturday 10 October

Fresh breezes with hazy weather and misty rain. Took in top-gallant sails and staysails. Set top-gallant sails and spanker. Fine starlight weather. Let the 2nd reef out of the main topsail, and set the fore and fore-top mast studding sails. Moderate breezes and fine weather. At daylight, let out all the reefs, and set all the small sails that would draw. *Ditto* weather. Cleaned the ship below and aired with stoves. Took in royals and top gall*ant* studding sails. Exercised the ships company in firing at a target with small arms. Moderate breezes with fine weather. Pintado-birds and albatrosses about the ship.

Me*ridian* alt*itude* ☉ Lowe*r* Lim*b* Circl*e* Di*rect*	61°22′0″N
Latitude	34°56′14″S

	By log		Latitude South		Longitude East							
Course	Distance	DR	Obs	DR	TK	Var allowed	Set or current	Ther	Barom	Bearing & distance	Error of TK
N82°E	139½	35°7′	34°56′	1°36′	4°36′	19W	6N 5E	53° 56° 62°	– 30.13 30.14	Cape of Good Hope N88°E 226½ leagues	–11′

[f. 76] **Sunday 11 October** *Investigator* **from Madeira**

Fresh breezes with fine weather. Set the fore and fore top mast stu*dding* sails, and the spanker. Squally. Took in the studding sails, treble-reefed the fore, and took two reefs in the main and mizzen top sails. Fresh breezes and squally. Handed the main top-gall*ant* sail and spanker. Moderate breezes and fine weather. At daylight, let one reef out of each top-sail, and set the spanker. Set the fore and fore-top mast studding sails. Cleaned the ship below and aired with stoves. Mustered the ships company and saw them clean. Set the staysails. Moderate breezes and fine weather. Many birds of different kinds about the ship. Weeks expenditure of water 2⅔ tons: Remaining 36⅓ tons.

Me*ridian* alt*itude* ☉ Center Circl*e*	62°15′45″N
Latitude	34°41′10″S

	By log		Latitude South		Longitude East							
Course	Distance	DR	Obs	DR	TK	Var allowed	Set or current	Ther	Barom	Bearing & distance	Error of TK
E1°N	170	34°55′	34°41′	5°3′	8°6′ 7°50′ by ☉ west ☾	22°W	14N 3E	58° 50° 57°	– 30.22 30.24	Cape of Good Hope N88½°E 169 leagues	–11′

Monday 12 October

Fresh breezes & fine w*eathe*r. Hauled up for a short time to get lunar observations. Took in studding sails and double-reefed the m*izzen* topsail. Hauled down the spanker. Moderate breezes and fine weather. Let the 2nd reef out of the fore, and the whole out of the m*izzen* topsail; and set the fore-top-mast and fore studding sails, and spanker. Set

royals, top-gallant studding-sails, and mizzen top-gallant sail. People employed working up junk. *Ditto* weather, with a long swell from the *westward*. Took in the royals.
Meridian alt*itude* ☉ center by Circle   62°38′7″N
Latitude   34°47′12″S

		Latitude South		Longitude East							
Course	Distance	DR	Obs	DR	TK	Var allowed	Set or current	Ther	Barom	Bearing & distance	Error of TK
S82°E	154	35°3′	34°41′	8°8′	11°16′ By SF JT	24W	22N 5E	55° 54° 62°	– 30.23 30.20	Cape of Good Hope N88°E 117 leagues	−12′

[f. 77] Tuesday 13 October towards the Cape of Good Hope

Moderate breezes and fine weather. Saw a stream of birds resembling pigeons coming from the eastward. A cross swell running from the south westward, which occasions the ship to roll considerably. Took a reef in the *mizzen* top-sail, and sent down the top-gallant sail. Light breezes with fine weather. Took in the studding-sails and braced up the yards. Fresh breezes and cloudy weather. Took in staysails and top-gallant sails. At 7, tacked ship to the southward, and double-reefed the topsails. Treble-reefed the fore and mizzen top sails, and sent down top-gall*ant* yards, there being a considerable headswell which makes the ship plunge. Fresh and strong breezes alternately, with cloudy weather; and an uncomfortable swell from the south-westward. Pintado-birds, carey chickens,[1] and small blue petrels about the ship: one of the pintados was caught with a hook and line.

		Latitude South		Longitude East							
Course	Distance	DR	Obs	DR	TK	Var allowed	Set or current	Ther	Barom below	Bearings & distance	Error of TK
S83°E	59	34°48′	–	9°20′	–	24W	12S 8W	56° 55° 56°	– 30.13 30.20	Some observations were taken this AM but too uncertain for dependence	−12′

Wednesday 14 October

Fresh breezes and cloudy, with a southerly swell. Moderate breezes. Let out 3rd reefs, sent up top gall*ant* yards, set the sails and the top staysail. At 6, wore ship, the southerly swell having made her miss stays. Fresh breezes and squally weather. Took in top-gallant

---

[1] i.e. storm petrels, often called Mother Carey's chickens.

Plate 1. A bay on the south coast of New Holland, January 1802, by William Westall. Oil on canvas. © National Maritime Museum, Greenwich, London. Ministry of Defence Art Collection.

Plate 2. *Cephalotus follicularis*, Australian pitcher plant, by Ferdinand Bauer. © Natural History Museum, London.

Plate 3.   *Stylidum scandens*, climbing trigger plant, by Ferdinand Bauer. Plate 82 from his *Botanical Drawings from Australia* (1801). © Natural History Museum, London.

Plate 4.   *Phascolarctos cinereus*, koalas by Ferdinand Bauer. Plate 5 from his collection of
49 original watercolour drawings of animals. © Natural History Museum, London.

sails. Fresh breezes and cloudy weather. At daylight, set top gallant sails, let out 2nd reefs, and set staysails. Moderate breezes and cloudy weather. People employed working up junk. Several birds about the ship, and some pintados were caught with a hook and line. Noon, moderate breezes with fine weather; but the swell from the southward makes the ship plunge a little.

Meridian altitude ☉ Lower Limb Circle direct	62°42′35″N
Latitude	35°5′32″S

By log		Latitude South		Longitude East							
Course	Distance	DR	Obs	DR	TK	Var allowed	Set or current	Ther	Barom	Bearing & distance	Error of TK
N83°E	56	34°41′	35°6′	10°28′	13°20′ 13°3′ by ☉ west ☾	25W	13S 8W	55° 55° 58°	– 30.22 30.21	Cape of Good Hope N82E 84 leagues	–12′

[f. 78] **Thursday 15 October *Investigator* from Madeira**

Moderate breezes and cloudy, with occasional clear intervals. Some pintado birds caught. Double-reefed the fore and mizzen top sails. Light breezes. Took in the staysails and spanker to keep them from beating about with the rolling of the ship. The watch scrubbing their hammocks. At daylight, let out 2nd reefs and set the fore and fore top-mast studding sails. Moderate breezes and cloudy weather. Set the spanker. Mustered the ships company and saw them all clean, afterwards took an account of their clothing. Moderate breezes and cloudy; and the water tolerably smooth.

Meridian altitude ☉ Lower Limb Sextant 483	63°15′46″N
Latitude	34°54′37″S

By log		Latitude South		Longitude East							
Course	Distance	DR	Obs	DR	TK	Var allowed	Set or current	Ther	Barom	Bearing & distance	Error of TK
N82°E	107	35°21′	34°55′	12°37′	15°32′ 15°15′ ☉ west ☾	26W	26N 3E	53° 54° 57°	– 30.22 30.16	Cape of Good Hope N79°E 143 miles (TK)	–12′

Friday 16 October

Moderate breezes and cloudy, with spitting rain and squalls at times. Took in the staysails and spanker. Took in the studding sails and 2nd reefs. Fresh breezes and cloudy, with spitting rain at times. Squally. Took in top-gallant sails and *Mizzen* top-mast stay sail. Saw the land through the haze bearing ENE: the weather squally at times with rain, so that we had but a very partial view of the land. Bent the cables, unstowed the anchors &c. At noon, the west extreme of the land NbyE and the high land towards Cape False ESE.[1] The weather hazy, but finer than before. At this time we have no person on the sick list.[2]

Meridian altitude ☉ center Circle   64°16′28″N

Latitude   34°32′2″S

	By log	Latitude South		Longitude East							
Course	Distance	DR	Obs	DR	TK	Var allowed	Set or current	Ther	Barom	Bearing & distance	Error of TK
N88°E	157	34°49′	34°32′	15°45′ ☉ west ☾	18°42′ 18°26′	27W	17N 1W	57° 57° 58°	– 30.05 30.11	Cape Point in sight bearing true North distant 3 or 4 leagues	–12′

[f. 79] **Saturday 17 October in False Bay Cape of Good Hope**

Fresh breezes with finer weather. Hauled up for the Cape Point[3] so soon as the observation for the latitude was calculated, and passed close without side the rocks that lie off it, the wind then becoming very variable in flaws[4] off the land. At 3hours 30′ saw the ships in Simons Bay[5] and at 4 the guard boat came on board. Soon after the master of HM ship *Lancaster* came on board to conduct the ship to her anchorage, where we came

---

[1] At 8 a.m. Flinders first saw the high land of the Cape of Good Hope. When the ship was 8 leagues from the Cape, he noted that Earnshaw's pocket timekeeper suggested it was only 5 leagues away whereas his own uncorrected lunar observations of 14 October indicated it was 12 leagues away. Britain had seized the Cape from the Dutch in 1795. This partly arose for strategic reasons (mainly to block French plans to occupy it) during the French revolutionary wars. But it also occurred because the Dutch at the Cape were a threat to Britain's commerce and settlements in India and the Pacific. A strong British military and naval presence was then established on the Cape Peninsula. On 1 October 1801, in accordance with the Treaty of Amiens, the Cape was restored to Dutch control, but British troops and a naval presence remained there because of Boer sympathy with the French. Flinders held instructions from the Admiralty to put in at the Cape of Good Hope for water and provisions. He had previously been at the Cape for seven weeks in 1791, when sailing with William Bligh, and later in January 1797, when he successfully took an examination for the rank of lieutenant at the Cape. The 'high land' refers to the Cape Peninsula between the Cape of Good Hope (34°20′S, 18°25′E) and Cape Town. Cape False was situated next to False Bay, which served as an anchorage when northerly gales made the entry to Table Bay hazardous. Vallance, Moore and Groves, eds, *Nature's Investigator*, pp. 77–8; Arkin, 'John Company at the Cape', pp. 177–344. Flinders, *A Voyage to Terra Australis*, I, pp. 36–8, describes the arrival at the Cape.

[2] Flinders wrote that he had closely followed James Cook's example in dealing with provisions, anti-scorbutics, cleanliness and shipboard discipline. Flinders, *A Voyage to Terra Australis*, I, p. 144.

[3] i.e. the Cape of Good Hope.

[4] i.e. gusts of wind.

[5] Off Simon's Town (34°12′S, 18°26′E), an embayment within False Bay.

to at six oclock in [*blank*] fathoms, furled the sails, and moored ship: Noahs Ark[1] bearing SE½S and the wharf SW½W about half a mile. The commander went on shore to wait upon the commander in chief. Ships draught of water Forward 13 feet 6 inches Aft 13 feet 10 inches. There were riding in Simons Bay, His Majestys ships *Lancaster*, *Jupiter*, *Diomede*, *Imperieuse*, *Hindoostan*, *Rattlesnake* and *Euphrosyne*, under the command of Vice Admiral Sir Roger Curtis Baronet and the *Countess of Sutherland* extra indiaman.[2]

Variable winds with occasional slight showers of rain. AM. Sent an officer on shore to pitch upon a watering place on the north side of the bay under the sand hills and sent two launch loads of empty casks on shore. Received on board a gang of caulkers from the squadron, who began immediately upon the quarter deck. Received 219 lbs of fresh beef. During the morning, slight showers of rain at times, but the weather in general fine.

This day continued to 36 hours, carrying the time on to Civil Account.[3]

PM. Moderate breezes and cloudy. A party of men on shore fetching water. Sent the tent-observatory & some astronomical instruments on shore to the astronomer and another tent with a small guard of marines under the charge of lieutenant Flinders. Sent on shore to the cooperage several packs and staves to be set up for water and provisions.

Thermometer   59°
Barometer   30.87

Additional remarks

Being unacquainted with the time that the kings ships usually leave False Bay to go around to Table Bay, but knowing that the *Sceptre*[4] had been lost in the latter place on the 5th of November, I had some time determined to put into False Bay, should we not learn by any ship that the squadron had already quitted it.[5] No person on board, in whom I could put confidence, had been in False Bay, and we were in some danger of mistaking Cape False for the Cape Point before the observation for the latitude was obtained at noon; and even then we were in some doubt, for the Cape Point is laid down in the Requisite Tables in 34°29′S, and as it bore due north should have been only 3 miles from us, instead of

---

[1] A large offshore rock in the Simon's Town area, on the False Bay side of the Cape peninsula (34°11′S, 18°27′E).

[2] The *Lancaster* was an East Indiaman launched in 1797 and hulked in 1807. It was a 64-gun vessel that served as the flagship at the Cape under the command of Sir Roger Curtis. It was returned to the Admiralty in 1832. The *Jupiter* was a 50-ton two-decker launched at Rotherhithe in 1778. It was wrecked in Vigo Bay in 1808. The *Diomede* was a 50-gun two-decker launched in 1798 from Deptford dockyard. It was broken up in 1815. The *Imperieuse* was originally a French vessel built at Toulon 1786–8 and taken by Britain at La Spezia in 1793. It was a fifth-rate 18-pounder frigate. The *Hindostan* was an East Indiaman purchased in 1795. It was a fourth-rate 56-gun two-decker, reregistered as a storeship in May 1801. The *Rattlesnake*, a ship-sloop with a quarterdeck, was launched in 1791 at Chatham dockyard. It was hulked in 1811. Curtis served in the navy in the American revolutionary and French revolutionary wars. He was appointed commander-in-chief of the Cape of Good Hope station in May 1800. He flew his flag in the *Lancaster* from 8 June 1801 to 24 February 1803. He was promoted to full admiral in 1804. Lyon, *The Sailing Navy List*, pp. 77, 115, 239, 241, 243, 260; Winfield, *British Warships in the Age of Sail*, pp. 104–5, 111, 118–19, 121, 159, 250–51; Knight, 'Curtis, Sir Roger (1746–1816)', pp. 778–9.

[3] This began at midnight (as distinct from nautical time which began 12 hours beforehand): see above, p. 90.

[4] HMS *Sceptre* was lost in Table Bay on 5 November 1799. Vallance, Moore and Groves, eds, *Nature's Investigator*, p. 78.

[5] This implies that Flinders wanted the safeguard of calling upon the naval vessels should any navigational difficulty arise at the Cape of Good Hope.

which we guessed its distance to be eight or nine. The point must certainly lie from 4 to 6 miles further north than it is laid down, and on consulting Cook's third voyage (Vol. III p. 484) I find it was made to lie in 34°23′S by the observations of captain King and Mr Bayly.[1]

In going up the bay we saw several whales; and some other fish which the sailors call a thrasher,[2] furiously engaged in combat with one of them at a less distance than half a mile from the ship. The thrasher threw himself frequently out of the water, [f. 80] apparently for the purpose of bruizing his opponent by falling upon him, and with his large shark-like tail he otherwise beat the poor whale unmercifully, who seemed to have no other defence than the great bulk of his body and the thick coat of fat that covered it.

On getting up to Simons Bay, I understood that Sir Roger Curtis, the commander in chief, had just arrived from Cape Town, and it was thought probable that he would return this same evening; I therefore left the ship working up to the anchorage under the charge of the master of the flag ship as pilot, and went on shore to wait upon the admiral before he should be gone. On shewing my orders, and explaining the various supplies and the necessary work requisite to put the *Investigator* into the same state as when she left England, I found that the naval stores could with difficulty furnish some part, and were utterly incapable of furnishing other supplies; but with great consideration for the service in which we were engaged, the Vice-Admiral ordered us to be supplied with everything wanted, either in the articles specified, or by substitution; and a thorough caulking, both without and within side being the principal part of the work necessary to our refitment, a gang of caulkers, collected from the different ships, were ordered immediately, and came on board in the morning.

Water is conducted down to the wharf in pipes for the convenience of ships, but we were informed this did not keep well at sea, and that which drains out at the bottom of the sand hills on the north side of the bay was recommended to us as being much superior in this respect. The officer whom I sent to examine the place found, that by sinking a cask in the sand with its head out and the upper hoops off, the water would drain in through the spaces between the staves, sufficiently clear and fast enough for our purpose; casks were therefore immediately sent on shore, and we began to fill with all expedition. This and some other necessary duties being set forward under the proper officers, I accompanied Mr Crosley, the astronomer, on shore to search for a convenient place to set up the tent observatory and a marquee. About three hundred yards from the magazine on the south side of the bay towards the town, and near a small rill of fresh water, was the situation we thought most convenient; and after obtaining the permission of the military commandant, the observatory, marquee, and part of the astronomical instruments were sent on shore and set up in the afternoon. The marquee and guard of marines I put under

---

[1] Lieutenant James King (1750–84) and William Bayly both served as astronomers on Cook's third Pacific voyage on the *Resolution* and *Discovery* in 1776. King ended up as commander of the *Discovery* and contributed to the authorship of the official account of this voyage published after Cook's death: see Cook and King, *A Voyage to the Pacific Ocean*. Bayly witnessed Cook's death in Hawaii. See Williams, 'King, James', pp. 412–13, and Howse, 'Bayly, William', p. 468.

[2] Correctly, the thresher shark, genus *Alopias*. A large and voracious shark whose name derives from the great length of the upper lobe of its tail, with which it beats, or thrashes, its prey. There are in fact three species, of different sizes.

the charge of Mr Flinders, the second lieutenant, who was also to assist Mr Crosley in his observations, for which he is qualified.[1]

Sunday 18 October
Civil account
Moderate and cloudy. Employed filling the coal hole out of the fore hold, watering the ship, picking oakum for the caulkers, and unbending the sails to be sent on board the *Lancaster* to be repaired. PM. Fine weather. Struck the lower yards and unrigged them. Received 230 lbs of fresh beef.

[f. 81] Monday 19 October
Moderate breezes and fine weather. The gang of caulkers on board and employed upon the ships bows. People employed in the holds. At noon, fresh breezes at times, with cloudy weather and occasional rains. Employed PM in sending on shore packs, staves, and casks to the cooperage, and as before.

Tuesday 20 October
Moderate and cloudy. Employed mostly in rafting off water and stowing it away, both AM. and PM. Caulkers upon the ships sides.

Wednesday 21 October
Light breezes and cloudy. Received 130 lbs of mutton. Discharged four men into H.M. ship *Lancaster* in lieu of four received.[2] Completed our provisions as we left England by receiving the requisite quantities of pease, sugar, and spirits, and rice in lieu of bread, from the *Lancaster*. PM. Moderate and cloudy. Employed in the holds and upon other necessary duties. Caulkers on board as before.[3]

Thursday 22 October[4]
Fresh breezes and squally. Received 57 lbs of fresh beef. Struck top gallant masts, cleared hawse, and got the sheet anchor over the side. Entered Mr Denis Lacy, midshipman, from the *Lancaster*. PM. People employed in the holds &c. Boats of the squadron assisting the ship *Countess of Sutherland*, who in preparing to sail had driven too far over to the north side of the bay, and touched the ground. Squally weather.

---

[1] Flinders hoped that he and his brother Samuel would have enough knowledge to continue this work. He did not intend to apply to the Board of Longitude for a replacement astronomer because nobody could reach Port Jackson in less than twelve months. Work continued at the observatory on shore until 1 November. Some of the scientists and naturalists – Robert Brown, John Allen and Ferdinand Bauer – also went ashore on this day. Estensen, *The Life of Matthew Flinders*, p. 174; Vallance, Moore and Groves, eds, *Nature's Investigator*, p. 79. For the botanical work undertaken, see Rourke, 'Robert Brown at the Cape of Good Hope', pp. 47–60.

[2] For the changes in the ship's company, see Appendix 1, vol. II, pp. 506–10.

[3] On this day Flinders wrote to Sir Joseph Banks to explain that he had 'thus far advanced prosperously in the voyage.' He has not yet heard about the arrival of the *Lady Nelson* at Port Jackson. He does not expect that the *Investigator* will arrive at Port Jackson before April 1802. Flinders to Banks, 21 October 1801, in Brunton, ed., *Matthew Flinders*, p. 77.

[4] On this day Flinders wrote a letter to his father, describing the ship's arrival at the Cape of Good Hope, noting that Samuel Flinders may turn out to be a successful assistant, approving of his father's retirement, and anxiously awaiting news from his wife. See Lincolnshire Archives, Flinders Papers, Matthew Flinders to Mr Flinders, 22 October 1801.

Friday 23 October
Moderate breezes and fine. Received boatswains stores in lieu of old returned, and 120 lbs of fresh beef. Our cooper employed on shore at the cooperage. Caulkers on board as before, and our carpenters working with them as usual. PM. Light breezes and sultry. Received boatswains stores, and also salt beef, pork, suet, raisins and vinegar to complete the ship in those species of provisions. Sent a boat to assist H.M. ship *Diomede*, as per signal.

Saturday 24 October
Moderate and dull cloudy weather. Received 130lbs of fresh beef. Answered the signal for all lieutenants. Employed rafting off water and stowing it away. At noon, fresh breezes with frequent small rain and thick weather. Sailed for England the ship *Countess of Sutherland*. The caulkers employed upon the lower deck, having finished the upper one and the outside of the ship.

Sunday 25 October
Moderate and fine weather. People employed scraping the outside of the ship, painting the masts, and stowing the holds. The caulkers at work upon the lower deck. PM. Fresh breezes and cloudy. At 1, fired a royal salute in commemoration of His Majestys accession to the throne, as did the squadron.[1]

Monday 26 October
Strong breezes with rain at times. Received 131 lbs of mutton. Caulkers employed upon the lower deck and under the counter. People employed principally in scraping the ships sides and upper deck. PM. Strong gusts of wind at times off the hills, with dull cloudy weather. Employed as in the morning.

[f. 82] Tuesday 27 October
Fresh breezes with small rain. Sailed H.M. ships *Diomede* and *Rattlesnake*. Got up the cables from the lower deck, and scraped, washed, and aired it well with stoves; then recoiled the cables over the part of the spare rudder. Received 132 lbs of fresh mutton, with fruit and vegetables as usual. PM. Fresh breezes and cloudy. Paid the ships company for their savings of bread between August 1 and October 20, amounting to £43/6, together with an advance of ten per cent. Struck the fore-top mast, fitted new cross trees, swayed up the mast, and sent up the top-gallant mast. Discharged all the caulkers except two, kept to repair ladders, gratings &c. Carpenters began painting the ship on the outside.

Wednesday 28 October
Fresh breezes and cloudy weather. Gave the upper deck a second scraping. Punished William Job and Edward Coward, seamen with twelve lashes each, for drunkenness and neglect of duty. Received our sails from the *Lancaster* where they have been repaired. Carpenters employed painting the ship, repairing ladders, and in other jobs. PM. Fresh breezes and cloudy. Swayed up the lower yards and bent sails. Fresh gales and fine weather, with some haze.

---

[1] George III acceded to the British throne on 25 October 1760.

Thursday 29 October

Moderate and fine weather. Stayed the masts and set up the rigging. Cut up two casks of pork and one of beef to their contents, and returned the casks. Carpenters employed painting the ship and as before. At noon, almost calm, but afterwards moderate breezes and fine. Employed in occasional jobs preparing for sea.

Friday 30 October

Moderate and fine. Employed principally in the holds. Discharged Mr N[athaniel] Bell into H.M.S. *Hindoostan* for a passage to England, per order.[1] Received boatswains and carpenters stores, and 132 lbs of fresh beef. PM. Got off the larger astronomical instruments from the observatory. Carpenters employed as before.

Saturday 31 October

Moderate breezes and fine. Received 170 lbs of fresh beef. Stowed the sheet anchors and swayed up top gallant masts. Employed fitting the studding sail geer [*sic*] and preparing everything for sea about the rigging. Cloudy weather.

Sunday 1 November

Fresh breezes and clear weather. Received 69 lbs of fresh beef. Struck top gall*a*nt masts. Employed refitting the studding sail geer, and securing everything for sea. PM Fresh gales and fine weather, with some haze. The commander brought off the timekeepers and remaining astronomical instruments.[2] Struck top-gallant masts and pointed the yards to the wind.

Monday 2 November

Moderate breezes. Received 230 lbs of fresh beef, and a weeks allowance of fruit and vegetables from the hospital.[3] Swayed up top-gall*a*nt masts, hoisted in the launch and prepared to unmoor so soon as the wind should permit. PM. Moderate and fine weather. Employed preparing for sea at night, it became calm.

[f. 81 extra] Tuesday 3 November[4]

Light airs. Sent up top gall*a*nt yards, cleared hawse, unmoored ship and hove short; but the wind freshening up again, blowing into the bay, the ship drove, and obliged us to drop the second anchor and send down top-gallant yards. Received 200 lbs of fresh beef, making the whole quantity received here from the Victualling Office to be 2200lbs. PM Light winds with variable weather. Hove up the best bower and veered to a third of a cable on the small bower, waiting for a wind to get out. Employed in the

---

[1] Nathaniel Bell left the voyage after claiming that he was unfit for service. His brother Thomas Bell remained on board. Estensen, *The Life of Matthew Flinders*, p. 174.

[2] The observatory and tents were also taken down this afternoon and stowed on board ship ready for departure. Vallance, Moore and Groves, eds, *Nature's Investigator*, p. 84.

[3] A naval hospital in Cape Town. Flinders, *A Voyage to Terra Australis*, I, p. 147.

[4] On this day Flinders wrote warmly to his wife, hoping that she will write to him regularly while he is absent. He misses her company but notes 'how miserable should I be as an idle man, I certainly should not live a twelve-month'. This letter was to be taken back to London by John Crosley, the astronomer who left the voyage at the Cape. Flinders to Ann Flinders, 3 November 1801, in Brunton, ed., *Matthew Flinders*, p. 78.

holds and securing everything for sea. At 6, a breeze sprung up, but it was then too late to move.[1]

Wednesday 4 November <u>Consisting of 12 hours only</u>
Moderate and fine weather. At 5, cloudy. Sent up top-gallant yards. Discharged Mr John Crosley, astronomer, by request, on account of ill health.[2] Set the sails, weighed the anchor, and cheered the vice admiral as we passed under the *Lancasters* stern. Tacked ship occasionally working down False Bay, with a boat towing ahead occasionally, the wind being light and variable. Heavy clouds hanging over the high land, and drizzling rain falling at times. Set royals and top-gallant studding sails. At noon, light breezes and fine. Cape Point WSW 2 or 3 leagues.

<u>Additional remarks</u>
Since leaving Madeira, Mr Crosley has been frequently unwell, and after trying the effect of a few days stay on shore he decided to remain at the Cape of Good Hope. He had imparted to me the probability of this event on our arrival, and therefore I had made use of every leisure moment to improve my knowledge in the department of science, and particularly to become familiar with the use of the larger instruments supplied to him by the Board of Longitude.[3]

The loss of the astronomer attached to the expedition could not be otherwise than severely felt by me, both on account of the improvement that I hoped to acquire from the conversation of a man of science, and also from the additional labour that must necessarily devolve upon me in those situations where time could be least spared to execute it. With respect to the voyage and the expectations that general science may entertain from it, the effect of this loss will be of more extensive import. Experiments and observations in this department cannot be made so often, or with that degree of nicety that might be expected from a professional man whose sole business it was to make them; and it is to be feared, that the situations of those places where the observatory may hereafter be set up, will want much of the accuracy that might have been attained; and since to fill up this important vacancy lies with me, so far as I may be able to accomplish the task, the loss will also be felt by the marine surveys, to which that portion of my time, which must be necessarily dedicated to the observatory, would have been otherwise wholly appropriated. With the assistance of my officers, however, especially of the second lieutenant, and an increase of exertion on my own part, I was not without hope that the most material part of the instructions from the Board of Longitude to the astronomer would be executed. Of these instructions Mr Crosley permitted me to take a copy, which is as follows.

[f. 82 extra] Instructions for Mr John Crosley, going as astronomer on board His Majestys ship *Investigator* to New Holland[4]

---

[1] The south-easterly gale had abated long enough for the ship to be unmoored but its departure from Simon's Bay was delayed by the return of the winds referred to here. Flinders, *A Voyage to Terra Australis*, I, pp. 41–3.
[2] Crosley had been frequently ill on the voyage from rheumatism and gout. Estensen, *The Life of Matthew Flinders*, p. 174.
[3] See below, pp. 211–12, for the list of these instruments.
[4] A draft version of these instructions is included in CUL, RGO 14/185, Royal Greenwich Observatory, Board of Longitude Papers, ff. 4r–4(b)r, Board of Longitude to John Crosley, 1 March 1801.

Observations to be made on ship board

1st You are every day, if the weather will permit, to observe the meridian altitudes of the sun, for finding the latitude: and other altitudes of the sun, both in the morning and afternoon, at a distance from noon, with the time between measured by a watch, and the sun bearing to the azimuth compass at the first observation, in order to determine both the apparent time of the day, and latitude, for fear the sun should be clouded at noon: You are moreover to observe distances of the moon from the sun and fixed stars with the Hadleys sextant,[1] from which you are to compute the longitude of the ship by the nautical almanac.

2nd You are to wind up the watches every day, as soon after the time of noon as you can conveniently, and compare them together and set down the respective times; and you are to note also the times of the watches when the suns morning and afternoon altitudes, or the distances of the moon and sun or fixed stars are observed; and to compute the longitude resulting from the comparison of the watches with the apparent time of the day from the morning and afternoon altitudes of the sun.

3rd You are to observe, or assist at the observation of, the variation of the compass, and to observe the inclination of the dipping needle from time to time.

4th You are to note the height of one or more thermometers placed in the air, and in the shade, early in the morning, and about the hottest time of the day; and to observe also the height of the thermometer within the vessel near the watches; and to make experiments of the saltness of the sea and the degree of cold, by letting the thermometer to greatest depths, as you shall have opportunity; and to make remarks on the southern lights, when you are far to the south, if any should appear.[2]

5th You are to keep a ship journal, with the log worked according to the dead reckoning, allowing for leeway and variation, noting therein the log line and the time of running out of the sand glasses from time to time, by the help of the watches: and you are to insert therein also another account corrected by the last celestial observations, and a third deduced from the watches.

6th You are to teach such officers on board the vessel as may desire it, the use of the Hadleys sextant in taking the moons distance from the sun and fixed stars, and the method of computing the longitude from the observations.[3]

---

[1] John Hadley (1682–1744) invented the octant around 1730. Capt. John Campbell enlarged Hadley's octant to a sixth of a circle, thereby creating the sextant. The sextant allows its user to determine the elevation of celestial objects in relation to the horizon. If the position of the object in the sky and the time of the observation are known, the user can calculate latitude. The sextant became an important part of navigation and replaced the cross-staff. The term 'Hadley's sextant' seems to have been adopted by makers to distinguish the reflecting sextant, principally designed for navigation, from the non-reflecting astronomical sextant. It was Hadley's design for the octant which established the advantages of the reflecting instrument, and the reflecting sextant was simply an enlargement of Hadley's reflecting octant. Hadley did not set up a firm to make the instruments, but apparently made an arrangement with a number of mathematical instrument makers to produce them, presumably under licence as Hadley had secured a patent. Clifton, 'Hadley, John', pp. 428–9.

[2] A reference to the southern polar lights (aurora australis), which are only visible from high latitudes in Antartica, South America and Australasia.

[3] Refers to celestial navigation to determine longitude by lunar distances. The navigator precisely measured the angle between the moon and a select group of stars lying along the ecliptic, corrected the angle for various errors, consulted an almanac that listed angles in tables, found the angle measured in relation to Greenwich time, and by this means calculated the longitude.

7th   You are to settle the positions of head lands, islands, and harbours, in latitude and longitude, by the celestial observations; and also set down what longitude the watches give to them.

Observations to be made on shore

1st   When you land, if time permits, you are to set up the tent observatory and astronomical clock; either setting the pendulum exactly to the same length as it was of at Greenwich before the voyage, or noting the difference by the revolution of the screw and divisions of the nut at bottom; and you are to take equal altitudes of the sun and fixt stars with the universal theodolite[1] with Hadleys sextant, by reflexion from the surface of quicksilver in a basin, according to circumstances, for determining the rate of going of the clock, [f. 81 extra [2]] and for finding the time of noon, and fixing a meridian for the universal theodolite, which is after that to be used as a transit instrument and meridian circle. You will thus, also, by the difference of the going of the clock at the place from its going at Greenwich before the voyage, determine the relative force of gravity between the two places.[2]

2nd   You are to wind up the watches every day, as soon after the time of noon as you can conveniently, and compare them together, and with the astronomical clock at the time, and also about the times of the equal altitudes, if any were taken.

3rd You are to observe meridian altitudes of the sun, and also of the brighter fixt stars, some to north and some to the south, or with the Hadleys sextant by reflexion from the basin of quicksilver, according to circumstances, and note the height of the thermometer in the shade, and that of the portable barometer.

4th   You are to observe continually transits of the sun and brighter fixt stars, being nearest the equator, over the meridian, and of the moon occasionally with the universal theodolite; and to observe eclipses of Jupiters first satellite,[3] and occultations[4] of fixt stars by the moon; and to take distances of the moon from the sun and fixed stars with Hadleys sextant; from all which you are to compute the going of the clock and watches, and the longitude of the place by the nautical almanac.

5th   You are to observe the height of the tides, and the times of high and low water, particularly at the full and change, and quarters of the moon, and to note whether there be any difference and what, between the night and day tides.[5]

6th   You are to observe the variation of the compass and the inclination of the dipping needle; and 7th you are to note the height of one or more thermometers placed in the shade, early in the morning, and about the hottest time of the day.

---

[1] An optical instrument used for astronomical work in navigation and in surveying. It is used for measuring horizontal and vertical angles upon a graduated circle.

[2] Gravity observations often comprised a series of daily clock rate comparisons of a special pendulum clock timed against some astronomical observations (daily equal altitudes of the sun either side of midday) often aggregated over the course of a month.

[3] Refers to Io (Jupiter 1), the first of the four moons discovered by Galileo in 1609–10. It is the fourth largest moon in the solar system. Eclipses are relatively frequent for Jupiter because its moons are large and it has a low axial tilt.

[4] An occultation is an event that occurs when one object is hidden by another object that passes between it and the observer. Astronomical events that produce occultations include transits and eclipses.

[5] A reference to the lunar and solar tides. These both exert a tidal gravitational pull. Both the moon and the sun affect tides, but since the moon is much closer to the earth it has a greater effect on tides than the sun. Ruthven, 'Theory of the Tides', pp. 1490–502.

General directions

You are to take particular care, that all your nautical and astronomical observations and trigonometrical operations, with the results, whether made on ship board or on shore, be kept in a clear, distinct and regular manner, in a book or books prepared for that purpose; and that they be written therein, with all their circumstances, immediately after they shall be made, or as soon after as they can be conveniently transcribed therein, from the loose papers or memorandum books, in which they may have been first entered; which book or books are to be always open for the inspection and use of the commander and master of the vessel; and you are to send to the astronomer royal,[1] by every safe conveyance which may offer, the results of your several observations, and also the principal observations themselves.

The astronomical instruments with which Mr Crosley was charged by the board, he agreed to leave with me, after having consulted with the commander in chief upon the subject, and received his approbation: the list of them is as follows.

[f. 82 extra [2]] A tent observatory

An astronomical clock, by Earnshaw[2]

An assistant clock

An alarum clock

Two box-time keepers, No. 82 & 176,[3] by Arnold

Two *ditto* in jimbols,[4] No. 520 543, by Earnshaw

A universal theodolite by the late Mr. Ramsden[5]

An acromatic telescope[6] of 46 inches focus, with an object-glass micrometer, and an eye tube with moveable wires, and a stand

A Hadleys sextant, by the late Mr. Ramsden

A *ditto* made by Mr. Dollond, with his patent back observation piece[7]

A wooden trough to hold quicksilver, with an inclined glass roof, for observing double altitudes by reflexion from the surface of the quicksilver, with Hadleys sextant

[1] A senior post in the British royal household, established in 1675. The incumbent was Director of the Royal Observatory, Greenwich, until 1972. The Rev. Dr Nevil Maskelyne (1732–1811) held this position from 1765 to 1811. He was an advocate of the lunar distance method of determining longitude. Howse, *Nevil Maskelyne* and *idem*, 'Maskelyne, Nevil', pp. 155–8.

[2] A highly accurate long-case clock built by Thomas Earnshaw in 1791. Used by George Vancouver on his voyage between 1791 and 1795 and by Flinders to check the timekeeping of the chronometers on the *Investigator*. It is now on display at the Powerhouse Museum, Sydney. See www.powerhousemuseum.com/collection/database. Betts, 'Earnshaw, Thomas', pp. 576–8.

[3] Flinders would have been familiar with Arnold's No. 176 from Bligh's second breadfruit voyage. Rigby, '"The whole of the surveying department rested on me"', p. 265. For further information on this chronometer, see Harries, 'A Late 18th Century "Expedition" Chronometer', pp. 5–10.

[4] i.e. gimbals, pivots on which an instrument is suspended, so that it remains horizontal on board ship.

[5] For information on Ramsden's instruments, see Stimson, 'Some Board of Longitude Instruments in the Nineteenth Century', pp. 93–115. For a detailed study of Ramsden, see McConnell, *Jesse Ramsden*.

[6] An achromatic telescope is a refracting telescope that uses an achromatic lens to correct for chromatic aberration. John Dollond (see next note below) acquired patent rights over the achromatic telescope, which his son Peter exploited commercially. Bennett, 'The Era of Newton, Herschel and Lord Rosse', pp. 33–42.

[7] John Dollond (1707–61), his son Peter Dollond (1730–1820) and Peter's nephew George Dollond (1774–1852) were master astronomical instrument makers in London. This refers to a patent taken out by Peter Dollond in 1772 for a lever arrangement for adjusting the back horizon glass of a sextant or octant. This device allowed a wider angle to be observed than the 120° of the standard sextant or the 90° of an octant. Clifton, *Directory of British Scientific Instrument Makers,* p. 87.

Six pounds of quicksilver (only 4 received)
A marine barometer
Two portable barometers
Three thermometers
A dipping needle, by Nairne & Blunt[1]
A set of six-inch magnetic bars to touch the dipping needle & change its poles
A pocket compass
An azimuth compass and spare card
A 30 inch night glass, by Dollond[2]
A 4 feet hand perspective
Two buckets to fetch up sea water from a depth, in order for the trial of its temperature as to heat and cold, and specific gravity as a measure of its saltness
A hydrostatic balance with three glasses to weigh water in, and one solid glass
A theodolite[3] and stand
A gunters chain[4]
A plain table and stand
Two ten-feet deal rods with brass ends
A five-feet brass standard
A beam compass[5] and scale of equal parts
A circular protractor
A station pointer[6]
Books and charts
Taylors logarithms[7]
Mackenzie on marine surveying[8]
Wild on surveying[9]
Huttons mathematical tables[10]
Robertsons navigation[11]
Two copies of Garrards tables of difference of latitude and departure[12]

[1] Edward Nairne (1726–1806) and his apprentice Thomas Blunt flourished in London c.1774–93 as optical instrument makers. A dipping needle is a magnetic needle suspended at its centre of gravity, and moving freely in a vertical plane, in order to indicate on a graduated circle the magnetic dip or inclination.

[2] i.e. a large marine telescope.

[3] A precision instrument for measuring angles in the horizontal and vertical planes.

[4] A measuring device used for land survey.

[5] A compass with a beam and sliding sockets or cursors for drawing and dividing circles larger than those made by a regular pair of compasses.

[6] A charting instrument comprising a graduated circle and three arms, one of which is fixed (at 0° on the scale) while the other two can move around the circle and have fixing screws.

[7] Named after the English mathematician Brook Taylor's *Methodus Incrementorum Directa et Inversa* (London, 1715). Taylor's logarithms were used by navigators to calculate the sun's rising and setting.

[8] i.e. Murdoch Mackenzie, Sr, *Treatise of Maritim Surveying* (London, 1774).

[9] Probably Samuel Wyld, *The Practical Surveyor, or the Art of Land-measuring made Easy*.

[10] Charles Hutton (1737–1823) published his *Mathematical Tables* in 1781 for the Board of Longitude. His most famous work was *The Mathematical and Philosophical Dictionary*.

[11] The most complete treatise on navigation in Flinders's age was Robertson, *The Elements of Navigation*.

[12] William Garrard had worked at the Royal Observatory, Greenwich. This is probably a reference to his *Copious Trigonometrical Tables*.

Two copies of the nautical almanacs for the years 1801, 1802, 1803, 1804, 1805[1]
(One copy of 1801, 1802 excepted, which were kept by Mr Crosley)
Two variation charts[2]
Wales on the longitude by time keepers[3]
Nautical almanac for 1773
My receipt for them was a copy of that given by Mr *Crosley* to the board, as follows
Received the above instruments and books (those marked IC excepted) from Mr John Crosley, on account of the Board of Longitude, which I promise to return to the said board in the best condition I am able, on the expiration of the *Investigators* voyage, the dangers of the sea and other accidents excepted.
Given under my hand on board H.M.S. *Investigator* in False Bay, Cape of *Good* Hope, this 31 day of October 1801 Matt*hew* Flinders[4]
[f. 81 extra [3]] Equal altitudes of the sun taken by lieutenant Flinders in a quicksilver horizon showed the errors of the time keepers from the established longitude to be as follows

1801 October ☿ 31	Pairs of altitudes		Uncorrected noon by Earnshaw 543	Correction	Interval between the observations
	[blank]		[blank]	[blank]	[blank]
Comparisons with 543			Longitudes given by Time Keepers		
Earnshaw 465	Arnold 1736		Earnshaw 543	Earnshaw 465	Arnold 1736
+ 5′11.50″	– 17′50.90″		19°4′28.5″	18°36′4.2″	20°50′28.3″

But a fresh departure having been taken for *Arnold* 1736 at Madeira, calling the longitude of that place 17°6′15″W whereas I believe it to lie in 16°56′W according to the Connaissance des temps: there has consequently been an error to the west in the longitude of that *Time Keeper* of +10′15″

Longitudes by time-keepers of Simons Town[5]   19°4′28.5″   18°36′4.2″   21°0′43.3″
But supposing its longitude to be the same as }
that of the Cape Town and Point,[6] I call it in }   18°23′15″   18°23′15″   18°23′15″
Errors of the time keepers to the eastward   0°41′13.5″   0°12′49.2″   2°37′28.3″
Error of the time keepers per day to the east   25.8″   8.0″   2′3.0″

The errors of E 543 and 465 were contracted since July 17, or in 96 days; but that of *Arnold* 1736 since August 8, or in 76 days. It is from these errors that the preceding columns of Err*or* of *Time Keeper* have been filled up; as also the corrections to the longitude of Trinidad, found on Sept*ember* 24.[7]

[1] Published annually by HM Nautical Almanac Office since 1767. The tables enabled navigators to use celestial navigation to determine the position of their ship while at sea. The almanac states for each whole hour of the year the position on the Earth's surface (in declination and Greenwich hour angle) at which the sun, moon, planets and first point of Aries is directly overhead. The positions of 57 selected stars are specified relative to the first point of Aries. Forbes, 'The Foundation and Early Development of the Nautical Almanac', pp. 391–401.

[2] Charts for calculating magnetic declination (i.e. the angle between magnetic north on a compass and true north).

[3] William Wales (1734–98) was a Nautical Almanac computer who served as the astronomer on Cook's second Pacific voyage (1772–5). He carried out work on longitude for the Board of Longitude. Orchiston and Howse, 'From transit of Venus to teaching navigation', pp. 156–66.

[4] Crosley took home with him Earnshaw's watch no. 465 and Troughton's reflecting circle no. 74, both of which Flinders considered a loss to the voyage. Flinders, *A Voyage to Terra Australis*, I, p. 147.

[5] The three columns of figures here represent the three timekeepers as in the table above.   [6] Cape Point.

[7] I have deleted 'see page 67'. For the corrections, see 'Additional remarks', after the entry for 24 September 1801, above on pp. 189–90.

Before leaving the ship Mr Crosley gave me a paper containing an account of the rates of going of all the time keepers left behind, from October 21 to 27. To this I added a set of equal altitudes (which follows hereafter) and brought the rates up to November 1 as in the following table[.]

1801 October	Times of comparison by		E520 slower than 543	Interval between comparisons	E520 loses		Daily rates		Daily rates of other TKs found by similar tables			Ther
	E520	E543	543		on 543	in 24h	E543	E520	A82	A176	A1736	
	h ′	h ′ ″	′ ″	h ′ ″	″	″	″	″	″	″	″	°
☿ 21	22 22	22 39 45.3	17 45.3									70
♃ 22	22 34	22 51 55.5	17 45.3	24 12	10.0	9.92	−5.09	−15.01	−3.51	−12.71	−20.73	67
♀ 23	22 29	22 47 6.2	17 55.3	23 55	10.9	10.94	−5.09	−16.03	−5.49	−15.10	Let down	80
♄ 24	22 28	22 46 16.0	18 6.2	23 59	9.8	9.80	−5.19	−14.99	−3.89	−12.22	−10.99	67
☉ 25	22 22	22 40 27.4	18 16.0	23 54	11.4	11.45	−5.19	−16.64	−3.29	−9.60	−9.01	71
☽ 26	22 20	22 38 37.8	18 27.4	23 58	10.4	10.42	−5.19	−15.61	−2.58	−7.89	−8.79	63
♂ 27	22 23	22 41 47.9	18 37.8	24 3	10.1	10.08	−5.19	−15.27	−2.00	−7.58	−11.59	70
☿ 28	22 16	22 34 58.5	18 47.9	23 53	10.6	10.65	−5.57	−16.23	−3.26	−7.48	−11.57	62
♃ 29	22 26	22 45 9.2	18 50.5	24 10	10.7	10.63	−5.57	−16.20	−4.08	−8.05	Let down	64
♄ 30	22 25	22 44 19.8	19 9.2	23 59	10.6	10.60	−5.57	−16.17	−1.37	−10.30	−16.77	64
♄ 31	22 32	22 51 29.8	19 19.8	24 7	10.0	9.96	−5.57	−15.53	−2.98	−5.27	−15.67	
☉ Nov 1	21 59	22 18 40.7	19 29.8	23 27	10.9	11.14	−5.57	−16.71	1.18.68	−2.40	−19.17	64
				Mean daily rates			−5.34	−15.854		−8.971	−17.203	

Note: Arnold 1736 was taken to be worn in the pocket on October 25 and returned to its box on the 29th. Its mean rate is deduced from comparisons with Earnshaw 543, on October 30, 31, and November 1. No rate is found for Arnold 82 from its irregularity. The observations by which the rates are continued up to November 1 and the final errors from mean Greenwich time as ascertained, are as follows

1801 November	Pairs of altitudes	Uncorrected noon by E 543	Correction of equal altitudes	Interval between the observations	Comparisons of Time Keepers with 543			
					E 520	A 82	A 176	A 1736
☉ 1	Eight	22 h51′32.33″	5.73″	3 h25′52″	− 19′40.7″	+ 41′36.0″	− 36′23.8″	+ 35′56.1″

Time Keepers found to differ from mean Greenwich time					
	E 543	E 520	A 82	A 176	A 1736
	− 14′42.69″	− 34′23.59″	+ 26′53.31″	−51′6.49″	+ 21′13.41″
Proportional part of the mean rates to reduce the errors to the time of mean noon there November 1 1801	+ 0.29″	+ 0.82″	[blank]	+ 0.46″	− 0.89″
Errors of Time Keepers from mean Greenwich time at noon there – 1st	− 14′42.98″ − or slow	34′24.21″		51′6.95″	21′12.52″ + or fast

[f. 82 extra [3]] <u>General remarks</u>

Besides completing our provisions and stores in False Bay, to nearly the same state as when the ship left Spithead, we were supplied every day with fresh meat, beef and mutton alternately. Vegetables were so scarce that they could not be bought, but we several times received small quantities from the naval hospital, which were sent from Cape Town; and to these were joined oranges and lemons. A few days before we were expected to sail, I represented to the commander in chief, that the lateness of the season and the service which I had to perform did not permit me to remain the usual time to refresh my ships company, and requested he would order for us as great a supply of fruit and vegetables to carry to sea as could be spared. With this request Sir Roger Curtis was pleased to comply, as indeed he did with all [requests] that I found it necessary to make to him for His Majestys Service.

To bring the ships company to the Cape in such a state of health that it should be unnecessary to remain one day on this account, beyond the time that the refitment of the ship required, was always a primary object with me during the passage from England; and we were so fortunate, that on our arrival there was not one man in the sick list. The advancement of the spring in the southern hemisphere made it unavoidable that a part of the most favourable season for exploring the southern coasts of New Holland must be lost before our arrival upon it; but that as little of it as possible should pass by us was the principal cause of my earnest desire to complete the re-equipment of the ship and pass the Cape of Good Hope with all practicable expedition. On this account we deferred examining into the state of the fore and mizzen rigging until our arrival in King Georges Sound, as well as put off such other duties as could bear delay and might be executed by our own people. In that place our naturalist would have ample employment so long as it might be necessary to stay, and the survey of the neighbouring parts, with the duties of the observatory in that important station, would very usefully occupy my time for two or three weeks, and much more agreeably than any business or amusement that the Cape of Good Hope could afford.

The usual time that His Majestys ships quit False Bay and return to Table Bay is the latter end of September.[1] That they were now lying in the former place in November was owing, in the first place, to the arrival of the *Hindoostan* from England, with a large supply of naval stores, the greater part of which it was necessary to deposit in False Bay. To land these and see them in security required a number of men, and all the artificers of the squadron that could be spared were employed in refitting the large extra-Indiaman the *Countess of Sutherland* which had been towed in dismasted. To this I ought to add the assistance required by the *Investigator*, and so simply given as to enable us to be ready for sea in sixteen days: on the seventeenth we should have been at sea had the wind permitted.

[f. 81 extra [4]] Since the loss of the *Sceptre* it appears that False Bay has been more frequented than formerly; and was it not from the disadvantage of its distance from Cape Town it would no doubt be more resorted to than Table Bay. It was observed to me by captain Larcom of the *Lancaster* that instances of ships being driven from their anchors by the south-east winds which blow into Simons Bay were exceedingly rare. We had observed that the strain upon a ships cables was not at all equal to what it was with the same quantity of wind off the land. This he accounted for by the water which the south-east winds force into the bay rebounding from the shore and forming a counter current

---

[1] This presumably occurred because False Bay was exposed to south-easterly winds in summer.

below the surface, which assists to keep a ship up to her anchors, and the more so if she rides near the shore. This takes place in Simons Bay with a south-east wind, but not so in Table Bay with the wind from the north-west, which blows into it; for ships there ride considerably further from the land, and not in the head of the bay; whence it most probably is, that the rebound of water, which is familiarly known to seamen by the expression undertow, does not pass out by where the ships ride in Table Bay but to the eastward of the anchorage.

Simons Bay is a case in the north-west part of False Bay; but it is so well known and has been so often mentioned that it is unnecessary to give any kind of direction for it: The chart of False Bay published by Laurie and Whittle seems moreover to be correct.[1] The country is very sandy in the neighbourhood of the town, and with every wind that blew, a considerable quantity was in motion and did much injury to our instruments in the observatory. There is a small place to the southward of the town called the Companys garden,[2] and the way to it lay past the place where our tents were pitched. This is the only ride or walk in the neighbourhood which the inhabitants of the town, as well as the gentlemen belonging to the ships in the bay, can enjoy. There was an inconvenience attending our having chosen this situation that was not at first thought of; for, from those of the first rank, who took their mornings ride, to the sailor who staggered past on a Sunday, all stopped at the observatory to see what was going on. Ramsdens universal theodolite, which was set up with the intention of observing transits, excited its share of attention from the curious. Some wanted information, some instruction, and all wished to see how the sun appeared through the telescope: thus the astronomer and his assistant had many hours of intermission from the tedious dryness of astronomical calculation.

Although the Cape of Good Hope cannot now be supposed to furnish much novelty in the department of natural history, especially to transient visitors who cannot go far from the water, it yet continues to afford an ample field for amusement and instruction to English botanists. This was the case with our gentlemen who were almost instantly on shore upon the search, and their collections, intended for examination on the next passage, were tolerably ample.[3] They were sufficiently orthodox in their mode of proceeding to walk many miles in order to botanize upon the celebrated Table Mountain,[4] as what disciple [f. 82 extra [4]] of Linnaeus would visit the Cape of Good Hope without doing it?[5] In taking so early a departure, though it was to proceed to the untrodden and not less fertile region of botany, New Holland, I had to engage with the counter wishes of my scientific companions; so much delighted were they to find the richest treasures of the English hot-house properly scattered upon the sides and summits of these barren hills.

[1] Robert Laurie and James Whittle, Fleet Street, London, published a chart of False Bay in 1794. Laurie and Whittle's *The country-trade East India pilot* (1799) also included a map of False Bay.
[2] The Company's Garden was laid out by Cape Town's founding father Jan van Riebeeck by order of the Dutch East-India Company to secure the provisioning of the colonists with vegetables. Today it is a large public park and botanical garden.
[3] Details on the botanizing at the Cape can be found in Vallance, Moore and Groves, eds, *Nature's Investigator*, pp. 78–83; Rourke, 'Robert Brown at the Cape of Good Hope', pp. 47–60; and Rourke, 'Getting There', pp. 25–37.
[4] A flat-topped mountain which is a prominent landmark overlooking the city of Cape Town. It has a level plateau about 1¾ miles from side to side, surrounded by steep cliffs. Its highest point is 3,563 feet above sea level.
[5] Carl Linnaeus (1707–78), the renowned Swedish botanist, whose taxonomic system for naming, ranking and classifying organisms is still in use today in the biological sciences.

Figure 5.   Portrait of Robert Brown (1773–1858), botanist on the *Investigator*, artist unknown. © Natural History Museum, London.

[f. 83] Thursday 5 November From the Cape towards New Holland[1]

Moderate breezes and fine weather. Hoisted up the cutter and secured all the boats. At 2, observed the water to be very red, which seemed to arise from its being full of round animalcula[2] there being no ground at 40 fathoms.[3] Stowed the anchors and unbent one cable. At 6, the extremes of the land SE½E and NWbW½W: the last being the Cape Point, and distant about 4 leagues. At 11, found bottom at 40 fathoms: Wore ship, having missed stays. Sounded in 50 fathoms. At daylight, the furthest land towards Cape Agullus[4] SEbE; and Cape False NEbN about 4 leagues. Light airs. Sounded at 9 o'clock in 78 fathoms greenish mud: Cape False bearing NE¾N and the Cape Point NNW. At noon, Sounded with 70 fathoms but got no bottom. Cape False bearing NEbN and the Cape Point NbW. Extreme towards Cape Agullus SEbE¾E. A light air springing up from the westward.

Meridian altitude ☉ Lower Limb	483 70°45′50″N
Latitude	34°36′0″

		Latitude South		Longitude East							
Course	Distance	DR	Obs	DR	TK	Var allowed	Set or current	Ther	Barom	Bearing & distance	Error of TK
S48°E	25	34°40′	34°36′	18°46′	18°45′	27W	4N 1W	59° 57° 68°	30.13 30.14 30.06	By HMS Lion Amsterdam Island lies in 38°42′S and longitude 76°54′E	−18″

Friday 6 November

Light breezes and fine weather. Set top-gallant studding sails. Heard guns, supposed to be the salute fired by the squadron in False Bay, to commemorate the escape from gunpowder treason.[5] The land in sight, extending from N½E to E½N. Fresh breezes and cloudy weather. Took in the middle stay sails and spanker. Squally at times. At daylight set the staysails, and the fore-top and lower studding sails. Fresh breezes and hazy. Took in the top mast studding sails. A few birds about the ship. Fresh breezes and fine weather, with haze: Some sea running from the WSW. A strange brig in sight.

Meridian altitude ☉ Lower Limb Sextant 483	69°52′0″N
Latitude	35°47′57″S

---

[1] Flinders had made the 5,000 mile crossing from the Cape of Good Hope to New Holland three times before. He chose the 37th parallel for the voyage to catch a prevailing westerly and to avoid gales in the higher latitudes. He had previously experienced heavy gales from the north and the south when sailing in 42° latitude. Estensen, *The Life of Matthew Flinders*, p. 175.

[2] Minute or microscopic organisms similar to paramecia or amoebae.

[3] The water appeared red because of a plankton bloom. Vallance, Moore and Groves, eds, *Nature's Investigator*, p. 84; Edwards, ed., *The Journal of Peter Good*, p. 45.

[4] Cape Agulhas (34°50′S, 20°00′E), in the Western Cape, is the official dividing line between the Atlantic and Indian oceans. It was a traditional hazard for sailors.

[5] i.e. to celebrate Guy Fawkes Night.

		Latitude South		Longitude East							
By log											
Course	Distance	DR	Obs	DR	TK	Var allowed	Set or current	Ther	Barom below	Bearing & distance	Error of TK
S51°E	133	36°00′	35°48′	20°52′	20°56′	27W	12N 5E	57° 57° 66°	30.02 29.92 29.93	Isle Amsterdam S86°E 893 leagues	–21′

[f. 84] Saturday 7 November *Investigator* from the Cape of Good Hope
Fresh breezes and squally weather. Carried away the lower studd*in*g sail boom. Handed the fore-top-gall*an*t sail, double-reefed the main and mizzen, and 3rd reefed the fore topsail. The strange brig passed astern of the ship showing a blue flag which we could not understand. Moderate breezes and cloudy weather. Took in top-gallant sails. Fresh gales and cloudy, with a considerable sea from the westward. Squally weather. Hauled up the main sail. A few albatrosses and pintados about the ship. Fresh breezes and cloudy weather, with occasional fine intervals. The swell from the westward makes the ship roll unpleasantly.
Mer*idian* alt*itude* ☉ Lowe*r* Lim*b* Sex*tant* 483   69°22′3″N
Latitude   36°35′40″S

		Latitude South		Longitude East							
By log											
Course	Distance	DR	Obs	DR	TK	Var allowed	Set or current	Ther	Barom	Bearing & distance	Error of TK
S73°E	157	36°34′	36°36′	23°57′	24°2′	26W	2S 1E	60° 60° 64°	29.98 29.84 29.87	Isle Amsterdam S87°E 83 leagues	–2′

Sunday 8 November
Strong breezes and cloudy weather, with rain at times. Set the main top gall*an*t sail. Squally with rain. Handed the main top gall*an*t and mizzen top sails; treble-reefed the main and close reefed the fore top sail. Bunted[1] the main sail. Strong breezes and squally, with rain at times. A heavy sea rolling after the ship from the westward. Heavy squalls at times. Fresh breezes generally, but sometimes interrupted with strong squalls. The ship very wet below, the water coming through the ships sides notwithstanding our late caulking, and through at the ports &c. Mustered the ships company and saw them clean. Fresh gales and cloudy weather, with a following sea from the westward.
Mer*idian* alt*itude* ☉ Lowe*r* Lim*b* Sex*tant* 483   69°45′58″N
Latitude   36°29′16″

---

[1] i.e. shaped the middle part of the sail like a pouch to increase the effect of the wind.

	By log	Latitude South		Longitude East						
Course	Distance	DR	Obs	DR	TK	Var allowed	Set or current	Ther	Barom	
S87°E	114	36°45′	36°29′	27°33′	–	30W	16N 10E	60° 55° 57°	29.86 29.90 30.01	No observations for the TKs either AM or PM

[f. 85] Monday 9 November towards Cape Leuwen New Holland

Strong breezes and cloudy weather, with squalls at times. Unsettled weather. Moderate breezes and cloudy. Squally at times, with rain: the westerly swell has abated a good deal of its violence. Set mizzen top-sail, let out double reef of the fore and main top-sails, and set top-gallant sails, stay sails, and spanker. At 8, let out 2nd reefs and set the fore-top and fore studding sails. Cleaned the ship below, and aired with stores. Issued sour kraut & vinegar to the people. Light breezes with fine weather, and some swell from the WSW. A few pintado birds and brown albatrosses about.

Meridian altitude ☉ Lower Limb 483   70°20′57″N
Latitude   36°11′30″S

	By log	Latitude South		Longitude East							
Course	Distance	DR	Obs	DR	TK	Var allowed	Set or current	Ther	Barom	Bearings & distance	Error of TK
S87½°E	144½	36°36′	36°12′	30°32′	30°57′	32W	24N 10E	54° 54° 64°	30.12 30.29 30.27	Isle Amsterdam S86°E 731 leagues	–36″

Tuesday 10 November

Light breezes with fine weather. Set main top-gallant studding sail. Clear starlight night: set the spanker. Moderate breezes with fine weather and smooth water. Set stay sails. Moderate breezes and cloudy. Some swell from the WSW still remaining. Exercised the watch below in the use of small arms, and fired two rounds of powder. Took in studding sails and spanker. Fresh breezes and hazy weather. Some albatrosses, many pintados, and some other birds about.

Meridian altitude ☉ Lower Limb Sextant 483   78°19′27″N
Latitude   36°30′01″S

	By log	Latitude South		Longitude East							
Course	Distance	DR	Obs	DR	TK	Var allowed	Set or current	Ther	Barom	Bearing & distance	Error of TK
S78°E	128	36°39′	36°30′	33°8′	33°36′	53W	9N 3E	61° 59° 65°	30.25 30.11 29.97	Isle Amsterdam S86°E 687 leagues	–41″

[f. 86] Wednesday 11 November *Investigator* from the Cape of Good Hope

Fresh breezes and hazy weather. Double-reefed the top-sails. Took in top gall*a*nt sails. Treble reefed the fore and mizzen top sails. Strong breezes and squally. Took in the main sail, and the main top and rig stay sails. Squally with rain, accompanied with loud thunder and vivid lightening. Treble-reefed the main, close-reefed the fore, and handed the mizzen top-sail. Unsettled weather, with rain at times. Set the treble-reefed fore, single reefed main and close-reefed mizzen top sail; and afterwards the main sail and staysails. At noon, moderate breezes and cloudy weather. Set the main top-gall*a*nt sail.

Mer*idian* alt*itude* ☉ Lowe*r* Lim*b* 483   70°14′37″N

Latitude   36°51′32″S

	By log	Latitude South		Longitude East							
Course	Distance	DR	Obs	DR	TK	Var allowed	Set or current	Ther	Barom	Bearing & distance	Error of TK
S84°E	178½	36°48′	36°52′	36°37′	36°39′	33W	4S 26W	64° 61° 62°	29.73 29.75 29.84	Isle Amsterdam S87°E 637 leagues	−45″

Thursday 12 November

Moderate breezes and cloudy. Let the two reefs out of the fore topsail, and set stud*ding* sails forward. Squally with rain. Took in the lower stud*ding* sail. Light breezes and cloudy. Swell from the westw*ard*. Light airs. Puffs of wind at times, with rain. At 9, hove to and hoisted in the larboard cutter to be repaired. Sent down one of the hydrostatic buckets 150 *fatho*ms. The thermometer being immersed into the water brought up stood at 63°1 whilst in the surface water it stood at 63°6.[1] At 10¾, filled and made sail. Set the larboard fore top and main top-gallant studding sails. Noon, moderate breezes and cloudy. Some large albatrosses and some pintados and sooty petrels about the ship, and settling in the water.

Mer*idian* alt*itude* ☉ Lowe*r* Lim*b* by se*x*tant No 483   70°50′9″N

Latitude   36°32′29″S

	By log	Latitude South		Longitude East							
Course	Distance	DR	Obs	DR	TK	Var allowed	Set or current	Ther	Barom	Bearing & distance	Error of TK
S88°E	64	36°54′	36°32′	37°56′	38°32′	33W	22N 34E	58° 62° 64°	29.93 30.00 30.07	Amsterdam S86°E 600 leagues	−30″

[f. 87] Friday 13 November towards Cape Leuwen New Holland

Light breezes and cloudy weather. The carpenters employed repairing the cutter. *Ditto* weather. Moderate breezes and cloudy weather. Took in the larboard studding sails, the staysails, spanker, and main sail. Fresh breezes and fine weather. Set the larboard studding

---

[1] The bucket was sent down when there were light winds. The aim was to determine the temperature of the water at different depths. However, the thermometer was not of a proper size to go into the bucket. Flinders, *A Voyage to Terra Australis*, I, p. 46.

sails, main sail, and stay sails. Carpenters repairing the cutter. Washed and cleaned below. Moderate breezes and fine weather, and the water smooth.

Meridian altitude ☉ Lower Limb Sextant 488   70°31′51″N
Latitude   37°6′53″S

	By log	Latitude South		Longitude East							
Course	Distance	DR	Obs	DR	Obs TK	Var allowed	Set or current	Ther	Barom	Bearing & distance	Error of TK
S82°E	119	36°52′	37°7′	40°23′	41°32′ 41°39′ by ☉ west ☾	33W	15S 33E	65° 65° 73°	30.04 30.05 30.07	Isle Amsterdam S87°E 558 leagues	−54″

Saturday 14 November

Moderate breezes and fine weather. Let out the first reefs of the topsails to get aired. Single-reefed the topsails. Lightening in the northern quarter. Hazy weather. Set starboard main studding sails. Set the starboard main top-gallant, and the fore studding sail. Exercised the great guns and fired one round of powder. Let the reefs out of the mizzen top sail. Light airs and hazy weather, with smooth water.

Meridian altitude ☉ Lower Limb 483   70°28′58″N
Latitude   37°25′34″S

	By log	Latitude South		Longitude East							
Course	Distance	DR	Obs	DR	TK	Var allowed	Set or current	Ther	Barom	Bearing & distance	Error of TK
S76°E	107	37°77′	37°26′	42°34′	43°44′	31W	7N 1E	65° 66° 74°	30.07 30.05 30.07	Isle Amsterdam S87°E 523 leagues	−59″

[f. 88] **Sunday 15 November** *Investigator* **from the Cape of Good Hope**

Light airs and hazy weather. Moderate breezes with drizzling rain at times. Took in studding sails. Fresh breezes. Double-reefed the top sails. The water very smooth. Fresh breezes with hazy, moist weather. Took in the top gallant sails and small stay sails. Strong breezes. Took in the jib and main topmast stay sail, and 3rd reefed the top sails. Lightening to the north-eastward. The ship has leaked 18 inches of water in the last ten hours. Sent down the top-gallant yards. Mustered the ships company and saw them clean. Fresh gales and hazy weather; with a sea rising from the northward. Today at noon, lieutenant Flinders fell near the taffrel[1] with sextant No. 482 in his hand, supplied by the Navy Board, and it was unfortunately broken.[2]

[1] Tafferel or taffrail, the upper part of a ship's stern timbers.
[2] A note at the bottom of the page adds: 'This morning the thermometer usually kept upon deck, and from which the log board was marked, was broken by a man falling against it. It is the third that has been broken by one accident or other. In future the logboard will be marked from a thermometer kept below, at 8 PM, daybreak and noon, the same with barometer.'

Meridian altitude ☉ Lower Limb 483   70°8'0"N
Latitude   38°2'2"S

| By log | | Latitude South | | Longitude East | | | | | | | |
Course	Distance	DR	Obs	DR	TK	Var allowed	Set or current	Ther	Barom	Bearing & distance	Error of TK
S80°E	140	37°50'	38°2'	45°28'	–	31W	12S 22E	64° 65° 69°	30.01 29.80 29.72		

Monday 16 November

Fresh gales with thick hazy weather, and rain at times. Secured the cutter more firmly upon the starboard quarter. The wind more moderate, with cloudy weather. Let the 3rd reef out of the main top sail, and set up the jib and spanker. Fresh breezes and fine weather. Took in the spanker. Squally. Took in the jib and main top-mast stay-sail. Some albatrosses and other birds about. Fresh breezes: a flying shower passed over. Sent up the main top-gallant yard. Served sour kraut and vinegar as usual on banyan days.[1] Moderate breezes and fine weather, with some sea running from the north-west.

Meridian altitude ☉ Lower Limb 483   70°55'43"N
Latitude   37°29'24"S

| By log | | Latitude South | | Longitude East | | | | | | | |
Course	Distance	DR	Obs	DR	TK	Var allowed	Set or current	Ther	Barom	Bearing & distance	Error of TK
S83°E	171	37°40'	37°29'	49°2'	50°57'	32W	11N 23E	68° 65° 65°	29.71 29.76 29.85	Isle Amsterdam S86½°E 406 leagues	–1'8"

[f. 89] Tuesday 17 November towards Cape Leuwen New Holland

Moderate breezes with flying showers of rain. Let the third reef out of the fore top-sail, and sent up the top-gallant yard. Set both fore studding sails. Let 2nd reef out of the main top-sail, and set both studding sails. Squally at times with small rain. Took in all the studding sails. Set the jib, stay-sails and spanker, and the fore studding sail. Fresh breezes and cloudy. Strong breezes. Took in the spanker and fore studding sail. Moderate and cloudy. Set the spanker: and soon afterwards the fore studding sail. Moderate breezes, with flying showers at times. Some brown albatrosses and other birds about.

Meridian altitude ☉ Lower Limb with E 932   71°13'48"N
Latitude   37°26'4"S

---

[1] In British naval tradition, this referred to a day in the week when no meat was served on board ship.

	By log	Latitude South		Longitude East							
Course	Distance	DR	Obs	DR	TK	Var allowed	Set or current	Ther	Barom	Bearing & distance	Error of TK
S89°E	158	37°32′	37°26′	52°22′	54°17′	32W	6N –	65° 63° 64°	29.96 30.10 30.22	Isle Amsterdam S86°E 354 leagues	–1′12″

Wednesday 18 November

Moderate breezes with fine weather. Served sweet wort[1] to the ships company. Saw a whale close under the bows. Light airs. Took in the fore studding sail. Hauled up the courses and took in the spanker. Clear weather. On a breeze springing up, set the courses, stay-sails and spanker. Let out all the reefs of the top-sails. Moderate breezes and fine weather. Washed the ship below and aired with stoves. Moderate breezes with fine pleasant weather.

Meridian altitude ☉ Lower Limb 483	71°22′30″N
Latitude	37°31′53″S

	By log	Latitude South		Longitude East							
Course	Distance	DR	Obs	DR	TK	Var allowed	Set or current	Ther	Barom	Bearing &c	Error of TK
S86°E	81	37°32′	37°32′	54°4′	55°53′	30W	– 6W	63° 62° 65°	30.26 30.28 30.30	Isle Amsterdam S86°E 329 leagues	–1′18″

[f. 90] Thursday 19 November *Investigator* from the Cape of Good Hope

Fresh breezes and cloudy weather. Double-reefed the fore and mizzen, and took one reef in the main top-sail. Fresh breezes and cloudy, with haze. Took in top-gallant sails, and one more reef in each top-sail. Strong breezes and cloudy dull weather; the wind moderate at intervals. Mustered the ships company and saw them clean, as usual twice a week when the weather will permit. At noon, fresh breezes and cloudy weather, with haze, and tolerably smooth water. No birds about the ship.

Meridian altitude ☉ Lower Limb 483	71°18′50″N
Latitude	37°49′42″S

	By log	Latitude South		Longitude East							
Course	Distance	DR	Obs	DR	TK	Var allowed	Set or current	Ther	Barom	Bearing & distance	Error of TK
S85°E	182	37°49′	37°50′	57°52′	59°47′	29°W	1S 6E	66° 63° 66°	30.23 30.10 29.96	Isle Amsterdam S86°E 267 leagues	–1′24″

---

[1] i.e. malt extract.

Friday 20 November

Fresh breezes and hazy weather. Let the third reefs out of the fore and mizzen top-sails. Took in again the third reefs in the fore and mizzen top-sails. Carried away the jib stay and haliards.[1] Fresh gales, with thick weather. Trimmed sails to the shift of wind, and set top-gallant sails. Moderate breezes with thick weather, and rain. Let another reef out of each of the top-sails. Set the fore-top and fore studding sails, and spanker. Cleaned the ship below, and aired with stores. Light breezes with dull cloudy weather.

By Mr Thistle

Meridian altitude ☉ Lower Limb 488   71°20′6″N

Latitude   38°2′13″S

	By log	Latitude South		Longitude East							
Course	Distance	DR	Obs	DR	TK	Var allowed	Set or current	Ther	Barom	Bearing &c	Error of TK
S84°E	150	38°6′	38°2′	61°2′	63°7′	20W	4N 10E	67° – 63°	29.78 29.78 29.84	Isle Amsterdam S86°E 214 leagues	–1′28″

[f. 91] Saturday 21 November towards the south west cape of New Holland

Moderate breezes and cloudy weather. Shifted the fore studding sails to the larboard and set the spanker. Many albatrosses about the ship. Set the jib and main sail. Moderate breezes and fine weather, with haze. Some westerly swell still running. Let out all reefs, and set the stay-sails and top gallant studding sails. Set up the main and mizzen top-mast rigging. Served sweet wort to the ships company. Moderate breezes and fine, with haze: Took in the top-gallant studding sails.

Meridian altitude ☉ Lower Limb 483   71°40′23″N

Latitude   37°55′23″S

	By log	Latitude South		Longitude East							
Course	Distance	DR	Obs	DR	TK	Var allowed	Set or current	Ther	Barom	Bearing & distance	Error of TK
N88°E	145½	37°57′	37°55′	64°7′	66°2′	26½	2N 10W	64° 63° 64°	29.88 29.86 29.90	Isle Amsterdam S85°E 170 leagues	–1′32″

Sunday 22 November

Moderate breezes and fine weather. Took one reef in the top-sails. The fore top-mast-studding-sail yard being carried away, took in the studding-sails, spanker, and top-gallant stay sail. Fresh breezes and cloudy weather with haze. Took in the middle stay sail. Moderate breezes and fine weather. Cloudy weather. At daylight, set the larboard studding sails, spanker and main top-gallant stay-sail. Moderate breezes and cloudy.

---

[1] i.e. the ropes or tackles usually employed to hoist or lower any sail upon its respective masts and stays.

Cleaned the ship below, and aired with stoves. Mustered the ships company, saw them clean, read the articles of war, and punished William Donovan, seaman, with 12 lashes for drunkenness and irregularity. Noon, moderate breezes and fine weather. Sweet wort served to the ships company.

Meridian altitude ☉ Lower Limb 483   72°9'18"N
Latitude   7°39'33"

		By log		Latitude South	Longitude East						
Course	Distance	DR	Obs	DR	TK	Var allowed	Set or current	Ther	Barom	Bearing & distance	Error of TK
N87°E	171	37°46'	37°40'	67°43'	69°32'	25½W	6N 6W	67° 65° 66°	29.97 29.90 30.05	Isle Amsterdam S80°E 117 leagues	–1'36"

[f. 92] **Monday 23 November *Investigator* from the Cape of Good Hope**
Light breezes and hazy weather. Many petrels about the ship. Took in the stay-sails. Set the stay-sails and spanker. Set royals and top-gallant studding sails. Light breezes and cloudy weather. Carpenters employed repairing the cutter. Mustered the ships companys clothing, and got the slops up to air them. Noon, light breezes and fine weather.

Meridian altitude ☉ Lower Limb 483   72°6'36"N
Latitude   37°55'1"S

		By log		Latitude South	Longitude East						
Course	Distance	DR	Obs	DR	TK	Var allowed	Set or current	Ther	Barom	Bearing & distance	Error of TK
S81°E	109	37°57'	37°55'	69°59'	72°5'	24W	2N 17E	68° 68° 66°	30.14 30.18 30.20	Amsterdam Island S78°E 232 miles	–1'41"

Tuesday 24 November
Moderate breezes and cloudy weather. Took in the royals and fore studding sail. Took in top-gallant studding sails, and double-reefed the top-sails. Fresh breezes and cloudy: a heavy dew falling. Took in the fore-top-mast studding sail, and the small staysails. Fresh breezes: the water smooth. Set staysails, and the fore top-mast studding sail. Many small blue petrels (Procelaria Forstere)[1] about the ship. Bent the cables and turned in the stoppers.[2] Took in the fore-top-mast studding sail. Sweet-wort served to the people as

---

[1] These petrels inhabit the southern oceans, nesting on Antarctic islands but ranging north of there to South Africa, South America and Australia.
[2] Stoppers were usually knots that prevented ropes from unravelling, but they could also be lengths of rope belayed at one end and attached to a tension line using a friction hitch to slacken part of the tensioned line.

usual. Strong breezes and cloudy weather with haze, so that the sun could not be seen. Several whales seen this morning.[1]

No observations for the latitude, the ☉ being invisible

		By log		Latitude South		Longitude East						
Course	Distance	DR	Obs	DR	TK	Var allowed	Set or current	Ther	Barom	Bearing & distance	Error of TK
S82°E	171	38°19′	Double altitude 38°20′	69°59′	73°34′	23½W	1S 6W	65° 65° 66°	30.14 30.12 30.13	Amsterdam Isle S71°E 71 miles	– 1′45″

[f. 93] Wednesday 25 November Off Amsterdam Island in the way to New Holland
Fresh breezes and cloudy weather. Several whales seen. Took in top gallant sails, jib, stay-sails, and spanker. Judging ourselves to be nearly in the longitude of Amsterdam at 11 PM brought to, intending to make it in the morning. Note. This isle is laid down in longitude 77°40′E by H.M. ship *Providence* in 1792.[2] At 3, wore, and brought to with the ships head westward. At 5, filled and steered southward until we judged the ship to be in the latitude of the island, when not seeing it, steered eastward on our course; the weather being thick and hazy, so that we could not see more than two leagues. Some whales and many cape hens and petrels about the ship. Cleared below and aired with stoves. Took in top gallant sails and 3rd reefed the top sails. Strong breezes, with cloudy, misty weather. The set of 23′ east this day seems to be the principal cause that we did not see Amsterdam; nevertheless if it is in 77°40′ we must have been very near it when we bore away at 6 *hours* 30′ AM and should have seen it had the weather been less thick. I judge we drifted between the two isles whilst lying to in the night.[3]

Double altitudes for the latitude

543 Time	18h35′46.5″	19h41′50″
483 ☉ Lower Limb	71°47′11″	65°31′40″
☉ bore NWbN at last observation		
Latitude at 9′2.4″ (1st observation)	38°20′23″	
Azimuths at 5 PM		
☉ magnetic azimuth	N75°35′W	turned { 75°20′
low limb	22°20′	21°54′

[1] In the evening Flinders estimated the ship's position as 38°20′S, 76°26′E. The voyage across the Indian Ocean was uneventful and 'it was a great satisfaction that frequent pumping of the ship was not now required'. Flinders, *A Voyage to Terra Australis*, I, p. 46.

[2] Rough Journal, I, f. 205, adds: 'I believe it to be to the eastward of 76°54′ as given in Lord Macartney's voyage ... I did not think it worthwhile to lose time by steering out of our way for these two islands; but had the weather been fine, I wished to have sent a boat on shore with the naturalist, to one or both of them.' Flinders had a copy of Macartney's mission in Staunton, *An Authentic Account*. Amsterdam Island (37°50′S, 77°30′E) and the nearby St Paul Island (38°44′S, 77°30′E) were the two islands. Amsterdam Island, rising to 2,434 feet, is much more easily seen than St Paul (866 feet high). In 1791–2 Flinders was midshipman on William Bligh's second breadfruit voyage, from Tahiti to the West Indies, on HMS *Providence*. Vallance, Moore and Groves, eds, *Nature's Investigator*, p. 85; Estensen, *The Life of Matthew Flinders*, pp. 10–11.

[3] This indicates that the island remained unsighted by Flinders. The *Investigator* had proceeded at around 140 miles per day from the Cape of Good Hope to this point of the Indian Ocean. Flinders, *A Voyage to Terra Australis*, I p. 149.

Variation	22°22′	No 1	23°56′N
⊙ magnetic azimuth	76°33′		{77°35′
low limb	21°4′	turned	{20°31′
Variation	23°21′	No 2	22°43′N
⊙ magnetic azimuth	77°52′		{78°40′
low limb	19°51′	turned	{19°31′
Variation	22°56′	No 3	22°23′W
Mean variation, West,	23°7′		

Cape Chatham by captain Vancouver lies in latitude 35°3′S and longitude 116°35′E

	By log		Latitude South		Longitude East						
Course	Distance	DR	Obs	DR	TK	Var allowed	Set or current	Ther	Barom	Bearing & distance	Error of TK
S83°E	124	38°36′	38°40′	76°12′	78°35′	2 Pts	4S 23E	67° 65° 66°	30.12 30.09 29.98	Cape Chatham N83E 611 leagues	– 1′49″

Thursday 26 November

Strong breezes with dull misty weather. Took in the main top mast stay-sails. Set the stay sail again, and let the 3rd reef out of the main top-sail: the wind being more moderate. Fresh breezes and thick weather, with drizzling rain. Let the 3rd reef out of the fore top-sail, and set top-gallant sails. Moderate breezes and cloudy. Let out the 2nd reefs, and set the spanker and staysails. Set studding-sails. Mustered the ships company and saw them clean. Moderate breezes and fine weather. Not many birds about the ship.

| Meridian altitude ⊙ Lower Limb 483 | 72°27′4″N |
| Latitude | 38°10′29″N |

	By log		Latitude South		Longitude East						
Course	Distance	DR	Obs	DR	TK	Var allowed	Set or current	Ther	Barom	Bearing & distance	Error of TK
N80°E	163	38°12′	38°10′	79°37′	82°1′	21W	2N 1E	66° 65° 66°	29.99 29.95 29.95	Cape Chatham N84°E 556 leagues	– 1′54″

[f. 94] Friday 27 November[1] *Investigator* from the Cape of Good Hope

A freshening breeze with cloudy weather. Passed some bunches of sea weed. Took in the staysails, spanker, and top-gallant studding-sails. Fresh breezes and fine weather.

---

[1] On this day Flinders wrote a letter in which he reflected on the potential success of the *Investigator's* voyage and its social and cultural impact on his life: 'Should this voyage prove successful I shall not be unknown in the world; my acquaintance in Soho Square [i.e. Sir Joseph Banks] will introduce me to many of the first philosophers

Took in all the studding sails. Moderate & fine weather. At daylight, set the studding sails on both sides, and the main royal. Took in the starboard studding sails. Shifted the studding sails. Swayed the lower yards higher up. Exercised great guns and fired one round of powder. Moderate breezes with fine weather. A long silent swell following after the ship.

Meridian altitude ☉ Lower Limb 483		73°9′44″N	
Latitude		37°39′2″S	

By log		Latitude South		Longitude East							
Course	Distance	DR	Obs	DR	TK	Var allowed	Set or current	Ther	Barom	Bearing & distance	Error of TK
N81°E	140	37°48′	37°39′	82°32′	85°8′	20W	9N 12E	64° 63° 65°	30.00 30.02 30.04	Cape Chatham[1] N85°E 511 leagues	– 1′59″

Saturday 28 November

Moderate breezes and cloudy. Took in the stay-sails and spanker, and set the larboard studding sails. Set the spanker and staysails. Fresh breezes and cloudy weather. Took in studding sails and staysails, but set them again at daylight. Fresh and moderate breezes, alternately, with rain at times. Exercised small arms, and fired two rounds of powder. Served sweet wort to the ships company as usual. At noon, moderate breezes with fine weather; a long westerly swell setting after us. Some Cape hens hovering about the ship.

By log		Latitude South		Longitude East							
Course	Distance	DR	Obs	DR	TK	Var allowed	Set or current	Ther	Barom	Bearing & distance	Error of TK
N83°E	146	37°21′	37°15′ Double altitude by JT	85°34′	88°5′	18°W	6N 5W	64° 62° 64°	30.05 30.02 30.03	Cape Chatham N84½E 462 leagues	–2′4″

[f. 95] Sunday 29 November towards Cape Leuwen New Holland

Moderate breezes and fine weather. Let the reefs out of the top sails to get aired; and set top gallant studding sails. Moderate and cloudy. Took one reef in the fore and main, and two in the mizzen top-sail. Took in top gallant studding sails and spanker; and soon after, all the studding sails. Light breezes. Set studding sails, and shifted them occasionally.

---

and literati in the kingdom.' He expressed his diffidence about solely writing up a published version of the voyage after his return home, and hoped to enlist his cousin Willingham Franklin, then at Oriel College, Oxford, to help him. SLV, Flinders Papers, Flinders to Willingham Franklin, 27 November 1801.

[1] See below, p. 238.

Some tropic birds reported to be about the ship. Set stay sails and spanker. Mustered the ships company and saw them clean. Served sweet wort. Fresh breezes and hazy weather. Took in the studding sails.

Meridian altitude ☉ Lower Limb No 483   74°27′16″N
Latitude   36°42′40″S

	By log	Latitude South		Longitude East							
Course	Distance	DR	Obs	DR	TK	Var allowed	Set or current	Ther	Barom	Bearing & distance	Error of TK
N84°E	135	37°1′	36°43′	88°22′	90°59′ 91°33′ by ☉ east ☾	17W	18N 6E	65° 61° 65°	30.02 29.99 29.84	Cape Chatham N85½°E 416 leagues	−2′9″

Monday 30 November

Fresh breezes and cloudy. Squally, with rain at times. Took in spanker, top gallant sails, and stay sails. Double-reefed the top sails. Strong breezes. Third reefed the fore and mizzen top-sails. At 2 hours 45′ the wind fell nearly to a calm, and then shifted almost immediately to the other side; bringing thick weather with small rain. Set the main top-gallant sail. Squally at times with rain: Hauled up the main sail. Sour krout served to the ships company, and, as usual, sweet-wort. Fresh breezes with fine weather. A few birds about the ship, of the usual kinds.

Meridian altitude ☉ Lower Limb No 483   75°1′26″N
Latitude   36°18′37″S

	By log	Latitude South		Longitude East							
Course	Distance	DR	Obs	DR	TK	Var allowed	Set or current	Ther	Barom	Bearing & distance	Error of TK
N85°E	185½	36°27′	36°19′	92°11′ by ☉ east ☾	94°56′ 95°20′	16W	8N 8E	65° 61° 59°	29.60 29.70 29.78	Cape Chatham N86°E 354 leagues	−2′13″

[f. 96] **Tuesday 1 December *Investigator* from the Cape of Good Hope**

Fresh breezes and cloudy, with rain at times; and a high following sea. Set the jib, stay sails, spanker, and fore top-mast studding sail. Light breezes. Under double-reefed topsails &c. Changeable weather. Took in the studding sails and spanker. Light winds and fine. Let out the 2nd reefs, and set the fore-top and fore studding-sails, the spanker, and staysails. Fresh breezes and cloudy weather. Cleaned the ship below. Some albatrosses and pintado birds about the ship. Served sweet wort. Fresh breezes and fine weather, with a long swell following after the ship.

Meridian altitude ☉ Lower Limb 483   75°29′9″N
Latitude   36°0′34″S

By log		Latitude South		Longitude East							
Course	Distance	DR	Obs	DR	TK	Var allowed	Set or current	Ther	Barom	Bearing & distance	Error of TK
N86°E	144	36°9′	36°1′	95°9′	98°0′	15W	8N 6E	59° 56° 59°	29.93 29.97 29.94	Cape Chatham N86½°E 304 leagues	–2′17″

Wednesday 2 December

Fresh breezes and cloudy weather. Carried away the fore-top-mast-studding-sail boom. Took in the stay sails and spanker. Squally weather. Double-reefed the top-sails and furled top-gallant sails. Split the jib. Fresh gales with a high sea. Treble-reefed the fore and main and handed the mizzen top-sail. Fresh gales and cloudy. Hauled up the main sail, and set the main stay-sail. The fore top-mast stay-sail being split, took it in. Set the mizzen top-sail. Fresh breezes with fine weather; and a high sea running from the north-westward. Bent a new fore-top-mast stay-sail. Sailmakers employed repairing sails. Let the 3rd reef out of the main top-sail. Fresh breezes and squally weather, with a following sea.

Meridian altitude ☉ Lower Limb (not good)   75°42′36″N
Latitude   35°56′31″S

By log		Latitude South		Longitude East							
Course	Distance	DR	Obs	DR	TK	Var allowed	Set or current	Ther	Barom	Bearing & distance	Error of TK
N88°E	190	35°54′	35°57′	99°2′	101°58′	3S 5E	8N 6E	58° 61° 61°	29.75 29.60 29.61	Cape Chatham N86°E 239 leagues	2′21″

[f. 97] Thursday 3 December towards Cape Leuwen New Holland

Strong breezes and squally weather. Handed the mizzen top-sail. Third-reefed the main top-sail, and reefed and set the main-sail. Lost two log lines. Strong breezes and squally. Hauled up the main sail, and cleared down the top sails in a squall: afterwards set them again. Lightning all round. Let the third reefs out of the fore and main, and set the close-reefed mizzen top sail. Strong squalls, with rain at times. Set top gallant sails. Mustered the ships company and saw them clean. Served sweet wort. Fresh breezes and cloudy, with a considerable following sea.

By log		Latitude South		Longitude East							
Course	Distance	DR	Obs	DR	TK	Var allowed	Set or current	Ther	Barom	Bearing & distance	Error of TK
N89°E	177	35°54′	35°18′ by JT	102°39′	105°31′	12W	36N 4W	59° 57° 57°	29.65 29.75 29.88	Missed the meridian at observation today	– 2′20″

Friday 4 December

Fresh breezes and cloudy: a considerable sea following from the westward. Fresh breezes and hazy, with spitting rain at times. Thick weather, with drizzling rain. D*itto* weather. Let the reef out of the main sail, and the 2nd reef out of the main top-sail. Cloudy weather, with spitting rain at times. Washed between decks and aired with stoves. Fresh breezes and cloudy weather, and the sea very little gone down.

Mer*idian* alt*itude* ☉ Lowe*r* Lim*b* R 932 by Lt Flinders	76°43′36″N
Latitude	35°12′40″S
Supp*lement* alt*itude* U*pper* Lim*b* 483	102°41′16″S
Latitude	5°9′56″S
Mean	5°11′18″S

By log		Latitude South		Longitude East							
Course	Distance	DR	Obs	DR	TK	Var allowed	Set or current	Ther	Barom	Bearing & distance	Error of TK
N82½°E	163	35°39′	35°11′	105°57′	108°39′	1 Pt W	28N 10W	56° 61° 64°	29.88 29.86 29.83	Cape Chatham N89°E 124 leagues	2′38″

[f. 98] **Saturday 5 December *Investigator* from the Cape of Good Hope**

Fresh breezes and cloudy. The old fore-top-mast stay-sail being repaired, bent it again. Double-reefed the main top sail. Squally with rain at times. Let out 2nd reefs, and set the spanker and studding-sails. Moderate breezes and fine weather: the sea much abated of its violence. Cleaned the ship below and aired with stoves. Served sweet wort as usual. Light breezes with fine pleasant weather.

Mer*idian* alt*itude* ☉ Lowe*r* Lim*b* 483	76°37′19″N
Latitude	35°26′48″S

By log		Latitude South		Longitude East							
Course	Distance	DR	Obs	DR	TK	Var allowed	Set or current	Ther	Barom	Bearing & distance	Error of TK
EbyS	157	35°41′	35°27′	109°6′	111°42′	1 Pt W	14N 6W	66° 63° 66°	29.84 29.84 29.90	Cape Chatham N84°E 240 miles	2′35″

Sunday 6 December

Moderate breezes and fine weather. Shifted the studding-sails. Moderate and cloudy. A silent swell following the ship from the westwards. Light breezes and dull cloudy weather. At 10, took in studding sails and trimmed to the wind, in order to make the

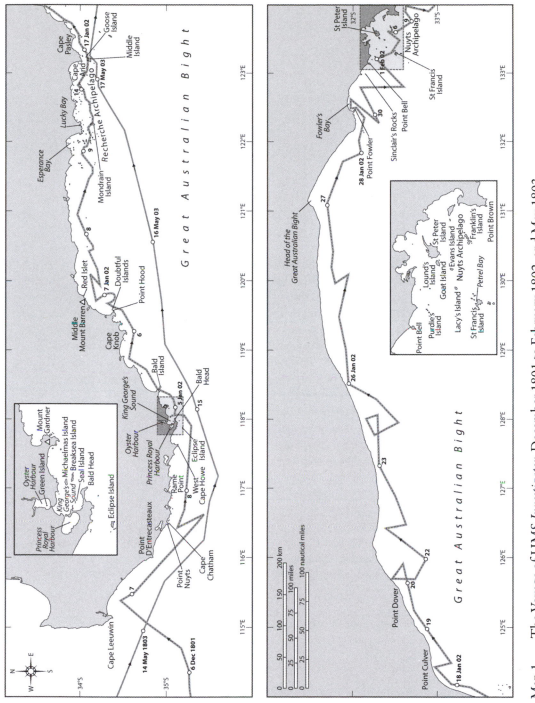

Map 1.   The Voyage of HMS *Investigator*, December 1801 to February 1802, and May 1803.

land.[1] Mustered ships company and saw them clean. Punished *Willia*m Beach, marine, with 12 lashes, for drunkenness and consequent neglect of duty. Moderate breezes and cloudy *w*eath*e*r. Served sweet wort.[2]

Mer*idian* alt*itude* ☉ *Lowe*r *Lim*b R 932   76°59′52″N

Latitude   35°11′48″S

	By log	Latitude South		Longitude East							
Course	Distance	DR	Obs	DR	TK	Var allowed	Set or current	Ther	Barom	Bearing & dist*ance*	Error of TK
N89°E	116½	35°25′	35°10′	111°29′	114°25′	11W	15N 20E	67° 65° 67°	29.91 29.91 29.92	Isles of Cape Leuwen N32°E 62 miles	–2′39″

[f. 99] Monday 7 December Off the south-west cape of New Holland

Moderate breezes and cloudy weather. Took in studding sails, and braced up, expecting to make the land before dark. Bent the cables. At 7, saw the land of New Holland from the masthead, bearing NNE. Sounded. Took in the jib, stay sails, spanker, & main sail. Sounded. Sounded; then wore ship and stood off under top-sails and top-gallant sails. Light winds and cloudy weather. Hove ship towards the land. At daylight made sail. At 5, saw the land in patches from NNW to EbS from the masthead. At 10, we were about 4 miles off shore, at the mouth of a bay,[3] in which were much breakers and apparently no shelter. At this time, wore ship and steered along the shore, keeping the wash of the surf upon the beach in sight. At 11, the weather squally. Double reefed the top sails and hauled something further off the shore. Sounded every hour as per column. At noon, the north extreme of the land (A[4] being the first seen) N48°W: a barren rock lying to the south of it not being now in sight.[5] Furthest extreme in sight ahead, S45°E. Country abreast, consisting of sandy hills, distant about 4 or 5 miles. On making the land I ordered the

---

[1] The first indication that the Australian continent was in sight. The ship had reached western Australia in a trouble-free 32 days from the Cape of Good Hope. Flinders reckoned that the latitude was 35°10′ and the longitude 114°19′ according to a traced copy of a chart by D'Entrecasteaux furnished to him by the Hydrographic Office of the Admiralty. Flinders, *A Voyage to Terra Australis*, I, p. 151.

[2] Flinders added in a note at the bottom of the page: 'Two isles off the SW cape are laid down in the chart of D'Entrecastreaux in latitude 34°18′S and about the longitude of 115°6′ East of Greenwich.'

[3] Marked as 'Dangerous Bight' in Flinders's chart accompanying *A Voyage to Terra Australis*, sheet 1. In 1829/30 it was renamed Flinders Bay.

[4] Cape Leeuwin (34°22′S, 115°08′E), a low round head joined to the mainland by a low swampy isthmus. This is the south-westernmost point of Australia. For Westall's sketch of the cape, see Flinders, *A Voyage to Terra Australis*, *Atlas*, plate XVII, view 1.

[5] Probably one of the St Alouarn Islands (34°24′S, 115°12′E) at the tip of Cape Leeuwin. In 1792 D'Entrecasteaux thought the cape was one of a group of islands which he named the Iles St Alouarn after his compatriot François de Saint-Alouarn, who was part of Yves-Joseph de Kergeulen-Trémarec's expedition that reached Cape Leeuwin in 1772. Flinders realized, however, that the cape was part of the mainland. Aware that the Dutch called the area Leeuwin's Land, after the Dutch ship which charted some of the nearby coastline in 1622, he renamed the feature Cape Leeuwin. Scott, *The Life of Matthew Flinders*, p. 147; Estensen, *The Life of Matthew Flinders,* p. 177.

gunner to keep the 2nd lieut*enant*s watch, the latter having engaged to assist me in the astronom*ical* department.[1]

Mer*idian* alt*itude* ☉ Lowe*r* Lim*b* by Mr Thistle	77°46′6″N
Latitude	34°32′40″S

		By log		Latitude South							
Course	Distance	DR	Obs	DR	TK	Var allowed	Set or current	Ther	Barom	Bearing &c	Error of TK
N53°E	43	34°44′	34°33′	112°10′	115°38′	11	11N 32E	66° 66° 68°	29.90 29.85 29.89		2′39″E

Additional remarks

The land first seen in the afternoon was not very distinct, but it seems to have been A [Cape Leeuwin], which I take to be the south-westernmost of Leuwens Land and of New Holland. From it the land trends easterly into a bight,[2] and then turns in the direction of SEbS. The land was visible all across at the back of the bight, equally sandy as the other part of the coast. A cape [Cape Leeuwin] seems to be rocky as well as sandy. From A SSE 3 or 4 miles lies a barren rocky island, a,[3] with much breaking water round it, and between them a lower sloping islet;[4] but they were all too far distant to speak particularly upon them. A ridge of sand hills with some small straggling trees upon them generally front the sea, and prevent anything of the interior part being seen, except here and there small parts of a higher back ridge of hills: upon these last, the wood seems to be larger and more abundant.

The coast ahead seems to be more regular, and no danger yet appears off the coast. The breakers in the bight [Dangerous Bight/Flinders Bay] to the eastward of A [Cape Leeuwin] I judge to belong to the barren islet a [Saint Alouarn Islet], but this island lies somewhat within the line of the coast. There is no appearance of natives, as yet. I judge A to be the land which, in D'Entrecasteaux's chart,[5] is marked to be islands.

[f. 100] Tuesday 8 December *Investigator* along the south coast

Fresh breezes and squally. Let out 3rd reefs. At 3, the southernmost extreme, C,[6] a steep cape S60°E without which was soon after seen a patch of breakers and induced me to haul a point farther off the shore. At 5 hours 40′ two small rocks, white at the top, S75°E. At 7 hours 15′ the rocks bore N29°E and the furthest land, seen indistinctly, N30°E. The wind heading, braced up and stood off, sounding as per column: under double reefed top-sails. Fresh breezes and squally weather, but it became finer afterwards. At 1, tacked ship, let out 3rd reefs, and set top-gallant sails. At daylight saw the land stretching to the

---

[1] This was Samuel Flinders.

[2] Now Flinders Bay (34°20′S, 115°12′E).

[3] Saint Alouarn Islet (34°24′S, 115°12′E). Godard and Kerros, *1772*, p. 117.

[4] Seal Island (35°05′S, 117°58′E), about 1½ miles from the shore.

[5] D'Entrecasteaux had followed this part of the shore in 1792, in the ships *Récherche* and *Espérance,* while searching for the lost explorer La Pérouse. Estensen, *The Life of Matthew Flinders*, p. 177; Scott, *The Life of Matthew Flinders*, p. 147.

[6] Point D'Entrecasteaux (34°50′S, 116°00′E). Flinders, *A Voyage to Terra Australis*, I, p. 50.

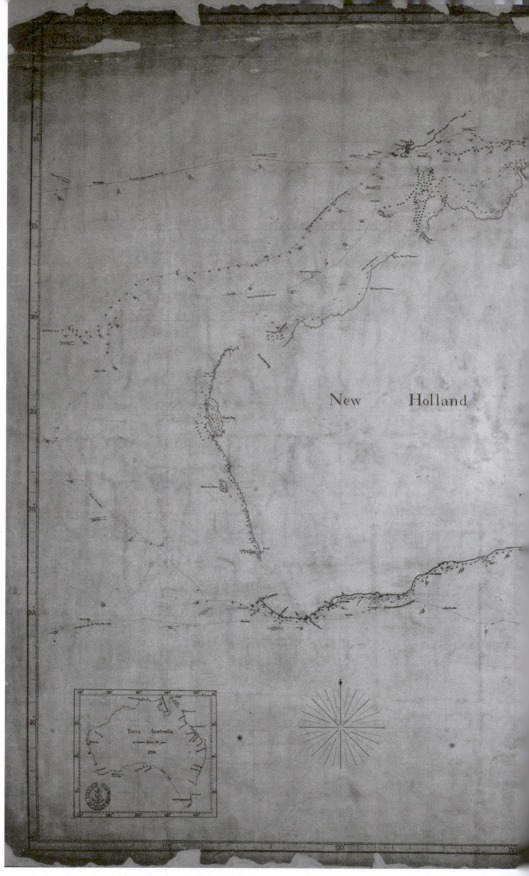

Figure 6.   Matthew Flinders, A General Chart of Terra Australis or Australia, ADM 352/477.
Courtesy of the National Archives, Kew.

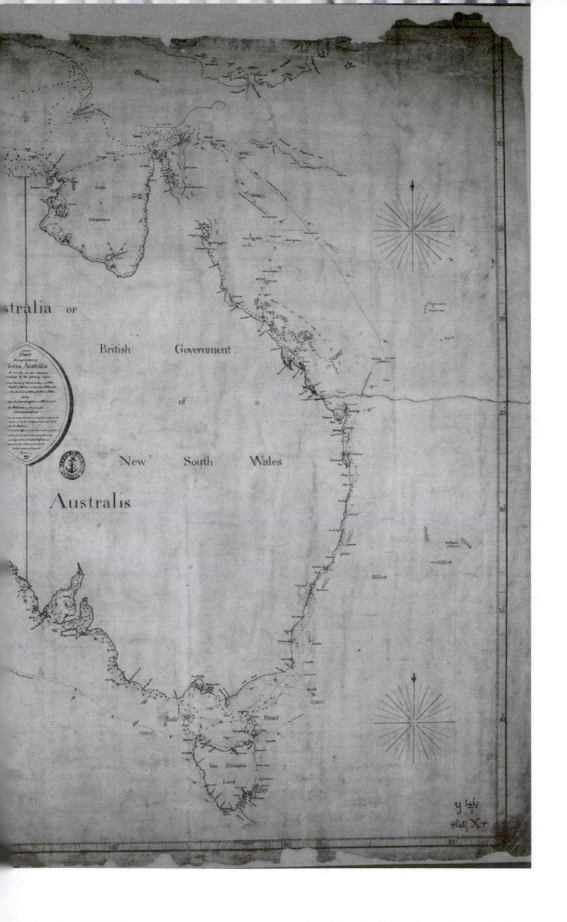

eastward, but cape C [Point D'Entrecasteaux], or the white-topped rocks, d,[1] not visible. At 5 *hours* 40′ a high steep head, D, N25°E 6 or 8 miles: this proved to be separated from the land, and is the Cape Chatham of captain Vancouver.[2] At 7 *hours* 15′ tacked, and steered along the shore: the rocks, a [Saint Alouarn Island], indistinctly seen at N60°W. Made more sail, keeping at from 3 to 6 miles off the shore and sounding as per column. At 10 *hours* 25′ kept more in towards the land, find it did not run to the southward. At noon, the shore abreast distant about four miles, divided into high heads and low points, with small sandy bights between them. Mod*erate* breezes & fine weather. F,[3] the furthest land ahead E4°S D [Cape Chatham] and E[4] in a line N65°W.

Mer*idian* alt*itude* ☉ Lowe*r* Lim*b* sext*ant* 483	77°17′45″N
Latitude	35°7′45″S
Supp*lement* alt*itude* ☉ U*pper* Lim*b* same sext*ant*	102°8′19″S
Latitude	35°6′25″S
Mean	35°7′5″S

		By log		Latitude South		Longitude East					
Course	Distance	DR	Obs	DR	TK	Var allowed	Set or current	Ther	Barom	Error of TK
S48½°E	57	35°11′	35°7′	113°2′	116°57′	7W	4N	68°	29.96	−2′49″E
							27E	66°	30.07	
								68°	30.18	

Additional remarks

The land continues to be sandy from the bight near A [Cape Leeuwin] unto the end of the steep cape C [Point D'Entrecasteaux]. On the east side of C is a sandy beach, but the land is higher there a little back, than what we have before passed. It was my intention to have come in again with C and the white rocks, d [Cow and Calf rocks], but the current, which appears to run more than a mile per hour, had drifted us to leeward.

D [Cape Chatham] is a smooth-surfaced bluff rock about one mile from the shore, and there is a bight in the shore behind it. From hence the shore trends eastward, forming

[1] Flinders called them 'the white-topped rocks' in his *Atlas*. They are now known as the Cow and Calf rocks, located about 8 miles offshore (35°01′S, 116°13′E). NAT MAP Pemberton Special; *Sailing Directions (Enroute): North, West, and South Coasts of Australia*, p. 140.

[2] Named after John Pitt, 2nd Earl of Chatham, First Lord of the Admiralty (July 1788–December 1794). George Vancouver (1757–98) discovered this feature in 1791 but thought it was part of the mainland. It was actually Chatham Island (35°02′S, 116°30′E). Flinders mapped it as an island but continued to call it Cape Chatham. Flinders's entries for December 1801 make numerous references to Vancouver's discoveries on the south-eastern coast of Australia during his voyage of Pacific exploration on HMS *Discovery*. Vancouver stayed in King George Sound for a fortnight and then sailed east as far as Termination Island (24°29′S, 122°00′E) before, meeting with contrary winds, he abandoned a survey of the south Australian coast and resumed his voyage to north-west America across the Pacific. On the *Investigator* Flinders had a copy of Vancouver, *Voyage of Discovery to the North Pacific Ocean*. Vallance, Moore and Groves, eds, *Nature's Investigator*, p. 89; Lamb, ed., *The Voyage of George Vancouver*, I, p. 333; Scott, *The Life of Matthew Flinders*, p. 147. Cape Chatham is drawn by Westall in the accompanying atlas to Flinders, *Voyage to Terra Australis*, plate XVII, view 2.

[3] Rame Point, now Rame Head (35°03′S, 116°52′E). Bearing Book, f. 3, refers to 'a Knob upon a head, resembling the Ram Head'.

[4] Bearing Book, f. 2, entry for 8 December 1801, identifies this as 'rather a steep cape'.

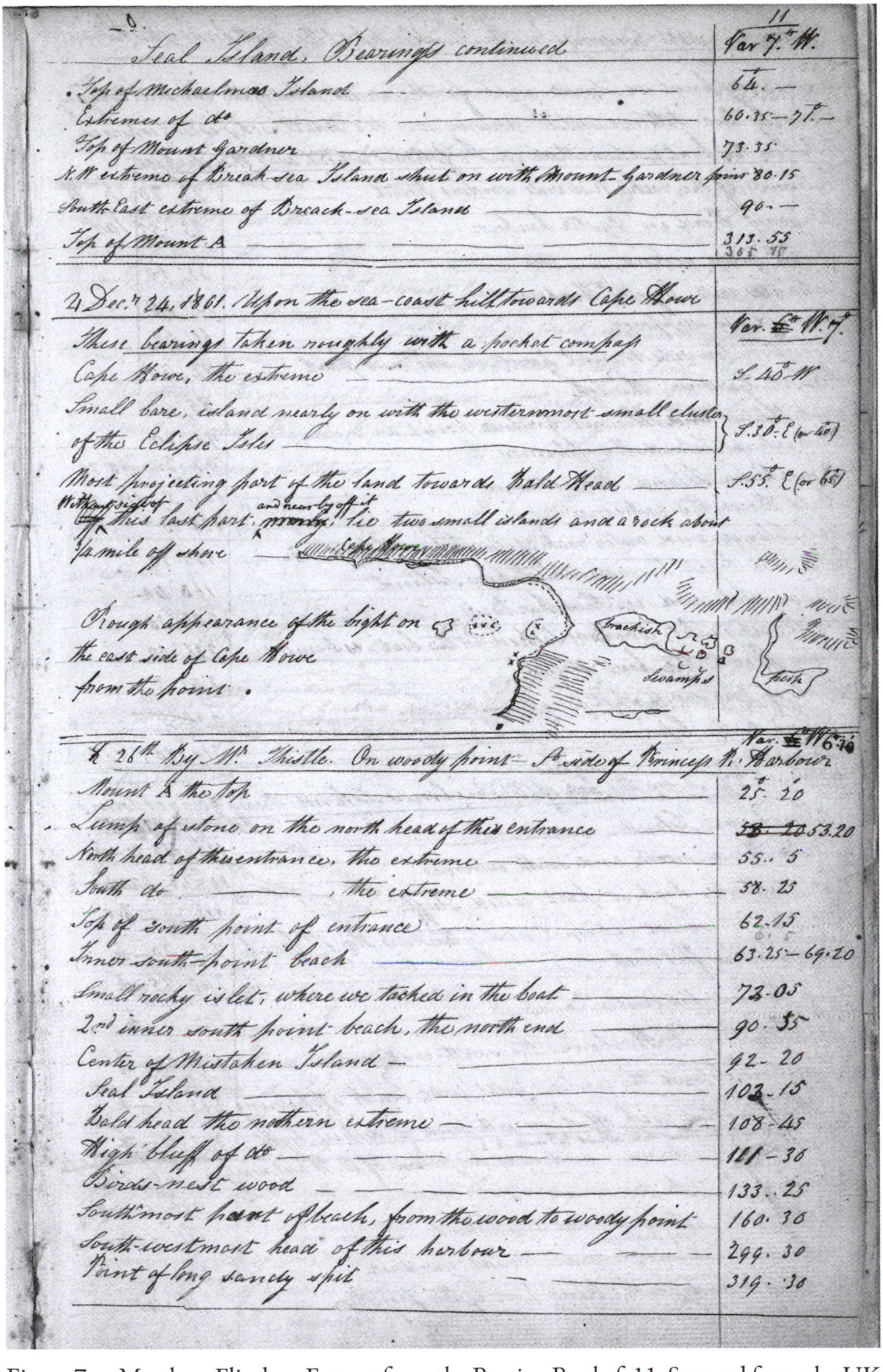

Seal Island. Bearings continued | Var 7.° W.

Top of Michaelmas Island	64. —
Extremes of do	60.35 — 71. —
Top of Mount Gardner	73. 35
N.W. extreme of Break-sea Island shut on with Mount Gardner pars	80.15
South East extreme of Break-sea Island	90. —
Top of Mount A	313. 55
	305. 45

2, Dec.r 24, 1861. Upon the sea-coast hill towards Cape Howe

Var. E.° N.° 7.

These bearings taken roughly with a pocket compass

Cape Howe, the extreme	S. 40° W
Small bare, island nearly on with the westernmost small cluster of the Eclipse Isles	S. 30.° E (or 40)
Most projecting part of the land towards Bald Head	S. 55.° E (or 65)

Without sight and nearly off it this last part. nearly lie two small islands and a rock about ¼ mile off shore

Rough appearance of the bight on the east side of Cape Howe from the point .

brackish
swamps
thistle

L. 28.th By M.r Thistle. On woody point — S.d side of Princess R. Harbour

Var. E.° N.° 11.6.70

Mount A the top	25.° 20
Lump of stone on the north head of this entrance	53.20
North head of the entrance, the extreme	55.. 5
South do the extreme	58. 25
Top of south point of entrance	62.15
Inner south-point beach	63.25 — 69.20
Small rocky islet, where we tacked in the boat	73.05
2.nd inner south point beach, the north end	90. 55
Center of Mistaken Island	92 — 20
Seal Island	102. 15
Bald head the northern extreme	108. 45
High bluff of do	111. 30
Birds-nest wood	133.. 25
Southmost part of beach, from the wood to woody point	160. 30
South-westmost head of this harbour	299. 30
Point of long sandy spit	319.. 30

Figure 7.   Matthew Flinders, Extract from the Bearing Book, f. 11. Sourced from the UK Hydrographic Office (www.ukho.gov.uk).

bights in some of which it is probable there may be shelter from most winds. They are not however above a mile or two or at most three deep. In general, the coast passed this morning has a difference [*sic*] appearance to the sandy shore of yesterday; it is higher, the shore is more steep and rocky, and the inland parts seem to be much better covered with wood; and near the shore a green coat of shrubs and other vegetation, though rather a shabby coat, covers the sloping hills down to the cliffs which form the higher heads. The sand shews itself through the herbage here and there, especially in those parts where the shore falls back and forms bays or bights.

Smokes were rising near a steep point which bore at noon N4°W 4 or 5 miles, and is the first yet noticed.

[f. 101] Wednesday 9 December into King Georges Sound New Holland

A freshening breeze, with fine weather. Made all sail in order to look into the bight behind Cape Howe[1] for anchorage before night. At 4, a sloping hummock, high in the center, came in sight wide off from the coast; this proved to be the Eclipse Isles.[2] At 5 *hours* Cape Howe north 3 or 4 miles. Finding a probability of getting into King Georges Sound[3] tonight, steered and made sail accordingly.[4] At half past six, the west end of the Eclipse Isles, Mount Gardner,[5] and Bald Head[6] were in a line, at N60°E. At 8, hauled up round Bald Head, and stretched over to Breaksea Island;[7] then tacked, and kept working up into the sound until 11½ *hours* when we came to anchor between Seal Island and the first beach round Bald Head, in 6 *fatho*ms sandy bottom, and furled sails.[8]

---

[1] 35°08′S, 117°36′E. Flinders named this West Cape Howe to distinguish this Cape Howe, named by Vancouver after Admiral Richard Howe (1726–99), from Cape Howe on Australia's eastern coast, named by Cook. Flinders, *A Voyage to Terra Australis*, I, p. 52.

[2] Eclipse Island (35°11′S, 117°53′E) and associated isles and rocks. Named by Vancouver who witnessed a solar eclipse here on 28 August 1791. Vallance, Moore and Groves, eds, *Nature's Investigator*, p. 90. The Eclipse Isles are drawn in the accompanying atlas to Flinders, *A Voyage to Terra Australis*, plate XVII, view 3.

[3] Originally called King George III's Sound after the reigning monarch. This is the location of the present-day town of Albany. The sound is sometimes still referred to as King George III Sound but is more commonly known today as King George Sound. Lamb, ed., *The Voyage of George Vancouver*, I, p. 337; http://:www.albany-baycityviews.com.au/albany_western_australia.html.

[4] Flinders gives a detailed account of the passage to the first anchorage in King George Sound (comprising 42 square miles) in *A Voyage to Terra Australis*, I, pp. 50–53. Flinders, Chart of Terra Australis, South Coast Sheet 1, states that there was high water once a day between 6 p.m. and midnight, and that the tides rose from 2′8″ to 3′2″. Semi-diurnal tides are frequent and diurnal tides are occasional at King George Sound.

[5] A peninsula on the east side of King George Sound (35°00′S, 118°11′E), named by Vancouver after his friend and patron Commodore Sir Alan (later, Admiral Lord) Gardner (1742–1809), Vallance, Moore and Groves, eds, *Nature's Investigator*, p. 108.

[6] The easternmost limit of the Flinders Peninsula on the west side of King George Sound (35°07′S, 118°01′E). Vancouver gave it this name because it lacked verdure. Vallance, Moore and Groves, eds, *Nature's Investigator*, pp. 90, 92; Lamb, ed., *The Voyage of George Vancouver*, I, p. 335. Bald Head is drawn in the accompanying atlas to Flinders, *A Voyage to Terra Australis*, plate XVII, view 3.

[7] An island of 255 acres (35°04′S, 118°03′E) in King George Sound, about 7 miles from Albany on the mainland. It was so called because of its battered appearance and resistance to the sea. Lamb, ed., *The Voyage of George Vancouver*, I, p. 335.

[8] Flinders anchored at King George Sound for nearly a month (8 December 1801–5 January 1802). The anchorage was off the Flinders Peninsula. During this time Robert Brown (the botanist) and Peter Good (the gardener) collected samples of over 500 plant species. Vallance, Moore and Groves, eds, *Nature's Investigator*, p. 91; NAT MAP Mount Barker Special.

AM. Moderate breezes and fine weather. At daylight sent the master to sound round the ship and to examine Seal Island: he brought on board four seals,[1] at 8 *hours*. Sent a boat to land the naturalist &c. near Bald Head, and went away with the master and draftsman to examine Princess-Royal Harbour[2] for a convenient place in which to wood, water, and refit the ship.[3]

Note: This day is continued to thirty-six hours, in order to bring the day to the civil or common account.

Noon, fresh breezes and fine weather. At sunset, sent down top-gallant yards, and the boats being returned, hoisted them up, but the naturalists remained on shore.

By log		Latitude South		Longitude East						
Course	Distance	DR	Obs	DR	TK	Var allowed	Set or current	Ther	Barom	Error of TK
S85°E	45½	35°11′	35°6′	113°57′	118°6′	7W	5N 14E	65½° – 66°	30.08 – 30.01	–3′3″E

Additional remarks upon the coast &c

The shore ran along this afternoon is of the same kind as the morning, a projecting head or point every 4 or 8 miles and sandy bights between them. The strong current that set along this shore carried us somewhat past our reckoning, so that when the Eclipse Isles appeared we only then knew that we were abreast of Cape Howe. The shore falls back on the east side of this cape 3 or 4 miles NNE: the cape consists of smooth brown cliffs, not very high.

We found Bald Head to be a more sloping projection than captain Vancouvers sketch shews it to be;[4] and it being dusk, the east end of Break-sea Island being more steep was taken for it; luckily, I had doubts of this, and determined to haul up into the weathermost bight, otherwise we had missed King George's Sound.[5]

[1] Probably the Australian sea lion (*Neophoca cinerea*). Dell, 'The Fauna Encountered in South-West Western Australia', p. 124.

[2] Named by Vancouver after Charlotte (1766–1828), the eldest daughter of George III (35°03′S, 117°53′E). A harbour on the west side of King George Sound, it is landlocked, with good protection from winds and heavy seas. Lamb, ed., *The Voyage of George Vancouver*, I, p. 337.

[3] Bearing Book, f. 4, adds: 'Deep water seems to be over on the north shore. A shoal spit with an isle or dry patch on it runs half way across from this to the north shore, furthest up the harbour. Head of the bay seems to be at least 5 miles further up, and the form not so round as given by Vancouver.'

[4] This is also mentioned in Flinders, *A Voyage to Terra Australis*, I, p. 53.

[5] Flinders selected King George Sound as the most suitable place to prepare for the examination of Australia's south coast for several reasons: it offered secure shelter; the masts could be stripped; the rigging and sails put in order; and communication could be made with the shore without the interference of the elements. King George Sound is recognized as one of the six major sheltered natural deep water harbours in the world and the best between Shark Bay and Melbourne. Ibid., I, p. 53; Milne, 'The Albany Perspective', p. 177. Westall produced coastal profiles, drawings, and pencil-and-wash views while the *Investigator* was anchored in King George Sound: see Stehn and George, 'Artist in a New Land', pp. 77–95. For the botanical discoveries in King George Sound, see Keighery and Gibson, 'The Flinders Expedition in Western Australia', pp. 105–13.

The anchoring place which we chose in the dark, proved to be as good almost as the sound affords, which shews captain Vancouvers survey to be good, as it certainly is in the main, although constructed with so much haste that he does not chuse to answer for it.[1]

In our way to *Princess* Royal Harbour in the morning, we stopped at Seal Island to look for captain Vancouver's bottle and parchment, but found no vestiges of it, or of the staff or pile of stones: which led me to suspect some ship had been here since.[2] From Seal Island the draftsmen and myself landed on the opposite shore to walk across to the harbour whilst the master beat the boat up. On the long beach there are some small drains of excellent water, but the surf would make it difficult for boats to get casks off them. The narrow neck of land which divides the harbour from the sound is more sand, with a few exceptions of rocky points. The south point of entrance is a sloping hill of quarry granite,[3] in many places bare of vegetation: from hence we had a good prospect of the harbour which is a large piece of shallow water, bounded by a low sandy shore with some rocky points. A woody projection to the WSW attracting my notice, we beat the boat up to it against a strong breeze. It was very shoal at a considerable distance from the shore, and no fresh water was found near it. Wood was plentiful and with some surprise we saw several trees which had been felled by saws and axes. Returning across, we found the deepest water to be near the northern shore, and in the entrance we found from 5 to 7 *fathoms* though in a narrow channel.[4]

[f. 102] **Thursday 10 December**

Light breezes and fine weather. At daybreak sent the master to examine the north side of Princess Royal Harbour for wood and water, and another boat for the naturalist and those with him who had remained on shore. At 7½ *hours*, got under weigh to work up towards the harbour. Tacked ship occasionally, keeping the lead constantly going and finding good regular soundings, for which see the survey.[5] At 10 *hours* 50′ anchored in 6 fathoms off the entrance of the harbour and about half a mile distant: the entrance of Oyster Harbour[6] being also open. Being doubtful of the masters success, I took a boat to examine the latter harbour and the depth of water into it.[7] At noon, the master returned

---

[1] For the use of Vancouver's chart, see Flinders, *A Voyage to Terra Australis*, I, p. 53.

[2] On 11 October 1791, to commemorate his visit, Vancouver had left a bottle sealed up, with the names of his vessels, their commanders, the name given to the Sound, and the date of arrival and departure. Another bottle was deposited on the top of Seal Island, with a staff on which was placed a medal of the year 1789. This second bottle was left because Seal Island was thought to be out of reach of any natives, which might not be the case on the mainland where the first bottle was left. Some ships had called at Seal Island between the voyages of Vancouver and Flinders. Two whaling vessels, the *Kingston*, Captain Thomas Dennis, and the *Elligood*, Captain Dixon, entered King George Sound in August 1800. Both were owned by Daniel Bennett of London. They had been sent to New Holland for whales, with instructions to examine King George Sound, then proceed to Shark Bay and the north-west coast before returning to London via Madagascar and southern Africa. Vancouver, *Voyage of Discovery*, I, p. 40. Vessels arriving at this vicinity between Vancouver and Flinders are discussed in Dickson, *To King George the Third Sound for Whales*, pp. 44–51. Seal Island is drawn in the atlas accompanying Flinders, *Voyage to Terra Australis*, plate XVII, view 4.

[3] Possession Point (35°02′S, 117°55′E). This is where Vancouver took possession of the area for George III on 29 September 1791. Flinders, *A Voyage to Terra Australis*, I, p. 54.

[4] Ibid., I, p. 54, adds: 'but the channel was too narrow to admit of getting in without a leading wind and much caution'.

[5] These are marked on Flinders's survey sheet of King George Sound in TNA, ADM 352/537.

[6] Oyster Harbour (about 35°00′S, 117°57′E), named by Vancouver because of the many oysters found there, was one of two harbours – the other being Princess Royal Harbour – in King George Sound. It was an inner cove to the north of the Sound. Lamb, ed., *The Voyage of George Vancouver*, I, p. 338.

[7] Flinders, *A Voyage to Terra Australis*, I, p. 55, notes that he was accompanied by his brother.

having found water, but no wood near it, [n]or could a boat come very near to the shore. Fresh breezes and fine.

PM. At 6, the Commander returned from Oyster Harbour, having found abundance of wood and some water near the entrance, but was not able to satisfy himself about the depth of water into it. Hoisted up the two cutters, and sent the gig to fish with hook and line: she had little success.

Additional remarks

Steering for the entrance of Oyster Harbour from the ship, I carried 6 and 7 fathoms until the south point of Michaelmas Island[1] came on with the north end of Break-sea Island, when it shoaled to 5, 4, 3, and 2¾. On hauling to the westward the water shoaled to six feet, but deepened again to 17 feet when we kept to the eastward: the east point of the entrance being then on with the center of some high land at the back. In this line I kept for the entrance, the water deepening to 3, 4, and 5 fathoms.

Within the harbour the channel divides: one part runs towards the little green island, but the deepest turns round towards the starboard shore.[2] There was nothing upon the island to indicate its having been visited by Europeans. It is full of holes which I judge to have been made by rats; and probably it is these animals that prevent the birds from laying their eggs here, for it does not appear that the natives visit it.[3] Shoal water surrounds the island, but a ship may lie in 3 or 4 fathoms at the distance of two cables lengths, if she could get into the harbour: there are more oysters upon the shoals.[4]

Having taken a set of angles from the top of this island,[5] I rowed over to the east side where the water appeared to be deep near the shore; but we could not approach it nearer than thirty yards with the boat. Wood was abundant here, but I could not see any fresh water: pieces of quartz and iron stone were scattered all over the shore.

Crossing over to a head[6] on the opposite side of the harbour, the boat could not come within a cables length of the shore. From this head I walked round to the south west point of the entrance, which is low and sandy. In the way I crossed two small streams of water, the one brackish, the other fresh but high coloured, and both inaccessible to boats. On the east side of the entrance, I found a patch of ground of six or eight feet square turned up, and on it was lying a piece of sheet copper marked 'August 1800 Christopher Dixson – ship *Ollegood*.'[7] Water being obtainable in this place by digging,

---

[1] Michaelmas Island (227 acres, 35°03′S, 118°03′E), named by Vancouver who sighted it on Michaelmas Day (29 September) 1791, is in the mouth of King George Sound. It has steep rocky shores along its northern, southern and eastern sides. Lamb, ed., *The Voyage of George Vancouver*, I, p. 60.

[2] Green Island (34°59′S, 117°56′E), only 820 yards from the mainland, is in Oyster Harbour. Flinders had read Vancouver's description of it 'as covered with luxuriant grass and other vegetables', but he found no grass there on his visit. Flinders, *A Voyage to Terra Australis*, I, p. 55, and *Atlas*, plate II, South Coast sheet I.

[3] The burrows were not made by rats but by the short-tailed shearwater. Abbott, 'Historic record of Australian Pelican', pp. 1–7.

[4] The flat or mud oyster, common on rocks and in soft sediments in embayments around Albany. Dell, 'The Fauna encountered in South-West Western Australia', p. 116.

[5] These are given in the entry for 10 December 1801, Bearing Book, f. 6.

[6] Marked as 'Bayonet Head' (34°58′S, 117°55′E) on Flinders, *A Voyage to Terra Australis*, *Atlas*, plate II, South Coast sheet 1. It is now an outer suburb of Albany.

[7] This refers to the whaling ship identified above on p. 242, n. 2. Flinders, *A Voyage to Terra Australis*, I, p. 56, notes that this 'solved the difficulty of the felled trees, and the disappearance of Captain Vancouver's bottle.'

wood being plentiful, and landing convenient, I considered it to be the best place we had yet found in which to refit the ship, if the depth over the bar would admit her into the harbour; the strength of the wind prevented me from ascertaining this point as I returned to the ship.

There was no fresh water at the south end of the long beach between the two harbours, but I found wood and further marks of axes and saws. At some distance behind the beach a lake of fresh water was afterwards found.

[f. 103] **Friday 11 December**

Light breezes and cloudy weather. Sent the master to sound upon the bar of the entrance into Oyster Harbour. Squally with rain at times afterwards moderate and cloudy. At 9 the master returned, but not being altogether satisfied with his report, went with him to examine further, but we could find no more than 13 feet in the shallowest part. In the evening sent a boat to Oyster Harbour to bring off the naturalist and other gentlemen who had been landed there in the morning. The boat collected a good quantity of oysters from the shoals and some of the large fan mussels,[1] but it was near high water and therefore a bad time for collecting them.

Additional remarks

Thinking it possible that there might be a deep part over the bar into Oyster Harbour which Mr Thistle the master might have missed, I went upon a hill near the entrance with some signal flags in order to direct him to the deepest part which was best seen from an eminence; it appeared however that 13 feet was now the deepest water upon the bar, which consequently precluded the *Investigator* from entering as she draws 14; but had there been 17 according to captain Vancouvers account, or even 15½ I would have preferred it to Princess Royal Harbour.[2]

Saturday 12 December

Light breezes and fine weather. Sent a party of men to cut wood at the south end of the long middle beach, and the launch with the same to fish. The wind coming fair for going into *Princess* Royal Harbour, made the signal with a gun for the launch to come on board. Put a kedge and hawser into her ready for use, and at 18 *hours* 25′ weighed and steered for the harbour under three top sails.[3] Passed through the narrow entrance, and at 11 *hours* 12′ anchored in 17 feet water abreast of the top of the highest hill on the north shore: distant from the beach about half a mile: the bottom muddy. Veered away and dropped the other anchor in 3 fathoms, having an open hawse to the southward, and Break-sea and Michaelmas Islands in the sound being on with the two points of the entrance into this harbour.[4]

Noon, moderate breezes and fine weather. Landed the naturalist and other gentlemen, and went on shore myself to look at the watering place and fix upon a situation for the observatory and tents. The wind freshening up in the evening, the launch was not able to

[1] Probably the large common razor clam, though other types of mussels are found at King George Sound. Dell, 'The Fauna encountered in South-West Western Australia', p. 116.

[2] Flinders abandoned the idea of refitting in Oyster Harbour because of the lack of water depth there. Flinders, *A Voyage to Terra Australis*, I, p. 56.

[3] Flinders had waited four days for the westerly wind to come around to the east to enable him to take the *Investigator* over the bar to anchor in Princess Royal Harbour.

[4] Breaksea Island is situated to the south of Michaelmas Island.

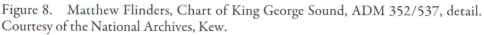

Figure 8.   Matthew Flinders, Chart of King George Sound, ADM 352/537, detail. Courtesy of the National Archives, Kew.

work into the sound for the wooders, but we sent to them to walk round abreast of the ship. Sent two tents on shore and pitched them near the watering place.[1] Employed otherwise repairing the rounding of the cables. Cut up beef No. [*blank*] to its contents. At sunset, sent down top-gallant yards.

Additional remarks

From our anchorage, into the harbour we carried 7, 6, 5, and in the narrowest part of the entrance 4 fathoms; then hauled up to SWbW½W to pass round the shoal which lies off the inner part of the north side, where we had 6, 7, and in the narrowest part between the shoals, 8 fathoms.[2] Abreast of the 3rd sandy beach on the north side the water shoaled to 3½ our course now being WNW. When Michaelmas I*sland* came nearly on with the middle of this entrance, we had 4 *fatho*ms: afterwards shoaler to the anchorage.

---

[1] The tents were set up at the foot of Mount Clarence (35°01′S, 117°89′E), which became in 1832 the site of the town of Albany. Vallance, Moore and Groves, eds, *Nature's Investigator*, p. 94.

[2] For the detailed soundings here, see the entry for 12 December 1801, Bearing Book, f. 7.

From the top of the hill at the back of the tents I had a tolerable view of the surrounding country. Amongst the bearings of remarkable objects taken from hence was a considerable extent of water to the westward, which I judged to be either a large lagoon, or an inlet from the head of the height near Cape Howe.[1]

[f. 104] **Sunday 13 December**

Light breezes and fine weather. Sent the observatory and astronomical instruments on shore. Sent the top-gallant masts down upon deck and a launch load of empty water casks on shore. Mustered the ships company, saw them clean, and gave a part leave to walk on shore. Fresh breezes & fine.

Monday 14 December

Light breezes with dull cloudy weather. Loosed the sails to dry and afterwards unbent them and unrove the running rigging. Cleared hawse. Received a launch load of wood from the first wooding place. The cooper employed at the watering place setting up and repairing casks, of which our holds were now cleared. Fresh breezes and squally. Struck the top masts and unrigged them to repair the rigging.[2]

Additional remarks

Some fires being seen at the head of the harbour, the naturalist and other gentlemen went towards them.[3] They met with natives who were rather shy, but did not seem to be afraid:[4] a man with whom they had some communication was admired for his manly behaviour: he received a bird, which had been shot, and a pocket handkerchief.[5]

As has usually been observed of the natives of other parts of New Holland these people did not wish for any communication, but made signs for the party to return back: they were not thought to be very black.[6]

Tuesday 15 December

Moderate breezes and fine weather. Sent a boat to Oyster Harbour, and the launch with the wooders to the south end of the middle beach again, the wood on the south side of this harbour being difficultly split: Unrigged the fore and mizzen masts and got the rigging on a stretch ready to be fresh served (: the main mast only was stripped at the

---

[1] This was Lake Powell (35°01′S, 117°44′E).

[2] Flinders, *A Voyage to Terra Australis*, I, p. 57, adds: 'our various duties commenced; the naturalists ranged the country in all directions, being landed at such places as they desired; whilst my own time was divided betwixt the observatory and the survey of the sound'.

[3] Aborigines deliberately started fires to procure game in the summer by surrounding an area and then setting fire to the grass and underbrush. The probable routes where Flinders and his party walked near King George Sound are drawn in Moore, 'Robert Brown on HMS Investigator', fig. 29, p. 52.

[4] In 1791 Vancouver had noted smokes, huts and drying fish here but he never sighted any people. Flinders's meetings with the Aborigines at King George Sound were notably friendly. Flinders was the first European to record meeting these people here. Milne, 'The Albany Perspective', p. 177.

[5] Samuel Smith added: 'On our first interview with them, they seem'd surprised, which gave us reason to think they had never before seen Europeans.' Monteath, ed., *Sailing with Flinders*, p. 35.

[6] Robert Brown's diary account for 14–16 December 1801 also commented on this first encounter with Aborigines during the voyage. See Vallance, Moore and Groves, eds, *Nature's Investigator*, pp. 96–8. Flinders, *A Voyage to Terra Australis*, I, p. 58, refers to the Aborigines as 'Indians', and includes detailed comments about them (pp. 58–9, 66–7).

Cape, for want of time.) The cutter returned in the evening loaded with oysters, which were issued to the ships company. Received two launch loads of wood.

Additional remarks

We were gratified this morning by a visit of [*blank*] natives to the tents. They approached very cautiously, one coming first with poised spear and many gestures, and much parleying.[1] One of our gentlemen[2] going to him unarmed brought about their confidence, and they became friendly; parting with some of their implements and receiving articles of iron and toys[3] in return.

Wednesday 16 December

Moderate breezes and fine weather: some passing squalls. Sent the cutter with the seine[4] to fish, but she returned in the afternoon without success. Fresh breezes and squally at times. People employed about the rigging. Sent the seine again in the evening with the cutter, and ordered them to kindle fires upon the beaches and haul the seine round them.

Thursday 17 December

Light breezes and fine weather. Two other natives came to the tents with one of our former visitors. The cutter returned very early with a few fish which were divided amongst the ships company. Employed on board principally about the rigging. Cooper at the tents setting up and repairing casks. Noon – light airs with sultry. Employed rigging the fore and mizzen masts. Many small mullet caught alongside with hook and line.

[f. 105] **Friday 18 December**

Fresh breezes and squally. Took the carpenter to the south side of the harbour to look for trees fit for plants and small spars; and walked up the hills to the sea shore to take bearings of the Eclipse Isles, Cape Howe &c but it came on to blow a violent gale of wind, with rain, and defeated my purpose. The top of the observatory was blown off by the first squall, and the instruments suffered some damage. Bent the sheet cable and unstowed the anchor. In the evening there were intervals of fair moderate weather.

Saturday 19 December

Fresh gales with frequent rain, and thunder and lightening; afterwards more moderate with fine intervals. People employed principally in refitting the rigging. At noon, fresh breezes with frequent showers of rain. Rigged the three topmasts.

Sunday 20 December

Fresh breezes and cloudy with drizzling rain at times. Mustered the ships company, as usual on this day, and saw them clean; afterwards the greater part were permitted to go on shore to wash their clothes and take a walk. Several large snappers caught alongside

---

[1] These Aborigines did not always carry spears in the encounters over these few days. As Samuel Smith explained, 'their spears being their chief commodity, they took care to hide them in their way to us'. Monteath, *Sailing with Flinders*, p. 35.

[2] Robert Purdie, the assistant-surgeon. Flinders, *A Voyage to Terra Australis*, I, p. 58.

[3] 'Toys' were manufactured metalware goods.

[4] A large vertical fishing-net whose ends are brought together and hauled.

with hook and line, and, as usual lately, many small mullet. Sent a boat to fish off the rocky points near the entrance of the harbour, but they had little success. Note. The snappers caught here seem to be exactly the same kind of fish as those caught near Port Jackson.

Noon, moderate breezes and cloudy weather. The launch, which had been sent to the south side of the harbour, returned with a log for sawing into plank, after having prepared another log and a saw pit[1] on shore. Dull cloudy w*eath*er.

Monday 21 December
Light breezes and cloudy. Fidded the topmasts[2] and set up the rigging. The cooper and some hands on shore repairing casks and filling water. Noon, moderate breezes and cloudy weather. People on board employed about the rigging. Carpenters sawing plank to make boxes for the naturalist, and for other purposes.

Tuesday 22 December
Fresh breezes and fine weather. A cutter employed surveying in the harbour. Rigged and crossed the top sail yards, and swayed up[3] the lower yards. At noon, *ditto* weather. People employed about the rigging. Cooper on shore as before.

Additional remarks

Accompanied by Mr Thistle, the master, I measured a base line[4] upon the long middle beach between the two harbours,[5] of 2.44 geographic miles, to serve as the foundation of a survey of the sound.[6] Having determined several fixed points by angles taken from different parts of this base, we ran over to Seal Island where another extensive set of angles were taken: the length of time taken to measure the base prevented us from doing more than returning to the ship before dark.

Wednesday 23 December
Fresh breezes with dull cloudy weather and heavy rain at times. A large party went into the country to visit some lagoons.[7] Employed getting coals out of the hold, and in other work preparatory to completing the water. Noon, *ditto* weather. People employed in the holds.

Additional remarks

Our party to the lagoon consisted of officers, the scientific gentlemen, and others to the number of thirteen, armed and provided for two days. Soon after leaving the head of

---

[1] A pit in which one sawyer stands while another stands above.

[2] i.e. used a square bar, with a shoulder, to support the weight of the topmasts.

[3] i.e. hoisted.

[4] An accurately measured line used as a base for triangulation. It involved using a surveyor's chain to lay down a base line running in a recorded compass direction; establishing the position of one end of the base line; and measuring the angle from there to a natural inland feature. Estensen, *The Life of Matthew Flinders*, p. 180.

[5] i.e. Oyster and Princess Royal Harbours.

[6] Flinders's main preoccupation here was a trigonometrical survey of King George Sound. He used Vancouver's survey as a basis for a more thorough investigation. Flinders's calculations for his survey are given in full in the Bearing Book, entry for 21 December 1801, ff. 9–10. His survey sheet for King George Sound is deposited at TNA, ADM 352/537.

[7] The lagoons were very close to one another. Flinders, *A Voyage to Terra Australis*, *Atlas*, plate II, South Coast, sheet 1.

Princess Royal Harbour a native was seen running before us, and an old man, who had before visited the tents, made his appearance, and was very resolute to prevent us from going into the country. He was not able to prevail, but we accommodated [f. 106] him by going round the part of the wood where it should seem his family were. He followed us through swamps and thick bushes, hollowing constantly for the purpose, as I suppose, of informing his friends of our movements. After we had passed some distance from the place where we met him, he fell behind and left us.[1]

From the head of the harbour to the lagoons, we steered a westerly course at the back of the sea coast hills, through a low swampy country. The hills consist of sand and rock, covered generally with small shrubs but without trees.

We found the first lagoon to be full of fresh water, the drainings from the low swampy country; its length is one-and-a-half miles, and one in width. Coasting around the north side of this towards a more western lagoon, we were stopped for a small serpentine stream which appeared to bring the water thrown from the *North* western hills, and obliged us to walk a further distance inland in order to cross it.

On Thursday morning we walked towards the head of the bight near Cape Howe with the intention of returning by the sea shore, but we came to a lagoon larger than the former whose water was brackish, proving it to have some communication with the sea. Fearing that this communication might be too large to be crossed, and our return by the sea shore therefore prevented, we were under the necessity of retracing our steps round the rivulet and eastern lagoon in order to reach the hills upon the sea coast. The descent from the hills being difficult, and there being doubts of the practicability of walking along the sea shore, we kept along the top of the ridge. After a wearisome walk, which was rendered distressing from the want of water, and still more so from the botanical draftsman being unable to proceed from excessive fatigue and thirst, the greater number of us reached the tents at eight in the evening: the rest of the party got in about midnight.[2]

Marks of kanguroos[3] were numerous about the lagoons, but not one was seen. The black swans were swimming in one of the streams.[4] The country has but little to recommend it, being either low and swampy, or rocky; and apparently with but a small depth of soil in every part.[5]

Thursday 24 December
Moderate breezes and fine weather. People employed watering the ship. Cut up beef No. [*blank*] and pork No. [*blank*] to their contents. At noon *ditto* weather. Received on board plank cut by the sawyers from the south side of the harbour. Light breezes and cloudy weather.

---

[1] Rough Journal, I, f. 237, adds: 'when a parroquet was shot he expressed neither surprise nor fear at the report of the gun but accepted the bird with apparent pleasure: he was curious to see what was doing when the gun was reloading'.

[2] Flinders, *A Voyage to Terra Australis*, I, p. 60, also mentions 'the excessive heat'.

[3] The western grey kangaroo (*Macropus fuliginosus*). Dell, 'The Fauna encountered in South-Western Australia', p. 123. 'Kanguroo' is Flinders's usual spelling for 'kangaroo'.

[4] The red-beaked black swan (*Cygnus atratus*) is common in the wetlands of this part of Australia. Perth's Swan River was named after this waterbird by Willem de Vlamingh in 1697.

[5] Flinders, *A Voyage to Terra Australis*, I, p. 60, notes that the soil was 'unfit for cultivation'.

Friday 25 December

Moderate breezes and fine weather. Employed cleaning the ship and in some other necessary duties. Sent the cutter to fish with hook and line, and at noon she returned with some success. Mustered ships company and saw them clean, afterwards part had permission to go on shore, whilst others volunteered to go fishing.

Saturday 26 December

Fresh breezes and cloudy. Employed stowing the after holds. A boat employed surveying in this harbour. PM Carpenters employed making garden boxes for the naturalist. Cooper on shore completing the water casks, which there are people kept ready to fill. Employed on board in the holds.

[f. 107] **Sunday 27 December**

Fresh breezes and cloudy. Employed stowing in the holds, the water brought off in rafts. One of the cutters employed surveying in the sound. At noon, moderate breezes and hazy. Employments PM as in the morning.

Monday 28 December

Fresh gales and squally with rain at times. Employed on board completing the holds with water. Sailmakers repairing sails. PM Fresh breezes and squally weather.

Tuesday 29 December

Light breezes and hazy. Bent sails. PM moderate and cloudy. Employed setting up the rigging fore and aft, and otherwise preparing for sea.

Wednesday 30 December

Light airs with cloudy weather. Punished William Donovan with 36 lashes for repeated drunkenness and fighting. Fidded the top-gallant mast and crossed the yards. Sent the marines on shore to be exercised in the presence of the natives; afterwards struck the tents. PM At 1 unmoored ship and hove short. Brought on board the tents, observatory, and astronomical instruments with the intention of running into the sound this evening; but the wind shortening upon us, and there being very little deep water to beat about in, we remained at anchor. Mod*erate* and dull w*eathe*r.

Additional remarks

The visits of the natives to our tents on shore have been very frequent. At first they always received presents of such things as appeared to be most agreeable to them; but they brought us nothing in return, and therefore we latterly broke off this practice. This morning five of them were almost persuaded to go into our boat to the ship, but in the end their fears got the better.[1] The landing of our small party of marines to be exercised, raised much astonishment amongst the natives, and apparently pleasure.[2] The red coats

---

[1] A note at the bottom of the page adds: 'and they made signs that the ship must come in shore to them'.

[2] This military exercise by the marines appears to have been staged to assess the Aborigines' responses. It was staged partly because the marines and the Aborigines lacked a common language. The Aborigines appear to have interpreted the military drill as an appropriate contact ritual. In 1908 the anthropologist Daisy Bates met an elderly man near Albany called Nebinyan. He told her that the Nyungar Aborigines of King George Sound

with white crossed belts were so much in their way of ornamenting themselves, that they absolutely screamed with delight on seeing the men drawn up; their vociferation and wild gestures could only be silenced by commencing the exercise, to which they paid the utmost attention. The fife, the drum, the motions of the exercise, all excited curiosity and astonishment; and the old man who had met us in our way to the lagoons was so absorbed with the latter, that with a stick in his hand he was, almost unknown to himself, imitating the marines in their exercise. Being apprized of the firing, the vollies did not raise much terror in the natives.[1]

We gained some words of the native language this morning with tolerable certainty,[2] and parted with our new friends after the tents were struck, with good humour, and without any quarrel having taken place during our intercourse; but it is remarkable, that when the marines returned to the ship, all the sensations which had been excited in the natives went also: such is the human mind when uncultivated; I believe, however, that they left us with higher ideas of our power than before, though from our desire to be friendly with them, which induced us to put up with little things from them which were not altogether pleasant. I suspect they took us for cowards; and had we remained longer should probably have been obliged to convince them that we were not to be insulted.[3]

[f. 108] Thursday 31 December

Moderate breezes and cloudy weather. The wind becoming more foul for getting out,[4] I sent the master to sound and take angles in Oyster Harbour; and I ascended the highest part of the sea-coast for the latter purpose also. Launch employed bringing on board some rough spars, and grass. At noon, fine weather with haze. Employed variously, preparing for sea.

---

believed that Flinders and his party were ghosts of their own dead ancestors who had returned from Kooranup, the home of the dead across the sea. They thought the full dress parade of the marines was a Kooranup ceremony. The ritual was considered sacred, to be handed down the generations. Vallance, Moore and Groves, eds, *Nature's Investigator*, p. 105; Carter, *Living in a New Country*, pp. 161–2; White, 'Birth and Death of a Ceremony', pp. 33–42.

[1] Samuel Smith's account of this encounter is as follows: 'At this time the Natives 5 in Number came up to their Middle in Water to meet the Boats signifying their Friendship, by Frightful Yels & Gestures, & seem'd surprised at our Marines in full regimentals. The Marines being form'd up was order'd to March; at this regiolur movement they seem'd surprised, but More so at the noise of the Fife & Drum. But they saw what it proceeded from & Made several attempts to take the Fife, but seeing the Obstinancy in giving it up they Desisted. They march'd from this on the sand & after several Maneuvers they Fired, which caused them to Dance & hollow unmercifully.' Monteath, ed., *Sailing with Flinders*, p. 35.

[2] Aboriginal words in this location were recorded by Brown and Good: see Vallance, Moore and Groves, eds, *Nature's Investigator*, p. 105, and Edwards, ed., *The Journal of Peter Good*, p. 52. Another version of the word list is given in Flinders, *A Voyage to Terra Australis*, I, p. 67.

[3] Robert Brown notes that William Westall showed an aborigine a drawing of him. The native 'appeard pleasd & bar'd his body to the waist that Mr West[all] might be able to finish his work. They appear[ed] clearly to understand our wishes to know their names for the different parts of the body & one of them unaskd began to run over them.' Peter Good reported that one of the natives permitted Brown and Bell to examine him physically, accompanying this with naming different parts of his body. Flinders reported a set of body measurements provided by Bell. This was the only time this occurred during the *Investigator*'s expedition. Flinders did not comment on, or analyse, the figures. Vallance, Moore and Groves, eds, *Nature's Investigator*, p. 105; Edwards, ed., *The Journal of Peter Good*, p. 52; Flinders, *A Voyage to Terra Australis*, I, p. 68; Dyer, *The French Explorers*, p. 52.

[4] The wind was blowing in a south-by-east direction. Flinders, *A Voyage to Terra Australis*, I, p. 61.

1802

Friday 1 January

Light airs and calms. A breeze springing up from the northward at 7, weighed and ran into the fair way of the entrance, intending to get into the sound by the first opportunity. Launch employed bringing on board grass and fire wood and the sailmakers in repairing sails. PM Fresh gales and hazy weather. Seeing the launch upset on the south side of the harbour, sent a cutter to her assistance. In the evening, more moderate breezes with cloudy weather.

Saturday 2 January

Moderate breezes and fine weather. Sent the cutter to fish with hook and line, and she caught sufficient fish to make a serving to those who had not caught enough on board for themselves. Sailmakers repairing the old sails. At noon, moderate and hazy. Employed preparing for sea.

Sunday 3 January

Light airs with dull cloudy weather. Hoisted in one of the cutters to be repaired. Mustered the ships company and read the articles of war. A light fair breeze springing up at 1, we weighed immediately and sailed through the entrance into the sound, finding from 7½ fathoms in the narrowest part between the shoals to 3¼ between the heads.[1] Stood backwards and forwards in the sound with the trawl[2] and dredge[3] overboard, and caught many subjects of observation for the naturalist, but not much fish for the ships company; but the small boat which had been sent to fish in the morning brought enough to serve everybody. At 7 *hours* 30′ PM came to with the small bower in 7 *fathoms*, near the flat rock on the south side of the sound, being exposed to the sea between Bald Head and Break-sea Island making an angle of ten degrees. Mod*erate* breezes and fine w*eather*.[4]

Monday 4 January

Fresh gales and hazy weather. Carpenters repairing the cutter. Cut up pork no. [*blank*] to its contents. Sent the master to take angles from Bald Head. At noon, d*itto* weather. Some fish caught with hook and line. Left a bottle upon Seal Island, containing a parchment to inform future visitors of our arrival and intention to sail on the morrow. Employed in jobs preparing for sea. At night, moderate breezes.

Ships draught of water for*ward* 14 *feet – inches* Aft 13 *feet* 10 *inches*.

Tuesday 5 January

Variable breezes with heavy rain: at 9, the weather cleared. Sent up top-gallant yards, treble reefed the topsails, and weighed the anchor.[5] Fresh gales and squally, with fine

---

[1] A change in wind direction enabled Flinders to take the *Investigator* out of Princess Royal Harbour into the Sound. Flinders, *A Voyage to Terra Australis*, I, pp. 61–2.

[2] An open-mouthed bag-net.

[3] A bag-net for raising deposits from under water.

[4] This was almost the same spot as Vancouver had chosen to anchor in September 1791. Flinders was able to anchor between Bald Head and Breaksea Island for several days because wood and water, 'though neither very good', were procurable there. Flinders, *A Voyage to Terra Australis*, I, p. 61.

[5] The *Investigator* made sail out of King George Sound 'to prosecute the further examination of the coast'. The coast immediately to the east of King George Sound had been seen by Vancouver in 1791 and D'Entrecasteaux in 1792. Flinders had copies of their charts. Ibid., I, p. 62; Vallance, Moore and Groves, eds, *Nature's Investigator*, p. 108; Marchant, 'Bruny D'Entrecasteaux', pp. 171–2.

intervals. Steered between Michaelmas Island and the main to ascertain the existence of a shoal lying off the NW end of the latter: passed it with 5 *fatho*ms water. At noon, sounded in 33 *fatho*ms, the east end of Break-sea Island SW½S. Steered for Mount-Gardner Point.

This day ends at noon, bringing the time to log account as before.

La*titude* obse*rved* by lieut*enant* Flinders 35°1′53″S

[f. 109] Distances of the Sun east and west moon, for the longitude of the observatory

Time 1801	Apparent time of observation	From calculation Sun true centre	From calculation Moon true centre	Apparent distance of times	Longitude deduced Sun west Moon	Longitude deduced Sun east Moon	Thermometer	Barometer
December	h ′ ″							
12	1 4 57.2	71 28 53	18 23 36	86 14 7	118 2 42		67°	30.20
	8 6.4	70 57 12	19 0 55	15 41	117 58 6			
13	5 20 8.8	20 51 23	48 43 32	100 43 34	117 56 12		68	30.20
	23 15.6	20 14 19	49 2 54	44 30	59 9			
31	20 23 59	*Observed* 41 53 54	77 35 50	45 2 28		118 4 15	68	29.90
	29 26.8	43 0 57	53 40	0 46		7 12		
	21 52 49.1	59 55 43	71 2 25	44 32 55		8 42		
	22 0 7.5	61 21 26	69 49 36	30 18		6 13.5		
					117 59 2	118 6.35 East of Greenwich		
					Mean longitude	118 2 49		
					From 12 sets taken by lieut*enant* Flinders	117 55 23		
					Mean of all	117 59 6 East		

The longitude of the observatory given on our arrival by the *Time Keeper*s was

E 543	E 520	A 176	A 1736
118°13′24.1″	117°57′3.1″	117°58′31.6″	118°0′49.6″

Whence the time keeper errors are

E 543	E 520	A 176	A 1736
+14′18.1″	−2′2.9″	−0′34.4″	+1′43.6″

Mean error + 3′21.1 or to the east which being contracted since Nov*ember* 1st or in an interval of 43.7 days gives a proportion of 4.6″ per day for the progress of the mean longitude to the east of the truth.

Dip of the south end of the magnetic needle (made by Nairne & Blunt)
1801 December 17th AM on shore

Marked end S°		Marked end N°	
Face East	Face West	Face East	Face West
64°40′	63°00′	63°20′	65°40′
64°25′	62°30′	63°20′	65°15′
64°32′	62°45′	63°20′	65°28′
Mean	63°38′	Mean	64°24′

Mean dip of the needle 64°15′

[December] 30 AM On board ship at anchor

Marked end S°		Marked end N°	
Face East	Face West	Face East	Face West
64°40′	62°25′	64°37′	68°00′
65°15′	61°45′	64°37′	67°35′
64°57.5′	62°5	64°37′	67°47.5′
Mean	63°31.2′	Mean	66°12.2′

Mean dip of the needle 64°51.7′

Observations with the universal theodolite

Time 1801 December	Meridian zenith distance ☉ Upper Limb	Latitude South	Theodolite
14	11°33′22″	35°2′25″	70½°
15	11°29′29″	[35°]2′4″	68°
29	11°28′43″	[35°]1′51″	64°

Mean latitude 35°2′7″ South

Azimuths taken off the mouth of Princess Royal Harbour, the ships head being South Easterly (binnacle)

Time	Sun mag azimuth	Sun cent altitude	Variation
December 11 A.M.	S 69°52′ E	24°33′	8°15′ W
	69°38′	25°8′	8°52′
	70°10′	25°57′	8°49′
	70°10′	26°32′	9°4′
	69°27′	27°33′	10°3′
	70°47′	31°2′	11°23′

From three compasses, both sides   Mean 9°28′W

Azimuths with the same three compasses on shore

☉ [December] 20 A.M.	S81°34′E	48°1′	7°7′W
	80°48.8′	50°58′	5°54.2′
	78°52.5′	53°39′	6°6.5′

From the compasses, both sides   Mean 6°22.6′W

Azimuths Theodolite at the observatory

[December] 29	S84°49.5′W	22°46′	8°3.5′
P.M	[84°]34′	21°37.8′	8°30′
		Mean	8°16.7′W

Ditto Theodolite upon the flat rock on the south side of the sound

1802 January 3	102°29.3′W	29°4.8′	3°45.3′
A.M			
	102°0.3′	30°40.3′	4°16.3′
		Mean	4°0.8′
		Mean by theodolite	6°8.8′

Result of equal altitudes taken at the observatory with *Troughton* sextant No. 483 on a stand; and a quicksilver horizon,[1] to find the rates of the time keepers, and final error from mean Greenwich time

Time	Pairs of observations	E543 corrected at noon	E543 slower than mean time	Comparisons of Time Keepers with No. 543			
				E520	A82	A176	A1736
1801 December 15	Nine	15h43′47.77″	8h11′27.32″	−26′18.5″	+35′15.5″	−38′10.2″	+28′30.5″
17	Two[2]	15h44′31.94″	11′41.51″	−26′39.0″	+34′38.8″	−38′19.2″	+28′17.2″
21	Five[3]	15h46′6.42″	12′5.75″	−27′20.0″	+34′0.5″	−38′32.0″	+28′3.5″
22		46′30.15″	12′12.43″	−27′28.0″	+33′26.7″	−38′31.5″	
24		47′17.62″	12′24.86″	−27′48.8″	+32′48.7″	−38′31.6″	+27′56.2″
1802 January 1	Nine	50′21.15″	13′17.09″	−29′12.9″	+28′49.0″	−38′58.0″	+27′37.0″

Daily rates of *Time Keepers* deduced

E543	F. 520	A 82	A 176	A 1736	Thermometer	Barometer
−7′10″	−17′34″	−25′44″	−11′59″	−13′74″	70°	30.06
					67	29.97
6′06″	16′31″	−15′63″	9′16″	9′48″	69	− .82
6′68″	14′68″	40′48″	6′18″	8′80″	68	30.00
6′21″	16′61″	25′21″	6′26″	8′80″	63	− .28
6′53″	17′04″	36′49″	9′83″	8′93″	67	29.95
−6′46″[4]	−16′72″	−29′19″	−9′27″	−9′60″		

[1] i.e. a mercurial artificial horizon.
[2] Zenith distances taken with the universal theodolite.
[3] Zenith distances taken with the universal theodolite.
[4] This row comprises 'Rates of time-keepers from the first and last days'.

The longitude of the observatory being taken as above, the errors of the time keepers reduced to Greenwich noon January 1st are as under

	E 543	E 520	A 82	A 176	A 1736
Timekeepers slower than mean time here at noon here January 1 1802	8h13′17.09″	8h42′29.99″	7h44′28.09″	8h52′15.09″	7h45′40.09″
Longitude in time	7h51′56.40″	7h51′56.40″	7h51′56.40″	7h51′56.40″	7h51′56.40″
Errors from mean Greenwich time	− 21′20.69″	− 50′33.59″	+ 7′28.31″	−1h0′18.69″	+ 6′16.31″
Part of the mean rates	+ 2.12″	+ 5.48″	− 9.57″	+ 08.04″	− 3.15″
Timekeepers slower than mean Greenwich time at noon there January 1 1802	− 21′22.01″	− 50′39.07″	+ 7′37.88″	−1h0′21.73″	+ 6′13.18″

[f. 110] <u>Experiments with the hydrostatic balance</u>

29th I took the bottle of sea water on shore, which had been taken up in latitude 36°30′S and longitude 38°30′E on November 12th (see the log of that day); and I found its comparative weight to be as under:

To balance the bulb of glass in air (the barometer standing at 29.96 and thermometer about 69°) it required to be put into the opposite scale 1748 grains.[1]

The bulb being suspended by a hair in fresh water, it required in the opposite scale 1206½ grains.

The bulb being suspended in the water from 150 fathoms deep, above mentioned, it required 1194½ grains.

When suspended in the surface water taken up at the same place, it required also 1194½ grains.

Also, when suspended in the water of Princess Royal Harbour, from alongside the ship 1194½ grains.

The water which had been taken up at sea smelt like bilge water, probably from not having been well corked up; and from its state of decomposition I suspect it might be lighter than when taken up on November 12. The fresh water that was used for the experiment was a little coloured by vegetable substances, none better for the purpose being to be procured near the tents.

<u>Of the tides</u>

We did not perceive any set of tide past the ship, either whilst lying in the sound or in Princess Royal Harbour; but in the entrance of the latter place we more than once, in a boat, found it running with considerable strength. According to the observations made by lieutenant Flinders,[2] during the 16 days that the observatory was on shore, there is only one high water in twenty-four hours, which always took place between 6 and 12 PM; for after, by gradually falling later, it had happened at 12, the next night it was high

---

[1] A note after this sentence adds: 'there appears to be an error of 2 dwts. in excess, in all these weights.' This refers to weights measured with the hydrostatic balance. Dwt can mean 'pennyweight' (⅟₂₀ of an ounce). Twenty-four grains make a pennyweight.

[2] Flinders's brother Samuel Ward Flinders, aged eighteen, undertook many astronomical observations as the Investigator sailed along the south Australian coast. Estensen, The Life of Matthew Flinders, p. 184.

water soon after six o'clock, and then happened later by three-quarters each night as before. The greatest rise observed was 3 feet 2 inches, and the least 2 feet 8 inches: It accumulated in this manner; after low water, it rose gradually for several hours, then ceased and became stationary, or perhaps fell a few inches; in a few hours it began to rise again and in about 12 hours after the first commencement it was high water.[1]

General remarks, upon the country and inhabitants

The basic stone of the country round King Georges Sound is granite, in which quartz is frequently pre-eminent; it appears bare in some places, both at the tops of the hills and by the water side, but is not uncommonly found to be covered with a crust of calcarious stone; and in Oyster Harbour there is also some iron stone.[2] The neighbouring country may, for the sake of description, be divided into hills and plains. The former are, near the sea coast, sandy and stony, and covered with a starving and small vegetation; but where they are sheltered from sea winds, there is a mixture of vegetable earth with the sand, and in such places trees of a tolerable size are produced. The plains are either covered with a thick and almost impenetrable brushwood, or they form, when low, lakes or swamps, the solid granite basis not seeming to permit the water to drain through into the earth. Considering the land with an eye to agriculture, it seems to be very bad; for I did not see five-hundred acres altogether that could have been sown with any kind of grain, in the expectation of getting back the seed. The borders of Oyster Harbour, of which I saw very little, are said to have a greater appearance of fertility. It seemed to obtain generally, that where the granite reached the surface the land was most barren; but more productive when the soil rested upon calcarious stone.

[f. 111] With the native inhabitants of this part of New Holland we were fortunate enough to obtain and preserve a friendly intercourse.[3] Our tents were frequently visited by small parties of men and latterly they always came without arms. The women were kept out of sight with seeming jealousy, and they seemed to suspect the same conduct in us, after being satisfied that even the most beardless of those they saw at the tents were of the same sex with the rest.

It was with surprise that I noticed the manners, actions, and customs of the natives of the east coast of New South Wales so nearly portrayed in those of the south-west coast of New Holland; and yet I heard but one word in which any fair similarity could be found. They do not indeed, like the indians of Port Jackson, knock out two of the front teeth at the time of puberty,[4] but their personal appearance is similar, their songs run in the same cadence, their manner of painting themselves is the same, their belts and fillets of hair are made in the same way, and of the same materials, and worn in the same manner.[5] The cloaks of kangaroo skin, which they wear over their shoulders, and is their only covering, is more

---

[1] Flinders, *A Voyage to Terra Australis*, I, pp. 71–2, adds: 'It was observed by Captain Cook upon the east coast of this country, and since by many others, including myself, that the night tide rose considerably higher than that of the day; which is conformable to our observations in King George's Sound; but with this difference, that in the day we had scarcely any tide at all.'

[2] This was mixed with quartz and granite. Ibid., I, p. 63.

[3] Ibid., I, pp. 65–7, has a detailed description of the Aborigines at King George Sound.

[4] This was a common Aboriginal practice. It was a feature only of male initiation and only a single tooth was knocked out. Collins, *An Account of the English Colony in New South Wales*, I, p. 458.

[5] Flinders had had previous contact with Aborigines on earlier voyages, notably on the *Tom Thumb* voyage south of Sydney in March 1796, on which he sailed with George Bass, and on the *Norfolk's* voyage north from Sydney to Hervey Bay in July 1799. Estensen, *The Life of Matthew Flinders*, pp. 57–9, 99–106.

in the custom of a wood native than of an inhabitant of the sea shore, and I agree with captain Vancouver that they appear to live more by hunting than fishing.[1] We could not make them understand the use of fish hooks, although upon many subjects they seemed to understand our signs very well; and nothing like a canoe was seen amongst them.

In manners, these Indians are quick and vehement, and their conversation is vociferous like most uncivilized people. They seemed to entertain no idea of any superiority that we possessed over them; but on the contrary they left us, after their first visit, with some apparent contempt for our pusillanimity, which was probably occasioned by the comparative mildness of our manners and the desire we shewed to be friendly with them.

Their language, as before observed, is very different to that at Port Jackson, but this is not to be wondered at, since even at Botany Bay and Broken Bay it is so.[2] The Port Jackson word of calling Coowee! was, however, used here with a little difference of pronunciation: it was here (as well as my recollection now serves me)[3] Cauwa!

I could only collect, with any degree of certainty, the names of some parts of the body (which are given in the margin) and indeed we found their pronunciation difficult to be imitated; more so, indeed, than they found ours to be, for they repeated many English words very perfectly, whilst of others they could make but little; thus their imitation of King George was Ken Jagger, and of ship yhip.[4]

Head	Kāāt[5]	Belly	Kobul[13]
Hair	Kaat-jou[6]	Posteriors	Walakah[14]
Nose	Moil[7]	Thigh	Dtoual[15]
Cheek or beard	Nyanūk[8]	Knee	Wonat[16]
Teeth	Yeaal[9]	Leg	Maat[17]
Ear	Duong[10]	Foot	Jain[18]
Lips	Urluck[11]	The sun	Djaat[19]
Nipple of the breast	Bpep[12]		

[1] For Vancouver's remark that the Aborigines' hunting grounds were much more important for their subsistence than fishing, see Lamb, ed., *The Voyage of George Vancouver*, I, pp. 354–5.

[2] Aboriginal language and dialects varied considerably in different parts of Australia. Therefore different groups of indigenous people did not necessarily understand one another. Flinders here came across Aborigines who spoke the Nyungar language. He was the first European to record samples of this language.

[3] A note adds: 'October 1804.'

[4] Flinders, *A Voyage to Terra Australis*, I, p. 67, adds: 'In the difficulty of pronouncing the f and s, they resemble the Port-Jackson natives; and the word used by them in calling to a distance, cau-wah! (come here) is nearly similar to cow-ee! The word also to express eye, is nearly the same.'

[5] Ibid., I, p. 67, also gives the equivalent words used by Aborigines at Port Jackson and Van Diemen's Land. In that account, Flinders drew upon information in Collins, *An Account of the English Colony in New South Wales*, I, pp. 506–13, and Rossel, *Voyage de D'Entrecasteaux*, I, pp. 552–6. Flinders adds: 'the words collected by Captain Cook at Endeavour River bear no resemblance to any of them.' 'Kaat' is the correct spelling. Several of the words in this list are identified in Dench, 'Nyungar', pp. 173–92.

[6] The correct spelling is 'kaat djaw'.

[7] The correct spelling is 'muuly'.

[8] The correct spelling for beard is 'ngarnak'.

[9] This is actually the word for 'eye'. The correct spelling is 'myaal'.

[10] The correct spelling is 'dhwongk'.

[11] This is actually the word for 'teeth', not 'lips'. The correct spelling is 'ngorlak'.

[12] The correct spelling for breast is 'biip'.

[13] The correct spelling for belly is 'korbal'.

[14] This word remains a mystery.

[15] The correct spelling is 'dhawul'.

[16] The correct spelling is 'bwonitj'.

[17] 'Maat' is correct.

[18] The correct spelling is 'djen'.

[19] 'Djaat' is correct.

[f. 112] Wednesday 6 January[1] HMS *Investigator* exploring along the south coast of New Holland

Squally at times with rain. Running generally under the topsails. At 2 *hours* 30′ steered to pass be[twe]en island I[2] and the main. The passage about one mile wide: soundings in passing through were as per column. Having passed through, we got into smooth water in a bight of the coast, but it is open to the eastward. Steered along a low sandy coast for a lump of rock, K,[3] which at 6 *hours* bore NNW ½ mile. Outer part of I [Bald Island] S40°W, and L,[4] a cape ahead, N43°E. At this time hauled off shore for the night under topsails and courses, sounding as per column. Fresh breezes and fine weather. At 1, wore ship towards the land. At daybreak, fresh breezes and cloudy. Let the 3rd reefs out of the topsails. At 6, the round rocky islet K [Haul-off Rock] N72°W 2½ miles: bore away and steered along the shore. At 7, hauled up to look into a bight[5] behind L [Cape Knob] in which is an island, but finding no anchorage bore away again along the coast. At 9, hauled further off shore, seeing a projection further out than the present line of the coast. Passed two large rocks lying near to the sandy shore. At noon, a rugged stony projection, Cape Knob, bore N20°E 3 miles. On the east side is a large sandy bight, and on the west a smaller in which lies a rocky islet.[6] Furthest land visible ahead N63°E.

Meri*dian* alt*itude* ☉ Lowe*r* Lim*b* T*roughton* No 483	77°44′33″N
Latitude	34°35′7″S
Supp*lement* ☉ U*pper* Lim*b*	101°43′28″S
Latitude	34°35′46″S
Mean latitude	34°35′26″S

		By log		Latitude South		Longitude East					
Course	Distance	DR	Obs	DR	TK	Var allowed	Set or current	Ther	Barom	Error of TK
N65°E	45½	34°43′	34°35′	119°00′	119°21′	6W	8N	64°	29.89	–
							21E	62°	29.98	
								65°	30.10	

Additional remarks

Island I [Bald Island] is about two miles long, it seems to be barren, and its stone to be of granite. The passage between it and the main is a short mile wide, and free from danger: I passed within the island because the French ships *Recherche* and *Esperance* passed without side.[7] Inland upon the opposite part of the main we see a ridge of irregular-shaped

---

[1] Flinders, *A Voyage to Terra Australis*, I, p. 73, notes that, in proceeding along the south coast of King George Sound, he had endeavoured to keep close to the land so that the breaking water on the shore would be visible from the ship's deck. Thus no river, or opening to a possible river, could escape being seen.

[2] Bald Island, called Ile Pelée by D'Entrecasteaux (34°55′S, 118°27′E). It is separated from the mainland by a channel that is ¾ mile wide. Ibid., I, p. 75; *Sailing Directions (Enroute): North, West and South Coasts of Australia*, p. 145.

[3] Flinders called this Haul-off Rock (34°42′S, 118°39′E). Flinders, *A Voyage to Terra Australis*, I, p. 75.

[4] Flinders called this Cape Knob (34°32′S, 119°14′E) because it had two lumps of rock at the top. Ibid.

[5] 'Beyond Cape Riche.' Ibid. This is Dillon Bay, a sandy bight.

[6] One of the four Doubtful Islands (named by Vancouver). Flinders was in Doubtful Island Bay, a series of shallow embayments extending from Hood Point north to the vicinity of Mid Mount Barren, about 34°04′S, 119°41′E. Ibid.; Vallance, Moore and Groves, eds, *Nature's Investigator*, p. 109.

[7] D'Entrecasteaux's ships (see above, p. 235, n. 5).

mountains, the most remarkable peak upon which lies N3°W by compass from the passage. The shore is low and sandy from the point opposite to I , to the high lump of rock K [Haul-off Rock], but it there rises gradually to a moderate height: K is about one mile from the main.

In the morning we came in again with K in order to continue the survey. The island I [Bald Island] was also in sight, as well as *Moun*t Many peak, which is visible from the sound.[1] Until 8 o clock, the shore we passed is rocky and of moderate height, but it then becomes sandy and continues so to Cape Knob. The front of this cape is about two miles long east and west, and there are sandy bights on each side of it: it has its name from the stony lumps upon its top. The irregular-shaped rugged mountains were in sight this morning, and from bearings seem to be seven leagues from the coast, and other mountains, distinct from the former, are coming in sight: except these, we see nothing inland. We observe but little wood near the shore.

[f. 113] Thursday 7 January the south coast of New Holland

Light breezes with fine weather. Passed to other bights in the land, rather deep. At 4, bore away to pass between the Doubtful Islands and Point Hood,[2] of Vancouver. At 4 *hours* 53′ being in mid-channel had 20 *fatho*ms. Hauled up into a deep and large bay[3] with the intention of anchoring. Sent the master to sound an inner passage between the isles and Point Hood by which it might escape if the wind should come to the eastward; but there proving to be only 2 *fatho*ms in it. Tacked and stretched out of the bay. At 8, tacked to the southward and weathered the Doubtful Islands. At 12, light airs with fine weather. At daybreak, the outer island N65°W 7 or 8 *miles*. As the wind came round, hauled up to look at the north side of the great bight or bay. Light airs and fine weather. Cleaned below and aired well with stoves. Sour krout and vinegar issued to the people, and as usual every day sweet wort. At noon, the Doubtful (now doubtless) Isles S66°W 4 leagues. A distant high hummock at the NEastern part of the great bight, bore N34°10′E, being the furthest extreme in sight. Light breezes and fine weather.

Meridian altitude ☉ *Lowe*r Limb & sup*plement* of *U*pper Limb 77°56′11″   101°31′49″
Latitudes   34°16′21″   34°16′59″
Mean latitude S   34°16′20″

By log		Latitude South		Longitude East						
Course	Distance	DR	Obs	DR	TK	Var allowed	Set or current	Ther	Barom	Error of TK
N69°E	27	34°25′	34°17′	119°30′	119°55′	9W	8N	66°	30.09	–
							4E	64°	29.99	
								68°	29.98	

[1] Flinders gave the peak this name because it had a number of small peaks on top of the ridge. Flinders, *A Voyage to Terra Australis*, I, p. 74. It is now called Mount Manypeaks.
[2] 34°22′S, 119°34′E. Vancouver named Point Hood after Admiral Lord Hood (1724–1816). Lamb, ed., *The Voyage of George Vancouver*, I, p. 343.
[3] Doubtful-Island Bay. This provides shelter from winds between S and SW. Flinders, *A Voyage to Terra Australis, Atlas*, plate II, South Coast, sheet 1; *Sailing Directions (Enroute): North, West, and South Coasts of Australia*, p. 146.

Additional remarks

The land from Cape Knob to Point Hood consists of two deep bights with beaches,[1] and a moderately high projection between them.[2] From captain Vancouvers chart[3] I expected to find the isle lying off Point Hood to be very small, but the two[4] which form the east side of the passage are two miles in length, and that on the west side is nearly as long. Between the easternmost of the two deep bights on the west, and the great bight on the north side of Point Hood,[5] that piece of land is almost insulated. It, as well as the islands, is steep rocky land, but the isthmus behind it is low, and possibly there may be a water communication through it. The passage through <u>which we sailed is nearly a mile wide, is deep</u>, and clear, but the inner passage is smaller, which the master was sent to sound, and shoal. A small sandy, rocky, islet lies on the north side of the isles, and had some seals upon it.[6] We hauled up within this islet and found deep water: when we tacked out of the bay at 5 *hours* 35′ our distance from the north side of the Point Hood was about a cables length and we had then 7½ fathoms. The land in the west and north sides of the great bight is mostly low and sandy, but there are some barren, peaked, and apparently granite mountains, standing but little way back from the water side.

[f. 114] **Friday 8 January**

Light breezes and fine weather. At 1 *hour* 30′ bore away to examine what appeared to be an opening in the NW part of the great bight; but it proving to be nothing, at 2 *hours* 30′ hauled to the wind along the shore, at the distance of two leagues. At 7, rocks were seen from the masthead bearing SEbE¼E, and some breakers, SSW distant about 4 miles. At 7 *hours* 30′, tacked off shore. Moderate breezes and cloudy weather. Drizzling rain at times. Tacked ship. Light breezes and cloudy: a southerly swell. At 5 *hours* 25′, bore away along the shore at the distance of 3 leagues, and soon after saw the breakers set last night at south SSW. Saw other breakers bearing ENE 5 miles from the former. Passed without the whole, the French ships having passed within them.

Saw a smooth rocky island O,[7] between which and the main I intended to pass, but breakers were seen to extend so far from the isle to the NEward, that we hauled up between the isle and a patch of rocks and breakers, the passage being about 2½ miles wide. At noon, island O [Red Islet] S72° W 3 leagues. A cluster of small rocky islets S68½E. Low land seen from the mast head ENE. Fine weather.

---

[1] These were Bay Sparkling and Bremer Bay (34°39′S, 119°37′E).

[2] Point Henry (34°28′S, 119°23′E).

[3] Flinders presumably consulted either the 1798 edition of Vancouver, *A Voyage of Discovery to the North Pacific Ocean*, which includes an atlas, or the octavo version of 1801, which has engravings of this and other charts.

[4] i.e. the Doubtful Islands.

[5] Doubtful Island Bay.

[6] Flinders, *Voyage to Terra Australis*, I, p. 78, writes: 'The island is low, smooth, and sterile, and is frequented by seals; its latitude is 34°6′ and longitude 120°28′ , and it lies eight or nine miles from the main land.' This is now known as Seal Rock. *Sailing Directions (Enroute): North, West, and South Coasts of Australia*, p. 146.

[7] Red Islet (34°2′S, 119°46′E), situated 5 miles ENE of Middle Mount Barren. Ibid., p. 146.

Meri*dian* alt*itude* ☉ Lowe*r Lim*b T*roughton* No 483   78°2′59″N
Latitude   34°1′58″S
Supplement ☉ U*pper Lim*b   101°24′4″S
Latitude   4°1′39″S
Mean latitude   34°1′48″S

	By log		Latitude South		Longitude East						
Course	Distance	DR	Obs	DR	TK	Var allowed	Set or current	Ther	Barom	Error of TK
N80°E	42½	34°10′	34°2′	120°21′	120°48′	9W	8N	68°	29.90	–
							2E	67°	29.90	
								67°	29.95	

Additional remarks

In the north-westernmost part of the great bight or bay, the land formed as if there was a harbour there, and there being smokes rising from the inland part behind we bore away to examine it, but finding nothing more than a small indent in the coast with low land at the back, I stood no nearer to it than would allow us to lie along the coast afterward[.] Hummock N[1] is a barren mount at the east extremity of those hills which lie close along that part of the shore which we passed this afternoon; on the east side of the hummock a low sandy shore again commences and continues further eastward than our situation this day at noon.

In the morning we came in with N [Middle Mount Barren]; and two other hills, (East and West M*oun*t Barren)[2] which are fixed points in the survey, were also in sight. I found the two patches of breakers very well placed, as also the island O [Red Islet] and rocks near it, in the French chart by M*onsieur* Baupré.[3] Past this island the shore is so low and sandy that at the distance of two leagues I cannot find any distinguishable parts to use in the survey.

Upon isle O there were many seals. From it the breakers extend 3 or 4 miles to the north and NNE but I think there <u>may</u> be a passage between it and the main, although there appeared to be other breakers extending southward from the main and almost meeting the former. I judge island O to be about seven miles from the main land.

All these hills appear to be granite.

[f. 115] **Saturday 9 January**

Moderate breezes with fine weather. Sailing along a low sandy shore at the distance of 6 or 7 miles. Fresh breezes: double reefed the *Top* sails. Passed within a cluster of rocky

---

[1] Middle Mount Barren (34°4′S, 119°37′E). Ibid.

[2] Flinders, *A Voyage to Terra Australis*, I, p. 76, refers to three masses of high land on the northern and north-western sides of Doubtful Island Bay, which he called West, Middle and East Mount Barren. East Mount Barren was visible at 14 leagues. Ibid., *Atlas*, Chart II, South Coast, sheet 1.

[3] Charles François Beautemps-Beaupré (1766–1854) was a skilled hydrographer who sailed with D'Entrecasteaux. After D'Entrecasteaux's death, at Java on the return voyage to France, Lt Rossel took charge and instructed Beautemps-Beaupré to prepare three sets of charts of the expedition, with the route marked in blue ink. Flinders appreciated Beaupré's skill in charting a coast that was so little known. Chapuis, *À la mer comme au ciel*; Scott, *The Life of Matthew Flinders*, p. 148.

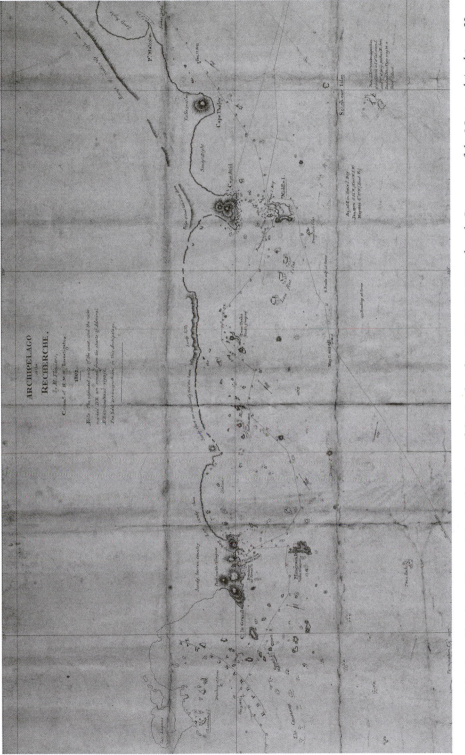

Figure 9. Matthew Flinders, Chart of the Archipelago of the Recherche, ADM 352/537, detail. Courtesy of the National Archives, Kew.

islets,[1] which were only visible from the tops. Passed two places having the appearance of opening in the land. Saw the land ahead, part of the islands forming D'Entrecasteaux Archipelago.[2] At 7, hauled to the wind; and at 8, tacked to the westward, the islands being 6 or 8 [miles] distant. Moderate breezes and fine weather. At 1, tacked to the eastward. Light breezes. At 5 *hours* 15′ bore away to run thro*ugh* the archipelago: the isles seen last night now bearing N72°E 5 or 6 miles.

Set studding sails, with the hope of getting through the cluster of dangers before night. At 8, we had passed the westernmost isles: many others in sight to the north and eastward and extensive breakers to the southward.[3] At 11, hauled more in for the land of the main. Saw the isle of Port de l'Esperance.[4] At noon, the isle bore N34°W 5 miles. Hove to, to take bearings of the isles, rocks and breakers, which surround us on all sides except about one point of the compass where we came in. Fine weather.

Mer*idian* alt*itude* ☉ Lowe*r Lim*b T No 483	77°55′56″N
Latitude	34°1′00″S
Supp*lemen*t ☉ Upper *Lim*b	101°30′14″S
Latitude	33°59′48″
Mean lat*itude*	34°0′24″S

		By log		Latitude South		Longitude East					
Course	Distance	DR	Obs	DR	TK	Var allowed	Set or current	Ther	Barom	Error of TK
S81°E	56	34°10′	32°0′	121°26′	121°57′	9W	13N	68°	29.95	–
							4E	65°	29.99	
								68°	30.03	

Additional remarks

Nothing of the interior country appeared above the low sandy shore along which we sailed this afternoon, until 4 o'clock; at that time the land abreast became higher. The two breaks in the land which had the appearance of being openings may probably be inlets into lagoons which the sea closes occasionally by throwing up sand before the mouths of them, and they remain shut until the water in the lagoon again rises high enough to force a passage.

The islands of the archipelago are moderately high and rocky. We were obliged to lie to for some little time, at noon, on account of the difficulty of taking distinct bearings of such a number of large and small islands, rocks above water, and separate patches of breakers as then surrounded us; and after all I cannot assert that even two-thirds of them were set; for without some arrangement into portions it was almost as

---

[1] The Rocky Islets (34°04′S, 120°54′E), two small islets about 17 miles south-west of Shoal Cape. *Sailing Directions (Enroute): North, West, and South Coasts of Australia*, pp. 146–7.

[2] The D'Entrecasteaux islands are better known as the Archipelago of the Recherche, comprising 105 islands off the coast of Western Australia. They cover a distance of 143 miles from east to west and stretch up to 31 miles offshore. Flinders was the first person to chart and explore these islands.

[3] Robert Brown noted in his diary for this day: 'Entrecasteauxs islands: their number more considerable than laid down in the French chart.' Vallance, Moore and Groves, eds, *Nature's Investigator*, p. 110.

[4] D'Entrecasteaux visited Esperance Bay (33°54′S, 121°58′E) in December 1792.

difficult for a stranger to describe or take accurate bearings of the whole before the ships position was materially changed as would be to describe the stars without the division into constellations.[1] Moreover, it was not my intention to lose much time in exploring this part of the south coast, both because I find M. Baupré's chart very accurate so far, and because I am desirous of getting to the unknown part[2] before the summer is too much advanced. This archipelago seems indeed to be very dangerous, and I wonder not at the dread expressed by the botanist Labillardiere on being here in a SW gale.[3]

[f. 116] Sunday 10 January At anchor in No 1 [Lucky] bay D'Entrecasteauxs Archipelago

Moderate breezes and cloudy. Having taken bearings, at 0 hours 30′ bore way through the middle of the islands, sounding every half hour. At 2 hours 12′ we were in the middle of a passage 1½ miles wide between some of the larger islands which lie off a cape of the main land. Luffed[4] to windward of some and bore away occasionally for other islands and breakers, in order to get to clear ground before night; but towards the evening finding the breakers increasing in number, and many islands in sight ahead as far as could be seen from aloft, I judge it most advisable to bear away for the main land at 5 hours 30′ where the appearance of some beaches behind the other islands made it probable we might find anchorage. Passed several rocks and breakers, and between two small (passage) islands ½ mile asunder; and at 7 steered into a small sandy bay, sheltered by islands from the south, and the easterly winds, and elsewhere by the main, being open only to the south-westward, in which direction also there are many islands, rocks, and breakers, at different distances in the offing.[5] Came to with the best bower, furled sails, hoisted out the cutter and sent the master to sound round the ship before dark, and in the north-west corner of the bay: he found it to be shoal there. Light breezes and fine.

AM. At daylight landed the scientific gentlemen. Sighted the anchor, but found it to be clear. Sent a cutter to fish off the rocky islands: she had little success, but saw several seals and some geese. Employed setting up the fore and fore top-mast rigging. Noon, moderate breezes and fine weather. Employed as in the morning, and the boats with the officers examining the country, surveying, getting observations for longitude &c. Hazy weather.

This day is continued to 36 hours, bringing the account to civil time.

Meridian supplement of ☉ Upper Limb No 483	101°47′34″S
Latitude	33°59′49″S

---

[1] Flinders, *A Voyage to Terra Australis*, I, p. 79, notes that charting was difficult on this part of the coast owing to a 'labyrinth of islands and rocks'.

[2] This refers to the south Australian coast beyond the Great Australian Bight.

[3] Jacques-Julien Houton de Labillardière (1755–1834) was the botanist on D'Entrecasteaux's voyage on the *Récherche* in 1792. Duyker, *Citizen Labillardière*. Flinders had a copy of de Labillardière, *Relation du Voyage à la Récherche de La Pérouse*, issued in an English translation by J. Stockdale in 1800.

[4] i.e. sailed closer into the wind.

[5] Refers to sailing between the small islands and breakers of the Archipelago of the Recherche towards the shore at Lucky Bay, named by Flinders (34°00′S, 122°14′E).

By log		Latitude South		Longitude East						
Course	Distance	DR	Obs	DR	TK	Var allowed	Set or current	Ther	Barom	Error of TK
East	17	34°1'	34°0'	121°46'	122°23'	9W	6E 1N	69° – 70°	30.07 – 30.03	–

Additional remarks

The naturalist and other scientific gentlemen having expressed a desire for the ship to remain a short time in this bay, that they might examine the productions of the surrounding country, I readily agreed to stop a day or two, considering that it would also enable me to obtain a better knowledge of this archipelago than could be gain[ed] by a hearty run through it, and also of examining into the accuracy of our time keepers.

Early in the morning the scientific gentlemen landed, and so soon as my rough chart was brought up I followed them.[1] Having taken the first observations for equal altitudes of the sun, in order to try the rates of the time keepers, I ascended the hill Δ[2] at the back of this little bay, and found the botanizing party there regaling upon palm nuts.[3] I did not much like these nuts, and fortunately eat but little of them, for those who had taken plentifully were taken very sick the rest of the day: Mr Brown thought, on turning to captain Cook's account, that they were the same kind that had poisoned his hogs on the east coast and affected many of the seamen.[4]

The hill would have afforded an extensive view of the eastern part of the archipelago, had not the haze prevented me from seeing beyond eight or nine miles. I counted, however, fifty-six Islands[5] and rocks above water, independent of numerous patches of breakers, where nothing above water appeared; and yet the major part of those through which we had already passed were either invisible from their distance or hid behind the projecting cape of the main land.

[f. 117] On turning from the view of the reefs, rocks, and scattered islands, so obnoxious to the seamans eye, to that of the interior country, the prospect improved but little; sand and stone with the slightest covering of vegetation everywhere presented themselves on the lower lands, and the more shining sides of the hills showed the granite of which they consist to be still more bare. The vegetation indeed consisted of an abundant variety of plants, and yielded a plentiful harvest to our botanists:[6] but to the herdsman and humble cultivator it promised nothing; not a blade of grass fit for cattle to

[1] Their shore work is described in Vallance, Moore and Groves, eds, *Nature's Investigator*, pp. 110–14.

[2] In 1841 this was named Mississippi Hill (about 33°59'S, 122°16'E) after the explorer Edward John Eyre and an Aboriginal companion were rescued nearby by a French whaler called the *Mississippi*. The hill is now part of Cape Le Grand National Park. Ibid., p. 110.

[3] The plant that produced these nuts was a species of *Zamia*, which was 'a class of plants nearly allied to the third kind of palm found by Captain Cook on the East Coast, the fruit of which produced the same deleterious effects on board the *Endeavour*'. Flinders, *A Voyage to Terra Australis*, I, pp. 80–81.

[4] For those affected with sickness from eating the nuts, see Vallance, Moore and Groves, eds, *Nature's Investigator*, p. 110, and Edwards, ed., *The Journal of Peter Good*, p. 54.

[5] Flinders, *A Voyage to Terra Australis*, I, p. 81, states forty-five.

[6] The specimens found at this locality are referred to in Vallance, Moore and Groves, eds, *Nature's Investigator*, p. 112, and Edwards, ed., *The Journal of Peter Good*, p. 54.

eat or a square yard of soil that could be expected to return the grain sown upon it, attracted the eye in its glance over the arid plains.

The stone near the sea shore as well as the mountains consist mostly of granite, in which streaks of pure quartz sometimes appear; and some pieces of granite were picked up which shewed marks of containing iron.

In returning by the back of the hill we found a large nest similar to those seen in King Georges Sound. It contained masses similar in external appearance to those containing the hair and bones of mice which the owls in England disgorge after having digested the flesh; but these consisted of the hair of seals, feathers of penguins, hair of land animals, and the bones of birds and small quadrupeds. The diameter of the nest was about 3¼ feet; and I judge its owner to have been an ospray [*sic*] or some bird of the eagle kind.[1]

Civil account
Monday 11 January
Moderate breezes and cloudy weather. Sent a boat to fish and kill seals upon the Passage Isles:[2] she brought on board three seals and a goose. Sent the master in the other cutter to examine a small bay about one mile to the westward. Employed on board making mats, repairing sails, and in other necessary jobs. PM. In the evening the master returned having found the bay of sufficient size to receive one ship and keep her in security. She would lie in the west corner with her bower anchor towards the entrance and the stream anchor on her quarter, and with hawsers on shore from her starboard bow and quarter; so secured she would lie in from 3 to 5 *fatho*ms, almost near enough to lay a stage to the shore. Moderate breezes and cloudy. A goose[3] and some ducks were brought on board by the shore parties.

Additional remarks
The little bay mentioned above could supply one ship with a sufficiency of wood for fuel, and at the back of the beach which surrounds the bay is a lake of fresh water about one mile in circumference, in which some ducks were shot. This lake is less than a hundred yards from the shore and a small stream runs from it into the little bay; but there is a stream of good water coming more into the west corner of the bay from the hills, which would better suit the purposes of a ship.[4]

At noon, I landed to observe the altitude of the sun for the latitude, as given hereafter. I observed that the granite of the islands which form the east side of the bay was in a state of decomposition. Its surface is scaling off in pieces from the smallest size to masses of the bigness of a ships hull. These last form large caves in some places, in one of which I find two swallows nests of the common kind. Mr Brown afterwards informed me that the head of the high peak had scaled off in the same way, and was lying loose like a cap upon it underneath: this prevented him from ascending to the very top of it.

---

[1] This is further described in Flinders, *A Voyage to Terra Australis*, I, p. 82.
[2] These islands (33°58′58″S, 122°25′58″E) were 2 miles to the westward of Lucky Bay. Ibid., I, p. 82.
[3] This resembled the barnacle goose, frequenting Furneaux's Islands in Bass Strait. Ibid., I, pp. 83–4.
[4] Flinders named this 'useful discovery' after John Thistle, the master of the ship, who found it. Ibid., I, p. 82.

[f. 118] Tuesday 12 January *Investigator* exploring the south coast of New Holland
Civil account

Light breezes and cloudy, but afterwards fine weather. Sent one boat to kill seals and the master in the other to examine the coast and islands to the eastward. Three large sharks were swimming about the ship this morning, one of which was caught and with some difficulty got on board. Carpenters employed sawing plank, and the seamen in making mats and other necessary businesses. In the evening the boats returned; the first bringing three seals; and the master with another, and the information that the archipelago was as dangerous to the eastward as the part through which we had already passed. He went about eight miles to the eastward to an island[1] whence he took bearing of many others farther on. Fresh easterly winds with fine weather, but rather hazy. Rock fish caught alongside as usual at such times as the sharks are not seen about the ship.

Additional remarks
The dimensions of the shark caught this morning were as follows

	Feet	inches
Extreme length	12	3
Greatest girth	8	–
Distance of the back fin from the nose	4	8
Outer part of the jaw bones, forming the diameter of his mouth	1	10
Length of each breast fin	2	4
Breadth of *ditto*	1	5
Height of the back fin	1	5
Breadth of the flukes of the tail	4	8

Number of gills on each side were five
He had either four, five, or six rows of teeth, but the number in each I do not know.

In the stomach was found a tolerably large seal bitten in two – one whole one which had been skinned and thrown overboard and many pieces, besides other various matters, amongst which was the end of a native spear, which he had swallowed at the same time with the seal which it had probably killed, for there was a horrifying hole in the back of the seal. The stench of the shark was great even before he was dead, but when the stomach was opened it was intolerable.[2]

Wednesday 13 January

Civil account

Fresh breezes and fine weather. The wind not allowing us to proceed on our voyage, I sent the cutter with the 1st lieut*enant* and master to the island U,[3] which is about seven miles in the offing, and the largest of this archipelago yet seen. They brought

---

[1] One of the islands east of Lucky Bay. Ibid., I, pp. 82–3.

[2] Flinders has further information on the 'monstrous sharks' seen to the east of Lucky Bay in ibid., I, p. 113.

[3] Mondrain Island (34°09′S, 122°14′E), situated 6¾ miles offshore, is the second largest island in the Archipelago of the Recherche. *Sailing Directions (Enroute): North, West, and South Coasts of Australia*, p. 150.

back some small kanguroos and seals. People on board employed occasionally. Fresh gales and hazy.

Additional remarks

The kanguroos brought from the island U [Mondrain Island] are very small and of a different species to any I have seen near Port Jackson: they most resemble the small mountain kangaroo called by the natives wering.[1] Seals were abundant upon the island as well as the kangaroo; they are of the fur kind, but the fur is red and very poor.[2] The island consists mostly of granite, and a micacious[3] piece was brought to me in which were sticking many garnets of tolerable size. The island was thickly covered with brush wood, which one party either from mischief or accident set on fire; and the wind being fresh, in the evening there was a general blaze near the island, and great volumes of smoke were rising from it next day.

[f. 119] No 1 [Lucky] bay, D'Entrecasteauxs Archipelago – General Remarks

Distances of ☉ west ☾ with sextant No. 483 on the NE side of the bay

Time 1802	Apparent time of observation	Apparent altitudes observed Sun center	Apparent altitudes observed Moon center	Apparent distance of the limbs	Longitude deduced	Observer	Thermometer	Barometer
January 10	1h53′0.8″	62°12′53″	28°21′14″	80°43′25″	122°28′15″	Commander	68°	30′10
	59′37.3″	60°54′8″	29°28′45″	46′11″	28′15″			
	2h4′48.8″	59°52′21″	30°21′27″	48′10.5″	32′12″			
	9′49.5″	58°52′1″	31°11′19″	50′11″	33′34.5″			
	14′20.3″	57°57′37″	55′41″	51′51″	38′15″			
	18′39.5″	5′33″	32°37′41″	53′30″	40′55.5″			
				Mean	122°33′32.2″ East			

By six sets of distances of the Sun east Moon taken afterwards on the 27th the longitude reduced by Time Keepers back to this bay, was   122°21′27.7″
                                                    No. 1 bay from 12 sets   122°27′30″ East
But the last six sets not being then procured, on leaving No. 1 bay, I took the longitude 122h 22′35.2″ as given by the three time keepers to be true.

With No. 483 near the same place

Time 1802	Sup of Sun's meridian Altitude to S	Latitude S deduced	Thermometer
January 11	101°47′34″	33°59′49″	71°

[1] Probably a western grey kangaroo.
[2] Several islands in the Archipelago of the Recherche were breeding grounds for seals.
[3] i.e. aluminum silicate minerals.

Azimuths on shore with three compasses both sides being used

Time 1802	Sun mag azimuth from both sides	Time altitude Sun's centre	Variation deduced
January 12	94°55'	35°29.2'	0°58'W
	95°37'	36°52'	2°31.2'
	94°23'	38°43'	2°29.2'
	N89°32'W	37°39'	2°45.5'
	90°12'	36°41'	2°53.6'
	89°36.2'	35°40'	3°55.8'

Mean variation 2°35.5'W

By Walkers new invented compass,[1] it was 4°55'W

12th AM Dip of the needle on shore

Marked end *South*		Marked end *North*	
Face *East*	Face *West*	Face *East*	Face *West*
67°50'	62°20'	65°45'	68°20'
68° 0'	62°55'	65°50'	67°50'
South end	65°16'	*North* end	66°56'

Mean dip of the south end 66° 6'

Azimuths on shore with theodolite

Time 1802	Sun mag azimuth from *North*	True altitude Sun cent	Variation deduced
January 13 P.M.	267°15'	28°27'	0°45'W

With the theodolite No. 1 on shore

[January] 12 AM	95°36'	33°16'	0°15'W

Mean variation from the theodolite 0°30'W

The compasses seem to be affected by some magnetic bodies[.]

Result of equal altitudes taken with *Troughton* sextant No. 483 on a stand on the NE side of No. 1 bay [Lucky Bay], from a quicksilver horizon, to find the present rates and errors of the time keepers.

				Comparisons of *Time Keeper* with No. 543				Daily rates of Time Keepers deduced						
Time 1802	Pairs of observations	E543 corrected at noon	E543 slower than mean time	E520	A82	A176	A1736	E543	E520	A82	A176	A1736	Ther mometer	Baro meter
January 10	Eight	15h35'49.62"	8h31'50.94" -	–30'35"	——	–39'36.9"	+27'4"						70°	30.03
13	Nine	15h36'39.45"	8h32'12.01"	–31'1.8"	——	–39'45.4"	+26'59"	–7.02"	–15.96"	——	–9.89"	–8.69"	71°	29.94

---

[1] Ralph Walker's meridional compass, made available in 1793.

The longitude of No. 1 bay [Lucky Bay], being taken at 122°22′35.2″, to find the errors of the time keepers from mean Greenwich time at noon there Jan*uary* 13th

	E543	E520	A82	A176	A1736
Timekeepers slower than mean time here, on January 13th at noon here	8h32′12.01″	9h3′13.81″	———	9h11′57.51″	8h5′13.01″
Longitude in time	8h9′30.35″	8h9′30.35″	8h 9′30.35″	8h9′30.35″	8h9′30.35″
Errors from mean Greenwich time	−22′41.66″	−53′43.46″	———	−1h2′27.16″	+4′17.34″
Part of the mean rates	+ 2.39″	+ 5.43″	———	+ 3.36″	− 2.95″
Time keepers slower than mean	0h22′44.05″	0h53′48.89″	———	1h2′30.52″	0h4′14.39″
Green*wich* time at noon there	– or slow	– or slow		– or slow	+ or Fast
January 13 1802					

The rates of the time-keepers deduced above being from an interval of three days only, would not have been put in competition with those found in King Georges Sound, but that they do not differ much from them, and shew moreover evident marks of being nearer to the present rates of their going than the former, and probably are exact.

The rise of the tide appeared to be so trifling here that under the circumstances of our stay, we did not pay any attention to it.

[f. 120] **Thursday 14 January AM log account *Investigator* from No 1 bay [Lucky Bay]**
Light variable breezes with cloudy weather. At 6 *hours* 40′ weighed and made sail out of the bay. Passed between the same two small islands as when we came in, and steered over towards the large isle U [Mondrain Island]. At 9, hauled to the eastward round U3,[1] which is a cluster of rocky islets and breakers. Moderate breezes, with weather so hazy that islands at a very few miles distance were scarcely visible. Passed by, and amongst, many small islands and patches of breakers, hauling up towards the main, that no opening of any magnitude might escape us. At noon, moderate and hazy. Hove to, to take bearings, the objects being too numerous to get them accurately without it. Some small high islands distant 1½ mile to the northw*ar*d and others in sight to the eastward.[2]

Meri*dian* alt*itude* ☉ Lowe*r Lim*b No 483   77°8′19″N
Latitude   34°2′4″S

		By log		Latitude South	Longitude East					
Course	Distance	DR	Obs	DR	TK	Var allowed	Set or current	Ther	Barom	Error of TK
S84½°E	15	34°1′	34°2′	122°41′	122°44′	9W	1S 3E	68° 71°	29.92 29.89	–

Additional remarks
The number of islands of different kinds as well as breakers in this archipelago make it absolutely impossible to describe them otherwise than by a chart, and even that I cannot

[1] The main island is now known as Finger Island (34°06′S, 122°20′E).
[2] Among these were two islands with peaks which, from their similarity, Flinders named the Twins. They are now called North Twin Peak Island (33°59′S, 122°50′E) and South Twin Peak Island (34°0′S, 122°48′E). Flinders, *A Voyage to Terra Australis*, I, p. 86.

offer as at all accurate, both from the haziness of the weather and the number of objects to be noticed. I did not make the surveying of the archipelago a main object; but I wished to run through it, and the chart contains what I was able to collect whilst so doing. The interior part of the archipelago is very defective in M. Baupré's chart, as it must necessarily be from their passing so far round to the southward.[1]

Friday 15 January

At 15′ past noon, made sail to the eastward, along the south side of several islands and breakers.[2] At 1 *hour* 30′, steered towards the main land to look for shelter between it and a cluster of islands before night. At 2 *hours* 30′ passed through the cluster, and hauled to the eastward along the shore, at the distance of from 3 to 5 miles. At 3¼, the water shoaling suddenly, we passed over where we could distinctly see the bottom, and expected the ship to strike. Hauled up to the wind and deepened the water; but the passage which I meant to take, between two low islets, appearing to be shoal, brought to, and sent the master in the cutter to sound. On his making the signal, filled and stretched after him: reached the boat at 5 *hours*.

At 5 *hours* 40′ bore away to look behind D, a large high island,[3] between which and the main land there appeared to be many small islands and passages. Finding there was shelter under the lee of the island, shortened sail, at 6½ *hours*, to run in easily, and at 7 *hours* came to with the best bower in 7 fathoms; sandy bottom; the large island sheltering us from NE round by the south to WbN. Sent the master to sound round the ship, and in the passage out to the NEward: he reported but 3 *fatho*ms in this passage; still it was possible to escape if it should blow hard from the westward.[4]

		Latitude South		Longitude East						
Course	Distance	DR	Obs	DR	TK	Var allowed	Set or current	Ther	Barom	Error of TK
S75°E	23½	34°8′	34°5′	123°8′	123°19′	9W	3N	70°	29.88	–
							8E	65°	29.85	
								70°	29.90	

[1] With the aid of Beautemps-Beaupré's chart of the Archipelago of the Recherche, Flinders was able to sail closer to the coast in the *Investigator* than D'Entrecasteaux's ships. One of Flinders's survey sheets of this archipelago marks parts copied from Beautemps-Beaupré's chart in red; another one uses double lines to represent the parts borrowed from the French hydrographer. Pearson, '"Nothing left undone": The hydrographic surveys of Beautemps-Beaupré', p. 22; TNA, ADM 352/538 and ADM 352/535. The NLA has manuscript copies of Beautemps-Beaupré's chart of the Archipelago of the Recherche (http://nla.gov.au/nla.map-ra82-s16) and of Flinders's chart of the same archipelago (http://nla.gov.au/nla.map-t571). Beautemps-Beaupré's charts of Australia were published in his *Atlas du voyage de Bruny Dentrecasteaux* (1807).

[2] D'Entrecasteaux's Archipelago.

[3] Middle Island, called Ile du Milieu by D'Entrecasteaux (34°06′S, 123°11′E). It is situated 5 miles SSE of Cape Arid. Flinders, *A Voyage to Terra Australis*, I, pp. 86–7; *Sailing Directions (Enroute): North, West, and South Coasts of Australia*, p 151.

[4] Flinders decided to stop at Middle Island for a couple of days to accommodate his botanists and to improve his chart of the archipelago. Flinders, *A Voyage to Terra Australis*, I, p. 87.

[f. 121] Log account, continued to 36 hours or civil account in D'Entrecasteauxs Archip*elago*

AM Fresh breezes with flying showers of rain. Sent a cutter with the seine to fish, but she had no success. Another boat which landed upon the lowish island[1] which shelters us from the northward had better success from finding it to be frequented by geese, nine of which were brought on board. On making another examination into the NE passage, the master found that after passing over the 3 *fatho*m bar, the water deepened from 5 to 7 *fatho*ms: a rock, dry at low water, lies in the middle of the passage, but there is 7 *fatho*ms about it. Noon, flying showers at times, but in the afternoon it cleared up and became steadier weather. Boats employed surveying and sounding, and attending the scientific gentlemen.

Additional remarks

At the back of the longest beach on the north side of D [Middle Island] Mr Thistle the master found a small lake so saturated with salt that quantities of it were chrystalized upon its banks, and the whole lake assumed a fine flesh colour.[2]

For the sake of improving my chart of this archipelago, and to give the botanists an opportunity of examining the islands, I determined to stop here for a day or two.[3] In the morning I landed upon the northern island and found that it consisted of a granite basis, upon which in many places, and on the northern part of the island in particular, was a thick crust of calcarious stone. Vegetation has not made sufficient progress upon this island to produce trees, but a tufty coarse grass with some low shrubs mostly covers the island. Penguins harbour amongst the shrubs, and I found geese amongst the tufts of grass and about the shores of the island; we killed nine of these, and a boat which afterwards landed got 16 more.

Having taken the bearings of various rocks, breakers and islands, as well those we had passed as those before us, I went to the north extremity of the island and took the annexed observation for the latitude; but as there were rocks too near to have a good horizon, it cannot be depended on nearer than a mile or two. From hence I crossed over to the large island D [Middle Island], and ascended its high smooth granite hill. The furthest visible mainland from thence bore 62°15′, and is the projection marked E[4] in the chart; to the southward, only one distant island was visible, but almost the whole space between this D and the opposite part of the main, C,[5] is occupied by small islands, low rocks, and breakers. On attentively viewing our track into this bay, I saw two small spots of breakers which had not been seen in the ship, and one of them lying in near, that I cannot be certain on which side of it we passed.

The mountain D[6] is a solid mass of granite; smooth, generally bare of vegetation, and of rather dangerous ascent; but almost every other part of the island is thickly covered

---

[1] Goose Island (34°06′S, 123°11′E), situated ½ mile off the north coast of Middle Island. Ibid.

[2] For a description of this lake and the salt water, see ibid., I, p. 88. This is Lake Hillier: see the photograph of it at http://www.panoramio.com/photo/3738103.

[3] Flinders noted that the tides were insignificant in the Archipelago of the Recherche. TNA, ADM 352/537.

[4] This cape was not seen by D'Entrecasteaux. Flinders named it Cape Pasley (33°55′S, 123°33′E) after the late Admiral Sir Thomas Pasley, under whom he had entered the naval service. Flinders, *A Voyage to Terra Australis*, I, p. 87.

[5] Cape Arid (34°01′S, 123°10′E).

[6] The north-western hill of Middle Island. It is now known as Flinders Peak. Flinders, *A Voyage to Terra Australis*, I, p. 87; *Sailing Directions (Enroute): North, West, and South Coasts of Australia*, p. 151.

with brush wood, and there are some few trees not far from the water side, growing under the mount.

The flesh-coloured lagoon added an uncommon, but beautiful, appearance to the view in that direction from the top of D [now Flinders Peak]; indeed the prospect was altogether fine and extensive, and afforded much assistance to making my survey more correct.

Meridian altitude ☉ Lower Limb 483	76°54′24″N
Latitude	34°5′26″S

[f. 122] **Saturday 16 January Civil account *Investigator* in No 2 [Goose Island] bay**[1]
Moderate breezes with fine weather. Sent a small party of men on shore to cut wood; and the master again to sound and examine the passage out to the eastward, having an intention to go out that way. Roused up the best bower cable, cleaned well below, sprinkled with vinegar and aired the ship with stoves. A boat employed by the Commander in surveying &c. Noon, ditto weather. The master returned from sounding out to the eastward where he found a safe passage for the ship, and he brought 27 geese with him which had been killed on one of the small clusters of islands. Received a boat load of wood. Cut up pork No. 1288 short of weight 12 lbs. Fine weather. Prepared to weigh AM.

Additional remarks
The geese obtained here are the same kind as those which I have before met with upon the islands in Bass' Strait.[2] We procured 65 of them, the greatest part of which were given by an equal distribution to the ships company, which made roasted geese and giblet pies very abundant between decks for three days. These birds abound more or less upon all these islands, and are very tame, the first of them being knocked down with sticks. There are a good number of small kanguroos amongst the thick brush upon D [Middle Island], if we may judge from their marks, for we did not kill any of them.

Our botanical gentlemen picked up very little upon either D or the goose island. On walking around the former it was found that the surface about the southern part was covered with a crust of calcarious stone the same as upon Goose Island, though there was none on the north side of either. Upon one of the points, a piece of plank was found, thought to have been part of a ships deck.

From the flesh-coloured lake, a ship might have procured a load of salt; which with the geese, and the fire wood which may be got, render No. 2 (Goose-Island Bay) a good place for a vessel to touch at; and it is most likely that there is fresh water upon the opposite part of the main.

Astronomical observations 16 civil account
Azimuth AM. on board No. 1

☉ magnetic azimuth N80°34′E Lower Limb	55°27′ = 3°26′W
☉ magnetic azimuth N74°18′ Lower Limb	56°38′ = 1°30′E
Mean variation	0.54W
Ships head WSW	

---

[1] Off the northern shore of Middle Island. It is sheltered from the swell and from all except north winds. *Sailing Directions (Enroute): North, West, and South Coasts of Australia*, p. 152.

[2] A reference to barnacle geese (see above, p. 267, n. 3).

Upon the north side of island D [Middle Island] middle beach

At app*ar*ent time	21°33′15.07″
Time E543	13°6′51.07″
Sun center 932	55°14′2″
Longitude	123°19′17.5″
E520	19′0.3″
A176	18′32.2″
Mean	123°18′56.7″E
Mer*idian* alt*itude* ☉ Lower Lim*b*	76°44′01″N
Latitude	34°4′45.5″

This observation is to be preferred to that upon Goose Island yesterday[.]

The glass of the watch *Arnold* No. 1736 having been broken, some sand stopped the hands, which is the reason that no longitude is given by it above; or cannot be used again as a time-keeper until a new error and rate are obtained. He did not perceive any tide running past the ship, although if there had been any set, it is reasonable to suppose we should have felt something of it in this passage.[1]

Nothing was found upon any of these islands that could induce us to think they had ever been previously visited, either by Europeans, or the natives from the opposite part of the main: it may be inferred from this that the natives have no canoes or even rafts in use amongst them.

[f. 123] Sunday 17 January AM Log account and along the south coast

Light breezes and cloudy. At daylight washed decks, sent up top gallant yards, and at 6 *hours* 30′ weighed. Ran over the bar under the topsails having only 17 feet, but it immediately deepened, and abreast of the middle rock we had 7 fathoms. At 7 *hours* 20′ passed from amongst the islands into a clearer sea, hoisted up the cutter, and made sail. Mod*erate* & fine w*eather*.

Passed 1¼′ on the north side of some breakers at 9 o'clock, and saw some low distant islands to the southward. Steered to pass between a cluster of small isles, g3,[2] and the projection E of the main land; which we did at 11, the passage being 3 miles wide, and clear. At noon, the furthest part of the main, a low point, N44°E. The nearest sandy shore distant 5 miles to the NW, with some small low islands in the same direction, distant two or three miles. Fine weather.

Supp*lement* of Mer*idian* alt*itude* ☉ Upper Limb 483	102°44′1″S
Latitude	33°54′8″S

		Latitude South		Longitude East						
By log										
Course	Distance	DR	Obs	DR	TK	Var allowed	Set or current	Ther	Barom	Error of TK
S72°E	21½	33°58′	33°54′	123°45′	123°46′	6W	4N	65°	29.99	–
							1E	67°	29.99	

---

[1] The tide was difficult to detect because the channel was narrow. Flinders, *A Voyage to Terra Australis*, I, p. 89.

[2] The south-east Isles of the Archipelago of the Recherche, including Pasley Island. Ibid., I, p. 90, and *Atlas*, plate II, South Coast, sheet 1.

Monday 18 January exploring Nuyts Land New Holland

Moderate breezes and fine w*eathe*r with haze. Set the fore top mast stud*ding* sail, but at 2 took it in again, seeing a sunken rock near us: still on our course along the shore: soundings as per column. Left a straggling cluster of islands[1] from 5′ to 10′ on the right. At 4, sailed close to a patch of high breakers, and soon after the water shoaled to 6 *fatho*ms, but trusting to a good look-out from the mast head, we hauled to the northward as the shore trended, and by that means got the water so much smoother that at 7¼ *hours*, we anchored upon a bottom of quartzoze sand, about 4 miles from the open coast: the north end of some bare sand hills bearing N10°W. At midnight, mod*erat*e and cloudy. Kept everything prepared to get under weigh at a moments warning; but nothing disturbed us till daylight, when we got up anchor and made all sail, continuing our course along the shore.

Took in stud*ding* sails on its falling calm. At 11, a sea breeze set in: trimmed to the wind. At noon, moderate breezes and fine weather. The northernmost of a number of sand hills N34°E. Nearest shore distant 4 miles. Low and sandy Land seen from the masthead as far out as NEbE.[2]

Supp*lemen*t to Mer*idian* alt*itude* ☉ Upper Lim*b* sextant 483   102°11′6″S

Latitude   33°9′21″S

		By log		Latitude South		Longitude East				
Course	Distance	DR	Obs	DR	TK	Var allowed	Set or current	Ther	Barom	Error of TK
N33°E	44	33°17′	33°9′	124°13′	124°21′	6W	8N	68°	29.99	–
							7E	68°	29.95	
								70½°	29.91	

Additional remarks

The shore along which we sailed this afternoon, and indeed since passing E [Cape Pasley], is very low and generally sandy, being in some parts totally uncovered by vegetation. A few miles behind this shore is a level and moderately high country, and some more island hills of considerable height peeping above it. The principal sea swell being from the SW the northerly trending of the land in the evening conducted us into smoother water, and the night being fine I preferred anchoring to standing off and on, from its greater advantage to my survey. Many dog fish[3] were caught by the people on watch during the night.

The coast passed this morning is still more sandy than that of yesterday, being commonly yellow hills without the least vegetation upon them. The back range continues.

---

[1] The Eastern Group (33°47′S, 124°05′E), which D'Entrecasteaux thought terminated the Archipelago of the Recherche. They consist of eight rocky islets, most of them low and barren. D'Entrecasteaux's supposition was correct. Dow Island is the largest in this group. In December 1792 D'Entrecasteaux was in Esperance Bay with low reserves of fresh water and with no significant source of fresh water found. He therefore abandoned his survey of south-west Australia and sailed directly to Van Diemen's Land in search of replenishment. Flinders, *A Voyage to Terra Australis*, I, p. 90; *Sailing Directions (Enroute): North, West, and South Coasts of Australia*, p. 153; Duyker, *Citizen Labillardière*, pp. xxix, 129–32.

[2] Flinders noted that he could not claim that all the great number of islands, rocks and reefs were all that existed; nor that he had placed every feature correctly: 'The Chart which I have constructed of this extensive mass of dangers is much more full, and in many parts should be more accurate than that of D'Entrecasteaux.' Flinders, *A Voyage to Terra Australis*, I, p. 91.

[3] A type of shark.

[f. 124] **Tuesday 19 January** *Investigator* **exploring the coast of Nuyts Land**

Moderate breezes and hazy weather. Passed through amongst some blubbers, such as are found in half saltwater, and much red scum was also sailed through.[1] Being only 1½′ from the shore, tacked off. At 5½ *hours*, tacked and stood towards the land until dusk, when we stood off for the night, a steep cliffy projection P[2] N64°E and the nearest shore 3½′ dist*ant*.[3] Double reefed the topsails: the wind moderate and weather cloudy. Light airs. Tacked ship towards the land. Saw the cliffy projection P [Point Culver] to leeward of us at daylight, and from it a cliffy shore continues without intermission to the NEward and P was soon indistinguishable, being lost amongst other similar projections.

We had kept away for the land since 5 *hours* 20′, having all the light sails set to a light breeze with fine weather. Washed and aired the ship well below. Issued sweet wort to the ships company; and sour krout with vinegar continue to be issued three times in the week, as usual.

At noon, moderate breezes and fine w*eathe*r. The furthest entrance of the land ahead, part of the same cliffy shore, N46°E from the deck. The furthest cliffs visible astern, which are near P [Point Culver], S85°W. Our distance off the shore being 5 or 6 miles.

Mer*idian* alt*itude* ☉ Lowe*r* Lim*b* 483	77°21′6″N
Latitude	32°52′31″S
Supp*lement* Upper Lim*b*	102°6′39″S
Latitude	32°52′52″S
Mean	32°52′41″S

		By log		Latitude South		Longitude East					
Course	Distance	DR	Obs	DR	TK	Var allowed	Set or current	Ther	Barom	Error of TK
N72°E	41	32°57′	32°53′	124°59′	125°9′	6W	4N	70°	29.85	–
							2E	69°	29.81	
								70°	29.85	

Additional remarks

The red scum mentioned above covered the water; and when taken up in a bucket had much the appearance of hay seeds. Being subjected to the action of spirit, these grains separated into fine tubes which appeared to be jointed like a reed.

The range at the back of the low sandy shore approaches close to the water near the furthest part of our track PM: and soon after no sand was to be seen, the ridge there forming steep cliffs, the first projecting part of which is marked P [Point Culver]: other cliffs opened beyond P at N69°E which is considerably different to the line of the shore in M. Baupré's chart, the nearest cliffs being further north than anything there laid down in this part.

Our track this morning lies wholly along the cliffy shore, which appears to be calcarious, the thin horizontal laminae which compose the two strata being very

[1] Flinders, *A Voyage to Terra Australis*, I, p. 93, refers to 'a number of pale red medusas' in the water.

[2] Point Culver (32°54′S, 124°42′E). Ibid., I, p. 93.

[3] As the ship sailed into the Great Australian Bight, a considerable change in coastal topography and geology occurred, with limestone coastal cliffs being common in the Eucla Basin. Vallance, Moore and Groves, eds, *Nature's Investigator*, p. 118.

distinguishable. The upper of these two is brown, and the lower almost white: above the cliffs, nothing appears from the inland part.[1] In some places the stone of the cliffs seems to have mouldered and fallen down, and by this only is the uniform perpendicularity of the shore at all broken. The brown sand brought up by the lead I judge to be calcarious.

[f. 125] **Wednesday 20 January south coast of New Holland**

Moderate breezes and cloudy weather. Carrying all sail, steering along the same cliffy shore as before. Fresh breezes. Distance off shore 4 miles. Took in small sails. Double reefed the topsails and hauled to the wind. Extremes of the land bearing N47°E to Q[2] at N85°W and our distance off the nearest shore about 6 miles. At 9 *hours* 15′, tacked ship. Fresh breezes and squally. Moderate and cloudy. Set top-gallant sails and staysails. Tacked ship to the eastward. At 5, the extremes of the land N60°E to S80°W and our distance from the shore 4 miles. Let out 2nd reefs, and at 6 tacked ship from the land; but owing to a considerable swell which rolls in upon the shore from the southward, the ship makes very little way. Light breezes and fine weather. Cleaned below. The carpenters employed putting the boats into good order.

Ditto weather. A part of the cliffs projecting somewhat beyond the line of the shore, bears N32°W six or eight miles: this is marked Q [Point Dover] in the chart, and at this time is the nearest land.

Meridian altitude ☉ Lower Limb Troughton 483   77°21′31″N
Latitude   32°39′35″S

	By log	Latitude South		Longitude East						
Course	Distance	DR	Obs	DR	TK	Var allowed	Set or current	Ther	Barom	Error of TK
N76°E	31	32°45′	32°40′	125°35′	125°45′	5W	5N	70°	29.90	–
							–	67°	29.90	
								68°	30.04	

Additional remarks

The little windings in the cliffy shore make separately like so many steep heads as they first come in sight, but they project so little from the general line of the coast that long before the ship comes up with them they are lost in the uniform range, and except Q [Point Dover], which remained distinguishable until the ship came abreast of it, I have had no fixed point which could be set a second time, whence my survey suffers much inconvenience: the course and distance seen, corrected by the observations and bearings of the extremes, together with our guessed distance from the shore abreast, being all that I have to lay down the land from.[3] Q [Point Dover] is whiter, as well as more projecting, than its neighbouring cliffs, whence I judge the old front of it has lately fallen off into the water.

---

[1] The high cliffs effectively blocked sight of the wastes of the Nullabor Plain, which lay inland from this part of the South Australian coast. Vallance, Moore and Groves, eds, *Nature's Investigator*, p. 118.

[2] Point Dover (32°21′S, 125°31′E), about 47 miles ENE of Point Culver. *Sailing Directions (Enroute): North, West, and South Coasts of Australia*, p. 153.

[3] Flinders did not have a fixed baseline from which he could measure angles to determine his location.

[f. 126] Thursday 21 January *Investigator* **exploring the south coast of New Holland Nuyts Land**

Moderate breezes and fine weather. Steering along the shore as well as the wind would allow us to lie up. At 4, the extreme astern, probably Q [Point Dover], bore S56°W, our distance being one mile off the shore: tacked ship off, until six, when we stood in again. At 7 h*ours* 35′ tacked off the same cliffy shore for the night. Fresh breezes and fine. Took in top gallant sails, staysails and spanker. Broke a deep-sea line and lost the lead. At 11, wore ship, having missed stays, arising from the south-easterly swell. Stood in shore till 2, expecting the wind to come more off the land, and then tacked off, a long stretch, until we found the wind was backing round again.[1] At daylight, hazy weather: no land in sight. Set top-gallant sails &c. and at 8 h*ours* 30′ tacked towards the land. Cleaned below and aired the ship with stoves. Let out 2nd reefs. Mustered the ships company and saw them clean, as usual on this day and on Sunday, when no particular duty intervenes. At noon, moderate breezes and fine weather. The land distinguishable through the haze, bearing NNW but whether the same cliffy shore as before cannot be known.

Supp*lemen*t to mer*idian* alt*itude* ⊙ Upper Lim*b*   102°23′4″S
Latitude   32°43′49″S

By log		Latitude South		Longitude East						
Course	Distance	DR	Obs	DR	TK	Var allowed	Set or current	Ther	Barom	Error of TK
N82°E	19	32°38′	32°44′	125°57′	125°59′	5W	6S 8W	69° 67° 70°	30.02 29.91 30.00	–

Friday 22 January

Moderate breezes with hazy weather. Fresh breezes and hazy. Continued steering in towards the shore. Double reefed the top sails. At sunset, the land distinguishable through the haze from West to NE: dist*ance* 6 or 8 miles at NWbN. Tacked off shore, and took in top-gall*ant* sails, jib, and spanker, and 3rd reef in the fore topsail. At 11, tacked towards the land, having a fresh breeze with fine weather. At 2, saw the land at NbE and tacked off, setting the jib and spanker. Moderate and cloudy. Employed repairing some of the rigging. Carpenters employed putting the boats into order, and sailmakers making a cutters fore sail. At 9, wore ship towards the land. Sweet wort and sour krout issued. At noon, light breezes and hazy. The land distinguishable from N85°W to N28°E appearing to be more irregular and sandy than the cliffs of yesterday PM. There are now many smokes upon the shore, and one of them so far out as NEbN.

Mer*idian* alt*itude* ⊙ Lowe*r* Lim*b* 483   76°55′49″N
Latitude   32°38′44″S

[1] Rough Journal, I, f. 277, adds: 'From this days experience as well as from former observation, I find that the wind draws round from the southward towards noon, becoming a sort of sea breeze, and towards midnight it comes more off the land. On this account it is, that I stretched in shore till 2 A.M. when the wind drawing more off shore enabled us to lie up better on the larboard tack; and on the winds heading at 8, tacked towards the land, for which, according to my expectation, the wind allowed us to lie up better each hour.'

By log		Latitude South		Longitude East					
Course	Distance	DR	Obs	DR	TK	Var allowed	Set or current	Ther	Barom
N70°E	26	32°35′	32°39′	126°28′	126°20′	5W	4S	71°	29.91
							10W	69°	29.87
								73°	29.82

[f. 127] Saturday 23 January *Investigator* exploring the south coast of New Holland Nuyts Land

Moderate breezes and cloudy weather. Got the anchor higher upon the bows and the boats upon the quarters, and fresh secured them, expecting that the wind would come from the SW ward and probably blow hard: the barometer is my prophet. At 5 *hours* 30′ tacked ship to the south*war*d the shore being only 2 miles distant. The extremes seen through haze WbN to E5°S. Double reefed the topsails. At 10 *hours* 30′ the wind took us aback, upon which we shortened sail and hove to on the larboard tack. Treble reefed the top-sails. At 11, wore round and lay to on the other tack, sultry w*eathe*r.

The 2nd lieutenant not having given me all the assistance in the astronomical and surveying departments that I expected, he was ordered to keep his own watch during the night. From the stimulus of pride, he chose to keep it in the day also, and to continue giving me the same proportion of assistance as he had done before.[1]

At 1, set the fore sail and filled; and at 2 *hours* 30′ wore ship: at 4 wore ship again having missed stays. Var*i*able winds and squally weather. At 5 bore away to make the land; let out the second reefs, set T*op* gall*ant* sails &c. At 8, saw the land, sandy and of a moderate height, through the haze; and at half past steered along the shore at the distance of 3 miles. Cleaned the ship below and aired with stoves. Sweet wort issued as usual every day. At noon, a freshening breeze with thick hazy weather. Handed top-gallant sails, double reefed the topsails and hauled two points more off shore: the nearest part now distant 4 or 5 miles. By bad observation

Suppl*eme*nt to the Mer*idi*an alt*itude* ☉ U*pper* L*im*b 483   102°24′27″S
Latitude   32°21′57″S

By log		Latitude South		Longitude East						
Course	Distance	DR	Obs	DR	TK	Var allowed	Set or current	Ther	Barom	Error of TK
N78°E	46	32°30′	32°22′	127°21′	127°12′	4W	8N	74°	29.65	–
							1W	73°	29.79	
								74°	29.84	

<u>Additional remarks</u>

The land from which we tacked at 5 *hours* 30′ PM is very different from the cliffs of the 21st PM being now low and sandy. There were some low hills a little to the westward which produced vegetation only in patches, giving them a variegated appearance. Many

---

[1] Refers to a disagreement between Flinders and his younger brother over the latter's duties. Estensen, *The Life of Matthew Flinders*, p. 184.

smokes were rising at the back of the shore; the time we have been beating off this part of the coast seeming to have attracted the notice of the natives and given them time to collect.[1] At the distance of 4 or 5 miles from the shore is the edge of a bank which goes off from 7 to 14 and 17 *fatho*ms rather suddenly; but our run this morning shows the soundings upon the bank to be tolerably regular.

The different parts of the coast in this neighbourhood so much resemble each other that it was impossible to know whether we came in with the same land in the morning that we tacked from overnight; it is, however, the same kind of shore, and cannot be far distant. A sandy beach runs along the front of the small hilly bank as far as we can see, but even the bank affords me no marks to assist in forming the survey: whether anything higher exists behind it, the haze will not permit us to see.

[f. 128] Sunday 24 January *Investigator* exploring the south coast Nuyts Land New Holland

Fresh breezes and cloudy weather, with haze. Set top-gallant sails &c. and a fore top-mast stud*ding* sail; and at 2 kept more in towards the shore. Strong breezes. Took in the small sails; but continued steering along the low sandy shore as in the morning, at the distance of 5 or 6 miles. The bank at the back of the beach is almost as level as the horizon; and might be taken for it at 3 or 4 leagues distance. At 7, treble reefed the topsails and hauled to the wind: the land being 7 or 8 miles distant, and the extremes bearing NE. and WbN. Reefed the main sail. Fresh breezes and fine weather. Wore ship to the westward. D*itto* weather. At daybreak, saw the land from WbN to NEbN and bore away for it. Let out 3rd reefs and made more sail. At 6, hauled up along the shore, which is the same kind as that from which we hauled off PM, but we cannot fix upon any certain spots. At 8 *hours* 25′ the shore being 2½ miles distant, tacked ship. Upon the bank at the back of the beach we now see some wood, and nothing from the interior part appears above this. At 11 *hours* 20′ set top-gall*ant* sails and staysails, and tacked ship towards the land. At noon, light breezes and fine. The nearest land NNW 4 or 5 miles. Extreme astern W 10°N distant perhaps 3 or 4 leagues. Ships company mustered, and, as well as the ship, seen to be clean, as usual.

Mer*idian* alt*itude* ☉ Lowe*r* Lim*b* 483   77°1′21″N
Latitude   32°5′52″S

By log		Latitude South		Longitude East					
Course	Distance	DR	Obs	DR	TK	Var allowed	Set or current	Ther	Barom
N82°E	53	32°14′	32°6′	128°23′	128°20′	5W	8N	70°	29.95
							6E	68°	30.07
								70°	30.16

Monday 25 January

Moderate breezes with fine weather. At 0 *hours* 45′ tacked ship from the land, it being then distant about 2 miles: it is a woody level bank with a sandy beach before it, and nothing appears above it. At 4, tacked ship along the shore. At 6 *hours* 30′ we were obliged to tack off again, the water becoming shoal. The head swell[2] makes the ship plunge and labour

---

[1] Deleted: 'a few were seen with our glasses'.

[2] Swells are waves that have left the area of wave generation and travel under their own energy.

considerably, and stops her way. At 10, tacked towards the land hoping to get the wind more from the northward. At 12, tacked and stretched off again. From the labouring occasioned by the head sea, the old leaks are beginning to open again and the ship now admits between one and two inches of water per hour. Found the main top-gallant mast to be sprung, which obliged us to get it down and another up. At 7 *hours* 30′ tacked to the northward, there being no land in sight or any shift of wind in our favour. Moderate breezes and fine weather. Sweet wort issued as usual every day. At noon, the land in sight to the northward from deck, distant eight or nine miles. Our observations give a mortifying confirmation to our fear of having gained nothing during this 24 hours. We ought to have been in with the land at 8 AM could we have known the course of the wind. By Mr Thistle

| Meri*dian* alt*itude* ☉ Lowe*r Lim*b No 488 | 76°40′59″N |
| Latitude | 32°11′53″ |

By log		Latitude South		Longitude East					
Course	Distance	DR	Obs	DR	TK	Var allowed	Set or current	Ther	Barom
SE	7	32°11′	32°12′	128°29′	128°18′	5W	1S	68°	30.15
							8W	66°	30.07
								68°	29.95

[f. 129] **Tuesday 26 January *Investigator* exploring the south coast Nuyts Land New Holland**

Moderate breezes and cloudy weather, with a short swell from the eastward. Having missed stays at 1 *hour* 45′,[1] wore ship off shore, being three miles distant. Set top gall*ant* sails and staysails, and at 5¾ *hours*, tacked towards the land. Light breezes and fine weather, with haze. At 10, tacked off shore. Light breezes and cloudy, with a swell from the eastward which impedes the ships progress. At daybreak, let out the 2nd reefs out of the topsails and set staysails. On the wind shifting at 8 *hours* 15′, hauled up for the land. At 10, it was 8 or 9 miles distant, and we bore away along it, but edging in withal. Made more sail: carried away a studding sail boom. Sweet wort issued as usual. Cleaned the ship below. At noon, fresh breezes and hazy weather. Double reefed the topsails and hauled a little further off the shore: its distance being 6 or 7 miles to the NNW.[2]

Meri*dian* alt*itude* ☉ Lowe*r* & Supp*lement* of U*pper Lim*b 483	76°46′29″	102°40′44″
Latitudes	31°51′42″	31°51′29″
Mean lat*itude*	31°51′35″	south

By log		Latitude South		Longitude East						
Course	Distance	DR	Obs	DR	TK	Var allowed	Set or current	Ther	Barom	Error of TK
N56°E	43	31°48′	31°52′	129°11′	128°58′	4W	4S	70°	29.84	–
							2W	69°	29.73	
								71°	29.76	

[1] Possibly because of the ship plunging during a head swell: see entry for 1 February 1802, below, p. 289.

[2] The entry for this and the previous day indicate that strong winds prevented Flinders from following his course along the coast.

Additional remarks

Upon that part of the shore whence we tacked at 1 *hour* 45′ PM there was a fire made close down upon the beach, which seemed to be intended for our observation. The natives had probably observed the ship standing off and on these two days past, for we had noticed smokes rising from behind the bank, where it is probable the country was on fire.

The land seen this morning is a few miles to the eastward of any extreme land seen distinctly PM and the direction of the wind when it shifted did not allow us to haul much to the westward for it, so that there is unavoidably a small part of the coast which we have only seen distantly through the haze and indeed about 2 leagues of which we have scarcely seen anything.[1] Abreast of our noons place, the level bank before mentioned is somewhat higher and retires a little from the water. In front of the bank the shore is low and sandy, but at a little distance ahead we see some hills of bare sand close to the water side. The top of the bank is not quite so woody as before, but is still tolerably well covered.

[f. 130] Wednesday 27 January *Investigator* exploring Nuyts Land on the south coast of New Holland

Strong breezes and cloudy weather. Running under double reefed topsails and foresails, steering as the shore trended at the distance of 4 or 5 miles. At 2½ *hours*, the bank at the back of the beach abreast comes close to the waterside, forming steep cliffs[.] At 6, the shore distant 5 miles. Treble reefed the topsails and close reefed the fore and mi*zzen* topsails, & reefed the courses. At 7 *hours* 30′ hauled to the wind, being then 5′ or 6′ offshore, and the furthest extremes seen through the haze bearing N70°W to N70°E. Strong breezes with fine weather. At 1, wore ship to the westward. At 3, made more sail and at 4 bore away for the land. At 5, the cliffy shore was distant 6 or 7 miles and we bore away along it. Let out 3rd reefs, set top gallant sails and a for[e] top mast studding sail. Moderate breezes and cloudy weather. Sweet wort issued today as usual, and sour kraut three times in the week. Cleaned below as usual. At noon, the nearest land NbW½W 6 or 7 miles. A projecting part of the cliffs, which seems to be the east extremity of them, bore N14°E. The furthest extreme ahead N30°E and astern N70°W. Fine w*eathe*r, but hazy.

Mer*idian* alt*itude* ☉ Lo*wer* & sup*plemen*t of U*pper* Lim*b* 483	76°41′51″	102°44′44″
Latitude	31°41′16″	102°40′25″
Mean latitude	31°40′50″	south

	By log		Latitude South		Longitude East						
Course	Distance	DR	Obs	DR	TK	Var allowed	Set or current	Ther	Barom	Error of TK
N88°E	100	31°49′	31°41′	131°8′	131°11′	4W	7N 16E	71° 67° 68°	29.85 29.84 29.94 in the cabin as usual	–

[1] Flinders added in a note: 'This supposition, made at the time, proved to be a mistake on laying down the log and observations. No part of the coast was missed.'

Additional remarks

The cliffs which commence abreast of our situation at 2 *hours* 30′ PM are from 400 to 600 feet high.[1] The upper third part is brown, and the lower two-thirds white; but whether they consist of lime or gritstone I cannot be certain: no other stratification appears at our distance from the shore except what is mentioned above. On coming to the sea side, the bank which was before well covered with wood becomes destitute of that covering and forms a surface almost as level as the sea horizon. At the conclusion of our afternoons track, the upper brown part of the cliffs had gradually increased until it occupied one half of the whole height; and in the morning I observed that it kept still increasing upon the lower white part. In the cliffs of this latter colour we observe several excavations, occasioned most probably from the falling down of pieces, which leads me to think that that part of the cliffs consists of sand or gritstone, whilst the upper brown part I judge to be calcarious. The land seen at noon beyond N14°E consists of sandy hills which trend to the NEward, towards the head of what may be called the great bight or gulph of New Holland.[2]

[f. 131] **Thursday 28 January** *Investigator* **exploring Nuyts Land on the south coast of New Holland**

Moderate breezes and hazy weather. At 1 hour 30′ the coast ceased to run northerly, and turned southward the head of the bight bearing north 3 or 4 leagues: Hauled along the shore as it trended. Moderate and cloudy: the shore dist*ant* 6′ or 7′ NE. At 6, breakers were seen lying out from the land at SE½S; at the same time a long swell was rolling in upon the shore from the south-west; on tacking, therefore, at 6, to the westward, I continued stretching off almost the whole night, with a light breeze and cloudy weather, and making but little way on account of the swell. At 3, wore ship, but it now became calm. At 4, a light variable breeze sprung up, with which we steered towards the land; and at daylight it was seen to the NE distant 3 or 4 leagues. Let out the 2nd reefs. Light breezes with cloudy weather. Set studding sails. Long swell from the south-westward. At noon, fine weather. The extremes of the land now bore from N12°W to S80°E the nearest shore being 7 or 8 miles distant. Breakers N45° to 25°E distant from 2 to 4 miles, and are the same seen bearing SE¼S at night[.]

Mer*idian* alt*itude* ⊙ Lowe*r Lim*b 483	76°5′31″N
Latitude	32°2′15″S

	By log	Latitude South		Longitude East						
Course	Distance	DR	Obs	DR	TK	Var allowed	Set or current	Ther	Barom	Error of TK
S57°E	35½	32°1′	32°2′	131°43′	132°4′	4W	1S 18E	70° 68° 69°	29.95 29.93 29.95	–

[1] Refers to the high cliffs in what is now the Nullarbor National Park (*c.*130°30′E). These are slightly to the west of the head of the Great Australian Bight.

[2] The *Investigator* had now reached the head of the Great Australian Bight.

Additional remarks

The head of the great bight[1] falls but little back from the general line of the coast, being formed by the bending of the coast from an ENE direction to SE. The most northern part lies in or near the latitude 31°27'S and longitude by our time keepers 131°24'E. The shore round the head is low and sandy, but the land rises very gradually inland, and continued to do so until it was obscured from our sight by the haze. The land becomes higher near the shore on the coast taking its direction to the south-east, but is still very sandy, the hills being quite bare and the other parts very lightly covered with vegetation. The land rises gradually from the water side into the country but not to any considerable height. The breakers near our situation at noon seem to stretch SSE about 2 miles in their front, and I think it probable that they may be so far connected with the shore as not to admit a ship passing between them. There are two large and remarkable patches of bare sand upon the rising shore at the back of these breakers. The examination of admiral D'Entrecasteaux terminates here at the place of our situation this afternoon, and these breakers were not seen by him.

Distances of ☉ east ☾ taken AM with No 483

Time No 543	Apparent altitude Observation ☉ lower limb	☾ upper limb	Apparent distance of limbs	Longitude
13h5'16.7"	60°25'1"	40°7'23"	77°54'00"	132° 4'10.5"
10'49"	61°29'54"	38°57'7"	51'29"	131°53'45"
15'5.2"	62°20'8"	38°5'50"	49'49"	53'49.5"
19'11.7"	63°8'11"	37°13'33"	48'3"	49'55.5"
23'30.8"	57'43"	36°21'33"	46'26"	53'19.5"
28'5.5"	64°49'33"	35°24'11"	44'41"	55'51"
			Mean longitude	131°55'8.5"

T Ks to the east of these observations	– 1'8"	
Difference of longitude by TKs from	No 1 [Lucky] bay	9°33'40"
(see page before January 14 last)	No 1 [Lucky] bay	122°21'27"

[f. 132] Friday 29 January *Investigator* exploring the coast of Nuyts Land on the south coast of New Holland

Moderate breezes and fine weather. Passed within two small clusters of rocky islets which have breakers round them: and there were other breakers and small islets near the shore within our track. Passed two projecting rocky heads and two bights with breakers in them.[2] At 5 *hours* 30', hauled round a third head, B,[3] into a wide bay[4] which promised

---

[1] Flinders gave the position of the head of the Great Australian Bight as 31°29'S and 131°10'E whereas D'Entrecasteaux's chart suggested it was at 31°36' and 131°27'. Flinders, *A Voyage to Terra Australis*, I, p. 98. Flinders' calculation was the more accurate of the two: the coordinates for the head of the Great Australian Bight are 31°30'S, 131°10'E.

[2] Flinders called these features Nuyts' reefs because they are in Nuyts' charts. Ibid., I, p. 99.

[3] Point Fowler (32°02'S, 132°29'E), a promontory that extends about 3 miles from the coast. Named after the 1st lieutenant, Robert Fowler. Ibid., I, p. 104.

[4] Fowler's Bay (31°30'S, 131°6'E).

shelter from southerly winds. On shoaling the water to 3 fathoms hove all aback and sent the master ahead in the boat to sound, but as he did not make the signal for deeper water, and we were already tolerably well sheltered, I dropped the small bower anchor in 3¼ fathoms the extreme of the cliffy head B [Point Fowler] bearing S34°¼E 2 miles. Distant land in sight at east, between which and B [Point Fowler] this bay seems to be exposed. Furled sails and sent down top gallant yards. AM Light breezes and cloudy. Washed the ship, squared the yards &c &c. Boats employed landing the botanists to examine the country, and by the commander in surveying.

Prepared to get under weigh after dinner.

Ships draught of water *Fore 14 feet 8 inches* Aft 14 feet 10 *inches*
On shore 1′ south of the anchorage

Meridian altitude ☉ Lower Limb 483	75°51′59″N
Latitude	32°0′3″S

	By log		Latitude South		Longitude East					
Course	Distance	DR	Obs	DR	TK	Var allowed	Set or current	Ther	Barom
East	24½	32°2′	31°59′	132°12′	132°39′	4W	3N	71°	29.95
							6E	69°	29.99
								71°	30.02

Additional remarks[1]

The part of the coast along which our track lies this afternoon is dangerous from the small rocky islets and breakers which lie off it. Our track however is sufficient to show that, with caution, it may be safely approached in the day time: The first projecting head is A, a steep rocky cape.[2]

On landing in the morning in this No. 3 bay,[3] I found the head which shelters it from the westerly and south winds was almost insulated, the neck which joins it to the main not being more than half a mile in breadth: the rock is all calcarious.

The shelter in this bay is something similar to that afforded by Torbay.[4] It is open to all winds from SE to east, but I do not apprehend that even these throw any great sea into it. From the bottom being shallow and covered with small weeds, and from plants growing close to the high-water mark it is, that I am inclined to form this opinion.

There is no appearance of fresh water, [n]or I believe can wood of a sufficient size for fuel to be procured, but the bay may be useful to ships going along the coast to the westward, since the security it affords against winds which would be foul for ships to proceed is complete.

Amongst other marks of natives we found some decayed spears, but no huts or anything that shewed them to have been here lately. There were tracks of dogs upon the

---

[1] The voyage had now reached the extremity of that part of the south coast explored previously. Flinders, *A Voyage to Terra Australis*, I, p. 100.

[2] Cape Nuyts (32°02′S, 132°21′E), which is 194 feet high.

[3] Fowler's Bay. Named by Flinders after his 1st lieutenant. From this point the coast had not been charted before. Thus the ship was entering unnavigated waters. Flinders, *A Voyage to Terra Australis*, I, p. 104; Scott, *The Life of Matthew Flinders*, p. 150.

[4] i.e. in South Devon.

beach, and some marks of the emu or cassuary.[1] A few small fish were caught alongside the ship with hook and line, and from the shore, two small ducks and as many sea-pies[2] and gulls were shot. The scantiness of plants was found to equal that of other productions.[3]

A large nest, similar to what is mentioned page 117 was found in a hole of a low cliff, but it had been long deserted.

[f. 133] Saturday 30 January *Investigator* exploring the coast of Nuyts Land on the south coast of New Holland

Moderate breezes and fine weather. At 1¼ *hours*, got under weigh, set all the plain sails, and tacked ship occasionally working out of the bay. Behind some cliffs which had been set at east from the anchorage, there appeared to be a bight in which I was desirous of getting the ship before dark. At 5 *hours* 30′, the cliffs N70°E 3 miles, but not being able to weather them in order to look into the bight, tacked ship, and there was not time to stretch in again before dark. At sunset the head B [Point Fowler] in a line with the western shore bore W3°S. Double reefed the topsails and handed top gall*ant* sails.

Fresh breezes with fine weather. Wore ship towards the land: a heavy swell from the southward. At 3, tacked ship. Light breezes and fine weather. At daylight, the lands A [Cape Nuyts] and B [Point Fowler] in sight, shewing our situation to be far to leeward. Wore ship, let out 2nd reefs, and set top gallant sails.

Expecting the wind would come more from the sea as the day advanced (the weather being fine) at 7 *hours* 30′ tacked and stood off before that should take place. At 10¾ *hours*, tacked ship towards the land, on her falling off. Noon, moderate breezes and fine weather. A [Cape Nuyts], the cliffy land about it, NbW about 5 leagues. Land in sight at NE for which we now look well up. Beyond this nothing has yet been seen.

Mer*idian* alt*itude* ☉ Lowe*r L*imb 483	75°18′16″N
Latitude	32°17′42″S

	By log		Latitude South		Longitude East					
Course	Distance	DR	Obs	DR	TK	Var allowed	Set or current	Ther	Barom
S16°E	16	32°15′	32°18′	132°44′	132°42′	3W	3S	70°	30.02
							2W	69°	30.01
								72°	29.96

Sunday 31 January

Moderate breezes with hazy weather. Kept a point free in order to get in with the land before dark.[4] At 4, the cliffs before mentioned were a due beam.[5] At 5, our distance from

[1] Robert Brown's diary entry for this day refers to 'a few old spears & very recent prints of dogs feet, uncommonly large'. The dogs were probably dingoes. Vallance, Moore and Groves, eds, *Nature's Investigator*, p. 121.

[2] The oyster catcher, a limicoline bird of the genus *Haemotopus*.

[3] Flinders had no reason to stay long in Fowler's Bay because the botanists found the fauna and flora scanty. Vallance, Moore and Groves, eds, *Nature's Investigator*, p. 122.

[4] Rough Journal, I, f. 299, adds: 'The land, with which we came in this afternoon, is that which runs from behind the cliffs which had been taken for an island. These cliffs I saw very distinctly, but no bight of any depth appeared to be eastward of it. The land is moderately high and generally covered with vegetation, but as usual the sand shews itself frequently, and towards the eastern extreme it is almost bare.'

[5] This means that the cliffs were at right angles to the keel of the ship.

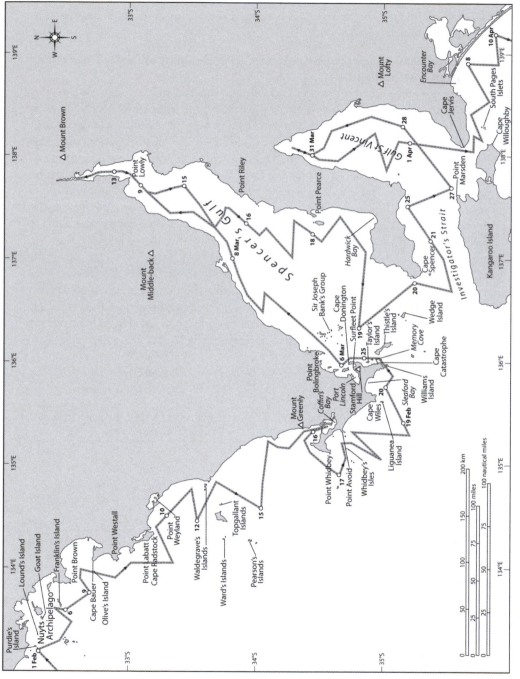

Map 2.   The voyage of HMS *Investigator* February to April 1802.

the shore was about two miles, and the furthest extreme bore S60°E; but from the mast head it is seen further south, with breakers. No bight of any consequence appears behind the cliffs. Tacked off at 5, and at 10 stood in shore again. Moderate breezes and cloudy weather. Tacked to seaward, and at 4 back again towards the land. At 7, the land was seen to the NEbE. Tacked to seaward, to be ready for the sea breeze. The shore distant 5 or 6 miles and its eastern low extreme EbS½S from the top. Three low islets with breakers about them were seen lying under the shore. Mustered and saw the ships company clean. At 11 *hours* 30′ the wind headed and we tacked towards the land, which at noon was in sight as far as ahead, but nothing that could be distinctly set.

Meri*dian* alt*itude* ☉ Lowe*r* Li*m*b 483   75°4′8″N
Latitude   32°15′27″S

By log		Latitude South		Longitude East						
Course	Distance	DR	Obs	DR	TK	Var allowed	Set or current	Ther	Barom	Error of TK
N86°E	22	32°16′	32°15′	133°9′	133°0′	2W	1N	72°	29.96	–
							7W	72°	29.98	
								72°	29.96	

[f. 134] Monday 1 February *Investigator* exploring the furthest part of Nuyts Land on the south coast of New Holland

Fresh breezes and fine weather with haze. Double reefed the topsails & took in the spanker and staysails. At 2, a small islet, c,[1] bore N36°E 1¾ mile. At 3, the main land was distant about 3 miles to the NE and the furthest extreme bore S42°E. Tacked off shore in 7 fathoms water. At 6 *hours* 30′, having missed stays from the ships plunging so much to the head swell, wore ship. Strong breezes and hazy. Tacked ship from the land. The labouring of the ship occasions her leaks to open more and more: she now makes 3 inches of water per hour. I am not however uneasy at this, because I suppose the leaks to be in the upper works, and that when the cause ceases, the leaking will cease also. At 1, wore ship towards the land; at daylight it bore ENE. The wind more moderate and the weather fine.

Our situation at 8 was nearly the same as at 3 PM, the islet c [Sinclair's Rocks] bearing N8°S 2 miles. A broad flat islet with heavy breakers round it[2] bore S34°E without the extreme of the main land, which is D;[3] and through the haze we see land further distant to the SEward. Tacked at 8, in 7 fathoms coral bottom and stretched off for the sea breeze. Cleaned the ship well below and aired with stores. Sweet wort, sour kraut, and vinegar issued as usual. At noon, fresh breezes and hazy weather. No land distinguishable. A heavy head swell running, which makes the ship plunge deeply, and leak much.[4]

[1] Sinclair Island (32°7′S, 133°0′E), named Sinclair's Rocks by Flinders in 1814. The name commemorates Kennet Sinclair, a midshipman on the *Investigator* who was also a cartographer. Vallance, Moore and Groves, eds, *Nature's Investigator*, p. 123.

[2] The breakers appear on modern maps as Flinders Rock (about 32°13′S, 133°12′E).

[3] In 1814 Flinders named this Point Bell (32°12′S, 133°08′E) after the surgeon Hugh Bell. Vallance, Moore and Groves, eds, *Nature's Investigator*, p. 123.

[4] Rough Journal, I, f. 301, adds: 'The swell from the southward, which the ship has bowed so much since leaving Bay no. 3 has been the cause of her leaks increasing considerably. She now appears to make about 3 inches per hour; but I attribute it entirely to the strain arising from her plunging to the head swell.'

Meridian altitude ☉ Lower Limb 483   74°42′39″N
Latitude   32°20′14″S

		By log		Latitude South	Longitude East					
Course	Distance	DR	Obs	DR	TK	Var allowed	Set or current	Ther	Barom	Error of TK
S55°E	15	32°23′	32°20′	133°24′	133°2′	2W	3N 13W	71° 70° 72°	29.93 29.98 29.97	–

Additional remarks

From the cliffs near No 3 bay [Fowler's Bay], off which we tacked in the evening of the 30th to our situation this morning, the shore takes a SEerly direction and runs nearly straight. Immediately behind the cliffs, there is a bight as mentioned before,[1] but no other remarkable indent. The shore is in general sandy, but there are some few rocky cliffs which do not project much from the line of the coast. From the shore the land rises by a gentle acclivity to a very moderate height: further than this the horizons of the weather and our distance did not permit us to discriminate.

Between the island, c [Sinclair's Rocks] with the breakers near it, and the main, I judge there is a ship passage which might be attempted in an emergency. From this part the shore takes a very easterly direction, but only to form a bight, for it comes out again to D [Point Bell], which is a projecting point, low at the extremity but the land immediately at its back is moderately high[.]

The shore in this part of Nuyts Land[2] must be approached with caution.

[f. 135] Tuesday 2 February

Fresh breezes and fine weather with haze. At 1 hour 10′ tacked ship towards the land. Saw the land at N50°E through the haze. Passed to windward of the broad flat islet and breakers. At 6 hours 30′, tacked ship off shore. Another island, d,[3] S37°E beyond which there is other land seen indistinctly through the haze. After the ship was about we distinguished a sunken rock within half a mile of the place where that evolution was performed. Moderate breezes and fine weather, with haze. At 1, tacked towards the land. At daylight, saw the land to windward of us as before. At 5 hours 40′ tacked towards the offing to be ready for the sea breeze.

Out 2nd reefs and set the staysails. Removed four tons of iron ballast forward from the after part of the ship, supposing that she was getting too much by the head. At 11 hours 30′ tacked ship towards the land, on the winds heading. At noon, moderate breezes

---

[1] Fowler's Bay is a coastal inlet near the head of the Great Australian Bight.

[2] In 1627 a Dutch East India Company vessel mapped around over 900 miles of the southern coast of Australia from Albany, Western Australia, to Ceduna, South Australia. The captain of the ship named this coast Pieter Nuyts' Land after the highest-ranking official on board the ship. Frequent strong winds, summer haze and a plethora of rocks and breakers made navigation challenging off this part of the South Australian coast. Klaassen, 'Nuyts, Pieter', pp. 310–11.

[3] Purdie's Island (32°16′S, 133°14′E), named by Flinders after Robert Purdie, the surgeon's assistant on the *Investigator*. Flinders, *A Voyage to Terra Australis, Atlas*, south coast, sheet 3; Scott, *The Life of Matthew Flinders*, p. 340.

with hazy weather; so as to make the horizon very indistinct. The swell from the southward considerably gone down.

| Meridian altitude ☉ Lower Limb No 483 | 74°14′14″N |
| Latitude | 32°31′39″S |

	By log		Latitude South		Longitude East						
Course	Distance	DR	Obs	DR	TK	Var allowed	Set or current	Ther	Barom	Error of TK
S48°E	20	32°33′	32°32′	133°42′	133°9′	–	1S 11W	72° 70° 72°	29.93 29.87 29.83	–

Additional remarks

From D [Point Bell], the furthest point of the main seen yesterday morning, the land curves to the eastward to another point E,[1] and then falls back, forming a bight whose extent is yet unknown. From this bight the shore projects out again, more to the southward. Calcarious cliffs and a low sandy shore still continue to divide the country between them, the abrupt part of the shore consisting of the first, and the low and level coast of the other.

The island d [Purdie's Island] is of a moderate height, and is almost environed with rocks and breakers, a long ridge of which extend NEerly from the island.

The perseverance of the wind to blow against us does not permit me to add anything further this day, relative to the land; for on finding we must pass to leeward of what had been before seen if we continued to stretch on in the morning, I stood off again to sea, with the hope of coming in more successfully in an advanced part of the day, when the wind might be expected to blow upon the shore nearer to a right angle from its direction.

[f. 136] Wednesday 3 February *Investigator* exploring Nuyts Archipelago on the south coast of New Holland

Moderate breezes and fine weather with haze. Came up with a cluster of islands some of which are weathered. On drawing near to an island (f)[2] with two smaller isles[3] and breakers near it, at 4 *hours* 40′ tacked ship to work up to the larger islands which lie a few miles to windward. Mod*erate* breezes, with weather so hazy that nothing can be seen beyond 6 or 7 miles. Tacked ship occasionally, working up to e,[4] the largest island, under which there appeared to be shelter. Passed over a bank which runs off from the NW point of the island upon which there was 6 *fatho*ms, the water deepening immediately to 10;

[1] Point Peter (32°12′S, 133°29′E), the north point of the entrance to Denial Bay. Flinders, *A Voyage to Terra Australis*, Atlas, south coast, sheet 3; *Sailing Directions (Enroute): North, West and South Coasts of Australia*, p. 159.

[2] In 1814 Flinders named it Lacy Island (32°24′S, 133°22′E) after Denis Lacy, a midshipman who joined *Investigator* at the Cape of Good Hope. It is one of a group known today as the Lacy Islands. *Sailing Directions (Enroute): North, West and South Coasts of Australia*, p. 160; Vallance, Moore and Groves, eds, *Nature's Investigator*, p. 125.

[3] Possibly Egg Island (32°28′S, 133°19′E) and Dog Island (32°29′S, 133°20′E).

[4] In 1814 Flinders named this 'Isle St Francis' (now St Francis Island, 32°31′S, 133°18′E), believing it to be the place so called by Nuyts in 1627. Vallance, Moore and Groves, eds, *Nature's Investigator*, p. 123. It is now part of the Nuyts Archipelago, off Ceduna, South Australia, at the eastern end of the Great Australian Bight.

when finding the bottom to be good, dropped the small bower anchor and furled sails, the water being smooth as in a mill pond.

AM. Light breezes with very hazy weather. At daylight we found ourselves in a secure bay and about ½ ′ [mile] from the shore in the best sheltered part. The extremes of the island S75°E and round by the south to N30°W. Four other islands distant 2 or 3 miles covered us from East to N43°E.[1]

Sent the master to sound about the bay,[2] and the other boats were employed landing the naturalists to examine the island, and the commander to survey and observe the situations of the neighbouring islands.

Swayed the lower yards higher up. Sailmakers repairing the spanker. At noon, light breezes with hot sultry weather; the wind off the land.

Meridian altitude ☉ Lower Limb No 483	73°52′21″N
Latitude	32°36′13″S

Note: From the extreme haziness of the weather, I do not put much confidence in the accuracy of these observations.

	By log	Latitude South		Longitude East						
Course	Distance	DR	Obs	DR	TK	Var allowed	Set or current	Ther	Barom	Error of TK
S82°E	20	32°35′	32°36′	134°6′	133°31′	0	1S 2W	73° 73° 75°	29.80 29.75 29.74	–

Additional remarks[3]

Great flocks of the sooty petrel, called by captain Hunter and the people of Norfolk Island[4] Mount Pitt birds,[5] had been seen within these few days, which I had conjectured must belong to some islands not very far distant, and it now appears that this and the neighbouring isles are their habitations. I have little doubt but that these isles belong to the cluster amongst which is marked Saint Peter and St. Francis in the charts, and discovered by Peter Nuyts in 1628. His discovery finishes with these islands, and as far as I know, the coast abreast of the islands and further eastward is totally unknown.[6]

[1] Three of these were Lacy's Isle, Evans' Isle and Franklin's Island. Flinders, *A Voyage to Terra Australis*, I, p. 108. The fourth island is unnamed in ibid., *Atlas*, south coast, sheet 3. The modern names are Lacy Island, Evans Island and the Franklin Islands.

[2] The master sounded Petrel Bay, on St Francis Island, and its environs. Flinders, *A Voyage to Terra Australis*, I, p. 109, states that this afforded 'excellent shelter for two or three ships'.

[3] Rough Journal, I, f. 305, adds: 'The haze was so thick this afternoon that scarcely anything but the looming of the islands could be seen until we came close to them. We counted 9 islands besides rocks, two of which appeared to be large. Under one of the large ones, where there seemed to be sandy beach, and very smooth water, I intended to anchor for the night not being able to do anything towards surveying the islands whilst the weather remained so thick. It was quite dark before we got to an anchor, but the shelter afforded us fully equalled my expectations.'

[4] John Hunter, a naval officer and Governor of New South Wales (1795–1800), who lived on Norfolk Island for eleven months after his ship HMS *Sirius* was wrecked there in February 1790. Auchmuty, 'Hunter, John', pp. 566–72, and Frost, 'Hunter, John (1737–1821)', pp. 906–8.

[5] Mount Pitt birds (*Procellaria norfolkiensis*) were burrowing Norfolk Island petrels which were hunted to extinction there by hungry European settlers. Vallance, Moore and Groves, eds, *Nature's Investigator*, p. 125.

[6] After the voyage on which Pieter Nuyts sailed reached this part of the south Australian coast, it turned back, sailed westwards, and returned to Batavia. No navigator between Nuyts and Flinders had explored or charted this unknown coast.

In the morning I landed to take angles of all that could be seen from two stations on this island e [Isle St Francis], the NW point and a sandy hill 1¾ miles to the S 4°15′W of it. I now make out twelve islands of this archipelago, besides rocks, although the haze allows us to see but to a small distance: of these, this island e is the largest, its circumference being by guess 8 or 10 miles. From the naturalist I learn that the stone which forms the basis of the island is porphyry;[1] but on all the upper parts the stone is calcarious and mostly lies in loose pieces. Upon it is a covering of sand, deeper in some places than in others, and mixed with as small a portion of vegetable earth as may be, but producing a coat of small shrubs, and here and there a bush. Wherever the sand and soil is six or eight inches deep amongst these shrubs, it is burrowed into by the Mount Pitt birds. In walking, one frequently steps into these holes, and not infrequently gets thrown down from it. Part of these burrows, [f. 137] especially those near the waterside are occupied by the penguins. Some small kangaroos were seen this day but none shot: they are of the same size as those upon island U [Mondrain Island] of D'Entrecasteaux's archipelago. Geese appear to frequent this island in some parts of the year, but it seems now to be too dry for them, the vegetation being almost burnt up by the heat of the sun. A few straggling seals were seen upon this and the neighbouring isles.

The reflected heat from the sand and rock made it intolerably hot walking, and the fatigue was not a little increased by frequently falling over the bird holes upon the hot sand. In the shade the thermometer stood at 98°, and the island does not in any one part promise to supply a mouthful of water.

On all parts of this south coast of New Holland hitherto, I find an easterly wind to have the same effect on the barometer as at the Cape of Good Hope, which is to make it rise: and although this wind should blow strong, the barometer will seldom stand lower than 30 inches. At 29.9 and lower, I have seldom been disappointed in my expectation of a westerly wind, which is usually stronger as the barometer stood lower; and on its reapproach to 30, I knew that the westerly wind was almost expired; but within these few days this statement does not at all answer: the easterly wind continues to follow its common routine although the height is not more than 29.80. No rain or any great quantity of wind follows this, but the atmosphere is loaded with so dense a haze that we cannot see the highest land more than 7 or 8 miles, and sometimes the sea horizon is undefinable. Whether the haze is the corresponding cause of the fall in the barometer, I cannot yet say with any degree of certainty.[2]

Thursday 4 February

Fresh breezes and hazy weather. On the haze clearing away a little saw land to the northward supposed it to be the main land. At sunset, sent down top gallant yards. Sent the boats on shore with a party of men to collect Mount Pitt birds: they returned in about an hour and half bringing 400, which were divided equally amongst the officers and ships company.

AM Light airs and calms, with hazy weather. Sent a cutter to fish and to collect more birds. She caught no fish, and being too late the birds had all gone off to sea for the day.

[1] An igneous rock with large crystals in a fine-grained matrix, or associated mineral deposit.
[2] Flinders, *A Voyage to Terra Australis*, I, p. 109, adds: 'That there was no entrance to a strait, nor any large inlet near these islands, was almost demonstrated by the insignificance of the tides; for neither in Fowler's Bay, nor at this Isle St Francis, could any set be perceived; nor was there any rise by the shore worthy of notice.'

Cut up pork no. 31 marked 53 pieces, but was short nine or 52 lbs. Roused up the small bower cable, cleaned well in the tier[1] and everywhere below, and recoiled the cable. Prepared to get under weigh on the setting in of the sea breeze.

Additional remarks

The great heat of the weather on shore deterred our gentlemen from any further examination of the island this morning. The party that went to haul the seine caught a small kangaroo, and a second yellow snake was also taken.

The horizon becoming somewhat clearer this morning than it had hitherto been, I landed at the north-east part of the island to examine more minutely the appearance of land which extended round to the southward of east. I could see little but took the bearing of two new islands, o[2] and p,[3] lying several miles to the eastward, and were now distinguishable through the haze.

The calcarious stone at this point forms some caverns in which I found pieces of good salt in cakes, sticking in the crevices of the stone. The immediate stone to which it adheres is not calcarious [n]or does it seem to be porphyry, but nearer allied to quartz.

[f. 138] General remarks

The shelter afforded by this bay is very good, for I apprehend that no wind whatever could raise much sea in it. From all parts of the compass, except between north and east, the island itself would shelter a ship properly placed; and from north east to east the islands would break off the surges that might rise within the main, for at the distance of seven leagues the main land extends entirely round the open part of the bay.

No wood or water can be obtained here, so far as we examined; but some hair seals[4] and any number of the petrels called Mount Pitt birds may be procured. If limestone was any object, it is sufficiently abundant. We felt no set of tides in this bay, nor did the shore present the appearance of any rise worth noticing.[5]

Friday 5 February *Investigator* in No 4 bay, island e [Isle St Francis] of Nuyts Archipelago on the south coast of New Holland

Light breezes with sultry weather. At 1 *hour* 30′ weighed, and steered out of the bay. At 2 passed between the small isles g and h,[6] ½ mile asunder, steering towards the main. At 4, passed island o [Evans' Island] and steered towards q[7] and I,[8] behind which the land

---

[1] The compartment below decks where cable and rope were stored.

[2] Evans Island (32°23′S, 133°29′E). Flinders, *A Voyage to Terra Australis*, I, p. 110.

[3] One of the two adjacent Franklin Islands (32°27′S, 133°39′E). Cooper, *The Unknown Coast*, p. 134.

[4] These are dark brown to brownish grey with a mane of coarse hair.

[5] Rough Journal, I, f. 310, adds: 'There being not the least appearance of water on this island or of wood, I proposed to leave it as soon as the breeze should set in from the southward, and intended to repeat my observation for the latitude, which on account of the haze yesterday I considered to be very uncertain; but although it was somewhat clearer than before, yet I found it impossible to distinguish the land from the horizon.'

[6] Smooth Island (32°29′S, 133°18′E) and Egg Island. These islands, just over half a mile apart, are among the Franklin Islands. Flinders, *A Voyage to Terra Australis*, I, p. 110.

[7] Goat Island (32°18′S, 133°31′E), about 3 miles NNE of Evans Island. *Sailing Directions (Enroute): North, West, and South Coasts of Australia*, p. 161.

[8] St Peter Island (32°17′S, 133°35′E), the largest island in the Nuyts Archipelago. Ibid.; Flinders, *A Voyage to Terra Australis*, I, p. 127.

seemed to be the main. In attempting to pass between q [Goat Island] and I [St Peter Island] for the purpose of anchoring for the night, we shoaled to 2¾ *fatho*ms, which obliged us to wear round suddenly and stand back. We were thoroughly prepared to wear, and the ship came round exceedingly quick, which alone saved us from striking the rocks. At 8, hove to, having tolerably clear water to the southward. Light breezes and fine weather. At 4 *hours* 30′ filled and made sail towards the eastern land.

At 8, the land was seen as far as S40°E and other lands round by the N to the center of e [Isle St Francis] which bore N 60°W. Tacked ship to the northward, but on the wind heading us, at 9 *hours* 45′, tacked again to the eastward. A flurry of hot wind obliged us to take in top gall*ant* sails, jib and staysails. Served lemon juice and sugar in lieu of sweet wort, as more suitable to the hot wea*the*r. At noon, F cape[1] N21°W 3 or 4 miles. Island s[2] and the main to the south-east in sight; but ahead we see no land there being an opening of some kind there, which we are now steering to examine.

Supplem*ent* to Mer*idian* alt*itude* ☉ Uppe*r* Lim*b* No 483   106°11′49″S

Latitude   32°37′27″S

This observation bad, from the haziness of the horizon, as all the preceding

Mr Thistle's observ*ation* was   32°40′42″S

By log		Latitude South		Longitude East					
Course	Distance	DR	Obs	DR	TK	Var allowed	Set or current	Ther	Barom
N86°E	23	32°34′	32°41′	134°33′	134°1′	2°W	7S	82°	29.67
							3E	76°	29.70
								65°	29.65

Additional remarks[3]

The islands g [Smooth Island] and h [Egg Island] appear to be porphyry covered with a calcarious crust. In the neighbourhood of I [St Peter Island] many grass-hopper shaped insects were flying about the ship, and also in the morning. About 20 small birds all of the same kind, which appeared to be driven off the land by the northwesterly wind, were taken in different parts of the ship[.][4]

Seeing that the mainland was very much broken in this neighbourhood, I judged it necessary to return to D [Point Bell] and I [St Peter Island] and explore every part onward, lest any river should escape us. The haze has been so thick since we quitted that

---

[1] Point Brown (32°32′S, 133°52′E), the north entrance point of Streaky Bay. Named after the botanist on the *Investigator*. Bearing Book, entry for 5 February 1802, f. 39; Flinders, *A Voyage to Terra Australis*, I, p. 110; Scott, *The Life of Matthew Flinders*, p. 340.

[2] Olive Island (32°44′S, 133°58′E), 4.5 miles west of Cape Bauer. Named after Flinders's clerk, John Olive. Flinders, *A Voyage to Terra Australis*, I, p. 111, and *Atlas*, south coast, sheet 3.

[3] Rough Journal, I, f. 313, adds: 'All the islands of this archipelago yet seen are much lower than those of D'Entrecasteauxs; but except amongst these latter islands, reefs do not seem to be so abundant. The land seeming to be very much broken and divided, I judge it necessary to return to the part of the main which we quitted on the evening of the 3rd. The dense haze that has prevailed since does not allow us to form a correct judgment of anything beyond 4 or 5 miles.'

[4] These birds were probably tawny-crowned (or yellow-tufted) honeyeaters. Cooper, *The Unknown Coast*, p. 65.

part, that beyond 5 or 6 miles no correct judgment can be formed of any land. There were many smokes from the mainland near our situation this day at noon.[1]

[f. 139] **Saturday 6 February**

Hot sultry winds with hazy weather. Steering up an opening, between F [Point Brown] and H:[2] much seaweed and refuse floating about. At 2 *hours* 25′ saw the land all round ahead about 5 or 6 miles distant, forming a bay and not a river as we had hoped; and there being shoal (or discoloured) water within half a mile of us,[3] bore away towards H [Cape Bauer], passing behind s island [Olive Island], and steered to the southward along the shore, at the distance of from 1 to 4 miles.

At 6 *hours*, G[4] cape NEbE and a further part S55°E 5 miles. Seeing the land now took a more easterly direction, hauled round to the northward again to explore the part between E [Point Peter] and F [Point Brown], of which very little has yet been seen. Kept away from the wind until 9 in order to give the island s [Olive Island] and the breakers round it a good berth; afterwards kept to the wind under three topsails, but keeping the mizzen topsail aback to give time for wearing round in case of danger.

Moderate breezes & fine, with haze. Saw a fire upon the shore to the ENE ward. At 5 *hours* 30′, white cliffs in island e [St Francis Island] bore N80°W and G [Point Westall], the southern extreme, S45°E. F cape [Point Brown] on the north side of the PM bay, N49°E 6 or 7 miles. Made all sail, hoping to pass between F and the p isles [Franklin Islands]; but at 7 *hours* 30′ finding we should not weather the isles, tacked ship. Moderate breezes and hazy. At 9, tacked again trying to weather the islands, but the wind heading as we approached, at 10 bore away to pass round them to leeward.

Light winds and fine weather, but so hazy that the shape of the land is altogether altered by it: sandy beaches seeming to be white cliffs. Land supposed to be e [St Francis Island] W8°S the isle p [one of the Franklin Islands] N20° to 55°E one mile, pp [one of the Franklin Islands] being shut behind it, and apparently no passage between them.

Mer*idian* alt*itude* ☉ Lowe*r* Lim*b* 483	72°59′36″N
Latitude	32°35′21″S
Supp*lemen*t to U*pper* L*imb*	106°8′41″S
Latitude	32°16′10″S

This last observation can have no confidence put in it

		By log		Latitude South		Longitude East					
Course	Distance	DR	Obs	DR	TK	Var allowed	Set or current	Ther	Barom	Error of TK
N38°W	17	32°27′	32°35′	134°20′	133°54′	–	8S	82°	29.62	–
							6E	76½°	29.64	
								82°	29.60	

[1] Flinders, *A Voyage to Terra Australis*, I, p. 112, adds: 'The number of smokes rising from the shores of this wide, open place, induced me to give it the name of SMOKY BAY.' Its coordinates are 32°18′S, 133°49′E.

[2] Cape Bauer (32°44′S, 134°04′E). Named after the botanical draughtsman of the *Investigator*. Flinders, *A Voyage to Terra Australis*, I, p. 110; Scott, *The Life of Matthew Flinders*, p. 340.

[3] Flinders named this Streaky Bay (32°35′S, 134°04′E) after the discoloured water which appeared to shallow rapidly towards the shore. Vallance, Moore and Groves, eds, *Nature's Investigator*, p. 126.

[4] Point Westall (32°55′S, 134°03′E). Named after William Westall, the landscape painter on the *Investigator*. Flinders, *A Voyage to Terra Australis*, I, p. 111; Scott, *The Life of Matthew Flinders*, p. 340.

Additional remarks

The land which forms the bay into which we steered PM is low and sandy, and there were three smokes on different parts of it. We stood so far into this bay as to be tolerably certain that no opening exists near its head into which the *Investigator* could be taken: indeed there was no appearance of any opening and the water seemed to be shoal all round the head of the bay. The direction of the wind prevented me from steering back towards D [Point Bell] this afternoon, therefore on hauling out of the bay I took the opportunity of exploring a part of the coast to the southward during daylight, and at dusk hauled to the northward to be ready for the wind next morning.[1]

We lost some time in trying to weather the isles p and pp [two of the Franklin Islands], which at last we were obliged to give up. These isles are each about 1¾ [miles] in length, and between them lie many low rocks and much broken water.

The very great uncertainty of the horizon creates many difficulties in my survey, more indeed than arises from the thickness of the haze preventing me from seeing land at a distance. This day at noon we had 6 or 7 different latitudes, the greatest and least differing ten miles from each other and all were observed to the north: the haze forming so many horizons that no person can be certain that he has the true one.

[f. 140] Sunday 7 February *Investigator* **to No 5, anchorage, island q [Goat Island] of Nuyts Archipelago on the south coast of New Holland**

Moderate breezes and fair weather, but very hazy. Hauled up round p islands [Franklin Islands] into a large bay, but finding the water to shoal, hauled up the main sail & at 2 *hours* 25′, having seen the bay nearly all round, we bore away to go round q [Goat Island] being then in 5½ *fatho*ms. Having passed between o [Evans' Island] and q, hauled up round the latter into another bay. Many insects and birds about the ship and much refuse floating upon the water. At 5 *hours* 15′ we were obliged to wear round and stand back, the water having shoaled to 3 *fatho*ms and no appearance of any channel leading further up, or of any opening in the head of the bay which was distant about 6 miles. At 6 *hours* 15′ tacked ship and worked up to a little beach on the north side of the island q [Goat Island] where we came to with the small bower, being ½ mile from q and something more from I [St Peter Island] the island or main on the other side of the passage: we were sheltered except from S60°W to N80°W. Saw great flocks of Mount Pitt birds coming in from sea. Light breezes with sultry weather.

AM. Moderate breezes with cloudy weather: lightening in the NE. Sent a boat very early to collect birds and kill seals, but she was too late for the first, and got only 3 or 4 seals of the hair kind. Other boats landing the naturalists upon I [St Peter Island], and the Commander upon q [Goat Island] to survey and examine the country. People on board employed as necessary. Light breezes with very warm and sultry weather: much haze about.

Meridian altitude ☉ Lower Limb No 483   72°55′20″N
Latitude   32°21′9″S
Differing six miles from most of the latitude lately taken

---

[1] The *Investigator* anchored at Goat Island. Vallance, Moore and Groves, eds, *Nature's Investigator*, p. 127.

| By log | | Latitude South | | Longitude East | | | | | | |
Course	Distance	DR	Obs	DR	TK	Var allowed	Set or current	Ther	Barom	Error of TK
north	7	32°28'	32°21'	134°20'	133°48'	–	7N 6W	83° 81° 83½°	29.62 29.65 29.70	–

Additional remarks

The last bay examined this afternoon gave us greater promise of an inlet into the country than anything we have before met with. The numerous smokes in the neighbourhood, the insects which usually frequent rivers and lakes of fresh water, the birds, and the grass and other refuse in the water, all tended to excite hopes. I considered that if any considerable river emptied itself in this neighbourhood, that the water ought to be fresher here than out in the open sea: and therefore that the hydrostatic balance would almost with certainty solve the question: the result of my experiment is annexed, and shews our hopes to be unfounded, in as much as the water is one 356th part saltier here than in *Prince George* Harbour, which I attribute to the exhalation of the lighter parts of the sea water by the present great heat of the sun and no rain having fallen for some time past. We have indeed ascertained now very nearly by actual observation that there is no considerable opening into the country near this point, a very small space only now remaining to complete the examination from G [Point Westall] back to D [Point Bell] and E [Point Peter] when we quitted it on the 2nd PM.

To balance the bulb of glass in air, it required in the oppos*ing* scale   1621 grains
    (the barometer standing at 29.60)
To balance the bulb in water out of our scuttle cask   1080 gr*ains*
In the water taken up alongside of the ship   1065 gr*ains*
Whence the sea water is heavier than that in Princess Royal Harbour as 1060 is to 1065, or one 356th part, consequently so much saltier.

[f. 141] Additional remarks continued

From my survey of the coast and islands in this neighbourhood, I have reason to suspect that the uncommon haziness of the weather has rendered our astronomical observations erroneous, and that not one of them taken from the sea horizon since the 3rd PM ought to have the least confidence in it. This being the case I determined to use the quicksilver horizon and take the observations on shore; and with this view I landed at 8 in the morning and took the altitudes before given: but the sun being too high at noon for the sextant to measure its double altitude, I was obliged to use the sea horizon, getting as close down to the water as the surf on the shore would permit in order to bring the horizon very near to me; by this means I avoided much, if not all, of the error that arises from the vast increase of horizontal refraction in the present state of the atmosphere.[1]

The surface stone of the island q [Goat Island] I found to be calcarious, but the lower rocks of the shore are of granite, in which I observed small veins of quartz as usual. Over the granite the calcarious crust is in some parts 50 feet thick. The top of the island is

---

[1] i.e. the refraction (which displaces astronomical objects) at the astronomical horizon.

298

covered with one kind of plant, a species of what we call Botany Bay greens,[1] amongst which the sooty petrels called *Mount* Pitt birds, or sheerwaters, burrow, undermining all the surface. From the excessive heat of the sun, the reflection from the sand, and from continually stepping mid-leg into these holes, I found a walk to the top of the island as much as I had strength to perform. I had no thermometer with me, but should suppose the temperature to be 130°, and there was not a breath of air moving. From this place where I had taken a station with the theodolite, I overlooked the eastern land Y,[2] which I was somewhat surprised to see divided from the main by a passage which communicates between the two bays we had been partly examining the preceding afternoon.

On returning to the boat, a flock of teal presented themselves, of which I shot four, and after observing the suns meridional altitudes, before given, I returned on board the ship with the intention to finish the examination up to d island and the cape D [Point Bell]; and then to work back to No. 4 bay,[3] in island e [Isle St Francis], where it was necessary to get better observations for reconstructing my chart of this archipelago entirely afresh.

Upon I [St Peter Island] the holes made by the sooty petrels were numerous, and also a small kind of kangaroo, of which four were killed of the size of a hare; they were something different to any before seen, were miserably thin, and infested with insects. No marks of natives were seen, [n]or did I furnish either wood or water, being fully as barren as its neighbour q [Goat Island]. No other than calcarious stone was seen upon I; and indeed as it is not so high as q, the granite would not appear if the upper stratum is of an equal thickness in both.

There was no set of tide past the ship whilst lying at this ⅃age, but I perceived that the tide had risen a foot or more from the time I landed in the morning to noon: nothing however can be decided upon the tide during such a short stay.

Besides the teal, I saw white bellied shags,[4] gulls of three kinds, numbers of crows, a greenish parrocquet[5] and two smaller birds. A black snake[6] was killed upon q [Goat Island] but its appearance did not bespeak it to be venomous.[7]

[f. 142] **Monday 8 February *Investigator* exploring Nuyts Archipelago on the south coast of New Holland**

Moderate breezes and fine weather, with haze. Made the signal for the boat with the naturalists party to return, and fired a gun. At 2, weighed and made sail along the coast towards D [Point Bell]. At 4½ hours a small island, t,[8] S30°E 1½ miles and the nearest part of the main NNE 3 miles. D and d [Purdie Island] in sight and zz[9] an islet lying 3 or 4 east

---

[1] Australian seashore plants (*Atriplex cinerea*) with an almost woody stem and scurfy foliage.

[2] Eyre Island (32°23′S, 133°50′E).

[3] Petrel Bay (32°30′S, 133°16′E) on the north side of Isle St Francis. Cooper, *The Unknown Coast*, p. 134.

[4] i.e. cormorants.

[5] i.e. parakeet.

[6] Probably the black tiger snake. Vallance, Moore and Groves, eds, *Nature's Investigator*, p. 128.

[7] Flinders added at the bottom of the page: 'Note. Although it does not appear that there is any inlet of consequence in this neighbourhood, I suspect there is some considerable lake or lagoon, at no very great distance from the sea shore.'

[8] Lounds Island (32°16′S, 133°22′N). Flinders named it after midshipman Sherrard Lound. Cooper, *The Unknown Coast*, p. 135; Vallance, Moore and Groves, eds, *Nature's Investigator*, p. 129.

[9] NAT MAP Nuyts does not name this islet.

from the latter. At 5 *hours* 15′ tacked ship being close to zz [unnamed]. Variable winds, with spitting rain at such times as the flows come from the northward. Having seen the continuation of the main land up to D, at 7 made sail for No. 4 bay [Petrel Bay], in isl*and* e [Isle St Francis]; but the wind becoming light and baffling we did not get to anchorage till 12 *hours* 45′ near our former place. Light airs and fine: lightening all round.

Note f [Lacy Island] bore east, about half past 8 o'clock.

AM Light airs and calm with sultry weather. Brought the sails afresh to the yards, after washing decks in the morning, and afterwards set up the fore-top-mast rigging. Sent a boat to fish with hook and line and she caught a few rockfish. A large shark was harpooned this morning, but got away. Light airs with sultry weather. A boat employed by the Commander.

Mer*idian* alt*itude* ☉ Lowe*r Lim*b No 483   72°24′14″N
Latitude   32°33′33′S

By log		Latitude South		Longitude East						
Course	Distance	DR	Obs	DR	TK	Var allowed	Set or current	Ther	Barom	Error of TK
S50°W	15	32°30′	32°34′	134°6′	133°35′	–	4S	82°	29.73	30″E
							1E	80°	29.60	
								82°	29.70	

Tuesday 9 February[1]

Light breezes and sultry weather with clouds rising at times. My survey of these islands requiring to be reconstructed I determined to remain at anchorage till the next morning. Employed getting water to hand in the holds and in jobs about the rigging. A boat employed fishing with some success. At dusk sent a party of men on shore to collect *Moun*t Pitt birds, which, though not equal to ducks, are desirable to men living on salt provisions, and had mostly reconstructed my survey of this part; nothing further remained, therefore, to prevent us from going on along the coast.

At 5, got up the anchor, and made sail with a moderate breeze for the head G [Point Westall] and that part of the main which we quitted on the 6th PM. Served out more than eight birds to every man in the ship. Passed between e [Isle St Francis] north-east point and K;[2] soundings as per column. Hazy weather, with a light breeze which dwindled away to a calm; but at 9½ the wind again freshened up from the westward. Served out sour krout and vinegar. Lime juice and sugar continue to be issued daily. At noon, fresh breezes and hazy weather, so that no land is in sight. Many of the sooty petrels and gannets about.

---

[1] Rough Journal, I, f. 322, adds: 'In the morning *Lieutenan*t Flinders took altitudes from the artificial horizon, which gave the longitude as opposite; and clearly shews how much we were deceived in the horizon when here before. At noon, we both observed the latitude from the beach, and clearly saw the double horizon ... The wind being light and foul, and having much work with my chart to correct a mass of errors, contracted between the times of being in this bay, from the haziness of the horizon; I deferred getting under way until the morning, proposing to collect a good quantity of the sooty petrels, and as much fish as could be caught by hook and line: there being rather too much surf on the beach for hauling the seine.'

[2] Cape Radstock (32°12′S, 134°19′E), the north entrance point of Anxious Bay. Named after Admiral Lord Radstock. Flinders, *A Voyage to Terra Australis*, I, pp. 120–21; Scott, *The Life of Matthew Flinders*, p. 340; *Sailing Directions (Enroute): North, West, and South Coasts of Australia*, p. 165.

Meridian altitude ☉ Lower Limb No 483	71°35′16″N
Latitude	32°43′34″S
Supplement of Upper Limb	107°31′9″S
Latitude	32°42′31″S
Mean	32°43′2″S

By log		Latitude South		Longitude East					
Course	Distance	DR	Obs	DR	TK	Var allowed	Set or current	Ther	Barom
SE	23	32°50′	32°43′	131°25′	134°6′	–	7N	83½°	29.73
							12E	80°	29.70
								77½°	29.77

[f. 143] **Wednesday 10 February**

Fresh breezes with thick hazy weather. At 0 hours 45′ saw the looming of white cliffs through the haze, probably of H [Cape Bauer]. At 1 hours 40′ saw the head G [Point Westall] distinctly, and at 2 hauled along the shore, 4 or 5 miles distant. Double reefed the topsails. At 4, high land, J,[1] bore N30° to 60°E 5 or 6 miles. Bore away a short time to see better an indistinct part of the shore. At 6, a high steep cape, K [Cape Radstock], bore N75°E 6 or 7 miles beyond which no land is visible. Hauled to the wind and shortened sail. At 8, tacked ship to the northward, having a moderate breeze with dull hazy weather, and a swell from the WSW. At 12, tacked to the southward. Lost a deep-sea lead.

Moderate breezes and dull cloudy weather. Tacked ship to the northward and at 5 bore away for the land which was soon after seen, K [Cape Radstock], bearing N60°E. At 7, bore away, to look into a bight behind K, but finding it full of breakers at 8 hours 45′ hauled along the shore again toward L2,[2] the extreme steep end of the cliffs from K. Passed several steep heads and small hollows in the coast between K and L2 [Point Weyland]: these two bore at 10 o'clock N78°W and S67°E.

Seeing the shore fall back from L2 into a bight, at 11 edged away to look into it, and finding there was an opening in it, soon after bore round up for it, hoping to find anchorage. As we approached the opening it appeared to be very small, and to be still further contracted by rocks and broken water, and the probability of finding shelter being too small to risk any uncertainty of being able to weather the land upon one tack or the other, at noon wore round and hauled the wind to the southward L2 bearing NW 1¼ mile. Head of the bight N5°E. At EbyN the shore was distant 2½ miles. Moderate breezes and dull cloudy weather. A long swell from SW.

Bad observation

| Supplement meridian altitude ☉ Upper Limb 483 | 108°23′9″S |
| Latitude | 33°15′23″S |

---

[1] Cape Blanche (33°02′S, 134°07′E). Cooper, *The Unknown Coast*, p. 135.

[2] Point Weyland, a cliffy point (33°15′S, 134°38′E), close to the SW entrance of Venus Bay. Bearing Book, entry for 9 February 1802, f. 43; Flinders, *A Voyage to Terra Australis*, I, p. 121; *Sailing Directions (Enroute): North, West, and South Coasts of Australia*, p. 166.

By log		Latitude South		Longitude East						
Course	Distance	DR	Obs	DR	TK	Var allowed	Set or current	Ther	Barom	Error of TK
N52°E	51	33°14′	33°15′	135°13′	134°53′	–	1S 1W	73° 73° 73°	29.74 29.78 29.87	1′51″

Additional remarks

The heads G [Point Westall] and J [Cape Blanche] are moderately high and cliffy, and seem to be calcarious. From the latter the shore becomes lower and takes a more southerly direction to K [Cape Radstock], but it then becomes higher than before and as far as L2 [Point Weyland] forms an almost uninterrupted continuation of steep cliffy shore, which is stratified and seems to be calcarious. A tolerably deep bight is formed here which for a short time gave a hope of finding anchorage, but the bight and opening round L2 still more so, inducing me to bear away for it before the wind, and with an awkward swell sitting upon the shore. We ran as far as was at all prudent, and almost further before we hauled round to the wind again. The opening then seemed to be very narrow and to lead only into a lagoon, the water of which we saw over the low front shore.

[f. 144] Thursday 11 February *Investigator* exploring Nuyts Archipelago and the neighbouring unknown part of the south coast of New Holland

Strong breezes and cloudy weather. At 1½ *hours* land appeared out to the westward of south, much beyond what we could weather. Kept stretching along parallel with the low sandy shore until 3 *hours* 40′ when the shallowing of the water obliged us to tack: distance off shore 2½ miles. Finding we were not likely to weather the cape K [Cape Radstock], tacked again. Islands were now seen reaching out to SWbW. At 7, tacked from the sandy shore again, nearly in the same place as before, having weathered little. Saw many breakers amongst the islands making it doubtful whether there was any passage between them. It was my wish to work up to the inner island u[1] and anchor for the night, but even this being impossible we stretched off towards K until 12 and then stood back again: the weather squally with rain.

Seeing the land under our lee bow at 4, we were obliged to tack again towards K and L2 [Point Weyland]. At daylight L2 N19°W. Southern main land S65°E and islands from thence to SWbS. At 5½ *hours* tacked ship in order to get under the inner island u [now East Island] for anchorage.

Strong breezes with squally weather. At 7 *hours* 30′ got up under the lee of island u and anchored with the small bower in 7 fathoms upon a bottom of calcarious sand; being well sheltered except from WbS to about NNW. Sent away the master to sound in the passage between point M[2] and the island u, which he found to be too shoal for the ship to pass. Employed setting up the standing rigging fore and aft, for which purpose

[1] There were two islands: a larger eastern one (33°36′S, 134°48′E) and another one about 33°36′S, 134°45′E. In 1814 Flinders called them Waldegrave's Isles to commemorate Admiral William Waldegrave (1753–1825), first Baron Radstock. The larger island is now called East Island; the smaller one is called West Island. Vallance, Moore and Groves, eds, *Nature's Investigator*, p. 131.

[2] McLachlan Point (33°35′S, 134°48′E).

principally I had anchored here. Another boat employed by the Commander and naturalist. Strong breezes and squally weather.

Meridian altitude ☉ Lower Limb 483   70°23′28″N

Latitude   33°36′48″S

Note: The latitude 33°36′48″ is rejected, the sun not having been quite up when it became clouded

	By log	Latitude South		Longitude East						
Course	Distance	DR	Obs	DR	TK	Var allowed	Set or current	Ther	Barom	Error of TK
S26°E	22	33°35′	33°37′	135°24′	135°5′	–	2S 1E	70° – 68½°	29.86 – 29.94	2′33″E

<u>Additional remarks upon the land &c</u>

Our situation this afternoon and night was very far from being a pleasant one; the shore curving round so much to the westward disabled us from clearing the shore on the starboard tack and on the other side we could not weather cape K [Cape Radstock]. It blew strong during the night and in the morning, but necessity obliged us to carry all the sail that the ship could bear, and at daylight we had gained so far that although we could not weather the isles u [now East Island] and v [now West Island], which lie off from the point M [McLachlan Point], yet we were able to fetch up under their lee; and as the press of sail carried in the night shewed us that the standing rigging was not sufficiently stiff I determined to anchor there and get it set up. The master was dispatched immediately after breakfast to sound the passage to leeward of us between M and u, for if the wind should come round to the northwestward and blow hard we had no chance of escaping but by cutting our cable and running out that way. Should the channel prove impracticable, I intended to get under weigh immediately after noon; but on considering afterwards, that with the present wind we should scarcely be able to keep our offing from the shore, the dread of passing such a night as the last, or perhaps a worse, induced me to remain at ⚓ and run the risk of a shift of wind.

Whilst the people on board were employed about the rigging, the naturalist and our party landed to examine the island, and soon after I landed also for the [f. 145] purpose of taking the observations before given, and from the highest part of the island the bearings of all such objects as should present themselves.

The passage between M [McLachlan Point] and this island I saw to be from three-quarters to one-and-quarter mile wide, but the water was breaking mostly across. Beyond M distant land appeared bearing 129°30′ or S50°30′E from which it would be impossible for us to keep our offing with the wind at SSW. To the westward were visible the small high island w[1] and the larger island x[2] and some rocks and breakers.

---

[1] Top Gallant Isles (33°43′S, 134°37′E) comprise an islet and several nearby bare rocks. They are situated 3½ miles east of Flinders Island. Flinders, *A Voyage to Terra Australis*, I, p. 121; *Sailing Directions (Enroute): North, West, and South Coasts of Australia*, p. 167.

[2] 33°43′S, 134°31′E. In 1814 Flinders named it Flinders Island after his brother Samuel. It is the largest island of the Investigator Group. Vallance, Moore and Groves, eds, *Nature's Investigator*, p. 132; *Sailing Directions (Enroute): North, West, and South Coasts of Australia*, p. 167.

The island u [now East Island] is about two miles long, and much resembles q [Goat Island] in its height, as well as in its basis of granite, its superstratum of calcarious stone, its vegetable productions, and in its surface being mostly excavated by the burrowings of the petrels; it has also, like q, been frequented by geese at some preceding time of the year, and there were marks of its having been a breeding place for them. At present, this island as well as all other islands of this archipelago visited by us, seems to be too much dried up to afford a vegetable subsistence to any animal. The spring I judge to be the time when geese frequent these islands. Crows of a fine dark, shining, blue colour were numerous. The bills of two that I shot were surrounded at the base with small feathers which extended one-fourth of the length towards the extremity. No quadruped, except one rat,[1] was found upon the island, or any marks of the inhabitants from the main having ever visited it. Some hair seals[2] were killed upon the shores.

The naturalist observes nothing remarkable concerning this island, but that it is the first upon which no one novelty in natural history presented itself.

Friday 12 February
Fresh breezes with strong squalls at times, accompanied with rain. A considerable swell rolling in and making the landing on shore bad. Employed in the holds getting water and provisions to hand. Cut up pork no. 13, being 11 lbs short of the marked weight. At 5, sent down top-gallant yards and veered to a whole cable. Strong squalls with rain at times during the night, but the wind being off the land we rode very safe. AM At daylight the wind moderated a little, and the weather became something finer. Got up the ⚓ and secured it before making sail; at 7 stretched over towards the island x [Flinders Island], the wind not permitting us to lie along the coast to the south-eastward.

On coming out from under the lee of the islands, the swell from the southwest-ward made it necessary to treble reef the fore topsail in order to case the ship in her plunging. The wind becoming more moderate again, let out the reef, sent up top-gallant yards and set the sails. At 11, tacked ship to work up under the lee of the island x. At noon, fresh breezes and cloudy. The island x for which we are now beating up, S5°W to 33°W 8 or 9 miles. Center of the small high island w [one of the Top-Gallant Islands] S16°E, on the south side of which are those rocks appearing like ships under sail.

Meri*dian* alt*itude* ☉ Lowe*r Lim*b 483   70°5'56"N
Latitude   33°34'40"S

	By log	Latitude South		Longitude East							
Course	Distance	DR	Obs	DR	TK	Var allowed	Set or current	Ther	Barom	Error of TK
N81°W	9	33°36'	33°35'	135°13'	–	–	1N	68½°	29.74	0'54"E
							–	66°	29.78	
								67°	29.87	

[1] The native bush rat. Flinders, *A Voyage to Terra Australis*, I, p. 123.
[2] Probably the Australian sea lion (*Neophoca cinerea*). Vallance, Moore and Groves, eds, *Nature's Investigator*, p. 131.

[f. 146] Saturday 13 February *Investigator* **exploring Nuyts Archipelago**
Fresh breezes and cloudy weather. At 1, tacked ship, and afterwards occasionally, working up under the lee of the island x [Flinders Island] in order to anchor. Out 2nd reef of the main top sail, and set the stay sails. At dusk we were still some distance short of the island, but there being apparently good shelter from the present wind, and no particular danger in the way to it, we continued to work up in the dark, and at half past nine came to with the best bower in 7 fathoms, about half a mile from the northern beach of the island x, whose extremes bore S85°E to S67°W. Veered to half a cable, furled sails, and sent down top-gallant yards. Fresh breezes and cloudy.

AM. Moderate breezes. Saw a small patch of broken water not more than ½ mile distant to the westward, which we must have passed very near to about 9 PM. The master found 6 feet upon this afterwards. Sent a boat away to sound, kill seals &c. The other cutter employed landing the scientific gentlemen to examine the island, and the commander to survey and take astronomical observations.[1]

Carpenters employed putting new timbers into the main top and otherwise securing it. Sailmakers repairing the main sail; and the people improving the stowage of the booms, for snugness and beating winds. Noon, moderate breezes and fine.

Meridian altitude ☉ Lower Limb 483   69°39′45″N
Latitude   33°40′57″S
From the sea horizon same place

		By log		Latitude South		Longitude East					
Course	Distance	DR	Obs	DR	TK	Var allowed	Set or current	Ther	Barom	Error of TK
S8°E	8	33°43′	33°41′	135°14′	134°47′	–	2N	67½°	30.04	1′44″E
							–	67½°	30.05	
								68°	30.08	

Additional remarks
I found the island x [Flinders Island] to consist of a basis of granite covered to a considerable thickness with calcarious stone; but between these was a stratum of grit or sand stone, in some places twenty feet thick: the sand of the beaches consists of this and of calcarious sand mixed together. The vegetation of this island is different from that of the other islands in the archipelago which we here visited, the lower parts being covered with bushes of considerable height. Very little of that small kind of Botany Bay greens under which the petrels burrow, or of the tufted wiry grass in which the geese delight, is seen here; yet the island is little better than a bed of sand upon a granite basis.

After taking the altitudes for the longitude, I walked to the highest part at the NE end of the island. Many small kangaroos were started in the lower parts, and during the day I killed five of them whose size was nearly that of a cat. From the hill I distinguished an island z,[2] bearing 217°30′, distant about four leagues. It appeared to be two or three miles

---

[1] Robert Brown provides detailed notes on the soil, flora and fauna and animals of Flinders Island: see ibid., pp. 132–4.

[2] One of the Pearson Islands (33°57′S, 134°15′E), the SW and outermost of the Investigator Group. Ibid., p. 135; *Sailing Directions (Enroute): North, West, and South Coasts of Australia*, p. 167.

in length and two peaks upon it seemed to be sufficiently high to produce a run of water from them to the low land, and water is an article of which we are now in want. A smaller island and rock y[1] and y1,[2] at the distance of eight or nine miles were visible to the SWbW and off the west side of this island were lying two patches of breakers, besides those that run off to some distance from the NW and western points.

This island x [Flinders Island] forms bays on every side, but those on the east and west sides as well as that on the north-west have many breakers and much shoal water about them: [f. 147] this bay on the north side affords good shelter from all southerly winds.[3] We examined over a considerable space of the island for water, but our nearest approach to success was in finding dried-up swamps; and in these the vegetation was all tinged of a red colour, whence I think that the water had been brackish. Small wood for fuel might with much difficulty be picked out from the largest bushes.

The boats crews killed several seals which were all of the hair kind and found upon the beaches. Families of these animals were usually lying asleep every two or three hundred yards, each consisting of a male, four or five females, and as many young ones. Some of these last were almost as large as the mother who was lying asleep before them and at whose teats they were sucking. I approached several of them very closely, unobserved and without disturbing their domestic tranquillity.

I did not make any observation upon the tide here, having much other business to occupy my time and the rise appearing to be as inconsiderable as we have hitherto found it along the south coast.

Sunday 14 February

Fresh breezes with fine weather. Several seals and small kangaroos brought on board by the boats crews, and the parties from the shore. At sunset, sent down top gallant yards and veered to a whole cable. AM Moderate breezes with cloudy weather. At 5 *hours* 30′ we weighed and made sail, with the intention of beating round this x [Flinders Island] and up to z island [one of the Pearson Islands], to search for water, as well as that the wind did not permit us to proceed with the examination of the coast.

In passing by the north-east point of x [Flinders Island], the water shoaled very quick to 5 fathoms, but deepened again to 13, as quickly. At 7 *hours* 25′ tacked ship, but instead of weathering the island x we could scarcely have fetched back to our last ⚓age,[4] the winds having been light and baffling: the weather fine but hazy. At 8 *hours* 30′ tacked to the eastward. At 10 *hours* 15′ tacked to the southwestward. Mustered the ships company and saw them clean as usual on this day, after cleaning and airing the ship well below. At noon, light breezes and fine weather. Our former anchorage now bore south about two miles, which distance we have lost since getting under weigh, owing to the baffling winds and the ship being now light. Tacked ship again to the eastward.

Mer*idian* alt*itude* ☉ Low*e*r Lim*b* 483	69°22′21″
Latitude	33°38′13″

---

[1] One of the Ward Islands (33°45′S, 134°15′E), comprising two islets. Cooper, *The Unknown Coast*, p. 135.

[2] Ibid.

[3] This is now known as Flinders Bay (on Flinders Island). Vallance, Moore and Groves, eds, *Nature's Investigator*, p. 132.

[4] On the north side of Flinders Island.

By log		Latitude South		Longitude East						
Course	Distance	DR	Obs	DR	TK	Var allowed	Set or current	Ther	Barom	Error of TK
N78°E	3½	33°40′	33°38′	135°18′	134°47′	–	2N	68°	30.09	2′36″E
							3W	65°	30.09	3′55″
								65°	30.12	

[f. 148] **Monday 15 February**

Fresh breezes and fine weather. On the ships lying higher up, kept stretching on, and passed to the southward of island u [now East Island] and point M [McLachlan Point] at 4 o clock. At 4 hours 30′ the cliffy shore distant 3 or 4 miles: tacked ship and double reefed the topsails. At 6, tacked back not being able to weather the rocks which lie off the small high island w [one of the Top-Gallant Islands]. At 8, tacked again towards w. Fresh breezes and fine weather. Passed to windward of w and the rocks, and stretched on until 12, at which time we wore ship, having missed stays. Moderate breezes and cloudy weather. At 4, tacked ship to seaward in order to be ready for the sea breeze from the southward, with which we might make a good stretch along the main coast. At 5 hours 40′ Isle w N68°N 6 miles. Furthest visible land E20°S. Let the 2nd reefs out of the topsails. Tacked ship on the wind coming ahead. A cluster of rocky islands near z [one of the Pearson Islands] from West to N77°W. At noon, moderate breezes and fine weather. Saw land to the south-eastward, supposed to be islands.

Meridian altitude ☉ Lower Limb 483   68°10′54″N
Latitude   33°59′20″S

By log		Latitude South		Longitude East						
Course	Distance	DR	Obs	DR	TK	Var allowed	Set or current	Ther	Barom	Error of TK
S44°E	22	33°54′	33°59′	135°36′	135°0′	–	5S	66°	30.14	3′27″E
							5W	65°	30.16	
								66°	30.13	

Additional remarks

The uncertainty of finding water on the island z [one of the Pearson Islands], or an ⚓ ing place, appeared to be such that so soon as I saw a prospect of being able to prosecute the examination of the main, the intention I had formed of visiting the island was superseded. The small spots of land in the neighbourhood of z may be either all one island or a cluster of very small islands. I incline to the latter opinion, but in the chart they are represented as we saw them.

[f. 149] **Tuesday 16 February**

Moderate breezes and fine weather high land appearing on the lee bow. Many smokes rising from the land ahead and to leeward. At 4 a small isle, &.[1] bore N33°E, 5 miles, and land was seen from the deck as far as S30°E. Being only 3 miles from the land at 6, tacked ship to seaward: a projection N, bearing S13°E about 5 miles: rocky isle &. N40°W. At 8,

[1] Rocky Island (34°16′S, 135°15′E) is about 3½ miles offshore. *Sailing Directions (Enroute): North, West, and South Coasts of Australia*, p. 168.

shortened sail on the wind permitting us to lie along the shore. A heavy dew falling. At 8 brought to on the larboard tack until daylight, the wind being light and weather fine. At 4 *hours* 30′ filled, keeping up for the land which bore N11°E to S12°W. At 5 *hours* 30′ set the main sail, staysails &c. and steered along the shore for a bay which appears ahead, O,[1] the outer cape bearing SWbS at 6 *hours* 30′ and a small islet N4°E 5 or 6 miles. Light breezes and fine weather. At 8 *hours* 30′ the water became so shoal on the east side of the bay that we hauled the wind for the other side; and the water continuing very shoal we tacked at 8 *hours* 50′ to the northward: and at this time we saw shoal water all round at the head of this bay. Saw natives on the west side of the bay, and others upon the hills on the east side.

Lime juice and sugar served daily as usual, and sour krout and vinegar three times a week. At 10 *hours* 30′ tacked ship into the bay and at noon tacked back, working to the westward round cape O [Point Sir Isaac] which now bore N66°W. A sandy projection in the bay dist*ant* 2′ or 3′ to the south.[2]

| Mer*idian* alt*itude* ☉ Lower Lim*b* 483 | 67°51′18″N |
| Latitude | 34°28′26″S |

		By log		Latitude South		Longitude East						
Course	Distance	DR	Obs	DR	TK	Var allowed	Set or current	Ther	Barom	Error of TK
S40°E	44	34°33′	34°28′	136°10′	135°32′	1E	5N 7W	68° 67° 69°	30.08 29.96 30.00	4′18″E

Additional remarks

The weather being sufficiently clear this afternoon to give us a general sight of the land from point M [McLachlan Point] to the extreme set from island u [now East Island] as there appeared to be no bight or inlet of any kind in it, I did not think it worthwhile to run to leeward to examine it more minutely, but fetch as far along the coast to the southward as we could.

The small rocky island marked e [Isle St Francis] lies 4 or 5 miles off the coast and about 3 leagues to the northward of N point.[3] The other rocky islet lies 5 or 6′ north of N [Mount Greenly] and 3 or 4 from the nearest shore. The east side of the great bay rises from the sandy shore, suddenly, to hills of a considerable height which are well covered with wood; but cape O [Point Sir Isaac] and the west side of the bay, which proved to be a peninsula of land,[4] is rather low and very sandy.[5]

---

[1] Point Sir Isaac, the most northerly point of Coffin Bay (34°27′S, 135°18′E). In 1814 Flinders named it after Admiral Sir Isaac Coffin (1759–1839), who had been resident commissioner at Sheerness and 'had taken so zealous a part in the outfit of the *Investigator*'. Bearing Book, entry for 15 February 1802, f. 47; Vallance, Moore and Groves, eds, *Nature's Investigator*, p. 135; Flinders, *A Voyage to Terra Australis*, I, p. 127 (quotation).

[2] Refers to a sandy peninsula on the west side of the bay.

[3] Mount Greenly (34°21′S, 135°22′E). Named after Sir Isaac Coffin's fiancée. Flinders, *A Voyage to Terra Australis*, I, p. 128.

[4] The Coffin Peninsula.

[5] Rough Journal, I, f. 337, adds: 'The wind blowing almost along shore during the night we kept our situation and had a large bay open before us in the morning. Three natives were seen round a fire under the trees, a little

[f. 150] **Wednesday 17 February**

Light breezes with fine pleasant weather, the water very smooth. At 3, tacked ship and at 5 *hours* 30', being taken aback, trimmed sails accordingly and steered for O [Point Sir Isaac] the outer point of this bay. At 6 *hours* 30' we passed the point with soundings as per column. At dusk the furthest part of the main bore S10°W and two islands in the offing S56°W.[1] Hauled up along the shore keeping nearly parallel to it until 12 when we brought to. Light breezes and cloudy weather with haze: a heavy dew falling. Finding the ship drawing nigh to the island α[2] in the offing, filled, and at 3 tacked ship towards the main. At 5 *hours* 40', P,[3] a point to the southward of O being distant 2 miles, tacked ship: this is the furthest land seen bore S 59°E a little after tacking. Isle x [Flinders Island] S60°W. At 7 *hours* 25' tacked back towards the land on seeing that the main trends to the eastward from P [Point Whidbey], forming a bay on its east side.

At 10, P bore N76°W Q[4] a low point S49°E and mount N [Mount Greenly] on the east side of the bay of yesterday, bore N21°E over the sandy neck: tacked ship towards the small islands in the offing, of which there are several. Got two carronades down into the afterhold, which had stood near the binnacle and were thought to have affected the compasses. At noon, moderate breezes and fine weather. Tacked ship towards the main land, several small islands near us, of which the highest, which lies most in the offing, β,[5] bore W13°N. P point [Point Whidbey] N1°W. Isle β [one of the Whidbey Islands] E4°N 1½ mile distant.[6]

Meri*dian* alt*itude* ☉ Lowe*r Lim*b 483	67°15'16"N
Latitude	34°43'13"S
Supp*lemen*t U*pper Lim*b	112°11'44"S
Latitude	34°43'13"S
Mean	34°43'29"S

	By log		Latitude South		Longitude East						
Course	Distance	DR	Obs	DR	TK	Var allowed	Set or current	Ther	Barom	Error of TK
S5°W	21½	34°49'	34°43'	136°9'	135°26'	1E	6N	71°	30.08	5'8"E
							5W	68°	29.96	6'42"
								66½°	30.00	

Additional remarks

From the variety of smokes seen in the bay, and from the natives who appeared on both sides, it should seem that this part of the coast is more thickly inhabited than that which

---

way up the hills but they did not appear to attend to the ship. The country on the east side of the bay is hilly and well wooded, on the west side it is lower & consists of rocks and sand.'

[1] The Whidbey Islands. (34°44'S, 135°08'E). Vallance, Moore and Groves, eds, *Nature's Investigator*, p. 136.

[2] Greenly Island (34°38'S, 134°47'E). Cooper, *The Unknown Coast*, p. 135.

[3] Point Whidbey (34°35'S, 135°08'E). Named after his friend, Joseph Whidbey, the master attendant at Sheerness. Flinders, *A Voyage to Terra Australis*, I, p. 128.

[4] Point Avoid (34°40'S, 135°19'E). Named thus because it was exposed to dangerous southern winds. Ibid., I, p. 129; Cooper, *The Unknown Coast*, p. 135.

[5] One of the Whidbey Islands.

[6] This entry in the journal shows that Flinders was repeatedly trying to steer towards the shore against a south-easterly wind.

we have hitherto passed.[1] Pieces of shallow water, such as the head of this bay seems to be, does indeed afford them more subsistence than an open coast, for fish is the principal support of the greater number of the present known inhabitants of New Holland and upon bays, the entrances of rivers, and the borders of lagoons, they have always hitherto been found most numerous. The point O [Point Sir Isaac] has a basis of granite covered with a calcarious crust, similar to the islands of Nuyts Archipelago. At its extremity is a small bay which would afford shelter from winds between SE and west.[2] The islands in the offing [the Whidbey Islands] appear to be mostly granite, though all are not, and these are the highest and peaked.

Having at different times found a disagreement between bearings and azimuths taken on different tacks, which I thought might be occasioned by the two guns that stood upon the quarter deck near the binnacle, they were removed this morning into the hold. I have sometimes fluctuated in opinion between this being the cause, or the neighbouring land; having found the disagreements greater amongst D'Entrecasteauxs Archipelago and now within these few days than at other times, or I have thought so.[3]

[f. 151] **Thursday 18 February**[4]
Fresh breezes with hazy weather. Passed close to the leeward of isle β [one of the Whidbey Islands]. At 2, tacked ship, island γ[5] bearing S55°E 1 mile, and the main land distant 2 miles. Passed to windward of β, which was a little to windward of us when we tacked at noon. At 4, tacked back towards the main and weathered γ [one of the Whidbey Islands] and δ[6] islands: these 3 are calcarious. At 6 *hours* 30′ the main land was only one mile distant, and the furthest extreme seen through the haze bore S40°E. Tacked ship to seaward and double reefed the top sails.

Fresh breezes. Tried to tack at 12, but there being a disagreeable short swell running, the ship missed stays and we wore. At 2, saw a small island NW½N. Tacked ship to the southward, let out 2nd reefs and set staysails. At daylight, our situation was nearly the same as at 6 PM. Passed to the leeward of a patch of breakers, which at 7 *hours* 15′ had borne S60°E 1½ or 2 miles. Washed and cleaned the ship below, and aired with stoves. Mustered the ships company and saw them all clean as usual on this day and Sunday, when particular duty does not intervene. At 11 *hours* 40′ tacked ship towards the main land, which was only seen partially through the haze, and bearing about east. No islands are in sight, being obscured by the haze.

Meri*dian* alt*itude* ☉ Lowe*r* Limb 483	66°35′36″N
Latitude	35°2′29″S
Supp*lement* ☉ Upper Lim*b*	112°50′56″S
Latitude	35°1′29″S
Mean	35°1′59″S

[1] Flinders, *A Voyage to Terra Australis*, *Atlas*, south coast, sheet 3, notes that natives were seen near Mount Greenly.

[2] Ironically, this is known as Avoid Bay.

[3] Flinders's findings on the causes of the compass variations are set out in an appendix to *A Voyage to Terra Australis*, II, pp. 512–15.

[4] Off the southern Eyre Peninsula.

[5] One of the Whidbey Islands.

[6] One of the Whidbey Islands.

		By log		Latitude South		Longitude East					
Course	Distance	DR	Obs	DR	TK	Var allowed	Set or current	Ther	Barom	Error of TK	
S35°E	26	35°4′	35°2′	136°27′	135°33′	1E	2N	68°	30.38	5′59″E	
							11W	66°	30.10	7′24″	
								68°	30.05		

Additional remarks

The part of the main, off which we have been working the whole of this day, is that peninsulated piece of land between the large shoal bay of yesterday and the sea to the southward. From P [Point Whidbey] the land runs eastward and afterwards by a northerly curve a bight is formed in the peninsula which at first promised shelter.[1] The peninsula is only a ridge of sandy land, rather low upon the shore, but from Q [Point Avoid] where, after curving out another bight,[2] the shore trends more southerly, the land becomes higher; and in this part there are large fields of a yellow colour which have no vegetation upon them, but whether of rock or sand I cannot tell.

In observing the meridional altitude of the sun or any other celestial object both to the north and south, I see many advantages over a single observation, more especially when the weather is hazy and the horizontal refraction much exceeds that allowed in the dip tables; for in this as well as in the errors of the glasses, and indeed of the observer, the errors in the observation on one side correct those of the other; the other errors of the instrument also, whether arising from incorrectness in the center work, or in the line of collimation[3] of the telescope will nearly balance if the suns altitude is great. The only necessary corrections to obtaining the latitude from such observations are the refraction and parallax, and to take the mean of the results.[4]

[f. 152] Friday 19 February

Moderate breezes and hazy weather. Many albatrosses seen today: an unusual thing. At 9 tacked ship, the land being about 4 miles distant and tolerably high with whitish cliffs facing the sea. At 4 hours 40′ tacked back towards the land. At 7, tacked off shore: the furthest visible part of the main (R)[5] S71°E and land which appears to be an island (ε)[6] S44°E. Some breakers are distant 2 miles to the E10°S. Fine weather with haze: a heavy dew falling. At 1, tacked ship, but finding the wind to come ahead, tacked again towards the land at 3 o'clock. Light airs and fine weather: a swell running from the southward. No land seen at daylight. Nearly calm until 10, when a breeze sprung up. Tacked ship to the eastward, set studding sails and steered towards R [Cape Wiles] and the island ε [Liguanea

---

[1] The peninsula is between Cape Carnot and Cape Wiles.

[2] Sleaford Bay (34°54′S, 135°46′E).

[3] i.e.the accurate adjustment of the line of sight of a telescope.

[4] Atmospheric refraction and parallax of altitude can increase or diminish the calculated latitude.

[5] Cape Wiles (34°57′S, 135°41′E). Named after the botanist on the *Providence*. Flinders, *A Voyage to Terra Australis*, I, p. 131; Scott, *The Life of Matthew Flinders*, p. 340.

[6] In 1814 Flinders named it Liguanea Island (35°00′S, 135°37′E) after a place in Jamaica which became a botanical garden and received plants from Bligh's second breadfruit expedition on which Flinders had been a midshipman. Vallance, Moore and Groves, eds, *Nature's Investigator*, p. 138.

Island]. Cleaned below and aired with stoves. Employed clearing out the bread room in which was found a leak, and some bread damaged from it. At noon, light breezes with fine weather, but much haze. The land seen indistinctly from the mast head, to the eastward.

Meridian altitude ☉ Lower Limb 483   66°10′15″N
Latitude   35°6′44″S

By log		Latitude South		Longitude East						
Course	Distance	DR	Obs	DR	TK	Var allowed	Set or current	Ther	Barom	Error of TK
S35°E	12½	35°12′	35°7′	136°36′	135°39′	1E	5N 3W	69° 67° 69°	30.00 29.90 29.92	6′50″E

Additional remarks

The coast seen this afternoon is eight or ten miles to the southward of the yellow land mentioned yesterday: it is moderately high near the water, to which it generally presents a cliffy front. From the strata observable on these cliffs I judge them to be calcarious, as I believe all those of the main from the cape P [Point Whidbey] are as well as the isles β [one of the Whidbey Islands], γ [one of the Whidbey Islands], δ [another of the Whidbey Islands] which lie very near. The furthest extreme yet seen slopes off to a low projecting part, in this point of view; and the island which lies off it (ε) [Liguanea Island] is low and sloping also; but the haziness of the weather prevents us from distinguishing accurately to any considerable distance.

[f. 153] Saturday 20 February

Light breezes and fine weather, with a long swell from the south-westward. Took in studding sails and first reefs, hauled to the wind, and at 2 hours 40′ tacked ship, there being breakers not far distant to leeward. At 4, the wind fresher. Tacked to the eastward and weathered the breakers and the isle ε [Liguanea Island] to which they belong. At 5, kept away to look behind R [Cape Wiles] which in this view is a steep head. At 6 hours 30′ R bore N15°E and S,[1] the furthest visible part of the main E8°N. Hauled up to the wind, it being too late to look into the bight between these two projections. Light winds. Wore ship off shore, but the wind heading, we were not able to weather the isle ε, therefore at 1 hour 35′ tacked ship working off the bight ready to examine it in the morning. At 4, moderate breezes. Saw breakers on the lee bow and tacked ship immediately. At 5, tacked back and weathered the breakers. Not being able to see up into the head of the bight, at 6 hours 30′ bore away to run into it hoping to find shelter; but we soon saw there was no opening of any kind or any security for anchorage, and therefore hauled the wind to the SW until nine, when hoping the ship would weather the cape S [Cape Catastrophe] we tacked; but the wind failing we were obliged to wear at 11 and stretch further off. At noon, light breezes and fine weather. S, a peaked hill upon the western part of the cape (Cape Catastrophe afterwards) bore N73°E η,[2] an island lying off S N84°E and the island ε N79°W.

[1] Cape Catastrophe (34°59′S, 136°00′E).
[2] Williams Island (35°02′S, 135°58′E). Flinders, A Voyage to Terra Australis, I, p. 131; Cooper, The Unknown Coast, p. 135.

Meridian altitude ☉ Lower Limb 483   65°53′62″
Latitude   35°2′34″S

	By log	Latitude South		Longitude East						
Course	Distance	DR	Obs	DR	TK	Var allowed	Set or current	Ther	Barom	Error of TK
N88°E	20	35°6′	35°3′	137°0′	136°3′	1E	3N –	69° 68°	29.98 29.86	7′42″E

Additional remarks

The island ε [Liguanea Island] lies 2 or 3 miles off the cape R [Cape Wiles], and the breakers stretch off from the western side of the island: R is a steep cape in its south-east part, but its southwestern part is low: two high rocks and a further lower one lie off this cape. The bight on its east side seems to afford shelter from winds which do not blow from the south or eastward between SSW and NE but a long swell would roll in during a south-westerly gale. The back land, though not high, yet appears to be sufficiently so to promise fresh water to those who should dig in the lower parts, and it was our present want of this essential article that induced me to bear away into the bight, at some hazard, but not further than we had a good prospect of lying out again; for the recess of the sun to the northward is a constant monitor to us not to lose even one day in vain whilst so much of the unknown part of this coast remains before us. The coast eastward from R is not altogether so sandy as on its west side and in some spots about the hills there are some scattered trees.

[f. 154] **Sunday 21 February**

Light breezes and fine weather. At 1, tacked ship expecting to weather the cape S [Cape Catastrophe]. At 3, it bore N48½E 3 or 4 miles, and we could now pass to windward of the island η [Williams Island], but seeing a passage between it and the cape, at 3 hours 45′ bore away for it. Found the passage to be two miles wide but although the water was deep there was much rippling of tide in it. Round the east part of S, we found the shore trend N15°W and five other islands open off from it.[1] Steered to the north end of a more eastern piece of land, passing though much rippling, with unequal soundings. At 6, dropped the anchor in 3½ fathoms, weighed the anchor again, stood out into 7 fathoms and then let it go upon a bottom of grey sand. The north-east extreme of this uncertain land E by N 1¼ mile, from whence there is nothing in sight to the NE or round to the main at NbN½W: to the westward and southward we are moderately well sheltered by the main and islands. Furled sails and sent down top-gallant yards. AM Squally weather at times. Boats employed loading the scientific gentlemen to examine this uncertain land, and the commander to survey and inspect the neighbouring parts from the hills.

This day is continued to 36 hours, or civil account.

Moderate breezes with fine weather. Sent the master Mr. Thistle over to the main land to search for water. At 7, the boat was seen returning, but suddenly missed, upon which lieutenant Fowler was sent in another boat to look after her. At 9½, fired again, and soon

---

[1] They included Taylor's Island, Grindal's Island and Smith's Island. Flinders, *A Voyage to Terra Australis*, *Atlas*, south coast, sheet 3.

after the last boat returned without any intelligence of the other boat, but had near been swamped herself amongst the strong ripplings of tide.

Upon the north side of the Uncertain Island[1]

Mer*idian* alt*itude* ☉ Lowe*r Limb* No 483	65°38′18″N
Latitude	34°55′55″S

	By log		Latitude South		Longitude East						
Course	Distance	DR	Obs	DR	TK	Var allowed	Set or current	Ther	Barom	Error of TK
N74°E	15	34°59′	34°56′	137°18′	136°23′	1E	3N 2E	67° 65° 67°	29.86 29.93 29.94	8′39″E 9′37″

[Additional remarks]

In passing through between the island η [Williams Island] and the point or cape S [Cape Catastrophe], I observed the rock on each side to consist of granite. There is a small bay on each side capable of sheltering small vessels, from most winds.

The uncommon direction of the coast round the eastern part of S, no land being visible to the north-east, and the strength of the tides here all tend to raise interesting conjectures amongst us concerning what we are now to meet with: large rivers, deep inlets, inland seas, and passages to the Gulph of Carpentaria are the phrases most current in our conversations.[2] From the bottom being very uneven, the strength of the tides, and the shallowness of the water in some parts, our anchorage is not secure; but in a place like this, and with darkness approaching, there is not much time to chuse.

From the cliffs on the northwest part of the uncertain island [Thistle Island], I could see the main, extending to N5°W, but three small islands appeared without it, the outermost which bore N31°E. To the southward also there are three small islands lying a considerable distance out at sea.

On landing in the morning I found the shores were frequented by seals and further on, were numberless marks of kanguroos; these being united with [f. 155] the total want of any marks of men confirmed me in the opinion of its being an island. Some marks of a former fire were visible but from these assuming the same appearance everywhere, I suppose them to have arisen from some general conflagration, which might have been caused by lightening, or by the rubbing of two leaning trees, moved by the wind.

In walking up the hills, a snake of a yellow colour, speckled, lay in our way asleep. By pressing the butt end of a musquet upon his neck he was kept down, and we sewed up his mouth with a needle and thread, and brought it on board alive to the naturalist; but we found he had killed two others of the same species, one of which was seven feet and nine

[1] In 1814 Flinders named this Thistle Island (35°00′S, 136°09′E). It lies on the west side of the entrance to Spencer Gulf, about 4 miles east of Cape Catastrophe. Vallance, Moore and Groves, eds, *Nature's Investigator*, p. 139; *Sailing Directions (Enroute): North, West, and South Coasts of Australia*, p. 172.

[2] Flinders thought that the strength of the tide and the movement of the ship to the north, compared with its previous trend to the east and south, might be indications of a strait's existence. It was commonly believed at the time that New Holland and New South Wales might be separated by a strait, and that they might be two separate land masses. The examination of Spencer Gulf over the next few days showed that this was an incorrect speculation. Scott, *The Life of Matthew Flinders*, p. 152.

inches in length.[1] Some large hawks[2] or rather eagles were seen, and in two instances they advanced to attack us, taking us probably for kanguroos. It should seem that these eagles sit watching upon the trees for their prey, and if the harmless kangaroo should unsuspectingly come out to feed in the day time, in an open space, he is seized and torn to pieces by these voracious birds. This accounts for why we saw so few kanguroos,[3] when the marks of them everywhere exceeded all proportion; and those that were seen kept so much under the thick bushes that it was impossible to shoot them: they were almost as shy as upon the mainland where they are chased by the natives.

The rock of this island consists almost altogether of calcarious stone, but at the height of two hundred or more feet above the water I found many small pieces of granite which were rounded, to all appearance, by attrition in the water.

Besides the kanguroos, which are larger than what we have yet seen upon the islands, we did not find any quadruped. Gulls, sea pies and shags frequent these shores.

It had been my intention to get underweigh immediately after noon, but the observations which lieut*enant* Flinders had taken on board the ship for the longitude, while I was on shore in the morning, giving a different result to what my bearings gave, it became necessary to go on shore again and get others from the artificial horizon; which observation, together with a previous one for the latitude, is before given. This delay made it too late to move before the following morning; but as a great object with us was to procure water, which this uncertain island did not afford in order to forward our business, I sent the master over to the high main land after dinner to search for water, and an anchoring place where we could take it off.[4]

The sudden disappearance of the boat, and the dangerous ripplings of tide that lieut*enant* Fowler found about the place where she was last seen make us fear that she has been upset, or as she was under three lug sails, perhaps capsized over the people, only two of whom, unfortunately, were at all expert in swimming. The tide ran to the southward for an hour and a half after we missed the boat. It is therefore probable that she has drifted to seaward. Had it been daylight, there is no doubt that we should have picked up some or all of the people, but the hallooing and firing of musquets was ineffectual to procure any intelligence of their situation, and it was too dark to see anything. After the last boat had been gone two hours I became anxious for her safety, and fired a gun for her to return: it appeared that my fears had not been groundless, for she had narrowly escaped being swamped in a strong tide rippling.

[f. 156] **Monday 22 February**
Moderate breezes and cloudy weather. At 5 *hours* 30′ weighed the ⚓, and steered towards that part of the main land near which the lost boat was last seen. Saw many patches of rippling and of an uncommonly smooth-looking water; on sending the cutter to sound upon them she found 12 *fatho*ms but nevertheless we hauled to the northward round it all, and then hauled up. Seeing a little beach on the main steered for it, and it was in a nice

---

[1] Probably carpet pythons. Vallance, Moore and Groves, eds, *Nature's Investigator*, p. 139.

[2] Probably white-bellied sea eagles. Ibid., p. 140.

[3] Tammar wallabies. Ibid., p. 139.

[4] Flinders needed water to replenish the ship's casks but he also wanted to remain at this anchorage to repeat survey observations the next morning. Thus, he sent Thistle with a boat and crew to seek an anchorage by the mainland where water might be obtained. Ibid., p. 140.

cove which was open only to the north-eastward, stood into it and anchored in 10½ *fatho*ms sandy bottom, the extremes of the main bearing ESE and N6°W when we had veered to half a cable and several islands lying off to the north-eastward. Sent the cutter away in search of the lost boat and people, and two parties went to walk along the shores upon the same pursuit. The cutter soon returned towing the wreck of the other boat bottom upwards. She was stove all to pieces having to appearance been dashed against the rocks, nothing within side her remaining whole. One oar was afterwards picked up, but nothing was seen of the bodies of the unfortunate people. Sent the cutter away again upon further search and stationed a petty officer upon a head of land with a spyglass to watch everything that might drift past with the tide.[1] Moderate breezes and cloudy weather: at 4 nearly calm, shortened in the cable. At 5, the cutter returned with some small remnants of the boat found to the northward between No. 4 isle[2] and the mainland, but nothing was seen of the officers or people. Cloudy weather.

Additional remarks

The two parties that went to search along the shore were that of the naturalist to the northward and mine to the southward to the extreme of the land, and over to a bay between the two parts of cape S, which now I call Cape Catastrophe, and confine S to the hill on the west part of it; but we were not able to gain any intelligence of our unfortunate shipmates. At the back of the little beach in the cove I found many footsteps of our people, made I presume whilst they were searching here for water before the accident happened. My search to the same purpose in this place was ineffectual, although there were many huts and other marks of natives; [n]or did we find any water in the neighbourhood.

Of the land, I noticed that the basis is granite covered with a crust of calcarious stone. Tall brush wood covers all the northern and eastern sides of the hills, but it is not difficult of penetration. Four small kanguroos were seen, but no natives although I found very recent marks of them. The botanist made some addition to his collection of specimens of new plants.[3]

Tuesday 23 February

Light breezes and cloudy weather. Sighted the anchor and found it to be clear. The commander took the cutter to search for the unfortunate people lost in the boat or for pieces of the wreck, and at the same time to survey the parts to the northward. Variable airs with dull cloudy weather until near noon, when it cleared up and a fresh breeze set in.

Cut up a cask of pork No. 32, contents 53 pieces. About 4 the commander returned, having found nothing more than a small keg which belonged to Mr Thistle, and two broken remnants of the boat. At 8, flurries of wind came off the land which made it necessary to veer to a whole cable and strike top gallant masts.

---

[1] Edwards, ed., *The Journal of Peter Good*, p. 62, states that Robert Fowler found the wrecked cutter off the southern head of Memory Cove.

[2] Taylor Island (34°53′S, 136°01′E). Vallance, Moore and Groves, eds, *Nature's Investigator*, p. 143; Cooper, *The Unknown Coast*, p. 135.

[3] Brown notes that he found about 20 new plants. Vallance, Moore and Groves, eds, *Nature's Investigator*, p. 141.

[f. 157] Additional remarks

In the boat excursion of this day I followed all the little sinuosities of the shore for twelve miles to the northward of the ship, thinking it likely that the bodies of some of our unfortunate companions might be thrown on shore; but we had no success in the pursuit.

From three different stations upon the main I took bearings of the neighbouring lands. The farthest extreme of the main bore from the best station N10°35′E which is point U;[1] but between that and a projection T5[2] which bore N3°20′W three miles, is a space where some of our gentlemen from the highest land near the ship saw some small places of shelter along the coast, and behind the island No. 4 [Taylor Island] there seems to be tolerable ⟨L⟩age.

Wednesday 24 February

Strong breezes until 3 AM when it moderated and the weather became fine. Sent away lieutenant Fowler in the cutter to examine the outer southern islands for the remains of our unfortunate people, but he was not able to land or obtain the least information upon the object of his pursuit. Swayed up top-gallant masts, sent up the yards and hove in the half cable service. Noon, moderate breezes and fine weather. In the evening sent the cutter to haul the seine upon the beach of this little cove [Memory Cove], which she did with such success as to give all the ships company two meals of fish and some to be cured. At sunset, sent down top gallant yards. Moderate with fine weather.

Additional remarks

This afternoon I ascended the highest hill near the ship with a theodolite, whence our gentlemen had seen the water running inland to the westward; it appeared to be a bay or the wide entrance of a river, but I could not trace it further back than to 322° from this station.

About three leagues to the south-eastward of Uncertain Island [Thistle Island] several other small islands were visible, and from this place also I was able to see R [Cape Wiles] and the island η [Williams Island], and the great bight between them and Cape Catastrophe.[3]

The same barrenness of soil prevails upon the whole of these hills that I have before seen. A dry loose covering of calcarious stone usually composes the surface, but in the lower parts much sand is mixed with it; I found, however, some blocks of granite in the highest parts of the hills today.

General remarks

Of the tides near this great cape of New Holland, I calculate that the flood comes from the southward and runs until the time that the moon passes over the meridian. There are two regular tides in twenty-four hours, and the water appears to rise from 6 to 8 feet. I think it probable that the direction of the tide from the southward is influenced by the position of the islands that lie off the cape, and that it may probably run somewhat differently on the eastern side of the uncertain island, probably from the southeastward.

---

[1] Point Bolingbroke (34°33′S, 136°05′E).

[2] A summit west of Memory Cove (34°58′S, 135°59′E). Vallance, Moore and Groves, eds, *Nature's Investigator*, p. 142.

[3] Sleaford Bay. Flinders, *Voyage to Terra Australis*, *Atlas*, south coast, sheet 3.

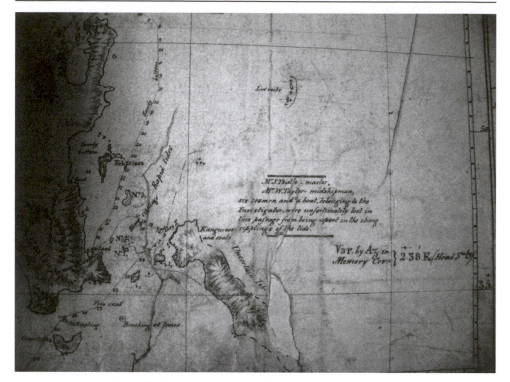

Figure 10.   Matthew Flinders, Chart of Memory Cove, ADM 352/356, detail. Courtesy of the National Archives, Kew.

[f. 158] As every search has now been made for our unfortunate shipmates that we could think had any prospect of being attended with success, I thought it would avail nothing to remain longer on this account; for there was only a small chance of obtaining these bodies when they might rise to the surface, from the number of sharks that we have constantly seen about. Even this small chance of obtaining their bodies would have induced me to wait a few days longer had not the want of water been so pressing to hurry us forward. I caused a stout post to be erected in the Cove, and to it was nailed a sheet of copper upon which was engraven the following inscription

Memory Cove
His Majestys ship *Investigator* Matthew Flinders Commander
Anchored here February 22 1802
Mr John Thistle the master
Mr William Taylor midshipman
and six of the crew were most unfortunately drowned near this
place from being upset in a boat. The wreck of the boat was
found, but their bodies were not recovered.
Nautici cavete![1]

[1] i.e. Sailors, beware! The copper plaque is now on display at the South Australian Maritime Museum. In Memory Cove there is a more recent memorial bearing the same words. To commemorate the loss, Flinders gave to each of the six islands near Cape Catastrophe the name of one of the seamen. Flinders, *A Voyage to Terra Australis*, I, p. 138.

I must take occasion to observe in this place that Mr Thistle was truly a valuable man, as a seaman, an officer, and a good member of society. I have known him since the year 1794, and we have mostly been together since that time. He was constantly one of those employed in the different excursions that were made from Port Jackson for the further discovery of the neighbouring coasts of New Holland; and for his superior merit and prudent conduct was advanced from before the mast to be a midshipman, and afterwards a master in His Majestys service. His zeal in the cause of discovery induced him to join the *Investigator* when at Spithead and ready to sail, although he had returned to England only three weeks before from a distant voyage of six years continuance.[1]

In a voyage like the present, his loss cannot be otherwise than severely felt and he is lamented by all on board, but more especially by his messmates who better know the goodness and stability of his disposition.

Mr Taylor was a young officer who promised to be an ornament to the service from his activity and attention to orders, and to society from the amicability of his manners and temper.

[f. 159] Thursday 25 February
Civil Account

Moderate breezes and cloudy weather. Ships draught of water. Sent the cutter on shore to set up the inscription and in the mean time at 8½ *hours* weighed and stood out of the cove. Hove to for the boat, and on her return hoisted her up. At 11 *hours* 30′ made sail to the northward between isles No. 3[2] and 4 [Taylor Island]. The best bower cable being much chafed at 13 *fathoms* from the clinch,[3] ordered it to be cut off and delivered to the boatswain for junk. At noon, Isle No. 4 [Taylor Island] WNW 1¼ mile. Moderate breezes and fine weather. At 1, hauled round gradually towards the great bay seen from the hills at the back of Memory Cove. At 2½ *hours* passed round T,[4] a peninsula forming the outer south point of entrance and hauled up into the bay. Passed two small islands,[5] and at 3 *hours* 10′ tacked ship, working up to the southern side of the bay.[6] At 3 *hours* 45′ came to an ⚓[7] upon a soft bottom of grey sand, being land-locked from N9°E, round by the west and south, to N38E, and one of the two islands occupying half the open space. Sent the cutter to sound round the ship, and on shore to dig for water at the foot of the hill T [Stamford Hill]. She saw many natives huts on shore, and dug a hole, but salt water flowed into it.

---

[1] Flinders and Thistle had served together on the voyage of the *Reliance* to Sydney in 1795 and also during the *Norfolk*'s circumnavigation of Van Diemen's Land and the survey run to Moreton Bay and Hervey Bay in 1799. Several months later Flinders wrote to his wife that 'it will grieve thee, as it has me, to understand that poor Thistle was lost upon the south coast. Thou knowest how I valued him; he is however gone.' Vallance, Moore and Groves, eds, *Nature's Investigator*, p. 141; NMM, Flinders Papers, FLI/25, Flinders to Ann Flinders, 31 May 1802.

[2] Wedge Island (35°10′S, 136°28′E). Bearing Book, entry for 24 February 1802, f. 55. This is the largest island among the Gambier Islands Group, situated between the tips of the Eyre and Yorke Peninsulas.

[3] i.e. a bolt.

[4] Stamford Hill (about 34°47′S, 135°56′E). Vallance, Moore and Groves, eds, *Nature's Investigator*, p. 145.

[5] One was Grantham Island (34°47′S, 135°52′E).

[6] Flinders later named this harbour Port Lincoln (34°43′S, 135°56′E) 'in honour of my native province'. Flinders, *A Voyage to Terra Australis*, 1, p. 142.

[7] Just west of Surfleet Point (34°46′S, 135°57′E). Vallance, Moore and Groves, eds, *Nature's Investigator*, p. 144.

Mr Thomas Evans masters mate, having done the duty of master since the loss of Mr Thistle, gave him an order to continue until further orders.

Meri*dian* alt*itude* ☉ Lowe*r Limb* No 483   64°14′6″

Latitude   34°52′32″S

Friday 26 February

Moderate breezes and cloudy weather. Sent the gig to examine a larger island in the NE part of the bay for water. Boats employed landing the naturalists to examine the country, and the commander to inspect into the bay from the hill T [Stamford Hill] and to take bearings. A lake was discovered to the westward about two miles from the head of this bay.[1] The boats being returned and the flood tide made at 10 *hours* 30′, weighed and steered up the bay with soundings as per column, and soft bottom, keeping nearest to the northern shore.

At noon, light breezes and fine weather. Saw many smokes at the head of the bay. Steered different courses occasionally to find the deepest water. At 1¼ *hour* we came to an anchor, finding we could not get higher up, in 3¾ *fatho*ms soft bottom; being about ¾ of a mile from the southern shore and 1½ mile from the head of the bay.

Took the cutter to examine the lake, in company with the naturalist, but it was found to be brackish and the way to it too stony to roll casks over. On digging in the lower parts about 100 yards from the beach at the head of the bay we found fresh water; there being a white clay about 3 feet under the surface at which the water lodged.

	By log	Latitude South		Longitude East						
Course	Distance	DR	Obs	DR	TK	Var allowed	Set or current	Ther	Barom	Error of TK
N47°W from Uncertain I*s*land	10	34°50′	34°48′	136°14′	136°9½′	2E	2N 5W	66° 67° 67°	30.20 30.11 30.15	12′47″E

Additional remarks

The land from the head of the bay to the lake is low, and covered with loose calcarious stones. Whence it is that the water in this lake is not fresh I can scarcely conjecture. Its shores consist of a white hardened clay covered, at the dry time, with a thin crust, in which salt is a component part. The length of the lake to the SSW is two or three miles and its greatest breadth half as much. That we find water so abundantly in this dry season, where there are no hills of considerable eminence in the neighbourhood is materially different from what our experience in New Holland led us to expect. I think it may be attributed to the consistence of the substratum which is whitish clay, below which the water does not penetrate, but either runs into the sea in that parallel or it lodges in lakes.[2]

[1] Sleaford Mere (about 34°50′S, 135°44′), named by Flinders. Westall drew Sleaford Mere. Ibid., p. 145; Perry and Simpson, *Drawings by William Westall*, no. 15. For an online version of the picture, see http://nla.gov.au/nla-pic-an4561807.

[2] There is a description and illustrations of the evaporitic carbonates of Sleaford Mere (derived from ground water, not infiltrating sea water) in Warren, *Evaporites*, pp. 222–3.

[f. 160] **Saturday 27 February**

Moderate breezes and fine weather. Sent a party of people on shore with spades to dig a long hole at which to water the ship; sent also the timekeepers, astronomical instruments and two tents on shore under the charge of lieut*enant* Flinders. Moored ship a cable each way, hoisted out the launch, and sent a raft of empty casks on shore. Some clear fine water being found to drain through the beach, a hole was dug at high water mark, into which the fresh water flowed, but on digging a little deeper it became salt and we found it necessary to return to the first hole, although the water was thick and white, but well tasted: this hole is about a hundred yards behind the beach near the head of the bay. PM Sent another raft of empty water casks on shore, and the gunners with a party to fill them. Employed on board in the main hold. Light breezes.

Sunday 28 February

Thick hazy weather until sunrise, when the haze dispersed. Light breezes and fair. A cutter employed by the Commander in surveying the bay. Received 17 puncheons of water from the tents. Employed putting provisions into the after hold and stowing water in the main hold, all the empty casks being now out of the ship. At noon, light breezes and fine weather. Received another raft of water casks from the tents. In the evening, the boats being returned, hoisted them up as usual, the launch excepted.

Additional remarks

In the boat excursion of this day I steered from the ship towards the high hill on the north side of the bay, the water shoaling gradually until we passed over the end of a spit from the NW part of the head of the bay, when it deepened again to thirteen feet.

The hill afforded a good view of the bay and islands, and of the lake; a small lake also was conspicuous on the south side of the bay below the ship, which had the same white salt-like appearance surrounding it. Some hills, which seemed to be those near Mount N [Mount Greenly], were visible to the north-westward, and one which might be the mount itself bore 306° yellow land, like that of the sea coast mentioned on the 18th and 19th, was seen bearing 270°15′.

From the shore under the hill we steered between the small isle (No. 3 of this bay [Wedge Island]) and the low point of the middle land, the passage being shoal and the bottom sandy; but from thence towards the large island in the lower part of the bay the water soon deepened to 7 fathoms. I ascended the highest part of the large island, but the trees and brushwood were so thick as to obstruct the view in every direction. I had left orders on board to fire three guns upon my making a signal from this place, and had provided a half second pendulum of 1.8 inches in length to measure the interval between the flash and report of the guns for the purpose of obtaining a base line to my survey, but was entirely disappointed.

From the west side of the large island we sounded in 9, 8, 7, 6 and 5 fathoms to the ships track up the bay, so that the channel out at the back of the island may not be the deepest.

Monday 1 March

Light airs and calms. Received two rafts of water, which employed us on board in stowing away. Noon, sultry weather with haze. Received another raft of water from the tents and stowed it away in the holds. At such times as the pitts[1] require to be left to replenish themselves, a part of the people on shore are employed cutting fire wood. In the evening, variable weather.

[f. 161] Additional remarks

Mr Brown and a party visited the large lake today;[2] they found that where we had supposed it to terminate there was a branching off into two parts, each of which runs to within a hundred yards of the sea in the bight on the east side of cape R [Cape Wiles].[3] They saw a boats sail and yard floating near the shore in that bight, belonging no doubt to our wrecked cutter: no other fragments were seen.

Tuesday 2 March

Light breezes, with calms and hazy weather. A cutter employed by the Commander in surveying the bay. Employed as before in watering the ship. At noon, moderate breezes with thick hazy weather until the evening, when it became clearer.[4]

Additional remarks

My expedition this day in the boat was again directed to the large island near the bottom of the harbour.[5] I counted 85 swings of a half-second pendulum between the flash and report of three different guns, allowing 1″ = 1142 feet and 6060 feet = a geographical mile, which makes the difference to be 8.01 miles.[6] Afterwards by the time-keepers and the angles taken on shore I made it something more than 8 miles.

This island appears to consist wholly of granite, scarcely any other calcarious stone has been seen upon it in two visits. Some marks of former fires were visible upon the fallen wood, and that which we made as a signal to the ship for firing the three guns was burning furiously and has spread over great part of the island before dark.

Wednesday 3 March

Light breezes and cloudy weather. Received the greater part of the remaining water casks from the tents and stowed them away, as also some firewood. Sent lieutenant Fowler in the cutter out of the bay and round to Memory Cove and the neighbouring islands in search of the bodies of our unfortunate shipmates, the boat being armed and provided for two days. Fresh breezes until the evening, when the wind became light: weather cloudy.

Thursday 4 March

Light airs with dull cloudy weather and rain. Received on board and stowed away the remaining part of our water casks, completing the holds to sixty tons. Ships draught of

---

[1] They had dug shallow wells on the beach, and had to wait for groundwater to replenish them.

[2] Sleaford Mere.

[3] It should be noted that in this journal Flinders only allotted 14 names to features of the shores of South Australia, whereas *A Voyage to Terra Australis* and the accompanying charts, published in 1814, provide a list of 140 coastal features. Cooper, *The Unknown Coast*, pp. 42, 134.

[4] Rough Journal, I, f. 364, adds: 'I found the soundings about the bay to run tolerably regular in this day's excursion, from 4 fathoms near the shores to 9 fathoms in the deepest.'

[5] Boston Island (34°42′S, 135°56′E). Vallance, Moore and Groves, eds, *Nature's Investigator*, p. 148.

[6] This calculation can be explained as follows: $85 \times 1 \div 2 \times 1142 = 48{,}535$ feet $\div 6{,}060$ feet $= 8.00$ miles. A geographical mile is equal to one minute of arc of longitude along the Equator, or 6,087.08 feet.

water *Fore* 13 *feet* 10 *inches Aft* 13 *feet* 8 *inches*. Cloudy weather with spitting rain at times until a little before noon, when it cleared up and enabled me to observe an eclipse of the sun[1] at the tents with a focus and a power of about 200 telescope of 46 inches. The beginning took place at apparent time[2] 1 *hour* 12′ 37.5″ and the end at 3 *hours* 36′ 11.5″. Immediately after the eclipse, brought on board the tents, astronomical instruments &c from the shore: hoisted in the launch and prepared everything ready for going down to the entrance of the bay in the morning. Light breezes and cloudy.

Additional remarks

This morning some natives were heard calling, as we supposed, to a boat which had just then landed at the tents, and two of them were seen at about half a mile from us; but they soon walked away, or perhaps retired into the woods to watch our motions. No attempts were made to follow them, as I have always found of the natives of New Holland that they avoid those that seem anxious to communicate with them, but if left entirely alone will usually come down after having watched our actions four or five days. These are the first natives seen at this place, and no great proportion of huts have been found; but the path which leads round the head of the bay must have been long and frequently trodden to have been so much worn as it is, by naked feet.[3]

[f. 162] Observations of Sun east Moon by *Lieutenant* Flinders with *Sextant* No. 932

	No. of sights	App*arent* time	App*arent* double altitudes		Distance of limbs[4]	Longitude *East*
February 1802			Sun Lower Limb (proportion)	Moon Upper Limb observ*ation*		
26	Six	22h20′48.6″	111°15′05″	48°25′6″	71°13′24″	136° 6′12″
26	Six	26′30.2″	112°56′2″	47°17′27″	10′46″	135°58′13.5″
26	Six	31′12.3″	114°16′22″	46°21′38″	9′45″	56′20.5″
					Mean	136° 0′18″

Mer*idian* altitudes in artificial horiz*on*

Time 1802	Mer*idian* alt*itude* lower limb	Latitude South	Observer
February			
27	64° 5′52″	34°48′34″	Lt Flinders
March			
3	62° 2′45″	48′32″	Lt Flinders
3	62°19′6″ centre	48′21″	Commander
4	61°39′57″ *Lower Limb*	48′22″	Lt Flinders
	Mean	34°48′27″ south	

[1] Flinders and his crew observed a 97 per cent partial eclipse from what is now Port Lincoln. http://eclipse.gsfc.nasa.gov/SENL/SENL200403.pdf. Further details of this solar eclipse are presented in CUL, RGO 14/68, Royal Greenwich Observatory, Board of Longitude Papers, f. 81r.

[2] Apparent solar time is the calculation of time based on the relative position of the sun.

[3] Flinders's experience of the shyness of the Aborigines led to his observation that they would have approached his party if he had waited a few more days. Flinders, *A Voyage to Terra Australis*, I, p. 146.

[4] i.e. edge or border.

Result of observations for the errors and rates of the *Time Keeper*s

Time 1802	Apparent time	Corrected time by E 543	E543 slower than mean time	Comparisons of other *Time Keepers* with 543			Daily rates of the time keepers – Losing				Thermometer
				E520 slower	A176 slower	A1736 faster	E543	E520	A176	A1736	
February 27 Noon		*14h40'18.54"	9h32'53.10"	37'52.3"	40'44.1"	6h21'2.5"	E543	E520	A176	A1736	
28 Noon		39'59.35"	33'1.51"	38'2.9"	40'51.0"	21'3.1"	8.41"	19.01"	15.31"	7.81"	74°
March 1 Noon		39'40.61"	33'8.94"	38'12.0"	45'3.6"	21'3.8"	7.43"	16.53"	4.20.03"	6.73"	78°
2 Noon		39'19.74"	33'18.06"	38'22.9"	Stopped	21'7.2"	9.12"	20.02"	Stopped	5.72"	76°
3 Noon		38'58.75"	33'26.78"	38'33.5"		21'9.8"	8.72"	19.32"		6.12"	76°
4	2h39'31.73"	*17h18'8.02"	33'34.98"	38'44.6"		21'16.1"	7.33"	19.30"		1.90"	72°
				Mean rates			–8.19"	–18.43"		–5.53"	

* Taken by the Commander

The time keepers not being compared with No. 543 exactly at noon will make a trifling difference between the true rates and those put down: No. 543 is the exact daily rate. Some hours before 176 stopped it was heard to make an uncommon noise.

The observations taken in this place for the longitude not being sufficient to be depended upon, I am under the necessity of taking what the time-keepers gave on the first day to be the truth, until others can be taken and reduced back to No. 10 bay.[1] Considering the longitude of the tents then to be 136°8'47.6" as given by the time keepers on the 27th the errors from mean Greenwich time will be found as follows.

	E 543	E520	A1736
Timekeepers slower than the mean time here On March 4th at apparent time 2 *hours* 39'31.73" }	9 *hours* 33'34.98"	10 *hours* 12'19.58"	3 *hours* 12'18.88"
Proportional part of the mean rates to reduce the errors to Greenwich noon on March 4 1802 }	+2.19"	+4.97"	+1.48"
	9 *hours* 33'37.17"	10 *hours* 12'24.55"	3 *hours* 12'20.36"
Longitude in time	9 4'35.17"	9 4'35.17"	9 4'35.17"
March 4th 1802 Greenwich noon	0 *hours* 29' 2.00"	1 *hour* 7'49.38"	5 *hours* 52'14.81"
Time Keepers slower than mean time there			Faster

The rate of No. 1736 is not steady enough to connect its longitude with No 543 and 520

For the variation and dip of the needle: taken on shore

Time 1802 March	No. of sights	Sun's mag. azimuth theodolite	Apparent altitude Sun low limb	Variation deduced	Observer
1	Four	270°15'	16°9'	1°39' East	Commander

---

[1] Port Lincoln (34°43'S, 135°56'E), a large bay between Cape Donington and Boston Point. Cooper, *The Unknown Coast*, p. 48; *Sailing Directions (Enroute): North, West, and South Coasts of Australia*, p. 174.

No observations were taken on shore with the common azimuth compasses.

Time 1802	Marked end south		Marked end north		Observer
	Face west	Face East	Face west	Face east	
March					
4	63°20′	64°50′	66°12′	64°5′	Commander
	62°35′	64°40′	65°50′	64°5′	
	62°57′	64°45′	66°1′	64°5′	
	Mean	63°51′	Mean	65°3′	
	Mean dip of the needle		64°27′ south		

From lieutenant Flinders observations on the rise of the tide it appears that like Princess Royal Harbour there is only one high water in twenty four hours, which happens about 11 hours after the moon passes over the meridian, or 1 hour before she comes to the lower meridian. The tide does not rise more than two or three feet.[1]

[f. 163] **Friday 5 March**

At daylight, moderate breezes and cloudy weather. Unmoored ship, and at 7 *hours* 45′ weighed and made sail down the bay. On attempting to pass between isles No. 1 and 2[2] and the opposite point, the water shoaled and obliged us to tack and wear round to leeward. Hauled up between the two isles and the outer south point T,[3] and at 10 *hours* 20′ came to with the best bower and furled sails. Point T [Cape Donington] N15°E 1 mile, and the distant land shut on behind it. Bent a new main top-gallant sail. At noon, fine weather. Served slops[4] to the ships company. At 5 pm *Lieutenant* Fowler returned with the cutter from Uncertain *Island* [Thistle Island] and Memory Cove being unsuccessful.

Meridian altitude ☉ Lower Limb 483	61°20′53″N
Latitude	34°44′22″S

At 5 P.M. Head SbE

☉ magnetic azimuth	S 94°22′W	} 0°58′E
low limb	18°21′	
☉ magnetic azimuth	S 93°45′W	} 0°48′
low limb	17°16′	
Mean variation	0°53′E	

---

[1] Flinders was mistaken in thinking that Port Lincoln, on the western side of the entrance to Spencer Gulf, has only one daily tide; in fact, it has two. His error, however, was easy to make. The reason is that the tides there are subject to the phenomenon of diurnal inequality. This means that the noon and afternoon tides are not equal in height, one is much higher than the other: 'at Port Lincoln the observable daily tide is simply the higher one of the two daily tides, for owing to the direction of the outlet of the harbour the water cannot escape freely, as the ebbing tide from the Gulf retards its outward flow. The result is that the level of water in the large area of Port Lincoln Harbour falls very slowly, so slowly that the second and lower tide which follows in the course of the day does not appreciably raise the level of the water, and so is not apparent as a tide.' Chapman, 'The Tides of Australia', pp. 972–84.

[2] Bicker Islands (34°52′S, 135°52′E) and Surfleet Point (34°46′S, 135°57′E). Cooper, *The Unknown Coast*, p. 49.

[3] Cape Donington (34°44′S, 136°00′E). Ibid., p. 47.

[4] Clothing.

Additional remarks

Lieut*enant* Fowler rowed and walked together close along the shore from this bay to Memory Cove: he revisited Uncertain Island [Thistle Island], and on his return examined about the shores of the neighbouring islands, for the bodies of the lost people or for fragments of the wreck, but altogether without effect. Two or three kanguroos were killed upon Uncertain Island.

Note: A fresh departure is taken from the head of this bay for D[ead] R[eckoning].

Saturday 6 March

Light breezes and cloudy weather. A cutter employed by the Commander very early, in surveying. Sent the acting-master to sound across from point T [Cape Donington] to the small isles No. 1 and 2 [Bicker Islands] where we had tried to pass with the ship: he found a small 3 *fatho*m channel there. Hoisted in the boat, and at 10 weighed and made sail out of the bay toward the point of the main U [Point Bolingbroke], having light airs and fine weather, with haze. At noon, point T bore SSE 3 miles, and the extremes of the large [*blank*] in the lower part of the bay left S67° to 10°W.[1]

This day consists of 12 hours only, bringing the time again to the log account.

Mer*idian* alt*itude* ☉ Lowe*r* Lim*b* 483	61°1′16″N
Latitude	34°40′50″S

Additional remarks

Sounding from our last anchorage in No 10 bay [Port Lincoln], to point T1[2] found the water to shoal gradually, and there were 5 *fathom*s within a cables length of the shore. From TI [Surfleet Point] had bearings of several islands to the north-eastward, which seem to form a small archipelago.[3]

Sunday 7 March

Log account

Light breezes and fine weather with haze. Sold the clothes of the lost boats crew at the mast.[4] Find ourselves set to the northward between point U [Point Bolingbroke] and the small archipelago of islands; and on passing near one of the first the water shoaled to 5 *fathom*s upon which we tacked, and about 6 *hours* came to with the best bower and furled sails, being ½ mile distant from the isle π1,[5] which bore S20°W to 34°E. Hoisted out the cutter, sounded about the ship and landed to inspect the neighbouring islands. Hazy weather.

AM. Cleaned the ship above and below, and sent up top-gallant yards. The naturalist and other gentlemen landed to examine the productions of the island, and the Commander to take bearings, which from the number of small islands was rather perplexing: the furthest visible π1 [South Pages Islet] N9°40′E. At noon, light breezes

---

[1] Rough Journal, I, f. 369, adds: 'The point T consists of granite, with a loose and slight covering of calcarious stone, and a little vegetable mould. The formation of the 1st bay within the point promises fresh water at the back of the beach by digging, when the season is not so dry as at present.'

[2] Surfleet Point. Cooper, *The Unknown Coast*, p. 49.

[3] The Sir Joseph Banks Group (34°35′S, 136°18′E), comprising 20 islands, islets and rocks.

[4] This was a naval custom. The buyers' wages were debited in the ships' books to the amount of the purchase. Estensen, *The Life of Matthew Flinders*, p. 193.

[5] The South Pages Islet (35°47′S, 138°18′E). Cooper, *The Unknown Coast*, p. 135.

and fine weather. Sold the effects of Mr Thistle and prepared to get under weigh as soon as the latitude was obtained.

The commander found π1 to consist of a granite basis with a covering of calcarious stone. The island is without trees and almost without shoals. There were many marks of geese upon it, but none of the birds were seen. A few hair seals[1] were killed.[2]

Meridian Altitude ☉ centre	61°2′1″N
Latitude	34°33′2″S

	By log			Latitude South		Longitude East					
Course	Distance	DR	Obs	DR	TK	Var allowed	Set or current	Ther	Barom	Error of TK
N58°E	20½	34°37′	34°33′	136°30′	136°35′	2E	4N	70°	29.97	13′38″E
							5E	70°	29.94	
								70°	30.02	

[f. 164] Monday 8 March *Investigator* exploring the unknown part on the south coast of New Holland No 12 great inlet [Spencer Gulf]

Moderate breezes and cloudy weather. At 2 *hours* 5′ weighed, and leaving the island to the right steered for the outermost part of the main land. Ditto weather. At 6 *hours* 30′ our distance from the shore was 5 or 6 miles, the farthest extreme bearing NNE½E and an inland mountain N72°W.[3] Hauled off the shore upon a wind, under double-reefed topsails and courses. Fresh breezes and cloudy weather. Tacked ship towards the land. Wore round and brought to 'till daylight, with the ships head offshore. At 6 saw the land and bore away to make it more distinctly. At 7 *hours* 15′ the inland mountain [Mount Middleback] bore S8°W at which time we hauled up along the shore, its distance being 7 or 8 miles. Fresh breezes with dull cloudy weather. Cleaned below and aired with stoves. Hauled up as we found the land to trend until 11, when the shallowing off [*sic*] the water made it necessary to keep to the wind. Let out 2nd reefs and set top-gallant sails. At noon, moderate breezes and cloudy weather. The low sandy shore distant 3 or 4 miles; and a hill, V,[4] at the north-eastern corner of the back hills N62°W; and a small opening in the shore N by E leading apparently into a small lagoon.[5]

Supplement Meridian altitude ☉ Upper Limb	118°20′26″S
Latitude	33°48′19″S

---

[1] The Australian sea lion (*Neophoca cinerea*).

[2] Rough Journal, I, f. 371, adds: 'The situation in which we anchored affords good shelter, being surrounded by the main land and islands at different distances. The nearest island π1 is about ½ mile distant, bearing S20°W to S34°E. The basis of this island is granite as usual, and with a slight covering of calcarious stone. There is not a sufficient depth of soil or sand for petrels to burrow in it but the same kind of grey shrub almost covers it, under which their holes are mostly found. Many marks of geese were to be seen upon the island, and two of the birds were also seen, but not killed. Pidgeons, parroquets, shags, gulls and a large hawk or ?[*illegible*] were seen. Seals are the most numerous race of animals, but they are not abundant.'

[3] Now Mount Middleback (1,463 feet high, 33°10′S, 137°07′E). Vallance, Moore and Groves, eds, *Nature's Investigator*, p. 151.

[4] Elbow Hill, situated near Franklin Harbour (33°44′S, 136°46′E). Bearing Book, entry for 8 March 1802, f. 63; Cooper, *The Unknown Coast*, p. 50.

[5] Now known as Franklin Harbour. Vallance, Moore and Groves, eds, *Nature's Investigator*, p. 151.

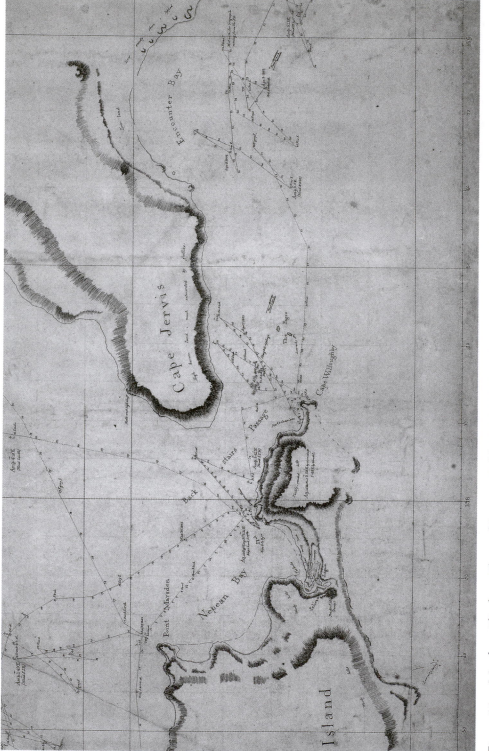

Figure 11.　Matthew Flinders, Chart of Spencer Gulf, ADM 352/524, detail. Courtesy of the National Archives, Kew.

By log		Latitude South		Longitude East						
Course	Distance	DR	Obs	DR	TK	Var allowed	Set or current	Ther	Barom	Error of TK
N53°E	42	34°8′	33°48′	137°10′	137°20′	2E	20M 5E	71° 69° 70°	30.08 30.10 30.13	13′38″E

Additional remarks

The cluster of islands [Sir Joseph Banks Group] which we now quitted are mostly small and low, having little vegetation upon them. From π1 [South Pages Islet] I took the bearings of 14 of them, but I believe there are some more to the south-eastward.[1] They do not occupy a large space, but for their relative positions and magnitudes, I refer to the chart which in this place, as in all others, I have taken particular pains to make as accurate a representation of what we saw as circumstances would permit. The tide ripples much amongst these islands.

From No. 10 bay [Port Lincoln] the shore of the mainland is mostly low for some miles past the point U [Point Bolingbroke], being partly rocky and partly sandy: but at that part which bore N9°40′E from π1 [South Pages Islet], it is of moderate elevation, of a smooth surface and bare of vegetation: it seems to be granite.

The mountain [Mount Middleback] whose bearing was set at night, and in the morning, is not much elevated above the front land: its top is flat and its north-east side steep. The shore becomes lower as we advanced northward on account of the hills retreating back a little from the water. V [Elbow Hill] forms a corner of these hills, their direction being then more northward, and further from the shore. The small lake a lagoon which was seen from the masthead over the front land, and into which the small opening seems to lead, lies a little to the eastward of V, and seems to be the draining of water from it and the other hills which form nearly a semicircle about it. No high land could be seen ahead at noon.

[f. 165] **Tuesday 9 March**

Moderate breezes with dull cloudy weather. Saw land like the main extending six points on the starboard bow and beam and dist*ant* about 5 leagues, at 4 o'clock: the shore on the other side then 5 or 6 miles distant. Kept hauling to the northward as the shore trended, and at 5 kept more in to look for ⚓age. On the water shoaling quick to 2¾ fathoms, wore round and stood back into 5 *fatho*ms, then ⚓ed with the best bower and furled sails. The weather being squally with spitting rain, veered to a whole cable and sent down top-gallant yards. The south extreme of the main bore S20°W and some hummocks like islands NbyE near to which the low land seems to extend from each shore. Fresh breezes and squally.

Sent up the top-gallant yards and at 9 weighed and steered to windward of the hummocks of land, which were soon found to be connected by low land to the western shore.[2] On the water shoaling suddenly from 12 to 7 *fatho*ms and the bottom being coral,

[1] For the bearings, see entries for 6–8 March 1802, Bearing Book, ff. 62–64.

[2] The hummocks included Mount Young, Middle Mount and Point Lowly. Flinders, *A Voyage to Terra Australis*, I, pp. 155–6.

tacked ship immediately, at 11 *hours*; but finding the depth to continue let the ship wear round off again and steered on as before, but under easier sail. Double reefed the topsails. At noon, fresh breezes and fine weather. A low point, W,[1] N43°E beyond which there appears to be some opening like a river within the eastern land.

Mer*idian* alt*itude* ☉ Lowe*r* Lim*b* 483	61°27′4″N
Latitude	33°5′15″S
Supp*lement* Upper Limb	118°1′14″S
Latitude	33°5′33″S

		Latitude South		Longitude East						
By log										
Course	Distance	DR	Obs	DR	TK	Var allowed	Set or current	Ther	Barom	Error of TK
N43°E	46	33°15′	33°6′	137°48′	138°3′	2°E	9N	71°	30.13	13′38″E
							5E	68°	30.16	
								67½°	30.18	

Additional remarks

From the shallowness of the water I had conjectured that this was not an open coast and the appearance of land this afternoon to the eastward seems to prove this to be only an inlet or perhaps river, though as yet we have no appearance of fresh water.[2]

The front land of the western shore is very low and seems to be sandy; as well as we can see from the distance at which the shoal water obliges us to keep; but the hills still continue to run behind it, and in some places, as near our anchorage, they approach near to the water side.

Our run up this inclosed piece of water (whatever it is) in the morning shewed us the connexion of the low western land with the different hummocks that were seen to the northward; so that there seems to be no opening on the western shore; yet it is likely there may be lagoons behind it. On both sides, the low land seems to be sandy and the higher parts to be but partially covered with wood.[3]

[f. 166] **Wednesday 10 March**[4] *Investigator* **exploring No 12 great inlet [Spencer Gulf] on the unknown south coast of New Holland**

Fresh breezes with fine weather. Saw a dry bank stretching along the western shore. At 1 bore away to leeward of the bank for what appears to be the entrance of a

[1] Point Lowly (33°00′S, 137°47′E). Cooper, *The Unknown Coast*, p. 135.

[2] Flinders added in *A Voyage to Terra Australis*, I, p. 156: 'Our prospect of a channel or strait, cutting off some considerable portion of Terra Australis, was lost, for it now appeared that the ship was entering into a gulph.' As the ship sailed past Point Lowly, Flinders noted that 'the gulph was found to take a river-like form, but the eastern half of it was occupied by a dry, sandy spit and shoal water'.

[3] Rough Journal, I, f. 375, adds: 'The front land to the westward is very low, and seems to be sandy. The hills retreat inland in some places; but near our anchorage, some considerable ones come near the sea shore. Three hummocks are particularly distinguishable[.] Our run up this inclosed piece of water (whatever it is) shewed us the connexion of the low western land with the hummocks, and almost as far as the high eastern land. This land seems to lie more to the eastward than that seen first, making the direction of this river or sound to be *North Easterly*. The low land is mostly sandy, and the higher land but partially covered with wood.'

[4] The botanist Robert Brown collected numerous plants in Spencer Gulf on 10–11 March 1802. These plants are listed and identified in the florula included in Vallance, Moore and Groves, eds, *Nature's Investigator*, pp. 157–60.

river.[1] Finding the soundings not to be very regular and much shoal water about, cleared down the fore and mizzen top-sails to be ready for ⚓ing at a short notice.[2] At 4, hauled more over towards the western shore for anchoring in better shelter, but we came suddenly into 2½ *fatho*ms upon a middle bank, which obliged us to wear instantly back, and on deepening the water to 7 *fatho*ms came to with the best bower and veered to a whole cable. Furled sails and sent down top-gallant yards; the wind blowing a fresh gale up the gulph. Our distance from each side of the river is about 1½ or 2 miles. The extremes downwards bear South to 30°E, and the head appears to be closed round, upwards, at the distance of 3 or 4 miles, but there seems to be small channels amongst the banks.

At sunset, dropped the small bower under foot and veered a fresh service into the hawse of the best bower. Tide running NNW one knot at 8 PM. AM Moderate breezes with fine weather. The scientific gentlemen landed on the east side in order to ascend the mountains which lie a little distance back and run parallel to the shore, and the Commander took the cutter upon a surveying expedition upwards accompanied by the surgeon, and taking the small time-keeper A No. 1736 and a sextant with him.[3]

Got the slops upon deck to be aired: found some of them bad from dampness and others eaten by mice. People employed making nippers[4] and otherwise in working up junk. Cut up pork No. 14 to 53, its contents.

This day continued to 36 hours or civil account.

Fresh breezes and fine weather. Employed in the holds and working up junk.

	By log	Latitude South		Longitude East						
Course	Distance	DR	Obs	DR	TK	Var allowed	Set or current	Ther	Barom	Error of TK
N27°E	22½	32°46′	32°45′	138°00′	138°15′	2°E	1N	69°	30.18	13′38″E
								65°	30.22	
								66½°	30.14	
								69°	30.04	

[1] This was not a river but an inlet which soon contracted to one mile wide and then became mud flats. Flinders, *A Voyage to Terra Australis*, I, p. 157.

[2] Rough Journal, I, f. 377, adds: 'At 2, we entered a part of the gulph or river which is much narrower than before being contracted by the approach of the western land. Its breadth here seems to be from 6 to10 miles and it contracts fast upwards. The land on both sides is moderately high at a little distance from the shore, especially on the eastern side where the mountain forms a sharp-topped ridge nearly parallel to the shore. The front land on each side is low and on the east side covered with wood. We see much smoke rising from it[.] At 4, the head appeared to be closed up by very low land in which some small channels of water were distinguishable. I wished to anchor on the western shore, but the water became so shoal suddenly, that before the ship wore round, they had only two *fatho*ms in the chains. It deepened again as suddenly on hauling to the eastward, although the shoal water appeared to extend to a considerable distance from that shore also[.]'

[3] Flinders found the results of his expedition discouraging, failing to find a major waterway penetrating the continent from No. 12 inlet. Estensen, *The Life of Matthew Flinders*, p. 194.

[4] Short pieces of rope nipped to the cables to bend an anchor warp around a capstan.

Additional remarks

The opening in the head of the gulph which we entered at 2 PM seems to be from six to ten miles wide, and it contracts upwards, rapidly. The shores are low, but at a little distance back the land rises, specially on the eastern side, where the hills rise into a high ridge, the highest top of which is the mountain X.[1] We s ee much smoke rising from the low lands near the water side, but as yet no inhabitants are seen. The shoal upon which we had 2½ *fathoms* (indeed the man in the chains said only 2) is a bank in the middle of the river, on each side of which is a deeper channel: this bank seems to be very steep to [*sic*] on its eastern side.

[f. 167] **Thursday 11 March**

Civil account: Light airs with fine weather. Cleaned below, saw the ships company clean and mustered them. Shortened in to half a cable. People employed working up junk. At noon, light airs and hazy. Party of scientific gentlemen who visited the eastern hills returned this afternoon; and at 10 PM the commander returned from his expedition up the inlet. He found the head of it to be in 32°25′ south and longitude by timekeepers 138°10′ east, being 20 miles in a straight line above the ship. No fresh water was found.

Meri*dian* alt*itude* ☉ Lowe*r Lim*b 488	61°0′45″N
Latitude	32°44′42″S

Additional remarks

The excursion of Messrs Brown, Bauer, and Westall, with attendants, to X [Mount Brown], the highest top of a ridge of hills on the east side of the inlet, proved to be a most laborious one; X proving to be about 15 miles distant, though it was thought to be not more than 6 or 7. They set off in the morning, and did not reach its top until 5 in the evening, and were then obliged to pass the night without water, nor did they find any until the following day in their way down.[2] They had an extensive view from the hill, but no rivers or lakes were visible inland, or anything of the sea to the southeastward, but one dead and almost uninterrupted flat everywhere presented itself. The stone of these hills is reddish, smooth, and close grained, and is thought by Mr Brown to be argillaceous.[3] The stone of the hill W1[4] on the other side of the inlet is of the same kind.

Previous to setting out on my excursion in the cutter, I made the annexed comparison of the pocket timekeeper 1736 with Earnshaws No. 543.

[Timekeepers]	h	′	″
E. 543 –	10	7	16.5
A. 1736 –	16	29	–
Difference	6	21	43.5

Stretching across to the west side of the inlet I had the following soundings, after passing over the middle shoal, 5, 7, 9, 10, 8, 7, 5, 3 fathoms, drawing near the mangroves on the

---

[1] Mount Brown (32°30′S, 138°00′E). Cooper, *The Unknown Coast*, p. 51.

[2] On this excursion see Grandison, 'Retracing the route taken by Robert Brown and company in a portion of the Flinders Ranges', pp. 105–7.

[3] i.e. rocks or sediments that are silt- or clay-sized.

[4] Flinders' Bluff, on the Fleurieu Peninsula (35°33′S, 138°37′E). Cooper, *The Unknown Coast*, p. 52.

west shore. Not being able to land from the muddiness of the bank, I steered upwards, carrying soundings as per Bearing Book,[1] and landed near W1 [Flinders' Bluff], a flat-topped hill on the west shore. After taking the annexed altitudes in the artificial horizon for the longitude, I walked to the top of W1 [Flinders' Bluff] and took angles of all the surrounding objects, as well as a rough sketch of the form of the stream upwards, the general line of which was 1°45′ in a flat country.

10 A.M. Civil account			
Ship bearing	137°	18′ (magnetic)	
X mount	52	15	
Apparent time	21h	49′	55.87″
Time 1736	18	39	56.6
543			
☉ apparent centre 483	48°	34′	12″
Longitude	138°	10′	48″ E
E.520		9	22
Mean	138	10	0.5

Returning to the boat we proceeded upwards, the stream being contracting to about 1½ mile in width, and much of it occupied by shoal water. Some time being lost in chasing ducks and other birds, we were about 14 miles above the ship when the setting sun made it necessary to prepare for passing the night. With some difficulty we found a dry place on the eastern shore, and from a small eminence near, I set the ships mast heads, which were visible over the low land, at 164°40′. High mount X [Mount Brown] bore 83°40′.[2] On Thursday morning we were proceeding downwards to the ship when a flight of black swans from the head of the stream made our mouths water for fresh food. The stream was very small and irregular at our sleeping place so that, as an object of utility, I had given up further examination; but having now an additional stimulus, the boats crew set off to row upwards with all their might. At 10 o'clock, we had ascended as far as a boat could get; the stream being there little better than a drain from a swamp, but it was [f. 168] still as salt, almost as at the ship. I made the requisite observations on the soundings and turnings in coming up and now took the annexed set of altitudes in the artificial horizon.

High mount X	106°	30′ (magnetic)	
Apparent time	21h	59′	57.4″
Time N°. 1736	18	49	28.9
N°. 543			
☉ apparent Centre 483	50°	5	17
Longitude	138°	10′	53.91″ E
E.520		9	4.5
Mean	138	9	59.2

[1] See Bearing Book, entry for 11 March 1802, f. 65.
[2] Its height is 3,173 feet.

X by theodolite	97°	25′ (magnetic)	
Meridian altitude ☉ Lower Limb (doubled)	122°	35′	00″
☉ Upper Limb	123	39	25
Latitude	32	28	8 S
X mount	69°	20′ by theodolite	
Meridian altitude ☽ Upper Limb (doubled) at 5h 56′	56°	53′	50″ N
Latitude —	32	35	26 S

Returning downwards we stopped at a red bank on the western shore where the annexed latitude was observed; from which, and the bearing of X [Mount Brown] from the ship, that mountain is in 32°38′26″S. At 1 PM I stopped on the west shore, about 9 miles above the ship, to observe the annexed latitude from the moon, according to which X would be 40″ further southward. Having missed our way in the dark among the mangroves and shoals on the east shore, we did not get on board before 10 o clock PM.

In wet seasons there is doubtless a good deal of water thrown from the hills which stand on each side, into the head of this stream; but at this time there is very little fresh water mixed with the salt. The tide overflows a considerable part of the shore, forming muddy swamps, where it is almost impossible to land. At least a hundred swans were seen, but not one that could not fly, and they all escaped us. A few ducks and red bills, or sea pies, were shot, the shoals being frequented by large flocks of them.

The rise of the tide appears to be from six to eight feet in common; and from its being high water at 9 AM the morning after our return on board (12 March) this should usually take place at 2½ hours after the moons passage over the meridian. There are two regular tides here in the day which makes it the more strange that there should have been only one in No. 10 bay [Port Lincoln].[1]

No natives were seen during our excursion, and but very few marks of them.

Friday 12 March civil account *Investigator* exploring the great inlet No 12 [Spencer Gulf] (downwards) on the unknown south coast of New Holland

Light airs and fair weather. Sighted the anchor, and finding it to be clear, dropped it again in 7 fathoms. Sent the gig to sound upon the middle shoal. Noon, variable breezes and fine weather. Sent the gig to fish with hook and line, and she had some success. In the evening, flurries of wind coming from the westward at times, which made it proper to veer to a whole cable. At 4 PM tide ran past the ship 1.4[2] NWbN.

Observations of ☉ west ☽ at this anchorage, taken by lieutenant Flinders, and reduced by means of the time-keepers to No. 10 bay [Port Lincoln] for fixing its longitude. Astronomical time.

---

[1] 'We had two flood tides in the day setting past the ship, and they ran at the strongest one mile and a half per hour; the rise appeared to be from six to eight feet, and high water to take place at two hours and a half after the moon passed the meridian.' Flinders, *A Voyage to Terra Australis*, I, p. 460. See above, p. 325, n. 1, for Flinders's error about the tides in No. 10 bay.

[2] i.e. 1.4 miles per hour.

Time 1802	No. of sights	Apparent time	Apparent altitudes from calculator		Apparent distance of limbs	Longitude	Sextant used
			Sun center	Moon center			
March 10	[blank]	1h29′28.6″	4°46′34″	12°28′54″	77°37′57″	138° 8′45″	R No. 932
″		35′3.6″	3°59′41″	13°16′26″	39′47″	23′45″	″
″		40′6.6″	53°15′31″	13°59′2″	42′20″	8′15″	″
″		55′16.0″	50°54′51″	16°3′24″	48′34″	0′0″	T No. 488
″		2h 0′56″	49°59′36″	16°48′8″	50′44″	137°59′15″	″
″		6′29″	49° 4′21″	17°31′4″	52′59″	53′15″	″
11		3h41′5.8″	31° 2′52″	20°41′48″	89°57′44″	138° 2′00″	″
″		47′20.8″	29°47′12″	21°19′47″	59′48″	1′15″	″
″		52′48.8″	28°40′42″	21°51′44″	90° 1′26″	137°53′30″	″
″		57′5.0″	27°48′34″	22°16′00″	2′42″	59′45″	″
″		4h 1′38.8″	26°52′45″	22°40′51″	4′20″	138° 2′45″	″
″		5′46″	26° 2′01″	23° 2′59″	5′32″	137°55′00″	″
					Mean	138° 2′18″ East	
		X of longitude by Time Keeper from the tents on No. 10 bay				2° 5′40″	
		Longitude of No. 10, from Sun west moon				135°56′38″	

[f. 169] **Saturday 13 March**

Moderate breezes with fine weather: at daylight, light winds. At 6, weighed and made sail down the inlet. In attempting to pass over to the east side, where there appeared to be a deep channel, the water shoaled very suddenly, and at 7 *hours* 45′ the ship took upon a shoal of soft mud covered with grass. Hove all aback, but the ship still sticking, hoisted out the cutter and dropped a kedge astern, with which we hove her off into deep water. At 8 *hours* 30′ made sail again downwards, and tried to get over to the eastern shore, along which we sail about 1½ mile distant, but as yet without effect.

At noon, light breezes and fine weather. Saw an extensive shoal, dry, and stretching out from a low point on the east shore, which obliged us to haul to the westward to pass round it.

This day ends at 12 hours, bringing the time back to log account.

Meridian altitude ☉ Lower Limb 483   60°1′4″N
Latitude   32°57′19″S

	By log	Latitude South		Longitude East						
Course	Distance	DR	Obs	DR	TK	Var allowed	Set or current	Ther	Barom	Error of TK
S13°E	12	32°57′	32°57′	138°18′	138°18′	2E		70° 69½°	29.77 29.78	13′38″E

Sunday 14 March

Moderate breezes and cloudy weather. Made several attempts to get close over to the eastern shore, but shoal water everywhere prevented us from succeeding. At low water there are two dry places upon these shoals. Tacked ship, bore away, and hauled to the wind occasionally. The weather becoming squally and the wind not permitting us to lay round the shoals, a little before 6 we came to ⚓ with the best bower, finding the water beginning again to shoal. W, hill[1] bore N79°W and mount X [Mount Brown] N18°E: no land being visible between SW and SSE. Sent the acting master to sound to the south-eastward on the edge of the great eastern shoal, where he found 3½ fathoms only about ¾ mile off, but not less than 4 everywhere else. Squally weather at night.

AM. Moderate and fine weather. At 6 hours 30' weighed and made sail to the southward under single reefed top-sails &c. Found the soundings to be irregular and shallow, but being desirous to get over to the eastern shore, we stood on as long as possible. Cleaned below and aired with stoves. Saw the ships company cleanly dressed and mustered them according to custom. At 11 hours 40' tacked ship from the eastern shoal in 3¼ fathoms. At noon, moderate breezes and fine weather. The low eastern shore distant 6 or 7 miles. W hill [Mount Young] N43°W. Southern extreme in sight S2°W.

Meridian altitude ☉ Lower Limb 483	59°12'06"N
Latitude	33°22'40"S
Supplement to ☉ Upper Limb	120°17'46"S
Latitude	33°24'46"S
Mean	33°23'43"S

	By log	Latitude South		Longitude East							
Course	Distance	DR	Obs	DR	TK	Var allowed	Set or current	Ther	Barom	Error of TK
S25°W	19	33°14'	33°24'	138°8'	138°12'	2E	10S	69°	29.83	11'38"E
							4E	69°	29.86	
								69°	29.94	

Additional remarks

The shoal which we have been constantly attempting to pass in order to get to the eastern shore of the inlet, I now judge to be connected with it. I wished to go down the inlet on this side as we went up on the other. The inland hills are high on the east side, but like the upper parts of the inlet, they are skirted by very low land which is not visible further than 9 or 10 miles. Some spits of white sand lie off from the shore, but it is not improbable that the water upon them is deep as in other places, this being the case higher up.

[f. 170] **Monday 15 March**

Fresh breezes and cloudy weather. At 1, tacked ship towards the eastern shore. At 3 hours 40' the water had shoaled to 3 fathoms. Tacked ship offshore, the land being 5 or 6 miles distant. X mount [Mount Brown] bearing N12°E. At 5, tacked again towards the eastern shore, and on the water shoaling to 4 fathoms came to with the best bower, veered to half a cable and furled sails: the wind being moderate and weather fine. Middle Hill N64°W. A hill on the east shore S77°E called Barn Hill.[2] No land visible from the deck between

---

[1] Mount Young (33°06'S, 137°28'E). Cooper, *The Unknown Coast*, p. 135.
[2] Situated about 12 miles from the shore. Flinders, *A Voyage to Terra Australis*, I, p. 162.

west and south. Sent down top-gallant yards and ranged both cables. At midnight, fresh breezes with rain, afterwards moderate breezes with dull hazy weather.

At 6½ hours, weighed and made sail down the inlet, upon a wind. The soundings being very variable, hauled the main-sail up to be ready for wearing off quickly. Fresh breezes and dull cloudy weather. At 10, tacked ship towards the eastern shore, but in 50 minutes the water had shoaled to 3 fathoms and obliged us to go about immediately: our distance offshore was 6 or 8 miles and Barn Hill N80°E.

At noon, fresh breezes and cloudy weather. A cask of wine purchased at Madeira for the sick, being found a little acid, we issued it, beginning this day, to the ships company: the lime-juice and sugar which had been regularly issued to this time being now stopped.

Meridian altitude ☉ Lower Limb 483			58°33′21″N
Latitude			33°37′48″S

	By log	Latitude South		Longitude East						
Course	Distance	DR	Obs	DR	TK	Var allowed	Set or current	Ther	Barom	Error of TK
S38°W	21	33°41′	33°38′	137°53′	137°52′	2E	3N 6W	60° 69° 68½°	30.05 30.15 30.22	13′38″E

Additional remarks

It appears that the great eastern shoal extends from the upper part, where the inlet takes a river-like form, to past our situation this day at noon, which is more than 40′ of latitude. In consequence of this, the eastern shore, thus far down, seems to be inaccessible, and indeed the greater part of the western shore presents a similar obstruction to ships. The first land seen on either side is the hills, though generally several miles behind the low front land. This low shore is covered with small wood so as to have rather a fertile appearance, but on a near approach it looks more sandy.

[f. 171] **Tuesday 16 March**

Moderate breezes and cloudy weather. The water shoaling gradually as we approached the western shore, it had got to 5 fathoms at 2 when the land was distant 6 or 7 miles to WNW; and we then tacked back to the eastward. At 4, double reefed the topsails.[1] The wind heading as we approached the eastern shore, so as to blow off the land, we came to with the best bower in ¼ less 5 fathoms at 5 hours 50′, there being no time to make another stretch before dark. Veered to half a cable, furled sails, sent down top-gallant yards, and set up the top-gallant rigging. The eastern shore extending out S12°W and its nearest distance 4 or 5 miles S60°E. The western land in sight to the WSW. Moderate breezes and hazy weather.

AM Moderate breezes and cloudy. At 6, weighed the anchor and made sail on the larboard tack down the inlet. At 8, moderate breezes and cloudy. Barn Hill N62°E and & Y, a low point on the eastern shore S57°E.[2] Cleaned the ship below. At times the wind

---

[1] Flinders added in a note inserted in the text: 'A hill which I take to be Middle Hill on the west shore bearing at N22°W.'

[2] Point Riley (33°53′S, 137°36′E). Cooper, *The Unknown Coast*, p. 53.

falling light. At noon, saw the eastern land as far as SbyE. The western land in sight, nearly upon the lee beam.[1]

Observations for the latitude taken on the following PM

Times 543 ☉ apparent Lower Limbs

| 14h33'53" | = | 57°41'31"N |
| 14h55'35" | = | 57°4'29"N |

Latitude at 6' past noon   34°3'58"S

		By log		Latitude South		Longitude East					
Course	Distance	DR	Obs	DR	TK	Var allowed	Set or current	Ther	Barom	Error of TK
S18°W	26	34°3'	34°4'	137°43'	137°40'	3E	1S 2W	70° 69° 69°	30.28 30.26 30.24	13'38"E

Additional remarks

The shore off which we anchored this evening is rather low and rocky, but still not near so low as the shores are higher up the inlet. A small range of black hills just peeps above the front land, but further southward this is lost, and nothing appears upon the land, which we sailed along in the morning, but what is in front of the shore: it is of moderate elevation and seems to be a level country by no means devoid of wood. At noon, we had passed the narrowest part of the lower extreme into the inlet, where its breadth is about 20 miles.

[f. 172] **Wednesday 17 March** *Investigator* **exploring No 12 great inlet [Spencer Gulf]**

Moderate breezes and cloudy weather. At 2, tacked towards the eastern shore. At 3 *hours* 30' saw breakers N78°E 1½ mile, and the water becoming shoal, tacked off: the nearest land bearing S52°E 7 or 8 miles. Tacked again towards the land at 5, but on drawing near the breakers at 6, tacked back and double reefed the topsails.

Fresh breezes with fine weather. Tacked ship to the eastward. Tacked from off the shore. Tacked again towards the land. At daylight, let out 2nd reefs and set top gallant sails. Saw the land to the ENE. Moderate breezes and fine weather. Cleaned below as usual. Tacked ship from the shore, its extremes then bearing S29°E to N10°W and its nearest part distant 3½ miles, a white sandy beach with low reddish cliffs at the back. At noon, moderate breezes and fine weather, with some haze. North extreme N14°E.

Meridian altitude ☉ Lower Limb 483	57°8'39"N
Latitude	34°15'11"S
Supplement to ☉ Upper Limb	122°20'14"S
Latitude	34°16'16"S
Mean latitude	34°15'43"S

---

[1] i.e. on the side sheltered from the wind.

	By log	Latitude South		Longitude East						
Course	Distance	DR	Obs	DR	TK	Var allowed	Set or current	Error of TK	Ther	Barom
S21°E	23	34°25′	34°16′	137°53′	137°49′	3°E	9N 1W	13′38″E	69° 69° 69°	30.25 30.22 30.19

Additional remarks

The breakers mentioned above lie some distance from the land, and as in this place there is not much sea breaking they are therefore dangerous, particularly to be approached in the night. On the shore behind them we noticed some white patches in the front land which appeared like cliffs, but I think it probable they are places upon the rising bank where the white sand shews itself through the vegetation. The land seen in the morning being but little distant from the former, it almost in every respect bears a resemblance to it: upon the whole it seems to be more sandy. No back hills appear upon this part of the coast.

[f. 173] **Thursday 18 March on the unknown south coast of New Holland**

Fresh breezes and fine weather. At 1, tacked ship towards the shore. At 3, tacked off; outermost land, like an island, or islands, as far out as S38°W (this is Z).[1] At 4 *hours* 30′ tacked again towards the shore. On drawing near, saw broken water and shoals stretching along the beach ahead; and the wind coming more round at 6, tacked and steered along the shore towards Z [Point Pearce]. It being dark at 7 and the shore low, with shoals lying off it, brought to in order to drift past Z island, or point, and thus expend a part of the night. Supposing ourselves far enough to leeward to pass clear of Z, at 9½ filled and stretching on to the SSW.

Light hazes and cloudy weather. At 3, tacked ship towards Z. At 5, the island or point was seen bearing ENE, and the water becoming shoaler tacked off in order to fetch to windward of Z and all its shoals; the extreme to the southward bearing SEbS. Tacked ship to the eastward. Moderate breezes and hazy weather. Cleaned the ship below, and afterwards the ships company cleaned themselves and were mustered as usual on this day. At 10 *hours* 30′ tacked ship offshore: Z bearing N26°W about 6 miles. The furthest land, supposed to be an island from the masthead, SWbS. At noon, fine weather with haze. Z bearing N22°E.

Meridian altitude ☉ Lower Limb 483	56°27′9″N
Latitude	34°33′1″S
Supplement Upper Limb	123°2′19″S
Latitude	34°34′41″S
Mean latitude	34°33′51″S

[1] Point Pearce, now Wardang Island (34°30′S, 137°21′E), named after a former chief clerk of the Admiralty William Pearce (?1751–1842). Point Pearce on modern maps is part of the adjacent mainland. Bearing Book, entry for 16 March 1802, f. 69; Cooper, *The Unknown Coast*, p. 135; Vallance, Moore and Groves, eds, *Nature's Investigator*, p. 162.

	By log	Latitude South		Longitude East						
Course	Distance	DR	Obs	DR	TK	Var allowed	Set or current	Error of TK	Ther	Barom
S16°W	26	34°41′	34°34′	137°44′	137°43′	3°E	7N 3E	13′38″E	67° 66° 68°	30.00 30.27 30.29

Additional remarks

It is uncertain whether Z [Point Pearce] is an island or a low projecting point. It had the appearance of being two islands, both when seen to the south and to the north, but I suspect that these more elevated parts are connected by a low sandy neck to the mainland. On the south side of this island or point, the shore forms a large bight facing the south.[1] The land is sandy round the bight, and even in the country the appearance is partly similar. Near the water the land is low, and although it continues to rise for some miles inland, the acclivity is so gentle that it is by no means high. The country has upon the whole a tolerable appearance for a sea coast, but I believe it to be mostly barren.

[f. 174] **Friday 19 March *Investigator* exploring No 12 great inlet [Spencer Gulf]**
Moderate breezes and fine weather. At 1, tacked ship. Passed through patches of discoloured water, having 8 and 9 *fatho*ms. At 4 *hours* 15′ tacked off shore, the land to the eastward being distant about 4 miles. At sunset, land seen from the mast head bearing SWbS appearing like an island, no land being seen to connect it with the main to the seaward. Kept steering on for the furthest land now that we had a fair breeze, the weather being moderate and fine. Saw a fire upon the westernmost land which served us to steer by. At 9 *hours* 40′ being at no great distance from the land, and the water having shoaled to 6 *fatho*ms came to with the best bower and furled sails. Heard the howling of dogs on shore.

AM. Light winds and fine weather. At daylight we found the land bore from east, round by the south to T [Cape Donington], the westernmost point, which bore S70°W about 3 miles. Having waited to get altitudes for the longitude, as per column, at 7 *hours* 30′ weighed and made sail past point T, and then hauled the wind to the westward in order to make some fixed point in the survey for trying the going of the timekeepers since leaving No 10 bay [Port Lincoln]. At 10 Uncertain Island [Thistle Island] was in sight, and a wedge-shaped island seen before from Memory Cove hills then bore S33°W about 7 leagues. At noon, moderate breezes and cloudy weather. The main land behind Memory Cove in sight. The highest part of Uncertain Island [Thistle Island] S58°W about 7 leagues. Wedge *Is*land S11½°W.

Mer*idian* alt*itude* ☉ Lowe*r* Limb 483	55°47′6″N
Latitude	34°49′23″S
Supp*lemen*t *U*pper *Lim*b	123°42′19″S
Latitude	34°51′0″S
Mean lat*itude*	34°50′11″S

---

[1] Flinders named this Hardwicke Bay (34°56′S, 137°22′E), presumably after Philip Yorke, 3rd Earl of Hardwicke (1757–1834). Vallance, Moore and Groves, eds, *Nature's Investigator*, p. 162.

	By log	Latitude South		Longitude East						
Course	Distance	DR	Obs	DR	TK	Var allowed	Set or current	Error of TK	Ther	Barom
S36°E	32	34°53'	34°50'	137°12'	137°1'	2E	3N 10W	13'38"E	69° 67° 68°	30.15 30.10 30.13

Additional remarks

The situation where we anchored late in the evening is well sheltered from the southerly winds which are those only which seem to blow here with violence at this time of the year. The fire seen on the land and the howling of the dogs confirm us in the opinion of its being the main. From the lower sea shore the land rises a little gradually and seems to be well covered with wood of a moderate size. The rocks appear to be calcarious where they shew themselves in cliffs. The coast of the east side of the inlet has now brought us near to the large Uncertain Island [Thistle Island], which consequently will lie in the entrance of this inlet or gulph. From the west point T [Cape Donington] the shore stretches S22°W which is directly to windward, and as we could not consequently sail along the shore in prosecution of the survey, I thought it advisable to stretch over to our former known lands, and ascertain how the time-keepers had gone lately, since no time would be lost by it.[1]

[f. 175] **Saturday 20 March on the unknown south coast of New Holland**

Moderate breezes and fine weather. Continued stretching to the westward until 4 *hours* 30', when having ascertained our position by bearings and the time-keepers as per column, tacked back towards T [Cape Donington] shore. A ledge of rocks S72°W 3 miles. At 6, the isles π [South Pages Islet] λ² &c. were a few miles to the northward of us, and Wedge I*sland* bore S26½°E. The eastern shore not in sight, but the land and islands near Memory Cove distinctly visible. Moderate breezes, falling light at times, with fine w*eathe*r. At 9 *hours* 30' tacked ship on the wind heading; and at 11, tacked back again from the same cause. Wedge I*sland* then bearing SbyW, by supposition 4 or 5 m*iles*. At 2, tacked ship to the southward. Moderate breezes and cloudy weather. At 6, saw the point T bearing N62°E and Wedge Island S47½°W with other smaller islands near it. At 9, saw land to the southward through the haze, at a considerable distance, the west extreme bearing S1°W: the furthest visible part of the main that we can be certain is so S42°E.

People employed working up junk and trimming sails to a variable wind. At noon, T4,[3] which is the furthest part of the certain main, bore E1°N5 or 6 miles, having small

---

[1] The longitude deduced from these bearings was 30°22'E from the head of Port Lincoln. The longitude taken from timekeepers in the same place was 30°53'. Flinders concluded this small difference indicated that the timekeepers had worked correctly from 4 March at Port Lincoln, when the last observations were made. Flinders, *A Voyage to Terra Australis*, I, pp. 165–6. Rough Journal, I, f. 395, adds: 'The wind being very nearly in the direction which the coast assumes from the west point which shelters the anchorage I stretched to the westward towards Uncertain Island, having an object to accomplish of some importance to the accuracy of my chart of this great inlet.'

[2] Stickney Islet (34°41'S, 136°17'E). Cooper, *The Unknown Coast*, p. 135.

[3] Cape Spencer (35°18'S, 136°53'E), the eastern entrance point of Spencer Gulf. Ibid., p. 54; *Sailing Directions (Enroute): North, West, and South Coasts of Australia*, p. 183.

islands lying off it.[1] Westernmost part of the southern land S13°W. Light airs with hazy weather.

Meridian altitude ☉ Lower Limb 483	54°54′56″N
Latitude	35°17′51″S
Supplement Upper Limb	124°31′38″S
Latitude south	35°16′38″
Mean latitude	35°17′15″S

		Latitude South		Longitude East						
Course	Distance	DR	Obs	DR	TK	Var allowed	Set or current	Error of TK	Ther	Barom
S30°E	29	35°15′	35°17′	137°30′	137°13′	2E	2S	13′38″E	67°	30.13
							6W		67°	30.04
									69°	29.94

Additional remarks

The observation taken at 4 hours 23′ PM shows that the positions of all the places fixed by the time-keepers in No. 12 [Spencer Gulf] are relatively correct with No. 10 bay [Port Lincoln], but the longitude of this bay is still uncertain; nay it is wrong, more or less, without doubt: for the difference of longitude between the tents there and the place of observation on Uncertain Island [Thistle Island] being 20′40″ from good theodolite bearings shews that the timekeepers had erred 5′ eastward between the 21 and 27 of February for they made it only 15′34.5″ of west longitude. At present I consider the timekeepers rates to be correct from No. 10, but the correct longitude of that bay is still to be settled.[2]

The cape T4 [Cape Spencer] is steep, calcarious, and moderately high, and the land runs easterly from it: whether the southern land joins to it is yet altogether in doubt.

[f. 176] **Sunday 21 March** *Investigator* **exploring from No 12 great inlet [Spencer Gulf]**

Variable light airs with cloudy weather. At 3 hours 35′ tacked ship to the southward, having then a little breeze; but not being able to weather O,[3] the island lying off cape T4 [Cape Spencer], tacked off at 4 hours. Variable winds and uncertain weather. Before 7, a steady breeze set in with which we steered towards the southern land, leaving the coast

[1] The Althorpe Islands (35°23′S, 136°51′E), located 5 miles south of Cape Spencer. These three islands were named by Flinders either after Earl Spencer's country home, Althorp in Northamptonshire, or after his eldest son and heir. Flinders, *A Voyage to Terra Australis*, I, pp. 174–5.

[2] Rough Journal, I, f. 397, adds: 'the longitudes of places as now given by Time Keepers is nearly the same as they gave from bay no. 10. The position of all the places in the gulph are thereby verified. Bay No. 10 at present stands in the longitude 136°8′47.3″ East as given by the time keepers from the rates in Bay No. 1. These rates were found to be erroneous and consequently the longitude they gave in Bay No. 10 would be more so, than that at Uncertain Island given 6 days before. I ascertain by bearings that the true difference between these two places is, in longitude 20′40″ which being subtracted from 136°24′27″, the longitude of Uncertain Island, gives an error of 5′ in the longitude of Bay No. 10, which it has been taken too great, and consequently every longitude since is equally erroneous.'

[3] Kangaroo Island (35°49′S, 137°15′E) stands at the entrance to Gulf St Vincent. Vallance, Moore and Groves, eds, *Nature's Investigator*, p. 163.

beyond T4 for a future examination. At 8, isle O [Kangaroo Island] E½N 4 or 5 miles. Fresh breezes. At 10, tacked and brought to under double-reefed topsails. At 12, isle O NEbE. Wore ship, treble reefed the topsails and stood under them to the southward finding the wind coming round that way. Carried away the fore top mast spring stay. Fresh gales with a heavy sea from the SW. Saw the looming of the southern land, high and very near us: wore ship to the northward till daylight, when the southern land bore from South to EbS through the haze, and isle O NbW about 5 miles. At 6 *hours* 10′ wore ship to the southward, sent down top-gallant yards and close-reefed the topsails. The water getting smoother as we approach the southern land. At 9 *hours* 30′ shortened sail with the intention of coming to an anchor in a bight under the cliffy shore until the weather becomes more moderate, but finding the place not well sheltered, continued our course to the eastward along the high cliffy shore, under two close-reefed topsails and foresail. At noon, fresh gales with strong squalls at times. Extremes of the shore S83°E (Δ2)[1] to S62°W distant offshore 3 miles. Water smoother under the land.

Meri*dian* alt*itude* ☉ Lowe*r* Lim*b* 483	54°17′48″N
Latitude	35°31′23″S

		Latitude South		Longitude East						
By log										
Course	Distance	DR	Obs	DR	TK	Var allowed	Set or current	Error of TK	Ther	Barom
S39°E	22	35°34′	35°31′	137°47′	137°48′	2°E	3N 18E	13′38″E	69° 66° 65°	29.90 29.94 30.10

Additional remarks

The gale that came on about 12 o'clock at night blew the hardest that we have yet experienced upon the coast of New Holland. The unknown space between T4 [Cape Spencer] and the southern land we were afraid to steer for during the night, but kept off and on until daylight, when the wind had not gotten so far to the southward as to prevent us from fetching under the southern shore, which I had been afraid it would. No smoke or other mark as yet appears by which we can ascertain whether or not this land is a part of the main. The width of the inlet or passage is 24 miles according to the observed latitudes. The south land is high and cliffy and like cape T4 and isle O [Kangaroo Island] seems to be calcarious. The general line of the shore from the western extreme seen this morning to Δ2 [Point Marsden] the extreme at noon seems to be nearly N75°E.

[f. 177] **Monday 22 March eastward to No 13 ⚓age on the unknown coast**

Fresh gales and cloudy weather. At 1 *hour* 50′ hauled up to the wind round the cape Δ2 [Point Marsden], from which the land trends to the southward into a large bay.[2] Let out 4th reefs and set the main sail trying to fetch up into the bay for ⚓age. At 6 we approached the land on the east side of the bay, where we anchored with the best bower in 9 *fathoms* upon a fine sandy bottom and in smooth water. The southern land bearing from E7½S

---

[1] Point Marsden (35°34′S, 137°38′E), on the north side of Kangaroo Island. Cooper, *The Unknown Coast*, p. 135.

[2] Nepean Bay (35°40′S, 137°45′E). Flinders, *A Voyage to Terra Australis*, I, p. 168.

(cape Θ)[1] to N67°30′W (Δ2), our distance from a small sandy beach ½ mile. Another piece of high land (Λ)[2] N71½°E to NN38½E. Fresh breezes and squally weather. Found a tide running as per column.

AM Moderate breezes with squalls at times. The commander and scientific gentlemen landed to survey and examine the country, which they found great reason to believe to be an island notwithstanding its magnitude. Three kanguroos of a good size were brought on board by the return of the boat. Sailmakers repairing the fore and mizzen topsails. During the morning the weather was so cloudy, with spitting rain, and until past noon that no observations for latitude or longitude could be obtained.

| Course | Distance | By log | | Latitude South | | Longitude East | | | | | | |
		DR	Obs	DR	TK	Var allowed	Set or current	Error of TK	Ther	Barom
S72°E	24½	35°39′	35°42′	138°16′	138°24′	2°E	3S 7E	13′38″E	62½° 67°	30.22 30.25

Additional remarks

The space between Δ2 [Point Marsden] and cape Θ [Cape Emu/Kangaroo Head] is occupied by the large bight into which we were unable to fetch. It comprehends several smaller bights, but they appear to be mostly shoal, and are out of the strength of the tides.

After coming to an ⚓ some black substances were seen moving about on the shore by some of the younger gentlemen and were thought to be animals of some kind; but the wiser ones, who thought they were lumps of stone, and that imagination supplied them with motion, laughed at this, asking if they were not elephants. On landing in the morning however we were agreeably surprised to find a great number of dark brown kanguroos grazing upon a small patch of grass near the landing place, and our landing gave them no disturbance. I had with me a double-barrelled gun with a bayonet, and the gentlemen with me had musquets. It is impossible to guess how many of the animals were seen during the day, but I killed ten and the rest of the party made the number up to 31 during the day, the least weighing 69 lbs and the largest 125, uncleaned. These made a glorious feast to people who had been four months on salt provisions. I ordered that 50 or 60 lbs should be stewed into soup each day in the ships coppers, and that as much meat besides should be served to the messes as the people could eat. These kanguroos seem to resemble the largest kind found in the forest lands in New South Wales, except that their colour is darker.[3]

It may be supposed that kangaroo hunting left me but little time or inclination for surveying; nevertheless I ascended to the higher land with the surveying instruments, scrambling with some difficulty through the brushwood and over the fallen trees, but the thickness and height of the wood prevented me from seeing anything.[4]

[1] Cape Emu, also Kangaroo Head, on the north side of Kangaroo Island. (35°43′S, 137°54′E). Cooper, *The Unknown Coast*, p. 135.

[2] Cape Jervis (35°37′S, 138°06′E), on the south-western tip of Fleurieu Peninsula. Ibid.

[3] The western grey kangaroo. Vallance, Moore and Groves, eds, *Nature's Investigator*, p. 166. Flinders added: 'In gratitude for so seasonable a supply I named this southern land Kangaroo Island.' *A Voyage to Terra Australis*, I, p. 170.

[4] Rough Journal, I, f. 401, adds: 'The main object for which I landed was defeated by the thickness and height of the brushwood, which would not permit me to see round after I had been at the labour of ascending the higher land; but the kanguroos and seals satisfied me that it was an island.'

[f. 178] Tuesday 23 March *Investigator* at No 13 anchorage under Kanguroo Island
Moderate breezes and cloudy weather. All hands employed skinning and cleaning kangaroo; afterwards got the top-gall*ant* masts down upon deck and struck the masts, preparatory to shifting them for others. Showers of rain at times. AM Variable breezes with cloudy weather. Employed shifting the present topmasts, which are split in the heels, for others. A party of gentlemen on shore examining the natural productions of the island, and killing kangaroo. At noon, moderate breezes and fine weather.
On shore: anchorage bearing N40°W⅔
Meridian double altitude of ☉ lower and upper limbs
   (the mean) with sext*ant* 483   107°10′0″N
Latitude   35°43′0″S

Additional remarks

This land, which we believe to be insulated and denominate Kangaroo Island, appears to be calcarious in all its cliffs which shew themselves to the westward of our anchorage, but here the calcarious matter is found scattered in loose and small quantities only. The basis seems to be a slate which, in some parts, splits off like iron bars. The strata lie nearly horizontal, and in the interstices some streaks of quartz are sometimes seen. In some pieces a composition with mica[1] gives it a shining ore-like appearance.

A thick wood covers all this part of the island in sight of our anchorage, but none of the trees that I saw in a vegetating state were equal in size to the generality of those that were dead. Such abundance of the last were lying on the ground in all directions, besides many yet standing, that in penetrating inland to get upon the higher land, a considerable portion of the walk was performed upon them. These prostrated trees were lying in all directions, and therefore I judge they were not thrown down by any general violent wind; but they seemed to be nearly all of the same age and in the same state of decay. I am induced from all circumstances to believe that they have been killed by fire, which by some accident, seems to have prevailed all over this side of the island, and probably over the whole of it.

The kanguroos possess a dominion in this island which probably has never before been invaded: the seals share with them on the shores, but they seem to dwell amicably together. It not unfrequently happened that the report of a gun fired at a kangaroo brought out two or three bellowing seals from bushes that were further from the shore than the kangaroo at which the gun was fired. The seals, indeed, seemed to be the most discerning animal of the two, for they acted as if they knew us not to be kanguroos, whereas the latter appeared not unfrequently to consider us to be seals.

The party on shore today report themselves to have seen some large running birds at a distance, which from their account appear to be the emu or cassuary.[2] Eleven kanguroos were brought on board, but many of these were small, when compared to the first, and seem to be of a different species.[3]

---

[1] A silicate mineral.

[2] The Kangaroo Island emu. Though emus are of the same family as cassowaries, the only species of cassowary in Australia is found in northern Queensland. Vallance, Moore and Groves, eds, *Nature's Investigator*, pp. 172–3.

[3] This island had probably not been explored previously: 'Can this part of Terra Australis have been visited before, unknown to the world? The French navigator, La Pérouse, was ordered to explore it, but there seems little probability that he ever passed Torres' Strait.' Flinders, *A Voyage to Terra Australis*, I, p. 171.

[f. 179] **Wednesday 24 March on the unknown south coast of New Holland**

Moderate breezes and cloudy weather. Employed rigging the new top-masts and set up the rigging. Light breezes and cloudy weather. AM Fresh breezes, afterwards moderate. Employed stowing the booms afresh, and scraping the new top-masts; which being greased and the decks cleared, at 10 weighed the anchor and made sail to the north-westward for the cape T4 [Cape Spencer] quitted on the 21st PM in order to continue the examination of the coast up to the port abreast of Kanguroo Island, where we see smokes rising. At noon, moderate breezes and squally at times. Extremes of Kanguroo Island N81°W to S55°E. A small head near our anchorage S31°E. Under single-reefed topsails &c.

Meridian altitude ☉ Lower Limb with 483	53°2′34″N
Latitude	35°35′45″S

	By log		Latitude South		Longitude East						
Course	Distance	DR	Obs	DR	TK	Var allowed	Set or current	Error of TK	Ther	Barom
N23°W	6	35°36′	35°36′	138°13′	–	2°E	–	13′37″E	64°	30.24
									61°	30.23
									64°	30.24

Additional remarks

The soil of that part of Kanguroo Island which was examined by us was judged to be much superior to any yet seen, either upon the islands or main of this south coast, some small spots in Princess Royal harbour excepted. I did not ascertain its depth, but in general it cannot be very shallow; it consists of vegetable earth mixed with sand, but not in any great proportion, and I think it superior to some part of the land which is cultivated about Port Jackson.

From the appearance of the shores I judge the rise of the tide here is about six feet. The flood comes from the eastward and the time of the ships swinging to the ebb is about two-and-a-half hours after the moon passes over the meridian, but from after observations it appears that it is not high water until one hour and a half afterwards.[1]

The wood of Kanguroo Island is in abundance near the water, and is of sufficient size for fuel or for stowage in a ships hold, but it does not appear to be calculated for superior purposes.[2]

[f. 180] **Thursday 25 March *Investigator* exploring from Kanguroo Island northward, on the unknown south coast**

Moderate breezes and cloudy weather, with squalls at times. Trimmed sails occasionally. Land seen to the northward from WNW (Variation 7°E) to a low point bearing NbyE 3 or 4 leagues. Kanguroo Island S40°W to S3°E. Double reefed the topsails. At 8, hauled up to the wind intending to be off isle o[3] and cape T4 [Cape Spencer] at daylight. Moderate breezes and cloudy weather. At 2 hours 40′ saw isle o [Evans Island] bearing WbyN.

---

[1] Kangaroo Island has strong tides and is surrounded by many reefs and rocky cliffs. Tides reach six feet at the eastern end of Kangaroo Island. Chapman, 'The Tides of Australia', pp. 972–84.

[2] Flinders added at the bottom of the page: 'Note. The additional remarks of these two days, incorporated according to the marks of reference, are the general remarks upon Kanguroo Island, and ought to have followed the 24th under that title.'

[3] Evans Island (32°23′S, 133°29′E). Cooper, *The Unknown Coast (a supplement)*, p. 24.

Tacked ship, shortened sail and brought to on the starboard tack until daylight; isle o bearing NW. Let out 2nd reefs, and at 6 *hours* 30' T4 bore N43°W about 8 miles, when we filled and stored to the eastward along shore. Mod*erate* breezes with dull cloudy weather. Mustered the ships company and saw them clean: kangaroo issued to them as before. On the water shoaling to 4 *fatho*ms at 11 *hours* 15' tacked ship: saw a sunken rock very near the ship. At noon, the point from which the shoal water runs off, N18°E 5 or 6 miles, the shore in general being low and sandy. Dull cloudy weather T4 [Cape Spencer] W8°S.

By log		Latitude South		Longitude East						
Course	Distance	DR	Obs from bearings	DR	Obs TK	Var allowed	Set or current	Error of TK	Ther	Barom
N51°W	34½	35°14'	35°15'	137°40'	–	2°E	1N 6W	–	65° 62° 64°	30.33 30.38 30.45

Friday 26 March

Moderate breezes and cloudy dull weather. The sun has not once appeared this day notwithstanding the height of the barometer. At 1 *hour* 10' tacked to the eastward until 4, when we stood back again, not being able to weather a low point which bore East 4 m*iles*. Double reefed the topsails. Fresh breezes and cloudy. Continued stretching over towards Kangaroo I*sland* until 10 *hours* 30' when it bore SW to East distant about 3 miles: tacked ship. Saw the land on the lee bow at 4, and the water beginning to shoal tacked ship at that time. At 6, tacked to the northward in order to weather the low point which bore east at 4 PM but finding we could not accomplish it at 8, tacked again to the southward, let out 2nd reefs, and set top-gallant sails.

At 11 *hours* 30' tacked ship to the northward. We find ourselves set so much to leeward that we lose ground rather than gain. At noon, moderate breezes and fine weather with haze. The low point of the northern land which we want to weather to examine an opening there, bears N38°20'E.

Mer*idian* alt*itude* ☉ Low*er Lim*b 483   52°29'39"N
Latitude   35°21'27"S

By log		Latitude South		Longitude East						
Course	Distance	DR	Obs	DR	TK	Var allowed	Set or current	Error of TK	Ther	Barom
S31°E	17	35°24'	35°21'	137°57'	137°52'	2°E	2N 7W	13'13"E	63° 61½° 63°	30.45 30.46 30.46

[f. 181] **Saturday 27 March northward, on the unknown south coast**

Moderate breezes and fine weather. At 2 *hours* 30' tacked to the southward, finding we could not weather the island-like, low, point,[1] round which is the inlet to be examined.

[1] Probably Point Marsden. Ibid.

At 4 tacked again for the point, and at least we weathered it. At 6, the low, island-like point bore N12°E and the furthest extreme there N38°E, our distance off the nearest shore 5 or 6 miles: Δ2 [Point Marsden] bore at this time S2°E. Double reefed the topsails. At 8, tacked to the southward on finding the water to shoal: our distance from the low shore to leeward being about 3 miles. Fresh breezes and squally. Tacked ship to the eastward; but on the wind heading us, at 2 tacked again to the southward. Tacked ship to the northward until 6 when we found ourselves nearly in the same situation as at 6 PM: tacked to the southward and let the 2nd reefs out of the topsails. Tacked ship for the new opening, but the wind heading almost immediately, tacked again to the southward. Towards noon, it became calm with hazy weather. Lowered down the sails and dropped the kedge to prevent being drifted to the westward. Extremes of Kanguroo Island Δ1[1] W10°S to cape Θ S60°E [Cape Emu/Kangaroo Head]. Point Δ2 [Point Marsden] S24°W 2½ miles.

Meridian altitude ☉ Lower Limb 483   51°55′41″N
Latitude   35°31′57″S

		Latitude South		Longitude East						
Course	Distance	DR	Obs	DR	TK	Var allowed	Set or current	Error of TK	Ther	Barom
S50°E	21	35°34′	35°32′	138°16′	138°6′	2°E	2N 5W	13′0°E	63° 63½° 67°	30.43 30.38 30.38

Additional remarks

The part of the main land opposite to Kanguroo Island from T4 [Cape Spencer] to the low island-like point is generally low land, and seemingly sandy. The point is somewhat remarkable for a hummock upon it, which at a little distance appears to be an island. There is no particular point there, but the land from thence trends to the NEward, and no land is visible from thence to the high land of great No. 2 (cape Λ) [Cape Jervis], which hitherto we have supposed to be mainland. From comparing the ships and course with that given by the log, I suspect that the tides run differently on the two sides of this passage or strait,[2] and that some inlet on the north side is the cause of it. At the time of anchoring at noon, we ought to have had a tide setting to the eastward, judging from what is observed at the anchorage further eastward but this was not the case.

The land about point Δ2 [Point Marsden] seems to be more barren than cape Θ [Cape Emu/Kangaroo Head] further eastward; but a thick brush is not wanting at a little distance behind the cliffs of the shore.

[f. 182] **Sunday 28 March** *Investigator* **on the unknown south coast**
Light airs and calms with cloudy weather and haze. Found no observable drift of tide any way until 9 o'clock, when it made a little to the NE towards the new opening. Weighed the kedge ⚓ on a light breeze springing up, and steered toward the unexplored part of the main.

---

[1] Cape Cassini (35°35′S, 137°20′E). Cooper, *The Unknown Coast*, p. 135.
[2] Named Investigator's Strait after the ship. Ibid.

Fresh breezes with threatening weather. Handed top-gallant sails and double-reefed the top sails. Saw a fire upon the land ahead. Took in the spanker, the jib and the mainsail, ready to perform any evolution which the exigency of the case may require. Land seen ahead and on the weather bow, and several fires upon it. Wore ship, having missed stays. At 2, tacked again to the eastward. Nearly calm, with lightening on the NE. At daylight, the high eastern land extended from about N35°E to S20°W; a lofty mountain N65°E:[1] our distance offshore about 9 miles. At 7½, it became calm with very hazy weather, so that the land is not very definable. Hauled up the courses. Cleaned the ship; and afterwards the ships company cleaned themselves and were mustered and inspected as usual.

By the lead, tried at various times this morning, no tide could be observed. At 11, a light air sprung up, and we made sail along the shore, upwards. Noon, fine weather with some haze.

Meridian altitude ☉ Lower Limb 483	51°59′49″N
Latitude	35°4′23″S
Supplement ☉ Upper Limb	127°28′9″S
Latitude	35°4′29″S
Mean latitude	35°4′26″S

	By log	Latitude South		Longitude East						
Course	Distance	DR	Obs	DR	TK	Var allowed	Set or current	Error of TK	Ther	Barom
N55½°E	41	35°9′	35°4′	138°57′	138°47′	2°E	2N	12′48″E	62°	30.33
									66°	30.32
									68°	30.29

Additional remarks

The eastern shore, from Λ cape [Cape Jervis] northward, along which we ran in the night, and lay near, becalmed in the morning, is much higher than Kanguroo Island or the opposite shore, and generally presents two ridges of land to our view. The shore is mostly rocky or sandy, with a few small trees scattered about, but higher up a well-appearing forest clothes the country. From the fires seen during the night, the smokes observed before upon it, and from its general appearance, we believe it to be the main land. The space between it and the island-like point to the westward, being fully thirty miles, as appears from the observations with the timekeepers, it may be presumed that we are entering a large inlet of some kind, as the set of the tides before gave me cause to suspect there was such an opening in the land in this neighbourhood.[2]

[f. 183] **Monday 29 March exploring No 14 great inlet [Gulf St Vincent] New Holland**

Light breezes and hazy weather. Steered nearly parallel to the low sandy shore, up the inlet. Finding the water to be getting shoaler, at 3 hours 30′ hauled further off the shore. Low land seen from the mast head as far out as NbyW. Loftiest of the eastern hills S69°E:

[1] Mount Lofty (34°58′S, 138°42′E). Vallance, Moore and Groves, eds, *Nature's Investigator*, p. 169.
[2] The *Investigator* had entered Gulf St Vincent (35°00′S, 138°10′E). Ibid.

our distance off shore about 8 miles. At 5 *hours* 50′ (before sunset) came to with the best bower upon a bottom of sand mixed with pieces of dead coral. Veered to a whole cable, furled sails and sent down top-gallant yards the low eastern sandy shore 8 or 10 miles distant, and seen out as far as North; and the opposite west shore seen from W5°S to NWbW. Moderate breezes and fine weather; some swell coming in from the southward. Very little tide observable during the night.

AM. Light airs and fine weather. At daylight, the commander took the gig and went to sound upon a rippling near the ship, but there did not appear to be any difference in the depth, which upon it was 5¼ fathoms. Set up the fore and main topmast and top-gallant rigging, and at 8 sent up top-gallant yards, as in harbour. Very light airs and calms. At 9 *hours* 30′ weighed and made sail to proceed up the inlet, but we had no wind until 11, when we hauled more off to the westward finding the water continue to get shoaler. At noon, light breezes and fine weather, with haze. Saw some hills to the northward forming one mountain, the middle of which bore N19°W. The furthest part of the low, sandy western shore N4°E.

Meridian altitude ⊙ Lower Limb 483	52°5′55″N
Latitude	34°34′51″S
Supplement Upper Limb	127°20′37″S
Latitude	34°33′31″S
Mean	34°34′11″S

	By log			Latitude South		Longitude East					
Course	Distance	DR	Obs	DR	TK	Var allowed	Set or current	Error of TK	Ther	Barom
N18°W	28	34°38′	34°34′	138°47′	138°40′	2°E	4N 3E	12′36″E	71° 69° 71°	30.31 30.27 30.34

Additional remarks

The low eastern shore along which we have run this day is generally sandy, but is mostly covered with small trees. The breadth of this low land from the water to the back hills is various. It seems to be not more than 5 or 6 miles in the first part, but as they preserve nearly a north-north-east direction, and the low shore curves to the westward it becomes much broader. We notice much smoke on the low land which is, probably, at no great distance beyond the fire seen on the preceding night; and at noon also great smokes were rising from the hills further up.

The rippling upon which I went to sound in the morning was evidently the effect of tide, but the difference in depth upon, or on each side of it, was scarcely perceptible, and the run of this tide past the ship was very trifling: what little there was set to the north-westward.

[f. 184] **Tuesday 30 March** *Investigator* **exploring No 14 inlet [Gulf St Vincent]**

Light breezes and cloudy weather. Hauled up nearly to the wind towards the west side of the inlet, to get deeper water. At 1 *hour* 30′ kept more away, but the shoal water from the eastern shore obliged us soon to haul more up again. At 3 *hours* 30′ steered nearly in a direct line upwards, but the water shoaling off the western shore, steered various ways for the deepest channel, the ship being directed from the masthead as usual. Towards sunset the inlet appeared to be closed round at the distance of six or seven miles, and finding no deep channel further up it, we came to with the best bower in 5¼ *fathoms* upon a bottom of coarse sand, shells, and broken pieces of coral. Veered to half a cable, furled sails, and sent down top-gallant yards. Highest part of the hummocky mount at the head of the inlet N2°W. Mount Lofty on the eastern shore S42°E, the shore distant in its nearest parts 4 or 5 miles. Hoisted out the cutter to be in readiness in the morning to examine the head of the inlet.

AM Light breezes and fine weather. The cutter taken by the Commander up the inlet, accompanied by the naturalist. Roused the small bower upon deck, to clean the tier and to repair the rounding of the cable. Noon, light breezes and fine weather. (At 8 AM the tide ½ knot past the ship to the SSW.)

Meridian altitude ☉ Lower Limb 488	52°0′45″N
Latitude	34°16′39″S
Supplement ☉ Upper Limb	127°27′1″N
Latitude	34°16′31″
Mean latitude	34°16′35″S

By log		Latitude South		Longitude East						
Course	Distance	DR	Obs	DR	TK	Var allowed	Set or current	Error of TK	Ther	Barom
N27°W	12½	34°23′	34°17′	138°40′	138°31′	3°E	6N 2W	12′24″E	71° 69° 71½°	30.35 30.35 30.34

Additional remarks

Although the western shore appears evidently to be the deepest side of the inlet in this upper part, yet it should seem that three or four miles is as near as a ship can approach it. The land on that side rises gradually to a moderate elevation, but in general it has a smooth barren appearance: many large smokes appear upon it. The eastern shore seems more woody and also more sandy.

In going up the inlet, the soundings were not less than three fathoms for the first 4 miles, but we then came quickly upon a bank where it was necessary to row a little back to get into a small deep channel nearer the western shore. There were numbers of rays upon the flat, but being unprovided we lost an opportunity of getting a good meal of fish. The narrow channel carried us up to near the head of the inlet, but the boat would not then approach nearer than half a mile to the shore: the bottom consisted of mud and sand.

After taking angles, and observing the latitude in the artificial horizon as annexed, we walked up to the ridge of back land, from whence the head of the inlet was sufficiently conspicuous. There did not appear to be any constant drain of water, but in wet weather much will no doubt be thrown into it from the hills which surround the head in a semicircular form; these hills are of moderate elevation, and are a continuation of the same ridge which seems nearly parallel to the east shore of the inlet. The water of No. 12 inlet [Spencer Gulf] was hid by land something higher than that upon which we were: but probably it might have been seen from the Hummocky Mountain[1] which we had proposed to ascend had not its distance been found beyond the bounds of returning to the ship in the evening. We found the tide to be out at 10 o'clock, and therefore it should be high water about seven hours after the moon passes over the meridian, and the common rise seems to be about 6 feet.

Some few shags, gulls, and one black swan were seen upon the shoals. The country has a pleasant appearance round the head of the inlet at a distant view, but all that I saw was poor in fertility. The trees grow but in patches and the grass is thin.

| Meridian altitude ☉ center 483 | 52°24′35″N |
| Latitude | 34°8′52″S |

[f. 185] **Wednesday 31 March at anchorage 2 on the unknown south coast**

Fresh breezes with fine weather. Employed finishing the rounding of the cable and restoring the booms.[2] Towards evening, light breezes with fine weather. At 7 the commander and naturalist returned with the cutter. At 10½, ship swung to the flood tide, which soon after ran NbE ½ knot per hour.

AM After washing decks, sent up top gallant yards at daylight, and at 6 *hours* 30′ weighed and made sail down the inlet, with light winds. Hoisted the gig within board to be repaired. Employed repairing the puddening of the anchor.[3] Light breezes and fine weather, with haze. All the small sail set fore and aft that will stand upon a wind. Cleaned ship below. Saw a turtle upon the water. Sour kraut served as usual. Tacked ship at 11 *hours* 30′ on the ship falling off: the western shore being distant three or four miles. At noon, moderate winds and fine weather.

Meridian altitude ☉ Lower Limb 483	51°26′54″N
Latitude	34°27′12″S
Supplement to meridian altitude ☉ Upper Limb	128°0′34″S
Latitude	34°26′46″S

By log		Latitude South		Longitude East						
Course	Distance	DR	Obs	DR	TK	Var allowed	Set or current	Error of TK	Ther	Barom
S27°W	8	34°24′	34°27′	138°36′	138°28′	2°E	3S 1E	12′12″E	72° 67° 69°	30.41 30.41 30.36

Thursday 1 April[4]

Moderate breezes and fine weather. At 2 *hours* 5′ we had got into shoal water in the east side of the deep channel, and therefore tacked ship. At 5 *hours* 30′ being within half a mile of the western shore tacked to the eastward: the Hummocky Mount bearing N16½E and

---

[1] Flinders called this 'Hummock Mount'. It is now called South Hummocks (1,093 feet, 34°02′S, 138°05′E). Vallance, Moore and Groves, eds, *Nature's Investigator*, p. 171.

[2] Spars along the bottom of the fore and aft rigged sails.

[3] i.e. parcelling the rings of anchors with tarred canvas.

[4] On this day Flinders completed the examination of Gulf St Vincent. Flinders, *A Voyage to Terra Australis*, I, p. 181.

the south extreme S5°E. Hazy weather. On the ship breaking off tacked ship to the southward.

Mod*erate* breezes and fine weather. Saw a large fire on the eastern shore. On the wind coming round so as to be free, shortened sail, and at 3 o'clock brought to until daylight, when we wore round and made sail for the western shore. Mo*unt* Lofty bearing E1½N but the western shore not in sight. On seeing the land at 8, hauled towards the southern extreme; and at 9 *hours* 30′ hauled round up to the *South Eastwar*d to weather a dry sand bank lying off the southern extreme, which we did, but passed over several patches of discoloured water, and saw other near us more extensive, where the elevated banks of sand were very conspicuous under the water. At noon, the extreme of the eastern land (part of cape Λ) [Cape Jervis] S14°E, Mount Lofty N70°E and Kanguroo Island in sight from the masthead. Light breezes and fine weather. Mustered the ships company and saw them clean.

Mer*idian* alt*itude* ☉ Low*er Lim*b 483	50°20′9″N
Latitude	35°10′46″S
Supp*lemen*t U*pper* Limb	129°6′4″S
Latitude	35°9′2″S
Mean	35°9′54″S

By log			Latitude South		Longitude East						
Course	Distance	DR	Obs	DR	TK	Var allowed	Set or current	Error of TK	Ther	Barom
S2°E	45	35°12′	35°10′	138°38′	138°27′	2E	2N 3W	11′59″E	70° 68½° 70½°	30.33 30.33 30.31

Additional remarks

The land to which we approached so near this afternoon has a pleasant appearance, being grassy hills of a gentle ascent with clumps of trees interspersed; but from analogy I judge it to be rather barren than fertile. The shore is somewhat cliffy, and not quite so low as usual; and from allowing us to approach within half a mile of the shore, it seems deeper than would be expected in an inclosed inlet where there was no stream running of consequence. Lower down near the entrance on the west side, the shore is very low, being a sandy beach from which extends a sandy spit to some miles distant. I saw the island-like hummock from the masthead at noon, but could not set it or find any object to which I could reduce an angle from it. The contrast between this low land and the opposite shore is great, that being mountainous and stony.

[f. 186] Friday 2 April *Investigator* back from No 14 inlet [Gulf St Vincent] back to anchorage No 13 [Kangaroo Head]

Light airs and hazy weather, and afterwards almost calm. At 3 tacked to the southward on a light breeze springing up from the south-eastward. Fine weather, with haze. Steering to the southward for Kanguroo Island, the former ⚓age being in sight, and bearing south. At 11, passed our former anchorage and steered along the shore into the western bight. At 11 *hours* 40′ dropped the anchor in 7½ fathoms: cape ☉ [Cape Emu/Kangaroo Head], extreme bearing ENE and our distance offshore about ¾ of a mile. Veered to half a cable and furled sails. Hoisted out the cutter to be in readiness to go on shore early in the morning.

AM Light breezes and fine weather. The Commander and a party landed to survey and shoot kanguroos, but very few were seen and only one brought on board. A party sent on shore to cut firewood, and another to shoot. Cleaned the ship below and aired as usual.

This day continued to 36 hours, or civil account.

Light breezes and fine weather. Sufficient kanguroos brought on board to give a fresh meal to the ships company. Received a cutter load of wood and stowed it away. Fresh breezes and cloudy weather. Veered away the half cable which had been boused in.[1]

Meridian altitude ☉ Lower Limb 488   49°24'10"N
Latitude   35°43'35"S

By log		Latitude South		Longitude East						
Course	Distance	DR	Obs	DR	TK	Var allowed	Set or current	Error of TK	Ther	Barom
S11°W	30½	35°40'	35°44'	138°45'	138°21'	3°E	4S	11'48"E	70°	30.28
							3W		70½°	–
									70½°	30.35
									70°	30.27

Additional remarks

The objects I had in view in coming to Kanguroo Island a second time were, first to get to a known place of shelter for the night, 2nd to get a few more fresh meals for the ships company, and 3rd to ascertain generally whether our timekeepers were still keeping the rates found for them in No 10 bay [Port Lincoln]. The kanguroos were not now found in anything like the numbers that they were at the 1st anchorage; and besides, we now find them much shyer than before. Five emus or cassuaries were distinctly seen today, but by people who had no guns with them: and part of the skin of a porcupine, or of some animal like it, was found. This island affords the only instance of containing the emu of any of the present known islands of New Holland, Van Diemens Land excepted. Note: The emu is also found upon Kings Island[2] in Bass's Strait.

The above observation shews the timekeepers to have differed about 1'50" of longitude westward since we quitted the island on March 24; our present rates of losing are therefore seven-tenths of a second of time per day too great.

Saturday 3 April

Civil account

Moderate breezes and cloudy weather. At 6 hours 30' weighed, stretched in towards the shore, then tacked to the northward intending to work out from between cape Λ [Cape Jervis] and Kanguroo Island and so to proceed in the examination of the coast, eastward; but we now found the time-keepers had run down, having been neglected to be wound

---

[1] i.e. hoisted with a tackle.

[2] i.e. King Island (39°52'S, 143°59'E). Flinders knew that the southern part of this island had been discovered by Captain William Reid in a sealing vessel in 1798. At the time he did not know that the northern portion of the island had been seen and named by John Black (in honour of Philip Gidley King) in the brig *Harbinger* in January 1801, but he later found this out from Grant, *The Narrative of a Voyage of Discovery*, p. 86. Flinders, *A Voyage to Terra Australis*, I, p. 205; Scott, *The Life of Matthew Flinders*, p. 169.

up yesterday. Came to anchor nearby in the same place again, and on the tide making up into the bight, moored ship.

The commander landed to get observations for ascertaining fresh rates for the time-keepers. Hoisted out the launch and sent an officer in her to the eastern part of the island to kill seals and kanguroos. A party of men sent on shore abreast of the ship to cut wood. At noon, light breezes and fine weather. The launch returned in the evening with several seal skins for the service of the rigging: she left a party of gentlemen to examine that part of the island.

Thermometer	69°	72°	73°
Barometer	30.26	30.22	30.17

[f. 187] Sunday 4 April Kanguroo Island on the unknown south coast
Light winds and cloudy weather. The commander went away in the cutter, accompanied by the naturalist, to examine the head of the large bight in which the ship lies.[1] Carpenters with some other hands on shore cutting firewood. Roused up the best bower cable, cleaned well in the tier and recoiled the cable. At noon, light airs and fine weather. Received on board a turn [bundle] of wood by the launch and in the evening a second turn. Employed on board stowing it away and in other necessary duties.

Thermometer	69°	72°	71°
Barometer	30.16	30.16	30.15

Monday 5 April
Spitting rain at times, with light airs and calms. Sent some hands onshore to cut broom stuff. Cleaned the ship thoroughly above and below, and aired well with stoves. Sent the launch to the eastward to fish, and to bring on board a party that went to shoot kanguroos. At 11, the commander and naturalist returned on board from their excursion. At noon, dull cloudy weather. People employed mostly in putting the holds in order. At dusk the launch returned with the shooting and fishing parties who had had but little success: one of the boats crew returned very lame having been bitten by a seal. Hoisted in the launch and prepared to go to sea in the morning. At 4 AM, tide ran SW 1 knot. At 5 hours 30′ it ran ENE 1 knot.

Thermometer	69°	72°	71°
Barometer	30.15	30.15	30.12

Additional remarks
Richard Stanly (entered at Madeira) the man who returned lame, having been simple enough to attack a large seal with a small stick in an incautious manner, was seized upon by the seal and much bitten in the leg. As he attacked the seal without any useful object in view, he was not undeserving of some punishment for his malignity: he has paid severely, for it is probable that he will always be more or less lame from it.

The object of my excursion in the cutter was both to examine the head of the great bay or bight, and also to ascend a hill towards the center of the island, which seems to be the only one where the height and thickness of the brushwood does not altogether intercept the view.

On approaching the south-west corner of the bay, we were gratified to find a small opening which led towards the hill and which brought us within a mile of the foot of it.

[1] The boat expedition went to the eastern cove of Nepean Bay. Flinders, *A Voyage to Terra Australis*, I, p. 182.

After observing the suns meridional altitude in the artificial horizon, as annexed, we got through the brush without much difficulty, and reached the top of the hill at one o'clock.[1] To my surprise the sea appeared at a very little distance to the southward from this station. To the south-east and south-west were projecting cliffy heads, forming between them a wide open bay, the head of which approached so near to the head of the small inlet we had come up in the boat, as to leave an isthmus of only two miles in breadth. The shore on the south side appeared to be calcarious and cliffy, but not high.

Our inlet or rather lagoon spreads itself into two heads, of which the southern one is the smallest and shallowest.[2] It extends three or four miles from the small entrance, but except at high water does not afford water enough to swim boats of any size. The eastern head of the lagoon contains three islands, of which two seem to be breeding places for pelicans: on the third we did not land. These birds were in great numbers, and many of them too young to fly.[3] From the quantity of scattered bones and skeletons upon the islands, I infer, that the pelicans not only commence their being here, but that they have selected this retreat for the closing scene of their existence. Here, at a distance from man the great disturber of all, surrounded by his feathered progeny, and in the very same spot where he first emerged from his own shelly prison: in this retreat, the aged pelican can quietly resign his small portion of ethereal flame back to the great eternal source of vitality [f. 188] whence it emanated, without having his last moments interrupted, and perhaps without a pang. Requiescant ossa in pace, barbare![4]

Besides pelicans, this piece of water is frequented by flocks of the pied shag,[5] and by a few ducks and gulls. Some oysters were found upon the shoals.

The country round the water is everywhere thickly covered with brush wood. The soil seems to be nearly of the same good quality as in the neighbourhood of the first anchorage. Only two kanguroos were killed and but few seen.

The depth of water in the outer part of the small entrance into the lagoon is less than it is higher up, where a regular channel is formed. I cannot give the depth of water, a lead and line having been neglected to be put into the boat, but it appears to be sufficient for rowing boats of any size.

---

[1] Flinders named this Prospect Hill (35°14′S, 138°43′E). Ibid., I, p. 183.

[2] Flinders named the inlet Pelican Lagoon. It was situated on the eastern end of Kangaroo Island. Ibid.

[3] Refers to the Australian pelican (*Pelecanus conspicillatus*). Vallance, Moore and Groves, eds, *Nature's Investigator*, p. 175.

[4] 'This passage means 'May their bones rest in peace, O barbarian.' 'Barbarian' refers to the European interlopers, of which he was one. Flinders added here in a note: 'I am conscious that sentimental conjectures and exclamations are very much out of their place when found in a ships logbook, or even in the narrative of a voyage of discovery: and I request the reader to pardon this touch of the melancholy, though not unpleasing, reflections which took hold of my mind on viewing this uncommon cemetery where the young wingless pelican was seen scrambling over the bones of his parent.' Flinders recalled this passage when he wrote his published voyage account, poignantly noting that the arrival of Europeans in the waters surrounding Kangaroo Island also heralded the passing of what he romantically termed the golden age of the pelicans: 'Alas, for the pelicans! Their golden age is past; but it has much exceeded in duration that of man' (Flinders, *A Voyage to Terra Australis*, I, pp. 83–4). This passage inspired James Montgomery to write a prolix poem entitled *The Pelican Island* (1827), in which he mused lengthily about the barbarity of man in contrast with the pelican, which has religious symbolic meaning in that it was supposed to peck its own breast to draw blood to feed its young and is thus an image of the self-sacrifice of Christ. Wiley, ed., *The Poems of James Montgomery*, pp. 155, 161–89.

[5] A medium-sized member of the Cormorant family.

To have ascertained the breadth of this large island is a valuable part of the little knowledge we yet have of its form and extent; and is more than I expected to have gained from the moderate height of the hill which I call Prospect Hill. In consequence of the near approach of Pelican Lagoon to the shore on the south side, Kanguroo Island is separated into two parts of very unequal size, connected by an isthmus whose breadth is about two miles.

We found it to be high water in the lagoon at 6 o'clock on the morning of the 5th, which is near four hours after the moon passes over the meridian; but it appears from the log board that the tide made from the westward more than an hour before that time; so that the first hour and half of the tide from the westward makes high water; which is three hours earlier than at the head of No. 14 inlet [Gulf St Vincent]. The rise of tide seemed to be between four and eight feet.

Double meridian alt*itude* ☉ *Upper Limb* 98°7′13″
                  ☉ *Lower Limb* 97°3′18″
Latitude 35°50′53″

General remarks

The number of kanguroos found at the first anchorage must exceed what have been found in any other part of the island. They seem to be attracted to that place from its being bare of brush wood, and by some small grass plants which they keep exceedingly close cropped.

Although not less than thirty emus or cassuaries were seen at different times, yet it so happened that they were but once fired at, and we did not get one of them. They were mostly seen near cape ☉ (or now Cape Emu), where is a small drain of water to the east of our first anchorage; and where, with some difficulty a ship might procure that essential article. It will be found at both ends of the longest beach.

[f. 189] Astronomical observations on shore abreast of the ship

On finding that the timekeepers had been let down, I judged it necessary to remain a few days to get fresh rates for them; lest by stopping they might have altered.[1] In ascertaining their errors from mean Greenwich time, I take the longitude of the place abreast of the ship to be about 1′20″ of longitude to the west of our first anchorage, as it was made by the observations on the 24th last, and therefore use 138°23′00E or 9°13′32″ in making the reduction. By using the longitude given on our arrival the first time, we avoid the error made by the timekeepers since then; and consequently we leave this island with the same error in our longitude as when we sailed from No. 10 bay [Port Lincoln], which appears to be a quarter of a degree, easterly; but for this see the tables and reductions of errors to be made hereafter at Port Jackson.

The result of the observations for ascertaining the present rates and errors of the timekeepers are as follows: the observations taken with sextant 483, and from an artificial horizon.

---

[1] This was carried out as follows: 'The rates of the timekeepers were obtained, for the sake of expedition, from single altitudes of the sun's upper and lower limbs, taken from a quicksilver horizon with a sextant fixed on a stand; the time being noted from Arnold's watch, compared with Earnshaw's time keepers before going on shore and immediately after returning.' Flinders, *A Voyage to Terra Australis*, I, p. 185.

Astronomical time 1802 April	No. of sights	Time of observation by watch 1736	Apparent altitude of ☉ center*	Comparisons with No. 543**		Observer	Errors from mean Greenwich time			Daily rates***		
				E520	A1736		E543+	E520–	A1736+	E543	E520	A1736
♀-2	Four	17h42' 8.45"	31° 6.37"	–45'13.90"	+5h51'33.30"	Commander	0h2'30.68"	0h42'43.22"	5h54 3.98"			
♄-3		20'26.95'	27°10.0'	–45'22.40"	+5h51'38.8"	Lt Flinders	2'21.75"	43' 0.65"	53'59.75"	–9.07"	–17.70"	–4.29"
☽-5		16h54' 8.65"	22° 3.45'	–45'42.39"	–5h51'43.2"	Commander	2'05.83"	43'36.56"	53'49.03"	–8.03"	–18.12"	–5.91"
Proportional part of the mean rates to reduce the Errors up to mean Greenwich noon April 6th							–4.56"	+9.78"	–2.74"	–8.38"	–17.98"	–5.04"
April ♂-6th at Greenwich noon the errors are							+2' 1.27"	–43'46.34"	+5h53'46.29"			

At the same place by Commander ♄–3rd [April]
Double meridian altitude

☉ Lower Limb No 483	98°	2'21"N
☉ Upper Limb	99°	6'26"S
Latitude		35°43'30"S

☽5th [April] AM Azimuths on shore

☉ magnetic azimuth	N61°56'E
lower limb	18°18'
Variation by theodolite	5°48'E
☉ magnetic azimuth	N63°46'E
lower limb	19°24'
Variation by No 1 compass	2°58'E

* These are the mean of the two upper and two lower limbs.

** These are deduced from the comparisons before going on shore and after returning, and are approximated to the mean of the times when the altitudes were taken.

*** Mean rates deduced from the errors on the first and last days divided by 2.967 days.

The above rates being less than those of No. 10 bay [Port Lincoln], corroborate with what the longitude given by the timekeepers on our arrival here the second time shewed they had been during our absence; I therefore judge that the rates are not altered by the letting down, and that we have got them sufficiently good to proceed along the coast with tolerable accuracy. This being the case I complied with the exigency of the season, in not waiting a moment longer than was necessary to proceed in our survey onward towards Port Jackson.

Tuesday 6 April Log account consisting of 12 hours only
At 4 AM Slack water and at 5 the ship swung to the westward. Moderate breezes and fine weather. Unmoored ship, hove short on the best bower and sent up top gallant yards. The commander took the cutter on shore to get the last altitudes for the timekeepers rates, immediately after which it became thick hazy weather.

At 9, weighed and made sail to the eastward, having light airs. Found so bad a chafe in the best bower cable as to make it necessary to shift it, in doing which we were occupied all the morning. At noon, we perceived by the land that the tide was carrying us to the westward, and therefore we dropped the small bower and lowered down the sails, nearly in the place of our first ⚓age.

Thermometer	71½°	72°
Barometer	30.12	30.11
Meridian altitude ☉ *Lower Limb* 483		47°54′27″
Latitude		35°41′34″

[f. 190] **Wednesday 7 April *Investigator* from No 13 (Kanguroo Island)**
Light variable airs with fine weather. At 2, a breeze sprung up, on which we weighed and made sail to the eastward for the passage between Kanguroo Island and cape Λ [Cape Jervis] of the main.[1] Employed sounding and pointing the new best bower cable. At 4 *hours* 15′ finding we could not weather cape A,[2] which bore ENE 4 or 5 miles, tacked ship towards the island. At 6, tacked ship, being about ¾ mile from the island, and having weathered but little, on account of the lee tide.[3] Double reefed the top sails. At 7 *hours* 35′ tacked back, the main being about 2 miles distant. Soon after 9 *hours* stood in for the south-east part of the island in search of an anchoring place, but finding the little bay there not sufficiently sheltered, hauled out and steered northward for a larger sandy bay. At 10 *hours* 20′ hauled in for the bay, but the water shoaling fast, backed and dropped a little out, then came to with the small bower in 4½ *fatho*ms sandy bottom. Sent the acting master to sound round the ship, and on his reporting no less water near us than 3¼ fathoms, and it being near low water, furled sails. Fresh breezes and squally weather.

---

[1] The decision to sail from Kangaroo Island was influenced by several factors: 'The approach of the winter season, and an apprehension that the discovery of the remaining unknown part of the South Coast might not be completed before a want of provisions would make it necessary to run for Port Jackson, prevented me from stopping a day longer at Kangaroo Island than was necessary to obtaining rates for the timekeepers, and consequently from examining the south and west parts of that island.' Flinders, *A Voyage to Terra Australis*, I, p. 186.

[2] Cape Nuyts (32°02′S, 132°21′E). Cooper, *The Unknown Coast (supplement)*, p. 2.

[3] i.e. a tide which runs in the same direction as the wind is blowing.

AM *Ditto* weather. Found the bearings of the land to be as follows. Points of the bay in which we lie E6°N to N44°W. Western extreme of cape Λ [Cape Jervis] N9°N. Two low islands (π and π1 [South Pages Islets]) with rocks about them from N69°E to E5°N lying near the middle of the passage.[1] Hoisted the cutter within board, both to lighten the ships quarters, and also from expecting bad weather in our ensuing examination of this south coast. At 7 *hours* 45′ weighed and made sail close to the wind, out of the bay. Let out 2nd reefs. At 11 *hours* 10′ tacked ship to the southward, being distant from the shore of cape Λ ¾ of a mile. At noon, moderate breezes and cloudy. Two small rocky isles π and π1 S12° and 4°W distant about 4 miles. Cape Λ, SW extreme, N75°30′W and the furthest extreme ahead, Λ1,[2] N66°30′E.

| Meridian altitude ☉ Lower Limb 483 | 47°31′32″N |
| Latitude | 35°41′50″S |

		Latitude South		Longitude East						
Course	Distance	DR	Obs	DR	TK	Var allowed	Set or current	Error of TK	Ther	Barom
S88°E	11	35°42′	35°42′	138°36′	138°48′	3°E	– 12E	14′10″E	70° 67° 67°	30.09 30.10 30.10

Additional remarks

The bay in which we lay this night affords moderately good shelter with all winds, though I believe a SE gale would throw a considerable sea round the eastern head. The bottom is a hardish sand and perhaps might not hold a ship by one anchor when it should blow very hard. The water seems to shoal rather suddenly in this way, so that the shore must be approached with caution.

Except the very eastern points, this part of the island is mostly covered with the kind of thick brush as the other parts mentioned. Round the shores of the bay were several clear spots where it is probable the kangaroo will be numerous, and perhaps the emu; but the decline of the fine season and the rapid approach of winter induced me to forego any probable advantage of this kind, and for the more important one of finishing the examination of the south coast, if possible, before the weather and a want of necessaries shall oblige us to run away for Port Jackson.

The stone of the eastern capes of Kanguroo Island seems to be slaty.

[f. 191] Thursday 8 April along the unknown south coast

Moderate breezes and cloudy weather. Set the staysails. At 2 *hours* 10′ tacked towards the mainland. Passed through a strong rippling of tide like breaking water, upon which we had 12 *fatho*ms: bottom, stones and shells. ☉3[3] west extreme bearing S9°W. At 5, tacked ship being about one mile distant from the main; and at 7 *hours* 40′ tacked back

---

[1] Flinders added in a note at the bottom of the page: 'The bearings disagree with others, and I judge them to be not very correct.'

[2] Newland Head (35°39′S, 138°31′E), the west extremity of Encounter Bay. Cooper, *The Unknown Coast*, p. 135.

[3] Cape Willoughby (35°51′S, 138°08′E). Ibid.

being within one mile of Θ2,[1] the west point of the last bay: thus we have gained nothing since the morning, but the tide now begins to make to windward.

At 9, saw one of the isles, π or π1 [the South Pages Islets], bearing NEbE½E, which we passed and steered on along the coast under easy sail, and keeping a good lookout as usual. Moderate breezes and cloudy weather. Saw the land on the lee quarter and beam, and the ship now breaking off, tacked to the southward. At 6, tacked towards the land. Saw Kanguroo *Island* and its northern part bore west. The main land from N74° to 19°E. Set top gallant sails. Moderate breezes and cloudy weather. At 9 tacked off shore; the land now seen as far out as east. Employed in the after hold. Mustered ships company and saw them clean after they had cleaned the ship below. Light breezes and dull cloudy weather, so that no observation for the latitude could be obtained. A swell from the southward impedes the ships way. Cape Λ [Cape Jervis], south extreme, S85°W. Eastern land out of sight.

No observation was obtained for the latitude at noon, but cape Λ bore S 85°30′W lat*itude* 35°39′15″S

		By log		Latitude South		Longitude East					
Course	Distance	DR	Obs	DR	TK	Var allowed	Set or current	Error of TK	Ther	Barom
S84°E	31	35°45′	35°39′	139°14′	139°12′	3°E	6N 14W	14′52″E	67° 65° 66°	30.03 30.05 30.11

Additional remarks

Cape Λ [Cape Jervis] and the land some distance east of it is tolerably high, and much intersected by deep ravines and gullies leading down to the sea, and which seem to have been made by the descending waters. The stone seems to be slaty, as the opposite cliffs of Kanguroo Island are. A short scrubby brush is the only covering which the hills of the main land have on the side facing the sea.

The land seen to the eastward this morning assumes a very different appearance to that of cape Λ. Numberless small hummocks first appeared, and as the land rose they were found to be joined to each other, and soon after the connexion with the main became visible. The connecting space is a large sandy bight, round which the land is lower than the hummocks, although they are much lower than the more western land near the cape: they differ also in being sandy land, whereas Λ is almost altogether stony.[2]

---

[1] Cape St Alban (35°48′S, 138°08′E). Ibid.

[2] Rough Journal, I, f. 431, adds: 'The bay which we left on the A.M. preceding the day's log seems to afford secure shelter in all cases: how far the kanguroos or emus may be numerous in its neighbourhood, we did not stay to ascertain. The water seems to shoal rather suddenly in this bay, so that the shore should be approached with caution. The eastern points excepted, this part of the island is covered with the same kind of thick brush as in the other parts. On the opposite part of the main, near which our track mostly lies this P.M. the clothing of the hills is very different. A short scrubby brush everywhere covers the land, which is rather high, and much intersected by ravines and gullies, apparently cut by water, which they seem to have conveyed from the highest parts down to the sea. The stone appears to be slaty, as upon cape θ of the opposite island.'

[f. 192] **Friday 9 April 1802 *Investigator* exploring the unknown south coast of New Holland between Kanguroo Island and Bass's Strait – Interview with *Le Géographe***
Moderate breezes and fine weather. At *1 hour* 30' tacked ship to the eastward. Harpooned a porpoise.

Saw something ahead which was first taken for a pyramid rock, but it proved to be a ship. Cleared at quarters and shewed our colours. On their shewing French colours with an English jack forward, hoisted a white flag; and as the ship was steering free, towards us, shortened sail and hove to, being ready for action. On the stranger coming up at about 5 *hours* 40', found it to be *Le Géographe*, captain Baudin, upon a voyage of discovery from France, but last from Mauritius and Timor.[1] Hoisted out the cutter and the commander accompanied by the naturalist went on board, but whilst this was doing kept our broadside towards the ship.[2] At 7 *hours* 10' the commander returned. Hoisted up the cutter, and made sail upon a wind in company with the *Géographe*, backing the mizzen top-sail occasionally, to keep company. At 12, burnt a blue light, on which the *Géographe* wore, as we did after her.

At daylight bore down to the French ship, lowered down the cutter, and the commander and naturalist again went on board. At 8, the commander returned from the *Géographe*, hoisted up the boat, and at half past 8 wore to the southward, leaving the French ship steering to the North-west. Light variable airs and fine weather, with haze. At noon, light airs and cloudy. Furthest visible part of Cape Jervis bore W*est* 5° *North*. Land seen from the mast head as far out as south-east, apparently the same kind of sandy hummocks as those abreast of the ship.

Mer*idian* alt*itude* ☉ Lowe*r* Lim*b* 483   46°44'33"N
Latitude   35°43'49"S

	By log	Latitude South		Longitude East						
Course	Distance	DR	Obs	DR	TK	Var allowed	Set or current	Error of TK	Ther	Barom
S83°E	10	35°40'	35°44'	139°26'	139°28'	3°E	4S	14'52"E	66°	30.08
							4W		66°	30.08
									66½°	30.02

[1] This meeting occurred in Encounter Bay – named by Flinders – which was around 7 miles SSE of the mouth of the Murray River. Nicolas Baudin, hydrographer and naturalist, led a French expedition to the South Seas, backed by Napoleon Bonaparte, to complete the French survey of the Australian coastline and to make scientific observations. He commanded two naval corvettes, *Le Géographe* and *Le Naturaliste*. The vessels left Le Havre in October 1800, sailed into the Atlantic, provisioned at Tenerife, entered the Indian Ocean via the Cape of Good Hope, stopped at Ile de France (i.e. Mauritius) and sighted Cape Leeuwin, on the south-western tip of New Holland, on 27 May 1801. The vessels sailed north via Timor around the north coast of Australia, then down the east coast of the continent to Van Diemen's Land, where they arrived on 13 January 1802. Baudin surveyed around D'Entrecasteaux Channel for more than a month and then sailed westwards to South Australian waters, where he met Flinders on the *Investigator*. Between 27 January and 8 April 1802 Flinders had surveyed the Australian coastline from Cape Leeuwin in an easterly direction along the South Australian coastline, from the Nuyts Archipelago and to Encounter Bay. Marchant and Reynolds, 'Baudin, Nicolas', pp. 71–3. Further contemporary reports of the meeting between Flinders and Baudin are in Scott, *The Life of Matthew Flinders*, pp. 311–14; Edwards, ed., *The Journal of Peter Good*, pp. 72–3; *The Journal of Post Captain Nicolas Baudin*, trans. Cornell, pp. 379–80; Vallance, Moore and Groves, eds, *Nature's Investigator*, pp. 178–9; and Baldwin, 'Flinders and the French', pp. 53–4.

[2] The naturalist was Robert Brown, the chief botanist for the *Investigator* expedition. He was in Australia from December 1801 until May 1805, collecting around 3,400 species of flora and fauna. Burbridge, 'Brown, Robert', pp. 166–7; Vallance, Moore and Groves, eds, *Nature's Investigator*, p. 180.

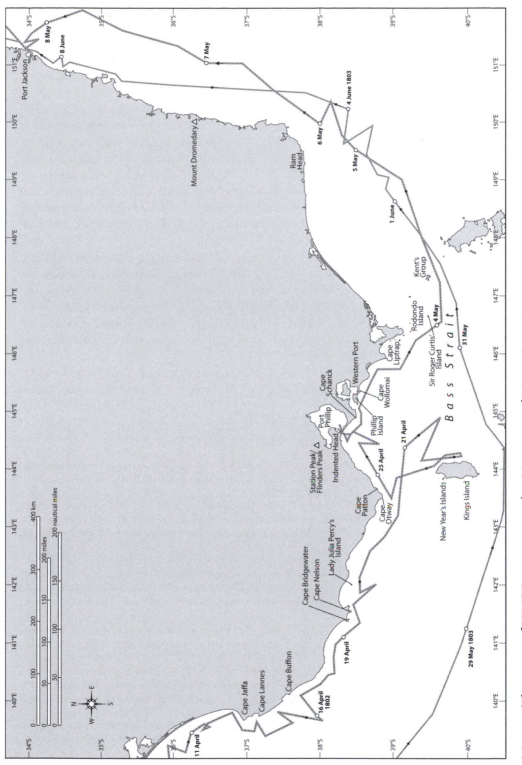

Map 3. The voyage of HMS *Investigator* April to May 1802 and May to June 1803.

Additional remarks

The French expedition on discovery to New Holland, under captain Baudin, had frequently furnished us with a topic of conversation; but when we first ascertained that it was a ship seen ahead, it was much doubted whether it was one of the French ships, or whether it was an English merchant ship examining along the coast for seals or whales.[1] On going on board I requested to see their passport which was shewn to me, and I offered mine for inspection, but captain Baudin put it back without looking at it. He informed me, that after exploring the south and east parts of Van Diemen's Land he had come through Bass's Strait, and had explored the whole of the coast from thence to the place of our meeting; that he had fine winds and weather since the strait, but had not found any place in which he could anchor along the coast there being no rivers, inlets, or places of shelter. I inquired concerning a large island in the western entrance of Bass's Strait, [f. 193] but he had not seen it and seemed much to doubt its existence. He had parted with the *Naturaliste* his consort in a gale of wind in the strait, and had not seen her.[2]

Captain Baudin was sufficiently communicative of his discoveries about Van Diemens Land, and of his remarks upon my chart of Bass's strait, many parts of which he condemned, but I was gratified to hear him say that the north side of Van Diemens Land was well laid down and the islands near it.[3] He had made Isle Waterhouse a rendezvous, thinking to find water there, but was much disappointed on finding in Steel's List a naval officer after whom it had been named by governor Hunter.[4] We parted with the intention of seeing each other in the morning.

In the morning I learned from different circumstances that the French had visited the west coast of New Holland, an unexplored part of which, between Cape Leeuwen and Edels Land, they had examined; but the opening of Dampier near the Rosemary Isles[5]

---

[1] After the English settlement of New South Wales in 1788, British merchants were active in the southern whale fisheries, where they concentrated on catching spermaceti whales, and in the Pacific sealing industry for peltry. Steven, *Trade, Tactics and Territory*, pp. 64–105.

[2] The 'large island' was King Island (see below, p. 376). Baudin had entered D'Entrecasteaux Channel on 13 January 1802. He then proceeded to explore parts of Van Diemen's Land, including Maria and Schouten islands and the River Derwent as far north as present-day Bridgewater. He charted much of the south and east coast of Van Diemen's Land.

[3] Rough Journal, I, f. 433, refers to Baudin having 'an imperfect copy' of this chart. Flinders and George Bass had charted the waters of Bass Strait in their longboat expedition of 1798 and 1799. Baudin had a copy of the English chart of this strait published by Arrowsmith in 1800, which showed that Van Diemen's Land was an island. This was supplied by the French government at the outset of Baudin's expedition. Flinders, *A Voyage to Terra Australis*, I, p. 190.

[4] Isle Waterhouse (now Waterhouse Island) (40°48′S, 147°38′E) lies off the northern coast of Van Diemen's Land, between Cape Portland and Port Dalrymple. It was named after Captain Henry Waterhouse of the *Reliance*, which sailed from England on 25 February 1795 to New South Wales. John Hunter, the second governor of New South Wales, was a passenger on this voyage. The Isle Waterhouse was discovered by Flinders in the *Norfolk* sloop in 1798. First published in London in 1780, Steel's lists were an unofficial guide to the ships, stations and commanders in the Royal Navy. There was no official Navy List until 1814. Auchmuty, 'Hunter, John', pp. 566–72; Clowes, *The Royal Navy*, II, *passim*.

[5] William Dampier had named the place he visited in August 1699 Rosemary Island. But whether it is the same place as the Rosemary Island (c.20°29′S, 116°35′) on modern maps in the Dampier Archipelago is debated. Vallance, Moore and Groves, eds, *Nature's Investigator*, p. 180.

they had left untouched.[1] Six of their scientific gentlemen had remained behind at Mauritius, and at Timor they had lost ten people from dysentery, amongst whom was their best botanist.[2] They had spent a considerable time upon the south and eastern parts of Van Diemens Land, on the last of which, his geographer, a boats crew, and their largest boat had been left, and probably lost: he recommended them to our care in case of meeting with them, or of their reaching Port Jackson.[3]

Captain Baudin was much more inquisitive this morning concerning the *Investigator* and her destination than before, having learned from the boats crew that our business was discovery; and finding that we had examined the south coast of New Holland thus far, I thought he appeared to be somewhat mortified. I gave as much information to him of Kanguroo I*sland*, the inlets No. 12 [Spencer's Gulf] and No. 14 [Gulf of St Vincent] and the bay No. 10 [Port Lincoln], as was necessary to his obtaining water; and I offered to convey any information he might wish to the *Naturaliste* in case of meeting with her; but he only requested me to say, that he should go to Port Jackson as soon as the bad weather set in.[4]

As Captain Baudin had an imperfect copy of my miscellaneous chart of Bass' Strait, I presented him this morning with a copy of the three charts lately published, and of the small memoir attached to them. His charts he said were yet unfinished, but that when he came to Port Jackson he should be able to make some return.[5] Upon my requesting to know the name of the commander of the *Naturaliste*,[6] before I went away, he, 'apropos', begged to know mine; and finding that it was the same as that of the author of the chart of Bass's Strait which he had been criticising, he expressed some surprise and congratulation; but I did not apprehend that my being here at this time, so far along the unknown part of the coast, gave him any great pleasure. I got information of a rock lying about two leagues off the coast, which has shoal water about it. It was reported to lie in latitude 37°1′ south and to be 22 leagues from the *Géographe*s situation yesterday noon.[7]

---

[1] Baudin anchored in present-day Géographe Bay, near Cape Leeuwin, on 30 May 1801. Here *Le Géographe* lost touch in a storm with *Le Naturaliste*. Baudin only surveyed the West Australian coast cursorily as far as Cape Leveque. He then sailed north to Timor whereas D'Entrecasteaux in late 1792 and Flinders in 1801 sailed eastwards from this part of the west Australian coast. Marchant and Reynolds, 'Baudin, Nicolas', pp. 71–3.

[2] Baudin spent 56 days in Timor. While there, many of his crew were ill from scurvy and dysentery. He himself was ill with a fever. The death reported here was of Baudin's friend, the gardener Anselm Riedlé, who had sailed with Baudin on an expedition to the West Indies (1796–8). Vallance, Moore and Groves, eds, *Nature's Investigator*, p. 181 n. 20.

[3] Baudin sent these men to survey the east coast of Van Diemen's Land, but they were lost. The geographer was Charles Pierre Boulanger. After waiting eight days for them to return, Baudin left Van Diemen's Land. Ibid., p. 178.

[4] Flinders was the first person to explore the central section of the South Australian coast. His survey showed that no major waterway entered the continent from Spencer Gulf or Gulf St Vincent. Baudin was the first explorer to see and record the shoreline from Cape Banks to Encounter Bay, a distance of 175 miles. Bladen, *HRNSW*, IV, p. 751; Estensen, *The Life of Matthew Flinders*, pp. 194–6, 204.

[5] The book mentioned by Flinders was his *Observations on the Coasts of Van Diemen's Land*.

[6] This was Jacques Félix Emmanuel Hamelin (1768–1839), second-in-command, under Baudin, of the French expedition to Australia. Estensen, *The Life of Matthew Flinders*, p. 124.

[7] Flinders named these the Géographe rocks in his journals, and marked this hazard on his own chart as 'Baudin's Rocks'. These are probably errors. The rock referred to was Margaret Brock Reef, about 10 miles off Cape Jaffa (36°58′S, 139°40′E). Ibid., p. 204.

[f. 194] Saturday 10 April 1802 *Investigator* exploring the unknown coast

Variable light airs and calms. We find by the lead that the ship drifts fast to the WNW which is probably from the flood tide. At 2, a breeze sprung up and we tacked to the eastward. Furthest visible land ESE. Double reefed the top-sails and tacked off shore. Moderate breezes with rain at times, and much lightening over the land. Tacked ship at nine, towards the land. Tacked offshore. Light airs and calms. At daylight, let out the second reefs, and set top gallant sails and staysails: having light uncertain winds. At 6 *hours* 45′ tacked ship towards the shore, which was 8 or 9 miles distant. Land near cape Jervis still in sight, bearing W10°N. Cut up pork No. 34 to its contents. Harpooned a porpoise. Aired the staysails. At 11 *hours* 20′ the shore was distant about 2½ miles to the NNE and the furthest extreme bore S60E: tacked off.[1] At noon, light breezes and cloudy. A long swell running from the southward.

Mer*idian* alt*itude* ☉ Lowe*r Lim*b 483   46°16′49″N

Latitude   35°49′17″S

		Latitude South		Longitude East						
Course	Distance	DR	Obs	DR	TK	Var allowed	Set or current	Ther	Barom	Error of TK
S60°E	22½	35°55′	35°49′	139°50′	139°41′	3E	6N	66½°	30.00	16′17″E
							3W	66½°	29.99	
								67°	29.97	

Additional remarks

The shore presents the same sandy, hummocky appearance so far as we could discern this day at noon as that of which we were abreast on the 8th AM and yesterday. These hummocks are none of them sufficiently remarkable from the rest to be known in different points of view, nor does anything inland appear above them, so that I have no object that can be taken as a fixed point in the survey; and therefore in this part, the bearing and distance of the nearest part of the beach, and the mast-head extremes form the substance of my bearing book. Having sent the two guns down below that were placed upon the quarter deck near the binnacle, I expected to have found a better agreement in the bearings by the azimuth compasses, and for some little time I thought an amendment had taken place; but for some time back I have again perceived a difference when the ships head has been different ways, and observations for the amplitude and azimuth have differed in the same manner.[2]

[f. 195] Sunday 11 April 1802 from No 13 ⚓age at Kanguroo I*sland* towards Bass' Strait

Light breezes and cloudy weather. At 2*hours* 15′ tacked ship towards the land.
Light breezes & fine weather. Land seen from the deck at SEbyE. Tacked ship off shore, the land being distant 3 or 4 miles. Moderate breezes and cloudy weather.

---

[1] The Younghusband Peninsula, which separates the sea from a lake system known as the Coorong. Vallance, Moore and Groves, eds, *Nature's Investigator*, p. 183.

[2] The azimuth compass measures in degrees an angle clockwise from the north. True North is 0° or 360°. East is 90°. South is 180°. West is 270°. This was part of important magnetic experiments that Flinders undertook along the coast of South Australia. Flinders, *A Voyage to Terra Australis*, I, p. 199.

At 2, tacked ship towards the land, but the wind now became light, and soon after died away. Perceived the ship to be drifted something to the north-west, by leaving the lead overboard. No land in sight from the mast head at daylight. At 6, a light breeze sprung up. Employed in getting the stream cable and anchor in complete readiness, and in cleaning the ship. At noon, saw land from NbyE to about S65°E from the masthead, and the nearest part bearing N60°E 7 or 8 miles.

At 6h 33′ PM

Meri*dian* alt*itude* ☽ Lowe*r Lim*b 483	27°27′17″N
Latitude	35°52′29″S

By log		Latitude South		Longitude East						
Course	Distance	DR	Obs	DR	TK	Var allowed	Set or current	Ther	Barom	Error of TK
S29°E	26	36°12′	36°13′	140°5′	139°55′	3E	1S 12N	66° 65° 66°	29.92 29.85 29.77	17′0″E

Monday 12 April 1802

Variable breezes with rain at times: short intervals of fine weather. At 1 steering more offshore. Saw a flock of sooty petrels. On a breeze springing up from the SE kept close up on a wind along the shore. At dusk, the same kind of sandy, hummocky land was distant 7 or 8 miles, and continues stretching south eastward. Double reefed the top sails, and at 7 *hours* 30′ tacked offshore. Tacked, at 10, to the eastward. Tacked ship to the westward. Rainy, with lightening in the western board. At 3, tacked to the eastward. Saw the land, on the weather bow; and at 5, brought to till daylight, when we saw the land extending from N½W to SE¼E and the nearest shore NE about 5 miles. Tilled & steered along shore with a light breeze and hazy weather. Got the anchors higher up, upon the bows. Lime juice and sugar served now again as usual.

At noon, light airs and hazy. The sandy shore distant 3 or 4 miles and trending nearly south, the farthest extreme visible from the masthead bearing SbyE.

Meri*dian* alt*itude* ☉ Lowe*r Lim*b 483	44°48′29″N
Latitude	36°33′26″S

By log		Latitude South		Longitude East						
Course	Distance	DR	Obs	DR	TK	Var allowed	Set or current	Ther	Barom	Error of TK
S44°E	17	36°25′	36°33′	140°20′	140°15′	3E	8S 5E	69° 65° 66°	29.74 29.70 29.70	17′42″E

[f. 196] **Tuesday 13 April 1802** *Investigator* **exploring the unknown south coast**

Light airs approaching nearly to a calm. Continued standing along, parallel to the low, sandy shore. Saw land as far out ahead as SbyW. Light airs and fine weather. Not being able to fetch further along the shore, at 5 *hours* 30′ tacked off, the beach being then distant

3 or 4 miles and Ξ[1] the furthest extreme bearing S34°W, but after tacking only 22°W. A small hummock standing at the head of a bight S5°W before, but S5°E after tacking. Fresh breezes and cloudy. Double reefed the topsails, and at 10, tacked towards the land.

Mod*erate* breezes with drizzling rain. Tacked from the shore. Squally with rain, and a considerable swell from SbyW. Tacked to the eastward until daylight, when Ξ [Cape Jaffa] outer part bore N9°E. The nearest shore NEbyE 5 miles and Π,[2] the southern extreme, S44°E. Tacked ship from the land. Fresh breezes with a confused sea from the southward. At 9 missed stays and wore ship towards the land. Saw a broad patch of rocks above water, to which we drew near at 11 o'clock. At 11 *hours* 30′ tacked ship offshore: the breakers which surround the rocks N55° to 71° distant 1¾ mile. At noon, moderate breezes and fine weather. Center of the rocks N64°E and the extremes to the north and south, Ξ and Π [Cape Lannes], N4°E and S44°E.

Mer*idian* alt*itude* ☉ Lowe*r Lim*b 483   43°52′47″N

Latitude   37°7′13″S

By log		Latitude South		Longitude East						
Course	Distance	DR	Obs	DR	TK	Var allowed	Set or current	Ther	Barom	Error of TK
S15°E	28½	37°1′	37°7′	140°11′	140°13′	3E	6S 7E	66½° 63½° 62½°	29.80 30.00 30.09	18′42″E

Additional remarks

The low sandy shore along which we steered this afternoon, differs from what we lately passed in not being hummocky, and in being more covered with bushes; and towards the evening, some higher ground shewed itself partially from behind the front bank. The projection Ξ [Cape Jaffa] is well covered with small wood and is higher than the sandy hummocky bank lately mentioned, as is the land as far as the projection Π [Cape Lannes] our present southern extreme.

The rocks from whence we tacked at 11 *hours* 30′ AM I judge to be those of which Monsieur Baudin gave me information. The latitude in which he placed them, to the best of my recollection, was 37°1′, but I make them to lie 4 or 5 miles more southward.[3] The breakers extend to some distance around them; but the rocks are well above water, and by supposition they are 3 or 4 miles from the shore.

[f. 197] **Wednesday 14 April 1802 from Kanguroo I*sland* towards Bass' Strait**

Fresh breezes and cloudy weather, with a jumbling sea from the south-westward. At 2 *hours* 55′ tacked ship tow*ards* the land, until 4 *hours* 20′, when we again tacked off, the outer part of point Π [Cape Lannes] bearing N82°E 3 miles, and the furthest extreme S36°E before, and 44° after tacking. Moderate breezes and fine weather; but the ship

---

[1] Cape Jaffa. Vallance, Moore and Groves, eds, *Nature's Investigator*, p. 183; Flinders, *A Voyage to Terra Australis*, Atlas, plate V.

[2] Cape Lannes. (37°12′S, 139°44′E). Vallance, Moore and Groves, eds, *Nature's Investigator*, p. 184; Flinders, *A Voyage to Terra Australis*, Atlas, plate V.

[3] Flinders later referred to these as 'Baudin's Rocks', but they are now usually called the Godfrey Islands (37°05′S, 139°43′E). Ibid., I, pp. 197–8; Vallance, Moore and Groves, eds, *Nature's Investigator*, p. 183.

uneasy from the motion of the sea. Tacked towards the land until 12, when we again stood off, and took in top-gallant sails, the wind being then fresh; but it soon became light, and showers of rain fell occasionally. Being taken aback at 3 *hours* 30′ filled on the starboard tack but soon after tacked to the southward, when it fell calm. On a breeze springing up, at 5 *hours* 40′ tacked ship to the south-eastward.

At daylight, let out the 2nd reefs and set staysails. Light breezes and cloudy weather: a long swell from the south-westward. At 9 *hours* 25′ tacked off the point Π [Cape Lannes], being little to windward of our situation at 4 *hours* 30′. PM Cleaned the ship below and aired with stoves. Sour krout served as usual three times per week, and vinegar once. At noon, light breezes and cloudy weather, with a long *South* Westerly swell. The land from N24°E near Ξ [Cape Jaffa] to S72°40′E the furthest extreme. Π [Cape Lannes] the nearest land N79°E 6 or 7 miles.

Mer*idian* alt*itude* ☉ Lowe*r* Lim*b* 483	43°24′57″N
Latitude deduced	37°13′20″S

By log		Latitude South		Longitude East						
Course	Distance	DR	Obs	DR	TK & bearings	Var allowed	Set or current	Ther	Barom	Error of TK
S10°W	15¼	37°22′	37°13′	140°8′	140°9′	3E	9N 1W	63° 61° 61°	30.26 30.34 30.42	19′7″E

Additional remarks

The projecting part Ξ [Cape Jaffa] is sandy, and is topped generally with bushes; in these respects much resembling the land about Π [Cape Lannes]. The north-eastern part of the point is rocky and the sea breaks upon it with much violence; there are also some black rocks straggling along the other parts of the projection. It is probable that the bight on the north side of Π, as well as that of Ξ, may afford shelter from southerly winds; but since they are open to west, no one would venture into either of them but in the last extremity; the depth of water and kind of bottom in these bights I do not know.

From the projection Π the shore takes a more easterly direction than before, being SE as far as we can see this day at noon. We make but little progress with the wind, as well as that the south-west swell drives us much to leeward.

[f. 198] Thursday 15 April 1802 *Investigator* exploring the unknown south coast

Moderate breezes and cloudy, with a long swell from the southwestward. At 3, tacked the ship towards the land. Breakers reported by the man at the masthead to be seen to the westward, but the commander went up immediately and could not see any, and probably it was a mistake. At dusk the land distinguishable from NE to ESE. Tacked offshore, the land being just visible. At 10 *hours* 30′ tacked towards the land. Tacked to the southward, the wind having come more off the land. Moderate breezes and cloudy weather. At daylight, the extremes of the land, as seen from the mast head, bore from NbyE to East, and it appears to be the same land set yesterday at noon; but it can scarcely be seen from the deck. Tacked ship towards the land. Mustered ships company and saw that they were clean and had clean linen on. At 11 *hours* 45′ tacked off shore: the sandy hummocky shore being about 4 miles distant. It trends to the SSE and the front bank is not so woody as to the northward of Π [Cape Lannes]; nothing inland appears above this bank. At noon, moderate breezes and fine weather. Extremes of the land from the deck N19°W to S65E. A patch of bare sand N79°E.

Mer*idian* alt*itude* ⊙ Lowe*r Lim*b 483   42°53′22″N
Latitude   37°23′19″S

		Latitude South		Longitude East						
	By log									
Course	Distance	DR	Obs	DR	TK	Var allowed	Set or current	Ther	Barom	Error of TK
S30°E	18	37°29′	37°23′	140°19′	140°22′	4E	6N 2E	60° 59° 60°	30.34 30.48 30.42	19′49″E

Friday 16 April 1802
Fresh breezes and fine weather. Tacked ship tow*ar*ds the land at 2, and took in the staysails. Double reefed the top-sails. The low, sandy, hummocky shore being distant 3 miles, tacked off at 5; the extreme in sight bearing S58°E afterwards point Σ.[1] Fresh breezes and fine weather. A southerly swell getting up. Tacked ship at 8 towards the land; and at 10, stood off again. Lost a log line. Fresh breezes and fine weather. Moderate breezes. At daylight let out 2nd reefs and set top-gallant sails. No land in sight, but we kept standing on to the southward, as the wind permitted us to lie well up. Finding the water becoming very deep, I suspected the coast had altered its direction, therefore at 9, tacked ship towards it; but the ship lay so very ill for it, that at 11 we tacked again to the southward. At noon, nearly calm. No land in sight from the mast head.[2]

Mer*idian* alt*itude* ⊙ Lowe*r Lim*b 483   41°58′12″
Latitude   37°57′4″S

		Latitude South		Longitude East						
	By log									
Course	Distance	DR	Obs	DR	TK	Var allowed	Set or current	Ther	Barom	Error of TK
S5°E	37½	38°1′	37°57′	140°23′	140°15′	4E	4N 3W	61° 63° 64°	30.37 30.37 30.35	20′42″E

[f. 199] Saturday 17 April 1802 from Kanguroo Island tow*ar*ds Bass' Strait
Fine weather with haze. A still, long swell rolling in from the southward. Light cats-paws of wind at times, sufficient to enable us to keep the ships head one way, but not to give the ship perceptible motion through the water. Fine weather with haze.

[1] Cape Buffon (37°35′S, 140°07′E).
[2] Rough Journal, I, f. 447, adds: 'From the soundings having increased to an unfathomable depth when our distance from the land cannot be more than 25 miles, I judge that the direction of the coast must now be altered; and it probably now runs eastward to Bass's Strait: the latitude at noon, being but little to the north of the north side of the strait.'

At 3 *hours* 45′, a light breeze sprung up, with which we steered to make the land near the furthest extreme Σ [Cape Buffon] seen yesterday PM. At daylight, saw high land seen from N½ E to EbyS 4 or 5 leagues. On the wind shifting to the northward at 7, braced up and took in royals: trying to fetch as far northward as the wind would permit. At 9, the point Σ the furthest extreme northward, and bore N33°W a small, sharp-topped peak N46°E the land being distant in that direction, and from thence to EbyS 2½ miles: Bore away along the shore with a light breeze; but on the wind reshifting to the westward hauled up to the wind again, for the furthest southern extreme.

At noon, light breezes and fine weather. The extremes of the land N30°W to S46°E the latter being lumps of rocks whose connexion with the main is not visible. The nearest shore distant 2½ miles, with scattered rocks lying along it. The land made this morning proved to be point Σ [Cape Buffon]. It projects something from the coast line; and on its north side there is a bight, the bottom of which we did not see more distinctly than just to ascertain that the point is connected with the other land.

The sea shore continues to be sandy and to be topped with hummocks as before; but whereas it has hitherto been so low as commonly not to be visible above 10 or 12 miles (from a ships deck, as usual) and nothing from the interior part appeared above it, it is now different in that we see land of considerable height looking over the front bank from the back country. The furthest extreme seems to terminate the direction of the coast to the SSE. There is much breaking water off it.

Mer*idian* alt*itude* ☉ Lo*wer Lim*b 483	41°46′22″N
Latitude	37°47′35″S

		Latitude South		Longitude East						
By log										
Course	Distance	DR	Obs	DR	TK	Var allowed	Set or current	Ther	Barom	Error of TK
N80°E	23	37°53′	37°48′	140°51′	140°48′	4E	5N	65°	30.23	21′14″E
							5E	62°	30.14	
								64°	30.18	

[f. 200] **Sunday 18 April 1802 *Investigato*r exploring the unknown south coast**
Moderate breezes and cloudy weather. On the wind coming ahead more than before, tacked ship at 1 *hour* 30′. The furthest rocks with breakers lying off. At 4 tacked towards the land, but on coming in with it find we had lost ground. At 6 tacked offshore. Light airs and cloudy weather. Calm, with light airs at times, just sufficient to keep the ships head one way. At day break, a light breeze sprung up with which we steered in for the land, and which we soon after saw bearing from NbyW to EbyS, but indistinctly on account of the haze. At 9, kept more away to pass round the rocky point and breakers; and on the wind becoming lighter hauled further off, there being a heavy south-west swell rolling in upon the shore. Mustered the ships company and saw them clean, after cleaning the ship well below. At noon, rocky islets which were the furthest extreme. PM bore N62°E 4 or 5 miles with extensive breakers round them. Sandy, hummocky extreme ESE.

Mer*idian* alt*itude* ☉ Lo*wer Lim*b 483	41°15′22″N
Latitude	37°57′27″

By log		Latitude South		Longitude East						
Course	Distance	DR	Obs	DR	TK	Var allowed	Set or current	Ther	Barom	Error of TK
S9°E	16	38°04′	37°57′	140°54′	–	4E	7N	63°	30.22	21′56″E
							15E	60°	30.29	
								61°	30.13	

Monday 19 April 1802[1]

Light breezes with a long rolling swell from the southward. At 3, an inland Table Hill[2] bore N68°E and the furthest extreme E5½S. We perceive from the bearings as well as from the lead that the ship is drifted to the eastward, in the calm. On a light breeze springing up at 7, took in top-gallant sails, and stretched off upon a wind until 9, when we brought to with the main top sail. Moderate breezes and cloudy. At 2, wore round and lay to with the ships head towards the land. Fresh breezes. On the winds heading, filled and stretched in for an hour and then brought to again. Double reefed the top-sails (the weather being squally) and at 6 made sail for the land. In a squall closed down the top sails, and before getting them again, took in the fore and mizzen topsails, the 3rd reefs. At 8, a cliffy point (Cape Northumberland of Lieutenant Grant)[3] which seems to have been the extreme at 3 PM, bore N34°W. (The rocks which lie off this point resemble the back fin of a shark.) Heavy breakers the land bore N25°W 3 or 4 miles, and the furthest extreme ESE: high and obscured by haze.

At 9 *hours* 45′ kept away as the land trended; it being now distant 3 or 4 miles. At 10 *hours* 30′, the wind suddenly shifted in a thick squall, with rain, and obliged us to haul close up to the wind to weather the land, which had been seen as far as SE. Let out the 3rd reefs of the fore and mizzen top sails, it being necessary to carry all possible sail: but the wind and sea are rising considerably, and the weather is so thick and rainy that no land is visible, although it is not further off than 4 or 5 miles under our lee and is rather high land.

By log		Latitude South		Longitude East						
Course	Distance	DR	Obs	DR	TK	Var allowed	Set or current	Ther	Barom	Error of TK
S55°E	22	38°10′	–	141°17′	141°45′	4E	1N	62°	30.05	22′39″E
							16E	62°	29.85	
								62°	29.76	

[f. 201] Tuesday 20 April 1802 from Kanguroo Island towards Bass' Strait

Strong breezes. 30′ past noon, the weather cleared a little and a bold cliffy cape Φ[4] bore S76°E5′, being the furthest land visible. At 2, kept away, and at 3 steered east along the

---

[1] On this day the *Investigator* passed east of 140°58′E into the waters of today's Victoria. Vallance, Moore and Groves, eds, *Nature's Investigator*, p. 185.

[2] Mount Schanck (37°56′S, 140°44′E).

[3] 38°04′S, 140°40′E, named by James Grant who had explored part of the south coast of Australia and Bass Strait on the *Lady Nelson* in 1800–1. McMartin, 'Grant, James', pp. 468–9.

[4] Cape Bridgewater (38°24′S, 141°25′E).

shore: the weather squally with rain and so thick that nothing can be seen, except at intervals. At 4, a double rocky islet bore N23°E 5 miles.[1] At 5 *hours* 30', the bold cape Φ (afterwards found to be Cape Bridgewater) bore N75°W being then falling behind the nearer cape Φ1:[2] the double rocky islet bore N45°W; and we now hauled to the wind off shore. Land seen indistinctly in the ENE (island p).[3]

Moderate weather at times, but squalls of wind and rain frequent, with lightening. Wore ship, having missed stays. Squalls of wind, hail, and rain. Treble reefed the topsails. At 5, wore ship; and at daylight bore away for the land, which was in sight to the northward. At 7 *hours* 30' a steep, flat-topped island[4] bore N10°E (its west end); Cape Φ [Cape Bridgewater] angled 82° to the left, and the double, rocky, islet 69° to the left. At 8 *hours* 17' hauled along the shore to the eastward. At 8 *hours* 30' the appearance of land was seen to the south-eastward upon which we hauled up to the wind, but finding in an hour that it was a deception, bore away again. (At 9, the center of island bore N4°W (or true north): it is 1½ miles long). Saw the land running along, eastward, from behind the island to a projection which bore east at 11 o'clock. At noon, strong squalls with frequent rain, and generally with thick weather.

AM by Lt Flinders at 1h 9'

Mer*idian* alt*itude* ☉ Lowe*r Lim*b 488		72°4'24"N
Latitude		38°35'51"S

	By log		Latitude South		Longitude East						
Course	Distance	DR	Obs	DR	TK	Var allowed	Set or current	Ther	Barom	Error of TK
S60°E	51	38°35'	38°34'	142°13'	142°49'	4E	–	59°	29.72	23'21"E
							8E	55°	29.64	
								57°	29.69	

Additional remarks

The shore along which our course has laid yesterday morning and this afternoon, is considerably higher than we have seen lately: it is sandy, but not so sandy as that part where the shore is topped with hummocks. For want of a latitude yesterday, the whole of the coast, eastward from the cliffy point at 8 AM (Northumberland) cannot be otherwise than ill laid down; when compared with the preceding parts of the coast: both in latitude and longitude, its form also is likely to be given imperfectly, for one thick squall succeeded another so fast, that generally, we were running in darkness, and common prudence made it absolutely necessary to keep at some distance in such weather.

The bold cape Φ [Cape Bridgewater] is nearly insulated, but I think not altogether so: a hummock upon it is the outermost of three which lie nearly in a line and near each other. The rocky islet consists of two small hummocks, whence it is called double. The island p [Lady Julia Percy Island] is cliffy & flat-topped but not high. The coast behind this island is either very low or it falls back to the northward, for we could see little of it.

[1] Lawrence's Islet. Flinders, *A Voyage to Terra Australis, Atlas*, South Coast, Sheet IV.
[2] Cape Nelson (38°26'S, 141°33'E).
[3] Lady Julia Percy Island (38°25'S, 142°00'E). Flinders, *A Voyage to Terra Australis*, I, p. 204.
[4] Ibid.

Further eastward we could see at intervals that the shore is sandy and rather low, as far as the projection set at 11 AM. A rock lies 7 or 8 miles westward from this projection and from 3 to 5 miles from the shore northward. Upon the whole, I will not presume to say anything certain of the coast passed today, except that the shore extends eastward as I have marked it nearby in the latitude and longitude.

[f. 202] **Wednesday 21 April 1802**[1]
Strong squalls with frequent rain. Clued down and set the treble-reefed top-sails occasionally. At 1 hour 40' a projection bore north, 5 or 6 miles, and land was seen as far as E¼S. Hauled up to the wind: close-reefed the topsails, reefed the main sail, and afterwards handed the mizzen top-sail. At 3, another projection seen, north 5 or 6 miles, and soon after, other land seen at ESE. Sent down top gallant yards, and handed the fore-top-sail, the wind blowing a strong gale, with thick weather; though it occasionally moderated for a few minutes, and then the ship drifted to leeward for want of sail. At 8 saw the land, during a clear interval, at no great distance under the beam, which obliged us to set the fore and mizzen top-sails and reefed main sail, if possible to weather the land; fortunately, no land appeared further ahead, and the wind now suffered us to lie better up for two or three hours.

The weather moderating at 2, let out 4th reefs and made more sail, but we were obliged almost immediately to take them in again, and to hand the fore and mizzen topsails, and take the reefed main sail off the ship; which kept us till daylight; at which time we were gratified to find no land in sight, for the ship could now scarcely make an east course good. Strong breezes with occasional squalls of wind and rain. Let a reef out of the main and set the fore and mizzen topsails; and the weather moderating still more, set the jib and spanker, and let out the close reefs. Saw high land astern, on the thick weather clearing away, which is no doubt main land. At noon, this land bore from NWbyW to NNW at the guessed distance 8 or 10 leagues. Moderate breezes with fine weather, and the high sea much gone down.

Mer*idian* alt*itude* ☉ Lowe*r* Lim*b* 483   39°0′19″N
Latitude   39°10′50″S

| | | Latitude South | | Longitude East | | | | | | |
By log										
Course	Distance	DR	Obs	DR	TK	Var allowed	Set or current	Ther	Barom	Error of TK
S62°E	91	39°16′	39°11′	143°57′	144°55′	5E	5N 22E	56° – 56°	29.58 – 29.60	24′4″E

Additional remarks
The land, which temporary cessations of thick squally weather permitted us now and then to get a sight of, this afternoon, seems to be rather a bold shore, but still it is sandy. The part seen under our lee at 8 PM by favour of a moonlight interval, appeared to be a head land of considerable height. Since we could not expect to weather the shore on the

---

[1] The *Investigator* entered Bass Strait, which had only been discovered in 1799 by George Bass and Flinders. Ibid., I, p. 205.

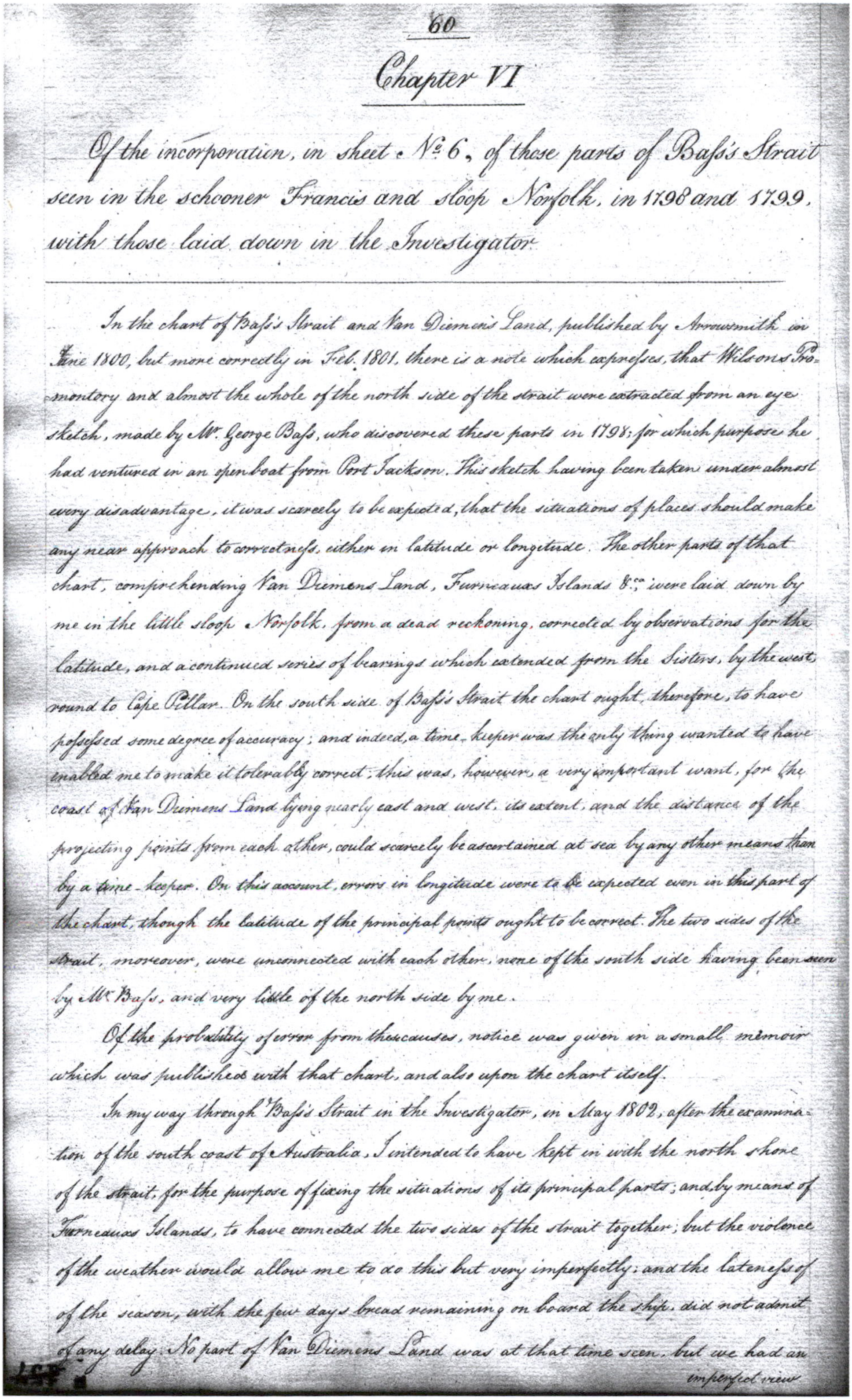

Chapter VI

Of the incorporation, in sheet № 6, of those parts of Bass's Strait seen in the schooner Francis and sloop Norfolk, in 1798 and 1799, with those laid down in the Investigator.

In the chart of Bass's Strait and Van Diemen's Land, published by Arrowsmith in June 1800, but more correctly in Feb. 1801, there is a note which expresses, that Wilsons Promontory and almost the whole of the north side of the strait were extracted from an eye sketch, made by Mr George Bass, who discovered these parts in 1798; for which purpose he had ventured in an open boat from Port Jackson. This sketch having been taken under almost every disadvantage, it was scarcely to be expected, that the situations of places should make any near approach to correctness, either in latitude or longitude. The other parts of that chart, comprehending Van Diemens Land, Furneaux's Islands &c. were laid down by me in the little sloop Norfolk, from a dead reckoning, corrected by observations for the latitude, and a continued series of bearings which extended from the Sisters, by the west, round to Cape Pillar. On the south side of Bass's Strait the chart ought, therefore, to have possessed some degree of accuracy; and indeed, a time keeper was the only thing wanted to have enabled me to make it tolerably correct: this was, however, a very important want, for the coast of Van Diemens Land lying nearly east and west, its extent, and the distance of the projecting points from each other, could scarcely be ascertained at sea by any other means than by a time keeper. On this account, errors in longitude were to be expected even in this part of the chart, though the latitude of the principal points ought to be correct. The two sides of the strait, moreover, were unconnected with each other, none of the south side having been seen by Mr Bass, and very little of the north side by me.

Of the probability of error from these causes, notice was given in a small memoir which was published with that chart, and also upon the chart itself.

In my way through Bass's Strait in the Investigator, in May 1802, after the examination of the south coast of Australia, I intended to have kept in with the north shore of the strait, for the purpose of fixing the situations of its principal parts; and by means of Furneaux's Islands, to have connected the two sides of the strait together; but the violence of the weather would allow me to do this but very imperfectly: and the lateness of the season, with the few day's bread remaining on board the ship, did not admit of any delay. No part of Van Diemens Land was at that time seen, but we had an imperfect view

Figure 12.   Matthew Flinders, Extract from the 'Memoir', ADM 55/76, f. 60. Courtesy of the National Archives, Kew. For transcript of this page , see Vol. II, p. 473.

other tack, we were obliged to keep on our course, at whatever risk along the unknown coast; and I determined now, if anything should bring us up during the night, to push on into Bass' Strait, and leave the remaining part of the south coast to a better opportunity. Not only the extreme danger at this time of year but the expenditure of our provisions forbid us keeping off the coast to wait for fairer weather to finish it; and besides I had nothing important to expect since Monsieur Baudin had been here before and given a bad account of it: still I quitted the space between cape Φ [Cape Bridgewater] and the Strait most unwillingly, without a thorough examination. That part of the main [land] seen at noon, will lie nearly in the latitude 38°45′S and by our time-keepers uncorrected, in the longitude 144°36′E from our bearing of it. By the assistance of the current we find ourselves at noon to be in the entrance of Bass's Strait, and according to Mr. Reeds position of the large island, concerning which I inquired of captain Baudin, we must be drawing under its lee; and from the water becoming so much smoother this is probably the case.[1]

[f. 203] **Thursday 22 April 1802 from Kanguroo I*sland* into Bass' Strait New Holland**

Moderate breezes and fine weather. Let out the third reefs, sent up top-gallant yards and set the sails. At 1, hauled close up to the southward intending to make Reeds large island, or if we should not fetch it, Hunters Islands.[1] Moderate breezes & cloudy. No land in sight at dusk. Light breezes and fine, but it soon became nearly calm. Tacked to the westward on the ship falling off. No land in sight at day light; but at 8, the land was seen to the southwestward, which is most probably the large island which was seen by Reed in 1798.[2] At 9, fresh breezes and cloudy. Handed top gallant sails. Mustered the ships company and saw them clean. At noon, the extremes of the island S6°W to the NW end which bore S62°30′W the nearest part being 8 or 9 miles distant. High land, which we suppose to be the same seen yesterday at noon, was seen from the mast-head, N35°W Fresh breezes and cloudy.

PM at 8 o'clock

Mer*idian* alt*itude* 483   36°26′56″N

Latitude   39°30′21″S

	By log	Latitude South		Longitude East						
Course	Distance	DR	Obs	DR	TK	Var allowed	Set or current	Ther	Barom	Error of TK
S20°E	27	39°36′	39°31′	143°56′	144°55′	6E	5N 13E	59° 55° 56	29.64 29.64 29.67	24′46″E

[1] Hunter Island (40°32′S, 144°45′E) is situated a few miles off the north-west coast of Van Diemen's Land.

[2] Still King Island.

Friday 23 April 1802

Fresh breezes and cloudy. At 3 tacked ship, the north-west extreme of Reeds island[1] S31½°W and high land to the northward N42°to 20°W. Continued standing on to the southward, but on the wind permitting us to lie well up, shortened sail. On the water shoaling to 16 *fatho*ms at 2 o'clock, brought to; but finding the water still shoaling, I was afraid of drawing near a reef which has been said to lie off the south-east end of the island: we therefore stretched back to the northward. Strong breezes at times with thick rainy weather. On the wind coming round to the southward, tacked off for an hour; at 4 o'clock, and at 5 stood in again. At daylight the island was distant 6 or 7 miles, and extended from WbyS to South. Let out 2nd reefs and made more sail. Moderate breezes. At 9, tacked to the SE ward, the shore being distant 4 or 5 miles, and the NW point bearing S46°W: a patch of breakers seen WbyS. Tacked to the westward, at 11, on the ship's falling off, with the intention of getting up under the island and ⚓ing.[2] At noon, fresh breezes and squally. The highest land near the north-west end and now bore true west; and the nearest shore was distant 4 or 5 miles, SW.

Mer*idian* alt*itude* ☉ Lowe*r Lim*b 483   37°53′49″
Latitude   39°36′8″

By log		Latitude South		Longitude East						
Course	Distance	DR	Obs	DR	TK	Var allowed	Set or current	Ther	Barom	Error of TK
S54°W	21	39°43′	39°36′	143°23′	144°44′	7E	7N	57°	29.68	25′28″E
							10E	57°	29.64	
								59°	29.86	

[f. 204] Saturday 24 April 1802 *Investigator* off Reeds large I*sland* in Bass' Strait and along the north side of the strait towards Port Jackson

Fresh breezes and squally. Double reefed the top sails. At 1, tacked ship, working up towards the land. At 1 *hour 45′* tacked again; and at 2 h*ours 45′* came to, with the small bower, upon a bottom of fine sand. Veered to half a cable, furled sails, and the extremes of the land then bore S43°E and N75°W the nearest shore S24°W a short half mile distant. Hoisted out the cutter, and the Commander and scientific gentlemen landed. At sunset they returned, bringing a kangaroo, two wom[b]ats, and a studding-sail boom which had been found washed up on the shore.[3] Hoisted in the cutter and prepared everything to get under weigh immediately, should a shift of wind take place in the night.

AM Fresh breezes and squally weather. Hoisted out the cutter at day light, and the naturalist and the other gentlemen landed, further to examine the natural productions of the island.[4] At 9, made a signal for the boat to return; and afterwards fired two guns to

---

[1] i.e. King Island.

[2] The difficulty of the prevailing winds in Bass Strait accounts for these various tacks.

[3] i.e. the common wombat. Vallance, Moore and Groves, eds, *Nature's Investigator*, p. 187. Here Flinders writes 'womat', as he does in *A Voyage to Terra Australis*, I, p. 206.

[4] Refers to Robert Brown. Rough Journal, I, f. 458, adds: 'A small lake of fresh water was found, half a mile distant from the beach, surrounded by a more fertile soil. Two very small streams of high-coloured, fresh, water had been found on the preceding evening, caused apparently by the late rains; these ran down to the beach.'

enforce it. At 11, weighed and made sail to the northward for the high land seen on the 22nd and 23rd at noon; the boat having returned at 10 *hours* ¾. At noon, fresh breezes and cloudy weather. Extremes of the island S50°W to S21°E. Breakers as far out as W½S the same as seen yesterday at 9 AM. They lie NbyE from the NW end of the island. [*marginal note*: 'no. of sick 6.']

Me*ridian* alt*itude* ☉ Lowe*r Lim*b 483		37°37′31″N
Latitude		39°32′39″E

		By log		Latitude South	Longitude East						
Course	Distance	DR	Obs	DR	TK & bearings	Var allowed	Set or current	Ther	Barom	Error of TK
N55°W	9	39°31′	39°33′	143°13′	144°58′	8E	2S	60°	30.05	26′11″
							4E	58°	30.28	
								59°	30.30	

Additional remarks

We landed upon this large western island without much difficulty, in a little bight behind a projecting rock. On stepping out of the boat, I saw one of those animals called Wom[b]ats, which I shot, and another was killed afterwards. Near the same place was lying a top-mast studding sail boom, not much injured, which I judge to have drifted from the wreck of the ship *Sydney Cove* at Preservation Island on the east side of the strait: it had no mark upon it.[1] The kanguroo killed here holds a middle place in size between the small kanguroo of the islands and the larger ones of the main, or of Kanguroo Island.[2] A seal of a different species to any yet seen by us was also killed. Its phlippers [*sic*] behind were double when compared to the common seal, and those forward were smaller and placed nearer to the head. The nose was very flat and broad and the quantity of fat upon the animal was at least treble in quantity: the hair much shorter, and of a blueish-grey colour.[3]

We found the island so thickly covered with brush wood that scarcely any one thought of attempting to penetrate it. The front bank next the sea is almost entirely of sand, which is either washed or blown up in great ridges, and it is partly held together by the roots of a long spreading grass which mostly covered them. We do not perceive anything much

---

[1] This merchant vessel had run onto the beach of the tiny Preservation Island in the Furneaux group in 1797. Flinders sailed on the last of three separate voyages in the colonial schooner *Francis* to rescue survivors and goods from the wreck of the *Sydney Cove* in 1797–8. While rescuing five survivors at Preservation Island and repairing the *Francis*, Flinders and his crew undertook a five-day expedition among the surrounding islands. Flinders produced a chart of the area, and speculated that he was situated in a strait dividing New South Wales from Van Diemen's Land. Estensen, *The Life of Matthew Flinders*, p. 66; Flinders, 'Narrative of an expedition to Furneauxs Islands', pp. 12–13.

[2] This may have been a red-necked wallaby rather than a kangaroo. Vallance, Moore and Groves, eds, *Nature's Investigator*, p. 187 n. 5.

[3] Here a note is added: 'I have since heard this animal called the sea elephant. On arriving at Port Jackson, I afterwards found that the ship *Harrington* had been sealing upon this island; and on the south-west side had found the wreck of a vessel; and it is more probable that the boom belonged to this vessel, than to the *Sydney Cove*.' Flinders thought this was the southern elephant seal, now extinct on King Island. It may have been this animal, which had a massive skull, but, alternatively, it may have been the Australian (or Tasmanian) fur seal. Ibid., p. 187; Flinders, *A Voyage to Terra Australis*, I, p. 206; Scott and Lord, 'Notes on the Sea Elephant', p. 93.

higher than these sandy ridges, except at the NW end of the island, where the hills seem to be stony, and not at all covered with wood: The small portions of stone which were found above the sand near the landing place seem to be granite. The naturalists having found a good harvest of new plants upon the island were desirous of a further examination. I therefore waited to give them another opportunity, and sent [f. 205] a boat with them again at daybreak. They found a small lake of fresh water at a little distance behind the bank of the shore, which was surrounded by a good vegetable earth, and their collection of balanced specimens received a good addition here, which kept them longer than was intended when they left the ship.[1] The lake is not sufficiently convenient for a ship to get water at except in great extremity; but I found two small streams of high-coloured water draining down to the shore, which I believe were merely the effect of the late rains.

Two wom[b]ats were killed in the morning, and a skull picked up which was thought to be that of a small dog, or more probably of an opossum.[2] The wind seeming to be now determinately fixed to the southward, my plan of making Hunters Isles in order to determine the relative position of them and of Van Diemens Land to that of the northern main[land] and this island, would be attended with much labour and loss of time: I therefore resolved to quit that object and make use of the wind as it was, to steer back to the main land, and trace it along to some known part, as Western Port[3] or Wilsons Promontory;[4] still continuing our progress towards Port Jackson. It may be thought strange that after escaping such imminent danger from a lee shore as we did in the evening of the 21st that I should now run directly, almost to the same place, before the wind: but the height of the barometer assures me that we shall not very soon have any bad weather and I put confidence in it.

Sunday 25 April 1802

Fresh breezes and cloudy. Saw two small islands round the north-west extreme of the large island: σ[5] opened off at S40°W and τ[6] at S26°W. (Note. I afterwards found that these two isles form a small roadste[a]d, in which was lying at this time the brig *Harrington*: they bear the name of New Years Isles.)[7] Lost sight of the large western island at 8 leagues distance (at 3 o'clock). Double reefed the topsails, and at 5 hauled to the wind: a bluff point Cape Otway,[8] bearing N65°W 3 or 4 leagues, and the extremes of the main land N69°W to N12°E.

---

[1] Rough Journal, I, f. 459, adds: the naturalist 'collected a greater variety of plants upon this island than upon any one we have yet seen'. Brown's page in his diary relating to these plants is blank. He only mentioned four species of plants found on King Island by name: *Eucalyptus*, *Styphelia acerosa*, *Fabricia loegivata* and *Casuarina stricta*. Austin, *The Voyage of the Investigator*, pp. 122–3.

[2] The animal was either a possum or a bandicoot. Vallance, Moore and Groves, eds, *Nature's Investigator*, p. 188.

[3] 38°21′S, 145°14′E.

[4] This is the southernmost point of the Australian mainland (*c.*39°08′S, 146°22′E), named by Flinders and Bass after Flinders's friend Thomas Wilson. Vallance, Moore and Groves, eds, *Nature's Investigator*, p. 181.

[5] One of the New Year's Isles (39°40′S, 143°50′E).

[6] Another of the New Year's Isles.

[7] These two small islands off the north-west side of King Island formed a small roadstead, in which the brig *Harrington* from Port Jackson 'had rode out the south-west gale; and was lying there at this time, engaged in a sealing expedition'. Flinders, *A Voyage to Terra Australis*, I, pp. 208–9; and Flinders, *Atlas*, plate VI.

[8] 38°52′S, 143°31′E.

Moderate breezes and cloudy weather. Tacked ship to the eastward. At daylight, bore away for the land, which was seen bearing NbyE to NNW. At 7, bore away along the shore, the bluff point ♈ [Cape Otway] bearing N52°W 8 or 10 miles, and the extremes N64°W to 18½°E the last being a square-topped projection lower than the back land west of it. Let out 2nd reefs, set the staysails, and the fore and fore topmast studding sails, steering along a high bold shore at the distance of about eight miles. Mustered the people and saw them clean, after cleaning the ship well below. At noon, light breezes and cloudy weather. Southern extreme of the land near point ♈ S72°W and that ahead N19°E from the deck. Nearest land N55°W about 8 miles. Water remaining in the ship 37½ tons.

Meridian altitude ☉ Lower Limb 483   38°4'20"N
Latitude   38°45'52"

	By log		Latitude South		Longitude East						
Course	Distance	DR	Obs	DR	TK	Var allowed	Set or current	Ther	Barom	Error of TK
N7°E	34	38°59'	38°46'	143°18'	144°34'	8E	13N 9W	60° 59° 61°	30.42 30.42 30.49	26'53"

[f. 206] <u>Additional remarks</u>
The land which we made this afternoon is, without doubt, the land seen on the 22 and 23 at noon: It is much higher than what we have usually seen near the sea side. I judge that the land seen at 8 PM on the 21st is 13 leagues to the westward of point ♈ [Cape Otway], but from the most western part seen at 5 o clock this PM. I think there is not more than 8 leagues left totally unexplored.[1] This very bold shore has a better appearance than almost any part of the south coast of New Holland; the upper ridges being well covered with wood and no bare sand or rock appearing in any part. On the west side of ♈ the shore falls back somewhat and then runs westward to our furthest extreme; whether anything more than a small indent is there formed we could not see, but I think not. On the east side of ♈ the shore runs north-eastward without any remarkable bight or projection, except indeed the square-topped projection,[2] set at 7 AM which however is scarcely distinguishable except in the direction it was then set.

Monday 26 April 1802 *Investigator* exploring on the north side of Bass' Strait
Light breezes and cloudy. At one, saw land bearing N59°E like an island: hauled more up: and seeing land running further to windward, at 2, hauled to the wind. The land appearing like an island has a bluff at its northern end: its extremes bore at dusk N59° to 79°E. Having light airs, bent the stream cable. Two small peaks of inland mounts N5°W. At 8, tacked to the southward, lest it should fall calm and the swell might drift us to near the shore.

[1] Rough Journal, I, f. 461, adds: 'From the height of the barometer I had but little doubt of the weather remaining fine, and therefore, notwithstanding that the wind blew nearly on the north coast of the strait, I steered over to trace as much of the remaining south coast of New Holland as we could, proceeding, at the same time, in our way towards Port Jackson.'
[2] Cape Patton (38°42'S, 143°50'E). Named by James Grant after Captain Charles Patton, RN (1771–1837). Lipscombe, *On Austral Shores*, p. 70.

Moderate breezes and fine weather. At 2, tacked ship to the northward until 4, and then tacked back until daybreak. At 5 *hours* 30′ tacked ship towards the land and soon after the bluff island-like land was seen to the north eastward.[1] On nearing the land, we found a low shore running along in the front of the bluff land, and continuing to the north-westward, apparently joining the other land. At 10 *hours* 45′, the eastern extreme, a cliffy head with rocks lying off it, ψ,[2] bore S69°E. Bluff hill or mount N71°E. and an irregular rocky point N9½°W. Bore away along the shore at the distance of 4 or 5 miles, in order to examine the head of this great bight between ♈ [Cape Otway] and ψ [Cape Schanck]. At noon, there was some appearance of an opening round the rocky point, but the water seemed to break across the Rocky Point. Bore N38°E 5 or 6 miles. ψ, the east extreme S78½°E. Bluff mount E10°N, a square-topped hill resembling an island at a distance N38°W near the head of the bight.[3]

Mer*idian* alt*itude* ☉ Low*er Lim*b No 483   38°8′31″N
Latitude   38°22′12

By log		Latitude South		Longitude East						
Course	Distance	DR	Obs	DR	TK	Var allowed	Set or current	Ther	Barom	Error of TK
N59°E	32	38°29′	38°22′	143°53′	145°7′	8E	7N	61°	30.46	27′36″E
							2W	60°	30.46	
								61°	30.47	

From the square topped point of yesterday the land trends to the north-north-east, becoming gradually lower until it is very low land, skirted with a sandy beach. The square-topped hill appeared like an island in the evening, and the peaked inland mountains like rocks. The cape ψ [Cape Schanck] is steep and one of the rocks lying off it appeared at first like a ship under sail.

I at first thought it possible that the bluff mountain might be the island lying in the mouth of Western Port, but after seeing the land joining round to the north-westward, I no longer expected to find any opening in this bight. If the opening seen at noon had been larger I should again have thought that it was the western entrance into Western Port since Monsieur Baudin had coasted along here and found no opening to the westward of that; this is indeed far from being conspicuous and there are yet doubts about it.[4]

---

[1] Not an island but part of a ridge of hills rising at Cape Schanck (38°30′S, 144°53′E). Flinders, *A Voyage to Terra Australis*, I, p. 210.

[2] Cape Schanck (38°30′S, 144°53′E). This is the southern point of the Mornington Peninsula. It was named after Captain John Schanck, a friend of James Grant. Bearing Book, entry for 3 May 1802, f. 95; Lipscombe, *On Austral Shores*, p. 79.

[3] Bluff Mount is Arthur's Seat (38°21′S, 144°57′E), named by John Murray because of its resemblance to the hill of that name near Edinburgh. Robert Brown and William Westall were respectively the naturalist and the landscape painter. Ferdinand Bauer, the botanical artist on the voyage of the *Investigator*, also joined this expedition. Brown's journal provides more detail here than Flinders. Flinders, *A Voyage to Terra Australis*, I, p. 212; Vallance, Moore and Groves, eds, *Nature's Investigator*, pp. 190–91; Edwards, ed., *The Journal of Peter Good*, pp. 75–6.

[4] Rough Journal, I, f. 463, states: 'The land like an island seems to be high land, more especially at its western end where it slopes off suddenly, and the land to the northward seems to be further distant; whence I judge that between them may be the Western Port of Mr. Bass, although its distance is not equal to what I supposed of that

[f. 207] **Tuesday 27 April 1802 Into no 16 port [Port Phillip], on the north side of Bass' Strait**

Moderate breezes and fine weather. The small opening round the Rocky Point assuming a more important form as we came more abreast, soon after noon bore away to examine it; and finding it led into a large piece of water, at 1 *hours* 30' we entered it, keeping nearly close to the wind ready for tacking out again, for there were strong ripplings of tide like breakers in the entrance, and some shoal banks towards the north side. At 2 *hours* 30' we came upon the edge of a shoal in the middle of the port, within the entrance, and tacked ship; as we did afterwards, occasionally, between the middle shoal and the south shore. At 4 *hours* 30' the water shoaled suddenly: Put the helm down; but before the ship came about, the tide hustled us upon a mud bank. Hove all about but the ship sticking fast, lowered down the gig and sounded round the ship: Finding the bank very shoal to the eastward, got the cutter out, dropped a kedge, and at half past six hove the ship into deeper water; but she again struck almost immediately against a bank, and we had only 10 feet over the bows; but getting her head towards the deepest water, she went off, and the water deepening quickly to 4, 6, and 10 fathoms, we dropped the best bower about 7 o'clock, and furled sails. The tide having been rising all the time, the banks being of mud, and the wind continuing light, with fine weather, it does not appear that the ship received the least injury.

AM Moderate breezes and cloudy. Find that the rocky south point of entrance bears W3°S and the dry middle bank N12° to 24°W. The Commander accompanied by the naturalist went up the port in the cutter. Employed drying sails which had gotten wet from the leakiness of the ships upper works during the late gale. A large shark caught this morning. Light airs and cloudy weather.

Meridian altitude ☉ Lower Limb 488	37°54'21"N
Latitude	38°17'0"S

		By log		Latitude South		Longitude East						
Course	Distance	DR	Obs	DR	TK	Var allowed	Set or current	Ther	Barom	Error of TK
East	8½	38°22'	38°17'	144°22'	145°24'	8E	6N	61°	30.42	28'18"E
							8E	60°	30.37	
								61°	30.43	

port. In the morning, the joining of low land to the bluff mount, prevented us from thinking any further that we were near the Western Port.' Baudin told Flinders that he had come upon no port or harbour between Western Port and Encounter Bay. Flinders thought he had come into Western Port. Brown notes this, too. However, the *Investigator* had instead come into Port Phillip Bay, on the coast of modern Victoria. Flinders did not know that the bay had been investigated about six weeks earlier by John Murray, acting lieutenant and commander of the *Lady Nelson*. Murray entered Port Phillip Bay for the first time on 14 February 1802 and spent more than a month surveying it. Murray had been sent by Governor Philip Gidley King (see below, pp. 397, n. 5, 399) to Bass Strait, in the hope that he might fall in with the *Investigator*. Flinders, *A Voyage to Terra Australis*, I, p. 211; Scott, *The Life of Matthew Flinders*, p. 172; Vallance, Moore and Groves, eds, *Nature's Investigator*, p. 189; Parsons, 'Murray, John', p. 272; Lee, *The Logbooks of Lady Nelson*, p. 127; Governor King to Sir Joseph Banks, 5 June 1802, in Bladen, *HRNSW*, IV, pp. 782–3.

Additional remarks

The entrance into this port is about two miles wide, but the deep channel between the rocks from Rocky Point and the shoals on the north side, is little more than one mile. It may be safely entered by keeping the rocks on the starboard hand close aboard; and afterwards near the south shore until the ship is sufficiently sheltered to anchor in safety. The port opens well to the view with a spacious expanse of water, the northern boundary of it not being visible from the mast head, when the weather is not very clear. The middle bank where we grounded is about 3 miles from the entrance, and the rocky tops of it seem to be dry at all times of tide. There appear to be deep channels up to the port both on the south side of this shoal, and also on the west side, but of what depth the latter is I cannot yet tell. We kept working in the southern channel and found the water deepest near the south shore; but to the eastward of the ship we see shoal water also in this southern channel.

Notwithstanding the narrowness of the entrance I thought for a long time that we had certainly got into Western Port, and that Mr. Bass, who discovered it, might have been under some mistake, as he only saw it from the shore; captain Baudins report biased my mind in this respect; and it is only from not being able to see any eastern entrance that I have altered my opinion, to believe now that this is a new discovery.[1] My expedition in the morning, with the scientific gentlemen, was directed to Bluff Mount [Arthur's Seat]. Its distance is about seven miles above the ship, and we carried from 7 to 4 fathoms all the way, passing a little to the south of the place where the ship grounded.[2]

[f. 208] Additional remarks – continued

The view from the Bluff Mount [Arthur's Seat] presented a large expanse of water, the furthest boundary of which was scarcely visible; and for the space of 60° to the northward could not be at a less distance than 15 miles, and may probably be twice that extent; and round the furthest visible projection on the western shore, an arm extends to the southwestward until the land hid it from our view. No island or other object above water appeared in the port to attract attention, except the dry tops of the middle shoal near the ship; but it seemed to be an immense basin of water, and since we do not find any considerable stream running out, it is probable, that the greater part of it is shoal water; yet we had tolerably regular soundings and depth both in going to and returning from the Bluff Mount.

Walking a little way back upon the mount we got sight of a considerable piece of water at the distance of 3 or 4 leagues to the eastward: It seemed to be mostly shallow; but as it also appeared to have communication with the sea, it is most probably the Western Port of Mr. Bass. We have not anywhere found upon the saltwater borders a soil equal to that which covers the sides and neighbourhood of the Bluff Mount [Arthur's Seat]: and indeed the shores of this port in general seem to possess a superior degree of fertility, and of general fitness for the purposes of the shepherd and husbandman; more probably, for the former than the latter, for I believe the soil is not generally very deep; as yet, however,

---

[1] Baudin had sailed along this coast in fine weather but had found 'no inlet of any kind'. Flinders, *A Voyage to Terra Australis*, I, p. 211.

[2] Flinders found the entrance to Port Phillip (38°18′S, 144°38′E) was less than two miles wide. Captain Flinders to the Admiralty, 11 May 1802, in Bladen, *HRNSW*, IV, p. 749. For further details of entering Port Phillip Bay, see Flinders, *A Voyage to Terra Australis*, I, pp. 210–12.

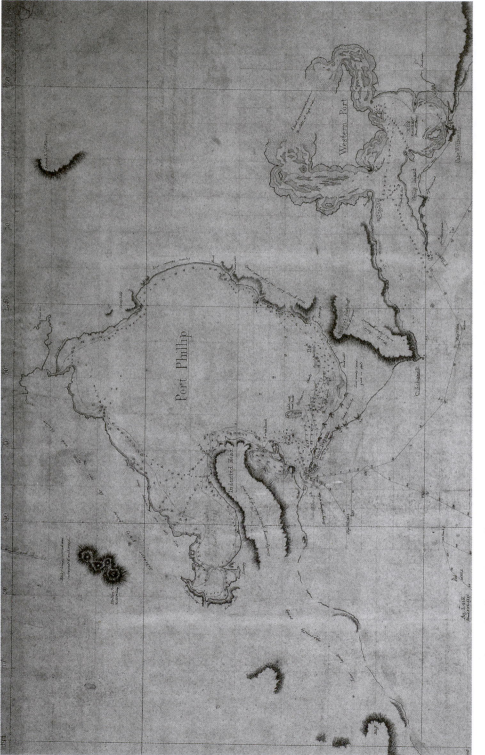

Figure 13.   Matthew Flinders, Chart of Port Phillip, ADM 352/518, detail. Courtesy of the National Archives, Kew.

we do not see any streams of fresh water falling into the port.[1] Marks of natives, such as fire places and heaps of oyster shells were numerous, but we did not see any of their persons, though there was a smoke between the ship and the mount, upon the peninsula which forms the south side of the port.

Quantities of very fine oysters were lying about the shores, between high and low water marks, washed up, apparently by the surf; a circumstance I never observed in any place before: it seems to show that the natives have not very lately visited the beach nearest to the mount, where we landed.[2] I found by the shore that the tide did not fall this afternoon above four feet or perhaps three; whereas its rise in Western Port is from ten to 14 feet according to Mr. Bass.[3] The latitude observed at the beach in the artificial horizon was as annexed, but it was from the top of the mount that the ship bore W7°15′ and the boat bore from thence 28°3½′ or W13°30′N. Seeing the place to be worth examination, I determined to coast round the borders of the port with the ship: or if that should be found impracticable, or too tedious, to get the ship as high up as might be convenient, and finish the examination in a boat; and with this resolution we set off back to the ship a little before sunset.

[f. 209] **Wednesday 28 April 1802**
continued to 36 hours or civil account

Light airs and cloudy weather. Having dried the wet sails, the people were now employed in making up and stowing them away. At 6½ hours, the Commander and gentlemen returned with the cutter. Moderate breezes and cloudy weather. Light breezes and fine, afterwards moist hazy weather. At 6 hours 45′ weighed and made sail further up the port. On coming near the middle shoal, tacked to the eastward steering along the south side of it and keeping a little off occasionally on account of shoal water. At 8 hours 25′, shortened sail, and it being now near high water, came to with the stream anchor. The rocky south point of entrance now bore W3°30′N the Bluff Mount [Arthur's Seat] S80°30′E; and the nearest sandy shore SW about 1½ mile. Sent the acting master to sound about the ship, and he found the tail end of the middle shoal to be about a cables length from us to the eastward, and that there was a deep channel between it and the shore under the Bluff Mount, leading to the north-eastward. On the tide slacking at 3 PM, weighed and made sail. At 3 hours 36′ tacked to the north-eastward, but the wind dying away, came to at 4 hours 30′ with the stream anchor and furled sails. Moderate breezes and cloudy weather, but falling calm occasionally.

Noon Meridian altitude ☉ Lower Limb 483	37°33′49″N
Latitude	38°18′22″

---

[1] Rough Journal, I, f. 466, adds: 'The soil about the mount was found to be much superior to any we have yet seen on any part of the coast of New Holland, and is equal to the middling ground in the best parts about Port Jackson, although upon the salt-water borders.'

[2] Flinders and his party came across Wathaurong Aborigines. The aboriginal club was a waddy, which was either used in the hand or as a thrown weapon. Among the plants was a species of mimosa. Vallance, Moore and Groves, eds, *Nature's Investigator*, pp. 191–2. Rough Journal, I, f. 466, adds: 'Several new plants were found, and a new kind of white cockatoo, whose under feathers were red, was shot.'

[3] See Bass's entry for 5 January 1798 in Bladen, *HRNSW*, III, pp. 323–4.

Thursday 29 April 1802

Moderate breezes and cloudy weather. At daylight the Commander took the cutter upon a three days excursion to examine the port, finding the proceeding of the ship upon that service to be too tedious.[1] At 7, weighed and made sail downwards with a beating wind. At 7 *hours* 50′ the ship touched the ground suddenly, and we had only ten feet on one side whilst there was 5 *fatho*ms on the other. Having swung the ship clear of the bank, at 8 came to in 7½ *fatho*ms and sent the gig to sound round the ship. The inner No*rth* point of entrance now bore WbyN½N. At 11 *hours* 30′ weighed, on the tide making downwards, in order to beat further down; but the wind coming directly against us and there being much danger of getting aground with the ebb, at 0 *hours* 45′ came to with the best bower: The entrance N77°W Bluff Mo*unt* [Arthur's Seat] East. Cloudy with rain. Lost overboard the iron stock of the stream anchor, from the fore lock coming out. Lightening about.

| Mer*idian* alt*itude* ☉ Lowe*r* Lim*b* 488 | 36°54′32″N |
| Latitude | 38°20′39″S |

Friday 30 April 1802

Fresh breezes and cloudy, with hail and rain at times. Cleaned the ship below, and scrubbed hammocks. Moderate and fresh breezes in the afternoon, and latterly calms and squalls alternately, accompanied with rain. Double reefed the mizzen top sail, to be used in swinging the ship.

| Mer*idian* alt*itude* ☉ Lowe*r* Lim*b* 488 | 36°54′32″N |
| Latitude | 38°20′09″S |

Saturday 1 May 1802

Light breezes and cloudy weather. People employed in the morning a getting a stream ⚓ out of the hold, ready for immediate use. Light airs and cloudy. At 2 PM weighed and made sail down towards the entrance of the port, keeping the gig ahead sounding. Hauled up and bore away occasionally to avoid shoal water. At 5 *hours* 30′ came to with the best bower and furled sails. The entrance of the port N85°W and Bluff Mount [Arthur's Seat] N84°E. The dry part of the middle shoal N45° to 55°E. Strong breezes and cloudy weather.

| Mer*idian* alt*itude* ☉ Lowe*r* Lim*b* 488 | 36°36′45″N |
| Latitude | 38°20′09″S |

[f. 210] Sunday 2 May 1802 *Investigator* **in No 16 port [Port Phillip] on the south coast of New Holland**

Strong breezes and cloudy. At daylight, fresh breezes. Weighed the ⚓ at 7 *hours* 15′ to drop a little nearer down to the entrance, and soon after came to in 9 *fatho*ms, fine brown sand. Veered to a third of a cable and furled sails: Points of the entrance bearing S86° and N85°W. Bluff Mount [Arthur's Seat] S85°E and our distance from the south shore being half a mile. Mustered the ships company and saw them clean. Moderate breezes and cloudy weather. At 4, the Commander returned in the cutter from his expedition to

---

[1] Flinders had a crew and provisions for two or three days. Edwards, ed., *The Journal of Peter Good*, p. 76.

examine the port: he brought two black swans. Light airs and moderate breezes at times: lightening in the western quarter.

Thermometer	61°	63°	66°
Barometer	29.83	29.84	29.84

Boat excursion to examine the port

To have circumnavigated the port with the ship would have been attended with this great advantage, that the examination of the shores and its productions by the men of science would have kept pace with my survey, and the duty of each department would have been better executed in that we should have had all our necessary implements and books about us; but the risk of repeatedly getting on shore with the ship, besides the tediousness attending such a proceeding, were such as made me give up the plan; and as I had no tender, a boat became the fittest and only substitute we had; with three days provisions, therefore, I set off in the cutter to make as complete an examination as three days would permit, leaving orders with lieutenant Fowler[1] to get the ship moved down towards the entrance, in the mean time that we might sail immediately on my return.

At 6 *hours* AM on the 29th I left the ship and proceeded along the eastern shore, round the point of the middle shoal, carrying from 6½ to 9 *fathoms* at the distance of 1¼ mile from the shore, and continuing that depth past the first and second eastern points above the Bluff Mount, and 4 *fathoms* close to the shore; for the westerly wind did not permit us to fetch further along the shore than about 2 miles short of the third eastern point. I had brought Arnolds watch No. 1736 with me,[2] having compared it with the time keepers, in order to determine the longitudes of the different places at which we might stop, and especially to determine the length of any river that we might find running near east or west, where observations for the latitude would be insufficient. On landing, I immediately took the annexed altitudes for the watch with the sextant 483 and an artificial horizon; and afterwards walked round to the third eastern point, through a good country, and took bearing with a theodolite of all the principal points and hills (for which see the Bearing book,[3] as well for all then taken on shore, as for those at sea, whether before or after this time.) I found a low sandy beach skirting along to the northward at the foot of some hills which had been seen from the ship, but it was lost from my sight before its direction had become very westerly.

---

[1] Robert Merrick Fowler (1778–1860), 1st lieutenant on the *Investigator*. Born at Horncastle, Lincolnshire, he had a long naval career, rising to Rear Admiral in 1846. His journal for the *Investigator*'s voyage is in TNA, ADM55/74 and 77. Flinders named Fowler's Bay and Point Fowler on the South Australian coast in his honour. Brunton, ed., *Matthew Flinders*, pp. 248–9.

[2] This was a pocket chronometer designed by John Arnold (1736–99) of London. Arnold was the first person to popularize the name chronometer. The watch was supplied to Flinders by the Navy Board. See his journal entry on the *Investigator* for 18 July 1801, above p. 144, and ML, Matthew Flinders letterbook (1801–6), Matthew Flinders to Dr. Maskelyne F.R.S., 25 May 1802. On Arnold, see Betts, 'Arnold, John', pp. 435–6.

[3] i.e. to record measures relating to the direction of a vessel. For details of the various points and hills in this vicinity, see the Bearing Book, entries for 29 and 30 April 1802, ff. 90–93.

Apparent time	21h45′31.9″
Time 1736	17h51′11.1″
E 543	11h59′05″
☉ supplement cente	28°53′11″
Longitude	145°40′52.5″
E 520	37′49.5″
Mean	145°39′21″E

2nd time and altitude for latitude

Time 1736	20h47′40.4″
☉ Lower Limb 483	36°22′36″
Latitude	38°14′24″S

I returned along the shore back to the boat with all expedition in order to observe for the latitude, but it was past noon, and therefore I took a second set of altitudes for the watch, forming the double altitudes as above.[1]

There being an appearance of a strong westerly wind, which would prevent us from either examining the port or returning to the ship so long as it should blow, unless we could [f. 211] get over to the weather side before it comes on, we set off immediately, after getting some dinner, to row across to the west shore which however was not distinguishable from the bank where we dined. In crossing, we found no less than 11 fathoms but generally no bottom with 12, until we drew near to that part of the west shore which, in the Bearing Book, is called Indented Point, and then there was 9 fathoms and near the shore 10 feet: at 9 o clock we landed and pitched the tent.[2]

30 [April] On looking round in the morning a fire was found at the distance of 200 yards from the tent; and from appearances I judged that natives had taken up their residence there in the evening, but had decamped upon our landing.[3] I walked a little distance to the north-easternmost part of the point in order to take bearings, and whilst so employed, a small body of natives appeared upon the shore a little to the westward. We got into the boat, and rowing there, landed and found a hut with a fire in it, but their utensils and arms as well as the natives were gone. I left some strips of stuffs of their favourite colour (red) hanging about the hut, and rowed westward along the shore into the arm leading south-westward, landing upon the most projecting parts to take bearings.

About 10 o'clock three men made their appearance abreast of the boat, and on our landing came to us without any hesitation. They received a shag and some trifles, with pleasure, and parted with such of their arms as we wished to possess without reluctance. On our quitting the shore they continued to keep abreast; and saw me shoot another shag which hovered over the boat; and when it was held up to them they ran down to the water side and received it without any question, acting apparently, without fear or

---

[1] A reference to taking two meridian observations of the sun to determine latitude. This also perhaps alludes to taking the observed altitude – the angle in degrees above the horizon – in order to make corrections to determine the calculated latitude.

[2] This refers to an expedition across Port Phillip Bay towards Indented Head (38°09′S, 144°43′E), on the Bellarine Peninsula, that Flinders undertook in a cutter with a small boat crew. Vallance, Moore and Groves, eds, *Nature's Investigator*, p. 193; Estensen, *The Life of Matthew Flinders*, p. 208. Bearing Book, entry for 1 May 1802, f. 92, provides a sketch drawing of Indented Head.

[3] Flinders spent the day examining the Bellarine Peninsula. Flinders, *A Voyage to Terra Australis*, I, pp. 214–16.

suspicion: they seemed well to understand the effect of firearms, which I thought they had acquired from seeing me shoot such birds as came near the boat.

It being now near noon, we stopped, and afterwards took the annexed observation for the latitude. The natives partook of our dinner and we left them on friendly terms to proceed along, up the south-west arm. About 1 mile or 1¼ westward, a number of birds induced me land upon a low sandy point, and here I took the annexed observation for the longitude.

Meridian altitude ☉ center 483	37°23′20″N
Latitude	38°7′8″S
Apparent time	2h12′6.4″
Time 1736	22h19′7.9″
E 543 from proportion	16h26′51.1″
☉ apparent double altitude center	57°28′56.5″
Longitude	145°16′42″E
E 520	13′54″
Mean	145°15′18″E

The water was now very shallow along the shore, and therefore I determined to strike north-westward across the southwest arm, both to try the depth across, and also for the purpose of ascending a high peaked mount which from Bluff Mount [Arthur's Seat] had borne 306° and is one of the two set on the 26 PM at N5°W. In going across, the soundings were at three-fifths of a mile from the shore, 4 fathoms; at one mile, 5; then 5½, 5½, 6, about mid passage, 5½, 5½, 4, 3½, about one mile from the northern shore,[1] and then shoal, water with dry mud banks, upon which were many ducks and other water fowl: the distance across is, by guess, six miles. We found the shore to be low and marshy, and had difficulty to find a place for the tent, and still greater to obtain firewood herewith to cook our ducks.

1 May 1802 At the dawn of the day in the morning I set off, with three men, for the top of the hill, supposing its distance to be six or seven miles, but it proved to be about ten to its foot.[2] On ascending the top, there was presented to my view the northern head of the port, the head of the south-west arm, and a considerable extent of surrounding country. I left the ships [f. 212] name upon a scroll of paper put into a pile of stones,[3] and after taking bearings of every remarkable object, we descended and returned to the boat but it was half past three PM before we arrived, having had our walk rendered exceedingly incommodious from not finding a drop of water. Mr. Lacy, the midshipman of the boat, gave me the annexed observation for the latitude, which he had made in the artificial horizon.[4]

Meridian altitude ☉ center 483	37°9′35″N
Latitude	38°2′24″S

---

[1] For these and other soundings, see the Bearing Book, ff. 93–94, entry for 2 May 1802.

[2] Flinders called this hill Station Peak (now known as Flinders Peak) because it was his station for taking bearings. Today it is part of the You Yang Regional Park, 12 miles north of Geelong. Flinders, *A Voyage to Terra Australis*, I, pp. 216–17; Lipscombe, *On Austral Shores*, p. 101.

[3] In January 1839 Flinders's disciple John Lort Stokes climbed Station Peak and found the pile of stones left by Flinders; but the message was no longer there. Lipscombe, *On Austral Shores*, p. 101.

[4] Denis Lacy, a midshipman who joined the *Investigator* at the Cape of Good Hope. Vallance, Moore and Groves, eds, *Nature's Investigator*, p. 125.

After taking some refreshment, we rowed back across the water to the place where I had observed the latitude yesterday. Coming near the shore after dark, some fires were seen moving along the shore, and on landing we found two newly erected huts, with fires and many of the utensils in them which the natives usually carry about with them, and which must have belonged to some of the men seen before, since there was found some rice in one of the baskets. We took up our quarters here, keeping a strict watch, but we received no disturbance.

2 [May] Soon after we had shoved off from the shore in the morning, seven natives shewed themselves on the brow of the hill, behind the huts. They immediately ran down to examine their habitations and finding everything as they left it, a little water excepted, of which we were in need, they went to our fire place where four of them stopped, but the other three followed us along the shore for some time. Along the whole of the shore of Indented Point, from the north-east part westward, we found the water to be very shoal, having no more than six feet at the distance of a cable length. Steering southward from the north east extreme, about half a mile from the shore, the soundings were 2, 2, 1¼, 1¼ past the easternmost projecting point; then 1½, 3, 4 at ⅔rds of a mile off shore; and continuing on for the low sandy peninsula, had from 3½ to 2¼. Upon this south-east part of the western shore of the port we were fortunate enough to find water and ducks, for our provisions were all out and we had had a very scanty breakfast; we also caught 3 black swans by chasing them with the boat. Upon two parts of this peninsula I took bearings, but no latitude could be observed at noon on account of the clouds.

I have said but little of what was observed as to the form of the port, because it is all delineated in the sketch, to which I refer.[1]

Steering towards the ship on the west side of the middle shoal, the soundings were from 2½ to 5 fathoms, which last I suppose to be in near the middle of the western passage. The water shoaled from thence gradually to 2½, which was probably owing to our passing over the tail of the middle shoal. The soundings afterwards to the ship were as follows, 3, 4, 5, 4½, 4¼, 5, 7 in the southern passage, 7, 7, 6½, 5, 4½, 7½, 8, 9, 8½ and alongside, where we came about 4 o'clock. The watch 1736 I found had gained 17.5″ upon Earnshaws No. 543;[2] by taking a proportional part of this quantity according to the interval of time, and applying it to the first comparison, I deduce what 543 shewed at the time of each of the preceding observations, and thence the longitudes by No. 543 and also by 520 are found as above.

[f. 213] The entrance into this port is so obscure, and, when seen, the tide appears so much like breakers running across, that I wonder not at Monsieur Baudin not having seen, or not venturing to enter it. I judge the general rise of tide to be from 3 to 5 feet, though towards the furthest parts it seems to be scarcely so much. From the swinging of the ship, which yet differed at different anchorages, the time of high water appears to be about 2½ hours after the moon passes the meridian. From the narrowness of the entrance and the large space of water within, it follows that the tide must run with much rapidity, which it does notwithstanding the small height to which it runs; and this is more

---

[1] This is the sketch in the Bearing Book, f. 92.

[2] Thomas Earnshaw, a pioneer constructor of precision timekeepers, invented his chronometer in 1780. He finalized the form of escapement (the 'spring detent') and the form of compensation balance to be used in the standard marine chronometer. Betts, 'Earnshaw, Thomas', pp. 576–8.

particularly the case just without the entrance where the water is much shoaler than it is directly in the passage; and here the strongest ripplings: Upon an ebb tide and a south-west gale it would scarcely be safe for a ship to pass it, and at all times of tide it would be dangerous to boats, except at slack water.[1] Concerning the middle shoal, and the passages on the south and west sides of it, I refer to the additional remarks of the 27th, and to the sketch.

The country that surrounds the port answers well to the description given by Mr. Bass of the borders of Western Port.[2] In every part the least elevated above the beach I found a good even grass covering the country, in some parts thickly covered with wood, in others the trees are but thinly scattered, and others again are intirely destitute of them. The sides and bottoms of the hills have the deepest soil; the plains which are uncovered with trees are extensive, but they have a stiffish and shallower soil: sand intermixes almost every shore, but generally in very small proportions. A friendly intercourse might easily be established with the natives, who already are acquainted with the effect of fire arms and are anxious to possess many of our conveniences. They are evidently the same kind of men as in King Georges Sound and Port Jackson, but I think them to be more fleshy and muscular than the former; perhaps they are better fed. Their arms and utensils differ little from those of the others already known. Of the language, no words are collected: it differs considerably and perhaps entirely from that spoken at Port Jackson.[3] Emu's, kanguroos, and a variety of water and other fowl may be found in the woods and about the borders of the port.

Observations of ☉ east ☾ taken on board by lieutenant Flinders

Time 1802	Apparent time	☉ lower limb	☾ lower limb	Distance with No 488	Longitude E
April 26	21h52′47.2″	30° 3′ 6″	53° 1′19″	66°15′35.5″	144°50′55.5″
,,	22h 0′ 2.2″	52′33″	51°52′ 4″	12′24.5″	42′48″
,,	6′44.5″	31°36′19″	50°46′20″	10′00″	51′16.5″
,,	12′33.7″	32°12′30″	49°48′11″	7′27.3″	46′30″
,,	18′22.1″	47′14″	48°50′18″	5′ 9.2″	49′13.5″
,,	24′46.3″	33°23′47″	47°40′39″	2′34.5″	49′40.5″
,,	34′35″	34°15′20″	45°56′15″	65°58′22″	47′19.5″
28	1h55′53.4″	31° 5′12″	13°12′39″	50°59′55″	145° 8′18″
,,	2h 1′41.9″	30°21′39″	12° 9′47″	56′36″	2′ 0″
,,	7′11.2″	29°43′49″	11°10′57″	53′32″	1′31.5″
,,	13′49.7″	28°56′31″	9°52′28″	49′49″	3′22.5″
,,	20′ 3.9″	10′54″	8°36′33″	46′26″	5′49.5″

[1] Flinders again refers to Baudin missing the entrance to Port Phillip. The violent rippling at its entrance has long been known as the Rip. Flinders notes the difficult navigation at the entrance to Port Phillip Bay in *A Voyage to Terra Australis*, I, pp. 210–12.

[2] This description is in George Bass, *Journal*, 5 January 1798, in Bladen, *HRNSW*, III, pp. 323–4.

[3] Flinders was interested in words and pronunciation among the Aborigines he encountered at King George Sound, Port Jackson and Van Diemen's Land. His difficulty in understanding the aboriginal language here stemmed from the brevity of his visit to Port Phillip and from being unable to distinguish between the twelve or so indigenous languages spoken in Victoria. Flinders, *A Voyage to Terra Australis*, I, pp. 66–7; Dixon, *Australian Languages*, p. 2.

Error of *Time Keeper* deduced 26 April	145°24′0.7″	
	144°48′14.7″	
	35′46.8″	TK to the east
Error of *Time Keeper*	145°30′43.5″	TK
	145° 2′36″	
	28′	TK to the east
	32′34.8″	Mean error

[f. 214] Monday 3 May 1802

Fresh breezes and fine weather, but at daylight the wind became light.

At 6 *hours* 40' weighed ⚓ to go out of the port with the last half of the ebb; backed, filled, and tacked occasionally, drifting out with the tide. At 8, the extreme rock off the south point of entrance S30°E two-thirds of a mile. The wind freshened up and blew strong immediately that we had gotten without side of the entrance. Double reefed the topsails. At 9 *hours* 45' kept away along the shore towards ψ [Cape Schanck], and at 11 *hours* hauled to the eastward round it. At noon, fresh breezes and cloudy. ψ N40°W 4 or 5 miles. A steep cape is now seen to the eastwards which I suppose to be Cape Wollamai:[1] the western entrance in Western Port is now open to the north eastward.

Meri*dian* alt*itude* ☉ *lowe*r *lim*b 483	35°45′24″N
Latitude	38°34′33″S
Dit*t*o obs*erve*d by Lt Flinders	38°33′46″
Mean	38°34′10″S

		By log		Latitude South		Longitude East						
Course	Distance	DR	Obs	DR	Observed TK	Var allowed	Set or current	Ther	Barom	Error of TK
S34°E	14	38°29′	38°34′	145°39′	145°36′	8E	5S	66°	29.84	32′32″E
							3W	61°	29.84	
								61	29.89	

Tuesday 4 May 1802

Strong breezes and cloudy weather. At 0 *hours* 50' hauled further off to clear a reef of rocks lying off the south-west end of that Port Island.[2] At 2½ passed by a patch of discoloured water, which we yawed to clear it. At 4, the eastern entrance in the port,[3] round C*a*pe Wollamai bore N55°W 7 or 8 miles. At sunset, Cape Wollamai, bore N54½W, and another projection seen through the haze, bore S65°E[4] At 5 *hours* 30' treble reefed the topsails and hauled to the wind off shore. At 8, fresh gales. Close-reefed the topsails, and reefed the main sail ready for setting. A considerable sea has now got

[1] Cape Wollomai [now Woolamai] (38°34′S, 145°20′E), the highest point of, and dominant feature on Phillip Island, at the entrance to Western Port. Lipscombe, *On Austral Shores*, p. 113.

[2] i.e. Phillip Island (38°29′S, 145°14′E).

[3] i.e. Western Port.

[4] Cape Liptrap (38°55′S, 145°55′E), a rugged headland on the Victorian coast overlooking Bass Strait. It is the northern head of the west side of Waratah Bay.

up from the south-westward. At 12, wore and stood towards the land for two hours, and then wore off again until 4. Squally weather with rain at times, and the wind blowing a fresh gale. At 4, wore towards the land, and at 6 saw a head E5°N through the haze, with some peaks of land off it: These proved to be the entrance of Wilsons Promontory, with the islands lying under it. At 9, a high peaked island,[1] about 6 miles from the promontory, bore N84½°E. Another high island S62°E which we now hauled up to weather.[2] At noon, fresh gales and squally weather, with fine intervals. Peaked island [Curtis Island] N21°W. Southern high island [in the Hogan's Group] N40°E 6 or 7 miles, near which are two remarkable peaked rocks. Steered to pass round these islands and Kents Group,[3] making the best of our way through the strait towards Port Jackson.

Breakers occupy a part of the west passage into Western Port, but it is wide and appears to be safe for ships to enter. One of the rocks lying off the SW end of the island is high and square-topped. There is a deep bight near the middle of the south side of the island, but the shore curves round again to the SE to Cape Wollamai, the extreme, which is steep, but the hand behind it low. Across the small eastern passage opposite to the cape the land is moderately high; but as the hills retire from the coast in their progress eastward, the shore soon becomes low and sandy. The island seems to be destitute of wood on its south side, and there are many rocks and breakers lying along that shore. Wilsons Promontory seems to be a very high, large, irregular shaped piece of land, but the thick haze and clouds much obscured it. Its latitude appears to be 39°12′ which is much different to its situation by Mr Bass; its longitude from Western Port is nearly correct.[4] The islands are rocky, and generally of moderate height: the greater number lie under the land on the west side of the promontory.

Meridian altitude ☉ lower limb 483   34°27′16″N
Latitude   39°35′4″S

| | By log | Latitude South | | Longitude East | | | | | | |
Course	Distance	DR	Obs	DR	TK	Var allowed	Set or current	Ther	Barom	Error of TK
S33°E	66	39°29′	39°35′	146°26′	147°13′	9E	6S	62°	29.90	33′15′E
							50E	65°	29.89	
								63	29.82	

[1] Curtis Island (c.39°28′S, 146°23′E). Named by James Grant after Sir Roger Curtis, who had passed instructions to Grant to sail through Bass Strait. Vallance, Moore and Groves, eds, *Nature's Investigator*, p. 198 n. 3; Lipscombe, *On Austral Shores*, p. 72.

[2] The highest island in the Hogan's Group. Flinders, *A Voyage to Terra Australis*, I, p. 224.

[3] Kent Group (39°25′S, 147°16′E). This includes six islands and islets. They now comprise Tasmania's northernmost national park. Flinders had previously seen these islands in 1798. Vallance, Moore and Groves, eds, *Nature's Investigator*, p. 198; http://www.parks.tas.gov.au.

[4] On his whaleboat voyage of 1797–8 Bass had used a damaged quadrant, and had not carried a timekeeper. A number of navigational errors were therefore made, including 12 to 14 miles in the longitude for Wilson's Promontory, which Flinders corrected here. Austin, *The Voyage of the Investigator*, p. 132.

[f. 215] Wednesday 5 May 1802 In Bass' Strait, steering for Port Jackson

Strong breezes and cloudy. Finding ourselves further to the south than expectation, at 0 *hours* 30′ bore away for Kents Group, which was in sight at 2 o'clock. Saw a small island to the northward from the masthead.[1] At 2 *hours* 55′ it bore north and Kents Group then bore N40° to 65°E. At 4, the pyramid S10°E and the passage through the group N28°E. At 5, saw a small unknown rock bearing E7°N. Small rugged island S74°E Kents Group N52° to 12°W and distant land S53°E; most probably a part of Furneauxs largest island.[2] At dusk the peaked unknown rock bore ESE and the body of Kents Group WNW.[3] No other land in sight. Continued steering to the eastward out of the strait, having one reef only out of the main top sail, so that we could haul to the wind if anything should be met with: The weather finer and wind more moderate than before.

Fresh breezes and cloudy. *Ditt*o weather. At daylight, let out the third reefs and set the main top gallant sail. No land in sight. Let the 2nd reef out of the main topsail.

Cleaned the ship well below and aired with stoves. Set the main sail and fore-top gallant sail and hauled more to the northward, finding the wind inclining that way.

Fresh breezes and cloudy weather. The appearance of land seen to the NWbyN from the mast head.

Mer*idian* alt*itude* ☉ Lowe*r Lim*b 484		35°13′2″N
Latitude		38°31′52″S

	By log		Latitude South		Longitude East						
Course	Distance	DR	Obs	DR	TK	Var allowed	Set or current	Ther	Barom	Error of TK
S73½°E	151	38°52′	38°32′ by RF	149°32′	150°15′	9E	20N 4W	61° 59° 61	29.89 29.88 29.86	33′57″E

Additional remarks

The high island No. 7 [Sir Roger Curtis Island] is peaked at its SW end, but the other part of it, though also high, has a more even surface. The more northern peaked island No. 1,[4] near the promontory, seems to consist of only one hill. I find, that in laying down Wilsons Promontory from Mr. Bass' account, and Kents Group and Furneaux Islands from my

[1] Possibly North East Isle (39°27′S, 147°22′E), part of the Kent Group.

[2] Now called Flinders Island (40°01′S, 148°02′E). The Furneaux Islands are between New South Wales and north-east Van Diemen's Land. On this night Flinders sailed into the Tasman Sea. Vallance, Moore and Groves, eds, *Nature's Investigator*, p. 198.

[3] Rough Journal, I, f. 481, adds: 'In passing through the strait this time I find some material errors in the relative positions of Kents Group & Wilsons Promontory with the islands between. These I shall be able to rectify, and to add a rock to the chart which had been imperfectly seen before.' Flinders refers to this rock in *A Voyage to Terra Australis*, I, p. 225.

[4] Rodondo Island (*c.*39°14′S, 146°23′E). This was named by James Grant owing to its resemblance to a rock known to all seamen in the West Indies. Vallance, Moore and Groves, eds, *Nature's Investigator*, p. 198; Lipscombe, *On Austral Shores*, p. 72.

dead reckoning in the *Francis* schooner and *Norfolk* sloop in 1798 and 1799, that several errors have been committed.[1] These I shall be now able to rectify, and also to add the small rock to the chart, which lies ESE from Kents Group, and had either not been seen before or its distance from the small rugged island had been mistaken. Being tolerably well satisfied that nothing lay in our way beyond the small rock which we passed soon after dusk, I thought it sufficiently safe to run all night, having such easy sail set that we could haul to the wind under it.

As near as I can ascertain our present longitude from the land, which is laid down according to lunar observations in Port Dalrymple,[2] our timekeepers are now 16′ to the east, but it remains to be proved whether this is correct, or whether the 32′ error according to the lunars in No. 16 port[2] is nearest the truth. The longitude shewn by the timekeepers on our arrival at Port Jackson will best determine how near these lands are correctly placed in longitude: I speak principally of Furneauxs largest island [Flinders Island], which is connected with Port Dalrymple by an unbroken series of angles.

[f. 216] Thursday 6 May 1802 *Investigator* from examining the south coast towards Port Jackson

Moderate breezes and cloudy weather. Set stay sails. Brought to, to sound: the land about Ram Head[3] being visible in patches from N½W to WbyN½N.

Moderate breezes and fine weather. On the ship breaking more off, tacked ship, at 3, to the westward. Lightening in the NW. Took in the top-gallant sails. Squally weather. Double reefed the topsails. Saw the land to the north-westward. At 11, tacked ship to the westward, after mustering the ships company and seeing them clean. At noon, the weather dull and cloudy, so that no observation could be procured.

		Latitude South		Longitude East						
By log										
Course	Distance	DR	Obs	DR	TK	Var allowed	Set or current	Ther	Barom	Error of TK
N33°E	53	37°48′	–	150°10′	–	10E	9S 1W	63° 63° 65	29.86 29.75 29.52	34′40′E

Friday 7 May 1802

Moderate breezes and fair weather. Let out the 2nd reefs and set top-gallant sails. The land in sight, in hummocks, from NbyW to West. Cloudy weather, with much lightening about, and other threatening appearances. Kept a point further off the land.

---

[1] Flinders corrected numerous errors made by Bass on his whaleboat voyage of 1797–8 and which he had himself had made on the *Francis* and *Norfolk*. Austin, *The Voyage of the Investigator*, p. 132.

[2] Port Dalrymple (41°08′S, 146°52′E) is on the north side of Van Diemen's Land overlooking Bass Strait and discovered by Flinders and Bass on their voyage on the *Norfolk* in 1798–9. Named after Alexander Dalrymple, the Hydrographer to the Admiralty, it is situated at the mouth of the Tamar River near Launceston. Vallance, Moore and Groves, eds, *Nature's Investigator*, p. 465.

[3] Port Phillip. Ibid., p. 189.

[4] Rame Head (37°47′S, 149°28′E).

Squally with rain at times. Double reefed the top sails. At daylight, set the top-gallant sails and stay sails. Lumps of land in sight from WbyS to NWbyW. Got the two twelve-pound carronades out of the hold into their carriages. Cleaned the ship below and aired with stoves. Sour krout served as usual. A piece of high land which we take to be Mount Dromedary bears W½S.[1] Other land from thence to north-west. Variable breezes and cloudy.

Meridian altitude ☉ lower limb 483   36°46′56″N
Latitude   36°23′49″S

| By log | | Latitude South | | Longitude East | | | | | | |
Course	Distance	DR	Obs	DR	TK	Var allowed	Set or current	Ther	Barom	Error of TK[2]
N27°E	116	36°6′	36°24′	151°17′	151°59′	10E	9S	64°	29.55	35′22″E
							–	61°	29.55	
								63	29.63	

[f. 217] **Saturday 8 May 1802**

Variable moderate breezes and cloudy weather. Served slops to the ships company. Fresh breezes. On the wind shifting suddenly to the southward, took in the main sail and top-gallant sails; afterwards the jib & 3rd. reef of the fore topsail. Fresh breezes and squally, with drizzling rain. The wind being now more steady and weather settled, made more sail. Let the 3rd. reef out of the fore topsail. Cut up pork No. 38 to its contents at daylight, and hauled up to the wind in order to make the land. Saw the land from the mast head, indistinctly. Handed top-gallant sails and spanker. Fresh breezes and cloudy. The land visible from the mast head, which I suppose to be near Hat Hill: it bore WbyS.[3]

Meridian altitude ☉ lower limb 483   38°42′11″N
Latitude   34°11′51″S

| By log | | Latitude South | | Longitude East | | | | | | |
Course	Distance	DR	Obs	DR	TK	Var allowed	Set or current	Ther	Barom	Error of TK
N9°E	139	34°7′	34°12′	151°43′	152°39′	11E	5S	65°	29.61	36′4″E
							14E	65°	29.80	
								65	29.87	

Additional remarks

If the land seen on the 7th at noon and this afternoon was Mount Dromedary, and I think it could be no other, it must be visible at a great distance. I take its longitude to be 150°4′ East whence, if our timekeepers are not more than 16′ too far to the east, its

---

[1] Named by James Cook in April 1770, this is the highest point on the south coast of New South Wales (36°18′S, 150°02′E). It is now called Mount Gulaga.

[2] Flinders added here: 'Port Jackson from lunars brought on N6°W 155 miles.'

[3] Named by Cook. Today known as Mount Kembla (34°26′S, 150°48′E) near Wollongong.

distance will be 28 leagues; which is immense for a mount to be so plainly distinguishable and high above the water;[1] and is such that I believed the error of the time-keepers to be much more considerable.[2] For this reason I ceased to steer in for the land at 10 PM; but at daylight we again hauled up for the land, as near as the wind would permit.

[f. 218] **Sunday 9 May 1802**[3]

Moderate breezes and cloudy weather. Set top-gallant sails and spanker, trying to fetch the heads of Port Jackson. Saw the heads bearing West, and soon after the colours were hoisted upon the south head. Shewed a white flag at the front top-gallant mast head, being a private signal to the governor. At 6, the flag staff SWbyW and our distance off shore 7 or 8 miles. Tacked towards the shore on the wind heading. A fire upon the south head bore WbyS: tacked ship.

Moderate breezes and fine weather. Let out 2nd reefs and set stay sails. Tacked ship to the north-west; but at daylight we found ourselves still to leeward of the port, the south head bearing WNW at 6 *hours* 30′, when we tacked to the southward, expecting the next shift of wind to be that way. Shewed our colours and private signal. At 9, tacked ship to the westward, the wind heading us. At noon, the entrance into the port bore NWbyW 2 or 3 miles; and we were now steering in for it with a free wind.[4]

		Latitude South		Longitude East						
Course	Distance	DR	Obs	DR	TK	Var allowed	Set or current	Ther	Barom	Error of TK
N70°W	35	34°59′	33°50′	151°03′	152°5′ Supposition	11E	9N 6E	65° 64° 62	30.05 30.08 30.13	36′47″E

Monday 10 May 1802

Moderate breezes and fine weather. At 1, entered between the heads of Port Jackson; tacked, took on board the pilot, and worked up to the mouth of Sydney Cove, in which we came to with the small bower in 5½ fathoms. At 3 *hours* 15′ furled sails, lowered down the cutter and the commander went on shore to wait upon His Excellency governor King. Found lying here His *Majesty's* armed vessel *Porpoise* and brig *Lady Nelson*; the French national ship *Le Naturaliste*, a south-sea whaler, and a brig privateer.[5]

---

[1] Flinders adds in a note: 'On arriving at Port Jackson, the error of the time-keepers, when reduced back to this time, was found to be 35′ 22″E so that the distance of the mount would be only 21 leagues.'

[2] Flinders noticed differences in the compass bearings which were caused by the ship's iron creating a local field of magnetic attraction. Together with the Earth's magnetic field, this was causing deviations in compass readings with each change in the ship's head. Flinders wrote in detail about variations in the mariner's compass in a paper printed in the *Philosophical Transactions of the Royal Society*, London, for 1806–7. Ingleton, *Matthew Flinders*, p. 155.

[3] Flinders, *A Voyage to Terra Australis*, I, pp. 227–39, only covers the period 9 May–21 July cursorily.

[4] Flinders added in a note in a box: 'No. of sick Four.'

[5] The brig *Lady Nelson* was commanded by Lieutenant John Murray. Flinders now found that this vessel had discovered Port Phillip Bay before him. In late 1801 and early 1802 Governor Philip Gidley King of New South Wales had sent Murray in command of the *Lady Nelson* to Bass Strait, expecting the ship to meet the *Investigator* en route. Murray did not come across the *Investigator* on his voyage, but he explored King Island and discovered

Light breezes and fine weather. Sent down the top-gallant yards at sunset. AM Light breezes and fine weather. People employed cleaning the ship, and in other occasional duties.

Additional remarks

From journals, sketches, and other papers put into my hands by His Excellency the governor, I learn the following particulars concerning a part of the south coast of New Holland and Bass' Strait. In the passage from the Cape of Good Hope to Port Jackson, lieutenant James Grant, in the brig *Lady Nelson*, made the south coast of New Holland in latitude 38° south, a projecting part of which he named Cape Northumberland.[1] This appears to be the cliffy rocky point mentioned on April the 19th; and the bold cliffy cape Φ he named Cape Bridgewater. The cape Υ obtained the name of Cape Otway, and the cape ψ he called Cape Schanck. Lieutenant Grant seems to have given the coast only a superficial examination, but he has undoubtedly the right of prior discovery to *Monsieur* Baudin, whereas I had hitherto given that credit to the French captain.[2]

Concerning the discoveries of the Dutch, French, and English upon the south coast of Terra Australis, or New Holland

It may be proper to point out the exact limits of the particular discoveries of lieutenant Grant, captain Baudin, and the *Investigator*, which I am able to do with sufficient accuracy. It is known that the French admiral D'Entrecasteaux did not pursue the coast of Nuyts Land [f. 219] so far as Nuyts himself had done; although Monsieur Labillardière, who may not be scrupulously nice in geographical matters, asserts the contrary; for the isles of St. Peter and St. Francis, which terminated the Dutch discovery, were not seen by him, or any islands that could have been mistaken for them: the French then have no claim to original discovery to the westward of these islands, although their contre-amiral D'Entrecasteaux and his geographer Baupré deserve much praise for their accurate delineation of these parts.[3]

Port Phillip on the mainland coast. Flinders told the captain of *Le Naturaliste*, which had been at Port Jackson since 24 April 1802, about Baudin's intention to come to Port Jackson. The *Porpoise* had taken King to Port Jackson in 1798. Governor King to Banks, 5 June 1802, in Bladen, *HRNSW*, IV, pp. 782–3.

[1] The *Lady Nelson*, commanded by Grant, had sailed from the River Thames on 13 January 1800. Its Australian landfall was at Cape Banks (near today's Mount Gambier, South Australia). The *Lady Nelson* reached Port Jackson on 16 December 1800. Lipscombe, *On Austral Shores*, p. 35.

[2] This portion of the south coast of Australia had been partially surveyed by James Grant and John Murray in 1800, 1801 and 1802 in the *Lady Nelson*. Baudin did not know this when he explored that part of the coast. Flinders only learned about these prior surveys when the *Investigator* arrived at Port Jackson in May 1802. Estensen, *The Life of Matthew Flinders*, p. 204.

[3] On 28 January 1802 Flinders named Nuyts Reef and Cape Nuyts and on 8 February 1802 he named the whole group of islands the Nuyts Archipelago after Pieter Nuyts, the Dutch discoverer of this part of the south Australian coast. Jean-Julien Houtou de Labilladière, a French botanist, was the naturalist on D'Entrecasteaux's expedition to Oceania in search of La Pérouse in 1791–3. In 1800 he published an account of the voyage. This reference shows that Flinders knew his work. Flinders also knew the charts made by Beautemps-Beaupré on the voyage which were under the control of Elisabeth-Paul-Edouard de Rossel, astronomer, surveyor and eventual leader of the expedition. See above, p. 262.

It is most probable that Nuyts did not see the main coast so far to the east as the islands which he named; be that as it may, it is certain that the *Investigator*s discovery will commence where that of the Dutch ends, and it will terminate where she met with *Le Géographe*. The western boundary of this space cannot be placed to the eastward of 135° east from Greenwich, and the place of meeting with captain Baudin was in 139°10′ (corrected). Within these limits are comprehended 1st the whole of that great projecting cape of which Cape Catastrophe is the south extreme, with its bays and neighbouring islands. 2nd the great inlet No.12 [Spencer Gulf] up to its head. 3rd the inlet No.14 [Gulf St Vincent]; and 4th the large Kanguroo Island, with the channel between it, and the middle main land and cape Λ [Cape Jervis] on the other side. To all these I apprehend the *Investigator* has an undisputed claim to affix names; and to her and the British Admiralty only can this right belong, so far as relates to European nations.

From the before-mentioned longitude of 139°10′ to Cape Northumberland, which I place in 140°50′, the claim of original discovery, so far as I am acquainted, is vested in captain Baudin and the French nation; nor shall I presume to call the headlands contained in this space by other names than such as shall be assigned to them in the French chart. The latitude comprehended in this space is from 35°43′ to 38°3′ south.[1] From Cape Northumberland to Western Port, lieutenant Grants priority of discovery cannot, I believe, be contested; or that of Mr Bass from Western Port to the situation of Point Hicks[2] in captain Cooks chart.[3] I find, also, that the large island on the west side of the strait had been visited since Reeds time by lieutenant Murray, who succeeded Mr Grant in the command of the *Lady Nelson*. But it had previously been seen by Mr Black, commander of the brig *Harbinger*, who named this piece of land King Island, which, as Reed gave it no name, seems to obtain generally, and I adopt it.[4] Lieutenant Murray also saw our port No. 16 [Port Phillip]; but not venturing to enter it with the brig, he ran to Western Port and sent a boat round to examine the entrance; afterwards, he went into it, and staying some time, made a rough sketch of its form: this port has obtained the name of Port Phillip, after the first governor of New South Wales.[5]

---

[1] Flinders and Baudin had discussed their respective discoveries along the southern coast of Australia when they met in Encounter Bay. See above, pp. 362–5.

[2] 37°48′S, 149°16′E.

[3] In 1798 George Bass in a whaleboat explored this part of modern Victoria's coastline. In 1800 Lieutenant James Grant, commander of the *Lady Nelson*, had only produced a rough eye-sketch of the Bass Strait area. Estensen, *The Life of Matthew Flinders*, pp. 68, 119; McMartin, 'Grant, James', pp. 468–9.

[4] King Island had been seen and named by John Black in the brig *Harbinger* in January 1801, and was charted by John Murray in the *Lady Nelson*. Flinders did not know these details when he confirmed the existence of the island. Estensen, *The Life of Matthew Flinders*, p. 206. Rough Journal, I, f. 524, notes that these details were gleaned from journals and papers furnished to Flinders by Governor King.

[5] John Murray originally named the Port Phillip area Port King after Governor Philip Gidley King, but he renamed it Port Phillip in honour of Governor Arthur Phillip of New South Wales. Currey, ed., *John Murray*, pp. 17–18.

Being upon the subject of names, it may not be improper to mention an agreement between captain Baudin and myself to call the south-west cape of New Holland, Cape Leeuwen; this we think the Dutch will not dispute.[1]

[f. 220] Tuesday 11 May 1802

Light airs and fine weather. People employed occasionally. AM At daylight the pilot came on board, and we weighed the anchor and warped up the cove into a convenient berth for being near Benilongs point (on the east side of the cove).[2] Moored ship a cable each way and hoisted out the launch. Light and moderate breezes alternately. PM. Sent two bell tents and a marquee to the east point, where we also began to land empty casks to be examined and repaired by the cooper. Unrove such part of the running rigging as was bad, in order to its being surveyed. Sent to the tents a corporal and three marines as a guard.

Wednesday 12 May 1802 <u>Civil account</u>

Sent the observatory and some of the instruments on shore to the tents, under the care of lieutenant Flinders.[3] Held a survey upon decayed boatswains stores, as also upon the barricading of the quarter deck. At noon fresh breezes with rain at times. Employed about the condemned stores, and in sending empty casks on shore to the cooper. Arrived the *Britannia* whaler, Turnbull, from a fishing cruize off New Zealand and this east coast.[4]

<u>Additional remarks</u>

The barricading of the quarter deck stood so high, although the hammock stantions upon it were exceedingly short that it was a great obstruction to any survey; for when the wind was upon the side next the land, I could only see over it by standing on the top of the binnacle. Before leaving Sheerness, I had requested to have it cut down, but as this was at a time when it was supposed all the carpenters work was done, the commissioner objected to it, and I did not chuse to make an application to the Navy Board, the ship being then ready for sailing, for I was too anxious to get away and commence my operations to throw anything like an obstruction in the way: The height of the barricade was also an obstruction to the ships beating to windward; I therefore stated these circumstances to His Excellency the governor, who is also the senior naval officer here, and he order[ed] lieut*enant* Murray of the *Lady Nelson*, Mr Moore the carpenter to this territory, and Mr Mart our carpenter, to survey the barricade, and report their opinions as to any injury which the ship might sustain from its

---

[1] This is the most south-westerly mainland point of the Australian continent. It appeared as 'Leeuwin' on Dutch maps *c*.1622.

[2] i.e. Bennelong Point, named after an Aborigine famous for his interaction with Governor Arthur Phillip of New South Wales. This is the site of the Sydney Opera House.

[3] Samuel Ward Flinders (1782–1842), younger brother of Matthew, was 2nd lieutenant on the *Investigator*. He acted as astronomer for most of the vessel's voyage around Australia. Estensen, *The Life of Matthew Flinders*, pp. 184–5.

[4] The *Britannia*, Robert Turnbull master, Enderby & Co. owners, 301 tons, brought in 1,300 barrels of sperm oil. Governor King promoted the activity of whalers, such as this vessel, at Port Jackson. Cumpston, *Shipping Arrivals & Departures*, p. 41; Steven, *Trade, Tactics and Territory*, p. 98. See also Aplin and Parsons, 'Maritime Trade: Shipping and the early Colonial Economy', p. 159.

removal. Their report being that the ships strength would not in the least be injured, and that her sailing would most probably be improved by its removal. His Excellency gave me an order to have it removed without delay, and he lent 4 convict carpenters from the colony to assist in taking it down and putting single, low, stantions with hammock nettings in its place.[1]

Thursday 13 May 1802
Fresh breezes and cloudy weather. Loosed sails to dry. Entered four carpenters as supernumeraries for victuals, to assist in taking down the barricade of the quarter deck. Cooper on shore repairing casks, and the people employed in the holds. Served greens to the ships company, which were given by the governor. Showers of rain at times about noon. PM Sent a suit of sails on shore to the tents, and the sailmakers to repair them. Employed otherwise as in the morning.

<u>Additional remarks – Astronomical time – General remarks on the errors of the time-keepers</u>[2]
Having ascertained the errors of the time-keepers, it will now be proper to enter into an analysis [f. 221] of their rates of going along the whole of the south coast of New Holland, in order to arrive at such corrections of the longitude of all its parts, as are requisite to bring the situation to such a degree of exactness as our materials will permit; and to fill up the columns of 'Error of Time Keepers' which have been hitherto left open.

The longitude of the boats in Princess-Royal Harbour, according to 20 nights of lunar observations, was 117°59′6″E (see page 109); but the four time-keepers brought from the Cape of Good Hope gave the mean longitude 118°2′27.1″, so that they had contracted an error of 3′21.1″ to the east, between November 1 at Greenwich noon, and December 15 at noon in Princess-Royal Harbour, or in 43.7 days, which gives a proportion of 4.60″ per day, to be applied westward to the longitude given by the time-keepers, in order to obtain the true situation, or rather an approximation to it.[3]

In this mode of correcting the longitude, there are three things taken as fixed data, two of which <u>may</u> be erroneous, and the third <u>most probably</u> is so. In the present case it is taken for granted, that when we left the Cape of Good Hope, the true longitude of that place was used in reducing the errors of the time keepers from mean time to the meridian of Greenwich; and also that the 20 sets of lunar observations gave us the exact longitude of Princess Royal harbour; but the Cape may not be laid down exactly correct, and still more probably may we not have the true longitude of the harbour.[4] But some longitude must be assumed in all cases, or otherwise the construction of charts and all business of this kind would be at a stand; therefore, it must be taken for granted, that

---

[1] These carpenters came from the dockyard to bring down the height of the barricade on the quarter deck.

[2] Flinders tabulates variations in longitude by the two Earnshaw timekeepers he used between the Cape of Good Hope and Port Jackson in *A Voyage to Terra Australis*, I, p. 268.

[3] The four timekeepers were Earnshaw's No. 520 and No. 543 and Arnold's No. 82 and No. 176. Ibid., I, p. 69.

[4] Flinders added in a note at the bottom of the page: 'Captain Vancouvers lunar observations gave it about 10′ further east; but the mean of his Kendals and Arnolds chronometers gave the longitude 3′ to the west, according to their rates brought from the Cape of Good Hope. See Vancouvers voyage Vol. 1 page 56.'

these situations are rightly determined, until it shall be found that they are not so. The third datum is still more liable to error than the two preceding: for it is assumed as a truth that the time-keepers have gone at the same equal rate during the whole interval in question, whereas the probability is that their average rate per week has altered gradually, and perhaps unequally, from that which was assigned them at the Cape to that which they were found to have in Princess Royal Harbour. Thus suppose the rate of the time-keeper No. 543 to have been 5.35″ per day on leaving the Cape of Good Hope, and that on arriving in Princess Royal Harbour, in 43.7 days, it was found to bear a longitude 3′21.1″ too far to the east; the application of the correction −4.60″ of longitude per day to every observation during that interval, supposes that the time-keepers real rate of losing had been 5.66″, but its rate of losing in the harbour being found to be 6.46″, it is more likely that it kept nearly its Cape rate for a great part of the interval, and that the major part of the error 3′21.1″ was contracted in the latter part of the time, probably during the last fortnight: But this can be only conjecture, and the sole datum that can be assumed with any degree of certainty is that the time-keeper did actually lose so much more than the rate allowed to it, that in 43.7 days the error amounted to 3′21.1″ of longitude. The apparent and most direct way, then, to get at the necessary correction to each days longitude, is, to divide the error by the number of days in which it was contracted: and this plan I have adopted, subject to such necessary alterations as may arise from the circumstances peculiar to each of the following cases.

[f. 222] I do not presume to say, that by means of these corrections the longitude deduced from the time-keepers at each observation will be exact, or even that it will be so near the truth as the fixed point may, in Princess-Royal harbour, No. 10 bay [Port Lincoln], or Port Jackson: We may not be able to do every error, but we may lessen it; and I think no one will be found to say, that because an error of 30 miles cannot be exactly corrected, that we are to reject a mode by which, in all probability, 25 of them may be done away. If, on the other hand, any are sufficiently exact and industrious to resort to an approximation by means of second differences or any other series, either regular or irregular, I will not oppose it; but for myself I do not take so much trouble with data which originate in conjecture; nor is it my intention to dispute for 3, 4, or 5 minutes of longitude; nautical utility upon an enlarged scale being more the object of my pursuit than the minutia of precision; especially when I do not see that any consequences, either certain or important, are likely to arise from a neglect of them.

The six sets of observations of the moon west of the stars, taken in No. 1 bay [Lucky Bay], and the six sets on the other side of the moon taken 17 days afterwards, gave the longitude of that place 4′54″ east of what the time-keepers shewed (see page 119) being then nine days from Princess Royal Harbour. At that time I was under the necessity of using the longitude given by the three time-keepers for the correct longitude, and from a consideration of after circumstances I think it to be preferable to that given by the lunar observations; therefore, on January 13, when leaving No. 1 bay, it is supposed that the time-keepers were correct and consequently no correction is required to the longitudes during the nine days between Princess Royal harbour and No. 1. The six sets of observations of stars east and west of the moon, on February 15, though not sufficient to ascertain precisely the error which the time-keepers had contrasted from leaving No. 1, will yet enable us to form some judgment upon it. They differ only 3′12″ from the time-keepers, on the east side, whence I judge, that as yet no great deviation from the truth had yet taken place.

No. 10 bay [Port Lincoln] is our second station upon the south coast. In it there were only three sets of lunar observations taken, but from the time of leaving that bay to March 26 the number was made up to 12 on each side of the moon; and the time keepers having been found to go nearly exact during that period, I have reduced the observations back to that station by their assistance, as on the following page. It appears there, that on February 27 the time-keepers were 13′37.6″ to the east of the truth, although the before-mentioned observations of the stars and moon shewed them to be, on February 15, 3′12″ on the other side; whence it is evident, that in order to get the correct error on each day, we must not, in this case, divide the error by the number of days from No. 1 bay [Lucky Bay], but in the first place search for something else to guide us in deciding at what time they began to deviate.

The observation on February 21 PM upon the north end of Uncertain Island [Thistle's Island] gave the longitude 136°24′26″, whereas after leaving No. 10 [Port Lincoln], with the new rates, it was found to be 4′50″ greater: whence I conclude, that the time-keepers had contracted 4′58″ of the error 13′37.6″ between February 21 P.M. and February 27 at noon; from whence it follows, if we allow the time-keepers to have been right on the 15th preceding, that the remaining part of the error, or 8′39.6″ must have been contracted between that time and the 21st PM.

[f. 222a] The results deduced from the solar eclipse of March 4th PM observed in this bay No. 10 [Port Lincoln] are as follows.[1]

		Beginning	End
Apparent time of observation		1 hour 12′37.5″	3 hours 36′ 11.5″
Nonagesimal degree	Longitude	11.16°43′37.5″	20°39′8″
	Altitudes	57.41.55	43.35.46
Parallaxes in	Longitude	3.39.5	25.26.2
	Latitude	32.9.7	43.50.4
Apparent times of conjunction		1 hour 56.69	1 hour 56.49.5

Mean longitude deduced: the
Greenwich time of ♂ being 16 hours 55′ 1.8″ } 135°26′51.7″ East

This longitude is 28′18.3″ west of that from the 24 sets of distance in the table, but as I can scarcely think the latter can be more than 10′, or at most 15′, wrong, it is probable, that in making the tedious and intricate calculation of the eclipse I have made some error; the longitude from the distance will therefore remain, until some more experienced astronomer shall re-calculate the eclipse.

[f. 223] Summary of lunar observations taken in No. 10 bay [Port Lincoln], discovered on the south coast, and of others reduced back to it by means of two time-keepers, to determine its longitude: the observations taken by lieutenant Flinders.[2]

[1] Observed by telescope at Port Lincoln. Vallance, Moore and Groves, eds, *Nature's Investigator*, p. 148, and Flinders, *A Voyage to Terra Australis*, I, p. 145.

[2] Flinders added in a note inserted vertically to the right-hand side of the table: 'Nota bene: It is to be particularly observed, that in this analysis I have noted the time according to the astronomical method, and not according to the sea mode, or the civil account; both of which last are occasionally used in all other parts of this log book.'

Time 1802	No. of sights	Longitude from observation	Place	Different longitude by time-keepers from No. 10 bay	Longitude of No. 10 bay From the position of the ship at noon west moon	Longitude of No. 10 Bay from the position of the ship at noon east moon	Sextant used
February 26	Six	136°6'12"	At the tents in the bay			136° 6'12"	Ramsdens No. 932
		135.58.13.5				135.58.13.5	
		56.28.5				.56.28.5	
March 10		138. 8.45	At anchor near the head of No. 12 inlet	2° 5'40"E	136° 3'5"		
		.23.45	Under sail, in the passage between Kangaroo Island & the main		18.5		
		.8.15			2.35		Troughtons No. 488
		.0. 0			135.54.20		
		137.59.15			.53.35		
		.53.15			.47.35		
March 11		138. 2. 0			.56.20		
		137.59.45			.54.5		
		138. 1.15			.55.35		
		. 2.45			.57.5		
		137.53.30			.47.50		
		.55. 0			.49.20		
March 25		.42.38		1°49'52"E		135.52.46	
		.52.45				136. 2.53	
		.43.15				135.53.23	
		.51.45				136. 1.53	
March 26		.44.45		1°59' 7"E		135.45.36	
		.44.15				.45. 8	
		.43. 8				.44. 1	
		.44.45				.45.38	
		.51.23				.52. 6	
				Means	135.56.38	135.53.42	East

Mean longitude of No. 10 bay [Port Lincoln] 135.55.10 East
The longitude of No. 10 by three time-keepers brought from No. 1 bay [Lucky Bay] is on February 27 by Earnshaw 543 136°13'57.15" [by] 520 136°16'5.02" [by] Arnold 176 135°56'20.55" [average is] 136°8'47.6East
Error of the timekeepers to the eastward 13'37.6"

21st P.M.; but as this is too great a proportion to be probable, I rather take the quantity 4′58″ between the 21st and the 27th to be the rate at which the time-keepers contracted the 13′37.6″ of error; which being taken, the commencement of the error will be on February 10 at 13 *hours* 5 of Greenwich time, from which time to the 27th or Greenwich time 26th at 14 *hours* 7 they erred at the rate of 50.94″ of longitude per day.

In order to ascertain how the time-keepers had kept their new rates whilst we had been exploring the great inlet No. 12 [Spencer Gulf], we crossed over again towards Uncertain Island, and on the 19th March PM when our longitude from bearings was 136°40′13″ (including the error 13′37.6″) the time-keepers shewed 136°41.10′; whence it was evident that they had kept their rates from No. 10 bay [Port Lincoln], almost exactly, and consequently the error 13′37.6″ still remained as the error of the time-keepers to the eastward. As it is impossible to ascertain the situation of a ship within a few seconds, from bearings taken under sail, I esteem the 57″ of longitude above, which the time-keepers gave to the east, to be of no material importance; and I also take it for granted, that they made no alteration before the 22nd and 23 AM when the longitude of the anchor 1 at Kanguroo Island was ascertained to be 138°24′20″East.

On arriving at the island the second time, we found on April 1st that the time-keepers *Earnshaw* 543 and 520 had erred about 1′50″ of longitude westward during our absence in the channel, and inlet No. 14 [Gulf St Vincent], or in an interval of 91 days; but in finding the new errors, [f. 224] after the time-keepers had been let down, the original longitude was used; and therefore it is taken for granted, that the error 13′37.6″ with which we had quitted No. 10 [Port Lincoln], still remained unchanged on April 6th at Greenwich noon, when we quitted the island and proceeded along the coast towards Port Jackson.

The six sets of observations of the stars and moon on April 16th seemed to shew that the error was then increasing, and the twelve sets of the stars east moon on the 26 and 28, taken by lieut*enant* Flinders in Port Phillip, shewed the same thing more forcibly; for according to them, the 13′37.6″ of eastern error had become 32′36.6″ at that time. If these last observations could have been paired with an equal number of the sun on the west side of the moon, they would have been sufficient to determine such an error to the time-keepers as would have been entitled to our confidence; but this not being the case, I referred the final decision of that point to Port Jackson.

On May 12 the longitude of the east point of Sydney Cove in Port Jackson, was, from the mean of 543 and 520, 151°56′37.3″E; but in 1795 and 1796 I had fixed its longitude at 151°17′12″E by 60 sets of lunar observations: the error of the time-keepers, therefore, had now become 39′25.3″. If from this we deduct the former error 13′37.6″ there will be remaining an error of 25′47.7″ contracted since leaving Kanguroo Island on April 6 at Greenwich noon, or in 36.5 days, giving a proportion of 42.4″ per day. To correct the longitudes, then, during the interval, we must apply the fixed error 13′37.6″, by subtraction, to each longitude shewn by the time-keepers, and afterwards the 42.4″ per day, from April 6 to May 12 AM; and we shall then have the correct, approximated, longitude at each observation; but still subject to the uncertainties mentioned in the beginning of this analysis.

Since we have some data at two points during the last interval, by which a judgment may be formed of the time-keepers errors, independent of the last proportional correction, let us try the accuracy of the proportion by them. The six lunar observations on April 16th gave the time keepers error to be 16′2″, but according to our proportion it was then 20′42″. Lieutenant Flinders' twelve sets of the sun east of the moon in Port Phillip gave the error on the 26 and 28 32′34″ whilst our proportion gives 28′29″. In the first case the lunars are 4′40″ on the east side of the proportion, and in the second they were 4′5.8″ on the west side. Every person much experienced in lunar observations will know that three sets on each side of the moon, taken on board a ship at sea, are insufficient to ascertain the longitude within 5 miles of the truth,[1] or even within ten miles to a certainty; and he will also know, that any number of observations on one side of the moon only are also insufficient; unless an instrument and an observer can be found more correct than I have yet seen them. Therefore, although the lunars do not agree with the proportion, yet as one gives on one side and the other on the opposite, they tend to shew that the proportion is not far from the truth.[2]

[f. 226] Friday 14 May 1802

Fresh breezes with showers of rain. Punished Andrew Robson (marine) with twelve lashes for using mutinous expressions. Held a survey upon the remains of Boatswains, gunners, and carpenters stores: employed otherwise in the holds and sending on shore empty casks. At noon, *ditto* weather. Employed as before upon the barricades, clearing the ship of empty casks, and getting pursers stores ready for survey.

Saturday 15 May 1802

Rainy unsettled weather. Sailmakers at the tents repairing sails. People on board employed as yesterday. Received a turn of water by the launch for present use.

Sunday 16 May 1802

Rainy unsettled weather. After cleaning the ship well below, mustered the ships company and saw them clean also; and afterwards gave part of them leave to go on shore. Fresh breezes and squally with rain.

Monday 17 May 1802

Ditto weather. Employed in the holds about the pursers stores and in sending on shore packs and staves; and at the tents in repairing sails and casks. Carpenters employed taking down the bulwark and refitting the rail.

Tuesday 18 May 1802

Variable weather. The French national ship *Le Naturaliste* having obtained a supply of bread, though of but little meat which was scarce, the colony being at a short allowance

---

[1] Flinders added in a note at the bottom of the page: 'I mean by this expression a longitude as true as can be ascertained from lunar observations excluding altogether any difference arising from errors in the lunar tables. I found that places which have been laid down from occultations of Jupiters satellites are usually about a quarter of a degree further west than I have made them by lunar observations.'

[2] f. 225 is blank in the original.

of it, sailed this morning to the southward.[1] Moderate breezes and cloudy. Employed as before about the barricade, repairing sails and casks, and in the holds.

Wednesday 19 May 1802
Moderate breezes and cloudy weather. Employed in the holds & as before. At noon, the same kind of weather. Received present-use water.

Thursday 20 May 1802
Moderate breezes and cloudy. Sent the different parts of the greenhouse on board the *Supply* hulk to be set up. Held a survey upon the remains of Pursers stores. Fresh breezes and cloudy with rain. PM Employed stowing away the provisions after being surveyed: otherwise as before.

Friday 21 May 1802
Moderate breezes and fine weather. Employed as before, but principally in the holds. At noon, cloudy with rain. Arrived the American ship *Arthur* – Jenckes, from Providence, with provisions and sundries.[2] Launch employed bringing on board water to complete the second tier.

Saturday 22 May 1802
Hard rain at times. Employed on board, in the holds and upon the barricade; and on shore in repairing sails and casks, and at the observatory. PM fresh breezes with hard rain. Employed as AM.

Sunday 23 May 1802
Frequent rain. Give part of the ships company leave to go on shore. PM Fresh breezes with hard rain.

Additional remarks
To captain Flinders Commander of H.M.S. *Investigator* By Philip G. King Esq*uire* captain of H*is* M*ajesty*'s ships and vessels in the Pacific Ocean &c. &c. &c.
    In consequence of your letter of the 18th inst*ant* stating your 'having experienced the utility of the presence of one of the natives of this country, in bringing on a friendly communication with the inhabitants of other parts of New Holland, and requesting my permission to carry two of them in the *Investigator* during her future examination of these

---

[1] *Le Naturaliste* reached Port Jackson on 25 April 1802, and sailed for the Ile de France (Mauritius) on 18 May. Severe storms off the south coast of Van Diemen's Land forced the vessel to turn back. It reached Port Jackson on 3 July 1802, and was reunited with Baudin and *Le Géographe*. Provisions were in such short supply at Sydney that fresh meat was extremely expensive and vegetables only available from the governor's garden. After reaching Port Jackson, Flinders complained that naval stores and salt provisions could not be procured except at exorbitant prices, and frequently not at any price, so he ordered additional provisions from London. Governor King used the Pacific Island trade in salt pork to protect the colony's valued herds of livestock free from being requisitioned by visiting ships. Flinders to Secretary Nepean, 15 May 1802, in Bladen, *HRNSW*, IV, p. 754; Austin, *The Voyage of the Investigator*, p. 139; Estensen, *The Life of Matthew Flinders*, p. 217; Horner, *The French Reconaissance*, p. 248.
[2] Scott Jenkes was the master and Brown & Co. were the owners of this vessel of 265 tons. Cumpston, *Shipping Arrivals & Departures*, p. 41.

coasts, if two proper persons, volunteers, can be found; and also that they may be borne as supernumeraries for provisions upon the books of His Majesty's sloop under your command.'[1] As I agree with you as to the great utility two natives would be of in furthering the service you have to perform You are hereby directed to make choice of two such natives as you may judge proper, bearing them upon your supernumerary list for provisions only, for which this shall be your order. Given under my hand &c May 21 1802. Philip Gidley King.

[f. 227] Monday 24 May 1802
Moderate and cloudy. Punished John Clark, seaman, with 12 lashes for leaving a boat when on duty. Employed in completing the water in the holds and in other occupations before mentioned. *Ditto* weather PM.

Tuesday 25 May 1802
Moderate and cloudy. Received 1078 gallons of rum from the ship *Arthur* for the ships use. Employed pumping it off into good casks and stowing it away in the after hold. PM Fine weather. Employed stowing away spirits.

Wednesday 26 May 1802
Moderate breezes and fine weather. Received 987 lbs of tobacco from the *Arthur*, for the ships use. (This cost 6d per lb. and the spirits 6/6 per gallon.) PM Employed on board upon the barricade and in the holds as before.

Thursday 27 May 1802
Moderate breezes and fine. Struck the main top-mast and unrigged the main mast. Carpenters employed refitting the barricade rails. Two men employed on shore painting hammock clothes, besides the cooper and sailmakers who continue at the tents with lieut*enant* Flinders as before. Sailed for Otaheite[2] H*is Majestys* armed vessel *Porpoise*, to fetch pork for the colony.[3] PM *Ditto* weather. Employed overhauling the main rigging. Sailed the *Cumberland* and *Francis*, colonial schooners, for Broken Bay.[4]

Friday 28 May 1802
People employed as before, and the armourer on shore fitting hammock stantions to the new barricade railing. PM Rigged the main mast, fidded[5] the top mast, and set up the rigging.

---

[1] Governor King gave Flinders permission to hire two aborigines, Bongaree and Nanbaree. Flinders, *A Voyage to Terra Australis*, I, p. 235.

[2] Tahiti.

[3] Listed in Cumpston, *Shipping Arrivals & Departures*, p. 39.

[4] Broken Bay (33°34′S, 151°22′E). The ships were both government vessels employed for the public service of the colony of New South Wales. The *Cumberland*, 28 tons, had been constructed by September 1801. The *Francis*, 40 tons, was used for voyages between Port Jackson and Norfolk Island, for bringing grain from the Hawkesbury River and coals from Hunter's River. Ibid., p. 40.

[5] Refers to the use of a square bar, with a shoulder, to support the weight of the topmast.

Saturday 29 May 1802
Moderate breezes and cloudy. Employed rattling down the rigging and in sundry other duties as before. PM Swayed up the main yard. Cut up beef No. 53 in the presence of the warrant officers, and it was found to be short of its marked weight. 32 lbs: pork No.19, cut up right.

Sunday 30 May 1802
Light breezes with rain. Mustered the ships company and gave part of them leave to go on shore. PM Calm, with drizzling rain: lightening about.

Monday 31 May 1802
Light breezes with fine weather. Sent the launch for a turn of water. People on board employed principally about the rigging. PM Moderate breezes. Employed on shore and on board as before.

Tuesday 1 June 1802
Blacked the yards and mast heads. Punished Richard Hetherly, seaman, for staying beyond his leave and for drunkenness, with 12 lashes; and for using mutinous expressions when brought on board, with 12 others. PM Cloudy with drizzling rain. Arrived here the brig *Harrington* – Campbell from a sealing expedition in Bass's Strait (see additional remarks to April 24 and a note in April 25 p. 205).[1]

Wednesday 2 June 1802
Moderate and cloudy. Employed tarring down the rigging, and getting on board present-use water. PM Fresh breezes. Employed painting the masts, and otherwise as before mentioned, on board and at the tents.

Thursday 3 June 1802
Fresh breezes and cloudy. Employed in various duties as before. PM Fresh breezes and fine. Employed clearing and cleaning the ship.

Friday 4 June 1802
Fresh breezes and fine. Dressed the ship with colours in honour of His Majestys birth day. Issued fresh beef to the ships company, in lieu of an equal quantity of salt meat returned to the colony. At 1 PM fired a royal salute and afterwards the Commander and officers dined with His Excellency the governor, to celebrate the birth day.

[f. 228] **Saturday 5 June 1802**
Fresh breezes and cloudy weather. Sent a masters mate and six men to cut wood on the north side of the harbour. Sailmakers and cooper employed at the tents as before, and the carpenters upon the barricade work. Washed and cleaned the ship below. At noon, ditto weather. Occupations going on as in the morning.

---

[1] William Campbell was the master and Chace & Co. were the owners of this ship. The *Harrington* brought in 500 gallons of elephant seal oil and 5,200 seal skins. Cumpston, *Shipping Arrivals & Departures*, p. 41.

Sunday 6 June 1802

Drizzling rain. Mustered the ships company and saw them clean; then paid them for their savings of bread, amounting to £54.5.3, and gave a part leave to go on shore. PM Sailed the ship *Speedy*, – Quested, for England by the way of Cape Horn.[1]

Additional remarks

By the *Speedy* I transmitted to the proper offices the ships monthly muster books, the survey of condemned stores and of the remains in the boatswains, gunners, carpenters, and pursers charge. To the Admiralty I transmitted an account of our proceedings and discoveries upon the south coast of New Holland, but the fair charts not being finished I was obliged to defer sending them to another opportunity. To the astronomer royal I transmitted, for the Board of Longitude, all the principal observations made upon the south coast, and an account of the going of the time-keepers and the mode I took to correct the longitudes given by them. The time-keepers No. 82 and 176, made by Arnold, I sent home by the same conveyance: and for all these I took receipts.

Monday 7 June 1802

Fresh breezes and squally with rain. Employed clearing the decks, and in other duties before mentioned. PM *ditto* weather.

Tuesday 8 June 1802

Fresh breezes and squally. Washed and cleaned below: employed otherwise as necessary. PM Moderate and cloudy weather, but rainy at times.

Wednesday 9 June 1802

Received on board present use water by the launch. Sailmakers, cooper, and armourer employed on shore as before. Carpenters having mostly finished the barricade, were now employed making arch pieces for the ports and completing the railing. The wooding party employed on shore as before: on board, the rest of the people employed upon occasional duties. Fresh breezes and cloudy.

Thursday 10 June 1802

Rainy at times. Employed as necessary. PM Fresh breezes and squally. Fired a salute of 17 guns on the coming on board of His Excellency, the governor and captain-general, to visit the ship.[2]

Friday 11 June 1802

Moderate and fine weather. Received a turn of wood by the launch. Dried the colours, and cleaned the ship. PM Fresh breezes and cloudy.

---

[1] In 1802 the *Speedy*, a South Sea whaler, was valued at £6,000. On this voyage Flinders sent back his letters, but not his charts, to the Admiralty as evidence of his voyage so far. He did not send the charts because they were numerous and extensive and he had not yet been able to finish them. Steven, *Trade, Tactics and Territory*, p. 134; Estensen, *The Life of Matthew Flinders*, p. 214.

[2] Flinders had written to the governor three days earlier, noting that he had not yet honoured the *Investigator* with a visit and asking him to do so. ML, Flinders to Governor King, 8 June 1802, Matthew Flinders letterbook (1801–6).

Saturday 12 June 1802

Moderate and fair. People employed picking oakum for the carpenters. PM The carpenters caulking the sheer plank about the timber heads.

Sunday 13 June 1802

Moderate breezes and fine weather. Mustered the ships company, and afterwards part had leave to go on shore. Sailed the ship *Britannia*, on a fishing cruize. PM Arrived the ship *Coromandel* – Sterling, with prisoners, 4 months from Portsmouth: She brings the 12 months provisions for which I applied on July 18, 1801, except the spirits.[1]

Monday 14 June 1802

D*itto*. weather. Employed as before in wooding, mending sails &c. PM Cloudy with rain at times and distant thunder. Armourer employed as before about the hammock stantions [stanchions].

[f. 229] Tuesday 15 June 1802

Fine weather. The launch employed wooding bringing on board wood from the party employed on the north shore. Punished Andrew Robson, marine, with 12 lashes for leaving his post when sentry. Entered Thomas Toney, seaman, being the third man entered here to replace the boats crew lost on February 22.[2] PM Calm and fine. Employed variously as before.

Wednesday 16 June 1802

Moderate breezes and fine weather. The launch employed bringing on board from the ship *Coromandel* part of our provisions, and in landing the remainder.[3] Entered Joseph Tuzo and John Simmonds. PM Cloudy weather. Employed principally in landing provisions as in the morning.

Thursday 17 June 1802

Thick foggy weather, afterwards clearer. Employed about the provisions. PM Fresh breezes and fine. A party of people stowing our provisions in a storehouse.

Friday 18 June 1802

Moderate breezes. Employed in the holds stowing away provisions, and in the government store house on shore. Entered Thomas Shirley. The launch employed bringing on board water to complete the third tier. Fine weather.

Saturday 19 June 1802

Moderate breezes and fine weather. Carpenters caulking the water-way seams upon the upper deck. PM Employed mostly in the holds completing the third tier.

---

[1] The master was Alexander Sterling. This was a ship of 522 tons. See Watson, ed., *HRA*, III, p. 641.

[2] John Thistle and a boat crew were lost trying to find an anchorage by the mainland where water could be obtained. Flinders, *A Voyage to Terra Australis*, I, pp. 133–6; and see above, p. 318.

[3] These were the supplies that Flinders had ordered at Spithead. Estensen, *The Life of Matthew Flinders*, p. 217.

Sunday 20 June 1802

D*itt*o weather. Mustered ships company and gave part leave to go on shore as usual on this day.

Monday 21 June 1802

Light airs. Sent a boat to assist in towing the French national ship *Le Géographe*, which came within the heads yesterday.[1] Employed in the holds completing with water. Entered Francis Smith. PM Moderate breezes and fine weather. Carpenters caulking on the upper deck. *Le Géographe* anchored in Neutral Bay.[2]

Tuesday 22 June 1802

Moderate and fine weather. Fired the morning gun, by general order of His Excellency the governor. The commandant of the French ship, captain Baudin, visited the ship.[3] PM Carpenters, cooper, sailmakers, armourers and wooders employed as before: other people employed as necessary. Fired the evening gun.

Wednesday 23 June 1802

Moderate and fine weather. Employed working up junk. The commander returned the visit of the French commandant on board *Le Géographe*. Employed working up junk and putting the rigging into order.

Thursday 24 June 1802

Moderate breezes and fine weather. Carpenters caulking upon the upper deck. Entered Tho*mas* Smith, seaman. PM People working up junk. Sent the launch and a coxon up to Parramatta on colonial service.[4]

Friday 25 June 1802

Fresh breezes and cloudy. Employed making points and gaskets. Entered Joseph Marlow. Came in, the ship *Greenwich* – Law, from a whaling cruize off New Zealand: the *Francis* schooner also arrived.[5]

---

[1] *Le Géographe* was in trouble navigating through the heads, and had a crew afflicted with scurvy. Flinders noted that Baudin informed him that only 12 out of 170 men on board were healthy enough to carry out their duties. After the encounter between Baudin and Flinders in Encounter Bay, *Le Géographe* had followed the south coast of Australia to the Nuyts Archipelago, then headed for Van Diemen's Land, before heading north to Port Jackson.

[2] Situated on the lower north shore of Sydney (33°50′S, 151°13′E).

[3] The meetings between Flinders and Baudin on 22 and 23 June 1802 are not mentioned in Flinders, *A Voyage to Terra Australis*. Baudin's journal stops on 17 June and does not resume until 17 November 1802., *The Journal of Post Captain Nicolas Baudin*, trans., Cornell, p. 423.

[4] Situated on the Parramatta River a few miles inland from Sydney (33°48′S, 151°00′E). Convicts and free people lived at Parramatta, which then had the largest population of settlers in the Sydney area after Port Jackson. Fletcher, *Landed Enterprise and Penal Society*, pp. 53, 55, 57.

[5] The master of the *Greenwich*, 338 tons, was Alexander Law. The owners were Enderby & Co. This ship was valued at £12,700 in 1802. Cumpston, *Shipping Arrivals & Departures*, p. 41; Steven, *Trade, Tactics and Territory*, p. 133. For the *Francis*, see above, p. 395.

Saturday 26 June 1802

Fresh breezes with rain. The carpenters having finished caulking the upper deck, the people were employed scraping them. PM Came in, the ship *General Boyd* from a whaling cruize; and the ship *Hercules* – Betts, with convicts, having sailed from Cork in November last.[1]

Sunday 27 June 1802

Fresh breezes and cloudy, with rain. Mustered the ships company and then gave a part leave to go on shore. *Ditto* weather. PM.

[f. 230] Monday 28 June 1802

Fresh breezes and cloudy with rain. Sent the launch up the harbour to collect logs of wood to be sawed into plank to make boxes for the green house. Entered John McDonald from the ship *Coromandel* and discharged Richard Stanley, a lame man, in lieu (see page 187). PM *Ditto* weather. Got on board the repaired sails from the tents. Employed otherwise upon occasional duties.

Tuesday 29 June 1802

Squally with rain. Carpenters employed repairing the scupper shoots &c. previous to painting the ship. PM the launch brought on board 5 logs for plank. The armourer and cooper employed on shore as before: the people as necessary.

Wednesday 30 June 1802

Fresh breezes and cloudy. Began painting the ship. Sent the carpenters on board the *Supply* hulk to fit up the green house.[2] Dried such sails as were wet on board and stowed them away. PM Received water by the launch, and afterwards sent her up to Parramatta upon the colony's service.

Thursday 1 July 1802 <u>Civil account</u>

Moderate breezes and cloudy weather. The cooper still employed on shore repairing casks, and packing the spare ones to be left behind. PM *Ditto* weather. Employed painting the ship and otherwise as necessary.

Friday 2 July 1802

Drizzling rain. Sent the carpenter into the woods to search for a proper piece of wood to make a back tiller. People employed upon occasional duties. PM Variable weather. Cut up beef No. 3 and pork No. 5 to their contents.

<u>Additional remarks</u>

From the weakness of the ships upper works, I saw that it would be very unsafe to carry the green house over our long tiller as it had been fitted at Sheerness. In order to take off

---

[1] The *General Boyd*, Owen Bunker master, Watson & Co. owners, was a whaler of 382 tons. In 1802 it was valued at £8,500. The *Hercules*, Lucklyn Betts master, was a convict vessel of 395 tons. Cumpston, *Shipping Arrivals & Departures*, p. 41; Steven, *Trade, Tactics and Territory*, p. 135; Watson, ed., *HRA*, III, p. 641.

[2] This was intended to store the plant specimens gathered.

some of the great strain in the working of the ship, I resolved to cut off the legs, and let it stand close down upon the deck; but to do this it was necessary to steer by a short tiller fitted abaft the rudder head; and to make up the want of power arising from its shortness, to lash blocks upon its extreme end through which to reeve[1] a purchase. Thus fitted I thought we should be able to carry it notwithstanding the weakness of the ship: but when it came to be set up I saw it was advisable to reduce it; and the naturalist agreeing that when so reduced it would be sufficient for the plants collected in one expedition, it was cut accordingly to two-thirds of its original size. I feared that if it was carried whole, any bad weather might oblige us to throw it overboard; but when reduced, the probability of such a circumstance would be greatly diminished.[2]

Saturday 3 July 1802
Moderate breezes and fine weather. Employed principally in painting the ship. Received 99 lbs of beef in lieu of an equal quantity of salt pork returned to the colony. The French ship *Naturaliste* having arrived some days since came up from the lower part of the harbour where she had been detained by foul winds.[3] Finished painting the ship and blacked the bends. Light breezes and fine weather.

Additional remarks
With the supply of provisions which the *Naturaliste* had obtained in this port, she had gone to the southward in order to get around Van Diemens Land and so to the westward to Mauritius; but the westerly and southerly winds would not permit her to do this at this season.[4]

Sunday 4 July 1802
Light breezes and fine. Served fresh beef to the ships company. Mustered the ships company, and read the articles of war to them. PM fresh breezes and cloudy. Came in the brig *Lady Nelson* from Broken Bay.[5]

[f. 231] Monday 5 July 1802 Civil account
Employed fitting new hammock clothes, and otherwise as necessary. The commander and lst lieut*enant* sitting as members of a Court of Vice Admiralty to try Mr. Lukyn Betts, commander of the *Hercules* for putting to death several convicts said to have been concerning [*sic*] in a mutinous attempt to take the ship.[6] Fresh breezes and fine. PM Received water for present use.

---

[1] i.e. pass a rope through a hole or channel.

[2] This is described in Flinders, *A Voyage to Terra Australis*, I, p. 231.

[3] *Le Naturaliste* came through the heads of Sydney Cove on 26 June 1802 but was wind-bound for eight days before joining *Le Géographe* in Neutral Bay. Estensen, *The Life of Matthew Flinders*, p. 219.

[4] The *Naturaliste* had left Port Jackson on 17 May 1802, after a stay of 23 days, but gale-force winter westerlies had forced her to return there on 26 June 1802 after failing to sail around Van Diemen's Land to take the southern route to Ile de France. Ibid., pp. 218–19.

[5] A 60 ton brig and a government vessel for the colony of New South Wales, the *Lady Nelson* had been used regularly since 1800 for surveys of the coastal areas of New South Wales and Bass Strait. Cumpston, *Shipping Arrivals & Departures*, p. 40.

[6] This case is referred to in Bladen, ed., *HRNSW*, IV, p. 796.

Tuesday 6 July 1802

Drizzling rain at times. Carpenters employed on board the *Supply* hulk fitting up the green house and sawing plank; and here in fitting the back tiller. Weather cloudy, and at times squally. PM Arrived the ship *Atlas* – Brookes with convicts: sailed from Cork in November last. The prisoners were very sickly and 60 had died; arising from the unnecessary length of the passage.[1] People employed occasionally.

Wednesday 7 July 1802

Fresh breezes and hazy. Employed in various necessary duties. PM D*itto* weather.

Thursday 8 July 1802

Moderate breezes and cloudy. Got the green house from on board the *Supply* hulk, and the Carpenters set it up in its place. People employed in various necessary duties. PM Armourer and cooper employed on shore as before.

Friday 9 July 1802

Fresh breezes and cloudy. Launch employed bringing on board biscuit from the shore. Arrived the American brig *Fanny* from Boston.[2] Employed as before.

Saturday 10 July 1802

Moderate breezes and fine weather. Received water by the launch. PM. Employed stowing away bread and in other necessary duties, as before.

Sunday 11 July 1802

D*itto* weather. Mustered the ships company previous to sending a large party on shore to attend Divine Service; afterwards some went upon leave.

Monday 12 July 1802

Light airs. Bent sails. Paid the carpenters, sawyers, armourer, cooper, and sailmakers for their extra work done in refitting the ship. *Le Géographe* warped up the harbour to be laid on shore for repairing some copper.[3] PM. Moderate and cloudy. Carpenters making boxes and otherwise fitting the green house.

Tuesday 13 July 1802

D*itto* weather. Sent paint on shore and a man to paint the new whale boat. Employed on board in various duties fitting the ship for sea, and in assisting the *Lady Nelson* brig.

Wednesday 14 July 1802

Calm hazy weather. Washed and cleaned the ship below. People employed working up junk. PM. Fired a salute of 11 guns on being visited by Monsieur Baudin, the French

---

[1] Richard Brooks was the master of this vessel of 435 tons. Cumpston, *Shipping Arrivals & Departures*, p. 42; Watson, ed., *HRA*, III, p. 641.

[2] E. Smith was the master of this ship of 185 tons. Cumpston, *Shipping Arrivals & Departures*, p. 42.

[3] Governor King gave permission for this to happen. The copper bottom of *Le Géographe* needed cleaning and repair, and the vessel was careened on the beach on the western side of Cattle Point. Estensen, *The Life of Matthew Flinders*, p. 219.

commandant, and by lieutenant-colonel Paterson, the lieutenant-governor of the colony.[1]

Thursday 15 July 1802

Moderate and cloudy. Roused up the small lower cable, cleaned the tier, stowed plank in it and recoiled the cable again. PM. Carpenters employed about the green house. John Davis, marine, being invalided by a medical survey, was discharged into the ship *Coromandel* for a passage to England, and Charles Brown was entered in his lieu.

Friday 16 July 1802

Moderate and cloudy. Employed setting the lower and topmast rigging fore and aft. Received 2,507 lbs of bread from the *Fanny* brig, being procured by the contractor to make up our quantity, and sent our launch back for spirits. PM. Rainy at times. Received 405¼ gallons of spirits from the brig. Employed pumping off this spirits into good casks and stowing it away.

[f. 232] Saturday 17 July 1802 Civil account

Rainy weather. Punished Francis Smith with 12 and Joseph Tozo with 6 lashes for fighting and drunkenness. PM. Calm with rain. Employed as necessary, cleaning the ship and preparing for sea.

Sunday 18 July 1802

Cloudy weather. Punished a man belonging to the ship *Greenwich*, with 18 lashes, at the request of the master, for mutinous expressions and striking the mate. Mustered the ships company previous to sending them on shore to attend Divine Service. PM. Gave part of the people leave on shore.

Monday 19 July 1802

Moderate and fine weather. Employed in getting biscuit from the shore, and preparing for sea. Cooper packing up spare staves. PM Got off this day 6,468 lbs of biscuit on board.

Tuesday 20 July 1802

Cloudy weather. Made the signal for sailing, with a gun. Employed restoring the booms. Sent all the spare packs and hoops on board the *Supply* hulk to be there lodged till our return to this port.

---

[1] William Paterson (1755–1810), soldier and explorer, was appointed lieutenant governor of New South Wales by Governor Philip Gidley King in 1802. He relinquished his duties, through ill health, in the first half of 1803 but later returned as governor in 1809–10. Between 1804 and 1808 he played a leading part in establishing European settlement in Van Diemen's Land. Baudin's two vessels and his ship's company and scientific officers remained at Port Jackson from July to November 1802. There were numerous encounters between the French visitors and their English hosts. Macmillan, 'Paterson, William (1755–1810)', pp. 317–19; Sankey, 'The Baudin Expedition in Port Jackson', pp. 5–36; Starbuck, *Baudin, Napoleon and the Exploration of Australia*, pp. 25–43.